The Moral Background

PRINCETON STUDIES IN CULTURAL SOCIOLOGY

Paul J. DiMaggio, Michèle Lamont,
Robert J. Wuthnow, and Viviana A. Zelizer,
Series Editors

A list of titles in this series appears at the back of the book

The Moral Background

An Inquiry into the History
of Business Ethics

Gabriel Abend

PRINCETON UNIVERSITY PRESS
Princeton and Oxford

Requests for permission to reproduce material from this work should be sent to
    Permissions, Princeton University Press
Published by Princeton University Press, 41 William Street, Princeton,
    New Jersey 08540
In the United Kingdom: Princeton University Press, 6 Oxford Street, Woodstock,
    Oxfordshire OX20 1TW

press.princeton.edu

Jacket art: Diego Lev, *Hombre Torresgarciano* (detail) 2008. Book paper and acrylic on
    cardboard.

Library of Congress Cataloging-in-Publication Data

Abend, Gabriel.
    The moral background : an inquiry into the history of business ethics / Gabriel Abend.
        pages cm. — (Princeton studies in cultural sociology)
    Includes bibliographical references and index.
    ISBN 978-0-691-15944-7 (hardcover : alk. paper) 1. Business ethics—History.
    I. Title.
    HF5387.A177 2014
    174'.4—dc23

                                                                        2013035034

British Library Cataloging-in-Publication Data is available

This book has been composed in Minion Pro and Trade Gothic

Printed on acid-free paper. ∞

Printed in the United States of America

10 9 8 7 6 5 4 3 2 1

a mis abuelos . . .

CONTENTS

The Moral Background

INTRODUCTION

That is the introduction. Writing one allows a writer to try to set the terms of what he will write about. Accounts, excuses, apologies designed to reframe what follows after them, designed to draw a line between deficiencies in what the author writes and deficiencies in himself, leaving him, he hopes, a little better defended than he might otherwise be. This sort of ritual work can certainly disconnect a hurried pedestrian from a minor inconvenience he might cause a passing stranger. Just as certainly, such efforts are optimistic when their purpose is to recast the way in which a long book is to be taken.

—Erving Goffman, 1974[1]

Occasionally some big business representative does speak less sanctimoniously and more forthrightly about what capitalism is really all about. Occasionally somebody exhumes the apparently antique notion that the business of business is profits; that virtue lies in the vigorous, undiluted assertion of the corporation's profit-making function. But these people get no embossed invitations to speak at the big, prestigeful [sic], and splashy business conferences—where social responsibility echoes as a new tyranny of fad and fancy.

—Theodore Levitt, 1958[2]

1. Moral Causes

In January 2011, the National Commission on the Causes of the Financial and Economic Crisis in the United States made public its final report. This commission "was established as part of the Fraud Enforcement and Recovery Act" of 2009. Chaired by Democrat Phil Angelides, it "reviewed millions of pages of documents and questioned hundreds of individuals—financial executives, business leaders, policy makers, regulators, community leaders, people from all walks of life—to find out how and why it [the worst financial meltdown since the Great Depression] happened."[3] Surely the commission was confronted with a most

---

1 Erving Goffman. 1974. *Frame Analysis: An Essay on the Organization of Experience.* Cambridge, MA: Harvard University Press, pp. 16–17.

2 Theodore Levitt. 1958. "The Dangers of Social Responsibility." *Harvard Business Review,* September–October 1958:41 50, p. 42.

3 *The Financial Crisis Inquiry Report: Final Report of the National Commission on the Causes of the Financial and Economic Crisis in the United States.* 2011. Washington, DC: U.S. Government Printing Office, p. 3.

difficult question and a most important assignment. What did it find? What was the cause of the crisis?

The final report presents six "major findings and conclusions."[4] First, "this financial crisis was avoidable"; second, "widespread failures in financial regulation and supervision proved devastating to the stability of the nation's financial markets"; third, "dramatic failures of corporate governance and risk management at many systemically important financial institutions were a key cause of this crisis"; fourth, "a combination of excessive borrowing, risky investments, and lack of transparency put the financial system on a collision course with crisis"; fifth, "the government was ill prepared for the crisis, and its inconsistent response added to the uncertainty and panic in the financial markets"; and sixth, "there was a systemic breakdown in accountability and ethics."[5] It sounds plausible that failures in regulation or excessive borrowing can be causes of a financial and economic crisis. Facts about regulation or borrowing seem to be the sorts of facts that account for financial and economic processes and outcomes. But what does ethics have to do with these issues at all? This is how the report spells out the relationship:

> The integrity of our financial markets and the public's trust in those markets are essential to the economic well-being of our nation. The soundness and the sustained prosperity of the financial system and our economy rely on the notions of fair dealing, responsibility, and transparency. In our economy, we expect businesses and individuals to pursue profits, at the same time that they produce products and services of quality and conduct themselves well.
>
> Unfortunately—as has been the case in past speculative booms and busts—we witnessed an erosion of standards of responsibility and ethics that exacerbated the financial crisis.

For example, the report continues, "major financial institutions" "knew a significant percentage of the sampled loans did not meet their own underwriting standards or those of the originators. Nonetheless, they sold those securities to investors." This "resulted not only in significant financial consequences but also in damage to the trust of investors, businesses, and the public in the financial system."[6] While the report's causal language is at times ambiguous, there is no doubt that it does mean to make a causal claim. Ethical phenomena are one of the causal antecedents, independent variables, or *explanantia*, and the economic and financial crisis is the causal consequent, dependent variable, or *explanandum*.

That moral facts can account for economic facts is in fact a familiar claim. The previous major earthquake in the U.S. economy took place at the dawn of the twenty-first century: a series of spectacular corporate scandals. As an article in the *New York Times* rightly observed, "[a]lmost every year, it seems, some scandal envelops a Fortune 500 company and causes a new spasm of public distrust of

---

4 These are actually the conclusions of the committee's majority only. The dissenting members issued their own report (actually two reports, since the dissenting members did not agree among themselves). Sewell Chan. 2010. "G.O.P. Panelists Dissent on Cause of Crisis." *New York Times*, December 14, 2010, p. B2.

5 *Financial Crisis Inquiry Report*, p. xi.

6 Ibid., p. xxii.

big corporations. This year's occurrence probably should not be surprising; in the competitive marketplace, the temptation to cut ethical corners can be hard to resist." This "scourge of scandals [was leaving] its mark": "a growing number of big companies are enacting strict ethical guidelines and backing them up with internal mechanisms to enforce them." "Lately . . . corporate America seems to be doing more than just paying lip service to standards of management behavior."[7] What is most remarkable about this otherwise unremarkable *New York Times* article about business ethics is its date: October 18, 2000, that is, one year before the Enron scandal erupted.

Stories of this sort, in the business-scandal-*qua*-morality-tale literary genre, would soon become ubiquitous. For, as we know with the benefit of hindsight, the news about Enron, Tyco, and WorldCom was just around the corner. Since their becoming public in 2001 and 2002, these cases have been insistently represented as morality tales, where ethical failures are one key causal factor. These tales afford considerable attention to moral villains, such as Jeffrey Skilling of Enron, Dennis Kozlowski of Tyco, or Bernard Ebbers of WorldCom, who are said to be causally and morally responsible. Eventually, they were sentenced to substantial prison terms, which, so the story goes, they fully deserved. Whether authored by high-status experts or by sensationalistic journalists, moral causation features prominently in public representations of these corporate scandals. For example, in December 2003, former SEC chairpersons Arthur Levitt Jr. and Richard Breeden reflected on "Our Ethical Erosion" in the *Wall Street Journal*. They expressed their expert concern about business immorality—that "standards of integrity and character seem to have slipped to dangerous lows at many firms"—and its harmful economic effects.[8] Trade books, magazines, and films have highlighted similar chains of causes and effects. We have then heard over and over about the "infectious greed" and "deceit" that "corrupted the financial markets," corrupted specific CEO's and corporations, and their disastrous results. We have heard scandals such as Enron described as an "all-American morality play."[9] It is itself culturally revealing that this might be due to the marketing appeal of morality tales and moral villains—say, Gordon Gekko in the 1987 movie *Wall Street*, or the Robber Barons of the Gilded Age, such as Jay Gould, J. P. Morgan, or Cornelius Vanderbilt.[10]

---

7   Amy Zipkin. 2000. "Getting Religion on Corporate Ethics." *New York Times*, October 18, 2000, p. C1.

8   Arthur Levitt, Jr., and Richard C. Breeden. 2003. "Our Ethical Erosion." *Wall Street Journal*, December 3, 2003, p. A16.

9   Frank Partnoy. 2003. *Infectious Greed: How Deceit and Risk Corrupted the Financial Markets.* New York: Times Books; Mimi Swartz, with Sherron Watkins. 2003. *Power Failure: The Inside Story of the Collapse of Enron.* New York: Doubleday, p. 346.

10   The historical record is rife with business-scandals-*qua*-morality-tales and Wall Street moral villains—from Richard Whitney's saga in the 1930s to the life insurance saga in the 1900s. For moral accounts of the latter, see "The Equitable Life Assurance Society." *The Independent*, June 8, 1905, p. 1313; "Life Insurance and the 'Equitable Life' Scandal." *Christian Advocate*, June 29, 1905, p. 1005; "The Gain and Loss." *Wall Street Journal*, November 27, 1905, p. 1; "The New York Life Indictments." *New York Times*, December 29, 1906, p. 8. Cf. Viviana A. Zelizer. [1979] 1983. *Morals and Markets: The Development of Life Insurance in the United States.* New Brunswick, NJ: Transaction Publishers, pp. 125, 147.

Even more revealing for my purposes is that moral causation also features prominently in more solemn and official accounts, such as the government's reactions. The government had to provide both an appropriate legislative and policy response and a well-founded explanation. Or perhaps the other way around: a well-founded explanation and an appropriate legislative and policy response based on it. Thus, the Sarbanes-Oxley Act of 2002 was based on an account of what happened, what went wrong, why, and hence why that was the causally appropriate response or causally effective antidote. Many things went wrong, but one of them recurrently framed explanatory accounts. Consider, for instance, the U.S. Senate's Committee on Banking, Housing, and Urban Affairs hearings regarding the implementation and impact of the Sarbanes-Oxley Act. On September 9, 2003, Republican Richard Shelby, chair of the committee, delivered his opening statement:

> When the "bubble" burst in the second quarter of 2000, it became apparent that the explosive growth in market capitalization in the late 1990's had been accompanied by egregious examples of corporate misconduct and an all too often disregard for business ethics. All too often, auditors turned a blind eye. As these problems came to light through a series of corporate scandals, investors lost confidence in corporate management and financial reporting and withdrew their money from the markets. The Sarbanes-Oxley Act was enacted, in part, to demonstrate to investors a commitment to fairness and integrity in corporate America.[11]

Bad business ethics can bring about bad economic outcomes—hundreds of millions of dollars bad. The expected effect of the Sarbanes-Oxley Act had to do with the "fairness and integrity in corporate America," upon whose improvement better economic outcomes were causally dependent. That this is a framing device that introduces Shelby's statement does not diminish its significance. Much to the contrary. This is how the chairman of the committee wishes to represent the problem in broad strokes; this is where the origins of the problem lie. As far as my argument is concerned, it is all the more significant for that.

All in all, the first decade of the twenty-first century saw more than its fair share of economic and financial unrest. Both the 2001–2002 events and the late-2000s events called for explanatory accounts—not only because "the public wants to know," but also because reform, legislation, and policy make them necessary. Many of these accounts have given business ethics an important causal role, at the individual and firm level, at the social or systemic level, or both. Hence, they may be called "moral causation" accounts. The issue here is not whether they are true, but that they are publicly valid accounts or representations. Now, what is neat about causal theories is that they allow us to manipulate the environment to our advantage: engineers use causal knowledge to design safer auto parts;

11 *Implementation of the Sarbanes-Oxley Act of 2002: Hearings before the Committee on Banking, Housing, and Urban Affairs, United States Senate, One Hundred Eighth Congress, First Session.* 2005. Washington, DC: U.S. Government Printing Office, p. 1.

pharmacologists, more effective drugs; psychotherapists more effective treatments; and educators more effective teaching methods. If you wish to get Y, then you need to introduce X. Assuming a linear and positive relationship, if you wish to get more of Y, then you need to increase the amount of X. With regard to the economy, this is the day-to-day job of central banks, ministers and secretaries of economic affairs, international financial institutions, economic advisers, and policy makers. But what if it turned out that one causal antecedent or independent variable belonged to the realm of ethics?

This is just how moral causation accounts would have it. If they turned out to be true, they should have significant implications for business and political life. If morality were a cause of economic and financial crises and instability, of the kind we have witnessed lately, then the stakes would be high indeed. If, in turn, economic and financial crises and instability led to social and political crises and instability, then the stakes would be even higher. Powerful individuals, corporations, and organizations would care about business ethics. The capitalist state would care, too. Unfortunately, though, not all causal manipulations are equally straightforward. A country's central bank may find it desirable and be able to increase the money supply or the cash reserve ratio, because of the effects it predicts these actions will have. Morality, however, does not seem so easy to increase at will. Differently put, an obvious policy recommendation follows from these accounts. We should improve the ethics of business; we should reduce the incidence of dishonesty, corruption, greed, unscrupulousness, and irresponsibility. But how in the world can we do that?

2. Business Ethicists

Fortunately, in our society there are people who are in precisely this business: business ethicists. In a nutshell, business ethicists' job is to increase the frequency of moral behavior in business—either in a business community as a whole, or within one or more particular companies. Their services may be required by governmental and nongovernmental organizations, as well as individual companies; they may advise on internal rules and norms, public policy, or legislation. From the perspective of moral causation accounts of economic and financial crises, it is fortunate that business ethicists typically place much emphasis on combating unethical practices. Their foes are, for instance, managers of large corporations who defraud their shareholders, resort to unethical competition methods, or cheat the tax authorities; or traders who "reserve the fairest and largest fruit for the top of the barrel, or mingle mahogany saw-dust with the cayenne pepper."[12] Yet, besides combating morally forbidden practices, business ethicists also promote morally good practices, and encourage businesspeople to take seriously their social and

12   Charles Rhoads. 1882. *Business Ethics in Relation to the Profession of the Religious Society of Friends. An Address Delivered before the Friends' Institute for Young Men, of Philadelphia, Second Month 9th, 1882.* n.p., p. 17.

environmental responsibilities. Business ethicists are the historical protagonists of this book. What do these people do, exactly? Where and for whom do they work?

Let us start with a snapshot of the present. Today business ethicists employ a variety of methods and work in a variety of settings. One of them is the business school, where business ethics professors teach courses to undergraduate and MBA students, do research, and (it is hoped) get their articles published in highly ranked business ethics journals. Other business ethicists work outside the university. For example, they "do things like compose ethics codes, run ethics workshops and retreats, do ethics audits, and set up lines of communication for whistle blowers."[13] There are organizations, such as the Center for Business Ethics at the Josephson Institute of Ethics, which "[help] companies improve their workplace culture. From ethics audits and consulting to ethics training and keynotes, the Institute's business ethics services have never been in greater demand."[14] There are also firms that offer "ethics education and awareness," and freelance business ethics consultants and speakers, who help you run "an ethical business . . . [which] will keep you on the right side of the law and in good stead with your clients and customers."[15] This is needed because "[i]n order to continue to survive and thrive, companies are increasingly required to demonstrate 'good' behavior in all that they do."[16]

In addition, a large corporation may have its own ethics officer, sometimes called ethics and compliance officer, chief compliance officer, or chief ethics officer.[17] Ethics officers multiplied as a result of the 1991 Federal Sentencing Guidelines, which reduced penalties if an organization had an "effective program to prevent and detect violations of law," including "[s]pecific high-level officer(s) . . . assigned the responsibility for compliance."[18] The following year, 1992, the Ethics & Compliance Officer Association was officially incorporated.[19] But ethics officers really became a "hot commodity in [the] post-Enron world."[20] Especially in the

---

13 Gordon Marino. 2002. "The Latest Industry to Flounder: Ethics Inc." *Wall Street Journal*, July 30, 2002, p. A14.

14 http://josephsoninstitute.org/business/overview/index.html.

15 This is taken from the website of Lauren Bloom, a "business ethics speaker and consultant," author of the e-book, *Elegant Ethical Solutions*. Her firm, "Elegant Solutions Consulting," promises that it "can resolve even the toughest business ethics issues!" http://www.businessethicsspeaker.com /consulting.php. The phrase, "ethics education and awareness," is taken from the website of EthicsOne: http://www.ethicsinc.com/about.htm.

16 http://www.goodcompanyindex.com/good-company/.

17 Linda K. Treviño and Katherine A. Nelson. 2011. *Managing Business Ethics: Straight Talk about How to Do It Right.* 5th ed. Hoboken, NJ: John Wiley & Sons, pp. 207–54.

18 Dan R. Dalton, Michael B. Metzger, and John W. Hill. 1994. "The 'New' U.S. Sentencing Commission Guidelines: A Wake-Up Call for Corporate America." *Academy of Management Executive* 8(1):7–13, p. 10; Diana E. Murphy. 2001–2002. "The Federal Sentencing Guidelines for Organizations: A Decade of Promoting Compliance and Ethics." *Iowa Law Review* 87:697–719. On the place of ethics, see pp. 714–16.

19 Formerly called the Ethics Officer Association, this is an association of "individuals responsible for their organization's ethics, compliance, and business conduct programs." Cf. http://www.the ecoa.org.

20 Jonathan D. Salant. 2002. "Ethics Officers Hot Commodity in Post-Enron World." *Pittsburgh Post-Gazette*, October 31, 2002, p. E-8.

post–Sarbanes-Oxley world.[21] If you wish to obtain formal training for these hot positions, you may enroll in Duquesne University's "Master of Science in Leadership, concentration in Business Ethics (MSLBE) program," whose business ethics core curriculum covers business ethics, information ethics, organizational ethics, global ethics, and an ethics elective, such as diversity or sustainability. Or you may enroll in the New England College of Business and Finance's "online Master of Science in Business Ethics & Compliance (MBE) program," which, according to its website, "was developed in timely response to disasters like the sub-prime mortgage crisis."[22]

According to moral causation accounts, business ethicists' intervention should have good economic effects, just like increasing the money supply. In the wake of the recent crises, business ethicists have indeed been asked to intervene. But they have also been blamed for what already transpired, just like a failure to increase the money supply could have. In this respect, business schools were singled out and harshly taken to task in the public sphere. Paul Volcker's statement at the 2003 Sarbanes-Oxley hearings sums up the critics' view: "I don't think our great schools of business can entirely escape responsibility. I was taken aback a while ago when one of the leaders of Wall Street, sharing with me his sense of distress about the perceived lapse of standards, commented 'What do you expect when our best business schools for twenty years have preached the doctrine that the only measure of success is the price of a company's stock, with the implication that any means of enhancing that price short of overtly criminal or unethical behavior is fair game?' As I overcame my surprise, I had to agree there was at least a grain of truth in what he said."[23] It does not matter whether there was a grain of truth in what he said or not. After all, why should "a leader of Wall Street" be qualified to speak about the history of business education? What does matter is that Volcker and his friend were expressing a publicly valid narrative. And Volcker's words—delivered both at these hearings in the senate and at Washington University's Olin School of Business a few days before—diffused it further.

The latest crisis provoked comparable complaints. As the *New York Times* reported in 2009, "with the economy in disarray and so many financial firms in free fall, analysts, and even educators themselves, are wondering if the way business students are taught may have contributed to the most serious economic crisis in decades." More specifically,

[c]ritics of business education have many complaints. Some say the schools have become too scientific, too detached from real-world issues. Others say students are taught to come up with hasty solutions to complicated problems. Another group contends that schools give students a limited and distorted view of their role—that they graduate with a focus on maximizing shareholder

21 Cf. David Hess. 2007. "A Business Ethics Perspective on Sarbanes-Oxley and the Organizational Sentencing Guidelines." *Michigan Law Review* 105(8).1781–1816.

22 http://www.duq.edu/leadership/mslbe/.

http://www.necb.edu/master-of-science-in-business-ethics-and-compliance-online.cfm.

23 *Implementation of the Sarbanes-Oxley Act of 2002*, p. 173.

value and only a limited understanding of ethical and social considerations essential to business leadership.[24]

This attribution of causal responsibility to business schools is historically familiar—which is precisely my point. In fact, it appears to repeat itself over time. Just like in the late 1980s, "[w]ith each new scandal, attention had been focused on business ethics—and, in turn, on what is being taught young men and women in business schools these days."[25] Just like in the late 1980s, "[e]thics is drawing new attention" and there is a "new focus on ethics."[26] Just like in the late 1980s, "[p]rompted by the insider trading on Wall Street and by reports of corporate misconduct, growing numbers of business schools have been offering a variety of ethics courses, seminars and lectures."[27] In short, in the wake of the recent crises business schools have felt a threat to their reputation—the reputation of the whole class, not only of the schools that awarded MBA degrees to unethical managers.[28] Their response was quick and conspicuously displayed: ethics courses, professorships, events, research projects, and public sphere statements. Funding was not an impediment, as corporations and philanthropic foundations lavishly supported these initiatives—just like Arthur Andersen and John S. R. Shad lavishly did in the late 1980s.

In sum, if moral causation accounts are accepted, the business ethicist becomes a key social actor and a key link in the causal chain. Her failure to act, or her failure to act effectively, can have dire economic and social consequences.[29] Conversely, for social and economic things to go well, her work is indispensable. In addition, her work is needed by individual companies, if they are to conduct themselves virtuously and responsibly, and thus stay out of legal trouble. When business ethicists are represented as having such causal powers and responsibility, they gladly embrace them. Indeed, they must gladly embrace them if their work is to have value and be demanded in the marketplace. For nowadays business ethicists sell their services, as consultants, professors, speakers, authors, ethics educators and trainers, writers of corporate social responsibility (CSR) reports and codes of ethics, and corporation officers. They run "Ethics Inc.," as one *Wall*

---

24   Kelley Holland. 2009. "Is It Time to Retrain B-Schools?" *New York Times*, March 15, 2009, p. BU1.

25   Sandra Salmans. 1987. "Suddenly, Business Schools Tackle Ethics." *New York Times*, August 2, 1987, p. EDUC64.

26   Elizabeth M. Fowler. 1987. "Industry's New Focus on Ethics." *New York Times*, August 11, 1987, p. D21. See also John S. R. Shad. 1987. "Business's Bottom Line: Ethics." *New York Times*, July 27, 1987, p. A19.

27   Eric N. Berg. 1988. "Harvard Will Require M.B.A. Ethics Course." *New York Times*, July 13, 1988, p. D2.

28   For a post-2001 example, see Ronald Alsop. 2003. "Right and Wrong: Can Business Schools Teach Students to be Virtuous?" *Wall Street Journal*, September 17, 2003, p. R9. For a post-2008 example, see Kelley Holland. 2009. "Is It Time to Retrain B-Schools?" *New York Times*, March 15, 2009, p. BU1.

29   I try to avoid gender-biased language, so I alternate masculine and feminine pronouns when referring to abstract persons, except where a feminine pronoun would be historically implausible and hence confusing.

Street Journal article pungently put it.[30] Hence, they must and do combat the skeptics according to whom they make no causal difference or have no effect—on the grounds that, for example, neither businesspeople nor MBA students can be made more ethical, because ethics cannot be taught, or because human nature is irreparably wicked.

There is another activity that business ethicists engage in. Not only are they assigned a moral enhancement job and expected to make a moral difference, *given* an accepted moral causation account. They may also provide that moral causation account in the first place. Or else, develop it, reinforce it, and help get it socially accepted. They are in the cultural business of designing, articulating, circulating, validating, and legitimating public understandings and accounts about social reality. Sociologists have long underscored the practice of validating understandings and defining situations, both in micro, face-to-face interaction, and in macro, public, and political contexts.[31] Business ethicists participate in fights over the correct representation of events in the public sphere, especially when it is unclear what happened, how to make sense of it, and what its causes were. They enter this arena having a vested interest in furthering understandings in which the economy and morality are inextricably intertwined, and in which morality is a causal factor. Yet, it is a case-by-case question whether their case ends up being persuasive, changes anybody's mind, or what effects their work ends up having.

This is a book about business ethicists, their practical work, and the cultural and institutional contexts in which they carry it out. More precisely, it is a book about the history of this work. Moreover, as we will see in section 4 of this chapter, this history is a means to develop a broader argument about morality and its scientific investigation. Historically, I focus on business ethicists' work in the United States, roughly from the 1850s until the 1930s. I examine who they were, where they worked, wrote, and spoke, and whom they addressed. I also examine what they recommended, prescribed, and demanded from businesspeople, politicians, the state, and society—and how all of these things relate to one another. This book is not a history of businesspeople's behavior. It does not explore the character and frequency of unethical practices, their changes over time, and what accounts for them. Needless to say, these are most important subjects in their own right, but they require data that I do not have. Instead, I investigate society's normative structure. I investigate the institutional and cultural mechanisms that establish what businesspeople are supposed to do, or morally ought to do. These are sociological facts, not psychological facts about intentions and motives—which presumably exist in individuals' minds, about which I have no data either.[32]

---

30 Gordon Marino. 2002. "The Latest Industry to Flounder: Ethics Inc." *Wall Street Journal*, July 30, 2002, p. A14.

31 Andreas Glaeser. 2011. *Political Epistemics: The Secret Police, the Opposition, and the End of East German Socialism*. Chicago: University of Chicago Press; Kieran Healy. 2006. *Last Best Gifts: Altruism and the Market for Human Blood and Organs*. Chicago. University of Chicago Press, esp. pp. 23–42.

32 Cf. Émile Durkheim. 1982. *The Rules of Sociological Method and Selected Texts on Sociology and its Method*. Edited with an Introduction by Steven Lukes. Translated by W. D. Halls. New York: Free Press.

Because of my historical approach, it makes most sense to cast a wide net and work with a broad definition of "business ethicist." Thus, by this expression I do not refer only to the full-time business ethics professors or chief ethics officers, with whom we are familiar today. Rather, I refer to several kinds of people who have concerned themselves with and worked to improve the ethics of business, in different capacities and with different degrees of devotion to the cause: ministers, journalists, pundits, politicians, professors, public intellectuals, among others. Businesspeople may be included, too, insofar as they publicly speak or write about the right and the good, and try to make the morals of their fellow businesspeople better. While they cannot be referred to as "business ethicists," I am also thinking of organizations that have business ethics projects or initiatives *qua* organization: trade associations, better business bureaus, civil society organizations, business schools, or business ethics associations. According to this definition, then, the colonial Puritan minister Cotton Mather, the nineteenth-century Episcopal minister Phillips Brooks, the Boston retailer Edward Filene, and the business school dean Ralph Heilman all count as occasional business ethicists.

3. History, Morals, and Markets

This book makes a contribution to the history of business ethics in the United States, or, more precisely, in the parts of the country where business ethicists were most active. This means primarily urban centers such as New York, Boston, Philadelphia, or Chicago. My narrative takes us to the various locations in which they could be found in action, say, a church in New York in the 1880s, or a business school in Chicago in the 1920s—taking into account the specific character of that location. Unlike many history books, however, a range of years does not appear in the title or subtitle: the boundaries of the period I examine are deliberately fuzzy. Roughly, it starts in the 1850s, that is, after the period Charles Sellers referred to as "the market revolution," and after the period Daniel Howe described as "the transformation of America."[33] In general, it does not go beyond the 1930s. Yet, I do sometimes discuss earlier and later events and sources, from corporate social responsibility in the twenty-first century to Cotton Mather in the seventeenth and eighteenth.

In the following chapters we will encounter different kinds of business ethics work and different kinds of business ethicists at work. We will see them urging businesspeople to be good and do the right thing, working out for them what the right thing to do is, giving them reasons for action, helping them realize when they are facing a moral issue, and helping them overcome "*akrasia*" or weakness

---

33 Daniel Walker Howe. 2007. *What Has God Wrought: The Transformation of America, 1815–1848.* New York: Oxford University Press; John Lauritz Larson. 2010. *The Market Revolution in America: Liberty, Ambition, and the Eclipse of the Common Good.* Cambridge, UK: Cambridge University Press; Charles Sellers. 1991. *The Market Revolution: Jacksonian America, 1815–1846.* New York: Oxford University Press.

of the will. We will see them encouraging businesspeople to pose ethical questions to themselves, such as what the point of a business life is, or what they owe to the community. In my narrative, business ethicists show up, too, trying to shape public opinion, set normative standards, and raise awareness about the urgent public problem of business ethics. They show up addressing politicians and policy makers in Washington, who can have an effect on business practice by introducing the right incentives and disincentives. We will see business ethicists speaking to the youth, who may be more receptive to both their questions and prescriptions—be it at a business school or at a church. Or speaking at business association meetings and writing for the business press, which are prone to be receptive to their questions, especially if the good name of business is at stake. Or publicly attacking real or fictional immoralists, who affirm that business ethics is an oxymoron, the buyer should beware (*caveat emptor*), the public should be damned, everyone's doing it, and business is business, therefore anything goes.

This book scrutinizes the content of business ethicists' understandings and prescriptions—taking into account their context, the audiences they were addressed to, and the cultural repertoires they drew from.[34] Because understandings are not Platonic ideas, I analyze the ways in which and the media through which business ethicists carried out their work. Much like sociologists and anthropologists of science, I am interested in the tools, devices, technologies, methods, and tactics business ethicists came up with and availed themselves of. Manuals of proper behavior, success manuals, pamphlets, biographies, obituaries, typologies, illustrations, and codes of ethics are not neutral, interchangeable containers of information. They are social things, with particular causal histories and social functions, and whose particular modes of operation, modes of existence, and materiality must be analyzed as well. They are not propositions but instruments.[35]

The first payoff of this book lies in the novelty of the history it tells, much of which is surprisingly unknown. Surprisingly, I say, because of the great attention the ethics of business receive these days. In light of recent events, this preoccupation is understandable. Yet, it is sharply at odds with our ignorance about the historical genealogy of the field of business ethics and business ethicists' work. I am not just talking about journalists and bloggers, whose job is to be timely and

34   Michèle Lamont. 1992. *Money, Morals, and Manners: The Culture of the French and the American Upper-Middle Class*. Chicago: University of Chicago Press; Michèle Lamont. 2000. *The Dignity of Working Men: Morality and the Boundaries of Race, Class, and Immigration*. New York: Russell Sage Foundation; Cambridge, MA: Harvard University Press; Ann Swidler. 2001. *Talk of Love: How Culture Matters*. Chicago. University of Chicago Press.

35   Davis Baird. 2004. *Thing Knowledge: A Philosophy of Scientific Instruments*. Berkeley: University of California Press; Gil Eyal. 2003. *The Origins of Postcommunist Elites: From Prague Spring to the Breakup of Czechoslovakia*. Minneapolis: University of Minnesota Press, pp. 80–86; Marion Fourcade. 2009. *Economists and Societies: Discipline and Profession in the United States, Britain, and France, 1890s to 1990s*. Princeton: Princeton University Press, pp. 28–29; Glaeser, *Political Epistemics*, pp. 165ff.; Bruno Latour. 1987. *Science in Action*. Cambridge, MA: Harvard University Press; Bruno Latour. 1993. *We Have Never Been Modern*. Cambridge, MA: Harvard University Press; Trevor Pinch and Richard Swedberg, eds. 2008. *Living in a Material World: Economic Sociology Meets Science and Technology Studies*. Cambridge, MA: MIT Press.

attention-grabbing, not historically accurate. Even professional business ethicists seem to have forgotten their mothers and fathers. One common mistake is to date the origins of their field to the 1960s.[36] Another common mistake is to announce that business ethics is a new or unprecedented phenomenon. For instance, in 1981 renowned management scholar Peter Drucker wrote:

> "BUSINESS ETHICS" is rapidly becoming the "in" subject, replacing yesterday's "social responsibilities." "Business ethics" is now being taught in departments of philosophy, business schools, and theological seminaries. There are countless seminars on it, speeches, articles, conferences and books, not to mention the many earnest attempts to write "business ethics" into the law. But what precisely is "business ethics"? And what could, or should, it be? Is it just another fad, and only the latest round in the hoary American blood sport of business baiting?[37]

Drucker went on to say that his "only qualification for making this attempt [to sort out what 'business ethics' might be] is that I once, many years before anybody even thought of 'business ethics,' taught philosophy and religion, and then worked arduously on the tangled questions of 'political ethics.'" Yet, in 1932, many years before Drucker worked arduously on the tangled questions of "political ethics," Carl Taeusch wrote:

> Several years ago there began to develop an interesting social-economic phenomenon, "business ethics," the like of which had not been seen since the days of the medieval guild. The symptoms of this more recent phenomenon consisted in the formulation of "codes of ethics," the establishment of "practice committees," and the publication of a number of books and articles on the subject. This situation has now perhaps settled down sufficiently to warrant an appraisal of the phenomenon and of the literature to which it gave rise.[38]

Taeusch was then an "Associate Professor of Business Ethics" at Harvard's Graduate School of Business Administration, where he was a faculty member since 1928. He had also written two learned books on the subject: *Professional and Business Ethics* (1926) and *Policy and Ethics in Business* (1931).[39] While his judgment about this "interesting social-economic phenomenon" is an improvement on Drucker's, it still falls short of its target. This interesting social-economic phenomenon began to develop many years before Taeusch worked arduously on the tangled questions of business ethics.

---

36   Gabriel Abend. 2013. "The Origins of Business Ethics in American Universities, 1902–1936." *Business Ethics Quarterly* 23(3):171–205. Cf. Arthur L. Stinchcombe. 1986. "Should Sociologists Forget their Mothers and Fathers?" Pp. 347–63 in *Stratification and Organization: Selected Papers*. New York: Cambridge University Press.

37   Peter F. Drucker. 1981. "What is 'Business Ethics'?" *The Public Interest* 63:18–36, p. 18.

38   C. F. Taeusch. 1932. "Business Ethics." *International Journal of Ethics* 42(3):273–88, p. 273.

39   Carl F. Taeusch. 1926. *Professional and Business Ethics*. New York: Henry Holt and Company; Carl F. Taeusch. 1931. *Policy and Ethics in Business*. New York; London: McGraw-Hill.

The bottom line is that our historical knowledge about business ethics has long been woefully inadequate. It has not been infrequent to hear or see downright false statements in both the public sphere and scholarly forums. This book begins to remedy this neglect. Indeed, my narrative shows that many of today's business ethics debates and many of today's solutions were already debated and already proposed one hundred years ago or so. The same or very similar obstacles were encountered then, the same or very similar objections and rejoinders were put forward, and the same or very similar cultural and institutional tools were appealed to. In this sense, I partake of an old historical trope: I show that things are older than is thought; what is thought to be new has already happened before; we have been there already. However, besides this (perhaps pedantic) pleasure, a history of business ethics may have practical implications. This is because societies' deliberations and decisions about what to do and how to live together should be oriented by adequate self-knowledge or self-understanding. In other words, what we should do should depend on who we are.

It is a typically modern view that social, political, and institutional arrangements can be based on abstract and rational plans or blueprints. It is a typically modern view that human reason is a priori or outside of history. Then, any society can be reorganized from top to bottom in accordance with it, even if that requires substituting ten-day *décades* for weeks and instituting ten-hour days, or designing rational cities that "could be anywhere at all."[40] However, experience has taught us that these modern views are illusory: social and political projects must rely on "local knowledge"; they must make sense in relation to local practices, institutions, narratives, and traditions. It is therefore crucial for a society to understand its particular character and the genealogy of its cultural and institutional configurations: how it has become what it is, how it used to be, and what happened to it in the meantime. Social and political action should take into account the particular people we happen to have become, and the idiosyncratic traditions that are built into our ways of being. This book's historical narrative hopes to contribute to this kind of societal self-understanding, which may help future practical and political projects.

Besides its historical value and potential practical value, business ethics embodies a key intersection and tension in modern Western societies: that between morals and markets, ethics and capitalism. This old tension, tackled by Mandeville and Smith in the eighteenth century, has recently garnered renewed scholarly attention. Both empirical and normative questions about it have been raised. If markets constitute an autonomous sphere and a morality-free zone, why would anyone opt for socially responsible mutual funds or companies, or only "buy American"? Why would consumption and spending choices be subject to moral scrutiny?[41] Why ought anything not to be bought and sold, if free

40   James C. Scott. 1998. *Seeing Like a State: How Certain Schemes to Improve the Human Condition Have Failed*. New Haven, CT: Yale University Press, p. 104. See also Wendy Nelson Espeland. 1998. *The Struggle for Water: Politics, Rationality, and Identity in the American Southwest*. Chicago: University of Chicago Press.

41   Daniel Horowitz. 1985. *The Morality of Spending: Attitudes Toward the Consumer Society in America, 1875–1940*. Baltimore: Johns Hopkins University Press.

individuals freely wish to do so?[42] What accounts for bread riots, and whence the idea of prices' fairness or justice to begin with?[43] How come market actors have normative motivations and engage in costly punishment of unethical behavior?[44] If money is a "neutral, impersonal, and interchangeable" medium, why do we actually find value built into it, earmarking, and "multiple currencies"?[45] What are the moral effects of the market and capitalism? Do they rest on a moral order or foundations?[46] These questions have also been central to economic and cultural sociologists who, since Zelizer's *Morals and Markets* (1979) and *Pricing the Priceless Child* (1985), have explored the moral dimensions of economic life.[47] This literature is topically diverse: from morally problematic markets to morally problematic workplaces;[48] from the effects of moral distinctions on economic policy and politics to the moral features of market society and capitalism.[49] Yet, taken together,

42   Michael J. Sandel. 2012. *What Money Can't Buy: The Moral Limits of Markets*. New York: Farrar, Straus and Giroux; Debra Satz. 2010. *Why Some Things Should Not Be for Sale: The Moral Limits of Markets*. New York: Oxford University Press.

43   James C. Scott. 1976. *The Moral Economy of the Peasant: Rebellion and Subsistence in Southeast Asia*. New Haven, CT: Yale University Press; E. P. Thompson. [1963] 1968. *The Making of the English Working Class*. Harmondsworth: Penguin; E. P. Thompson. 1971. "The Moral Economy of the English Crowd in the Eighteenth Century." *Past and Present* 50(1):76–136.

44   George A. Akerlof. 2007. "The Missing Motivation in Macroeconomics." *American Economic Review* 97(1):5–36; Joseph Henrich et al. 2006. "Costly Punishment Across Human Societies." *Science* 312(5781):1767–70.

45   Viviana Zelizer. 1997. *The Social Meaning of Money: Pin Money, Paychecks, Poor Relief, and Other Currencies*. Princeton: Princeton University Press, p. 202.

46   Albert O. Hirschman. [1977] 1997. *The Passions and the Interests: Political Arguments for Capitalism before Its Triumph*. Princeton: Princeton University Press; Steven Lukes. 1985. *Marxism and Morality*. Oxford: Clarendon Press; New York: Oxford University Press; Nico Stehr, Christoph Henning, and Bernd Weiler, eds. 2006. *The Moralization of Markets*. New Brunswick, NJ: Transaction Publishers.

47   Zelizer, *Morals and Markets*; Viviana Zelizer. 1985. *Pricing the Priceless Child: The Changing Social Value of Children*. New York: Basic Books. Cf. Rebekah Peeples Massengill and Amy Reynolds. 2010. "Moral Discourse in Economic Contexts." Pp. 485–501 in *Handbook of the Sociology of Morality*, edited by Steven Hitlin and Stephen Vaisey. New York: Springer; Frederick F. Wherry. 2012. *The Culture of Markets*. Cambridge: Polity.

48   Rene Almeling. 2011. *Sex Cells: The Medical Market for Eggs and Sperm*. Berkeley: University of California Press; Michel Anteby. 2010. "Markets, Morals, and Practices of Trade: Jurisdictional Disputes in the U.S. Commerce in Cadavers." *Administrative Science Quarterly* 55:606–38; Healy, *Last Best Gifts*; Robert Jackall. 1988. *Moral Mazes: The World of Corporate Managers*. New York: Oxford University Press; Sarah Quinn. 2008. "The Transformation of Morals in Markets: Death, Benefits, and the Exchange of Life Insurance Policies." *American Journal of Sociology* 114(3):738–80.

49   Jens Beckert. 2005. "The Moral Embeddedness of Markets." MPIfG Discussion Paper 05/6. Köln: Max-Planck-Institut für Gesellschaftsforschung; Luc Boltanski and Eve Chiapello. 1999. *Le nouvel esprit du capitalisme*. Paris: Gallimard; Marion Fourcade and Kieran Healy. 2007. "Moral Views of Market Society." *Annual Review of Sociology* 33:285–311; M. Fourcade, P. Steiner, W. Streeck, and C. Woll. 2013. "Moral Categories in the Financial Crisis." *Socio-Economic Review* 11:601–27; Lyn Spillman. 2012. *Solidarity in Strategy: Making Business Meaningful in American Trade Associations*. Chicago: University of Chicago Press; Brian Steensland. 2008. *The Failed Welfare Revolution: America's Struggle over Guaranteed Income Policy*. Princeton: Princeton University Press; Brian Steensland and Zachary Schrank. 2011. "Is the Market Moral?" *Review of Religious Research* 53:257–77; Richard Swedberg. 2005. "Capitalism and Ethics: How Conflicts-of-Interest Legislation Can Be Used to Handle Moral Dilemmas in the Economy." *International Social Science Journal* 57:481–92.

these sociological works foreground and problematize the uneasy interactions between the economic and the moral—which is precisely where the business ethicist is located. My study about this unique character hopes to contribute to this literature, and shed new light on the tension between markets and morals.

Thus far I have sketched out the major themes of this book. However, I have not stated its arguments yet—and there is a reason for that. This book has two main arguments: a conceptual or theoretical one, and an empirical or historical one. The latter has to do with the history of business ethicists' work, whereas the former has to do with the empirical investigation of morality in general. The catch is that the conceptual argument is logically prior to the empirical argument. In order to state the latter, it is necessary to grasp the former. It is only through this conceptual framework or lens that my historical claims can be made out at all. Subsequently, some significant and hitherto unknown facts about business ethics will come to light. So I turn now to what my conceptual framework is, and then to how I bring it to bear on the history of business ethics.

4. The Arguments

This book develops a framework for the scientific study of morality. The science of morality is a very old project.[50] However, in the past few years it has expanded in an unprecedented manner, and in several disciplines: psychology, neuroscience, anthropology, sociology, economics, and the burgeoning field of experimental philosophy.[51] Scholars have been turning out a large number of findings and theories about morality. Besides, there seems to be much excitement about the promise of the science of morality, which universities, publishers, and funding agencies seem to share, and which the media has been quick to pick up (and overstate). Perhaps as a consequence of this very excitement, though, little thought is being given to the nature of the object of inquiry of the science of morality. What exactly are these numerous new studies about? What exactly are these numerous

---

50   Gabriel Abend. 2010. "What's New and What's Old about the New Sociology of Morality." Pp. 561–84 in *Handbook of the Sociology of Morality*, edited by Steven Hitlin and Stephen Vaisey. New York: Springer.

51   In sociology, see, e.g., Steven Hitlin and Stephen Vaisey, eds. 2010. *Handbook of the Sociology of Morality*. New York: Springer; Steven Hitlin and Stephen Vaisey. 2013. "The New Sociology of Morality." *Annual Review of Sociology* 39:51–68; Jan E. Stets and Michael J. Carter. 2012. "A Theory of the Self for the Sociology of Morality." *American Sociological Review* 77.120–40, Iddo Tavory. 2011. "The Question of Moral Action: A Formalist Position." *Sociological Theory* 29:272–93.

In anthropology, see, e.g., Didier Fassin. 2008. "Beyond Good and Evil? Questioning the Anthropological Discomfort with Morals." *Anthropological Theory* 8(4):333–44; Didier Fassin. 2012. *Humanitarian Reason: A Moral History of the Present*. Translated by Rachel Gomme. Berkeley and Los Angeles: University of California Press.

In psychology and neuroscience, see, e.g., Jonathan Haidt. 2012. *The Righteous Mind: Why Good People Are Divided by Politics and Religion*. New York: Pantheon Books; Walter Sinnott-Armstrong, ed. 2008. *Moral Psychology*. 3 vols. Cambridge, MA: MIT Press; Paul J. Zak. 2012. *The Moral Molecule: The Source of Love and Prosperity*. New York: Dutton.

new theories theories of? No doubt, you may say that the object of inquiry of the science of morality is morality, in some sense. But this is not very helpful. The question is, precisely, in what sense.[52]

I argue that, taking the science of morality as a whole, three objects of inquiry should be individuated. Differently put, the science of morality comprises three distinct levels, each of which should be studied in its own right, and whose inter-relations should be studied as well. Two of them are already familiar to scientists of morality in sociology, psychology, and elsewhere. First, there is the level of behavior or practices. For example, to what extent people cheat, steal, and lie; under what conditions they are more likely to cheat, steal, and lie; or what social factors account for the likelihood of someone's cheating, stealing, or lying. Second, there is the level of people's moral judgments and beliefs, and societies' and social groups' moral norms and institutions. For example, given an individual, what practices he finds to be morally permissible, forbidden, or supererogatory; given a society, what practices are generally accepted to be morally permissible, forbidden, or supererogatory, and what institutional mechanisms reflect and enforce these collective tendencies.

In this book I introduce a third level, which up to now has not been recognized as a distinct object of scientific inquiry: the moral background. To offer a preliminary characterization of what this is, I discuss first one real case, and then one thought experiment. Madécasse is a company that produces chocolate in Madagascar, "from bean to bar." As the wrapper informs the interested chocolate lover, its American owners were "Peace Corps volunteers in Madagascar" who "fell in love with the country & people but we wanted to do more." Their company not only "[pays] farmers a fair price for their cocoa," but also makes the bars in the country (as opposed to shipping the cocoa elsewhere). The wrappers are themselves printed locally, too. The take-home message, printed in a larger and bolder type, is that "this creates 4 times the impact of fair trade cocoa." But what does "impact" mean in this context? Of course, a chocolate bar wrapper is not the place to look for ethical theory. Still, it does look like Madécasse is talking about moral stuff here. We might then assume, not unreasonably, that "impact" refers to something like good in a moral sense—having an impact means roughly doing good to Madagascar. Madécasse's wrapper is operating at the level of moral norms, judgments, and claims: it makes claims about the good. But we may further ask what this level of moral norms, judgments, and claims is underlain or enabled by. For a company to create four times more moral good than ordinary fair trade companies, it must be the case that moral goodness can be measured and quantified. What is more, the scale cannot be ordinal, as this would allow only for more and less good; it must be continuous if quadruples are to be possible. These are moral background properties. This Madécasse wrapper does not affirm but presupposes such understanding of moral goodness. Its claims are about the good they are

52   Gabriel Abend. 2013. "What the Science of Morality Doesn't Say about Morality." *Philosophy of the Social Sciences* 43(2):157–200.

bringing to Madagascar, not about the nature of goodness. That belongs to the background level.

A thought experiment can further explicate the point. Imagine a heated but civil debate about the moral status of contentious practice P. Suppose a person named Alice disapprovingly depicts P as cruel and brutal. Of course, for Alice to be able to offer this depiction, the concepts of cruelty and brutality must be available to her. Suppose Lewis responds that P is not morally wrong, because it maximizes the well-being of the disadvantaged members of society. Of course, for Lewis to be able to respond in this way, he must have an understanding of well-being as a quantifiable property, an understanding of society as a distinct entity, and an understanding of society such that it contains disadvantaged and non-disadvantaged members. Further, he must think that maximization of well-being makes a practice morally right. Suppose Carol interjects that the issue of whether P is immoral would be best resolved either by a show of hands or by flipping a coin. Predictably, everyone else first looks mystified and then dismisses her as insane. Clearly, this reaction is based on an underlying understanding about adequate and inadequate methods to deal with moral questions. Last, Dodgson argues that the practice P necessarily taints the soul and, therefore, creatures or beings that have a soul ought not to engage in it. Obviously, this is because Dodgson conceives of the world as containing immaterial entities called "souls," which causally interact with the material world and can be tainted by it. And he believes that these entities are possessed only by some beings—witches and dogs do not have souls, for example.

What lesson can be drawn from this thought experiment? The debate about the moral status of P depends on some elements that are not directly about the moral issue under discussion, and which do not necessarily come to the surface in the debate itself. More formally, the moral background is best explained vis-à-vis the two other levels of morality, the normative and the behavioral—which taken together constitute first-order morality. The moral background is the set of second-order elements that facilitate, support, or enable first-order morality. By "second-order" I mean that they do not belong to the realm of first-order morality; they do not belong to the realm of moral claims, norms, actions, practices, and institutions. Rather, they are "para-moral" elements: they are ancillary or auxiliary to morality. For example, the existence of particular concepts is a fact about the culture in which the debate about P takes place, not about P, nor about the debate about P. Yet, Alice's judgments about P's cruelty and brutality are dependent on that fact, just like her ability to order gazpacho at the restaurant is dependent on whether gazpacho is on the menu. To use another helpful analogy, a premise of liberal political theory is the individual who makes free choices. But individuals' purported freedom is in fact constrained by the conditions under which they are choosing, which are surely not up to them. Similarly, certain conditions need to be in place for you to be able to exercise your individual rights, and even for these rights to be intelligible in the first place. The study of the moral background is analogous to the study of these conditions, not to the study of first-order rights, freedoms, and choices.

This is just a brief introduction to the moral background; chapter 1 is wholly devoted to its nature and features. There, I distinguish six background dimensions: (1) the kinds of reasons or grounds that support first-order morality; (2) conceptual repertoires; (3) what can be morally evaluated; (4) what counts as proper moral methods and arguments; (5) whether first-order morality is assumed to be objective; and (6) metaphysical conceptions about what there is and what these things are like. My argument is that these six second-order, background dimensions underlie first-order morality. Societies and social groups may differ both in their first-order morality and in their second-order moral backgrounds. It is well known to sociologists, historians, psychologists, and anthropologists how radically first-order morality varies. There are pro-life and pro-choice people; there are societies where you can own a slave and societies where slavery is the most repugnant institution. Some people burn the corpses of their parents and some people eat them; some people are more likely to behave altruistically and generously than others; some situations encourage more altruistic and generous behavior than others. One of the core tasks of scientists of morality is to discover and explain these differences. For example, they may hypothesize and empirically test whether a person's religiosity or age has an effect on their moral convictions, or whether a society's religious composition or age distribution has an effect on its prevalent moral norms and institutions.

I argue that, much like first-order morality, the moral background varies as well. These variations scientists of morality should account for, too. For instance, societies and groups may differ in what is taken to be a good moral argument, what is taken to be a moral argument at all, and what objects can and cannot be morally evaluated. People may differ in the assumptions they make about moral objectivity and in the kinds of reasons with which they defend views, actions, and norms. Not possessing the apposite conceptual tools, the science of morality has been hitherto blind to these differences. Empirically, I argue that this kind of background variation lies at the heart of the history of business ethics—and, in particular, the history of business ethicists' work. If you look at the history of slavery or abortion, what is most salient is variation at the first-order level. By contrast, if you look at the history of business ethics, much of the action occurs at the background level. First-order morality is a monotonous and predictable affair, and this is so in three ways.

First, the story goes round in circles, periodically, as Chrysippus or Polybius might have predicted.[53] Every once in a while, one or more instances of terribly immoral behavior are discovered. The public is startled: "[t]he present season is as notable for moral as for physical earthquakes. A succession of defalcations among men of exceptional reputation has startled the country."[54] The degeneration of business morals is decried. Business ethicists and educators are urged to

---

53 Cf. A. A. Long. 1985. "The Stoics on World-Conflagration and Everlasting Recurrence." *Southern Journal of Philosophy* 23 suppl.:13–37; G. W. Trompf. 1979. *The Idea of Historical Recurrence in Western Thought: From Antiquity to the Reformation.* Berkeley: University of California Press.

54 "The Epidemic of Fraud." *New York Herald*, October 11, 1886, p. 8.

do something about it. Business schools reaffirm their commitment to "[inculcating] a more acute sense of social responsibility on the part of the next generation of business leaders."[55] Maybe a few corporations go bankrupt and a few businesspeople go to prison. Employees lose their jobs and shareholders lose their investments. Maybe new regulatory legislation is passed and public relations efforts are intensified. Eventually, the waters get calm. Some time later, one or more new instances of terribly immoral behavior are discovered.

Second, equally monotonous and predictable are the jeremiads about business ethics today—no matter what day the indexical word "today" refers to. We wish we did not have to complain about this issue, but sadly we are forced to, just like Cotton Mather was in eighteenth-century New England: "How Glad should I be, if the *Sermon* that I am going to make, might be one, of which the Hearer might Reasonably say, *There was no Reason for Preaching such an one!* But Either there is Reason for a *Sermon* to Detect and Decry the wayes of Dishonest Gain among us, or else there is no manner of Reason, for the loud Complaints about us, that are heard a Thousand Leagues off, and reach to the very Heavens."[56] Similarly, Herbert Spencer's complaints in "The Morals of Trade" (1859) would not be out of place in a present-day magazine or blog:

> It is not true, as many suppose, that only the lower classes of the commercial world are guilty of fraudulent dealings: those above them are to a great extent blameworthy. On the average, men who deal in bales and tons differ but little in morality from men who deal in yards and pounds. Illicit practices, of every form and shade, from venial deception up to all but direct theft, may be brought home to the higher grades of our commercial world. Tricks innumerable, lies acted or uttered, elaborately-devised frauds, are prevalent—many of them established as "customs of trade;" nay, not only established but defended.[57]

Like Spencer and his contemporaries, we worry about the morals of "the higher grades of our commercial world." We also worry about executive compensation.[58] Likewise, in 1905 the Boston magazine *The Arena* censured executives' "handsome private-car[s]," "the lavish waste of the policy-holders' money," and "the reign of extravagance, loot and waste that is one conspicuous feature of the management of the big New York companies." What is more, the "corruptionists of Wall street" were "gambling with trust-funds," "speculating or gambling

55 Leverett S. Lyon. 1932. "A Ten-Year Look Ahead in Business Education. *Journal of Business of the University of Chicago* 5(4):123–32, p. 125.

56 Cotton Mather. 1705. *Lex Mercatoria: Or, the Just Rules of Commerce Declared*. Boston: Printed and Sold by Timothy Green, pp. 3–4.

57 Herbert Spencer. [1859] 1888. "The Morals of Trade." Pp. 107–48 in *Essays: Moral, Political and Aesthetic*. New and enlarged edition. New York: D. Appleton and Company, pp. 107–8.

58 Lucian Bebchuk and Jesse Fried. 2004. *Pay without Performance: The Unfulfilled Promise of Executive Compensation*. Cambridge, MA: Harvard University Press; Rakesh Khurana. 2002. *Searching for a Corporate Savior: The Irrational Quest for Charismatic CEOs*. Princeton: Princeton University Press; Philippe Steiner. 2011. *Les rémunérations obscènes*. Paris: La Découverte.

with watered stocks," and "defrauding the millions and placing their earnings in jeopardy."[59] Curiously, though, *The Arena* did not summon its readers to occupy Wall Street.

Third, even more monotonous and predictable is the history of business ethicists' prescriptions and principles in the manuals and pamphlets they write, and the lectures and speeches they deliver. The business ethicist urges the businessperson not to cheat, steal, or lie. He ought to be honest and truthful, act with integrity, care about his community, not shortchange his customer, not misrepresent his products, not mistreat his employee, and not falsify his books. This is true today, as much as in the business ethics manuals and pamphlets of the early twentieth century, and as much as in Richard Steele's seventeenth-century business ethics manual.[60] Whether the business ethicist is the president of a trade association, a public servant, policy maker, university professor, or church pastor, their prescriptions have seldom been discordant. True, there are differences regarding terminology, sophistication, the types of firms considered, what practices are actually deemed permissible and impermissible, how to implement and enforce principles, and so on. Still, the normative bottom line has been remarkably stable. The overall picture is one of normative continuities and consensus, and only sporadic, minor differences and outliers.

In this book I show that, underlying these first-order, normative continuities, there lie major second-order background differences. To use an evocative but not perfectly accurate metaphor, different business ethicists have reached similar normative endpoints through different background paths. At present, we know much more about the endpoints than about the paths. This book begins to fill this gap by bringing out a set of historical variations at the background level. Specifically, on the basis of my historical analysis of business ethicists' work, I identify two types of moral background, which I label Standards of Practice and Christian Merchant. How these types differ and what their main traits are I discuss briefly in the next section, and at length in chapters 6 and 7.

5. The Plan

To sum up, in this book I undertake two tasks. First, I put forward a conceptual framework for the scientific investigation of morality. Second, I use this framework to look at the history of business ethicists' work in the United States from the 1850s until the 1930s. The moral background is an empirical tool, so I do some empirical work with it. In this regard, I distinguish and characterize two types of moral background: Standards of Practice and Christian Merchant. These

59 "Great Insurance Companies as Fountain-Heads of Political and Commercial Corruption." *The Arena*, vol. 34, no. 192, November 1905, pp. 514–23, pp. 516 and 523.

60 Richard Steele. 1684. *The Trades-man's Calling: Being a Discourse Concerning the Nature, Necessity, Choice, &c. of a Calling in General: and Directions for the Right Managing of the Tradesman's Calling in Particular*. London: Printed by J.D. for Samuel Sprint.

types differ in many ways: from their understandings of the good to their preferred concepts and methods; from their metaphysical pictures to the social loci where they are more likely to be empirically found. More formally, this book advances two arguments: "there is X" and "A differs from B with respect to X." At such level of generality, my arguments have a pretty simple form. Furthermore, I do not intend to offer an explanation of the differences between A and B. As usual, however, the devil shall be in the details.

I contend, too, that one important part of the history of business ethics is invisible to studies about first-order morality. What is most remarkable about this history is that so much normative continuity and consensus is underlain by divergent moral background elements. Therefore, the eye must be conceptually prepared to perceive these differences, which historical research is one good way to bring out. To paraphrase Kuhn, history, if viewed as a repository for more than anecdote or chronology, could produce a decisive transformation in the image of business ethics by which we are now possessed.[61] But this book makes a broader point, too. The history of business ethics can produce a decisive transformation in the image of morality by which we are now possessed. It can suggest to the up-and-coming science of morality that there is more to morality than its ordinary objects of inquiry: behaviors, beliefs, judgments, and institutions. Empirical research about these objects has produced valuable results. But it is also key to realize that they are facilitated, supported, and enabled by second-order or para-moral background elements—even though these are more difficult to see. Then, this book looks at business ethicists' work from a particular perspective. For example, it attends to which questions they raise, which questions they do not find worth raising, the form of their moral arguments, and the presuppositions of their moral prescriptions. It is more interested in asking what kind of thing moral evaluations are about than in their substance.

It goes without saying that there are many facets of the history of business ethics that this book does not deal with. As Goffman felicitously said once, "[t]his book will have weaknesses enough in the areas it claims to deal with; there is no need to find limitations in regard to what it does not set about to cover."[62] I would like to underscore, then, what this book does not set about to cover. As I said earlier, my subject is not what businesspeople did or did not do, but what they were advised, urged, and expected to do and not to do. What morally good businesspeople were expected or supposed to do, be, and believe. My data and arguments are about society's normative structure, or what I want to call "public moral normativity." These are public facts. They can be best observed in socially prominent and prestigious loci, which is where normative standards are set. Thus, this book is largely about what business ethicists publicly did, said, and wrote, especially when they spoke from high-status stages and pulpits. It is not about what they really believed, or what their true intentions were. As I show,

61   Cf. Thomas S. Kuhn. [1962] 1996. *The Structure of Scientific Revolutions.* Chicago: University of Chicago Press, p. 1.

62   Goffman, *Frame Analysis*, p. 13.

there is nothing new to the frequent present-day criticism that business ethics and corporate social responsibility are but public relations or marketing ploys. Yet, whether they really are public relations or marketing ploys, or, rather, their motivations and intentions are genuinely selfless, this book does not help find out at all. In Goffman's terms, my account is about the public front-stage, not the private backstage.[63]

Let me turn to the organization of the book. I take it that a book is not just a longer article, or collection of thematically connected chapters. A book is a qualitatively different kind of writing, in which much turns on how the narrative and arguments unfold, and how its parts hang together and relate to one another—a common theme is not enough. Much turns on how claims are given support—the evidence is not a separable appendage, which might as well be given as supplementary online material. Therefore, a book's architecture and construction are important not merely for aesthetic and rhetorical reasons, but also for substantive reasons. This is in any case true of the present volume. Chapter 1 is the "theory" chapter, which unpacks my conceptual framework. I discuss what the moral background is, how empirical researchers can benefit from it, and what sociological and philosophical ideas it builds on. Readers who like history more than theory may choose to skip this chapter and go straight to chapter 2 (but I reserve the right not to like their choice). In the rest of the book, three narrative and argumentative threads coexist, which approach business ethicists' moral background from complementary empirical angles.

The first thread is the historical genealogy of the doctrine that honesty is the best policy, or, in contemporary terms, the doctrine that business ethics and corporate social responsibility are good business. Chapter 2 and chapter 3 are specifically organized around this theme. The basic question is what reason a businessperson has to be moral—especially if the odds of getting caught happen to be low. I begin by distinguishing two claims: (1) the empirical claim that acting ethically pays, and (2) the normative claim that because acting ethically pays, you should act ethically. Next, I examine how they show up in the popular literature on business ethics in the early twenty-first century. It turns out that (1) and (2) similarly show up in the popular literature on business ethics in the early twentieth century. Chapter 2 presents several illustrations of this, from a trade association leader's discussion about "business ethics and balance sheets" in the 1920s, to Rotary's motto, "he profits most who serves best," in the 1910s.[64]

The conjunction of (1) and (2) seemed to offer a win-win solution to the business ethics problem—as it still seems to many commentators nowadays. Yet, there is a tradition of business ethicists who reject this purported solution. Chapter 3 turns to Christian ministers for whom the key business ethics issue was businessmen's motives or "springs of action." To begin with, "honesty is the best policy" is no guarantee that they will act honestly in a reliable fashion. Whenever

---

63 Erving Goffman. 1959. *The Presentation of Self in Everyday Life*. Garden City, NY: Doubleday.
64 Ernest F. Dubrul. 1926. "Business Ethics and Balance Sheets." *Nation's Business*, February 1926, p. 76.

dishonesty happens to be the best policy, they would have reason to be dishonest. Most important, policy is not an acceptable motive. If it were, then appearing to act morally would be no different from actually acting morally. Then, chapter 3 analyzes Christian business ethics in more detail, and in particular the tension between two kinds of motives: act always from love of God and love of rightness, or because it is right; and act because it pays in the hereafter, your soul will be saved, or you will not end up *chez* Lucifer. In the end, a good Christian business-man should not even ask whether business ethics pays or not; some questions are better left unasked.

In this first argumentative thread I am exploring the dimension of the moral background that chapter 1 names "grounding": the grounds or reasons given to support moral claims and the ethical theories on which they are based. Alongside this background issue, I am delving into the social science issue of reason-giving: individuals and organizations are often urged, well advised, or even required to produce reasons.[65] In my historical case, part of business ethicists' job is to give reasons as to why business activities should be conducted in an ethical manner. But giving good reasons to this effect is no easy job. The book's second argumen-tative thread speaks precisely to this difficulty. The business ethicists featured in chapter 2 emphasize that business ethics benefits the individual businessman. In chapter 2 and chapter 3 the individual is in the foreground. The business ethicists featured in chapter 4 and chapter 5, respectively, emphasize how American busi-ness and American society can benefit from business ethics (for whom and why this is a reason to act morally is a further question). Thus, chapters 2 through 5 can be grouped together as successively presenting a broader beneficiary from business ethics: an individual, business, and society as a whole.

The story of chapter 4, "The Good of American Business," revolves around the Chamber of Commerce of the United States, the influential business associa-tion founded in 1912. In 1924, Secretary of Commerce Herbert Hoover came to its annual conference in Cleveland with a simple message: "business must end its wrongs or law will."[66] The syllogism was straightforward. Fewer wrongs will prevent government regulation. Less government regulation is good for business. Therefore, business ethics is good for business. Because the business of a national business association is to advance the interests of business, this gave it a good reason to promote business ethics. Chapter 4, then, deals with a familiar subject in business history: the battles of business against regulation, whether through lobbying strategies or through public opinion strategies. In that 1920s context, one of the tools used by the Chamber was an officially sanctioned code of ethics, the Principles of Business Conduct. Like other ethical codes that proliferated at the time, the Principles should help business be recognized as a profession.

65 Luc Boltanski. 1990. *L'Amour et la justice comme competences*. Paris: Métalié; Luc Boltanski and Laurent Thévenot. 1991. *De la justification: les economies de la grandeur*. Paris: Gallimard; Charles Tilly. 2008. *Why?* Princeton: Princeton University Press.

66 "Business Must End its Wrongs or Law Will, Hoover Warns." *Washington Post*, May 8, 1924, p. 1; Herbert Hoover. 1924. "If Business Doesn't, Government Will." *Nation's Business*, June 5, 1924, p. 7.

At the same time, chapter 4 makes an argument specifically about the moral background. It argues that all of this business ethics work was enabled by an underlying ontological process: the conceptual and organizational constitution of business or American business as a distinct entity. Business became capable of being both a moral agent and a moral object: it could do things and have things done to it. Then, this entity was used in a popular causal story, in which *it* was accused of bad business ethics, bad business ethics had bad consequences for *it*, and *it* was called to act to minimize these bad consequences. This argument explores the sixth dimension of the background, metaphysics. It has to do not with first-order business ethics, but with the constitution and existence of American business as a fact about social ontology.

The story of chapter 5, "The Good of American Society," revolves around the university-based business schools that emerged in the late nineteenth and early twentieth centuries. I begin by characterizing the establishment of business schools as an archetypal public reason-giving situation. Universities, especially high-status universities, had to play the game of public moral normativity. New policies and changes had to be publicly justified as the kind of thing that a distinguished higher-education institution does. What is more, universities are typically conceived of and perceived as contributors to the common good (although not always in the same way and to the same degree). Then, the question was why universities should have a business school at all, which a priori seemed to fit neither with their scholarly objectives and spirit, nor with their social or moral objectives and spirit. Not only were reasons needed if a business school was to gather enough local support at a university to be founded. Reasons were also needed afterward to legitimize the young business schools and assuage critics and skeptics in the public sphere. In this chapter I show how business ethics and social responsibility were brought into play for this purpose, focusing on the history of the Wharton School of Finance and Commerce, the Harvard Graduate School of Business Administration, and the Northwestern University School of Commerce. The business school had, should have, or would have social and moral aims. That was their point or *raison d'être*. They would turn out more ethical and responsible businessmen than those whose training was merely experience. They would turn out professionals, like doctors and lawyers, who care about society and the community, not only about making fat profits.[67] Per this book's methodological orientation, my arguments are neither about the weight given to social and moral reasons in closed-doors decision-making processes, nor about the weight given to business ethics in actual business school policy. Instead, they are about the role of moral considerations and proposals in public accounts, and the representation of business ethics as one of the main aims of these schools.

At the same time, chapter 5 makes an argument specifically about the moral background. Business schools claimed that they could make a contribution to

---

67 Cf. Rakesh Khurana. 2007. *From Higher Aims to Hired Hands: The Social Transformation of American Business Schools and the Unfulfilled Promise of Management as a Profession.* Princeton: Princeton University Press.

society through business ethics and social responsibility. They underscored that advances in business ethics would benefit American society as a whole. This necessitated a concept of the good and a conception of what is good for American society. I show how the common good was associated with safeguarding the American way of life and institutions, and ultimately the capitalist system, which the profusion of unethical and irresponsible business practices seemed to undermine. Attacks on business corruption, greed, and selfishness pulled on the same cultural rope as local strikes and international revolutions. They created doubts and anxieties about the health of capitalism. Except for the international revolutions part, anyone who keeps up with current events should be familiar with the feeling. In addition, business schools highlighted the moralizing and civilizing effects of business—much like one lineage of political economists had long been doing.[68] This was an added reason why business ethics was good for American society.

The third argumentative thread of this book is deployed in chapter 6 and chapter 7. In these chapters I approach my evidence about business ethicists' work from a different perspective and in a different way. On the basis of an analysis of the data in terms of my background dimensions or categories, I distinguish two conjunctions of elements: the Standards of Practice and the Christian Merchant types of moral background. The latter I find mostly in the sermons and writings of Christian business ethicists and in Christian periodicals. The former I find in a more diverse set of places, which cannot be located in one organizational setting or cultural milieu only. It includes much of the business press, popular business books and manuals, and the speeches and writings of some leaders of business associations, business schools, and state agencies. While they do admit of exceptions, I argue that these are recognizable patterns into which business ethicists' work can be classified. Yet, I make no arguments about their relative incidence in society or the culture at large. My focus throughout remains on the character and significance of these differences. Then, while chapters 2 through 5 read as narrative history, chapters 6 and 7 may read more as an analytical discussion and comparison of the distinctive features of each type. Table 6.1 summarizes these features, providing an easy visualization of how the two types differ. However, my account in chapters 6 and 7 is not comprehensive of all the dimensions of the moral background, as itemized in chapter 1. It only covers the most instructive ones for a history of business ethics.

The first task of chapter 6 is to inspect one of the pillars of the Standards of Practice type: its faith in science and the applicability of scientific methods to human affairs. Even more, business ethics should become a branch of science: "For the present scientific age we cannot deduce the laws of conduct from abstract principles, or from the words of an authoritative teacher. To do so would be as futile as to take our astronomy on authority, or to learn anatomy from some

68 Hirschman, *The Passions and the Interests*; Fourcade and Healy, "Moral Views of Market Society."

arbitrary notion of the human body."[69] Given these commitments, it makes sense that this 1926 book, titled *The Ethics of Business*, was advertised in the press as follows: "NOT a sermon but an exposition of FACTS."[70] The emphasis on "facts" was not accidental; the contrast with a sermon was not accidental either. Next, I show that in the early twentieth century business schools were on board with these metaphysical leanings. After all, they were themselves made possible by the idea that business could and should be scientifically investigated.

Business schools are partly responsible for another key feature of the Standards of Practice type: business ethics should concern itself with ethical "cases." From a moral background point of view, placing cases at the heart of ethics is not an innocuous move. It does have major implications for what ethics can and cannot do, and what it can and cannot reach. Business ethics cases call for a judgment or decision, so the main problem of business ethics becomes what the morally right decision or judgment is. More technically, business ethics associates itself with the "ethics of doing," the approaches that ask what you should do. It disassociates itself from the "ethics of being," the approaches that ask what you should be or become. The most noteworthy developments occur again at the second-order background level, which fixes what morality comprises and how to go about tackling it. In the next section of chapter 6 I examine the fifth background dimension, metaethical objectivity. While the Christian Merchant type affirms or assumes some version of moral objectivism, the Standards of Practice type affirms or assumes some version of moral relativism. According to the latter, as Edward Filene's 1934 lecture on the morals of trade at the University of California illustrates, "[m]orals are temporal and local. They are local because people live in different times and times change."[71] Finally, I continue this explicit comparison by presenting two tools that both types helped themselves from, and which were indeed ubiquitous in business ethics work of all stripes: the concept of service and the Golden Rule.

The first task of chapter 7 is to introduce "the Christian Merchant," a moral exemplar that Christian business ethicists often appealed to. The Christian Merchant is not simply a merchant who was baptized and goes to church, even if he does so regularly. Rather, the Christian Merchant always conducts his business piously; he "installs" "the Bible in the counting-house."[72] Protestant ministers thus managed their anxieties and "lasting ambivalence" vis-à-vis Mammon.[73] While business is a morally acceptable activity, not any business activity is morally acceptable. Hence, these ministers—many of whose parishioners were in business or would soon go into business—were well advised to get more involved in the business world. They had to technically understand these activities in order to

69   Edgar L. Heermance. 1926. *The Ethics of Business: A Study of Current Standards*. New York and London: Harper & Brothers, p. 192.

70   [*Ethics of Business* Ad.] 1926. *The Rotarian*, vol. 28, no. 6, p. 54.

71   Edward A. Filene. 1935. *Morals in Business*. Berkeley: University of California Press, p. 13.

72   H. A. Boardman. 1853. *The Bible in the Counting-House: A Course of Lectures to Merchants*. Philadelphia: Lippincott, Grambo & Co.

73   Robert Wuthnow. 1998. *God and Mammon in America*. New York: Free Press, p. 26.

morally regulate them. They had to judge what was pious and what was impious for a Christian to do.

I go on to analyze the strong metaphysical commitments of the Christian Merchant type. We are divine creatures living in a divine universe. We have a heart into which God can see. Consequently, the motives of the businessman wind up at the center of moral arguments, prescriptions, and reasons for action. Policy considerations are unbefitting (as chapter 3 shows). Since God owns his creation, we are only temporary stewards of what may seem to be our property—but in fact is not ours at all. Time is God's, too. Hence, it is not up to us to decide what to do with it. Further, there is a metaphysically laden hierarchy of ends and pursuits, the highest of which are spiritual. Lower pursuits, such as business, should be subordinated to higher ones. So business is not a separate, morally autonomous sphere. That business is business is baloney. Chapter 7 also shows that, unlike the Standards of Practice type, the Christian Merchant type pays much attention to the ethics of being. Businesspeople should be or become a particular kind of person. They should be a Christian, or, more precisely, a Christian merchant, such as the moral exemplars with which that chapter begins. Finally, these background elements generally underlay the work of clergymen who belonged to a *longue durée* Christian tradition. This is a tradition of thought about abstract questions of metaphysics and ethics, as well as concrete questions of social and economic life. It is a tradition of moral action, organization, and persuasion, too. Typically, Christian business ethicists had been socialized into this tradition, so its understandings about the universe, human beings, and morality were natural sources for them.

These three argumentative threads jointly bring out the value of the moral background for a historical and sociological account about business ethics. But the moral background is a concept of more general ambitions. In the conclusion I consider its potential contributions to the scientific investigation of morality, whatever the thematic focus or substantive area might be. Specifically, I analyze a widespread approach in present-day moral psychology and neuroscience, which conceives of morality as a hardwired and evolved capacity, and whose object of inquiry is an individual's moral judgment. I then raise two sets of questions about this approach. First, how far can it take us in understanding morality? Can it help us understand not only morality's building blocks, but morality proper as well? Second, how might the moral background affect psychologists' and neuroscientists' prevalent conception of morality? I cannot hope to answer these hard questions in a brief concluding chapter, though. I simply hope to encourage scientists of morality to think harder about their conception of morality, its effects on their theories, and, more generally, to think harder about what understanding morality should entail.

1

The Moral Background

1.1 Morality as an Object of Inquiry

What is the moral background? How does it differ from other familiar moral objects, such as moral judgments, beliefs, and norms? Let me begin to address this question by means of an analogy between science and morality. Consider a journal article in molecular biology or political science, which advances the empirical claim, "*X* causes *Y*." According to a traditional conception of science, this claim aims at the truth, understood roughly as correspondence to the world. Science makes progress by accumulating more and more truths about what the world is like and how the world works. In the history of molecular biology and political science, each individual scientist has made a small contribution to the human store of truth—a timeless, placeless, universal collection of propositions. This traditional conception of science has been questioned on many grounds and for many reasons, especially after Kuhn's 1962 classic, *The Structure of Scientific Revolutions*. For my present purposes, one of these lines of criticism is most relevant. Kuhn and later many philosophers and sociologists of science (and earlier, Polanyi, and much earlier, Fleck) have argued that scientists belong to and work within communities. This is what Fleck calls "thought collectives" ("*Denkkollektiven*") or "thought communities" ("*Denkgemeinschaften*").[1]

Unlike the universal community of science imagined by the traditional conception, these thought communities are historically specific. For instance: Newtonian physics, Einsteinian physics, U.S. structural-functionalist sociology, or Paraguayan Marxist sociology. Like any community, they have common practices, languages, and understandings. What is it that members of a scientific community share, exactly? For one, they likely share many social and demographic characteristics. That helps account sociologically for their having become members of that community in the first place. More important, they have common epistemological and ontological intuitions, dispositions, or assumptions. They agree on how you go about answering a scientific question, and what kind of evidence and how much of it you need to corroborate a hypothesis. Even more: they agree on what is a scientific question and what is not, and what is an interesting and important scientific question, and what is a stupid or ridiculous one. To quote Kuhn, "what is a problem and what a solution" is internal to each thought community.[2] For example, whether *X*

1 Ludwik Fleck. [1935] 1979. *Genesis and Development of a Scientific Fact*. Translated by Fred Bradley and Thaddeus J. Trenn. Chicago: University of Chicago Press; Michael Polanyi. 1958. *Personal Knowledge: Towards a Post-Critical Philosophy*. Chicago: University of Chicago Press.

2 Kuhn, *The Structure of Scientific Revolutions*, p. 109. Cf. Nicholas Jardine. 1991. *The Scenes of Inquiry: On the Reality of Questions in the Sciences*. Oxford: Clarendon Press; New York: Oxford University Press.

causes *Y* is a worthwhile question for the above-mentioned molecular biologists and political scientists, partly because they are in the causal business: the business of unearthing the causal structure of the natural and social worlds, respectively.

Further, members of a thought community generally agree on what there is, that is, what the world contains. They generally agree, too, on what there is not, that is, what does not exist. And they share an inventory or repertoire of concepts that is at their disposal—that is, the set of concepts they may choose to use. For instance, after Becher and before Lavoisier, scientific chemists believed that the world contained phlogiston. Contemporary physicists believe that the world contains quarks (which have different flavors). Contemporary biologists believe that the world contains animal species. Similarly, both Newtonian and Einsteinian physicists believed that an object had a "mass," even though they did not mean the same thing by that word. To return to the molecular biologists' and political scientists' claim, "*X* causes *Y*," *X* and *Y* must be real entities or classes of entities for them—say, genes, memes, information, classes, public spheres, political cultures, or economies. Moreover, both of these communities must have the concept of causation, that is, they must believe that causation is a real relationship that can obtain between two entities.

This Kuhnian line of argument can be taken in various directions. You may investigate the shared epistemologies of particular thought communities.[3] You may build on Wittgenstein's ideas about linguistic communities and ways of life.[4] You may build on Kuhn's and Feyerabend's ideas about incommensurability.[5] Or you may add a critical edge to the argument—critical of science's self-understanding as the final arbiter of truth.[6] What matters here is that all of this work is based on a distinction between the empirical claims of a community of scientists—e.g., "It is the case that *p*," or "It is the case that *X* causes *Y*"—and its ontology and epistemology. The empirical claims are necessarily explicit and thus easy to see. They are first-order claims, sets of statements that occur in journal articles and conference presentations. Their subject matter might be molecular biology, social stratification, or avian ethology. In contrast, ontologies and epistemologies are either more hidden from view or completely hidden from view. They underlie, support, and make possible first-order molecular biology, social stratification,

---

3   Gabriel Abend. 2006. "Styles of Sociological Thought: Sociologies, Epistemologies, and the Mexican and U.S. Quests for Truth." *Sociological Theory* 24(1):1–41; Karin Knorr Cetina. 1999. *Epistemic Cultures: How the Sciences Make Knowledge*. Cambridge, MA: Harvard University Press; Owen Whooley. 2010. "Organization Formation as Epistemic Practice: The Early Epistemological Function of the American Medical Association." *Qualitative Sociology* 33(4):491–511; Owen Whooley. 2013. *Knowledge in the Time of Cholera: The Epistemic Contest over Medical Knowledge in Nineteenth Century United States*. Chicago: University of Chicago Press.

4   David Bloor. 1983. *Wittgenstein: A Social Theory of Knowledge*. New York: Columbia University Press.

5   P. Hoyningen-Huene and H. Sankey, eds. 2001. *Incommensurability and Related Matters*. Dordrecht: Kluwer; H. Sankey. 1994. *The Incommensurability Thesis*. Avebury: Aldershot.

6   Sandra Harding. 1991. *Whose Science? Whose Knowledge? Thinking from Women's Lives*. Ithaca: Cornell University Press; Sandra Harding. 1998. *Is Science Multicultural? Postcolonialisms, Feminisms, and Epistemologies*. Bloomington: Indiana University Press.

and avian ethology claims. But they are not themselves about molecular biology, social stratification, or avian ethology.

Having looked at science, I can now turn to the promised analogy with morality. In this book I argue that first-order morality is underlain by a second-order moral background. Just like any first-order scientific theory is underlain by a second-order understanding about the nature of knowledge, any first-order moral prescription, norm, value, institution, or action is underlain by a second-order understanding about the nature of morality. Just like any first-order scientific theory is advanced with the help of certain scientific tools and concepts, any first-order moral prescription is advanced with the help of certain moral tools and concepts. For example, the epistemological commitments of a scientific community answer this question:

(i) In virtue of what is something—e.g., an empirical claim or theory— acceptable or good, scientifically speaking? Is it in virtue of its truth, explanatory power, predictive power, parsimony, simplicity, beauty, or all of the above? Differently put, what makes it scientifically good?

Analogously, the epistemological commitments of a moral community answer this question:

(ii) In virtue of what is something—e.g., a normative claim or institution— acceptable or good, morally speaking? For instance, assume that helping strangers is a morally good thing and slavery is a morally bad thing. Then, what makes them good and bad things, respectively? Is slavery morally bad because it decreases the total amount of utility or pleasure in the world, because it is intrinsically wrong, because nobody can rationally desire to be a slave, because it is against the will of God, or all of the above?

The background provides the theories and tools that people and organizations employ to ascertain goodness in the realm of morality—implicitly or explicitly, in their day-to-day life, interactions, institutions, law, and elsewhere. In practice, these theories and tools offer them acceptable moral grounds or reasons, which they may use if needed. What is more, the background provides the criteria for morality's or moral considerations' being relevant in a situation in the first place. In some situations morality is not applicable. Say, if a pig, a horse, or a rat harms a person—for it obviously cannot be morally responsible. But in some other situations morality is applicable. Say, if a pig, a horse, or a rat harmed a person in medieval Europe—for it obviously was morally responsible.[7] I use the word "obviously" to highlight an important fact about the background: while this difference about what can be responsible stems from complex moral, religious, and metaphysical views, it generally manifests itself as an intuition. You do not need to be

---

7   Cf. Peter Dinzelbacher. 2002. "Animal Trials: A Multidisciplinary Approach." *Journal of Interdisciplinary History* 32(3):405–21; E. P. Evans. 1906. *The Criminal Prosecution and Capital Punishment of Animals.* London: William Heinemann.

aware of these moral, religious, and metaphysical views to know that, today, it would be crazy to morally evaluate a pig's behavior. It just feels crazy.

As we will see shortly, that is one dimension of the moral background: what can and cannot be evaluated from a moral point of view. The analogy between science and morality helps us see yet another dimension of the background, which the next section also spells out. The quantum physics paradigm offers a particular repertoire of concepts: superposition, uncertainty, tunneling, nonlocality, entanglement, decoherence, duality, wave function, and so on. Naturally, the experiments, claims, and theories of quantum physicists are made possible by these concepts. Physicists working under a different paradigm would simply be unable to make them. For all their genius, neither Newton nor Aristotle could have made them. Similarly, a community's moral background offers a particular repertoire of concepts. Sadly, we are all too familiar with exploitative, materialistic, chauvinistic, and sexist people, and with despotic, oppressive, and fanatical regimes. These moral concepts have complex institutional and cultural preconditions, which do not obtain in all societies. Where they do not obtain, these sad observations cannot be made. In this sense, the moral background is comparable to the quantum physics paradigm, except that in physics, conceptual innovation is a deliberate undertaking, for which a Nobel Prize may be awarded. Now, there being *these* moral concepts for us to use (rather than some others) is not a fact about first-order morality. It is a fact about the second-order, enabling, and constraining moral background level.

I have given a preliminary depiction of the moral background and its relationship to first-order morality. To better see this relationship, table 1.1 represents my tripartite conceptual framework. The second column presents some empirical questions at each of the three levels. It does so in a general form, which applies to any moral area or issue. The third column presents some empirical questions specifically about business ethics—some of which the following chapters of the book empirically investigate. However, neither column is intended to be exhaustive of the issues each level covers; they only provide a few illustrative examples.

Why care about the moral background? Why is it worth studying empirically? The first-order normative level and the first-order behavioral level are no doubt worth studying, because of their contributions to both theory and practice. Yet, current scientific understandings of morality are impoverished because of their neglect of the moral background, what it contains, how it varies, and how it affects the normative and behavioral levels. Starting our empirical investigations at the level of people's first-order morality is like arriving to the theater only for the second act—to use another evocative but not perfectly accurate metaphor. Scientists of morality have looked at practices and institutions that produce and reproduce moral norms and values. They have looked at people's moral convictions, evaluations, and actions. But they have not looked at what makes these *moral* norms, values, convictions, evaluations, and actions, nor what accounts for our being able to have *these* moral beliefs and perform *these* moral actions (rather than those that could be had and performed in other places and times). In brief, currently we see organizations and individuals who carry out actions, endorse and enforce

Table 1.1: The Three Levels of the Science of Morality

Level	Empirical Questions	Business Ethics Examples
First-order normative	(i) Given a society or group, what are people's moral views and understandings, e.g., about what is right, good, permissible, obligatory, admirable, etc.? What moral norms and institutions are there? (ii) What accounts for first-order normative differences within a society or group and across societies or groups?	(i) Given a society or group, what business practices are deemed morally right and wrong? For example, how is the distinction between advertising and misrepresentation drawn? Do companies have obligations to the community, their competitors, and the environment? (ii) What accounts for differences across groups and societies and over time in the business practices deemed morally right and wrong? What accounts for a practice moving from one category to another (e.g., from advertising to misrepresentation)? What accounts for differences across groups and societies and over time in the degree to which a practice is deemed morally reprehensible (e.g., borderline, pretty bad, hideous)?
First-order behavioral	(i) Given a society or group, what moral and immoral behaviors are carried out (whatever counts as moral and immoral there)? (ii) What accounts for first-order behavioral differences within a society or group and across societies or groups? What accounts for the frequency of ethical and unethical behavior in that group? What accounts for change over time? What factors affect the odds of someone's engaging in ethical or unethical behavior?	(i) Given a society or group, what unethical business practices are most and least common? How are they actually carried out? (ii) Under what conditions are particular unethical business practices more and less likely to occur? What accounts for differences across groups and societies and over time in their occurrence? (iii) What individuals and organizations perform business ethics work (e.g., schools, universities, families, business associations, state agencies, the media, religious organizations, etc.)? What does their work consist of?
Moral background	(i) Given a society or group, what counts as a moral action and a moral reason? What counts as a moral problem and as an important moral problem? (ii) How do you go about asking and answering moral questions? What are moral questions primarily about? (iii) What objects can and cannot be morally evaluated? (iv) What kinds of reasons do individuals and organizations use to support moral views and actions? What kinds of ethical theories are these reasons based on? (v) Is morality taken to be capable of objectivity? (vi) What metaphysical assumptions underlie first-order morality? (vii) What repertoire of moral concepts is available in that society? What concepts do individuals and organizations use frequently and successfully?	(i) Given a society or group, which business ethics problems, projects, and proposals are forceful in the public sphere? Which ones are not forceful, not important, implausible, or ludicrous? (ii) What is business ethicists' starting point and main interest? For example, do they focus on what businesspeople do or on what businesspeople are? (iii) Can a company be morally responsible? Can business (that is, business as a whole) be morally evaluated? Is business a moral agent? (iv) What kinds of reasons are used to support business ethics institutions and understandings? For example, given a particular morally wrong practice, what makes it morally wrong? How are contentious norms and policies morally justified? (v) Is it up to each business community to decide what is right and what is wrong in business? (vi) Do societies have a *telos* or ultimate end? Do individuals have a *telos* or ultimate end? Do people in general and businesspeople in particular have an intrinsically selfish and wicked nature? (vii) Are there concepts of corporate social responsibility, fiduciary duty, service, exploitation, market freedom, or just price? How are they used? What are they used for?

norms, and hold convictions. But we do not see the background that underlies and makes possible all of this. We do not see the first act, which sets the stage for the second act.

The history of business ethicists' work is a good empirical setting to bring out the limitations of current understandings of morality. As I mentioned in the introduction, the most conspicuous aspect of the history of slavery is behavioral and normative variation. In many places and times, the institution of slavery has been legally tolerated and morally defended. In many other places and times, it has been rejected and combatted—and sometimes deemed the worst moral error in human history. Likewise, the most conspicuous aspect of the history of women's rights is behavioral and normative variation. Women have had an inferior social, moral, and legal status in many places and times. In many other places and times, women's inferior status has been rejected and combatted—and sometimes deemed the worst moral error in human history. If a scientist of morality decides to investigate the history of slavery, or women's rights around the world, she will surely be expected to account for these conspicuous first-order differences. By contrast, business ethics prescriptions, duties, norms, and complaints are largely constant over time. The first-order level is relatively uneventful. It is monotonous and predictable, as I put it earlier. The moral background level is much more interesting and rife with significant differences. Without my conceptual framework, we would be blind to them. We would miss where the action is.

1.2 What the Background Comprises

I undertake now a deeper examination of the moral background by distinguishing the six dimensions that it comprises (or, which is the same, six classes of background elements): grounding; conceptual repertoire; object of evaluation; method and argument; metaethical objectivity; and metaphysics. Since the moral background is my own conceptual creation, there is no fact of the matter as to whether it really comprises six, three, or nine dimensions. Rather, these are six areas that seem to me most important for the science of morality in general and for my study about business ethics in particular. I take them in turn.

(1) GROUNDING

In the first chapter of *Sources of the Self*, Charles Taylor analyzes how "moral reactions" differ from "visceral reactions," such as "our nausea at certain smells or objects." Much work in moral philosophy and moral psychology has played up their similarities. Taylor argues that this way of thinking is misguided. Suppose a person smells rotten meat and is nauseated by it. The connection between her nausea and the object that causes it is a "brute fact." It makes no sense to ask whether that was an appropriate reaction on her part, or whether that piece of rotten meat merits her reaction. By contrast, Taylor says, this is precisely one essential characteristic of moral reactions: "Thus we argue and reason over what and who is a fit object of moral respect, while this doesn't seem to be even possible for a reaction like nausea."[8]

Taylor's contrasting moral and visceral reactions suggests a broader point: moral understandings, views, judgments, practices, institutions, and actions are always open, in principle, to a demand for reasons or grounding. If you say that an action is wrong, an institution is exploitative, a practice is indecent, or a regime is brutal, you may be asked what makes them wrong, exploitative, indecent, and brutal, respectively. In other words, what makes them merit your evaluation or judgment to that effect. Likewise, if you tell your friend that she should refrain from a morally questionable course of action, she may ask you why she should do so, if she does not feel like it at all. My point is not empirical. As a matter of fact, these questions may not arise very often. When they do arise, people's responses may be confused, unhelpful, or incomprehensible. Further, while sometimes people's reasons and deliberations are causally efficacious, in some situations they do not even know what to say.[9] Still, unlike the case of nausea, in the moral case it always makes sense to ask what grounds you have or what criteria you use. And it will not do to respond, "I just don't like that institution," or, "I just don't like that action." Your imagined interlocutor already understands that you do not like them. But your not liking them does not entail that the action is wrong and the institution is exploitative. If your personal dislike is all there is to it, could you still be said to be assessing them morally or from a moral point of view?

The moral background contains resources for people and organizations to address these demands for reasons or grounding. More specifically, it contains resources to address two distinct questions: (a) What makes things moral and immoral? and (b) What reason do you have to do what is moral and, more generally, to be moral at all? Thus, the background provides people and organizations with understandings and accounts they can invoke if they need to—the need here might be due to demands from social interaction or conversation, the legal system, education, introspection, or something else. Regarding (a), they specify in virtue of what a wrong action is wrong, an unjust institution is unjust, a despicable person despicable, and so on. For instance, what property do all wrong actions have that makes them wrong actions—e.g., causing more pain than pleasure, being at odds with one of the 613 *mitzvot*, being at odds with the will of one's husband, being at odds with tradition? Regarding (b), they specify in virtue of what morality and moral things are preferable to, or worth choosing over, immorality and immoral things. And, hence, why you ought to or have reason to choose them.

Take a practice that seems to Jones to be discriminatory, such as employment decisions based on racial stereotypes. She may want to get her friend, family,

8 Charles Taylor. 1989. *Sources of the Self: The Making of the Modern Identity*. Cambridge, MA: Harvard University Press, p. 6.

9 Jonathan Haidt. 2001. "The Emotional Dog and Its Rational Tail: A Social Intuitionist Approach to Moral Judgment." *Psychological Review* 108(4):814–34.

community, or country to change that practice. In such a situation, Jones needs to be able to say why she finds that practice to be discriminatory, and why discriminatory practices are bad and ought to be changed. So, this dimension of the moral background provides Jones with grounds or reasons for her first-order normative views, action proposals, and policy recommendations. Alternatively, you may say that it provides justifications for her first-order normative views. In this context, unlike in ordinary English and in moral psychology, the word "justification" has no pejorative connotations. It does not mean a false story a person retrospectively makes up as an excuse, or something along these lines. It means the reasons that, in many social situations, people and organizations must give to other people, organizations, and even themselves. As Boltanski and Thévenot have argued, these justifications have consequential effects; an account of social life should not neglect them.[10]

What is the content of these understandings and accounts the moral background provides Jones with? This is an empirical question: there are no a priori substantive constraints. For instance, regarding (a), "There are certain things that just *are* morally wrong, period: here's a list of them (and discrimination is one of them)," is just as legitimate as, "An action is wrong if and only if it diminishes my niece's pleasure or increases my niece's pain (and discrimination does both)." Regarding (b), "Do what is moral because it pays (and not discriminating pays)," is just as legitimate as, "Do what is moral because God commands it (and He commands us not to discriminate)." In terms of form, these accounts can be as short as one short sentence, or a couple of short sentences. Or they can be a story or parable, whose lesson is not a formal principle. Or they can be full-fledged, elaborate normative theories, along with a clear-cut litmus test that tells morality from immorality. For instance, if you traveled to eighteenth-century Königsberg to ask Kant what is wrong with lying to your partner about an important matter, he would probably answer by deploying a set of sophisticated and internally consistent arguments. Yet, while many people agree that it is wrong to lie to their partner about an important matter, few people will give the elaborate accounts that a professional philosopher would as to why that is wrong. In fact, as mentioned previously, not everyone can even produce a reasonably coherent account.

The moral debates friends have in cafés over coffee and in bars over beer are much unlike the moral debates philosophers have in seminar rooms over water (or wine if they are French). The former debates deal with specific, applied issues, prompted by practical concerns, and rarely address abstract issues or utilize fancy words (German or otherwise). So, my first point is to deny that a philosophical normative theory, say hedonistic utilitarianism or Kantian deontology, is the prototype of these accounts. An account may be a philosophical or theological theory, but it need not. My second point is to draw attention to a group that is of special interest here—neither philosophers nor ordinary folks. In some societies there are people and organizations that engage in practical ethics work.

---

10 Luc Boltanski and Laurent Thévenot. 1991. *De la justification: les economies de la grandeur.* Paris: Gallimard; Boltanski and Chiapello, *Le nouvel esprit du capitalisme.*

In contemporary Western societies, for example, they include politicians, policy makers, and some parts of the state, religious organizations and leaders, newspaper editorialists, teachers, and business ethicists. Unlike ordinary folks, practical ethicists are compelled to produce persuasive moral arguments beyond a mere statement of what is wrong or what should be done. This is the case in both senses of the verb "to produce": to create and to exhibit. Even when they are not literally compelled to, they are encouraged and incentivized to do so by the nature of their job. And sometimes it is literally true that there is compulsion, e.g., due to bureaucratic and organizational requirements for a policy or course of action to be implemented. In turn, practical ethicists' moral arguments rely, explicitly or implicitly, on accounts about (a) and (b).

My last point is that people and organizations do not invent these accounts privately, from scratch. Indeed, they would not be able to do that at all. Rather, they draw on a common cultural store of accounts. To be sure, substantively speaking, there is no agreement about the validity of these accounts. But there is an underlying agreement as to what counts as grounding for a normative view, as opposed to an irrelevant consideration, an answer to a different question, or a bunch of nonsense.

In sum, a scientist of morality who wishes to investigate the first dimension of the moral background should ask: What understandings and accounts about (a) and (b) underlie people's and organizations' first-order morality? What accounts do they invoke and mobilize when they need to? How are these distributed across individuals, groups, and situations?[11]

(2) CONCEPTUAL REPERTOIRES

Conceptual repertoires are the set of concepts that are available to any given group or society, in a given time and place. This second dimension of the moral background raises the questions of how, when, where, how often, by whom, and for what purpose each of the actually existing concepts is used. For example, consider first a few concepts that have nothing to do with morality. In some societies you find a concept of furniture, of precious metals, of strolling, of hipness, and of gifted children. In some other societies there is nothing like that. In turn, this is partly due to a well-known sociological fact: societies differ in how things are

---

11 This first dimension of the background is consonant with Davenport's approach in *Friends of the Unrighteous Mammon*. Davenport argues that "the three main 'Christian' responses to the development of market capitalism fell along the lines of the three main ethical traditions of Western philosophy: utilitarianism, deontology, and virtue ethics. What antebellum Christians thought about market capitalism depended a great deal on which of these three traditions they inhabited; and which of these traditions they inhabited depended largely on their self-appointed social '*characters*'" (p. 11). Drawing on Taylor (including the idea of "'frameworks,' 'horizons,' 'traditional boundaries,' or even 'background pictures'" [p. 14]) and MacIntyre (from whom it borrows the word "*character*"), the book "explores the 'richer background languages' that informed antebellum Christians as they responded in print to developing market capitalism" (p. 15). Stewart Davenport. 2008. *Friends of the Unrighteous Mammon: Northern Christians and Market Capitalism, 1815–1860*. Chicago: University of Chicago Press.

classified and grouped, what things are generally perceived and noticed and what things are generally missed, how things are perceived and noticed, and the institutions that rubberstamp systems of perception and classification.[12] Consider now some moral concepts. Some societies have a concept of nobleness, such that certain courses of action are noble, and thus are fitting of a noble person. Some others do not. Some societies have a concept of integrity, of piety, of exploitation, of materialism, of humanness, and of objectification. Some others do not have anything like that. My point is not that in one society slavery is widely viewed as an exploitative institution, while in another society it is not. Rather, my point is that both societies have a concept of exploitation, even if they do not apply it in the same way and to the same things. By contrast, in a third society there might not exist such a thing as a concept of exploitation at all.

To capture this empirical phenomenon I speak of conceptual repertoires, roughly in the same sense that Lamont, Lamont and Thévenot, and Swidler speak of cultural repertoires.[13] It is uncontroversial that repertoires of moral concepts vary across time and place. For instance, in contemporary Western societies we have concepts of exploitation, objectification, materialism, fanaticism, barbarism, integrity, decency, moderation, and humanness. What do they do for us? We have radio shows, newspaper editorials, café conversations, parliamentary debates, laws, and court cases that are about the humane treatment of non-human animals, the exploitation of workers, and the objectification of women. Fanaticism and intolerance are two moral problems contemporary Western societies are struggling with, legally, politically, and culturally. And so on. None of this would be possible in a society or group that did not have concepts of humanness, exploitation, objectification, fanaticism, and intolerance. The repertoire of concepts, a moral background property, enables and constrains first-order morality. In this sense, it is comparable to a restaurant menu, which enables you to order dish X, but prevents you from ordering dish Y. What you order is up to you, but what is listed on the menu is not.

Social actors have access to a repertoire of moral concepts. This repertoire enables and constrains their thought and speech, their laws and institutions, and, importantly, the actions they may undertake. This might sound counterintuitive. Is not moral action a concrete, tangible occurrence in the physical world, like somebody actually doing something? How can it be dependent on conceptual repertoires? There are two main reasons. First, a body, bodies, or body parts moving in certain ways do not suffice to individuate actions. Bodily movements are

---

12   Geoffrey C. Bowker and Susan Leigh Star. 1999. *Sorting Things Out: Classification and its Consequences.* Cambridge, MA: MIT Press; Mary Douglas. 1966. *Purity and Danger: An Analysis of Concepts of Pollution and Taboo.* London: Routledge & K. Paul; Émile Durkheim and Marcel Mauss. 1903. "De quelques formes primitives de classification." *L'Année sociologique* 6:1–72.

13   Lamont, *Money, Morals, and Manners*; Michèle Lamont and Laurent Thévenot, eds. 2000. *Rethinking Comparative Culture Sociology: Repertoires of Evaluation in France and the United States.* Cambridge, UK: Cambridge University Press; Ann Swidler. 2001. *Talk of Love: How Culture Matters.* Chicago: University of Chicago Press.

physical events that can be described by equations of motion and can be captured by video cameras. However, they cannot by themselves elucidate what the agent is doing. What an agent is doing is not a concept-independent question, nor is it independent from her mental states.[14] This argument is not limited to moral action: all actions depend on what there is to do. These are the "doables" that Velleman, drawing on Sacks, Schegloff, and Schutz, has recently discussed: "An agent cannot invent an entire ontology of actions from scratch; for the most part, he must choose from a socially provided repertoire of action concepts. Just as he sees things of kinds that he has been taught can be seen, so he does things of kinds that he has been taught can be done."[15] Comparably, Taylor notes that there is a "'repertory' of collective actions at the disposal of a given group of society"; "the common actions that they know how to undertake, all the way from the general election . . . to knowing how to strike up a polite but uninvolved conversation."[16] Yet, my argument is not just about what people know how to undertake, but what they are conceptually able to undertake.

Second, moral actions depend on what there is to do that will count as a *moral* action, and hence depend on a particular concept of the moral. Besides the question of what an agent is doing, there is the question of whether what she is doing can be correctly described as a moral thing. Here moral is not the opposite of immoral but of non-moral: obviously, not all actions fall within the province of morality, just like not all issues, judgments, and views do. They may have to do with neighboring provinces, such as etiquette, prudence, convention, religion, politics, or the law, but not with morality. To tell the difference, you need second-order criteria about the boundary between the moral and the non-moral. And these criteria are not established individually but socially.

It is an important fact about people's moral lives that they are shaped in these ways by conceptual repertoires. It is an important fact about conceptual repertoires that there are two kinds of moral concepts: thin and thick.[17] Thin moral concepts include right and wrong, good and bad, appropriate and inappropriate, permissible and impermissible, and ought and ought not. Thick moral concepts include dignity, decency, integrity, piety, responsibility, tolerance, moderation, fanaticism, extremism, despotism, chauvinism, rudeness, uptightness, misery, exploitation, oppression, materialism, humanness, hospitality, courage, cruelty, chastity, perversion, obscenity, lewdness, civility, clemency, and friendship. One key difference between thin and thick moral concepts is this. You can apply a

---

14   G.E.M. Anscombe. [1963] 2000. *Intention.* 2nd ed. Cambridge, MA: Harvard University Press; Clifford Geertz. 1973. "Thick Description: Toward an Interpretive Theory of Culture." Pp. 3–30 in *The Interpretation of Cultures.* New York: Basic Books.

15   J. David Velleman. 2013. "Doables." *Philosophical Explorations* 16(3):1–16.

16   Charles Taylor. 2004. *Modern Social Imaginaries.* Duke and London: Duke University Press, p. 25; Charles Taylor. 2007. *A Secular Age.* Cambridge and London: Belknap Press of Harvard University Press, p. 173.

17   Bernard Williams. 1985. *Ethics and the Limits of Philosophy.* Cambridge, MA: Harvard University Press. Cf. Gabriel Abend. 2011. "Thick Concepts and the Moral Brain." *European Journal of Sociology* 52(1):143–72.

thin concept to anything you wish. Suppose someone says that torturing babies is permissible, or that Pinochet was a good man. She may be mistaken morally speaking, but she has not made any conceptual or semantic mistake. This is because statements such as, "X is wrong" and "Y is impermissible," do not convey any further information about X and Y—aside from their being said to be wrong and impermissible.

By contrast, the application of thick concepts is constrained by what the world is like. Statements such as, "A is a cruel act" and "B is a materialistic act," do tell you something about A and B, in addition to their negative evaluation. Roughly, B must have something to do with material goods and possessions, something like placing too much importance and worrying too much about money and making money, in detriment of other pursuits and concerns. If B had nothing to do with these issues, but you still said, "B is a materialistic act," then you would not understand the meaning of the English word "materialistic." To be sure, two individuals may disagree as to whether B is a materialistic act, not so much, or not at all. More generally, two individuals may disagree as to the criteria for the application of the concept of materialism—e.g., how much importance and worrying is too much, or where to draw the line between reasonable financial security and materialism. Yet, despite these disagreements, both individuals must be talking about the same set of issues, which the word "materialistic" points toward. Hence, "cruel" and "materialistic" are unlike "wrong" and "impermissible," which do not limit in any way what they can refer or apply to.

Last, pace Plato, concepts are not immutable or eternal: they come into being, change over time, and sometimes disappear. Thick moral concepts make this point especially obvious. Then, the empirical study of the conceptual repertoire comprises the history of moral concepts. It investigates how present-day repertoires have come about historically and what their genealogical lineages are. The science of morality is in this regard in good company: it partakes in the time-honored project of conceptual genealogists, from Nietzsche, Canguilhem, and Foucault to Hacking, Davidson, Somers, and Koselleck and the Begriffsgeschichte group.[18]

In sum, the second dimension of the moral background raises three empirical questions for the science of morality: what concepts are on the menu; which ones are ordered most often, when, and by whom; and how the conceptual menu got historically constituted.

---

18   Arnold I. Davidson. 2001. The Emergence of Sexuality: Historical Epistemology and the Formation of Concepts. Cambridge, MA: Harvard University Press; Ian Hacking. 1995. Rewriting the Soul: Multiple Personality and the Sciences of Memory. Princeton: Princeton University Press; Ian Hacking. 2002. Historical Ontology. Cambridge, MA: Harvard University Press; Reinhart Koselleck. 2002. The Practice of Conceptual History. Translated by Todd Samuel Presner and others. Stanford: Stanford University Press; Margaret R. Somers. 1995. "What's Political or Cultural about Political Culture and the Public Sphere? Toward an Historical Sociology of Concept Formation." Sociological Theory 13(2):113–44. Cf. Brian Epstein. 2010. "History and the Critique of Social Concepts." Philosophy of the Social Sciences 40(1):3–29.

(3) OBJECT OF EVALUATION

Moral evaluations are a first-order morality phenomenon. Like any kind of evaluation, they must be made by someone or something. And they must be of or about someone or something.[19] More specifically, they must be of or about something whose nature makes it capable of being evaluated from a moral point of view. It is a common feature of moral life that things are evaluated as morally good, wrong, admirable, indecent, cruel, or humane. Yet, how is it established which things can and which things cannot be evaluated in this way? Take tigers and toddlers.[20] A tiger may devour your friend; your baby may shatter your friend's precious vase. They caused harm. But are they morally responsible? Can they be evaluated morally? Can you evaluate morally the Jim Crow laws, the institution of slavery, American business, the rain, a sleepwalker, a psychopath, a robot, and God or the gods? This problem reaches all the way down to a widespread intuition: "the person" seems the quintessential object of moral evaluation and the quintessential source of moral agency, but it is not always clear what a person is.[21] Further, "the person" means a "normal" person, but the distinction between the mentally sane and the mentally ill is even less clear.

Whatever one's intuitions about these issues are, the bottom line is that societies and groups may differ in the objects that are capable of being morally evaluated. This is the third dimension of the moral background, which comprises two distinct empirical questions. Given a society or group: first, what objects are capable and incapable of being morally evaluated; second, among the objects that are capable of being morally evaluated, which ones are evaluated more often, when, where, by whom, and for what purpose. To take an example my historical narrative will explore, moral evaluations may be mostly about individual action or decision. Or they may be about a person's character or life as a whole. Or they may not be about properties of individuals, but about institutions, situations, or states of affairs. What is more, if evaluations are mostly about actions and decisions, what kind of actions and decisions are they mostly about? And what about them? What aspect of an action or decision is most commonly evaluated?

In this regard, the oversights of current moral psychology are instructive, because its choice of objects of evaluation arguably reflects larger trends in the society in which it operates. In their research moral psychologists have focused

---

19   Cf. Michèle Lamont. 2012. "Toward a Comparative Sociology of Valuation and Evaluation." *Annual Review of Sociology* 38:201–21.

20   Cf. Charles Tilly. 2008. *Credit and Blame*. Princeton: Princeton University Press, p. 12.

21   For example, Nagel's paper about brain bisection concludes that "it is possible that the ordinary, simple idea of a single person will come to seem quaint some day, when the complexities of the human control system become clearer and we become less certain that there is anything very important that we are *one* of." Thomas Nagel. 1971. "Brain Bisection and the Unity of Consciousness." *Synthese* 22:396–413, p. 411. See also Michael Carrithers, Steven Collins, and Steven Lukes, eds. 1985. *The Category of the Person: Anthropology, Philosophy, History*. Cambridge: Cambridge University Press; Marcel Mauss. 1938. "Une catégorie de l'esprit humain: la notion de personne, celle de 'moi'." *Journal of the Royal Anthropological Institute* 68:263–81.

on one kind of object of inquiry: experimental subjects' moral judgments about the rightness, appropriateness, or permissibility of an imagined person's course of action. What is it right for this person to do? What morally ought she to do? Consider this oft-cited story, devised by Lawrence Kohlberg:

> In Europe, a woman was near death from a very bad disease, a special kind of cancer. There was one drug that the doctors thought might save her. It was a form of radium that a druggist in the same town had recently discovered. The drug was expensive to make, but the druggist was charging ten times what the drug cost him to make. He paid $200 for the radium and charged $2,000 for a small dose of the drug. The sick woman's husband, Heinz, went to everyone he knew to borrow the money and tried every legal means, but he could only get together about $1,000 which was half of what it cost. He told the druggist that his wife was dying, and asked him to sell it cheaper or let him pay later. But the druggist said, "No, I discovered the drug and I'm going to make money from it."[22]

At this point, Kohlberg and many experimental psychologists have asked their subjects: "Should Heinz steal the drug?" "*Is it actually right or wrong for him to steal the drug?*" or "Does Heinz have a duty or obligation to steal the drug?" These questions are hard because of the conflict between two strong moral pulls—which is what makes a moral dilemma a dilemma. Yet, what I wish to stress is what they are about. They are questions about a person's action, and, more specifically, a particular decision about how to act. This is the object of moral evaluation in this dilemma and in moral dilemmas in general. The story leads to a momentous point in time, at which a person must make a choice and take one or another course of action: either shove a fat man onto the train tracks to save the lives of five workers or stay put,[23] either join the *Forces françaises libres* in England or stay at home to look after one's ailing mother,[24] either tell the truth or lie to a murderer about the whereabouts of his intended victim.[25]

These choices about action are one kind of thing that can be morally evaluated in Western societies today, from both the first-person and the third-person perspectives: my action and somebody else's. Perhaps contemporary Westerners evaluate it frequently. Perhaps they see it as a prototypical moral problem (though perhaps this is so in psychology labs and philosophy lectures more than in ordinary people's lives[26]). However, this is neither the only kind of thing that can be

22   Lawrence Kohlberg and Carol Gilligan. 1971. "The Adolescent as a Philosopher: The Discovery of the Self in a Postconventional World." *Daedalus* 100(4):1051–86, pp. 1072–73.

23   Philippa Foot. 1967. "The Problem of Abortion and the Doctrine of Double Effect." *Oxford Review* 5:5–15.

24   Jean Paul Sartre. [1946] 1996. *L'existentialisme est un humanisme.* Paris: Gallimard, p. 41.

25   Immanuel Kant. [1797] 1949. "On a Supposed Right to Lie from Altruistic Motives." Pp. 346–50 in *Critique of Practical Reason and Other Writings in Moral Philosophy.* Translated and edited by Lewis White Beck. Chicago: University of Chicago Press.

26   Gabriel Abend. 2013. "What the Science of Morality Doesn't Say about Morality." *Philosophy of the Social Sciences* 43(2):157–200.

morally evaluated, nor the only kind of thing that is worthwhile to morally evaluate. In some societies the most frequent and important moral questions may not be about what a person should do in a particular situation. Rather, they may be about what ends or purposes she should have, what kind of person she should be, or what kind of life she should lead.[27] For example, "How ought I live?" or "What should my life be like?" was the fundamental ethical question in some ancient societies. As Annas notes, "[t]his is not taken to be in origin a philosopher's question; it is a question which an ordinary person will at some point put to herself."[28] Mayo makes a similar observation in his description of Plato's and Aristotle's ethics:

> Justice, for Plato, though it is closely connected with acting according to law, does not *mean* acting according to law: it is a quality of character and a just action is one such as a just man would do. Telling the truth, for Aristotle, is not, as it was for Kant, fulfilling an obligation; again it is a quality of character, or, rather, a whole range of qualities of character, some of which may actually be defects, such as tactlessness, boastfulness, and so on—a point which can be brought out, in terms of principles, only with the greatest complexity and artificiality, but quite simply and naturally in terms of character. [...] The basic moral question, for Aristotle, is not, What shall I do but, What shall I be?[29]

To use Mayo's terms, Plato and Aristotle represent the "ethics of being," whereas most modern moral philosophy, consequentialism and deontology alike, represent the "ethics of doing."[30] Whether or not Plato, Aristotle, and other Greek scholars actually reflect prevalent patterns in society is an empirical question. In either case, the idea is that in some societies and groups, people might not see reflection and discussion about the ethics of doing as a very useful, enlightening, or interesting exercise. Nor would they be interested in trying to come up with general moral principles under which individual action cases can be subsumed. Much more fruitful is to look at and reflect on lives as wholes, these people might say. This is what their newspapers write about, radio and TV shows talk about, people find worthy of their time, funding agencies find worthy of their money,

27 Douglas V. Porpora. 2001. *Landscapes of the Soul*. New York: Oxford University Press, pp. 8–10, 72–73, and *passim*.

28 Julia Annas. 1993. *The Morality of Happiness*. New York: Oxford University Press, p. 27. Annas continues: "Many ordinary people may of course be too unreflective, or too satisfied with convention, or just too busy, to pose the question. But it is assumed that people of average intellect with a modicum of leisure will at some point reflect on their lives and ask whether they are as they should be."

29 Bernard Mayo. 1958. *Ethics and the Moral Life*. London: Macmillan; New York: St. Martin's Press, pp. 209–10. Cf. Victor Brochard. 1901. "La morale ancienne et la morale moderne." *Revue philosophique* 36:1–12; Gregory Fernando Pappas. 1997. "To Be or To Do: John Dewey and the Great Divide in Ethics." *History of Philosophy Quarterly* 14(4):447–72.

30 Mayo (p. 213) adds that "according to the philosophy of moral character, there is another way of answering the fundamental question 'What ought I to do?' Instead of quoting a rule, we quote a quality of character, a virtue: we say 'Be brave,' or 'Be patient' or 'Be lenient.' We may even say 'Be a man': if I am in doubt, say, whether to take a risk, and someone says 'Be a man,' meaning a morally sound man, in this case a man of sufficient courage. (Compare the very different ideal invoked in 'Be a gentleman.' I shall not discuss whether this is a *moral* ideal.)"

and legislators and judges appeal to in support of their arguments and decisions. Ought you to strive to be a loving and caring person, a frugal and industrious one, a respectful and obedient one, or a pious and god-fearing one? What is the moral standing of the life of the army general who risks his life for his nation? How about the life of the hedonist, the aesthete, or the ascetic? What virtues ought you to cultivate in you and your children?

The object of evaluation is then a background dimension or property that underlies first-order morality. It works as a constraint by limiting what moral evaluations can be about. This is the case in two ways. First, whether a moral evaluation is about a person, state of affairs, organization, group, non-human animal, another sort of entity, or nobody in particular (e.g., via a passive construction or an impersonal pronoun). Second, where applicable, what about these things can and should be morally evaluated. For instance, whether what they are, their being, or what they do or have done, their doing.

This brings us back to moral psychologists' current work. I said that their investigations are about one possible object of evaluation. But they do not seem to have realized that there are many other possibilities, and that their choice is not a neutral one. Indeed, their choice may itself be shaped by their own moral background. Arguably, the background of these scholars in North America and Europe privileges the rightness and permissibility of individuals' actions as an object of moral evaluation. That is what morality is about. In terms of my earlier metaphor, on this restaurant's menu this is the most conspicuous dish. It is today's special, except that it is today's special every day. I argue, then, that the science of morality can benefit from the moral background reflexively as well. First, it should realize that its methodological choices might themselves be affected by an enabling and constraining moral background level. Second, it should empirically investigate how moral backgrounds vary, comparatively and historically, and how these variations affect first-order variations—including scientists of morality's own understandings about what morality is and encompasses, and what counts and does not count as a moral object.

(4) METHOD AND ARGUMENT

Science is essentially characterized by its method, the scientific method: the way in which scientists should go about addressing their research problems and questions. Certain procedures ought to be followed, such as meticulous and systematic observation. Certain procedures ought not to be followed, such as looking for witchcraft substance in the intestines of deceased individuals. Not all pieces of information, data sources, and considerations are relevant in science. They must be the right kind of thing, and they must have been obtained in the right kind of way.[31] Scientific arguments, too, must abide by specific rules, such as the law of

---

31   On "evidential cultures," see H. M. Collins. 1998. "The Meaning of Data: Open and Closed Evidential Cultures in the Search for Gravitational Waves." *American Journal of Sociology* 104(2):293–338; H. M. Collins. 2004. *Gravity's Shadow: The Search for Gravitational Waves.* Chicago: University of Chicago Press.

identity and the law of the excluded middle. Within the class of formally valid scientific arguments, there are more and less plausible ones, and more and less forceful ones. Not all forms of argument and not all argumentative tools are acceptable. And an army of vigilant methodologists makes sure that violators do not get away with it. If push comes to shove, they will have to be excommunicated, since they are not doing science anymore. This is one boundary that demarcates science from non-science.[32]

Likewise, a society, social group, or organizational field may have a characteristic way of going about addressing moral questions and making moral arguments. As Jonsen and Toulmin might say, moral reasoning has a history.[33] What moral method and evidence may be used—e.g., empirical and scientific, introspective, or spiritual and religious? What formal features do plausible moral arguments have—e.g., analogical or deductive? What is a relevant piece of evidence in a moral argument (as opposed to a relevant piece of evidence in, say, a historical or culinary argument)? "Characteristic ways" does not mean absolute consensus or perfect convergence in methodological, argumentative, and evidentiary practices. There are outliers and objectors. Moral disagreements can turn into meta-disagreements about moral method, argument, or evidence. Yet, you may still be able to identify a society's or group's core agreements or central tendencies regarding moral method and argument: what is clearly beside the point and irrelevant, what is literally laughable or even insane, and what clearly does not work (as opposed to what may or may not work).

Moral method and argument is a property of the background, not a property of first-order morality. Normative claims, arguments, practices, institutions, and behaviors do not state what their own method is. They just use it or are based on it. Few people are aware of the kinds of considerations or facts they dismiss as morally irrelevant or laughable, or how they generally go about doing so. They just go ahead and dismiss them as morally irrelevant or laughable on a case-by-case basis. Few organizations could articulate what kind of moral arguments and evidence ought to be produced to give sufficient support for institutional innovations. They just go ahead and argue for one institutional innovation at a time.[34] Yet, the usage of these methodological and argumentative tools and strategies is

---

32 Thomas F. Gieryn. 1983. "Boundary-Work and the Demarcation of Science from Non-Science: Strains and Interests in Professional Ideologies of Scientists." *American Sociological Review* 48:781–95; Thomas F. Gieryn. 1999. *Cultural Boundaries of Science: Credibility on the Line.* Chicago: University of Chicago Press; Michèle Lamont and Virág Molnár. 2002. "The Study of Boundaries in the Social Sciences." *Annual Review of Sociology* 28:167–95.

33 Albert R. Jonsen and Stephen Toulmin. 1988. *The Abuse of Casuistry: A History of Moral Reasoning.* Berkeley and Los Angeles: University of California Press. See also John H. Evans. 2002. *Playing God? Human Genetic Engineering and the Rationalization of Public Bioethical Debate.* Chicago: University of Chicago Press.

34 This is interestingly unlike the law, because procedural or adjective law and the law of evidence ascertain these conditions in formal and general terms. It is interestingly unlike science, whose methodological rules are formally laid out as well. Still, the methodological and scientific levels are analytically distinct; so are substance and procedure in the law. This is comparable to the distinction between morality and the moral background, except that moral background rules are rarely codified.

socially patterned. And these patterns emerge most clearly when we make comparisons across societies, groups, organizational fields, and historical periods.

Let me illustrate this idea with a thought experiment. Imagine two remote islands of the South Pacific—call them "Paraguay" and "Uruguay." In Paraguay, the moral arguments that work best are analogical or contain key analogies. Analogies seem to carry a special weight in moral contexts. For example: (i) Much like you cannot choose your personality, you cannot choose your sexual orientation; (ii) You can no more win a war than you can win an earthquake; (iii) "You can no more hear the cries of an animal as mere noise than you can the words of a person;"[35] or (iv) "[O]ne can no more obtain a correct idea of a city or nation from its newspapers, than one can get a correct idea of a man from two or three pimples on his face or a half dozen warts on his hand" in the context of an argument about discrimination on the basis of national origin.[36] By contrast, in Uruguay analogies rarely carry the day in moral contexts. In fact, they are rarely used to begin with. For analogies strike Uruguayans as legerdemains or attempts to change the subject. It is true that you cannot get a correct idea of a man from two or three pimples on his face. But how does this help establish that you cannot get a correct idea of a nation from its newspapers? The belief that men:pimples is analogous in the relevant respects to nations:newspapers is on as secure bases as the belief that you cannot get a correct idea of a nation from its newspapers. Further, the choice of men:pimples is arbitrary. What makes *that* the chosen analogy rather than any other? Why should you be permitted to cherry-pick the one you please?

In Uruguay, the moral arguments that work best are deductive, or arguments that have a prominent deductive component. Their major premise establishes a general moral principle, and their minor premise establishes that the empirical conditions are such that the general moral principle does apply. Differently put, the minor premise establishes that the situation, act, or practice under consideration does belong to the class or category of situations, acts, or practices to which the major premise refers. For example, Uruguayans believe that one should always welcome foreigners and accept them as fellows, as long as they intend to contribute to the country's overall welfare and be responsible members of the community. Argentine immigrants do intend to contribute to Uruguay's welfare, and have indeed been responsible members of the communities in which they live. Therefore, Uruguay should welcome Argentines, treat them as equals, and not discriminate against them. They deserve the same opportunities and benefits native Uruguayans have. This conclusion is logically entailed by the premises. Yet, much like Uruguayans are not persuaded by Paraguayans' analogies, Paraguayans are not persuaded by Uruguayans' deductions. From a Paraguayan perspective, Uruguayans' fixation on deductive logic seems out of place in moral matters. Because real-life moral situations are so complex and involve so many factors, deductive logic and general principles will not deliver the goods. Rather than

35 Christine Korsgaard. 1996. *The Sources of Normativity*. Cambridge; New York: Cambridge University Press, p. 153.
36 *The Chautauquan*, December 13, 1913, p. 290.

algorithms, one needs judgment, discretion, and discernment. Bending the rules and using rules of thumb are unavoidable.

In addition to particular kinds of arguments, moral backgrounds also privilege particular kinds of evidence. For example, Paraguayans often invoke their intuitions as evidence to support their moral claims. They claim that a course of action or state of affairs is morally questionable, because it conflicts with their intuition or "gut feeling," as they are more likely to say in their broken English. Thus, intuitions are accepted as valid evidence. Never does one hear a response such as, "Well, that's just your intuition, you haven't even thought much about it, so it's totally irrelevant," or, "What in the world have your gut feelings to do with it?"

However, this is just how Uruguayans feel about the role of intuitions as evidence for or against moral arguments. That something relevant might be gained by looking inside oneself seems to them preposterous. So does the idea that a moral claim or principle should be consistent with people's intuitions: people may be mistaken, or deluded by unconscious, morally irrelevant biases. Instead, Uruguayans' moral arguments tend to make use of scientific evidence. They make use of it in various ways. Obviously, scientific evidence can support the non-moral premises of their moral arguments—e.g., the most up-to-date sociology on the effects of educational policies on learning in disadvantaged neighborhoods, and the most up-to-date psychology on the factors that increase and decrease stress and anxiety. More interestingly, Uruguayans use scientific evidence to support their moral conclusions themselves.[37] For example, some of them argue for more social inequality and against public policies that mitigate it, because ethologists have shown that all animal species are highly unequal.

While this is only a thought experiment, its point is to invite social scientists to empirically investigate the kinds of moral evidence that are acceptable and forceful in actual societies and groups (including actual Paraguay and Uruguay). These criteria of acceptability and forcefulness are second-order moral background elements.[38]

(5) METAETHICAL OBJECTIVITY

Scientific work normally assumes that it can attain objectivity and truth. While there might not be much talk about epistemology in their laboratories, scientists take it for granted that their theories and conclusions are not determined by their preferences and opinions. Rather, they are determined by what the world is like. How about morality? Do ordinary moral actors, individuals and organizations,

---

37 The expression "their moral conclusions themselves" is problematic. Roughly, it could be objected that in the following examples scientific evidence gives support to the factual premises, but the moral or value component of the argument comes from elsewhere. How to respond to this objection depends on what the distinction between facts and values is thought to amount to.

38 Besides intuitions and scientific findings, there are many other kinds of evidence that moral arguments may draw on: stories and narratives, fictional or not (parables, children's stories, popular myths, folkloric tales, scholarly history, novels, and movies); people's own senses, experiences, and feelings (their own, as opposed to someone else's story or someone else's scientific finding); and so on.

assume that first-order morality can attain objectivity or truth? Roughly speaking, the empirical question here is whether morality is taken to be: a matter of objective fact; or a matter of subjective opinion, preference, or taste; or something else. Then, the ensuing empirical questions are by whom, where, and when this is taken to be so. For me to be able to speak less roughly about this issue, though, I need to introduce four technical terms: "metaethical," "realism," "skepticism," and "relativism."

Moral philosophy can be classified into three areas: applied ethics, normative ethics, and metaethics. Applied ethics analyzes concrete problems from a moral point of view: euthanasia, abortion, or the estate tax. Normative ethics analyzes more general views about what kinds of actions ought not to be done, what kinds of institutional arrangements are just, and what kinds of lives are worth living. Metaethics analyzes the nature of morality and moral language. One influential metaethical view is moral realism. In Brink's words, it "asserts the existence of moral facts and true moral propositions." Moreover, it is "committed to moral facts and truths that are *objective* in some way."[39] Moral realists argue that moral questions have correct and mistaken answers, just like the questions, "Who won the Battle of Hastings? and "Is the moon made of blue cheese or volcanic rock?" Take the moral question, "Is it wrong to torture a child for the fun of it?" Moral realists argue that there is a fact of the matter about it. The fact of the matter is, presumably, that it *is* wrong to torture a child for the fun of it. Anyone who disagrees with this answer is in error.

Opponents of realism are many. Here the philosophical jargon gets quite messy and quite strange quite fast: there are many kinds of moral subjectivism, skepticism, relativism, non-cognitivism, emotivism, expressivism, prescriptivism, quasi-realism, quasi-quasi-realism, and anti-realism. Yet, for present purposes I am content with singling out two families of views, without worrying about their philosophical genealogy or metaethicists' preferred terminology. First, there is the view that answers to moral questions cannot be correct or mistaken at all; moral claims are not capable of truth or falsehood. I refer to this view as "moral skepticism." Consider the sentences, "Please shut the door," "Hurrah to Athletic Bilbao!" "The Pixies are better than Joy Division," or "Apples are yummier than oranges." These sentences do not seem to be truth-apt. In the former two, it does not even make sense to ask whether they are true or false, correct or mistaken. For they are, respectively, a request and an expression of support for a Basque soccer team (objectively good and deserving of support though that team is). In the latter two, you may say that their actual meaning is, respectively, "I like The Pixies better than Joy Division," and "I like apples better than oranges." These *are* truth-apt propositions. However, they are not about music and fruits, but about me—about my preferences in music and fruits. By contrast, their original formulations cannot be true or false (though most music and food critics would disagree). According to this argument, the same is true of moral claims, such as "It is wrong to torture children," or "Pinochet was a wicked man." They do not try to

39 David Brink. 1989. *Moral Realism and the Foundations of Ethics*. Cambridge; New York: Cambridge University Press, p. 14.

get at facts about the world. Rather, they are something like personal preferences or expressions of approval or disapproval. They could be restated as, "I do not like what Pinochet did," and "I do not like that children be tortured." Or else, as "Boo to Pinochet!" and "Boo to torturing children!"

Second, there is the view that answers to moral questions cannot be correct or mistaken *tout court*, but that they can be correct or mistaken relative to something. In particular, they can be true or false *for* one particular group, community, society, culture, and even person, yet not true for others. I refer to this view as "moral relativism." For example, you might say that "It is wrong to torture a child for the fun of it" is true for us, or true in the United States today. But it might not be true for another group of people, whose way of life is entirely different from ours. Moral relativism thus claims that moral claims are truth-apt in one particular way. This is not how the concept of truth is normally used with regard to factual matters, though. According to this more common usage, that a proposition is true necessarily entails its being true for everyone. Even more, the word "true" is sometimes said to mean true for everyone. Moral relativism denies that there is anything wrong with its usage of the word "true" to mean true for me only, or for you guys, or for the Azande, rather than for everyone.[40]

Moral realism, skepticism, and relativism are philosophers' metaethical views. In this book I turn this philosophical controversy into a tool for empirical research. Consider the following ordinary social phenomena: a state agency's new policy and its rationale for it, a criminal case and the jury's decision, the day-to-day practices of a non-profit environmental organization, the community service of a church, a minister's sermons and teachings, a business association's code of ethics, or a group of friends' conversation about the permissibility of abortion or the exploitation of Mexican workers in the United States. The empirical research question I propose about these phenomena is what metaethical objectivity assumptions they are underlain by. Almost certainly, the actors themselves will not spontaneously talk about them, just like most scientists do not spontaneously talk about epistemology. Nor will they be familiar with the philosophical jargon with which their assumptions can be described. Yet, empirical research can still unearth what they are.

For example, the informal routines and the formal rules and structures of complex organizations may have metaethical assumptions built into them. In particular, you may hypothesize that many organizations, agencies, and bureaucracies lean toward moral realism. For moral skepticism and moral relativism can have

---

40 "True-for" moral claims have gotten relativists into several difficulties. As a response, some of them have abandoned the concepts of moral truth, moral facts, and moral objectivity, and have tried to use instead some other concepts that do not carry such heavy epistemic and semantic loads. Unfortunately, the danger is that if you tone down your claims in this way, you may end up with descriptive, sociological facts about moral variation across cultures, which do not speak to the metaethical issue under discussion. And, metaethically, you may end up not having a distinct position anymore, but just a version of moral skepticism. Cf. Paul Boghossian. 2006. *Fear of Knowledge: Against Relativism and Constructivism*. Oxford: Oxford University Press; Paul Boghossian. 2011. "Three Kinds of Relativism." Pp. 53–69 in *A Companion to Relativism*, edited by Steven D. Hales. Malden, MA: Wiley-Blackwell.

costly practical consequences: they can make their goals difficult or impossible to realize. Similarly, ethnographic observation of social interactions—say, the interactions of a family in their home over a period of time—may reveal a tacit rejection of moral skepticism and moral relativism. At least where I come from, *patres familias* are unlikely to feel that any moral view is as good as any other. Rather, objective correctness does apply to moral matters, and they are always objectively correct and their wives and children always mistaken. Alternatively, while actors may not be aware of their metaethical assumptions, a skilled interviewer can bring them into view. Suppose the interviewer's research subject is filial duties to aging parents in Uruguay and Paraguay. Uruguayan and Paraguayan societies differ greatly at the first-order moral level. In Paraguay, elderly parents often move in with their children, whereas in Uruguay they often move to "assisted living facilities." The Uruguayan way of life does not condemn or ostracize people who neglect their elderly parents; in Paraguay that entails severe social penalties. Now, to get at second-order metaethical assumptions, the interviewer should carefully and patiently probe her Uruguayan subjects' feelings toward the status of filial duties in Paraguay (and vice versa). Are Paraguayans mistaken, or do they have a right to have their own opinion? Is it possible that you, Uruguayans, are mistaken about this issue? Is it possible that both of you are right? Do Paraguayans' rules and reasons apply in Uruguay? Are filial duties up to each family to decide? Are they up to each society? Up to each individual?

Finally, there are experimental options: just like a clever interviewer, cleverly designed experimental tasks can elicit subjects' metaethical assumptions. Indeed, a few experiments about this very question have been conducted recently. Sarkissian and his colleagues have asked: "Do people believe in objective moral truth, or do they accept some form of moral relativism?"[41] Similarly, Goodwin and Darley have asked: "How do lay individuals think about the objectivity of their ethical beliefs? Do they regard them as factual and objective, or as more subjective and opinion-based, and what might predict such differences?" While they use experimental methods and I use historical methods, my approach is comparable to Goodwin and Darley's in two ways. First, their research question is not metaethical—whether ethical beliefs are objective. Rather, it is social scientific—whether people believe ethical beliefs to be objective. Second, their research question is not about the psychology of ethics—what people's ethical beliefs are. Rather, it is about the psychology of metaethics—what people's beliefs about the status of their ethical beliefs are.[42]

---

41   Shaun Nichols. 2004. "After Objectivity: An Empirical Study of Moral Judgment." *Philosophical Psychology* 17(1):5–28; Hagop Sarkissian, John Park, David Tien, Jennifer Cole Wright, and Joshua Knobe. 2011. "Folk Moral Relativism." *Mind & Language* 26(4):482–505, p. 483; Joshua Knobe, Wesley Buckwalter, Shaun Nichols, Philip Robbins, Hagop Sarkissian, and Tamler Sommers. 2012. "Experimental Philosophy." *Annual Review of Psychology* 63:81–99; Jennifer C. Wright, Piper T. Grandjean, and Cullen B. McWhite. 2013. "The Meta-Ethical Grounding of Our Moral Beliefs: Evidence for Meta-Ethical Pluralism." *Philosophical Psychology* 26(3):336–61.

42   Geoffrey P. Goodwin and John M. Darley. 2008. "The Psychology of Meta-Ethics: Exploring Objectivism." *Cognition* 106:1339–66, p. 1339; Geoffrey P. Goodwin and John M. Darley. 2010. "The

No doubt, it may be hard to tell what metaethical assumptions underlie first-order morality. There are inherent practical difficulties. To make things worse, this background dimension allows for variation within a society or even within a group, which my thought experiment about Uruguay and Paraguay did not reflect. The difficulties seem even greater for historical research. Still, the historical scholar of the moral background can profit, for example, from records of moral debates and controversies. If she is fortunate, these controversies may reveal what the contenders thought they were doing, and in particular whether they thought that one of them must be mistaken, or rather everyone could be correct in some way (although it might be argued that the very fact of participating in a moral debate commits participants to moral objectivity—otherwise what would be the point?). In any case, even if discovering metaethical assumptions is really hard, this is not a reason, or not a sufficient reason anyway, to not try to do it.

(6) METAPHYSICS

Metaphysics is the branch of philosophy that deals with the most abstract and general philosophical questions, such as the nature of being, reality, space, time, causation, universals, modality, or infinity. Metaphysics includes but is not identical with ontology. While ontology asks what there is or what entities exist, metaphysics asks what the nature of the entities that exist is, what they are like, what their essence is, and what it is for something to exist at all. In this sense, metaphysics is a scholarly endeavor. A philosopher puts forward a metaphysical argument in a book or journal article. Other philosophers scrutinize the validity of her inferences or the plausibility of her premises. Some object to her interpretation of David Armstrong, if their mother tongue is English, or her interpretation of Heidegger, if their mother tongue is French. These arguments and counterarguments are discussed in university courses and academic conferences about metaphysics.

My moral background framework is not interested in these metaphysical arguments that professional philosophers put forward, but in social metaphysics. These are the metaphysical pictures or assumptions that ordinary people and social practices, institutions, and understandings manifest. Take democracy, communism, socialism, the modern state, the American constitution, social policy, economics, neuroscience, particle physics, the common law and the Roman law traditions, art museums, the Azande's rituals, Buddhism, Confucianism, and—last but not least—everyday social interaction. Each of these systems of practices, institutions, and understandings is underlain by metaphysical elements, even though they can be wholly tacit, built into practices, routines, and devices. More generally, societies or "cultures" taken as wholes might share specific assumptions about being, reality, space, or time. They might also share specific assumptions

Perceived Objectivity of Ethical Beliefs: Psychological Findings and Implications for Public Policy." *Review of Philosophy and Psychology* 1(2):161–88; Geoffrey P. Goodwin and John M. Darley. 2012. "Why Are Some Moral Beliefs Perceived to Be More Objective than Others?" *Journal of Experimental Social Psychology* 48(1):250–56.

about human beings, what they are like, what they are capable of, what they are for, and what is their essence. Differently put, they might have common "anthropological" assumptions.[43] Like metaethical stances, metaphysical pictures are to be inferred by the social scientist—even though this may not be easy and may not even be possible at times. For the most part, they cannot be articulated by the people who manifest them, who are not metaphysicians and rarely or never talk about metaphysics.

As an example, consider the metaphysical commitments of contemporary neuroscience (or what they seem to be anyway). Neurons and brain areas exist; souls do not. Brains and even brain areas can "make decisions or . . . be indecisive"; they can "be thoughtful or . . . be thoughtless"; they can "see, hear, smell and taste things."[44] Neural activity is not just correlated with but causally responsible for perception, experience, thought, and behavior. Then, neuroscience can in principle determine why we see what we see, why we believe what we believe, and why we do what we do. Consciousness is nothing but a neurobiological phenomenon. Ultimately, you are your brain.[45] That is where your essence lies. Suppose you are anesthetized and your brain is transplanted into another body; that person would still be you. Alternatively, consider Andreas Glaeser's account about the character and collapse of East German socialism. Glaeser argues that socialism had a "metaphysical core, its philosophy of history as a lawlike, preordained development toward an inevitably just human society, that is, communism as a secular paradise." Its reputation for abstraction and abstruseness to the contrary, in this case metaphysics had tangible, indeed earth-shattering, consequences: "One could say that in the end, socialism stumbled over its social ontology and its scientific pretensions."[46]

Or consider the interesting though peculiar example of present-day art practices and institutions, and their underlying understandings about what art is, what art is for, what counts as a work of art, and what is the nature of artistic value. Museums, teachers, award committees, and critics are ordinarily busy

43   Michel Foucault. 1966. *Les mots et les choses: une archéologie des sciences humaines*. Paris: Gallimard; Helmuth Plessner. 1928. *Die Stufen des Organischen und der Mensch; Einleitung in die philosophische Anthropologie*. Berlin: W. de Gruyter; Max Scheler. 1928. *Die Stellung des Menschen in Kosmos*. Darmstadt: Reichl; Christian Smith. 2003. *Moral, Believing Animals: Human Personhood and Culture*. New York: Oxford University Press; Christian Smith. 2010. *What is a Person? Rethinking Humanity, Social Life, and the Moral Good from the Person Up*. Chicago: University of Chicago Press; Christian Smith. 2014. *To Flourish or Destruct: A Personalist Theory of Human Goods, Motivations, Failure, and Evil*. Chicago: University of Chicago Press.

On the social consequences of understandings about people's nature, see George Steinmetz. 2007. *The Devil's Handwriting: Precoloniality and the German Colonial State in Qingdao, Samoa, and Southwest Africa*. Chicago: University of Chicago Press; Nicholas Hoover Wilson. 2011. "From Reflection to Refraction: State Administration in British India, circa 1770–1855." *American Journal of Sociology* 116(5):1437–77.

44   M. R. Bennett and P.M.S. Hacker. 2003. *Philosophical Foundations of Neuroscience*. Malden, MA: Blackwell, p. 73.

45   Cf. Alva Noë. 2009. *Out of Our Heads. Why You Are not Your Brain, and Other Lessons from the Biology of Consciousness*. New York: Hill and Wang.

46   Glaeser, *Political Epistemics*, pp. 560 and 561.

dealing with first-order issues, e.g., whether this particular piece or artist is good, how to exhibit someone's work, or how to make good or better art. However, from time to time they also take up second-order, background issues, e.g., what it is to be a work of art, or what makes an installation an installation. Indeed, not only art criticism but art itself may performatively ask what art is. Unlike most social actors, institutions, and practices, the contemporary Western art world is unusually metaphysically reflective. It is conscious, perhaps too conscious, of the second-order level, its metaphysical categories and vocabularies. The boundary between art on the one hand, and philosophy of art or philosophical aesthetics on the other, can be porous. Yet, in contrast to philosophical aesthetics, art practices need their metaphysical commitments right now. Museums must keep exhibiting works (hundreds of visitors are lining up outside), this year's prizes and fellowships must be awarded (hundreds of artists submitted their candidacies), and committee members must catch their flights home (hundreds of other duties await to be attended to).[47] Empirical research about the moral background explores these metaphysical pictures and assumptions—the metaphysics of neuroscience, socialism, art, particular groups, whole societies, and so on. It empirically investigates what they are and how they vary.

1.3 What Makes the Background a Background

In the preceding sections I talked somewhat imprecisely about the background as something that underlies morality, a distinct object that scientists of morality can and should empirically investigate. The word "something" in the preceding sentence is a suitable one. For up to this point I have avoided two unavoidable questions: what the moral background is, more precisely, and what it means to say that it "underlies" morality. Cunningly, I identified and discussed the dimensions of the moral background, all the while being vague about what these dimensions are dimensions of. However, my grace period is finally over. What sort of thing is the moral background? Where is it to be found? What makes the moral background a *background*? And what makes it a *moral* background?

The moral background comprises several heterogeneous elements, which the previous section sorted into six dimensions. This heterogeneity has a cost: there is no parsimonious way of encapsulating the essence of the background's six dimensions and how they work. In fact, moral background elements do not share one substantive characteristic. Instead, they have a comparable relationship to or position vis-à-vis first-order morality, moral action, norms, beliefs, institutions, and so on. This relationship may be preliminarily captured by saying that moral background elements are "para-moral" elements. To see what this means, consider the classic distinction in epistemology between experience and that which makes experience possible, the classic example of which is Kant's categories of

47   For an analogous situation, see Michèle Lamont. 2009. *How Professors Think: Inside the Curious World of Academic Judgment.* Cambridge, MA: Harvard University Press.

understanding. For Kant, this distinction marks an ontological difference: experience and the categories do not exist at the same level or in the same way; they are not the same sort of thing. The categories are *a priori*, whereas experience is *a posteriori*. The categories are prior to and the condition of possibility for experience. Alternatively, consider the distinction between claims about substantive scientific matters, and claims about the methodological and epistemological apparatus relied upon by claims about substantive scientific matters. This is not an ontological distinction, but there is still a difference between two kinds of claims. One of them—methodology and epistemology—is in one sense prior to and ancillary to the other—molecular biology or political science.

Analogously, moral background elements do not belong to the level or realm of first-order morality. Rather, they facilitate, support, or enable first-order moral claims, norms, actions, practices, and institutions. Hence, it is apposite to speak of para-moral elements or a para-moral apparatus. In contemporary English, the prefix "para-" is generally used to mean "beside," "alongside," or "related to." Sometimes it is used to mean more specifically "ancillary" or "auxiliary." For instance, as in the *Oxford English Dictionary* definition of "paramedical": "Associated with or related to medicine or the medical profession; *spec.* designating or relating to fields considered to be allied or auxiliary to medicine, such as physiotherapy, social work, etc." Or "parafiscal": "Ancillary to what is fiscal; containing elements not usually regarded as fiscal." Then, the moral background can reasonably be called the para-moral background, too. Note that here the prefix "para-" is more accurate than the prefix "meta-." Only some moral background elements are meta-moral in the most common sense of this prefix—something like "about," as in meta-data or meta-theory. But all of them are para-moral. Be that as it may, the moral background is still a relative of what Glaeser calls meta-understandings.[48] Whatever it gets called, the bottom line is that these elements are not moral, but auxiliary to morality.

As a consequence, moral background elements are not necessarily visible to the naked eye, so to speak. At least, they are not as easily visible as first-order, morally normative and behavioral elements. This is why the words "background" and "to underlie" seem fitting as well: they call to mind a suggestive picture. In the foreground or on the surface you can observe people talking about the life worth living, people helping strangers in distress, institutions that are oppressive, practices that are cruel, and so on. That is easy to see. Then, you have a moral background, that is, "the scenery or ground behind something" (as per the *Merriam-Webster Dictionary*), or "The ground or surface lying at the back of or behind the chief objects of contemplation, which occupy the foreground" (as per the *Oxford English Dictionary*). Therefore, it takes some excavation or probing to bring the background into view—to bring it to the fore or to the surface. Background elements are located, metaphorically, underneath or behind.

I said that the moral background facilitates, supports, or enables morality. I had to juxtapose three verbs, because the relationship between first-order morality

48   Glaeser, *Political Epistemics*, pp. 26–28.

and second-order background cannot be parsimoniously captured. Both the class of moral background elements and the class of moral elements are heterogeneous. There is much diversity on both sides of the equation. Therefore, different permutations will yield instances of the former facilitating, supporting, or enabling the latter. Some moral life is made possible by the background; however, some moral life is only facilitated or supported by it. In this respect, there is one kind of relationship and terminology that I decided to downplay in this book. Some social theorists and philosophers would like to say that the background makes moral life intelligible, or that moral life is only intelligible against a given background. I do not reject this phrasing and these ideas, and I even employ them in my discussion of Heidegger. On the other hand, the concept of intelligibility has implications I would rather not embrace here, and may open a can of worms I would rather not address.

One last facet of the moral background's heterogeneity must be noted: background elements may be discursive and overt, may be unspoken understandings, or may be non-propositional. First, there are overt discursive elements. Consider, for example, the first dimension of the background: the grounds or reasons that support a moral institution, practice, or view; the reasons given for its validity, worth, point, or *raison d'être*. Sometimes these can be directly accessed as marks on the paper or strings of sounds. They manifest themselves in loci such as parliamentary debates, sacred texts, parents' didactic accounts, community council meetings, newspaper editorials, and dinner tables. For example, imagine someone making a case on TV in favor of the "war on terror," or for the permissibility of torture, on the grounds that they can save many innocent American lives. Even though the speaker would not describe herself as making a consequentialist case, she is no doubt making a consequentialist case. The scientist of morality is fortunate to have direct access to these data—and without even leaving his own comfortable living room—which pertains to that dimension of the moral background. While the analysis of these data may be hard, their observation is generally unproblematic.

Second, there are unspoken understandings. To continue with the same example, sometimes grounds or reasons may be taken for granted by everyone, such that they are never overtly stated. As a matter of fact, in that society or social group they are unspoken. Still, they *could* be spoken if needed. Take the third and fourth dimensions of the moral background: object of evaluation and method and argument. It is probably unusual that these dimensions are overtly discussed *qua* second-order or para-moral elements. You can observe people and organizations going about advancing moral arguments in certain ways rather than others, and picking certain objects for evaluation rather than others. You can systematically repeat these observations under different conditions, which may license inferences about typical moral methods, arguments, and objects of evaluation. On the other hand, few ordinary actors actually reflect on moral method, object, and argument. They only do so when something seems to be amiss.

Third, understandings about moral object, method, and argument need not be propositional, representational, or discursive. They may not come in that format or be that sort of thing at all, much like Aristotle's virtue-as-*hexis*,[49] Mauss's *habitus*,[50] Bourdieu's *habitus*,[51] or Glaeser's emotive and kinesthetic modes of understanding.[52] They do not necessarily exist as propositions to the effect that such-and-such a method does not work, such-and-such an argument is invalid, or such-and-such a consideration is out of the question. Instead, they can be embedded in or built into social institutions and practices. Or they can be embodied in or inscribed into human bodies, and manifested in space-time bodily orientations.[53] In either case, they are unlike, say, a textbook's description of the methods of science or logic, which by their very nature must consist in sets of sentences—telling the reader about the methodological principles scientists do or should follow, or the rules of inference logicians do or should follow. However, these textbooks arguably do not ever guide the actual practice of scientists and logicians, who have instead embodied understandings of what to do in the lab, how to do it, what to laugh at, and so on. These activities do not involve thinking, intentionality, rules, and the like. They are effortless, just like Heidegger's carpenter's hammering.

While they obviously work differently, both social institutions and embodied dispositions can non-discursively make some things happen and prevent other things from happening. They have causal powers over social action patterns, and at the same time are expressed or reflected non-discursively. In this sense, inadequate or incompetent ways of going about talking or acting will not be argued against or objected to. Rather, they will spark negative emotions, discomfort, booing, or disgust. What is more, they may meet with downright incomprehension and puzzlement: puzzled facial expressions, inattention, frowning, and shoulder shrugging. These embodied and embedded understandings can render a practice or claim not just inadequate but unintelligible in that social context. Hence, they render it in effect impossible *qua* that practice or claim.

Not all background elements can work like this. But some do. People intuitively know what can and cannot be morally evaluated, what counts and does not count as a moral argument, and what is and is not a valid moral method. They have intuitions, dispositions, habits, or habits of action to that effect (nothing much hangs on what you call them). As long as things are going well, people will just act and speak and go about their lives in a competent fashion. They will not make nonsensical moral evaluations, or pause to wonder about meta-moral or para-moral issues. These are abnormal courses of action, just like breakdowns in ethnomethodology or in Heidegger's ordinary coping with reality. They require

---

49 *Nicomachean Ethics* 1105b25–28.
50 Marcel Mauss. 1934. "Les techniques du corps." *Journal de Psychologie* 32(3–4):271–93.
51 Pierre Bourdieu. 1980. *Le sens pratique*. Paris: Éditions de Minuit.
52 Glaeser, *Political Epistemics*.
53 Maurice Merleau-Ponty. 1945. *Phénoménologie de la perception*. Paris: Gallimard. See also Samuel Todes. 2001. *Body and World*. Cambridge, MA: MIT Press; Michal Pagis. 2009. "Embodied Self-Reflexivity." *Social Psychology Quarterly* 72(3):265–83; Michal Pagis. 2010. "From Abstract Concepts to Experiential Knowledge: Embodying Enlightenment in a Meditation Center." *Qualitative Sociology* 33(4):469–89.

an abnormal trigger, such as the doorknob's not turning, the hammer's being too heavy, the arrival of a stranger who does not understand how we do things around here, or the arrival of a student of Garfinkel's who intends that we become her unwitting research subjects.

1.4 Background Theorists

Thus far I have explicated the moral background in three steps. First, I provided a general introduction to what it is. Second, I discussed each of its six dimensions. Third, I analyzed the relationship between the moral background and first-order morality. This section takes a fourth step. It begins with a succinct review of the theoretical landscape to identify some concepts my concept is a family member of. Next, it further explicates the moral background by recruiting the help of Searle, Taylor, and Heidegger.

Something like the moral background occurs in the works of many authors, even if they might not talk about a "background" (or the closest word in their language), and even if they might not talk about morality but knowledge, understanding, or perception. Wittgenstein and Heidegger's Division I of *Being and Time* might spring to mind first. Readers steeped in phenomenology and ethnomethodology may think first of Husserl, Schutz, and Garfinkel, and their discussions about intersubjectivity, the lifeworld, the natural standpoint (*natürliche Einstellung*), and shared "methods of common-sense reasoning" and "background of mutually constituted intelligibility."[54] Readers steeped in science studies may link the background to Fleck, Polanyi, and Kuhn's paradigms; or to scholarship on *habitus*, *mētis*, and other forms of practical sense and practical knowledge.[55] Foucauldians may link the background to a discursive formation's "rules of formation," and the conditions of possibility set by the *episteme* of an epoch.[56] Another relevant French tradition is the history of social imaginaries, sensibilities, *mentalités*, and *outillages mentaux*, led by Bloch, Duby, Febvre, and Le Goff.[57] Equally relevant are the communitarians, for whom social life can make no sense without

54 Edmund Husserl. [1931] 2012. *Ideas*. London; New York: Routledge; Alfred Schutz. [1932] 1967. *The Phenomenology of the Social World*. Evanston: Northwestern University Press; John Heritage. 1984. *Garfinkel and Ethnomethodology*. Cambridge; New York: Polity Press, p. 306; Anne Rawls. 2002. "Editor's Introduction." In Harold Garfinkel. 2002. *Ethnomethodology's Program: Working Out Durkheim's Aphorism*. Lanham: Rowman & Littlefield, p. 25. See also Paul L. Jalbert. 1994. "Structures of the 'Unsaid'." *Theory, Culture & Society* 11:127–60.

55 Bourdieu, *Le sens pratique*; Marcel Detienne and Jean-Pierre Vernant. 1974. *Les ruses de l'intelligence: la mètis des Grecs*. Paris: Flammarion; Scott, *Seeing Like a State*, esp. pp. 309–41.

56 Michel Foucault. 1966. *Les mots et les choses: une archéologie des sciences humaines*. Paris: Gallimard; Michel Foucault. 1969. *L'archéologie du savoir*. Paris: Gallimard.

57 Marc Bloch. [1924] 1983. *Les rois thaumaturges: étude sur le caractère surnaturel attribué à la puissance royale particulièrement en France et en Angleterre*. Paris: Gallimard; Lucien Febvre. 1942. *Le problème de l'incroyance au XVIe siècle, la religion de Rabelais*. Paris: A. Michel. Cf. Jacques Le Goff. 1974. "Les mentalités: une histoire ambiguë." Pp. 76–94 in *Faire de l'histoire. Noveaux objets*, edited by Jacques Le Goff and Pierre Nora. Paris: Gallimard.

a context or tradition. Likewise, while he eschews the communitarian label, Mac-Intyre's *magnum opus* makes a distinction between our moral vocabulary and the "beliefs presupposed by [its] use"; currently, "we possess . . . fragments of a conceptual scheme, parts which now lack those contexts from which their significance derived."[58]

In short, the background is genealogically related to diverse scholarly traditions and a diverse conceptual family.[59] In Wittgenstein-speak, "we see a complicated network of similarities overlapping and criss-crossing."[60] I think this complicated network can be sorted into three groups. First, one line of the family consists of variations on the concept of knowledge: tacit knowledge, local knowledge, practical knowledge, *phronēsis*, non-observational knowledge, experiential knowledge, know-how, non-discursive understandings, meta-understandings, the taken-for-granted, the unsaid, and background knowledge. The second line consists of concepts that stress the body and embodied properties: skill, practical sense, habit, *habitus*, *hexis*, disposition, *mētis*, and kinesthetic understanding. The third family line turns to the macro level and stresses collective or shared properties in a group or community: paradigm, shared assumptions, shared presuppositions, social imaginary, *mentalité*, *outillages mentaux*, *episteme*, *Lebensform*, *Lebenswelt*, frame, framework, scheme, tradition, and horizon of significance.

The conceptual map is already quite complex, but that is not all. Numerous overlapping and criss-crossing adjectives are used to qualify these nouns: unspoken, unstated, unsaid, unarticulated, taken-for-granted, non-discursive, implicit, tacit, and unconscious. And it is not always clear whether unspoken is supposed to mean unspeakable, i.e., necessarily unconscious, ineffable in principle.[61] Ineffability suggests some seductive paths, which writers like Fleck and Lovejoy were willing to traverse, at least to some extent. Fleck compared a style of thought to breathing, although he did not say it was unconscious, but only "almost unconscious."[62] Likewise, in his discussion of the "objects of the interest of the historian of ideas," Lovejoy did not say that mental habits were unconscious, but only "more or less unconscious":

On social imaginaries, see Bronisław Baczko. 1984. *Les imaginaires sociaux: memoires et espoires collectifs.* Paris: Payot; Cornelius Castoriadis. 1975. *L'institution imaginaire de la société.* Paris: Seuil; Jacques Le Goff. 1985. *L'imaginaire médiéval.* Paris: Gallimard.

58   Alasdair MacIntyre. [1981] 2007. *After Virtue: A Study in Moral Theory.* 3rd ed. Notre Dame: University of Notre Dame Press, pp. xiv and 1–2.

59   Besides, the family is not without its problems. For example, Turner objects to "the idea that there is something cognitive or quasi-cognitive that is 'behind' or prior to that which is explicit and publicly uttered that is implicit and unuttered." While he mentions "presuppositions," "tacit premises," "ideology," "structures of knowledge," and "*Weltanschauungen*," his main foe is the concept of practices and their purportedly being shared or common. Stephen Turner. 1994. *The Social Theory of Practices: Tradition, Tacit Knowledge, and Presuppositions.* Chicago: University of Chicago Press, p. 29.

60   Wittgenstein, *Philosophical Investigations*, §66.

61   Cf. Harry Collins. 2010. *Tacit and Explicit Knowledge.* Chicago: University of Chicago Press.

62   Fleck, *Genesis and Development of a Scientific Fact*, p. 141.

There are, first, implicit or incompletely explicit *assumptions*, or more or less *unconscious mental habits*, operating in the thought of an individual or a generation. It is the beliefs which are so much a matter of course that they are rather tacitly presupposed than formally expressed and argued for, the ways of thinking which seem so natural and inevitable that they are not scrutinized with the eye of logical self-consciousness, that often are most decisive of the character of a philosopher's doctrine, and still oftener of the dominant intellectual tendencies of an age.[63]

It is not my aim to bring real order to this theoretical landscape: the genealogical lineages of the background and kindred concepts are complex, and they are complexly related to one another. I rest content with stressing one simple point, which aptly introduces the subsequent subsections. There are evident dissimilarities across and within family lines. However, all the members of the extended family make a distinction between two realms or levels, and pay special attention to the one that lies underneath or behind the other. In this regard, I find some arguments advanced by Searle, Taylor, and Heidegger to be particularly helpful. They will help us discern what this distinction amounts to, and how it can contribute to the empirical investigation of morality.

SEARLE

Searle can help us sharpen the relationship between two levels, A and B, where one of them does the enabling (A enables B), and the other one is enabled (B is enabled by A).[64] Searle's "Background" is a concept in the philosophy of mind, and his aim is to give an account of literal meaning and intentionality (the property of mental states of being directed at or about something). In his book, *Intentionality*, Searle defines the Background as "a set of nonrepresentational mental capacities that enable all representing to take place" (p. 143). According to him, understanding the literal meaning of a sentence or "[forming] the intention to go to the refrigerator and get a bottle of cold beer to drink" would be impossible without the Background. Why is that?

The Background is "a set of skills, stances, preintentional assumptions and presuppositions, practices, and habits. And all of these, as far as we know, are realized in human brains and bodies" (p. 154; see also p. 151).[65] Two subcategories can

---

63 Arthur Oncken Lovejoy. 1936. *The Great Chain of Being: A Study of the History of an Idea*. Cambridge, MA: Harvard University Press, p. 7.

64 John Searle. 1979. *Expression and Meaning: Studies in the Theory of Speech Acts*. New York: Cambridge University Press; John Searle. 1983. *Intentionality: An Essay in the Philosophy of Mind*. New York: Cambridge University Press; John Searle. 1995. *The Construction of Social Reality*. New York: Free Press.

65 Here Searle is in fact trying to prevent metaphysical interpretations of his Background: "The Background, therefore, is not a set of things nor a set of mysterious relations between ourselves and things, rather it is simply a set of skills, stances, preintentional assumptions and presuppositions, practices, and habits. And all of these, as far as we know, are realized in human brains and bodies. There is nothing whatever that is 'transcendental' or 'metaphysical' about the Background, as I am using that term." However, he immediately observes that his own talk is imprecise: "The reader by now

be distinguished. There is a "deep Background," "which would include at least all of those Background capacities that are common to all normal human beings in virtue of their biological makeup." And there is also a "'local Background' or 'local cultural practices'" (pp. 143–44). Searle then argues that

> the literal meaning of any sentence can only determine its truth conditions or other conditions of satisfaction against a Background of capacities, dispositions, know-how, etc., which are not themselves part of the semantic content of the sentence. You can see this if you think about any sentence at all, but it is perhaps most obvious with sentences containing simple English verbs like "cut," "open," or "grow." [. . .] If you consider the sentence "Cut the grass!" you know that this is to be interpreted differently from "Cut the cake!" [. . .] Yet nothing in the literal meaning of those sentences blocks [the] wrong interpretations. In each case we understand the verb differently, even though its literal meaning is constant, because in each case our interpretation depends on our Background abilities.[66]

Then, how does Searle depict the relationship between the Background on the one hand and intentionality and representation on the other? The former is sometimes described as a "presupposition" (p. 148) or a "precondition" of the latter: "The Background is 'preintentional' in the sense that though not a form or forms of Intentionality, it is nonetheless a precondition or set of preconditions of Intentionality" (p. 143).[67] Sometimes he says that the Background "underlies" intentional states: "Intentional states are underlain by nonrepresentational, preintentional capacities" (p. 144). Or he says that it "*permeates* the entire Network of Intentional states; since without the Background the states could not function" (p. 151). In his 1995 *The Construction of Social Reality*, he also speaks of "facilitation": "*the Background facilitates certain kinds of readiness*" (p. 136).

Most important, both in *Intentionality* and in *The Construction of Social Reality*, Searle's Background also "enables": "the Background provides necessary but not sufficient conditions for understanding, believing, desiring, intending, etc., and in that sense it is enabling and not determining." Thus: "On the conception I am presenting, the Background is . . . the set of practices, skills, habits, and stances that enable Intentional contents to work in the various ways that they do, and it is in that sense that the Background functions causally by providing a set of enabling conditions for the operation of Intentional states."[68] The examples of a constitution and the rules of a game suggest what he has in mind:

---

will have noticed that there is a real difficulty in finding ordinary language terms to describe the Background: one speaks vaguely of 'practices,' 'capacities,' and 'Stances' or one speaks suggestively but misleadingly of 'assumptions' and 'presuppositions'" (p. 156). Why this is so is telling: "There simply is no first-order vocabulary for the Background, because the Background has no Intentionality. As the precondition of Intentionality, the Background is as invisible to Intentionality as the eye which sees is invisible to itself. [. . .] The price we pay for deliberately going against ordinary language is metaphor, oxymoron, and outright neologism" (p. 157).

66 Searle, *Construction of Social Reality*, pp. 130–31.
67 See also Searle, *Construction of Social Reality*, p. 132.
68 Searle, *Intentionality*, p. 158.

The Background provides a set of enabling conditions that make it possible for particular forms of Intentionality to function. Just as the Constitution of the United States enables a certain potential candidate to form the intention to become President, and just as the rules of a game enable certain moves to be made in the game, so the Background enables us to have particular forms of Intentionality. [. . .] In traditional terms, the Background provides necessary but not sufficient conditions for understanding, believing, desiring, intending, etc., and in that sense it is enabling and not determining. (pp. 157–58)

While Searle differentiates the Background from rules, because it is not representational, a constitution and the rules of a game still illustrate its enabling function. No constitution, no president, no intention to become president. This is precisely the role that my moral background sometimes plays. It enables morality; it enables people to utter moral utterances and to perform moral actions. Unlike Searle, I am not worried about background elements' being representational or non-representational, linguistic or non-linguistic: I have already said that both are comprised. Unlike Searle, I do not want to speak of causation here, because I do not want to be sidetracked by the hard questions it would force me to address—e.g., what is the difference between "*A* causes *B*" and "*A* enables *B*" (or, "*A* provides the conditions for the possibility of *B*"). But my conceptual framework still draws on Searle's distinction. On the conception I am presenting, moral life, institutions, and claims are analogous to Searle's intentionality, and my moral background is analogous to Searle's Background.

TAYLOR

Taylor's usefulness for my conceptual argument is twofold. First, while Searle develops the idea of the Background, Taylor develops the idea of a *moral* background. Second, Taylor argues that, given a distinction between two levels, differences on one level do not necessarily entail differences on the other. In particular, convergence at the level of moral principles and first-order morality may coexist with divergence at the background level. If my arguments in this book are correct, this is just what much of the history of business ethicists' work in the United States looks like.

In *Sources of the Self* Taylor discusses the idea of a "background picture," which he understands in a particular way: "I want to explore the background picture of our spiritual nature and predicament which lies behind some of the moral and spiritual intuitions of our contemporaries. In the course of doing so, I shall also be trying to make clearer just what a background picture is, and what role it plays in our lives."[69] Taylor thus makes a distinction between two levels, one of which is behind the other: the background is behind moral and spiritual intuitions. Next, he makes his point more precise:

---

69 Taylor, *Sources of the Self*, pp. 3–4. See also Charles Taylor. 1995. "Lichtung or Lebensform: Parallels between Heidegger and Wittgenstein." Pp. 61–78 in *Philosophical Arguments*. Cambridge, MA: Harvard University Press; Taylor, *Modern Social Imaginaries*, p. 25 and *passim*.

I could now rephrase this and say that my target is the moral ontology which articulates these intuitions. What is the picture of our spiritual nature and predicament which makes sense of our responses? "Making sense" here means articulating what makes these responses appropriate. . . . What is articulated here is the background we assume and draw on in any claim to rightness, part of which we are forced to spell out when we have to defend our responses as the right ones. (pp. 8–9)

Taylor sees an ontological, second-order level, which underlies and "makes sense" of people's first-order responses, intuitions, reactions, beliefs, or reasons. As Stephen Mulhall puts it, "[w]ithout such an ontology . . . those [moral] judgments [characteristic of modernity in the West] can neither secure their distinctive content nor receive a truly rational assessment of their strength and limitations."[70] Judgments about, say, respect, dignity, or honor have the sense that they do because of their underlying ontology—as well as a set of practices, institutions, and a way of life. They "repose" on a "background understanding" (p. 25). More generally, "[f]rameworks provide the background, explicit or implicit, for our moral judgements [sic], intuitions, or reactions" (p. 26). Taylor also emphasizes the background's not being necessarily conscious or explicit, so that the "agent himself or herself is not necessarily the best authority, at least not at the outset." In fact, there may even be a "lack of fit" between what "people as it were consciously and officially believe . . . and what they need to make sense of some of their moral reactions" (p. 9).

In short, whereas Searle's Background underlies intentionality and meaning, Taylor's background picture underlies morality. What Taylor actually does to unearth background pictures and social imaginaries is in the style of political and social philosophy, not that of empirical social science, as Craig Calhoun has observed.[71] His main sources are great books. But he can still orient the social scientist toward an empirical object: ordinary people's moral ontology or background pictures. While my moral background departs from Taylor's substantive foci—what this thing is made out of—he has still shown the way to any effort in this direction.

Moreover, there is a more specific line of argument of Taylor's that can give us a sense of what moral background differences may look like. In *Sources of the Self* Taylor looks at the history of the "notion of a right, also called a 'subjective right'." He observes:

The revolution in natural law theory in the seventeenth century partly consisted in using this language of rights to express the universal moral norms. We began to speak of "natural" rights, and now to such things as life and liberty which supposedly everyone has.

70 Stephen Mulhall. 2004. "Articulating the Horizons of Liberalism: Taylor's Political Philosophy." Pp. 105–26 in *Charles Taylor*, edited by Ruth Abbey. Cambridge, UK, and New York: Cambridge University Press, p. 105.

71 Craig Calhoun. 1991. "Morality, Identify, and Historical Explanation: Charles Taylor on the Sources of the Self." *Sociological Theory* 9(2):232–63, p. 233.

In one way, to speak of a universal, natural right to life doesn't seem much of an innovation. The change seems to be one of form. The earlier way of putting it was that there was a natural law against taking innocent life. Both formulations seem to prohibit the same things. But the difference lies not in what is forbidden but in the place of the subject. (p. 11)

People used to be "*under* law." After this change, people had rights, "something which the possessor can and ought to act on to put it into effect." A change of "form" is only a preliminary or superficial way of describing this, though. What has happened is, first, that another conceptual network has been brought into play. For example, the concept of rights involves the concept of autonomy in a particular way. Yet, Taylor continues, there is a deeper process going on:

Beyond this lie various richer pictures of human nature and our predicament, which offer reasons for this demand. These include, for instance, the notion of ourselves as disengaged subjects, breaking free from a comfortable but illusory sense of immersion in nature, and objectifying the world around us; or the Kantian picture of ourselves as pure rational agents; or the Romantic picture . . . where we understand ourselves in terms of organic metaphors and a concept of self-expression. [. . .] Here again, a generalized moral consensus breaks into controversy at the level of philosophical explication. (p. 12)

I would not call this "philosophical explication." You do not need to have read Kant's ethical work to have this background picture of yourself as an independent, rational agent—as is suggested by Taylor's own argument to the effect that "[operating] without a philosophically defined framework" does not mean "[being] without a framework at all" (p. 21). In either case, the point is that a major shift has occurred underneath an apparent continuity. The moral and legal prohibitions against, say, "taking innocent life" have remained the same. That fact anyone can see, and much of social science consists of documenting and accounting for these sorts of continuities or changes, as the case may be. However, the "pictures of human nature and our predicament" that underlie these prohibitions have not remained the same at all. Therefore, a social scientist's account of morality and law would be unsatisfactory were she unaware of this other level. This is the level in the context of which or against the background of which moral understandings and legal norms exist.[72]

Taylor's argument has practical implications, which his paper, "Conditions of an Unforced Consensus on Human Rights," forcefully brings out.[73] His starting

---

72 Formally analogous is Taylor's argument in *Modern Social Imaginaries* about "different ways of erecting and animating the institutional forms" of modernity; "different understandings . . . animate similar institutions and practices even in the West." So these institutions look the same superficially, but under the surface they are "animated" by different understandings. Taylor, *Modern Social Imaginaries*, pp. 195–96.

73 Charles Taylor. 1999. "Conditions of an Unforced Consensus on Human Rights." Pp. 124–44 in *The East Asian Challenge for Human Rights*, edited by Joanne R. Bauer and Daniel A. Bell. Cambridge, UK; New York: Cambridge University Press. (I thank Steven Lukes for bringing this paper to my attention.) See also Jonsen and Toulmin, *The Abuse of Casuistry*, pp. 16–19.

point is again the distinction between two levels—one of which he describes as "underlying," a "background," or a "basis," and sometimes as the "starting point" or "starting place" for the other level. But here Taylor's concerns are narrower. Substantively, the question is specifically about human rights. Theoretically, the question is specifically about the distinction between moral "norms" on the one hand, and on the other "why they [are] the right norms," or their "underlying justification." Essentially, the argument is that consensus on the former does not require consensus on the latter. Building on Rawls's "overlapping consensus,"[74] Taylor writes:

> [D]ifferent groups, countries, religious communities, and civilizations, although holding incompatible fundamental views on theology, metaphysics, human nature, and so on, would come to an agreement on certain norms that ought to govern human behavior. Each would have its own way of justifying this from out of its profound background conception. We would agree on the norms while disagreeing on why they were the right norms, and we would be content to live in this consensus, undisturbed by the differences of profound underlying belief. (p. 124)

Is, then, an international consensus on human rights possible? Agreement on this question has been perennially elusive, and Taylor thinks his approach can help overcome this standoff. Some people see such consensus as impossible, precisely because of cross-cultural incompatibilities about theology, metaphysics, human nature, and so on. But Taylor has one additional resource: he can analytically distinguish the above-mentioned two levels, and then, resuming the discussion in *Sources of the Self*, show how it applies to the idea of a right. Thus, the modern West "contrasts with many other cultures, including the premodern West, not because some of the same protections and immunities were not present, but because they had a quite different basis" (p. 128). In this way the modern West can agree about human rights with, say, Confucian or Theravāda Buddhist societies. For instance: "The human rights doctrine based on this [Western] humanism stresses the incomparable importance of the human agent. It centers everything on him or her, makes his or her freedom and self-control a major value, something to be maximized. [. . .] The Buddhist philosophy that I have been describing starts from a quite different place, the demand of *ahimsa* (nonviolence), and yet seems to ground many of the same norms" (pp. 135–36). While this consensus would be at the more superficial level only, this is precisely what we care about politically: "what really matters to us, the enforceable norms" (p. 129).

From the perspective of my moral background, note that Taylor explicitly speaks of "levels" and "planes." Further, his level of "underlying justification" is roughly what I refer to as grounds and grounding—the first dimension of the moral background. For instance, the reasons and arguments produced by business ethicists as to what makes it wrong for a businessperson to, say, shortchange their customers. Taylor's language in this paper fluctuates between the narrower

---

74 John Rawls. 1993. *Political Liberalism*. New York: Columbia University Press.

"underlying justification" (p. 126) or "underlying philosophical justification" (p. 133), and the broader "underlying picture of human life," "underlying philosophy of the human person in society" (p. 128), "ideals," "notions of human excellence," "reference points" (p. 136), "spiritual basis" (p. 137), and "philosophical and spiritual backgrounds" (pp. 137, 143). Yet, his idea throughout is that one level is based on the other. In this very spirit, my historical account about business ethics will examine how grounds for moral norms, principles, injunctions, and doctrines rely on broader moral and metaphysical "reference points" and "pictures."

HEIDEGGER

From Heidegger my conceptual framework borrows a simple insight. Heidegger and the Heideggerian tradition argue that people encounter an intelligible world in which things show up *as* something to them. Cartesians have gotten it wrong: we are not subjects who, through a series of mental operations, experience raw sense data, then sort them into categories, and eventually grasp them as this or that object with these or those properties and functions. Rather, things are already encountered as what they are for us. The starting point is the world, with things and us coping with them already in it. Then, what things show up as can and should be sociologically understood and accounted for. This is a fundamental Heideggerian (as well as late-Wittgensteinian) point: intelligibility is a function of the social context; A's-showing-up-as-B is a function of local practices and understandings.[75]

As Hubert Dreyfus summarizes Heidegger's idea:

A culture's understanding of being allows people and things to show up *as* something—as heroes in Greece and as saints in the Middle Ages, for example. That is, the shared practices into which we are socialized provide a background understanding of what counts as an object, what counts as a human being and what it makes sense to do—on the basis of which we can direct our actions towards particular things and people.[76]

This is essentially a sociological idea, and one of Dreyfus's examples is hence reasonably drawn from sociology: "sociologists point out that mothers in different cultures handle their babies differently and so inculcate the babies into different styles of coping with themselves, people, and things." For instance, a "rattle-thing" reputedly shows up differently to babies in the United States and Japan: "[f]or an American baby, a rattle-thing is an object to make expressive noise with and to throw on the floor in a willful way in order to get a parent to pick it up." By contrast, "generally we might suppose a rattle-thing is encountered [by a Japanese baby] as serving a soothing, pacifying function, like a Native American rain stick."

75   Martin Heidegger. [1927] 2010. *Being and Time*. Translated by Joan Stambaugh. Revised and with a Foreword by Dennis J. Schmidt. Albany: State University of New York Press.

76   Hubert L. Dreyfus. 1996. "Being and Power: Heidegger and Foucault." *International Journal of Philosophical Studies* 4(1):1–16, pp. 2–3.

A rattle is not prior to a rattle-showing-up-as-this-thing. Differently put, "no bare rattle is ever encountered"; there is no rattle in itself. Dreyfus's larger conclusion is that "a style governs how anything can show up *as* anything." Examples such as mothers' ways of handling their babies illustrate "the way the background practices work to grant intelligibility"; importantly, "[e]ach specific style is a specific mode of intelligibility and so is a specific understanding of being."[77]

These arguments have a direct bearing on my conceptual framework—and their profits may be reaped without committing oneself to the whole Heideggerian approach. To put it in terms of my framework, a thing's showing up as a moral object is a function of the moral background. To put it slightly differently, moral objects are intelligible *qua* moral objects only in relation to the moral background. This "showing up as" includes the demarcation of moral issues from non-moral issues—i.e., what counts as a moral issue rather than an issue of etiquette, convention, or prudence. It includes, too, what entities we must have a moral attitude toward, or to what entities moral considerations apply—e.g., what persons we owe which duties to, and what counts as a person in the first place.

Thus, Heidegger can help the scientist of morality notice what she might be prone to oversee. Much social science starts with its objects already constituted: individuals, concepts, subject matters, and kinds of actions, for example. Similarly, much social science of morality has started with its objects already constituted. However, if we limit our empirical analyses to the level of first-order morality, we are missing not only this level's conditions of possibility, but also one important kind of variation. This level is made possible or intelligible by something else—social practices, understandings, assumptions, frameworks, or backgrounds (or whatever you wish to call them)—which also call for empirical examination. In turn, as we will see in the conclusion, this is one fundamental difference between morality and the emotions, and between human morality and non-human animals' reciprocal altruism or cooperation.

Significantly, the fact that most present-day scientists of morality are unaware of this argument about the conditions of possibility of morality can itself be accounted for by a psychological consequence of it. Phenomenologically, we experience moral objects as given. We experience them as moral objects immediately, not after giving some thought to the matter and coming to the conclusion that that is what they are. Despite some exceptions, this is how they naturally show up for us. Our fellow human beings—or human-being-like-things—generally show up as moral beings, worthy of respect, whom suffering should not be inflicted to, and so on. This is so due to cultural background elements, which, however, are ordinarily invisible to us, much like the seeing eye cannot see itself. Yet, that they are at work can be seen comparatively and historically, since not all "human-being-like-things" have always morally shown up in this way. These are historically specific phenomena, like something's showing up as a hero in Greece, or as a saint in the Middle Ages. The contemporary science of morality has not properly

---

77 Hubert L. Dreyfus. 2005. "Foreword." In Carol White. 2005. *Time and Death: Heidegger's Analysis of Finitude*. Burlington, VT: Ashgate, pp. xi–xii.

identified these background conditions of possibility, because its stance is internal to a particular set of background elements. This background sets the stage both for ordinary Western moral life and for ordinary Western science of moral life. It is not surprising that scientists of morality have investigated what is immediately apparent to them as moral objects.

1.5 What the Background Is For

What is it that scientists who investigate morality investigate? First, they investigate the behavioral level. For instance, the distribution and predictors of someone's helping a stranger or a businessperson's engaging in unethical practices. Second, they investigate the normative level. For instance, the distribution and predictors of what people find morally right and wrong, admirable and despicable; the moral goods they pursue; and a society's moral institutions and norms. I have argued that scientists of morality have failed to recognize a third level: the moral background. In this chapter I have explained what the moral background is and what it comprises. In section 1.2 I discussed what the dimensions of the background are; in section 1.3 what makes the background a background; and in section 1.4 how my framework draws on Searle, Taylor, and Heidegger.

The moral background is intended to orient scientists of morality toward novel empirical questions—as it orients my own research on business ethics in this book. These novel empirical questions are mostly sociological, historical, and anthropological, because the background is the product of social and historical processes. For example, it is an outcome of such processes that in a particular social context or group there are only so many valid methods to go about making a moral claim, only so many concepts with which to make it, and only so many objects for it to be about. It is also an outcome of such processes that in a given social context you can tell apart moral actions, non-moral actions, and reflexes; and that you can tell apart sounds that count as an acceptable moral reason, sounds that count as a reason for being locked up in a mental hospital, and sounds that are not even meaningful. Even where there are individual differences within a society or group, an individual can only go so far. Similarly, diachronic changes are not due to individuals' crusades but deeper social trends. In brief, the background is essentially a social object (though how this is the case depends on the dimension—more on this shortly). Therefore, it calls for sociological, historical, and anthropological research about specific configurations of background dimensions in specific societies and groups, along with their causes and consequences—which eventually should be integrated to assess if any general patterns emerge.

Needless to add, this chapter left many problems unresolved, which hence lurk in the background. I wish to mention four of them, so as to own up to the gaps and limitations of my analysis. While I am unable to do justice to these problems here, I still wish to hint at what my arguments might look like if I tried to address them. I hope that this may encourage other scholars to try to do so as well. First, because my discussion of the ontology of the background was far from thorough, someone may raise a "metaphysical queerness" objection.[78] This is the objection that backgrounds and kindred concepts are metaphysically mysterious. They are entities that somehow enable or guide action, cognition, representation, and even life, but they are nowhere to be actually found. At least, it is unclear where they are to be found. What would my response be? Roughly, I would stress that the concept of the moral background has no ontological ambitions; it is metaphysically modest. Instead, I am a nominalist and a pragmatist about it. The moral background does not exist anywhere as such. By "moral background" I just mean a particular collection of para-moral elements that seem to me worthy of empirical investigation, or whose empirical investigation may produce valuable outcomes. Indeed, the background has six parts, each of which has its own specificities and mode of existence. I have devised some tools with which to apprehend these aspects of moral life, and that is all there is to it. Whether or not this response is philosophically satisfactory, I think the concept can still do its job as an empirical tool.

The unresolved ontological problems do not end there. I did not satisfactorily consider what the moral background is a property of, whether of individuals, brains, groups, societies, utterances, pieces of writing, situations, or something else. Discussions about backgrounds, mentalities, paradigms, the taken-for-granted, and the social imaginary sometimes take them to be ontologically emergent entities.[79] They are supposed to get at irreducibly social-level or collective-level phenomena; a *sui generis* level, as Durkheim would say.[80] Fleck's account of science in terms of thought communities and styles of thought is a good example. A full-fledged holist, Fleck proposes the analogies of "a soccer match, a conversation, or the playing of an orchestra," which would "lose [their] meaning" if regarded as "individual kicks one by one," or "the work only of individual instruments."[81] However, *pace* Fleck, any of these concepts admits of both holistic and individualistic interpretations. Take Le Goff's "*mentalité*," which he describes as "that which Caesar and the last soldier of his legions, Saint Louis and the peasant in his domains, Christopher Columbus and the sailor on his ships have in common."[82] However holistic this sentence may sound, you can also read it in an individualistic fashion: "*mentalité*" is an individual property, each person has her own "*mentalité*," but it so happens that everyone on that ship, or in that domain, or in that society, has an identical one.

What about my moral background? Due to its heterogeneity, not all of its dimensions are alike in this regard either. The repertoire of moral concepts is a

78   The expression comes from Mackie's argument about the queerness of values. J. L. Mackie. 1977. *Ethics: Inventing Right and Wrong.* Harmondsworth: Penguin.

79   David Chalmers. 2006. "Strong and Weak Emergence." Pp. 244–54 in *The Re-Emergence of Emergence,* edited by P. Clayton and P. Davies. New York: Oxford University Press; Paul Humphreys. 1996. "Aspects of Emergence." *Philosophical Topics* 24(1):53–70; Jaegwon Kim. 2006. "Emergence: Core Ideas and Issues." *Synthese* 151:547–59.

80   Durkheim, *Rules,* pp. 39 and 54; Margaret Gilbert. 1989. *On Social Facts.* London; New York: Routledge; Steven Lukes. 1973. *Individualism.* Oxford: Blackwell.

81   Fleck, *Genesis and Development of a Scientific Fact,* pp. 46 and 99.

82   Le Goff, "Les mentalités," p. 80. My translation.

collective-level property. This is much like the English lexicon, which in principle cannot be an individual-level property. However, other dimensions—especially metaethical objectivity, method and argument, and grounding—are trickier. To begin with, they are associated with specific actions and events—one organization's code of ethics, one person's case in a court of law. In fact, the proper unity of analysis can be as specific as one utterance, because there is no guarantee that, say, a person will keep using the same moral method on different occasions or even throughout one address. Then, if you take one society or group, there will very likely be differences regarding the kinds of moral arguments made, the methods used, the reasons given, and the objectivity assumptions held. For example, not all U.S. undergraduates hold the same metaethical beliefs about the status of their ethical beliefs.[83] On the other hand, given a society or group, not any grounds, method, or reason are possible. There are social- or group-level constraints on, say, which noises will be seen as irrelevant considerations or sheer nonsense, and which noises will be seen as a moral reason or a moral argument.

Then, we must distinguish two stages or planes. First, what reasons, methods, and grounds are available, and will count as reasons, methods, and grounds. This is a property of a group or society. Groups and societies are the units of analysis of research projects about this first plane. Second, the likelihood of using one or another is a property of individuals and subgroups, probabilistically. Then, within a society or group, these moral background elements can be represented as a distribution, just like other individual outcomes or attributes. In all likelihood, there will be patterns as to who uses what and when, which can be sociologically accounted for.

Third, methodological problems were left unresolved, too. For empirical research about the moral background, unspoken understandings are obviously more troublesome than overt statements. Some of them may be elicited through ingenious methodological tactics—at least where "unspoken" means not actually spoken. For instance, I mentioned social psychologists Goodwin and Darley, who try to elicit the metaethical status of people's moral claims experimentally. Few people ever think about that issue, but they may be able to do it on the spot, in the laboratory. Ethnomethodologists may unveil taken-for-granted assumptions by means of breaching experiments. Ethnographers' observations may unearth embodied dispositions and kinesthetic understandings, which are by definition nondiscursive. Historians are unfortunately forced to make inferences from voiceless and motionless objects, such as sheets of paper and archaeological remains. But there are more and less ingenious and reasonable ways of trying to get at unspoken understandings with historical data. To be sure, all of these tactics are subject to the usual criticisms: you have made subjective judgments and your results are not replicable. To be sure, all of these methods have weaknesses. But so does any scientific method. Perhaps the only "sane response" to this critic is that that kind of objectivity and certainty is not available to us, human beings. We are not gods, so "such uncertainty is an ineradicable part of our epistemological predicament."[84]

---

83   Sarkissian et al., "Folk Moral Relativism."
84   Charles Taylor. 1971. "Interpretation and the Sciences of Man." *Review of Metaphysics* 25(1):3–51, p. 6.

Fourth, my discussion about the moral background may make a thoroughgoing Heideggerian or a thoroughgoing late-Wittgensteinian uncomfortable. For, according to them, people do not adopt background beliefs or subscribe to background understandings. As Dreyfus's Heidegger puts it, the focus should not be beliefs and minds, but artifacts and bodies:

> The case of child rearing helps us see that a cultural style is not something in our minds but, rather, a disposition to act in certain ways in certain situations. It is not in our beliefs but in our artifacts, our sensibilities and our bodily skills. Like all skills it is too embodied to be made explicit in terms of rules. Therefore it is misleading to think of a cultural style as a scheme, or conceptual framework. Our cultural style is invisible both because it is manifest in everything we see and do, and so is too pervasive to notice—like the water to the fish—and because it is in our comportment, not in our minds.[85]

As suggested by his tacit reference to Merleau-Ponty's *"comportement"*—a third way between action and bodily movement—what Dreyfus has in mind cannot be captured by propositions.[86] Cultural styles and backgrounds are not like implicit knowledge or rules, which could be made explicit in the form of knowledge or rules, even if generally nobody does. They are more like "sensibilities" and "bodily skills." As Dreyfus says, a cultural style is "in" them. Sensibilities and skills do not try to represent, describe, or affirm anything. They have a different sort of relationship to the world.

This line of thinking may be seen as an objection to the empirical investigation of people's moral backgrounds, as I have presented it in this chapter. But I think that upon careful inspection it is compatible with my arguments. First, that something is not a proposition or representation does not entail that it is ineffable or cannot be represented linguistically. It may be difficult to speak about sensibilities and bodily skills, partly because of our defective lexicon in these areas, and partly because of our lack of practice. It is surely more difficult than to speak about ordinary beliefs or actions, which we are used to speaking about. Yet, it does not follow that something that is "too embodied," a disposition, or an emotion cannot be talked about at all.

Second, my concept of the moral background does comprise propositional elements, even if they may partly manifest themselves in artifacts, buildings, institutions, emotions, dispositions, bodily movements, and so on. If this makes

---

In fact, "even to characterize it as 'uncertainty' is to adopt an absurdly severe criterion of 'certainty,' which deprives the concept of any sensible use."

85 Dreyfus, "Foreword," p. xii. Comparably, Wittgenstein says in *On Certainty* §110 that at bottom there are ways of acting: "As if giving grounds did not come to an end sometime. But the end is not an ungrounded presupposition: it is an ungrounded way of acting." Ludwig Wittgenstein. 1969. *On Certainty*. Translated by G.E.M. Anscombe and D. Paul. Oxford: Blackwell.

86 Maurice Merleau-Ponty. 1942. *La structure du comportement*. Paris: Presses universitaires de France. For Dreyfus's reading of Merleau-Ponty, see Hubert L. Dreyfus. 2000. "A Merleau-Pontyian Critique of Husserl's and Searle's Representationalist Accounts of Action." *Proceedings of the Aristotelian Society* 100:287–302; Hubert L. Dreyfus. 2002. "Intelligence without Representation—Merleau-Ponty's Critique of Mental Representation." *Phenomenology and the Cognitive Sciences* 1:367–83; Hubert L. Dreyfus. 2007. "The Return of the Myth of the Mental." *Inquiry* 50(4):352–65.

my background the black sheep of the theoretical family, so be it. Furthermore, while I hope this book will encourage ethnographic research on the moral background, this is not the kind of empirical work I have done on the ethics of business. Ethnographic research can shed light on bodily dispositions and movements and space-time orientations in a way that historical research cannot—or at least generally cannot. Naturally, my arguments in the following chapters deal with what my evidence allows me to. However, the moral background encompasses propositions, representations, and beliefs, as well as non-propositional components, dispositions, sensibilities, and artifacts. Several methods—including but not limited to historical and ethnographic ones—should work together toward a comprehensive account of it.

All in all, the concept of the moral background is a tool for empirical research. As everybody knows, tools are not objects of contemplation: their value lies in their practical utility. Therefore, in the following chapters I put the moral background to use. My empirical field is the history of business ethics, or, more precisely, the history of business ethicists' work, projects, and activities. As mentioned in the introduction, in this book the expression "business ethicists" refers to people who engaged in such work whatever their occupation or profession was: from university professors to business association leaders, from politicians to journalists, from clergymen to businessmen. Their work, projects, and activities included sermons, speeches, editorials, meetings, conferences, classes, popular writings, academic writings, ethical codes, and organizational reforms. And I talk about not only individuals, but also organizations that engaged in business ethics work, in ways that went beyond the work of their individual members. Crucially, my primary goal is not to give a historical account of the first-order normative level, such as business ethicists' prescriptions and recommendations (although I do some of that as well). Rather, my primary goal is to give a historical account of the second-order moral background, which facilitated, supported, and enabled business ethicists' prescriptions and recommendations.

2

Ethics as a Business Proposition

> Social and environmental initiatives should not be something that firms do in addition to making profit: instead, they should become a central part of the strategy for corporate prosperity.
>
> — *Doing Good: Business and the Sustainability Challenge*, 2008[1]

> In the past twenty years the service idea in business has grown to be the predominant policy; the standard of both profit and reputation. This has come about through no ethical revolution, but through the cold demonstration of business success. Service standards bring success, and only the unwise and unsuccessful today belittle them.
>
> —J. George Frederick, 1925[2]

2.1 Glaucon's Challenge

Business ethicists of all eras and persuasions have vocally held that businesspeople should not cheat, lie, or steal. So have organizations and state agencies concerned about business ethics and their consequences. They have time and again exhorted businesspeople to conduct their affairs in an ethical fashion—in their relations with customers, competitors, employees, the state, the community, the public, and the environment. They have asked businesspeople to refrain from falsifying financial statements and insider trading; from "[mingling] mahogany saw-dust with the cayenne pepper,"[3] and from "mixing . . . starch with cocoa," and "[diluting] . . . butter with lard."[4] These demands have been made by social, political, religious, and business actors and organizations of all types and varieties. And every so often, particularly in the aftermath of business scandals, they receive a great deal of public attention. The problem for these business ethicists and organizations is that their demands require a satisfactory response to a prior problem. Why should a businessperson not cheat, lie, or steal? Why should she be moral rather than immoral, really? In other words, if you say that she should not cheat, lie, or steal, what kind of "should" is this?

One possible response is that a businessperson should not lie about the quality of her products or her firm's annual financial performance, because that is illegal and she may end up in prison. Besides the personal costs thereby incurred, this is probably a bad business decision, as a consultant's risk analysis might show. These

---

1 Economist Intelligence Unit. 2008. *Doing Good: Business and the Sustainability Challenge*, p. 42.
2 J. George Frederick. 1925. *Book of Business Standards*. New York: Nicholas L. Brown, p. 48.
3 Rhoads, *Business Ethics in Relation to the Profession of the Religious Society of Friends*, p. 17.
4 Spencer, "The Morals of Trade," p. 107.

are rather prudent prudential reasons, which businesspeople care a lot about. And legislators and enforcement agencies know that businesspeople care a lot about them. Yet, for the sake of the argument, let us put prudence to one side. Suppose it is certain that a businessperson will get away with her deception. It is certain that nobody will ever find out. Alternatively, suppose that a particular unethical practice happens not to be contemplated by the law of the country. Does she still have reason not to engage in it? Put differently, this businessperson grants that lying to a client, partner, or shareholder would be morally wrong, but she still wonders what reason she has to listen to what morality says in the first place.

Whether or not she has reason to listen to what morality says, this businessperson does have reason to listen to what Plato says. For she is in fact grappling with a version of the challenge that Glaucon and Adeimantus pose to Socrates in Book II of the *Republic*.[5] The central subject of this dialogue is what justice is (the Greek word, frequently used in scholarly discussions in English, is *"dikaiosunē"*—which here means "justice," but in other contexts is translated as "righteousness").[6] In Book I, Socrates hears and refutes the argument of the immoralist sophist Thrasymachus. But Glaucon and Adeimantus, Plato's brothers in real life, are still not persuaded. Then, Glaucon challenges Socrates' account of justice by means of an ingenious thought experiment.[7] He recalls the story of Gyges, a Lydian shepherd who accidentally discovered a gold ring that made him invisible at will: "He [Gyges] was astonished at this, and again touching the ring he turned the collet outwards and reappeared; he made several trials of the ring, and always with the same result—when he turned the collet inwards he became invisible, when outwards he reappeared. Whereupon he contrived to be chosen one of the messengers who were sent to the court; where as soon as he arrived he seduced the queen, and with her help conspired against the king and slew him, and took the kingdom."[8] Glaucon then cuts to the moral chase of the story:

> Suppose now that there were two such magic rings, and the just put on one of them and the unjust the other; no man can be imagined to be of such an iron nature that he would stand fast in justice. No man would keep his hands off what was not his own when he could safely take what he liked out of the

5 There are hundreds of commentaries on this intervention of Glaucon and Adeimantus. For a succinct recent presentation, see Stanley Rosen. 2005. *Plato's Republic: A Study*. New Haven, CT; London: Yale University Press, pp. 60–76.

6 One important such context is the New Testament. Cf. Christopher D. Marshall. 2001. *Beyond Retribution: A New Testament Vision for Justice, Crime, and Punishment*. Grand Rapids, MI: Wm. B. Eerdmans, p. 38; Charles H. Talbert. 2004. *Reading the Sermon on the Mount*. Columbia: University of South Carolina Press, pp. 62–63; Nicholas Wolterstorff. 2008. *Justice: Rights and Wrongs*. Princeton: Princeton University Press, pp. 110–13.

7 *Republic* 357a–362c.

8 The story of Gyges had been told earlier by Herodotus in his *Histories*; on the relation between Plato's and Herodotus's accounts, see Andrew Laird. 2001. "Ringing the Changes on Gyges: Philosophy and the Formation of Fiction in Plato's *Republic*." *Journal of Hellenic Studies* 121:12–29. See also Katherine Philippakis. 1997. "See No Evil: The Story of Gyges in Herodotus and Plato." Pp. 27–40 in *Justice v. Law in Greek Political Thought*, edited by Leslie G. Rubin. Lanham, MD: Rowman & Littlefield.

market, or go into houses and lie with any one at his pleasure, or kill or release from prison whom he would, and in all respects be like a God among men. Then the actions of the just would be as the actions of the unjust; they would both come at last to the same point. And this we may truly affirm to be a great proof that a man is just, not willingly or because he thinks that justice is any good to him individually, but of necessity, for wherever any one thinks that he can safely be unjust, there he is unjust.

Why be just if you can be unjust and get away with it? To be sure, if the magic ring bearer already cares about being just or a morally good person, then he has good reason not to seduce the queen, not to slay the king, and to keep his hands off what is not his own. But then the question would be just pushed one step further: what reason does he have to care about being a morally good person to begin with? The reasonable fear here is circularity. On the one hand, it seems that an argument that appealed to moral considerations would be circular. On the other hand, maybe there is nothing else to appeal to but moral considerations, considerations internal to morality. If so, then a total skeptic or amoral person just cannot be won over: Thrasymachus earlier in the *Republic* and Callicles in the *Gorgias* will always remain unmoved. This is, then, the big predicament for the ethicist. Is it possible to demonstrate that one should pursue justice and be just *not* because of its good consequences, but for its own sake, as Socrates would have it? Is it possible to demonstrate that justice is intrinsically good or valuable?[9] Can virtue be shown to be its own reward, as the proverb due to Claudian and Seneca has it? Or, rather, is it inevitable to eventually fall back to consequentialist arguments, e.g., about afterlife punishments in Tartarus and rewards in the Islands of the Blessed, as in the eschatological myths at the end of the *Gorgias* and the *Republic*? In light of the sheer number of pages written about it throughout the history of philosophy, Glaucon's challenge has definitely been a challenging one.[10]

The implications of Glaucon's challenge for business ethics "are momentous."[11] For it forcefully brings out the contrast between being a moral person and being believed to be a moral person. Business ethicists have long underscored the advantageous effects of being moral on a businessperson's business. As this chapter will document, they have urged that business ethics is good business, it pays, it

---

9   Noah Lemos. 1994. *Intrinsic Value: Concept and Warrant.* New York: Cambridge University Press.

10   Characteristically for a philosophical conundrum, part of the challenge has been to agree on what exactly the challenge is and what it would take to adequately meet it. Also note that these are not incompatible alternatives. It is possible to maintain, as Plato through Socrates actually did, that justice, piety, or morality both has good consequences and is intrinsically good (cf. *Republic* 357b–358a). As Annas and Russell show, though, Plato's myths of judgment can be interpreted in different ways, and in any case the myths in the *Gorgias*, the *Phaedo*, and the *Republic* do not all try to make the same point. Julia Annas. 1982. "Plato's Myths of Judgment." *Phronesis* 27(2):119–43; Daniel C. Russell. 2001. "Misunderstanding the Myth in the *Gorgias*." *Southern Journal of Philosophy* 39(1):557–73.

11   Max L. Stackhouse, Dennis P. McCann, and Shirley J. Roels, with Preston N. Williams. 1995. *On Moral Business: Classical and Contemporary Resources for Ethics in Economic Life.* Grand Rapids, MI: William B. Eerdmans, p. 116.

is the best policy, it has dollars-and-cents value, it makes business sense, and it makes bottom-line sense. They have claimed that being moral is in your enlightened self-interest; being good is good business; you can do well by doing good. Yet, this does not seem to be quite right. As far as advantageous effects are concerned, a businessperson only needs the appearance of or reputation for being moral. There is no need for her to actually be moral *as well*—on top of the appearance, as it were. Indeed, as far as advantageous effects are concerned, actually being moral without the appearance of or reputation for being moral will not help. In brief, it seems that actually being moral is neither a necessary nor a sufficient condition for being believed to be moral. The conclusion is Machiavellian through and through.[12]

Business ethicists of all eras and persuasions have had to confront a most difficult problem, then. They have emphatically told businesspeople to conduct their business in a moral manner. But they have also had to tell them—just in case one of them is a bit too curious and wonders—why they should be moral. Thus, Glaucon's challenge has hung over the heads of business ethicists like a sword of Damocles—even over the heads of those business ethicists who have never heard of Glaucon (or of Damocles). True, businesspeople are fortunately incapable of availing themselves of magic rings, regardless of how much they would be willing to pay for them. On the other hand, sometimes the empirical conditions are such that for all intents and purposes it is as though a businessperson were indeed invisible. For sometimes the odds of being seen are really, really low. And the odds of being seen by someone who it would be deleterious to be seen by are even lower. True, if a businessperson wishes to be believed to be a moral person, sometimes the easiest method may be to actually be a moral person always—along with a good amount of publicity to make her morally praiseworthy behavior widely known. This may be cheaper than, for example, keeping track of whether someone is watching, who is watching, and so on. However, most times this is not the case: moral action is normally more costly than cutting moral corners. Finally,

---

12 In fact, it is more Machiavellian than Machiavelli, whose notorious advice in *The Prince* is only that unethical courses of action are *sometimes* necesary: "There is therefore no necessity for a prince to possess all the good qualities I have enumerated, but it is indispensible that he should appear to have them: I will even go so far as to say, that it is sometimes dangerous to make use of them, though it is always useful to seem to possess them. It is the duty of a prince most earnestly to endeavour to gain the reputation of kindness, clemency, piety, justice, and fidelity to his engagements. He ought to possess all these good qualities, but still to retain such power over himself as to display their opposites whenever it may be expedient. I maintain it that a prince, and more especially a new prince, cannot with impunity exercise all the virtues, because his own self-preservation will often compel him to violate the laws of charity, religion, and humanity. He should habituate himself to bend easily to the various circumstances which may from time to time surround him. In a word, it will be as useful to him to persevere in the path of rectitude, while he feels no inconvenience in doing so, as to know how to deviate from it when circumstances may require it. He should, above all, study to utter nothing which does not breathe kindness, justice, good faith, and piety: the last quality is however that which it is most important for him to appear to possess, as men in general judge moreby their eyes than by their other senses." Niccolò Machiavelli. [1532] 1810. *The Prince*. London: Printed for Sherwood, Neely, and Jones, pp. 102–3.

because morality is always open to the possibility of a demand for grounds, Glaucon's challenge has been sometimes anticipated (as opposed to confronted *ex post facto*). Some business ethicists have produced reasons and grounds without there being any actual pesky Glaucon and Adeimantus around, probably suspecting that the effectiveness of their work would thus increase.

This and the next chapters look at business ethicists' responses to Glaucon's challenge, and thereby address themselves to the first dimension of the moral background: grounding. I pay special attention to the resources, understandings, and normative theories on which they have drawn for that purpose. In the rest of this chapter I examine one common response to the question of why be moral in business. In fact, it consists of two distinct claims:

(1) Empirical: Acting ethically pays.
(2) Normative: Because acting ethically pays, you should act ethically.

Claim (1) is an empirical claim about the causal connections that obtain in a businessperson's environment: business ethics, corporate social responsibility, integrity, honesty, etc., will in the short or long run result in material rewards. Claim (2) is a normative claim about a businessperson's reasons for action given those causal connections (it assumes (1) to be true): that business ethics will in the short or long run result in material rewards is the reason why she ought to be ethical (or at least *a* reason). As we will see, in the United States many business actors and organizations have militantly advocated (1). "Business ethics is good for you, American businessman!" has been their battle cry. The day-to-day work of many business ethicists has been to convince businesspeople and the public that (1) is empirically true. That has been hard work. However, in the next chapter we will see that some other business actors and organizations have militantly rejected (2). The day-to-day work of these business ethicists has been to argue that, even if claim (1) were true, businesspeople should not accept normative claim (2). That work has been even harder.

The narrative of this chapter is organized as follows. Sections 2.2, 2.3, and 2.4 focus on contemporary business ethicists who publicly defend and promote claims (1) and (2). In other words, what these days gets called the "business case" for business ethics, or its effects on the bottom line. Section 2.5 examines two genealogical lineages of the business case: the old idea that honesty is the best policy, and the old concept of enlightened self-interest. Finally, sections 2.6, 2.7, and 2.8 turn to the first few decades of the twentieth century. They focus on business ethicists who publicly defended and promoted claims (1) and (2) at that time— including leaders of trade associations, Rotarians, state officials, high-status businessmen, and business school deans. In other words, what those days got called the "cash value of ethics," or its effects on the balance sheet. Note how the arguments of this chapter set the stage for the arguments of the next one. Notwithstanding its popularity in several prestigious social settings, the conjunction of claims (1) and (2) has never been universally accepted. In particular, it is not acceptable to a good Christian merchant, who must act out of morally good motives or "springs of action." He ought not to be motivated by material gain, even when material gain would motivate him to perform morally good and socially desirable actions. The motives of the Christian merchant, along with Christian business ethicists' stance on claims (1) and (2), are the topic of chapter 3.

2.2 Today's Business Ethicists

Just good business. This is the catchy title of *The Economist*'s "special report on corporate social responsibility," published in January 2008. Penned by editor Daniel Franklin, the report looks "in detail at how companies are implementing CSR [corporate social responsibility]." It concludes that CSR, "done badly, it is often just a figleaf and can be positively harmful. Done well, though, it is not some separate activity that companies do on the side, a corner of corporate life reserved for virtue: it is just good business."[13] *Just Good Business* is also the catchy title of a 2008 book by Kellie McElhaney, faculty member at the Haas business school at the University of California at Berkeley, and a private CSR consultant. The book gives advice to businesspeople, using the second person, on "how to create a top-notch CSR strategy and how to brand and communicate your CSR strategy for maximum impact." Its take-home point is straightforward:

> If this book has any power, it is in convincing you that you can and should brand and communicate your CSR. Corporate social responsibility can help firms—particularly those in highly commoditized industry segments such as consumer products or banking and financial services—to differentiate their brand and stand out above the noise when price, quality, and convenience are relatively equal. This positive impact creates a competitive advantage for these firms both when markets are up and when they're down.[14]

The book's introduction asks, "Why CSR?" And the answer is, essentially, competitive advantage. It explains how to achieve "maximum impact" through good branding and communication. But what is this maximum impact an impact *on*? Not on society, the community, or the environment. What is maximized through good branding and communication is CSR's impact on the firm's bottom line. In any event, the good news is that, as of 2008, "many businesses leaders are realizing that CSR is also a viable component of their overall business strategy"; they are "beginning to realize that an effective corporate social responsibility goal can be much more than a feel-good public relations (PR) release for prospective customers, employees, shareholders, and other stakeholders; it can have a significant and positive impact on the bottom line."[15]

Thus, *Just Good Business* claims that CSR has—or, more precisely, "can have"—a significant and positive causal impact on the bottom line. *Just Good*

---

13 Daniel Franklin. 2008. "The Economist Report on CSR." *Just Good Business* (*The Economist* special report), January 19, 2008, p. 3.

14 Kellie A. McElhaney. 2008. *Just Good Business: The Strategic Guide to Aligning Corporate Responsibility and Brand*. San Francisco: Berrett-Koehler Publishers, pp. 169, 4.

15 Ibid., pp. 13, 16.

Business also touches on the reasons businesspeople may have to conduct their business ethically. As it happens, that causal claim is the best reason: "I still typically advise companies never to lead with their corporate citizenship. Corporate citizenship should instead be linked in some way to the attributes of price or quality or both. Hormone-free means higher-quality chicken. Compact fluorescent light bulbs mean lower power-company bills."[16] Luckily, hormone-free chicken means more humanely raised chicken, too. And compact fluorescent light bulbs mean less environmental impact, too. But these are not the considerations the author directs the attention of businesspeople to—reasonably enough, perhaps, in her capacity as a CSR consultant. Indeed, her piece of advice is independent of whether a businessperson cares about ethics at all. Rather, it is all about market competition: "Whether or not you support doing something about global warming, trying to feed the world, or finding a cure for AIDS, breast cancer, or autism, companies in increasing numbers are becoming involved in these and many other social and environmental issues"; "Your competitors are developing CSR strategies. Don't let them get ahead of you."[17]

Just Good Business is just a good example. It illustrates the claim that business ethics and corporate social responsibility make business sense or bottom-line sense. There is a "business case" for business ethics; "principled behaviour pays dividends—literally."[18] Both institutionally and culturally, business ethics and CSR are quite widespread in the United States today. However small might be the proportion of firms that actually have CSR objectives and programs, CSR is much present at the high end of the status distribution, and in the public sphere more generally. Thus, Glaucon's challenge cannot go unanswered. There is a need for a legitimate and persuasive reason as to why a company should engage in CSR activities—a reason that a manager may use to answer tough questions, justify her decisions, or make a public statement on behalf of her firm. The "business case" or "just good business" is one such reason.

While business ethics and CSR are quite widespread in the United States today, how widespread is the business case as a reason? To what extent is this claim prominent? According to David Vogel, very much:

> It is impossible to exaggerate the significance of the contemporary claim that there is a business case for corporate responsibility, business ethics, corporate citizenship, environmental stewardship, pollution control, sustainable development, and the like. [. . .] [W]hile profitability may not be the only reason corporations will or should behave virtuously, it has become the most influential.

According to the business case for CSR, firms will increasingly behave more responsibly not because managers have become more public-spirited—though some may have—but because more managers now believe that being a better corporate citizen is a source of competitive advantage. A more responsibly managed firms will face fewer business risks than its less virtuous competitors:

16   Ibid., p. 170.
17   Ibid., pp. 170–71.
18   Geoffrey Heal. 2008. "Principled Behaviour Pays Dividends." *Economic Times*, January 14, 2008.

it will be more likely to avoid consumer boycotts, be better able to obtain capital at a lower cost, and be in a better position to attract and retain committed employees and loyal customers.[19]

I think Vogel is right: that contemporary claim has been very significant and influential. It would be ideal to measure its significance and influence, especially vis-à-vis alternative claims, and most especially vis-à-vis the competing claim that there is *not* a business case for business ethics. Unfortunately, it is difficult to construct a good indicator based on large corpora of textual evidence, in which morphological electronic searches reliably pick out the contending arguments. Fortunately, my account does not depend on which idea has won the battle of ideas, or which one is the most influential. It is enough that today "business ethics is good business" be a reasonable candidate or contender, or a reasonably widespread idea. And that much is not controversial, I think. It is equally uncontroversial that this idea is more likely to be produced by socially visible and high-status actors and in visible and high-status settings—which shape what earlier I called public moral normativity.

Consider some examples: legislators' and state secretaries' speeches, policy makers' reports, proposals for public funding, corporations' annual reports and public statements, business schools' and consulting firms' presentations of self on their websites, newspaper editorials and business sections, interviews on TV, business ethics manuals and textbooks, and commencement addresses. The interest of the accounts produced, validated, and legitimated in these social loci lies not in their accuracy or insightfulness. Nor do they normally provide faithful representations of how business is actually conducted, or what businesspeople truly believe if they were to introspect candidly. Rather, their interest lies in what they reveal about normative guidelines or expectations in business: what one ought to do, what good people are said to do, what is well-regarded, what one would not be embarrassed to recount to strangers at a cocktail party, what is likely to result in reputational gains for a person or firm. As Boltanski and Chiapello write as regards their data sources in *The New Spirit of Capitalism*, "management literature can be read on two levels." "We certainly find in it a source of new methods of profit-making and novel recommendations to managers for creating firms that are more efficient and more competitive." However, it "simultaneously has a high moral tone, if only because it is a normative literature stating what should be the case, not what is the case."[20]

---

19   David Vogel. 2005. *The Market for Virtue: The Potential and Limits of Corporate Social Responsibility*. Washington, DC: Brookings Institution, pp. 16–17.

20   Management literature "cannot be exclusively orientated towards the pursuit of profit. It must also justify the way profit is obtained, give *cadres* arguments with which to resist the criticisms that are bound to arise if they seek to implement its abundant recommendations, and to answer the demands for justification they will face from their subordinates or in other social arenas. [. . .] It cannot stop at economic motives and incentives. It must also be based on normative aims, taking into account not only personal aspirations to security and autonomy, but also the way these aspirations can be attached to a more general orientation to the common good." Luc Boltanski and Eve Chiapello. 2005. *The New Spirit of Capitalism*. Translated by Gregory Elliott. London: Verso, p. 58. See also Francis X. Sutton et al. 1956. *The American Business Creed*. Cambridge: Harvard University Press.

The popular business ethics and CSR literature is an extreme case of this. It explicitly lays out normative guidelines about what is moral and what is not, and tells businesspeople to have their conduct guided by them. Its style and tone resemble those of self-help or self-improvement literature, which gives advice on what to do and how to live, harking back to Samuel Smiles's 1859 best seller, *Self-Help*.[21] In fact, this is a genre that, more than merely giving readers advice or educating them, tries also to encourage, embolden, cheer, and motivate them. It is a hortative genre. As one of these books concludes: "Now that you've finished reading this book, you know how to develop an integrated CSR strategy, and you know how to turn it into a brand, communicate it, and tell your CSR story. As you reflect on what you have learned, I ask you just one thing: *please don't do nothing*."[22] As another book concludes: "We encourage you to put these principles to work in your firm, building a great company and contributing to the creation of a good society."[23]

The implicit or explicit premise is that business and morality can be reconciled, everyone will win, capitalism is not morally bad even if there will always be a few bad apples among businesspeople (as among any other group), and the ethics of business can and should be improved through education, incentives, organizational design, or legislation. While economic growth used to come "at the expense of the natural environment and . . . sometimes at the expense of the under-privileged," "[n]ow things are changing." Even more: "we can see the outline of a new system in which we can enjoy the undoubted benefits of a competitive market economy without the social or environmental costs."[24] On the whole, this body of business ethics work conveys an "unabashedly positive and hopeful" message about the interaction and intersection between capitalism and morality, markets and morals, making profits and being good.[25]

2.3 The Business Case

If you browse through the latest issues of a business magazine, business section of a newspaper, or business blog, it should not be long until you run into a discussion about business ethics or CSR. Perhaps the author will be against it; perhaps she will be for it. Yet, whether she is a detractor or an enthusiast, she will probably broach at some point the relationship between corporate or financial performance on the one hand, and business ethics and CSR on the other. Do they pay? Do they have no effect? What is the nature of the relationship between these variables? Is there a "business case" for business ethics, environmental responsibility, or concern for the well-being of stakeholders? If you are a regular reader

---

21 Samuel Smiles. [1859] 1881. *Self-Help*. Chicago: Belford, Clarke, & Co.
22 McElhaney, *Just Good Business*, p. 179.
23 Ira A. Jackson and Jane Nelson. 2004. *Profits with Principles: Seven Strategies for Delivering Value with Values*. New York: Currency/Doubleday, p. 347.
24 Geoffrey Heal, "Principled Behaviour Pays Dividends."
25 Jackson and Nelson, *Profits with Principles*, p. 2.

of business magazines, business sections of newspapers, and business blogs, you may have realized how often the exact same points are rehashed. New case studies, data sources, or illustrations may be invoked, new experts may be consulted, and new jargon may be coined. However, you find few (if any) truly novel stances, arguments, or counterarguments, and little (if any) increase in argumentative sophistication.

These discussions often deal with the two claims singled out earlier: (1) ethics pays; and (2) because ethics pays you should be ethical. The former, (1), comes in several varieties. It might refer to the effects of business ethics, narrowly conceived—say, fairness and honesty in business relations. Or to the effects of CSR more broadly—say, attention to the welfare of stakeholders, that is, those affected by the company in one way or another. It might refer to good old philanthropy or charity—about which it is said that "smart giving is good business."[26] Or to sustainability or "environmental strategy," that is, the strategic use of environmental policy—where the examples to be followed are "smart companies" that "use environmental strategy" and "seize competitive advantage through strategic management of environmental challenges."[27]

These ideas have been phrased in various ways, but a common way of speaking is that business ethics, philanthropy, or CSR are sources of "competitive advantage."[28] One competitive advantage of "competitive advantage" is that it can be effortlessly weaved into standard management terminology, and ways of thinking, speaking, and teaching. So can discussions about the "alignment" of companies' social and financial goals. That is, how they may "align social, environmental and economic performance drivers with core business strategies," or how they may "[align] corporate responsibility and brand"—where CSR is seen in relation to business strategy, branding, and risk.[29] And so can discussions about "investment returns" and the "business case" for business ethics or CSR: "In business practitioner terms, a 'business case' is a pitch for investment in a project or initiative that promises to yield a suitably significant return to justify the expenditure. In what has become known as the 'business case for Corporate Social Responsibility (CSR)' the pitch is that a company can 'do well by doing good.'"[30] Of much historical significance (as we will see) is the expression "enlightened self-interest."

26 Curt Weeden. 2011. *Smart Giving is Good Business: How Corporate Philanthropy Can Benefit Your Company and Society*. San Francisco: Jossey-Bass.

27 Daniel C. Esty and Andrew S. Winston. 2009. *Green to Gold: How Smart Companies Use Environmental Strategy to Innovate, Create Value, and Build Competitive Advantage*. 2nd ed. Hoboken, NJ: John Wiley & Sons, p. 3.

28 On philanthropy in particular, see Michael E. Porter and Mark R. Kramer. [2002] 2003. "The Competitive Advantage of Corporate Philanthropy." Pp. 27–64 in *Harvard Business Review on Corporate Responsibility*. Boston: Harvard Business School Press.

29 Wayne Visser, Dirk Matten, Manfred Pohl, and Nick Tolhurst. 2010. *The A to Z of Corporate Social Responsibility*. 2nd ed. Chichester, UK: John Wiley & Sons, p. 370; McElhaney, *Just Good Business*.

30 E. C. Kurucz, B. A. Colbert, and D. C. Wheeler. 2008. "The Business Case for Corporate Social Responsibility." Pp. 83–112 in *The Oxford Handbook on Corporate Social Responsibility*, edited by A. Crane, A. McWilliams, D. Matten, J. Moon, and D. Seigel. Oxford: Oxford University Press, p. 84.

While perhaps less common today, business ethicists still use it occasionally. For example, in the aforementioned *The Economist* special report on CSR, the article concludes:

> One way of looking at CSR is that it is part of what businesses need to do to keep up with (or, if possible, stay slightly ahead of) society's fast-changing expectations. It is an aspect of taking care of a company's reputation, managing its risks and gaining a competitive edge. This is what good managers ought to do anyway. [...]
>
> So paying attention to CSR can amount to enlightened self-interest, something that over time will help to sustain profits for shareholders. The truly responsible business never loses sight of the commercial imperative. It is, after all, by staying in business and providing products and services people want that firms do most good. If ignoring CSR is risky, ignoring what makes business sense is a certain route to failure.[31]

CSR is what good managers ought to do anyway. For ethics causes profits; responsibility improves financial performance. Yet, if you are a business ethicist, how do you show that this is the case? In particular, how do you show this to an audience such as newspaper readers? How do you show this not to patient business scholars, but to busy business students who must hurry to their next class, or busy business executives who must hurry to the airport or the golf course? Ultimately, you are not trying to find out the truth about the size of a causal effect. You are not trying to win an academic debate, but to win over businesspeople and encourage them to follow your practical recommendations.

If you manage to get their attention in-between classes, meetings, flights, or swings, you may want to give them at least three things. Or so the popular business literature has done. First, it has offered examples of correlations between the two variables, that is, examples of companies that score high or low on both. Sizeable charitable contribution to Uruguayan banana farmers at time t_1, stocks went up at time t_2. No concern for the local community at time t_1, company went out of business at time t_2. The good news is that this is not a scholarly paper, so cherry-picked examples are tolerated, even desirable due to their evocative qualities. Like in everyday conversation, one case, anecdote, or experience may be used to give support to a general statement: met one courteous Uruguayan person, therefore Uruguayans are a courteous people. Complaints about logic or method are unlikely to arise.

Second, they have provided businesspeople with the opinion of their peers, either through interviews with opinion leaders, or aggregate survey data. Both kinds of support are meant to show the pervasiveness of the opinion that ethics pays. For instance, according to a 2008 Economist Intelligence Unit report on corporate citizenship: "Seventy-four percent of respondents to the survey conducted for this report say that corporate citizenship can also help to increase profits at

31 Franklin, "The Economist Report on CSR," p. 14.

their company."[32] Or consider what the executive summary of the Economist Intelligence Unit report, *Doing Good: Business and the Sustainability Challenge*, says: "*Sustainability does pay*. Most executives (57%) say that the benefits of pursuing sustainable practices outweigh the costs, although well over eight out of ten expect any change to profits to be small."[33] Now, this is a clear *non sequitur*: from most executives' belief that sustainability pays it does not follow that sustainability pays. Opinion surveys do not speak to this question at all. Yet, this statistical fact can be rhetorically powerful all the same. If the reader is a businessperson with no independent source of evidence or knowledge, what the majority of businesspeople believe may be a reason for him to follow suit.

Third, "ethics pays" is a causal claim, and causal claims require the identification of mechanisms. The question, then, is what are the mechanisms through which CSR, or business ethics more generally, may make a bottom-line difference. On this count, there is much agreement. For example, in their book, *What Matters Most*, Hollender and Fenichell identify "five key areas":

Here we make *The Business Case for Social Corporate Responsibility* by citing a wealth of research demonstrating convincingly that responsible businesses not only perform as well as values-neutral businesses but also in most cases actually outperform them based upon traditional financial metrics.

The following research represents a small sampling of evidence supporting the business case for CSR, which revolves around five key areas:

I. CORPORATE FINANCIAL PERFORMANCE
[...]
II. CSR INVESTMENT RETURNS
III. THE COST OF GETTING CAUGHT DOING THE WRONG THING
IV. MANAGING REPUTATION AND TRUST
V. IMPROVEMENTS IN EMPLOYEE LOYALTY AND PRODUCTIVITY[34]

Comparably, according to McElhaney, the "value of CSR" lies not in increase in share price but "human resources, reputation, branding, and operational cost savings." For instance, "changing photocopiers to double-sided will decrease operating costs."[35] Or the effect might be more indirect—e.g., CSR has an effect on the hiring and retaining of good employees, which in turn has an effect on financial performance. According to Weeden, who is specifically talking about "company donations," their effects include "enhanced company or brand name recognition, basic research that is a door-opener to discoveries that may have long-term commercial

32 Economist Intelligence Unit. 2008. *Corporate Citizenship: Profiting from a Sustainable Business*, pp. 5, 22.

33 Economist Intelligence Unit. 2008. *Doing Good: Business and the Sustainability Challenge*, p. 5 (cf. p. 31).

34 Jeffrey Hollender and Stephen Fenichell. 2004. *What Matters Most: How a Small Group of Pioneers Is Teaching Social Responsibility to Big Business, and Why Big Business Is Listening*. New York: Basic Books, p. 307.

35 McElhaney, *Just Good Business*, pp. 11–12.

potential, community services that improve a plant location so it becomes a more desirable site for new hires, and the list goes on."[36] Similarly, in *Corporate Social Responsibility: Doing the Most Good for Your Company and Your Cause*, Kotler and Lee discuss the following: increased sales and market share, strengthened brand positioning, enhanced corporate image and clout, increased ability to attract, motivate, and retain employees, decreased operating costs, and increased appeal to investors and financial analysts. Kotler and Lee add that these mechanisms do work: "[t]here is growing evidence that it [participation in corporate social initiatives] *does good* for the brand and the bottom line as well as for the community."[37]

In truth, though, the empirical validation of causal claim (1) is not good enough yet. This is because the mechanisms that connect causes and effects depend on accidental facts about their social and cultural context. For instance, imagine a society where almost nobody cares about the environment; educational, social, and political institutions do not thematize and problematize the future of the planet; and so on. Or imagine a society where knowledge about the future of forests, waters, and climate has not been produced at all, so people are not even aware that that might be a problem. If an environmentally conscious Danish or Canadian entrepreneur opens a branch of her business in one such society, her sustainability policies will not get her more business (nor will they get her less business, of course, provided they do not have adverse side effects). As a consequence, environmental strategy may or may not pay off; for instance, it may pay off if your customers are white, middle-class Green Bay women, but not if they are upper-class, Afro-Uruguayan men. From a bottom-line perspective, the relevant question is to what degree a firm's relevant others, the actors on which its profits depend, happen to care about business ethics.

Contemporary business ethicists tend to be optimistic on this count, too. The news is good, they tell us. The relevant others of business do care. For example, a recent textbook raises the question, "Why Is CSR Important?" Part of its answer is as follows:

CSR is important . . . because it influences all aspects of a company's operations. Increasingly, consumers want to buy products from companies they trust, suppliers want to form business partnerships with companies they can rely on, employees want to work for companies they respect, large investment funds want to support firms that they perceive to be socially responsible, and nonprofits and NGOs want to work together with companies seeking practical solutions to common goals. Satisfying each of these stakeholder groups (and others) allows companies to maximize their commitment to their owners (their ultimate stakeholders), who benefit most when all of these groups' needs are being met.[38]

36   Weeden, *Smart Giving is Good Business*, p. 3.
37   Philip Kotler and Nancy Lee. 2005. *Corporate Social Responsibility: Doing the Most Good for Your Company and Your Cause*. Hoboken, NJ: Wiley, pp. 10–11.
38   William B. Werther and David Chandler. 2011. *Strategic Corporate Social Responsibility: Stakeholders in a Global Environment*. 2nd ed. Thousand Oaks, CA: Sage, p. 19.

My concern is not whether any of this is empirically true or even reasonable to maintain. For instance, it seems reasonable to suppose that suppliers have always wanted to form business partnerships with companies they can rely on. What warrants the diachronic assertion that this is increasingly the case? And this is precisely the point. The point of much popular business literature is normative, prescriptive, and even motivational: to make claims about what a businessperson ought to do, and to persuade him or her to do that. Business ethics and CSR textbooks, in particular, have a particular practical use and goal. They are addressed to business students, they are used in business courses, and they try to make the case that CSR is a good and necessary thing. Even though it is in theory possible that a CSR textbook be against or cynical about CSR, such textbook would not sell many copies, and hence it is unlikely to get into print. This is analogous to the structural predictability of the opinions of corporations' ethics officers and ethics and compliance consultants. Then, the word "increasingly" has a rhetorical function. It looks descriptive or constative, but pragmatically it has a further function or point: to encourage and exhort. The authors' point is that the facts that are needed for the "ethics pays" mechanism to work do obtain today, will obtain even more tomorrow, and in light of this you, the reader, should get on board with the movement as well! Business ethicists need to proclaim this loudly to businesspeople and business students, in order to counteract the many CSR skeptics and cynics out there, whose voices are said to be loud as well.[39]

2.4 Do the Right Thing

Up to now I have discussed the contemporary claim that business ethics and CSR pay, that is, claim (1). With regard to claim (2), my narrative might have made it seem as if there were only one game in town. It might have made it seem as if ethicists, pundits, politicians, and manuals always unambiguously responded to "why be moral" in the same way. The reason why you should not cheat or you should give to the community is their eventual economic payoffs.[40] Yet, this is not accurate. There is another answer that also turns up sometimes, in certain contexts and situations. It goes like this. You will no doubt profit from doing this action

---

39 Similarly, Heal tells the reader that there is a trend: "there are growing forces that make it in a company's financial interest to be concerned about its social and environmental footprint. There is evidence that capital markets penalize companies for what is perceived as antisocial behavior, and that consumers are increasingly willing to do the same. To the extent that this is true, companies can gain financially from concern about environmental and social impacts of their activities." These forces are growing, so financial gain today, but more financial gain tomorrow. Geoffrey Heal. 2008. *When Principles Pay: Corporate Social Responsibility and the Bottom Line*. New York: Columbia Business School Pub., p. 2.

40 Claim (2) gives policy considerations to act in ways that are deemed ethical and to refrain from acting in ways that are deemed unethical. Can you still say that this is in some sense a moral reason? I do not need to normatively take sides on this issue, which depends on the moral theory you endorse. But I return to it descriptively in chapter 3.

that the business ethics and CSR perspective recommends. But this is the morally right thing to do *as well*. Luckily, the two kinds of considerations and points of view agree on what you should do. So you have two reasons to do it. Is life not great? As Jackson and Nelson put it in *Profits with Principles*:

> We are convinced that the companies playing a leadership role in address-ing these challenges [low levels of trust, high levels of inequality, and rising levels of environmental damage] will reap sound business benefits in terms of long-term competitive advantage, better risk management, and new mar-ket opportunities. At the same time, in a world where the private sector is increasingly powerful and influential, taking on a greater leadership is simply the responsible thing to do. This leadership role is about value and also about values; about competition and also about collaboration; about economics and also about ethics.[41]

"Right" or "morally right" in lieu of "responsible" would have probably sounded too moralistic in this businesslike context. But the point is the same. Both elements are at play at the same time: reaping sound benefits and doing what is right. Even if there is no explicit discussion of reasons for action, it is implied that both are good reasons for a businessperson to do what business ethics and CSR recommend.

Similarly, the "Executive Summary" of the Economist Intelligence Unit report on corporate citizenship affirms that "[t]he strategy [of leading companies] is characterised as much by a hunger for new business opportunities as by the urge to do the right thing." So, again, both money hunger and morality urge are at play. However, it then adds: "To convince senior executives that corporate citizenship is effective, the financial benefit must be clear. Companies must set ambitious goals, along with ways of keeping track of progress towards them." Not surpris-ingly, given the goals and audience of a report by *The Economist*, "we conclude by offering practical advice for firms wishing to use corporate citizenship in order to improve their bottom line."[42] While "the urge to do the right thing" is mentioned, the emphasis is on the bottom line. Indeed, recall the title of the report: *Corporate Citizenship: Profiting from a Sustainable Business*. The bottom line is also empha-sized in Jackson and Nelson's *Profits with Principles*. That an action is "simply the responsible thing to do" is mentioned, but, as the "product description" suggests, that is not where the book's priorities lie:

> At a time when unethical business practices continue to dominate the busi-ness press, PROFITS WITH PRINCIPLES offers persuasive proof that when businesses combine profit making with a concern for values and the greater good, they do better in the marketplace than those that concentrate only on the bottom line.

---

41 Jackson and Nelson, *Profits with Principles*, pp. x–xi.
42 Economist Intelligence Unit. 2008. *Corporate Citizenship: Profiting from a Sustainable Busi-ness*, p. 4.

In PROFITS WITH PRINCIPLES, Ira A. Jackson and Jane Nelson show the quantifiable and enduring business advantage to "doing the right thing." The companies profiled in PROFITS WITH PRINCIPLES . . . have implemented different strategies to build trust and gain a competitive advantage. What they share, however, are basic operating principles of making values integral to the way they do business. By focusing on creating societal as well as shareholder value, they have built market share, improved risk management, enhanced innovation, strengthened consumer loyalty, and attracted the best talent.

[. . .]

This breakthrough guide on how companies can build trust and grow market share by making a difference opens the door to a new kind of capitalism, providing a wealth of infinitely useful and practical recommendations a company of any size can adapt.[43]

The target audience of this book is active businesspeople, and the authors, as any rational *homo economicus* would, probably prefer to sell more to less copies. Then, "a wealth of infinitely useful and practical recommendations" that help "build trust and grow market share" is the kind of content that can increase sales and hence the authors' wealth. Further, the product description is precisely the place for a sales pitch. All of which makes the observed facts even more significant. The emphasis turns out to be on the long-term-profits reason, not on the just-doing-the-right-thing reason. More generally, in the contemporary business ethics documents I have analyzed, the two reasons are not on a par. While I lack a quantitative measure of this difference, it seems to me clear that "because it pays" takes precedence, both in terms of attention and argumentative importance.[44]

Then, why mention the because-it-is-the-right-thing-to-do reason at all? I cannot read the minds of business ethics speakers and writers, but let me make two observations. First, the two reasons are not logically incompatible, so it is not necessary to reject one to support the other. If mentioning this additional reason is seen as a cost, it is a relatively small one. It amounts to some space in a text, some time in a speech, some diversion of attention in both texts and speeches. Second, it can yield gains. As we will see, it may anticipate specific criticisms (though, as we shall see as well, it cannot silence them completely). It may mitigate the impression of materialism or excessive interest in the profit side of the equation, which may conflict with authors' self-understanding or "self-concept."[45] After all, these are people who worry about business ethics—so much so that they spend much time thinking, speaking, and writing about it. Moreover, the impression of

---

43   Jackson and Nelson, *Profits with Principles*.

44   For a similar situation, see Douglas V. Porpora and Alexander Nikolaev. 2008. "Moral Muting in U.S. Newspapers Op-Eds Debating the Attack on Iraq." *Discourse & Communication* 2(2):165–84, pp. 177–78.

45   Neil Gross. 2008. *Richard Rorty: The Making of an American Philosopher.* Chicago: University of Chicago Press.

materialism may be a turn-off for part of the audience. It is plausible to suppose that people come to a book or talk about business ethics with at least some interest in the ethics side of the equation; in order to learn about profit-making they go to other talks and books.

At the end of the day, however, "ethics pays" tends to predominate. The person to whom business ethicists primarily address themselves is the hard-nosed businessperson or the future hard-nosed businessperson, who wants to learn about the effects of ethics on profits, and who may view moral talk as irrelevant, something like moral window-dressing. It is imperative that this businessperson be persuaded; preaching to the choir is fun, but not equally urgent. Generally, then, that you should do what is right because it is the right thing to do gets only in-passing attention. It can even feel like a reverential or courteous hat tipping to ethics and purely ethical considerations. Generally, the main desideratum is to sound properly businesslike—use businesslike expressions, make businesslike, practical, no-nonsense, hard-nosed suggestions—even when talking about ethics. Or, maybe, *especially* when talking about ethics. Like social scientists whose main desideratum is to sound properly scientific, business ethicists sometimes sound defensive, too. An ethical, CSR, or environmental initiative or consideration is not merely a "feel-good digression from the real work of a company. It's an essential element of business strategy in the modern world."[46] The contrast between "feel-good digression" and "real work" is a familiar one. Men of affairs have long been fond of it, and have long used it to dismiss "idealistic," "impractical," and "lofty" projects and ideas. "Because it is the right thing to do" belongs to this category; it is not a properly businesslike consideration. Nor is "charity." As one anonymous businessperson illustratively said: "It's not about charity; it's about the fact that if you do the right things in the community, the community will do the right things for you. If you do the right things for the environment, you'll have a stronger business so that you can make more money."[47]

All in all, the general tenor and feel of popular business writing about claim (2) might be best illustrated by an unexpected source: an MBA student. The story is reported in a 2007 article about sustainability programs at business schools in *The Chronicle of Higher Education*. It comes from the University of Michigan at Ann Arbor, which "offers a master's degree in global sustainable enterprise that combines an M.B.A. with a master of science from the School of Natural Resources and Environment":

> This summer and next, two students from that program will take turns working as interns for the Dow Chemical Company and Environmental Defense, a New York City-based advocacy group. Marc Weatherill spent this summer helping the group identify partnerships like the one it forged several years ago with McDonald's, which resulted in more environmentally friendly hamburger packaging.

46 Esty and Winston, *Green to Gold*, p. 3.
47 Quoted in Kurucz et al., "The Business Case for Corporate Social Responsibility," p. 83.

"The idea is not to make a philanthropic proposal but to come up with one that makes solid business sense," says Mr. Weatherill, who will switch to Dow next summer. "There's something to be said for doing things because it's the right thing to do. But if businesses are going to go broke doing it, there are limits to what they'll be willing to accept."[48]

True, there is something to be said for it. But whatever that something is, what carries the day is and ought to be what makes business sense. *Solid* business sense. Whether you like it or not, that is the hard reality of the market today.

2.5 Policy and Self-Interest

In the preceding sections I looked at the business ethicists of today; in the rest of this chapter I look at the business ethicists of yesteryears. Vogel argues that it is impossible to exaggerate the significance of the contemporary claim that there is a business case for business ethics. I argue that it is impossible to exaggerate the significance of the claim that there is a business case for business ethics in the first decades of the twentieth century. However, as chapter 3 will show in detail, significance does not mean universal acceptance. I argue, too, that in the early twentieth century public attention to the business ethics problem increased, and new actors concerned themselves with it. In fact, a new configuration of actors and organizations came together in the business ethics field at the time—which is the focus of much of the historical narrative of this book.

These old business ethicists, then, may sound strikingly familiar to contemporary ears. Yet, to better understand the business ethicists of the early twentieth century, we must understand what they, in turn, were able to draw and build on. For the business case has much deeper and older roots. Because of their later relevance, the idea that honesty is the best policy and the concept of enlightened self-interest merit special attention as historical precursors. Take the former first: ancient children were already aware of the beneficial effects of honesty. For example, Aesop's fable "Hermes and the Woodcutter" (Perry Index 173) in the sixth century BC makes just this point. "The Merchant of Seri," one of the Jātaka tales of the Theravāda Buddhist tradition (originally collected in the fourth century BC), makes just this point. While only the latter has to do specifically with commerce, both tales uphold the relevant causal claim: ethics pays. What is more, they are meant to give people reasons for action. Even though they do not explicitly state normative claim (2) in so many words, keep in mind that these are popular tales and fables. Presumably, their pragmatic point is to urge children—and grown-ups—to behave ethically and honestly.

The idea that honesty pays has had many versions and incarnations, but one of them is especially noteworthy here. It originates in the eighteenth century and

---

48   Katherine Mangan. 2007. "People, Profit, and Planet." *Chronicle of Higher Education*, September 7, 2007, p. A14.

in the United States.[49] This is "that most important principle of the capitalistic ethic," which Weber identifies in *The Protestant Ethic and the Spirit of Capitalism*: "[W]e have already called attention to that most important principle of the capitalistic ethic which is generally formulated 'honesty is the best policy'. Its classical document is the tract of Franklin quoted above. And even in the judgment of the seventeenth century the specific form of the worldly asceticism of the Baptists, especially the Quakers, lay in the practical adoption of this maxim."[50] It is problematic to claim, as Weber does, that "the tract of Franklin quoted above" is "the classical document" of that principle. Neither Franklin's "Advice to a Young Tradesman" (1748) nor his "Necessary Hints to Those that Would Be Rich" (1736) properly fit the bill.[51] Philological niceties aside, and as any well brought-up American citizen knows, Franklin did relentlessly promote honesty, industry, and frugality. He represented the honest, industrious, and frugal businessman as a moral model. And he did hold that honesty is the best policy elsewhere, even if that relationship might not have been his central concern.

Whatever pedantic Franklin scholars may say he said, Franklin has come to be seen as representing that view, and has even been erroneously said to have coined the phrase, "honesty is the best policy"—including, e.g., in D. H. Lawrence's critical essay, "Benjamin Franklin." What is more, in Franklin you can clearly discern two gaps or tensions in that view, which this book is particularly interested in: the apparent gap between honesty and other virtues, and the apparent gap between honesty and the appearance of honesty. With regard to the former, consider Franklin's preface to his 1756 *Poor Richard's Almanack*. The author, "Richard Saunders," tells his "courteous reader" why the almanac he bought was worth buying: "I suppose my Almanack may be worth the Money thou hast paid for it," "for with a View to the Improvement of thy *Mind* and thy *Estate*, I have constantly interspers'd in every little Vacancy, *Moral Hints, Wise Sayings,* and *Maxims of Thrift*, tending to impress the Benefits arising from *Honesty, Sobriety, Industry* and *Frugality*; which if thou hast duly observed, it is highly probable thou art *wiser* and *richer* many fold more than the Pence my Labours have cost thee."

49   The phrase has been found in print in English as early as 1605. In the second half of that century we find titles such as Marchamont Needham's (1678) *Honesty's best policy*, the anonymous *Plain dealing is a jewel, and honesty the best policy* (1682), and Charlwood Lawton's (1689) *Honesty is the best policy*. A search in three large electronic collections of historical texts—*The Making of the Modern World, Sabin Americana*, and *America's Historical Imprints*—yields the following results. Between 1700 and 1850, "honesty is the best policy" occurs, respectively, in 162, 121, and 119 items.

50   Max Weber [1904–1905] 1930. *The Protestant Ethic and the Spirit of Capitalism*. Translated by Talcott Parsons. New York: Charles Scribner's Sons, p. 151. For a better translation, see Max Weber. [1904–1905] 2011. *The Protestant Ethic and the Spirit of Capitalism*. Translated by Stephen Kalberg. New York: Oxford University Press.

51   The "tract of Franklin quoted above" is "Advice to a Young Tradesman" (1748). "Advice to a Young Tradesman" may be considered a classical document of frugality, industry, or creditworthiness as capitalist virtues, but not of "honesty is the best policy." In fact, the papers of Benjamin Franklin, housed at Yale University, contain only three documents in which this phrase occurs: "Comparison of Great Britain and America as to Credit" (1777), a letter to Edward Bridgen (1779), and "The American Commissioners to Robert R. Livingston" (1783).

In this passage, honesty, sobriety, industry, and frugality are lumped together. Yet, they are in one sense dissimilar. It is easy to see that material benefits arise from sobriety, industry, and frugality. The causal mechanism at work is obvious. Going to bed early rather than going to the tavern and getting inebriated means more and better time devoted to work and decreased odds of cirrhosis and black eyes, both of which in turn increase the odds of financial success. Hence, "early to bed, and early to rise, make a man healthy, wealthy, and wise," as Franklin put it elsewhere. Besides, the cost of the almanac is not too high a bar anyway. By contrast, it is not obvious what material benefits arise from honesty alone. By lumping it together with sobriety, industry, and frugality, you can get away with not working this out—a frequent legerdemain in the history of the "ethics pays" doctrine.

The second tension in Franklin's work is the usual Achilles' heel of honesty-is-the-best-policy advocates. Consider Franklin's oft-quoted piece of advice in "Advice to a Young Tradesman," which calls the young tradesman's attention to the sharpness of creditors' eyes and ears:

> The most trifling Actions that affect a Man's Credit, are to be regarded. The Sound of your Hammer at Five in the Morning or Nine at Night, heard by a Creditor, makes him easy Six Months longer. But if he sees you at a Billiard Table, or hears your Voice in a Tavern, when you should be at Work, he sends for his Money the next Day. Finer Cloaths than he or his Wife wears, or greater Expence in any particular than he affords himself, shocks his Pride, and he duns you to humble you. Creditors are a kind of People, that have the sharpest Eyes and Ears, as well as the best Memories of any in the World.

Maybe creditors do have sharp eyes and ears. But if they were blind or deaf, or one day lost their sight or hearing, you could go to the tavern or play billiards as much as you felt like. You may own fine clothes as long as you do not wear them in their presence. Come to think about it, why not record the sound of your hammer and set it to play automatically at five in the morning to pretend you are already working? As Weber observed in his commentary on Franklin in *The Protestant Ethic*, something seems to have gone morally astray here:

> Now, all Franklin's moral attitudes are coloured with utilitarianism. Honesty is useful, because it assures credit; so are punctuality, industry, frugality, and that is the reason they are virtues. A logical deduction from this would be that where, for instance, the appearance of honesty serves the same purpose, that would suffice, and an unnecessary surplus of this virtue would evidently appear to Franklin's eyes as unproductive waste. And as a matter of fact, the story in his autobiography of his conversion to those virtues, or the discussion of the value of a strict maintenance of the appearance of modesty, the assiduous belittlement of one's own deserts in order to gain general recognition later, confirms this impression. According to Franklin, those virtues, like all others, are only in so far virtues as they are actually useful to the individual, and the surrogate of mere appearance is always sufficient when it

accomplishes the end in view. It is a conclusion which is inevitable for strict utilitarianism.[52]

Virtues are virtues because of their good or useful or profitable consequences of one kind or another. Alas, this stance opens the door to Glaucon's challenge: the appearance of virtue and actual virtue are morally indistinguishable, insofar as they serve the same practical purposes or have equally useful practical consequences. It also opens the door to accusations of hypocrisy. That is what critics of business ethics and CSR often say today. And that is what Weber remarked as well: "[t]he impression of many Germans that the virtues professed by Americanism are pure hypocrisy," illustrated, for example, by Ferdinand Kürnberger's "clever and malicious" 1855 novel, *Der Amerikamüde: Amerikanisches Kulturbild.*

In his defense, Franklin is not primarily talking about honesty per se or how to lead a good life. He is primarily talking about credit and creditworthiness. And he is giving advice about creditworthiness in popular pieces of writing, such as *Poor Richard's Almanack* and *Way to Wealth*, addressed to ordinary merchants, not moral philosophers. Like trustworthiness yet unlike honesty, creditworthiness is necessarily a relational property, which requires other people's perception (compare with honesty and acting honestly). Franklin is making conditional statements about this subject. If you wish to have good credit, then do thus and so. It is an empirical fact that reputation is the basis of credit; if you wish to have a good reputation, then do thus and so. Industry and the appearance of industry, or honesty and the appearance of honesty, are indeed undistinguishable as far as creditworthiness is concerned. However, *pace* Weber, Franklin does not hold them to be morally indistinguishable. He simply recommends businesspeople to publicize widely their own virtues, hard work, and honesty. Perhaps what made Europeans uncomfortable was Americans' comfortableness with tooting their own horn—their hard work, honesty, success, good deeds, charitable donations, or undergraduate GPA's and extracurricular activities.[53]

"Honesty is the best policy" conveys the message that being good, morally, is good for you, financially. An analogous message is conveyed by the concept of enlightened self-interest—which is also ubiquitous in the history of business ethics. What is this concept? Where does it come from? The story can begin with a problem faced by modern and contemporary political and social theorists: the tension, or seeming tension, between the good of the individual and the good of the collective. Is there a necessary conflict between individuals' or citizens' desires, goals, interests, rights, and freedoms on the one hand, and, on the other, the

---

52 Here the word "utilitarianism" can be confusing. Weber is not referring to the moral philosophy of Bentham, Mill, Henry Sidgwick, or (surely not) Peter Singer; instead, he means roughly what we mean by "consequentialism."

53 Weber discusses honesty and policy in *Ancient Judaism*, *General Economic History*, the essay "The Protestant Sects and the Spirit of Capitalism," and *Protestant Ethic*. Cf. Max Weber. 1952. *Ancient Judaism.* Translated and edited by Hans H. Gerth and Don Martinadale. Glencoe, IL: Free Press, p. 344; Max Weber. 1950. *General Economic History.* Translated by Frank H. Knight. Glencoe, IL: Free Press, pp. 366–67; Max Weber, *Protestant Ethic*, pp. 282–83.

public good, the interest of all, the general will, or the commonweal, represented by the modern state and other public institutions? If so, what is the nature of this conflict, why is it necessary, and what is to be done about it? These questions are of great political import, and they became more and more pressing as both modern states and individualistic cultural worldviews grew stronger.

One of political and social theorists' answers is that, appearances to the contrary, in fact there is no conflict. There is no need to worry. In fact, not only is individuals' pursuit of their selfish interests compatible with the public good. It actually brings about more public good than altruistic individuals would. Butchers, bakers, and brewers selfishly set out to make a profit for themselves, yet, as a result, we all end up better off: we have delicious food and drink on our tables, as well as democratic governments and international peace. Or so the argument goes anyway. Differently put, as Mandeville put it in *The Grumbling Hive* (1705) and *The Fable of the Bees* (1714), there is a causal relationship between bees' being privately vicious and hives' being publicly virtuous, or, more generally, a causal relationship between private vice and public virtue. In Mandeville's hive, "every Part was full of Vice / Yet the whole Mass a Paradice." Yet, if you let Jupiter turn knaves honest, the public good shall go to Hades. Moral of the story: you should stick with knaves.

The claims attributed to Mandeville, Adam Smith, and their numerous followers may be summarized as follows:

(M) Each individual does what is in her selfish interest or what self-interest recommends → Society as a whole ends up better off materially (or otherwise)
(M') Each individual acts morally or does what morality recommends → Society as a whole ends up worse off materially (or otherwise)

These arguments may seem counterintuitive and puzzling. Indeed, they look a bit like a magic trick: terrible starting point, terrific endpoint. These arguments have been very helpful to liberal understandings of how modern societies work, how they automatically work, what the rights of individuals are, and what the role of the state ought to be (basically, to be quiet). They have also been very helpful to understandings of markets as having good, "civilizing" effects on society.[54] And they have also helped resist gloomy Hobbesian accounts, according to which there is a necessary antagonism between individuals' desires and inclinations and the public good.[55]

Unfortunately, though, from the point of view of business ethics, the Mandeville and Smith approach is not all that helpful. For it appears to promote knavery and immorality. True, it may not actually promote knavery and immorality in the sense that business ethicists have in mind. Or it may be unclear what they promote, because the words "morally," "honesty," "knavery," and "self-interest"

---

54 Cf. Fourcade and Healy, "Moral Views of Market Society."
55 The Hobbesian claim may be expressed as follows: (H) Each individual does what is in her selfish interest or what self-interest recommends → Society as a whole ends up worse off materially (and otherwise).

are ambiguously used. At the very least, they do not explicitly promote morality. Fortunately, there is a relative of the approach of Mandeville and Smith that has picked up the tab, so to speak, and thus has been very helpful to business ethicists. It may be called the Tocquevillian approach, or the enlightened-self-interest approach, and it may be summarized as follows:

(T) Each individual acts morally or does what morality recommends → She herself ends up better off materially (or otherwise)
(T') Each individual acts immorally or does not do what morality recommends → She herself ends up worse off materially (or otherwise)

These arguments may also seem counterintuitive and puzzling. Indeed, their remarkable corollary is that an individual's acting morally or honestly, or doing what morality or honesty recommends, is identical with what is in her self-ish interest or what self-interest recommends. These are therefore most happy results for practicing business ethicists. What is more, when (T) and (T') are applied to business, the mechanisms that connect causes and effects may seem straightforward (though they are actually not). If you cheat, lie, and steal, your customers, partners, and suppliers, or else the cops and the Internal Revenue Service, will find it out. In either case you will soon go out of business. If instead you do business honestly, your customers, partners, and suppliers will know, they will tell others, and you will have a great deal of business. Obviously, then, claim (T) comes in much more handy than claim (M) if you are in the business ethics business. If this evening you have to give a speech at the annual dinner party of a renowned business association, or if this afternoon you have to teach a class at a top business school, urging your audience to follow enlightened self-interest, per (T), would be more adequate than urging them to follow plain selfishness, per (M).

To better explicate the concept of enlightened self-interest we may resort to the work of Tocqueville himself.[56] In one of the most famous chapters of *Democracy in America* (1835–1840), Tocqueville's topic is "how the Americans combat individualism by the doctrine of self-interest well understood [*l'intérêt bien entendu*]." He begins by observing a disparity between aristocratic and democratic societies with regard to morality. In "aristocratic ages," it was professed that "it is praise-worthy to forget oneself, and that good should be done without hope of reward, as it is by the Deity himself." Not that people in those times were in actual fact any more virtuous than at other times. But "they were incessantly talking of the beauties of virtue, and its utility was only studied in secret." By contrast, later moralists began to ask "whether the personal advantage of each member of the community does not consist in working for the good of all." In the United States, this perspective became predominant, the predominant answer was in the affirmative, and it eventually became a "general theory":

---

56 However, note that Tocqueville invented neither the idea nor the phrase. Also note that "*l'intérêt bien entendu*" has been translated into English as "enlightened self-interest," and permutations of "interest" or "self-interest," and "well understood," "rightly understood," or "properly understood."

I have already shown, in several parts of this work, by what means the inhabitants of the United States almost always manage to combine their own advantage with that of their fellow citizens; my present purpose is to point out the general rule that enables them to do so. In the United States hardly anybody talks of the beauty of virtue, but they maintain that virtue is useful and prove it every day. The American moralists do not profess that men ought to sacrifice themselves for their fellow creatures *because* it is noble to make such sacrifices, but they boldly [*hardiment*] aver that such sacrifices are as necessary to him who imposes them upon himself as to him for whose sake they are made.
[...]
They therefore do not deny that every man may follow his own interest, but they endeavor to prove that it is the interest of every man to be virtuous [*honnête*].[57]

The adverb "boldly" ("*hardiment*") is significant. That American moralists were "bold enough to say" what they said suggests that American moralists were touching a nerve with some people. In any case, the point is that virtue will yield profits to both parties: the person who does a virtuous act or a sacrifice and the person who receives it. Tocqueville goes on to point out that the doctrine of enlightened self-interest is not new, quoting Montaigne's sixteenth-century version in the *Essais*.[58] What Tocqueville finds remarkable is not its novelty, then, but its "universal acceptance" in the United States at that time:

The doctrine of interest rightly understood [*l'intérêt bien entendu*] is not then new, but among the Americans of our time it finds universal acceptance; it has become popular there; you may trace it at the bottom of all their actions, you will remark it in all they say. It is as often asserted by the poor man as by the rich. In Europe the principle of interest is much grosser than it is in America, but it is also less common and especially it is less avowed; among us, men still constantly feign great abnegation which they no longer feel.

The Americans, on the other hand, are fond of explaining almost all the actions of their lives by the principle of self-interest rightly understood; they show with complacency how an enlightened regard for themselves constantly prompts them to assist one another and inclines them willingly to sacrifice a portion of their time and property to the welfare of the state. In this respect I think they frequently fail to do themselves justice, for in the United States as well as elsewhere people are sometimes seen to give way to those disinterested and spontaneous impulses that are natural to man; but the Americans seldom

---

57   Alexis de Tocqueville. 1840. *Democracy in America. Part the Second, The Social Influence of Democracy*. Translated by Henry Reeve, Esq. New York: J. & H. G. Langley, pp. 121–22. I quote from this old translation because it stylistically represents the time of original publication. For a better one, see Alexis de Tocqueville. 2000. *Democracy in America*. Translated, edited, and with an Introduction by Harvey C. Mansfield and Delba Winthrop. Chicago: University of Chicago Press, p. 501.

58   See Montaigne's *Essais*, livre II, chapitre XVI, "De la gloire." Tocqueville fails to mention that Montaigne in turn quotes Quintilian's *Institutio Oratoria* i.12: "This gift Providence has given to men, that honest things should be the most agreeable."

admit that they yield to emotions of this kind; they are more anxious to do honor to their philosophy than to themselves.[59]

Not only are Americans driven by self-interest and love of themselves; they are proud of being driven by self-interest and love of themselves! They say so loudly, even when in reality they are driven by disinterested motives. That might have struck Europeans as strange, or might have made them uneasy. As John Stuart Mill says in his commentary on this passage, "in an aristocratic society . . . we hear chiefly of the beauty and dignity of virtue, the grandeur of self-sacrifice; in the other [a Democracy], of honesty the best policy, the value of character, and the common interest of every individual in the good of the whole."[60] However, unlike many of his fellow Europeans, Tocqueville is overall sympathetic to the doctrine of enlightened self-interest. He does see its drawbacks and weaknesses. Empirically, it is not always or all-around true. Morally, it discourages "extraordinary virtues" and extraordinary people. All things considered, though, he still approves of it as "the most appropriate to the needs of [his] contemporaries." It is good for a modern large society considered as a whole; "for the age of implicit self-sacrifice [dévouements aveugles] and instinctive virtues is already flitting far away from us."

The contemporary doctrines that business ethics and CSR pay are the descendants of the doctrines that honesty is the best policy and the concept of enlightened self-interest. In this section I have depicted these antecessors, which would continue to show up throughout the history of business ethicists' work. The contemporary doctrines that business ethics and CSR pay are frequently discussed as the "business case" for business ethics, the "triple bottom line," a firm's "social performance," or ethics or CSR as "competitive advantages." These are expressions characteristic of current management lingo. And they are frequently offered as reasons for a businessperson or company to behave ethically and responsibly. However, there is nothing new about their substantive point and arguments. In the next two sections I show how U.S. business ethicists made this very substantive point and arguments in the first decades of the twentieth century. Claims (1) and (2) have been at the center of business ethics for a long time indeed.

2.6 Yesterday's Business Ethicists

Business ethics issues were certainly not absent from the U.S. public sphere in the eighteenth and nineteenth centuries. Periodicals regularly wrote about "commercial morality," "commercial integrity," or "the morals of trade"—in general (though not always) complaining about how bad they were, or how bad they had gotten in recent years. Businesspeople and politicians occasionally contributed their opinions, too—in general (though not always) drawing more optimistic conclusions than journalists. Hagiographies and "lives" of American

---

59 Tocqueville, *Democracy in America*, p. 122.
60 John Stuart Mill. 1859. "M. de Tocqueville on Democracy in America." Pp. 1–83 in *Dissertations and Discussions: Political, Philosophical, and Historical*. Vol. 2. London: John W. Parker and Son, p. 51.

businessmen offered moral exemplars, "eminent for integrity, enterprise and public spirit," such as the "lives" written by John Frost and *Merchants' Magazine* editor Freeman Hunt.[61] What today goes by the name of "CSR" was occasionally broached at the time as well—sometimes framed in terms of duty or obligation, sometimes framed in terms of charity, giving, or stewardship. What does the successful, prosperous man of affairs owe to his fellows? What are corporations for? What is their relationship to the common good? Do they have any special obligations to society, given that society grants them special rights and legal status?[62]

However, in the early twentieth century the field of business ethics changed qualitatively and quantitatively. It changed qualitatively, because new actors started to get involved, such as business associations, business schools, and the group of writers collectively known as the muckrakers. Some Progressive businesspeople got involved, too. And Progressive politicians and policy makers got involved, too—and with them the regulatory and legal machinery of the state. These actors did not replace but rather supplemented an older but still robust presence: Protestant ministers, churches, and organizations. Predictably, new actors brought with them new tools and ideas. They brought with them new worldviews, perspectives, and understandings of what business ethics was all about—as my analysis of moral background types in chapters 6 and 7 will show. Furthermore, business ethicists of the early twentieth century addressed new social, economic, and political realities. For one, the business ethicists of the twentieth century had to address a new social actor: the large corporation or "big business." The unethical behavior of a large corporation had potentially much larger social consequences than the unethical behavior of a small, local store. The unethical behavior of big business was a national problem, which could negatively affect thousands of people, and which the state could not avoid paying attention to. In addition, the separation of ownership and management brought about its own share of new ethical problems. All of which took place under novel political conditions, including Progressive politics, civil service reform, a stronger socialist party, a stronger labor movement, the Great War, among others.

The field of business ethics changed quantitatively, too: the ethics of business became a more common public issue. From this fact about frequency it may be inferred that it became a more important public issue, a more worrisome one, worth attending to. Figure 2.1 is a Google Books Ngram Viewer chart comparing

---

61 John Frost. 1846. *Lives of American Merchants: Eminent for Integrity, Enterprise and Public Spirit.* 5th ed. New York: Saxton and Miles; Freeman Hunt. 1858. *Lives of American Merchants.* Vol. 1. New York: Derby & Jackson; Cincinnati: H. W. Derby & Co. Cf. Scott E. Casper. 1999. *Constructing American Lives: Biography and Culture in Nineteenth-Century America.* Chapel Hill: University of North Carolina Press, pp. 89–90; Lorman A. Ratner, Paula T. Kaufman, and Dwight L. Teeter. 2009. *Paradoxes of Prosperity: Wealth-Seeking Versus Christian Values in Pre-Civil War America.* Urbana: University of Illinois Press, pp. 72–84.

62 See, e.g., Ronald E. Seavoy. 1978. "The Public Service Origins of the American Business Corporation." *Business History Review* 52(1):30–60; Ronald E. Seavoy. 1982. *The Origins of the American Business Corporation, 1784–1855.* Westport, CT: Greenwood Press.

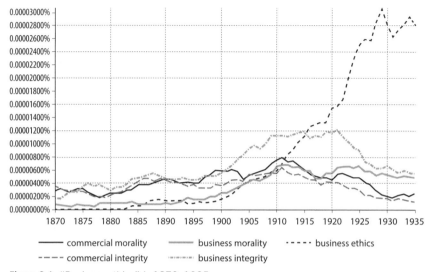

Figure 2.1. "Business ethics" I, 1870–1935.

Source: Google Books Ngram Viewer. Corpus: American English; Smoothing: 3. http://books
.google.com/ngrams

the usage frequency of the following two-word expressions or 2-grams: "commercial morality," "business morality," "commercial integrity," "business integrity," and "business ethics" from 1870 until 1935 in the "American English" corpus of books. This is a large corpus indeed: the Ngram Viewer database contains "about 4% of all books ever printed," digitized by Google Books. Usage frequency "is computed by dividing the number of instances of the n-gram in a given year by the total number of words in the corpus in that year."[63] The graph, then, shows diachronic trends in these frequencies, that is, how common a given n-gram is in the selected corpus.

On the one hand, figure 2.1 shows a linguistic pattern over time. Specifically, it shows variation in the lexical items and combinations of lexical items used to express one concept or idea (what some linguists call "onomasiology" or "*Bezeichnungslehre*"[64]). Granted, there are semantic differences between, say, "commercial integrity" and "business ethics": commerce is not synonymous with business, and integrity is not synonymous with ethics. But it is still reasonable to assume that, pragmatically, these five expressions served similar functions in the contexts in which they were used, at least most times. The usage of "business ethics" grew slowly in the late nineteenth century. In the early twentieth century

---

63 Jean-Baptiste Michel, Yuan Kui Shen, Aviva Presser Aiden, Adrian Veres, Matthew K. Gray, William Brockman, The Google Books Team, Joseph P. Pickett, Dale Hoiberg, Dan Clancy, Peter Norvig, Jon Orwant, Steven Pinker, Martin A. Nowak, and Erez Lieberman Aiden. 2011. "Quantitative Analysis of Culture Using Millions of Digitized Books." *Science* 331(6014):176–82, p. 176.

64 Joachim Grzega. 2002. "Some Aspects of Modern Diachronic Onomasiology." *Linguistics* 40(5):1021–45; Pavol Štekauer. 2005. "Onomasiological Approach to Word-Formation." Pp. 207–32 in *Handbook of Word-Formation*, edited by Pavol Štekauer and Rochelle Lieber. Dordrecht: Springer.

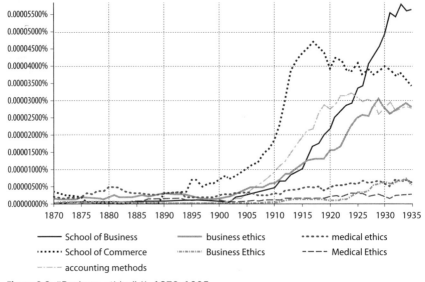

Figure 2.2. "Business ethics" II, 1870–1935.
Source: Google Books Ngram Viewer. Corpus: American English; Smoothing: 3. http://books
.google.com/ngrams

its growth grew steeper, and by the end of the 1910s it was more popular than the other expressions. This is simply a linguistic fact, like the fact that the past tense of the verb "to smell" used to be "smelt" and over time increasingly became "smelled."[65] However, figure 2.1 shows another pattern, too: besides linguistic change, interest in the subject seems to have grown as well. While the frequency of "commercial integrity," "business integrity," "commercial morality," and "business morality" did not increase much in this period overall, "business ethics" reached a frequency of 3×10^{-4} around 1930.

N-gram usage frequencies are easier to make sense of in comparative terms rather than by themselves. So, in order to provide a few points of comparison, figure 2.2 charts the frequencies of "business ethics," the capitalized "Business Ethics" (searches are case-sensitive), as well as "School of Business," "School of Commerce," "accounting methods," "medical ethics," and "Medical Ethics." I selected these other 2-grams somewhat arbitrarily, thinking about English expressions that were employed at the time, issues that belonged broadly speaking to the same realm as business ethics, and interest in which could be expected to grow throughout the period. Hence, these particular comparisons should not be given too much interpretive weight. Yet, at a minimum, they suggest that a usage frequency of 3×10^{-4} is not insignificant for a 2-gram in the American English corpus of books (in fact, it is more adequate to consider the sum of "business ethics" and "Business Ethics," which is about 3.5×10^{-4}). True, "School of Business" and "School of Commerce" surpass that frequency considerably, the former peaking

65 Michel et al., "Quantitative Analysis of Culture," p. 177.

at around 5.5×10^{-4} in the mid-1930s. But this difference should not be surprising, since this is a much broader concept, which many more people have reason to discuss, and which is (so to speak) quite book-friendly. In fact, this concept can also be expressed by other 2-grams, such as "Business School" and "business school," so a more accurate estimate would have to include them, too. Still, "business ethics" and "Business Ethics" perform reasonably well overall. For example, in the 1930s they surpass "accounting methods"—which is another book-friendly subject. And they surpass "medical ethics" and "Medical Ethics" considerably— even though this expression was not linguistically strange. It was, for instance, the title of Thomas Percival's influential code, on which the American Medical Association in turn based its own.[66]

I have claimed that in the first decades of the twentieth century the field of business ethics changed qualitatively and quantitatively, and I have provided some empirical support for this claim (even if my data are not conclusive but only suggestive). As I will later document, some steps toward formalization and institutionalization began to appear, too. To mention but two examples, the University of California established a regular series of business ethics lectures, the "Barbara Weinstock Lectures on the Morals of Trade," starting in 1904; and the National Civic Federation established a "Business Ethics Committee," starting in 1914. These facts suggest that business ethics was apprehended as a distinct subject matter or even field, such that there might now be lectures and committees about it. Yet, one thing that did not change was business ethicists' central normative message: a businessperson should not cheat, lie, or steal. As many generations of business ethicists had done in the past, they continued to urge businesspeople to be honest, truthful, and fair, and to discharge their obligations toward society, the community, and the public. You should do business in a moral manner. But why should you do business in a moral manner, again?

2.7 Balance Sheets

It is impossible to exaggerate the significance of the claim that there is a business case for business ethics in the first decades of the twentieth century. Just like in the first decades of the twenty-first century, morality, fairness, honesty, and service to the community were then said to be assets and have a cash value. While there were important exceptions—which will be discussed in the next chapter—the business case was advanced by many high-status actors and in many public settings. Business associations, state agencies, business schools, and publicly active businesspeople typically upheld it. The popular business literature and business press typically trumpeted it with enormous enthusiasm. For example, Ernest F.

---

66 Thomas Percival. 1803. *Medical Ethics, or, A Code of Institutes and Precepts, Adapted to the Professional Conduct of Physicians and Surgeons.* Manchester: Printed by S. Russell. See also Austin Flint. 1883. *Medical Ethics and Etiquette: The Code of Ethics Adopted by the American Medical Association.* New York: D. Appleton and Company.

Dubrul, general manager of the National Machine Tool Builders Association, wrote in 1926 in *Nation's Business* about "Business Ethics and Balance Sheets": "The cynic about business ethics pretends to believe that as a cold business proposition it does not pay to be ethical, and that the whole movement to establish better ethics in business is merely a futile gesture. But if the truth were known, it would be seen that ethical conduct in business is absolutely reflected in the balance sheet."[67] Ethical conduct was then a "cold business proposition."

Dubrul was the manager of a trade association, and he wrote this piece for the organ of a national business association, the U.S. Chamber of Commerce. In chapter 4 we will look at how national business associations, and in particular the U.S. Chamber, got involved in business ethics matters in the 1920s. In turn, the chamber was partly responding to the state, its regulatory apparatus, and in particular the Department of Commerce under Herbert Hoover (1921–1928). In turn, the Department of Commerce's threat of additional regulation was partly a response to the public sentiment that the morals of business were in a dreadful condition. They were so bad that someone had to do something about it. If business would not do it itself, then regulators would be forced to intervene. This was a common public representation of the Pure Food and Drug Act, the Sherman Act, and the Federal Trade Commission. Importantly, the state's claims and demands might be couched in bottom-line or balance-sheet terms. Regulation is surely costly (and annoying). In addition, business ethics is in and of itself profitable, aside from the costs (and annoyances) of regulation. So ethics should have a dual positive effect on a firm's bottom line.

The following polemic illustrates the point. In December 1929, John T. Flynn, of later fame as a critic of FDR and the New Deal, published an incendiary piece in the popular magazine, *The Forum*. Titled "Dishonest Business," it basically claimed that business was dishonest: "I lay down this proposition—that the ethics of business is on a very low plane."[68] Shortly afterward, Julius Klein, Assistant Secretary of Commerce, responded in defense of business. Klein was a "defender and champion of business ethics," as the caption under his crayon portrait in the magazine informs the reader: "Dr. Julius Klein. Scholar and economic expert, Hoover's lieutenant in the Department of Commerce, defender and champion of business ethics." Titled "The Dividends of Honesty in Business," Klein's article argues that honesty in business pays dividends. For him, "[b]usiness ethics these days simply must be—and are—sound; otherwise modern business could not continue to function as it does."

Klein's claims are instructive partly because they are, in one respect, slightly unusual. With regard to claim (1), they are not at all unusual: ethics pays. With regard to claim (2), however, his relative originality consists in explicitly dismissing motivations as inscrutable, and hence inconsequential or irrelevant. Klein begins

67 Ernest F. Dubrul. 1926. "Business Ethics and Balance Sheets." *Nation's Business*, February 1926, p. 76.

68 John T. Flynn. 1929. "Dishonest Business." *The Forum*, vol. 82, no. 6, December 1929, p. 351. For a later, more optimistic analysis, see John T. Flynn. 1935. "Post-Depression Progress in Business Ethics." *The Rotarian*, vol. 46, no. 1, January 1935, pp. 9–11, 50–51.

by making an empirical claim about business morality, and then considers the reasons for businessmen's actions:

To-day its [business'] ethics are not a bit worse than those of any other body in the community. In fact, for certain good reasons, they are apt to be a little better; and the first of those good reasons is that in modern business—in contrast to conditions existing even a decade or two ago—it emphatically does not pay to be dishonest. [. . .] If a business man has any hopes of prolonged existence as such, he soon discovers that his code of behavior has, if anything, to be a little above that of the rest of the community.

Whether this condition arises from some inward urge or because of various forces of compulsion, seems to me of little consequence. It is rather difficult, and quite academic and trivial, to prove just how much of Little Johnny's good behavior arises from his own inherent high morals and how much from the fear of promptly meted punishment. We are concerned with the actualities of the case and not with the utterly unprovable mysteries of the reasons for conduct.[69]

The first of those good reasons, even though there are others, is that honesty pays. Yet, Klein views "reasons for conduct" as "unprovable mysteries," as if he were a devotee of Watson's behaviorist psychology.[70] It even sounds like B. F. Skinner's radical behaviorism *avant la lettre*: "[w]hen what a person does is attributed to what is going on inside him, investigation is brought to an end."[71] While Klein was not speaking from a university or business school, his attitude and anti-metaphysical spirit were consistent with the scientific attitude and anti-metaphysical spirit that universities and business schools were bringing to bear on the problem.

Next, Klein shows why businesspeople in his day had to have an above-average code of behavior. That is, the mechanisms, which were new to his time, and hence could back up a causal attribution: they were causally responsible for a change for the better. Like the business ethicists of the 2000s, he aptly realizes that the truth of claim (1) is contingent on empirical conditions. His mechanisms include: "[t]he enormously increased significance of good will in our economic life"; the increased significance of credit and credit's requiring honesty and trust; "the very large part which advertising has come to play in business"; that "the means of communicating news as to delinquencies have become so much more alert and effective" (and he was not talking about the Internet or WikiLeaks!); and that "competition forces fair play"—and competition "is so intense that the slightest flaw in the product or the most trivial ethical shortcoming on the part of the manufacturer is promptly pounced upon and capitalized by an ever-watchful rival group."

In the end, Klein's piece is mostly about claim (1). While ostensibly reasons for conduct do not matter to him, and his tone is ostensibly descriptive, he implicitly

---

69 Julius Klein. 1930. "The Dividends of Honesty in Business." *The Forum*, vol. 83, no. 3, March 1930, p. 32.

70 John B. Watson. 1913. "Psychology as the Behaviorist Views It." *Psychological Review* 20:158–77.

71 B. F. Skinner. 1974. *About Behaviorism*. New York: Knopf, pp. 19–20.

gives a reason to be honest to businesspeople seeking to increase their profits. What is more, sometimes he does speculate on what people's reasons are, despite his supposed behaviorism. According to "our more successful department stores," "the customer is always right." "And that policy is followed; not necessarily because of any silly, milk-and-honey, millennial ideas as to the superior moral integrity of the mass of consumers, but simply because of the well-founded belief that such a policy pays." That is why that policy is followed. Furthermore, like the business ethicists of the 2000s, Klein, a champion of business ethics, seems to have little patience for ethics, or "silly, milk-and-honey, millennial ideas." Instead, he cares about "solid realities" and "dollars and cents" and "cold figures": "It isn't simply a vague generality, but a solid reality translatable into dollars and cents. Indeed, in many corporations, as recent merger operations have shown, the good will item is rated in cold figures, and at higher value than the physical assets of the firm." Dollars and cents and all, though, he seemed to resent that America be accused of materialism.[72]

Julius Klein was representing the Department of Commerce. He defended businessmen, and spoke about dollars and cents and cold figures quite like a businessman. But he was not speaking *qua* businessman. In fact, he was not really a businessman at all, but an academic by training—an economic historian of Spain and Spanish America, who had actually given up a promising academic career as Assistant Professor of Latin American History and Economics at Harvard University.[73] It is thus ironic—or perhaps predictable—that a former academic should dismiss a thought or suggestion as "academic and trivial." In any event, many active businessmen speaking *qua* businessmen expressed similar opinions in public statements of various kinds. Typically, it was big businessmen who spoke, public representatives of that central public actor in the Progressive Era: "big business," in the singular, as it came to be referred to.

Large corporations were in the eye of the storm in the late nineteenth and early twentieth centuries. Among other things, they were accused of unethical monopolistic and anti-competitive practices, unethical labor practices, unethical relationships with public servants, and, more generally, of lack of concern for

---

72   To which accusers he bitingly replied: "Our European critics, echoed by the mournful chorus of some of our expatriates in their midst, still have difficulty in suppressing their tear at the thought of our 'gross materialism,' our devotion to good plumbing, comfortable shoes, and nicely balanced ledgers. But when these transatlantic cynics find themselves in a position to acquire these very items of sordid worldly goods, they seem to have no hesitation whatever in doing so—though doubtless their motive is to utilize such acquisitions solely as aids to further 'cultural advance'—whatever that is."

73   Cf. Julius Klein. 1920. *The Mesta: A Study in Spanish Economic History, 1273–1836.* Cambridge, MA: Harvard University Press. Klein was "chief of the Commerce Department's Latin-American section" from 1917 to 1919, then commercial attaché in Buenos Aires from 1919 to 1921, Director of the Bureau of Foreign and Domestic Commerce from 1921 to 1929, and Assistant Secretary of Commerce from 1929 to 1933. "Foreign Trade Scouts Seek a Legal Status." *New York Times,* December 19, 1926, p. XX7.

As *Time Magazine* recalled: "Secretary Hoover brought him from Buenos Aires . . . to be his technician, his Ariel. People who think that every Jew is a commercial genius and vice versa every commercial genius a Jew have long believed Dr. Julius Klein a Jew. He is a Republican Protestant, born to Frederick and Katherine (Giebenhain) Klein at San Jose, Calif., in 1886, married to Dorothy Bates of Cambridge, Mass., in 1915. He is slender, brown-haired, and has a notably broad forehead." "Business and Finance: Potash and Klein." *Time Magazine,* July 19, 1926.

American society and democracy. The muckraking journalists' favorite targets were large corporations. Public opinion was not favorably disposed; big business did not have the "good will" of the public. In turn, bad reputation was believed to have financial consequences, through the actions of consumers, workers, or regulators. Thus, the field and profession of public relations emerged to try to solve this reputational problem—as Ivy Lee tried to solve John Rockefeller's reputational problems as of 1903.[74]

Big businessmen, then, and especially the visible faces of firms, seemed to have reputational reasons to jump on the business ethics bandwagon—either collectively through business associations, or independently on behalf of their individual firms. This could be perceived and received as a sign of unselfishness and cooperation, and hence their reputation could be improved. Whatever their reasons or motives were, that is in any case what some highly visible businessmen did, such as Elbert H. Gary. "Judge Gary," as he was ordinarily referred to, is a complex historical character. He had been a lawyer and a judge (hence his nickname), and then became a businessman. But not just *a* businessman. He was one of the organizers and chairman of the board of the biggest corporation in the world, the first billion-dollar corporation: the United States Steel Corporation (established in 1901). He was a representative of big business if anyone was. Moreover, he was the chairman of the board of a corporation whose relationships with both government and labor were not at all unproblematic—the former due to its anti-competitive practices, which President Taft went after; the latter due to its uncompromising anti-unionism. Gary refused to even talk to unions and defended the 12-hour workday, at the same time asserting that "there is at present . . . no necessity for labor unions."[75] Judge Gary and U.S. Steel did have many apologists who viewed the company as a "good trust."[76] However, its business practices were surely not beyond ethical reproach. "Ethics in Business" is precisely the subject that Judge Gary chose for the address he was invited to deliver at Northwestern University on June 17, 1922.

As reported in the *Chicago Daily Tribune* the next day, "yesterday [Judge Gary] journeyed out to Northwestern university—the school from which he graduated years ago—and, for the benefit of about 2,000 other alumni, drew a lesson

74 Cf. Morrell Heald. [1970] 1988. *The Social Responsibilities of Business: Company and Community, 1900–1960.* New Brunswick and London: Transaction Publishers; Ray Eldon Hiebert. 1966. *Courtier to the Crowd: The Story of Ivy Lee and the Development of Public Relations.* Ames: Iowa State University Press; Roland Marchand. 1998. *Creating the Corporate Soul: The Rise of Public Relations and Corporate Imagery in American Big Business.* Berkeley and Los Angeles: University of California Press; Richard S. Tedlow. 1979. *Keeping the Corporate Image: Public Relations and Business, 1900–1950.* Greenwich, CT: JAI Press.

75 "U.S. Steel Corporation Principles: Chairman Gary Speaks at the Annual Meeting." 1921. *Iron Age,* vol. 107, no. 16, April 21, 1921, pp. 1043–45, p. 1043. Cf. David Brody. [1965] 1982. *Labor in Crisis: The Steel Strike of 1919.* Westport, CT: Greenwood Press; Gabriel Kolko. 1963. *The Triumph of Conservatism. A Re-Interpretation of American History, 1900–1916.* New York: Free Press of Glencoe.

76 Arundel Cotter. 1921. *United States Steel: A Corporation with a Soul.* New York and Toronto: Doubleday, Page & company; Arundel Cotter. 1928. *The Gary I Knew.* Boston: The Stratford company; Ida M. Tarbell. 1925. *The Life of Elbert H. Gary: The Story of Steel.* New York and London: D. Appleton and company.

from the changing standards of 'big business'." Gary, who was a trustee of the university, had graduated from the law school in 1867. In 1922, in addition to this address before the alumni, Gary received "the honorary degree of LL.D. at the university commencement exercises," and was "the principal speaker at the annual dinner of the law school from which he graduated." According to Gary, "corporations of twenty years ago . . . gave little heed to moral dictates," but now "ethics has become the lode star of modern business."[77] He offered two explanations for why modern business attends to ethics. First, because of the influence of public opinion, which "has aroused and will always arouse the consciences of men and women." People—including businesspeople— have a "natural instinct" to care about their fellows' opinion: "[w]e dread the condemnation of the general public, especially if there is reason for it." Then, "[t]his natural instinct in the hearts of well intentioned men and women has had a decided influence in reforming business methods." Second, because it pays:

> There is another convincing reason for the noticeable changes resulting from the adoption of ethics in business. While the motives are not equally worthy with others, they are very practical and influential with many who would otherwise not be converted. Ethical management brings additional profits to business. Sooner or later it pays in dollars and cents. Any man or concern that firmly establishes a reputation for honesty and fair dealing which is not questioned has a business asset of great pecuniary value and profit.[78]

It is beautifully illustrative that Gary says that these motives "are not equally worthy with others." Yet, worthy or not, it is on these motives that he insisted a few minutes later: "From considerable experience I assert with confidence and emphasis that, taken as a whole, year after year, the pecuniary gains of a large or small business will be greater if it is fairly, humanely and honestly conducted. If this be true it alone furnishes a logic to every one which should be conclusive."[79] The worthier motives he did not find worthy of mention. Yes, they do exist. Yet they may still be neglected, bracketed, or forgotten, as a successful success manual put it in 1915: "'Playing people for suckers' is very poor business, and dishonest advertising is the MOST EXPENSIVE policy that foolish storekeeping permits. [. . .] Forgetting the matter of morals or religion, and considered merely from a strictly business (money-making) point of view, there never has been a sounder business maxim stated than this: 'HONESTY IS THE BEST POLICY'."[80]

The claim that business ethics had positive effects on the balance sheet was typically agreed to, too, by the then young business schools. These schools are the protagonists of chapter 5, so here I only highlight their support for claims (1) and (2), which the following story illustrates. Harvard University founded its business

77   "Business Virtue T. R. Monument, Gary Declares." *Chicago Daily Tribune*, June 18, 1922, p. 3.

78   Elbert H. Gary. 1922. *Address by Elbert H. Gary at Northwestern University. Evanston, Ill. June 17, 1922.* n.p., p. 10.

79   Ibid., p. 12.

80   W. R. Hotchkin. 1915. *The Manual of Successful Storekeeping.* Doubleday, Page & Company, pp. 21–22. See also W. R. Hotchkin. 1917. *Making More Money in Storekeeping.* New York: Ronald Press Company, pp. 240, 270.

school in 1908. By 1926 it was already a relatively well-established institution. That year the New York Edison Company asked Assistant Dean Deane W. Malott whether a faculty member could give a lecture at the company's Commercial School. The subject of the lecture was to be "Ethics of Business and the Service Rendered by the Salesman."[81] Malott, himself a graduate of the Harvard business school, decided to give the lecture himself. Beforehand, he sent a letter outlining his plan for it:

I am planning to open with a discussion of what is meant by the terms "Business Ethics" and "Sales Service", then to show the complexity of the ethical problems which business faces and that this complexity is largely a state of mind. I am then planning to show some of the misconceptions of business ethics and their cause and to analyze the real state of business in this country; to show that business ethics is really a concept and that the ethical practices which come within this concept are changing year by year and decade by decade. In other words, I am going to attempt to give them a look into the field as a whole to start them to thinking [sic] along the line [sic] of business ethics and then to show that after all the answer to ethical problems is sound business expediency and that good ethics in the long run is simply good business and vice versa.[82]

Malott's claim that good ethics is good business is clear. Malott's "vice versa" claim, that good business is good ethics, would require some more interpretation and analysis. I do not know how Malott's talk at the New York Edison Company actually went. Nor do I know how much time he actually spent spelling out and giving support to his claims about "business expediency" and the rewards of ethics. I do know that many other business educators shared his sentiment and preached this message to businesspeople and business students. Many described it as an ongoing historical process of increasingly better ethics in business, and increasing concern for the community, to which business schools were making a contribution, yet which was also a self-reinforcing process. As Willard Hotchkiss, dean of the School of Commerce at Northwestern University, explained in a public lecture in 1916: "advance in moral standards has been forced on unwilling victims through legislation, public opinion, or class struggle, and then men have discovered, as a happy surprise after the event, that 'good ethics' was profitable."[83] This *post hoc* surprise must have been a happy one indeed.[84]

81 Letter of Arthur Williams to Assistant Dean Deane W. Malott. July 21, 1926. HBS Dean's Office Correspondence. 1919–1942. Box 22. Folder 22–10.

82 Letter of Deane W. Malott to Marion Brainard. November 2, 1926. HBS Dean's Office Correspondence. 1919–1942. Box 22. Folder 22–10. Underlining in original.

83 Willard E. Hotchkiss. 1918. *Higher Education and Business Standards*. Boston: Houghton Mifflin, pp. 80–81. (The lecture took place in 1916, but it was published only in 1918, when Hotchkiss had already left Northwestern for Minnesota. "Dean Hotchkiss to Minnesota." 1917. *Northwestern University Bulletin. Alumni Journal Number,* vol. 18, no. 13, November 3, 1917, pp. 10–11.)

84 The unexpected-good-outcome trope was one of business ethicists' favorites. For instance, in his *Introduction to the Study of Business Ethics*, Everett Hood used it in connection to labor policies: "[The capitalist] has found that supposed concessions to workers have had the boomerang tendency. Employers have benefited by human kindness to workers to a greater extent than the employees themselves. When the twelve hour day was abolished there was a large amount of uneasiness. Ten hours of

2.8 He Profits Most Who Serves Best

The late nineteenth and early twentieth centuries saw the creation of hundreds of new business associations in the United States. Some of them hoped to have morally good effects. They spoke of codes of ethics, fairness, and standardization; "cooperation" that would prevent races to the bottom; and self-policing and self-regulation that would prevent "sharp" practices.[85] They spoke of "[t]he strengthening of business ideals, the reduction of the wastes and frictions of trade, the increased efficiency in production and distribution, the vast savings to the public."[86] The flip side of the coin was that "cooperation" could actually mean anti-competitive practices, price fixing, and restraint of trade—and in certain industries first and foremost cooperation against labor unions—which could hardly count as morally good effects. Either way, among the business associations that hoped to have morally good effects, the Better Business Bureau (also known as BBB) and Rotary were unique in their ethical mission.

Whence BBB? Advertising and marketing are susceptible to special business ethics problems, especially as regards truthfulness and honesty. A dramatic illustration of this is the history of the Pure Food and Drug Act of 1906. Yet, misrepresentation and misleading labels are no less morally questionable in the hosiery business than in the patent medicine business (if surely less lethal). In the early twentieth century false advertising had become a major public concern, and "advertising men" were often held responsible for it. Their response, lo and behold, was an advertising campaign: the "truth in advertising" campaign. It was orchestrated by the new national organization of advertising clubs, the Associated Advertising Clubs of America (established in 1904 as the National Federation of Advertising Clubs, renamed Associated Advertising Clubs of America in 1906). Under the leadership of Samuel C. Dobbs and George W. Coleman, the annual conventions of this national organization insisted *ad nauseam* on the importance of truthfulness and honesty, and made sure their pronouncements reached the public as the official stance of American advertisers. They called it a movement: the "truth movement."

In addition, a more practical policy was soon put into practice: local "vigilance committees" and an umbrella National Vigilance Committee (established in 1912, renamed National Better Business Bureau of the Associated Advertising Clubs of the World in 1921). The aim of vigilance committees and better business bureaus was "to promote high standards of business practice and thereby increase public confidence in business transactions."[87] In practice, they policed the ethics

---

labor would mean that five instead of six articles would be produced. Imagine the relief, surprise, even joy, with which industry noticed that the SAME AMOUNT was produced in ten hours!" Everett W. Hood. 1930. *An Introduction to the Study of Business Ethics*. Buffalo, NY: R. W. Bryant, p. 17.

85   See, e.g., Emmett Hay Naylor. 1921. *Trade Associations: Their Organization and Management*. New York: Ronald Press Company.

86   Franklin D. Jones. 1922. *Trade Association Activities and the Law*. New York: McGraw-Hill, p. vii.

87   "Better Business Bureau is Organized in New York." *Christian Science Monitor*, June 22, 1922, p. 3.

of advertising and selling, heard customers' complaints, and if possible arbitrated disagreements, thus avoiding suits, courts, and judges. All in all, advertisers were hoping to improve their reputation in the public sphere—"erase their Barnum image."[88] They hoped to convince the public that their self-policing was effective, and that they were not just paying "lip-service" to "lofty ideals."[89] More generally, they were hoping to turn advertising into a profession, as many other occupations were at that time. For this goal, good ethics—or, at least, not terrible ethics—was a necessary condition.

In the early twentieth century, then, a group of advertisers embarked on an ethical project: fight against misrepresentation of goods and deceitful labels and ads, and fight for truthfulness and honesty in advertising. Like many others, they asked themselves why one should be moral, that is, what reasons an advertiser had to be truthful and honest. Like many others, their answer was self-interest. For example, take Merle Sidener's speech at the 1919 National Advertising Convention in New Orleans—later published in *Printers' Ink*, the traditional "journal for advertisers." Sidener, chairman of the National Vigilance Committee at the time, maintained that "every man must realize the need of truth," and, quite radically, that "[t]here is no such thing as a white lie, especially in advertising. A statement is either true or untrue." Apparently, this leaves little leeway for what advertisers traditionally do. Then he asked: "Impossible idealism? No, merely applied common sense. We will all agree that only right survives and that only honesty builds permanently." Like many others, Sidener dismissed "idealism" as a bad thing, not a businesslike thing. Advertisers had "definite interest" in the movement: "Your dividends will come in the form of increased profits in your own individual lines because of the greater confidence the public will have in business generally."[90]

Whence Rotary? The first Rotary Club was founded in Chicago in 1905. In the retrospective words of its founder, Paul P. Harris, the "original aim" of the club was to promote "understanding and fellowship among business and professional men."[91] The time was apparently ripe for an organization of that sort, because it very soon and very fast spread to several cities in the United States and abroad, having particular success among small and relatively small businessmen. In particular, the "clubs attracted only those businessmen vitally interested in local economic life and thus appealed primarily to smaller businessmen and independent professionals, whose business success might depend on such in-

---

88 Roland Marchand. 1985. *Advertising the American Dream. Making Way for Modernity, 1920–1940*. Berkeley: University of California Press, p. 7.

89 H. J. Kenner. 1936. *The Fight for Truth in Advertising: A Story of What Business Has Done and Is Doing to Establish and Maintain Accuracy and Fair Play in Advertising and Selling for the Public's Protection*. New York: Round Table Press, Inc, p. 263.

90 Merle Sidener. 1919. "A Greater Truth Work of the National Vigilance Committee." *Printers' Ink*, vol. 108, no. 13, September 25, 1919, pp. 53–56, p. 53.

91 Paul P. Harris. [1945]. *An Interview with Paul Harris. Founder of Rotary*, p. 6. http://www.whatpaulharriswrote.org/. See also Paul P. Harris. 1948. *My Road to Rotary: The Story of a Boy, a Vermont Community, and Rotary*. Chicago: A. Kroch and Son, Publishers.

formal connections."[92] In 1910 a national organization was formed and annual conventions began to meet. Its official organ, *The National Rotarian* (later shortened to *The Rotarian*), began publication in January 1911, edited by Chesley R. Perry. Rotary's code of ethics was adopted in 1915.[93] In 1912, the organization changed its name to International Association of Rotary Clubs, and in 1922 to Rotary International, to take account of its international character. While trade associations and commercial clubs mushroomed at the time, Rotary was in some respects atypical. For one, it was atypical how central Rotary's moral project was in its presentation of self in public—whatever its "latent functions," its founders' unwritten aims, or its members' reasons to participate.[94]

Several business associations concerned themselves or claimed to concern themselves with moral issues of one sort or another, but Rotary put moral issues at the center of its mission. So did organizations modeled after Rotary, such as the Kiwanis (founded in 1915 in Detroit) and the Lions (founded in 1917 in Chicago). For instance, the "Objects of Rotary" were "to encourage and foster" the following:

a. High ethical standards in business and professions.

b. The ideal of *service* as the basis of all worthy enterprise.

c. The active interest of every Rotarian in the civic, commercial, social and moral welfare of his community.

d. The development of a broad acquaintanceship as an opportunity for service as well as an aid to success.

e. The interchange of ideas and of business methods as a means of increasing the efficiency and usefulness of Rotarians.

f. The recognition of the worthiness of all legitimate occupations and the dignifying of the occupation of each Rotarian as affording him an opportunity to serve society.[95]

Developing a "broad acquaintanceship"—that is, fellowship, or as we would now say, networking—is explicitly acknowledged. Even networking "as an aid to success" is acknowledged. At least in "fellowship" terms, Harris always emphasized it as one of the aims of the organization. Still, the emphasis is overall placed on "ethical standards," "usefulness," and "service."

---

92 Jeffrey A. Charles. 1993. *Service Clubs in American Society: Rotary, Kiwanis, and Lions.* Urbana: University of Illinois Press, p. 3.

93 J. R. Perkins. 1917. "History of the Rotary Code of Ethics." *The Rotarian*, vol. 10, no. 2, February 1917, pp. 119–21.

94 On latent functions, see Robert K. Merton. 1968. *Social Theory and Social Structure.* New York: Free Press, esp. pp. 114–27.

95 "Rotary and its Magazine." *The Rotarian*, vol. 13, no. 5, November 1918, p. 201. See also George Dugan. 1920. "The Objects of Rotary." *The Rotarian*, vol. 17, no. 2, August 1920, pp. 83–85; G. Frank Kelly. 1924. "Rotary at the Crossroads." *The Rotarian*, vol. 24, no. 6, June 1924, pp. 25–26. Note that from time to time the "Objects of Rotary" changed, its number ranging from three to six, even though the basic ideas did not change much.

"He Profits Most Who Serves Best," the Rotary motto, was adopted at the 1911 Portland convention, and was included as the concluding sentence of the Rotary platform. The phrase was coined by Arthur Frederick Sheldon, an early Rotarian who ran a business college in downtown Chicago, the Sheldon School of Scientific Salesmanship, and edited a business journal, *The Business Philosopher*. Sheldon used it in the report of the Committee on Business Methods, of which he was the author, and which was read in Portland—though he had used a very similar phrase the year before at the Chicago convention. Now, what does "He Profits Most Who Serves Best" mean, exactly? *Prima facie*, it seems to pithily summarize the doctrine of honesty is the best policy and enlightened self-interest, which business ethicists have always been so fond of. As Sheldon himself said elsewhere: "Service to others is enlightened self-interest. Selfishness is the road to self-destruction." Service is *"sound economics."*[96] Differently put, "He Profits Most Who Serves Best" seems to be simply a pithy phrasing of claim (1), suitable for organization building, communication, and publicity.

However, there is a further twist to the story, which makes it even more germane here. Rotary International was an organization rife with moral purpose, at least as far as its public self-representations went. As far as we can tell, its members appeared to support and work for these moral objectives and considerations. Certainly, that is what Rotarians expressed in public all the time. But then the Rotary motto's appeal to profit looks problematic. Does it mean that profit is the *summum bonum*, the highest good? Is it because of the hope of pecuniary gain that people join in? That would be inappropriate, inappropriately materialistic, for an organization like Rotary, would it not?[97]

This is just what some Rotarians wondered about—and feared—since the early days of the organization.[98] One such Rotarian was Joseph R. Naylor, of Wheeling, West Virginia. Speaking at his local club in 1918, Naylor discussed his misgivings about the slogan, "He Profits Most Who Serves Best":

Words are made to convey thoughts, but it is difficult to select one word like "profits" and be sure the meaning you intend is the one given by others.

Too many people think only of financial gain when they hear the word "profits," and for that reason feel that Rotary, having its motto what it is, really means a body of men gathered together for financial gain.

---

96 Arthur Frederick Sheldon. 1921. "The Philosophy of Rotary." Pp. 109–145 in *Proceedings: Twelfth Annual Convention of the International Association of Rotary Clubs. Edinburgh, Scotland. June 13–16, 1921.* Chicago: International Association of Rotary Clubs, p. 117.

97 In fact, Rotary used two slogans: "He Profits Most Who Serves Best," and "Service, not Self." At times they were presented combined as one, hyphenated: "Service, not Self—He Profits Most Who Serves Best." The phrase "Service, not Self" is due to Frank Collins, a Minneapolis Rotarian, who said it at the 1911 Portland convention. It eventually became "Service Above Self," which Rotary uses to this day.

98 Cf. Glenn C. Mead. 1934. "Service Begins at Home." *The Rotarian*, vol. 44, no. 3, March 1934, p. 49.

It is evident however, when we peruse the Code of Ethics and the Constitution, that this was not the meaning intended by the founders of Rotary or the maker of this motto. There is no question that the meaning was intended to be something higher and more important. It is a fact that good service, true service, will result in material gain, but it may not be in large amount.

If you can convince me that in your line you can provide me with better service than another, when I desire the thing that you sell, I naturally turn to you. This is the material profit that comes from good service, but the important profit, the great gain, the great benefit which comes to all of us because of unselfish service, and because of work well done, is that moral uplift and mental invigoration which follow.[99]

Naylor thought he had spotted a semantic confusion. The word "profit" is ambiguous. Perhaps its most intuitive meaning is something like financial or material gain. Perhaps that is what most competent English speakers will normally understand by it. But the word surely has another sense: moral and mental gain, "moral uplift and mental invigoration." And *this* is the "important profit," even though the unimportant one will also accrue to he who serves best (or at least well), even if only a small amount of it. Naylor's semantic analysis then turns to what the intended meaning was, that is, in which of its two senses the word "profit" was used by "the founders of Rotary or the maker of this motto." He is positive about that. It cannot possibly be financial gain. They intended to mean "something higher and more important" than mere money.

Or maybe not. The founder of Rotary is surely in a better position than Naylor to know what the founders of Rotary meant. In fact, not only did Paul Harris have epistemic advantages, that is, his being more likely to know that. Being the founder and unquestionable leader of Rotary, he also shaped the general understanding of the meaning of the motto and thereby its reception and transmission. As any socially or politically central actor, Harris had causal powers over the validity of interpretations, and over semantics more generally—even if more limited than the powers of the authors of the *Newspeak Dictionary* in Orwell's *1984*. In the present case, interpretation and validation of interpretations are particularly consequential, because Sheldon did not make himself very clear. His "The Philosophy of Rotary," a philosophical manifesto of sorts, is full of inconsistencies and confusions. As a consequence, what he really meant was up for grabs.[100] This is what Harris said about the meaning of the Rotary motto in his 1935 book, *This Rotarian Age*:

---

99 Joseph R. Naylor. 1918. "Our Responsibilities." *The Rotarian*, vol. 13, no. 4, October 1918, pp. 181–82.

100 There is no doubt that Sheldon thought about both "material gain" and "spiritual values." Yet, whether he cared most about one or the other is underdetermined by the evidence: "Yes, 'He profits most who serves best.' He 'profits' most *in material gain* as well as in *spiritual values*, who renders the best service to those with whom he deals." Sheldon, "The Philosophy of Rotary," p. 125.

The epigram, "He profits most who serves best," has been the object of much criticism as being too worldly, and also the cause of speculation as to what Sheldon had in mind, pecuniary or spiritual reward. The writer [Harris] believes that Sheldon, so far as he himself was concerned, was interested primarily in what might be termed the spiritual reward, but his aim was to bring the maximum of good to the largest possible number. He recognized the fact that the largest number were interested in pecuniary profits and therefore the pecuniary profit-seeking group was the group he desired to reach.

[. . .] If the world's thinking was to continue to be in terms of profits, he would at least bend his efforts to making profits legitimate. With what some might consider fanatical zeal he contended that profit was as inevitable a consequence of service as heat was the inevitable consequence of fire. The bigger the fire, the greater the heat; the greater the service, the more the profit.[101]

Harris claims to be himself speculating about what Sheldon had in mind, what Sheldon meant by the verb "to profit." Still, Harris claims that, while Sheldon was personally interested in spiritual rewards, his slogan was meant for large numbers, who were interested in pecuniary rewards. This empirical belief about what people want, along with the utilitarian principle, maximize the good of the greatest number, led Sheldon to use "profit" the way most people do. This passage is perhaps not entirely clear, though, and no evidence is provided as to whether Sheldon meant what Harris says he meant. Yet, the anecdote Harris tells next leaves no room for doubt or for a different interpretation (assuming of course that it is true):

A well-intentioned minister, introducing Sheldon to his congregation in Rochester, New York, once made the mistake of saying that to follow Sheldon's doctrine would of course not be to one's financial advantage but that he thought that one would be more compensated by the satisfaction he would experience in realization of the fact that he had done the right thing. This was not Sheldon's doctrine and it required most of the time allotted him for his speech to beat down the bad effects of his unfortunate introduction.

Sheldon was not forgetful of the spiritual advantage of service; he was keenly alive to it, but he felt that his own special mission was to reconcile man's prevalent and natural desire for profits with the highest possible ideal of service to humanity.

Now things are crystal clear. Make a note to yourself. Next time you are asked to introduce Fred Sheldon to your congregation, do not play down financial advantage and do not play up doing the right thing. Or else he will have to waste most of his allotted time rectifying your mistake. Sheldon's doctrine, encapsulated in the slogan, "He Profits Most Who Serves Best," is about profits, real profits. Not just "profits." Semantic gymnastics, like Naylor's, will not help. You

---

101   Paul P. Harris. 1935. *This Rotarian Age*. Chicago: Rotary International, pp. 96–97.

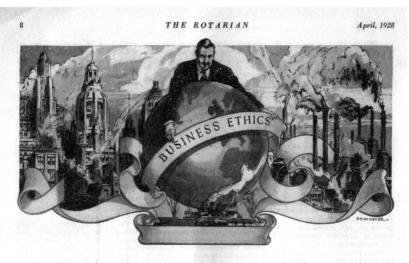

8   THE ROTARIAN   April, 1928

The Cash Value of Ethics

By John O. Knutson
Decorations by A. H. Winkler

" **E**THICS is the bunk!" Thus a successful business man expressed himself in my presence recently. He did not really mean that. But he had heard the word "ethics" misused and abused so much that it had lost much practice" means the same, but it is longer and is more of a definition than a synonym. So in spite of its abuse, the word "ethics" is the best word in the English language to convey what we mean by applying the Golden Rule to business or professional practices. commodities nor the medium of exchange have any significance without the human element represented by the buyer and the seller. The human element enters in at the very beginning—all the way back to the raw material in its crudest form—

Figure 2.3. The cash value of ethics.
Source: Illustration by A. H. Winkler. *The Rotarian*, vol. 32, no. 4, April 1928, p. 8. Thanks to Rotary International for permission to reproduce this illustration.

should serve best because you will profit most, financially. Or so the public, organizational understanding of the slogan is—that is, the understanding of Rotary itself, whose official voice is Harris.

The words of another active Rotarian, John Knutson, sum it up well: ethics has a "cash value." Indeed, the bombastic title of Knutson's article in the April 1928 issue of *The Rotarian* is, "The Cash Value of Ethics."[102] Figure 2.3 depicts a businessman spreading a banner across the globe. An inscription on the banner reads: "BUSINESS ETHICS." Here a picture is truly worth a thousand words.

In this chapter I have analyzed the work of various business ethicists who appealed in various ways to the "ethics pays," "enlightened self-interest," and "honesty is the best policy" doctrines. This is what the chapter's epigraphs illustrate, too. The 1925 *Book of Business Standards*, by "Research and Sales Counselor

---

102   John O. Knutson. 1928. "The Cash Value of Ethics." *The Rotarian*, April 1928, pp. 8–9, 59–60. See also Earnest Elmo Calkins. 1927. "The Practical Ethics of Sincere Advertising." *Advertising and Selling* 10(1):19–20, 64–66.

[*sic*]" J. George Frederick, puts the point thus: "In the past twenty years the service idea in business has grown to be the predominant policy; the standard of both profit and reputation. This has come about through no ethical revolution, but through the cold demonstration of business success. Service standards bring success, and only the unwise and unsuccessful today belittle them."[103] In this context, service means roughly ethics—which is warm and fuzzy, unlike cold demonstrations and business successes. Similarly, John D. Rockefeller, Jr. made this point in 1927, addressing "700 employes [*sic*] and guests of the Standard Oil Company of New Jersey at the Hotel Biltmore": "Today the vital matter to which business must needs [*sic*] address itself is the re-emphasizing of *high standards of business ethics*, for upon such a foundation only can business be permanently successful. [. . .] It is true that money is often made by trickery and sharp practice, but successful business is not established on a foundation so shifting."[104]

At the end of the day, though, the historical evidence taken together calls for a levelheaded assessment. Generally speaking, this is a matter of relative weight and emphasis. Plato in the fourth century BC and *The Economist* in the twenty-first century AD resemble in this respect the business ethicists of the first decades of the twentieth century AD, who were shown at work in this chapter. The alternatives are not mutually exclusive: business ethics may both be intrinsically good and have good consequences such as money and fame. This is not necessarily an either/or question. Then, reasonably, business ethicists could profit from these sorts of conciliatory stances.[105] As a consequence, for the analyst, the devil turns out to be in the details. Regarding individual business ethicists, the question becomes what he underscores and devotes more time to, what he expresses most excitement and enthusiasm about, and what he deals with more perfunctorily or only gestures toward and quickly moves on to other things. In more technical terms, which basket he puts most of his eggs in. Regarding the business ethics field as a whole, the question becomes what contexts, situations, and audiences make particular emphases more likely.

While conciliatory stances are comfortable and secure (and facilitate political careers), it is fortunate that not everybody desires comfort and security (nor political careers). The Protestant business ethicists showcased in the next chapter had such less comfortable desires. They had several problems with the connection between morality and profit. They deplored moral behavior motivated by policy considerations and calculations. There was also a more moderate wing, which, while uncomfortable with this connection, still looked for palatable versions of it. Thus, Christian responses, rejections, and amendments to empirical claim (1) and

---

103   Frederick, *Book of Business Standards*, p. 48.

104   John D. Rockefeller, Jr. 1927. *Character: The Foundation of Successful Business*. [New York?]: n.p., pp. 7, 13; "Rockefeller Urges High Trade Ethics." *New York Times*, December 2, 1927, p. 11; "J. D. Rockefeller, Jr., Talks on Business Life." *Wall Street Journal*, December 2, 1927, p. 12. See also S. J. Woolf. 1928. "A Champion of Honor in Business Life." *New York Times*, March 11, 1928, p. 75.

105   For a business education example, see J. Kahn and J. Klein. 1914. *Principles and Methods in Commercial Education: A Text-Book for Teachers, Students and Business Men*. New York: Macmillan, p. 44.

normative claim (2) were of many kinds. But they were all dealing with the same set of questions. If ethics pays, should Christian business ethicists preach that ethics pay? If ethics pays, does it pay in this world, only in the hereafter, or both? If good consequences are not a good reason for ethical action, what are some good reasons? Should they preach that the only worthy motive is love of God and righteousness? Should a good Christian businessperson even ask whether ethics pays or not?

3

Christian Motives

> Whilst others . . . are canvassing more doubtful Points in Doctrine or Worship, my present Province shall be to direct the Mind and Practice of the conscientious Christian in his daily Employment, where certainly he hath most Temptations, and without God's Grace falls into most Sins, and where he hath need of all the Assistance that God or Man shall impart unto him. For it is not sufficient to be devout in Prayer in the Morning, and at Night, and leave Conscience asleep all the Day.
>
> —Richard Steele, 1684[1]

> That "Honesty is the best *policy*," is a familiar and, perhaps, true adage; but in the outset, I wish to repudiate its soundness as a Christian rule of action [. . .] It is not *expediency*, nor the hope of temporal reward, but the love of God, and a reverent fear of breaking His commands, that are the foundation stones of true honesty, and the business ethics of the Christian.
>
> —Charles Rhoads, 1882[2]

3.1 Enlightened Scots

The previous chapter looked at business ethicists' approach to a pesky question: why should a businessperson be ethical at all? Business ethicists are not theoretical but practical moralists, who work for the improvement of ethics in business in various ways. So, their job requires that they deal with this pesky question. If you are going to go out and tell businesspeople to do what business ethics recommends, you should probably be prepared to tell them, too, the reason or reasons why they should do what business ethics recommends. Just in case somebody asks. In addition, being able to explain why your plea is to be followed should make it more persuasive. Next, I expounded one widespread answer to this pesky question, variants of which are common in the U.S. public sphere today, as well as many decades ago, and even in colonial times. Informally, this answer is that business ethics is materially beneficial for you. More formally, I summarized it as follows:

(1) Empirical: Acting ethically pays.
(2) Normative: Because acting ethically pays, you should act ethically.

---

1   Richard Steele. 1684. *The Trades-man's Calling: Being a Discourse Concerning the Nature, Necessity, Choice, &c. of a Calling in General: and Directions for the Right Managing of the Tradesman's Calling in Particular.* London: Printed by J D for Samuel Sprint.

2   Charles Rhoads. 1882. *Business Ethics in Relation to the Profession of the Religious Society of Friends. An Address Delivered before the Friends' Institute for Young Men, of Philadelphia, Second Month 9th, 1882,* pp. 3–4.

Normative claim (2) assumes the truth of empirical claim (1)—the because-clause explicitly endorses it. Thus, if you support (2) you are thereby supporting (1). By contrast, claim (1) does not logically commit you to (2) at all. Some business ethicists have made a case for both, first for (1), and then for (2). Some other business ethicists have spent all of their energies, time, and space on (1), without explicitly broaching (2). However, pragmatics suggests their utterances can be interpreted as intending to give support to (2), too. For their audience can be plausibly believed to take financial profit to be a good reason, or at least a good *pro tanto* reason. In any case, and despite their differences, the ideas that honesty is the best policy, corporate social responsibility pays, and sustainability makes bottom-line sense have all been put to the same sort of use. They have been used to encourage businesspeople to do business honestly, implement sustainability programs, or give to the community. That these ideas should be extremely attractive to business ethicists is evident. If they were correct, then the business ethics problem would become a pseudo-problem. An individual's acting morally and making profit would not be in conflict after all. Ethics and capitalism would not be in conflict after all. It is a Panglossian win-win situation, of which business-people just need to be made aware. Once they know the truth, any remnant of immoral behavior will vanish.

However, despite their public prominence and popularity, present and past, not everyone has agreed with claims (1) and (2). Objections have been raised against (1), against (2), and against (1) and (2) taken as a whole. To begin with empirical claim (1), how good is the empirical support it has actually gotten? Predictably, the evidence provided in political speeches, newspaper articles, and trade books is nothing but evocative stories and anecdotes. Yet, in recent years business scholars have tried to test (1) more systematically.

Scholars are divided, though. Some say ethical behavior and CSR overall pay. Or even that they always pay—as implied by an article having to ask rhetorically, "Do Good Ethics Always Make for Good Business?"[3] Some say they overall do not pay: they have no effect or their effect is even negative. Some do not want to ask whether they pay overall, always, everywhere, on average, net of all other variables. Instead, they explore the conditions under which they do and do not pay. For this depends on, say, demographic factors, the firm's line of business, the specific character of its CSR policies, and so on. Either way, the expressions "on average," "in the long run," "all things considered," or "*ceteris paribus*" introduce additional sources of disagreement. In addition, since there are innumerable sources of data and innumerable methods to analyze these data, the lack of agreement is partly a function of divergent methodological choices. It is also partly a function of divergent ways of specifying the question to be answered, the hypothesis to be tested, and the auxiliary hypotheses to be accepted—a standard Duhem-Quine situation.[4] All

---

3   Bernhard Schwab. 1996. "A Note on Ethics and Strategy: Do Good Ethics Always Make for Good Business?" *Strategic Management Journal* 17:499–500.

4   P. Duhem. 1906. *La théorie physique: son objet et sa structure.* Paris: Chevalier & Rivière.

in all, it is hard to tell where the truth lies. But claim (1) is at the very least very controversial.[5]

Objections to (1) are not new, however. Eighteenth-century Scottish philosopher Adam Smith did not have access to the extensive databases and statistical modeling techniques that business scholars have access to at present. Nonetheless, he mused over (1) in his Glasgow armchair, and he was not persuaded by it. In his *Theory of Moral Sentiments*, Smith makes this sensible observation as to whether honesty is the best policy, that "good old" proverb:

> In the middling and inferior stations of life, the road to virtue and that to fortune . . . are, happily in most cases, very nearly the same. In all the middling and inferior professions, real and solid professional abilities, joined to prudent, just, firm, and temperate conduct, can very seldom fail of success. [. . .] Either habitual imprudence, however, or injustice, or weakness, or profligacy, will always cloud, and sometimes depress altogether, the most splendid professional abilities. Men in the inferior and middling stations of life, besides, can never be great enough to be above the law, which must generally overawe them into some sort of respect for, at least, the more important rules of justice. The success of such people, too, almost always depends upon the favour and good opinion of their neighbours and equals; and without a tolerably regular conduct these can very seldom be obtained. The good old proverb, therefore, That honesty is the best policy, holds, in such situations, almost always perfectly true. In such situations, therefore, we may generally expect a considerable degree of virtue; and, fortunately for the good morals of society, these are the situations of by far the greater part of mankind.
>
> In the superior stations of life the case is unhappily not always the same.[6]

Smith sensibly observes that it is not necessarily or universally true that honesty is the best policy. It is true contingent on certain empirical conditions' obtaining. These conditions happen to obtain in "the middling and inferior stations of life," such as men's depending "upon the favour and good opinion of their neighbours and equals" for success. Likewise, because they "can never be great enough to be above the law," they must respect "the more important rules of justice." But these conditions do not obtain in "the superior stations of life," such as "the courts of princes" and "the drawing-rooms of the great." Hence, honesty is not the best

---

5 M. L. Barnett and R. M. Solomon. 2012. "Does it Pay to Be *Really* Good?" *Strategic Management Journal* 33:1304 20; A. B. Carroll and K. M. Shabana. 2010. "The Business Case for Corporate Social Responsibility." *International Journal of Management Reviews* 12(1):85–105; B. Lev, C. Petrovits, and S. Radhakrishnan. 2010. "Is Doing Good Good for You?" *Strategic Management Journal* 31:182–200; J. D. Margolis and J. P. Walsh. 2003. "Misery Loves Companies." *Administrative Science Quarterly* 48:268–305; M. Orlitzky. 2008. "Corporate Social Performance and Financial Performance." Pp. 113–34 in *The Oxford Handbook of Corporate Social Responsibility*. Oxford: Oxford University Press; P. Schreck. 2011. "Reviewing the Business Case for Corporate Social Responsibility." *Journal of Business Ethics* 103:167–88.

6 Adam Smith. [1759] 2002. *The Theory of Moral Sentiments*. Cambridge, UK: Cambridge University Press, p. 74.

policy in those places. It so happens that most people belong to the former groups or "stations of life." From a social and moral point of view, this is a fortunate fact about social stratification. But it is also a contingent one. Furthermore, Smith uses his quantifiers prudently: "almost always," "very seldom," "not always." The implication is that these rules do have exceptions: sometimes even in the middling and inferior stations of life honesty is not the best policy.

Smith thus rejects empirical claim (1) as it stands; he proposes a revised version, as it were. Yet, this revision has major implications for normative claim (2)— which as we saw assumes (1) to be true. If the reason a businessperson should act ethically is that it pays, and if acting ethically turns out to pay only sometimes, then a businessperson has reason to act ethically only sometimes: more precisely, whenever it pays, and only then. At other times, she has reason to lie, cheat, steal, engage in insider trading, and dilute butter with lard. From the point of view of business ethicists' interests, this is a disastrous outcome.

Adam Smith's friend David Hume makes this point more directly and pungently. In the *Enquiry Concerning the Principles of Morals,* or "second *Enquiry,*" Hume imagines a peculiar character: the "sensible knave." Over the years, this character became one of the classic moral skeptics, along with Plato's Gyges and Hobbes's "Foole."[7] The sensible knave argues that "honesty is the best policy" might be generally true, but it is not always true. Then, he sensibly and knavishly wonders why not act honestly when honesty is good policy, and act dishonestly when dishonesty is better policy:

> And though it is allowed that, without a regard to property, no society could subsist; yet according to the imperfect way in which human affairs are conducted, a sensible knave, in particular incidents, may think that an act of iniquity or infidelity will make a considerable addition to his fortune, without causing any considerable breach in the social union and confederacy. That *honesty is the best policy,* may be a good general rule, but is liable to many exceptions; and he, it may perhaps be thought, conducts himself with most wisdom, who observes the general rule, and takes advantage of all the exceptions.[8]

Hume is not talking about business or commerce in particular. But what he says is particularly pertinent in a business or commerce context. People engaged in business normally prefer making additions to their fortunes to not doing so, and sensible knaves seem to have greater chances of making greater additions than consistently honest people. Now, Hume's argument involves society as a whole, "the social union and confederacy." In this sense, it is a predecessor of what a couple of centuries later became known as the free-rider problem. But consider now the individual's situation and perspective. Taking advantage of all

7 David Gauthier. 1982. "Three Against Justice: The Foole, the Sensible Knave, and the Lydian Shepherd." *Midwest Studies in Philosophy* 7(1):11–29; Anita M. Superson. 2009. *The Moral Skeptic.* Oxford; New York: Oxford University Press.

8 David Hume. [1751] 1998. *Enquiry Concerning the Principles of Morals.* Edited by Tom L. Beauchamp. Oxford; New York: Oxford University Press, pp. 81–82.

the exceptions would "make a considerable addition to [your] fortune," without causing any damage to society. Then why not do it? It is a tough question. Indeed, Hume appears to give up on the sensible knave: "I must confess that, if a man think that this reasoning much requires an answer, it will be a little difficult to find any which will to him appear satisfactory and convincing."[9] Yet, because the goals of business ethicists are eminently practical, they cannot give up on sensible and knavish businesspeople. Their job is precisely to prevent potential Bernie Madoffs from behaving unethically, and even to prevent potential Bernie Madoffs from coming about in the first place (e.g., through good moral education).

In sum, the enlightened Scots get the better of enlightened self-interest. Hume and Smith—and many others after them—cast doubt on the force of the business case for business ethics and corporate social responsibility. Claim (1) has exceptions, perhaps many exceptions. Then claim (2) will not do anymore. The business case seems to fail. Then the practical project that (1) and (2) jointly push for—the project of promoting moral behavior—is in danger. Perhaps this is because the hope at the heart of this project is a chimera: too easy and too good to be true. That is, the hope that you can bring about morally good actions and outcomes in business, individual and collective, without requiring or fostering or worrying about moral motivations. You may pay a little lip service to them if you wish; that will not hurt. Yet the emphasis should remain on tangible payoffs, dollars-and-cents payoffs; that will do the trick.

Christian business ethicists generally think this is nonsense. Like Hume, Smith, and others, they think this is empirical nonsense. More important, they think this is ethical nonsense. Like Kant, Christian business ethicists generally tell businesspeople that they should act morally from a moral motive. Even if empirical claim (1) were true, normative claim (2) would be morally hideous. In this chapter I analyze these concerns and objections of Christian business ethicists, looking mostly at the second half of the nineteenth century—after Sellers's "market revolution"[10] and Howe's "transformation of America."[11] Next, I spell out the deontological theory and temperament these concerns and objections drew on. From this historical account a more fundamental conclusion will emerge. I will argue that the objections of Christian business ethicists to (1) and (2) bespeak deeper divergences between them and business ethicists who supported (1) and (2). Not only were they at odds regarding their reasons or grounds to be ethical. They were also at odds regarding other dimensions of the moral background, including their fundamental metaphysical premises.

9 Cf. Korsgaard, *The Sources of Normativity*, pp. 58–60; Gerald J. Postema. 1988. "Hume's Reply to the Sensible Knave." *History of Philosophy Quarterly* 5(1):23–40; Thomas Reid. 1788. *Essays on the Active Powers of Man*. Edinburgh: Printed for J. Bell [etc.], pp. 409–44.

10 John Lauritz Larson. 2010. *The Market Revolution in America: Liberty, Ambition, and the Eclipse of the Common Good*. Cambridge, UK: Cambridge University Press; Charles Sellers. 1991. *The Market Revolution: Jacksonian America, 1815–1846*. New York: Oxford University Press.

11 Daniel Walker Howe. 2007. *What Has God Wrought: The Transformation of America, 1815–1848*. New York: Oxford University Press.

One caveat is in order before moving on. My sometimes speaking of *the* Christian moral background, Christian worldview, and Christian business ethicists is a great simplification, intended merely as an analytical tool. No doubt, one could make numerous distinctions and find numerous differences within what I call one background and one worldview, just like the adjectives "Christian" and "Protestant" encompass numerous doctrines and practices, even in one country only—especially if this one country is the United States. What is more, "one country only" is not accurate either. While sometimes I use the adjectives "American" or "U.S.," in fact my data are mostly from a few states, such as Massachusetts, New York, New Jersey, Pennsylvania, and Illinois. Likewise, general statements about the second half of the nineteenth century would be for certain purposes unacceptably imprecise. Luckily, these are not my purposes. My goal is not a theological history or institutional church history, but to identify patterns in the moral background that underlies first-order morality. These patterns may be shared by people and groups that otherwise have little in common. That is what my analytical eye is on, even where my historical account could have been more fine-grained, substituting differences and particularities for similarities and generalizations. All of the usual disclaimers apply, then.

3.2 Springs of Action

Charles Rhoads was a successful businessman in mid-nineteenth century Philadelphia, working in the conveyancing and real estate business. Born in 1828 in Marple Township, Pennsylvania, he grew up in a traditional Quaker family, and received a traditional Quaker education.[12] While his better-known twin brother James Evans Rhoads decided to study medicine (and has gone down in history as the first president of Bryn Mawr College), Charles decided to enter business.[13] His Quaker upbringing notwithstanding, his self-described "wayward youth" was not free from "youthful failures" and the gratification of "carnal desires." As a biographical-cum-hagiographical account narrates: "About his twentieth year he engaged in business in Philadelphia, where coming into close relations with acquaintances who had not the strong conscientious convictions which had been felt by himself, he was led into some indulgences of fashionable life which delayed his spiritual progress."[14] God only knows what these indulgences of fashionable life were, but we mortals know that Rhoads soon felt God's call. "In 1859 [he] recorded a Divine visitation to his soul" in his diary: "I could not doubt my blessed Saviour [*sic*] had in great mercy, visited me with the presence of his Holy Spirit; so that I could say, 'Surely my Redeemer liveth, and will yet give me the victory

---

12　E. Digby Baltzell. 1958. *Philadelphia Gentlemen: The Making of a National Upper Class.* Glencoe: Free Press, p. 272.

13　Henry Hartshorne. 1895. "Memoir of James E. Rhoads, M.D., LL.D." *Proceedings of the American Philosophical Society* 34(149):354–57.

14　*Memorial of Charles Rhoads.* 1904. Philadelphia: Friends' Book Store, pp. 20, 4, 5. Also published as: "Charles Rhoads." *The Friend*, vol. 78, no. 25, Seventh-Day, Twelfth Month 31, 1904.

over the cruel adversary'." From then on, Rhoads turned his life more and more toward the Religious Society of Friends. He "received a call to the ministry" in 1866, after which he "continued to exercise his gift in the ministry as renewed calls to service were from time to time extended; and in the Ninth Month of 1872, the Elders of his Monthly Meeting decided to propose official recognition of his gift." As a result, "he concluded to break off from the active pursuit of business" to devote himself entirely to religious and philanthropic activities. By then he had moved to Haddonfield, New Jersey, a few miles southeast of Philadelphia across the Delaware River, where he became one of the town's notables.[15]

On February 9, 1882, fifty-four-year-old Rhoads delivered an address at the Friends' Institute for Young Men in Philadelphia—an organization whose aim was "to provide accommodations for 'closer acquaintance and association among the young men connected either by membership or community of interest with the Society of Friends'."[16] Rhoads's address was titled, *Business Ethics in Relation to the Profession of the Religious Society of Friends*, and it addressed the ethics of borrowing, trusts, monopolies, employers and employees, salesmen, insolvency, and contracts. It was addressed to young Quaker businessmen, and eventually it was "[p]rinted for distribution, especially among young men, already or about to be in business." In this respect, it was a typical morally didactic speech and later pamphlet. Rhoads rehearsed customary Christian business ethics themes, such as the condemnation of the "[m]odern greed of wealth, and of its *rapid* acquisition," and of "habits of extravagance in living, now so rife everywhere." He quoted customary Christian business ethics New Testament verses, such as "Ye cannot serve God and Mammon" (Matthew 6:24 and Luke 16:13); "Verily, I say unto you, that a rich man shall *hardly* enter into the kingdom of Heaven" (Matthew 19:23); "Take heed and beware of covetousness, for a man's life consisteth not in the abundance of the things that he possesseth" (Luke 12:15); and "Do good and lend, hoping for nothing again" (Luke 6:35).[17] In these respects, Rhoads was drawing on an extensive tradition of Christian thinking about "Mammonism," avarice, and usury (and occasionally any kind of interest-bearing loan). He was also drawing on a local source, the Philadelphia Yearly Meeting, where business ethics was a regular subject.[18]

---

15 *The Two Hundredth Anniversary of the Settlement of Haddonfield, New Jersey*, pp. 11–12, 13.

16 *The Friend*, Twelfth Month 24, 1881, pp. 159–60. Cf. Allen C. Thomas. 1891. *Edward Lawrence Scull: A Brief Memoir with Extracts from His Letters and Journals*. Cambridge: Riverside Press, pp. 148–49.

17 Rhoads, *Business Ethics in Relation to the Profession of the Religious Society of Friends*, pp. 10, 5–6, 11.

18 *Rules of Discipline of the Yearly Meeting of Friends Held in Philadelphia*. 1856. Philadelphia: T. Ellwood Chapman, pp. 104–10; Ezra Michener. 1860. *A Retrospect of Early Quakerism; Being Extracts from the Records of Philadelphia Yearly Meeting and the Meetings Composing It*. Philadelphia: T. Ellwood Zell, pp. 263–66. See also the series of notes on "Trade and Business" in *The Friend* in 1888: "A Friend has sent a series of short extracts from the approved writings of our Society, designed to call the attention of our readers to the caution respecting 'Trade and Business,' which have been issued from time to time, with a concern for the preservation of our members, and the reputation of the Truth we profess. The first of these is now presented.—ED." "Trade and Business." *The Friend*, vol. 61, no. 28, Seventh-Day, Second Month 11, 1888, p. 219.

Rhoads's speech made an unambiguous case against normative claim (2), the claim that you should be moral or act morally because it pays. Right at the outset, after quick deferential references to Quaker authorities George Fox and William Penn, Rhoads took the policy bull by the horns:

> That "Honesty is the best *policy*," is a familiar and, perhaps, true adage; but in the outset, I wish to repudiate its soundness as a Christian rule of action. If our honesty springs from motives of *policy only*, it will fail in the hour of temptation, because it is based on selfishness, not on the deep principles of right and justice. The man that sells a good article to his customers, only because he hopes to secure their future trade, will find occasions when the prospect of gain will blow from another quarter, and his *policy* will shift with it. It is not *expediency*, nor the hope of temporal reward, but the love of God, and a reverent fear of breaking His commands, that are the foundation stones of true honesty, and the business ethics of the Christian.[19]

In this passage Rhoads rejects both empirical claim (1) and normative claim (2). First he suggests that (1) may *perhaps* be true. Then he suggests that (1) may *sometimes* be true, because there are also "occasions when the prospect of gain will blow from another quarter." If so, then policy and expediency, "the hope of temporal reward," will not deliver the moral goods. Normative claim (2) fails as well. The reason, "because he hopes to secure [a customer's] future trade," is not a morally acceptable reason. "Selfishness" is not a morally acceptable motive, as theologians had long insisted. Instead, morally acceptable motives are "the deep principles of right and justice," "the love of God," and "a reverent fear of breaking His commands." These are obviously three different things—principles of right, love, and fear—but we can ignore these nuances for the moment. For the moment it suffices to stress three points. First, Rhoads tackles head-on the "why be moral?" question in the context of business. Second, he directs our attention to the motives or springs of action of businesspeople (or, as it was then also said, what they are "actuated" by). Third, Rhoads thinks there are morally good and morally bad motives. As we will see, this line of thinking has problematic implications, because ontologically it is not evident what or where people's motives are, and epistemically it is not evident how to find out what people's motives are.

Further light on the Christian business ethicists' approach to (1) and (2) is shed by another active clergyman of the second half of the nineteenth century, Reverend Joshua W. Wellman. Wellman, a Congregational, was born in 1821 in Cornish, New Hampshire, attended Dartmouth College and the Andover Theological Seminary, and was the pastor of the First Church in Derry, New Hampshire (1851), then the Eliot Congregational Church in Newton, Massachusetts (1856), and finally the First Congregational Church in Malden, Massachusetts (1873).[20] Like many of his contemporaries, Wellman expressed much concern

---

19 Rhoads, *Business Ethics in Relation to the Profession of the Religious Society of Friends*, pp. 3–4.
20 "Long and Active Life." *Boston Daily Globe*, November 29, 1903, p. 6; "Death of Oldest Dartmouth Alumnus." *Boston Daily Globe*, September 29, 1912, p. 16.

about the "immoralities of business" of his day; the "alarmingly intense craving after wealth," and the "rapidly multiplying" "temptations to dishonesty." Invoking the authority of Richard Whately (1787–1863), the influential Archbishop of Ireland, Wellman had issues both with empirical claim (1) and with normative claim (2):

> Times like the present prove that very much of that which is called "commercial integrity," is not that "integrity of the upright" of which the Scriptures speak, but simply that integrity of the politic, which the maxims of trade too often inculcate. Archbishop Whately is right when he says that "Honesty is the best policy, but he who acts from that principle is not an honest man." The man who is honest simply because it pays well, will be dishonest the moment dishonesty pays better. If there is a great increase of fraudulent practices in these tumultuous times, it simply discloses the previous hollowness of commercial virtue. What is needed is, more of that honesty that springs not from policy, but from principle; more of that integrity which is practised not because it will pay, but because it is right. Our only remedy is in the Gospel of Christ brought to bear, in its regenerating power upon the hearts of men, and faithfully applied in its precepts to their conduct in the sphere of business as in every other sphere of their action.[21]

Like Rhoads, Wellman thought that (1) was not always the case. It followed that (2) would not work as some expected it to. Policy will not work; principle will. Then, why be moral? "[N]ot because it will pay, but because it is right." That is the "integrity of the upright" that Proverbs 11:3 is talking about: "The integrity of the upright shall guide them: but the perverseness of transgressors shall destroy them." Or, as Brooklyn Presbyterian pastor Theodore L. Cuyler pithily put it some years later, "[t]he divine law never recognizes honesty as a 'policy,' but evermore as a principle."[22] Perhaps most eloquently, W. H. Van Doren, of the Reformed Church, advised "young men entering mercantile life":

> *Honesty* ought never to be named in the same category with *policy*. Honesty is sometimes practised with the same mechanical exactness with which a wheel, with its hundreds of cogs, meets the cogs of its fellow wheel. There is no jar nor violence, all move smoothly and harmoniously as the finest chronometer. But it is the mere form and features of honesty, a frame-work without a heart, a mask without a head. [. . .]

21   Wellman's article was originally published in the *Boston Recorder*, the traditional Congregational paper founded in 1816. However, here I am using its reprints in *Friends' Intelligencer* and *The Friend*. Much of the article consists of a discussion of a remark of Marsh's in *Man and Nature*, and of Spencer's essays, "The Morals of Trade" and "Railway Morals and Railway Policy." J. W. Wellman. 1865. "Immoralities of Business." *The Friend*, April 15, 1865, p. 260; J. W. Wellman. 1865. "Immoralities of Business." *Friends' Intelligencer*, May 20, 1865, p. 174. Cf. George P. Marsh. 1864. *Man and Nature; or, Physical Geography as Modified by Human Action*. New York: Charles Scribner.

22   Theodore L. Cuyler. 1892. *Stirring the Eagle's Nest and Other Practical Discourses*. New York: Baker and Taylor Company, p. 103.

Thus the young man who abstains from fraud only because it is for his pecuniary interest to be honest is in truth a thief. When the proper time arrives, when the *better policy*, as he thinks, will be advisable, he will steal. Hence the constant solemnity of the law which lays its fiery finger on the heart,—thou shalt not covet. [. . .]

Honesty is that state of mind which will stand the test of the eye of the All-seeing God.[23]

The bottom line is that Van Doren, Cuyler, Rhoads, Wellman, and Archbishop Whately were not satisfied with a morally acceptable behavior or outcome; springs of action had to pass a moral test, too. Indeed, Whately's words became an aphorism of sorts: "'Honesty is the best policy;' but he who acts from that principle is not an honest man, because he acts from policy, and not from the love of right.— Abp. Whately."[24] This aphorism was reproduced in several didactic collections and manuals in Britain and the United States, such as the *New Cyclopædia of Prose Illustrations* (New York, 1876), *Illustrative Gatherings for Preachers and Teachers* (Philadelphia, 1867), or *The Secret of Achievement* (New York, 1898). Then, Christian business ethicists were endowed with a crucial distinction between good and bad, worthy and unworthy, pious and impious motives. Not all of them identified, described, and evaluated the same set of motives, so the constituents of the two categories could vary. Further, the same words could stand for different motives, which becomes apparent when their meaning is spelled out or examples are given. Still, the category of morally acceptable motives generally included: principle, love of God, love to God and Christ, love of virtue, virtue its own reward, love of right, obedience to God, submission to God, and fear of God (in the sense of awe and respect, as opposed to fear of his punishment). The morally unacceptable motives generally included: policy, expediency, self-interest, self-love, pride, vanity, and love of praise. There was also a *sui generis*, problematic category of motives, which consisted of hope of reward and fear of punishment in this world. A second *sui generis* category consisted of hope of reward and fear of punishment

23 Wm. Howard Van Doren. 1852. *Mercantile Morals; Thoughts for Young Men entering Mercantile Life*. New York: Charles Scribner, pp. 49, 56, 57. "The Rev. William Howard Van Doren, son of the Rev. Isaac Van Doren," was at the time the "Pastor of the Second Reformed Dutch Church, of Piermont, N. Y." Earlier he had been the "pastor of the First Reformed Church of Williamsburgh." Cf. *A History of the Classis of Paramus of the Reformed Church in America*. 1902. New York: The Board of Publication, R. C. A., pp. 430–31; A. Van Doren Honeyman. 1909. *The Van Doorn Family (Van Doorn, Van Dorn, Van Doren, Etc.) in Holland and America, 1088–1908*. Plainfield, NJ: Honeyman's Publishing House, p. 562.

24 Elon Foster, ed. 1876. *New Cyclopædia of Prose Illustrations, Adapted to Christian Teaching*. New York: Thomas Y. Crowell, p. 244. See also G. S. Bowes. 1867. *Illustrative Gatherings for Preachers and Teachers*. Philadelphia: Perkinpine & Higgins, pp. 123, 231; Orison Swett Marden. 1898. *The Secret of Achievement*. New York: Thomas Y. Crowell & Company, p. 53. Cf. Richard Whately. 1857. *Lessons on Morals, and Christian Evidences*. Cambridge, MA: John Bartlett, p. 149. Reverend Van Doren similarly said: "Honesty to heaven and earth, God himself being judge, is 'profitable for all things.' But he who practises it for its profitableness or gain, deserves no higher name than 'No-thief'"; "although *honesty be the worst policy*, he alone is honest who is so from principle, or a sense of obligation." Van Doren, *Mercantile Morals*, pp. 53, 59.

in the hereafter—obviously not as worthy as love of God or love of virtue, but obviously not as unworthy as expediency. As we will see, these two *sui generis* categories of motives are key to understanding the predicament of Christian business ethicists.[25]

Last, because Christian business ethics approaches focus on motives, on the internal rather than the external, they can turn out to have a surprisingly good implication—surprisingly good if you are an employer or principal, anyway. True, you will have to be honest to your customers and to the tax authorities, because of your love and fear of God, even when dishonesty would have been more profitable. The good news is that your employees and agents will likewise have to be honest to you, because of their love and fear of God. In other words, religious motives "will keep the barytes out of pure white lead, and sand out of iron castings," and they will also "quicken the industry of the employee when no human eye could detect idleness."[26] Rhoads spells out this idea, quoting and praising the contentious New Testament passage, Ephesians 6:5–6:

> To the employed, he [the Apostle] says, "be obedient to your masters, in single-ness of your heart as unto Christ; not with eye-service as men-pleasers, but as the servants of Christ, doing the will of God from the heart." [. . .]
>
> What an exalted standard of action is here proposed! and [*sic*] how does it elevate the lowest station in life to dignity when the incumbent fills it on such principles! In singleness of heart as unto Christ, not with eye-service! The clerk actuated by such motives requires no watching to stimulate to duty. His employer's interest is regarded as his own. No grudging stint of care and pains to perform his work in the best style, although out of sight and observation.[27]

This implication complicates my account of Rhoads's and Rhoads-like business ethics approaches—and in particular his rejection of claim (2). From the clerk's point of view, if he is "actuated by such motives," he will be actuated by the right sort of motives. But recall the character of Rhoads's audience. Rhoads's words were addressed to young men who were more likely to become masters than servants. So he was in fact telling future employers that the "clerk actuated by such motives requires no watching to stimulate duty." From the employer's point of view, this consideration surely has nothing to do with "the deep principles of right and justice." It surely has to do with the financial effects of business ethics. On the other hand, Rhoads does not explicitly endorse this sort of consideration as a reason. In any case, the issue here is independent of what Rhoads's really meant or believed. Whatever he meant or believed, an obedient workforce is a

---

25 To be sure, several of these motives could be appealed to simultaneously. For instance, Georg Christian Knapp says in his *Lectures on Christian Theology*: "[T]he virtuous man is described in the Bible as *obedient* and *submissive*"; he "cheerfully bows to the authority of God." And then he adds that "[a]ll virtue should proceed from religious motives, from thankful love, and a spirit of obedience towards God." George [*sic*] Christian Knapp. 1850. *Lectures on Christian Theology*. Translated by Leonard Woods. Second American edition. New York: M. W. Dodd, p. 302.

26 Rhoads, *Business Ethics in Relation to the Profession of the Religious Society of Friends*, p. 17.

27 Ibid., p. 12.

capitalist's dream come true (more on this in chapter 5). So this could be a very useful motive. As the *Messenger* put it in 1878 in an article on "Business Morality": "The workman will not 'scamp' his work, or waste the time of his employer. Why? 'Because of the fear of God.'"[28]

All in all, Rhoads, Wellman, Cuyler, Van Doren, and Whately illustrate how Christian business ethicists protested against improper, unworthy, or ungodly motives. They required that ethical business conduct should spring from appropriate springs of action, such as the Christian's love of God. This is the true "business ethics of the Christian." And this is in keeping with Christian theology and the Christian worldview, and the moral centrality they have always granted to motivation, at the time as much as today.[29] Thus, normative claim (2) was clearly at odds with Christian morality. However, Christian business ethicists had issues with empirical claim (1), too. First, it is empirically unreliable; it only obtains sometimes. But there is a further concern. The problem is not merely that sometimes "the prospect of gain will blow from another quarter." At least in principle, laws and institutions could be redesigned in such a way that the prospect of gain always blow from the ethical quarter. The problem is more serious: claim (1) seems to be unable to tell apart reality from appearance. It seems unable to tell apart acting ethically from appearing to act ethically. Back to Glaucon and Adeimantus—and Machiavelli.

3.3 Machiavellian Appearances

Henry Augustus Boardman (1808–1880) was a reputed Presbyterian pastor and writer. From 1833 until 1876 he was the pastor of Philadelphia's Tenth Presbyterian Church, "that large Old School congregation located in the midst of the city's rapidly expanding business sector (Twelfth and Walnut)."[30] Boardman's sermons, lectures, and writings did not shy away from practical, this-worldly matters, such as the institution of slavery (*What Christianity Demands of Us at the Present Crisis*), the Civil War (*The Peace We Need*), and the intersection of religion and work (*The Claims of Religion upon Medical Men*).[31] His "course of

---

28 And not only the ethics of the "workman" would improve due to this motive: "And so, too, will this powerful motive, the fear of God, purify into a bright, honest, cheerful singlemindedness and considerate kindness, the reciprocal duties of employer and employed. The servant will not reason, 'My Lord delayeth His coming: I may do this trifling piece of commission, and no human eye will detect me.' The landlord will not hardly press his tenant, though long accepted precedents still flourishing around him may invite his imitation. The workman will not 'scamp' his work, or waste the time of his employer. Why? 'Because of the fear of God.'" "Business Morality." *Messenger*, January 9, 1878, p. 1.

29 Cf. Linda Zagzebski. 2004. *Divine Motivation Theory*. Cambridge; New York: Cambridge University Press.

30 Richard W. Pointer. 2002. "Philadelphia Presbyterians, Capitalism, and the Morality of Economic Success." Pp. 171–91 in *God and Mammon: Protestants, Money, and the Market, 1790–1860*, edited by Mark A. Noll. New York: Oxford University Press, p. 182.

31 Henry Augustus Boardman was born in 1808 in Troy, New York, the son of a Puritan father and a Quaker mother. "In the fall of 1830 he entered the Theological Seminary in Princeton, N. J., and

lectures to merchants" was published as *The Bible in the Counting-House* in Philadelphia in 1853, and later reprinted in England and Scotland. Boardman meant
it to be a "Hand-book on the moralities of Commerce," and his rationale was that
"[m]erchants have had too little help from the Pulpit. They have been left, very
much, to frame their own ethics, and to grapple, as they might, with the temptations and trials of business." Thus, he tried to fill that gap by discussing the ethics
of speculation, bankruptcy, principals and clerks, "the claims of Sabbath upon
merchants," "the true mercantile character," and why "hasting to be rich" was a
bad idea.

"It is not expediency . . . but the love of God . . . ," said Quaker Charles Rhoads
in the 1880s. The word choice is telling. "Expediency" was a key word in business
ethics projects and discussions. Some business ethicists endorsed and commended
it—recall how Harvard's Assistant Dean Deane Malott confidently asserted that
"the answer to ethical problems is sound business expediency" (chapter 2). By
contrast, for much of the Christian tradition "expediency" was, like "self-interest,"
a key evil word. Thus Boardman said: "There are, for example, in every great
trading community, individuals whose only rule of conduct is *Expediency*. Right
and wrong are with them mere professional technicalities. [. . .] If a transaction
promises to promote their interest, it is right; if not, it is wrong. If a lie will answer
a better purpose than the truth, it would be effeminate not to use it."[32] Along these
lines, one of the foes of Boardman's *The Bible in the Counting-House* is the motive
of "expediency" or "policy." But what was meant by "expediency," exactly? It referred to a rule of action that prioritizes its beneficial or profitable consequences;
what will "promote [one's] interest" or "answer a better purpose." The *Oxford English Dictionary*'s definition explicates this sense well: "The consideration of what
is expedient, as a motive or rule of action; 'policy,' prudential considerations as
distinguished from those of morality or justice. In mod. use often in a bad sense,
the consideration of what is merely politic (esp. with regard to self-interest) to the
neglect of what is just or right." As the dictionary suggests, "expediency" may by
itself involve a normative assessment.

Acting from expediency is therefore the opposite of acting from principle or
rightness. Crucially, unlike principle and rightness, the expediency of an action
in business may depend on other people's perception, such as the perceptions of

in April, 1833, was licensed to preach. In September, 1833, he was called to the pastorate of the Tenth
Presbyterian Church of Philadelphia, over which he was duly installed, Nov. 8, 1833, and of which
he continued in charge until May, 1876, when he became Pastor Emeritus. After an interval of feeble
health, he died in Philadelphia, June 15, 1880, aged 72 years. During his long and eminent pastorate,
he was repeatedly called to other fields of labor,—notably in May, 1853, to the chair of Pastoral Theology in Princeton Seminary. He published many volumes and pamphlets, on theological subjects.
The degree of D.D [sic] was conferred on him by Marshall College." *Obituary Record of Graduates of
Yale College. Deceased during the Academical [sic] Year Ending in June, 1880*. New Haven, CT: Tuttle,
Morenhouse & Taylor, pp. 388–89. See also John DeWitt. 1881. *A Sermon Commemorative of the Life
and Work of the Rev. Henry Augustus Boardman, D. D.* Philadelphia: n.p.; A. A. Hodge. 1881. *Address
at the Funeral of the Rev. Henry Augustus Boardman, D. D.* Philadelphia: The Chandler Printing House.
32   Boardman, *Bible*, p. 43.

a retailer's customers about her actions. Boardman made just this point in his second lecture, "The Standard of Commercial Rectitude":

> If they [individuals whose only rule of conduct is *Expediency*] can take advantage of a customer, without being detected, they would be faithless to themselves to let the opportunity slip. I say, "without being detected:" for it must not be supposed that this class of persons have cast off all outward decorum. Far from it. It is one of the elements which enter into their current calculations, how far they can go in this or that direction without being exposed, and whether any proposed measure can be adopted without a sacrifice of their reputation. They are so graphically delineated by the great Coryphæus of the school to which they belong, that I am tempted to quote his own words.[33]

The great Coryphæus of the school is the early-sixteenth-century Florentine political consultant, Niccolò Machiavelli. And the passage of *The Prince* that Boardman quotes next is the notorious passage I quoted earlier, which begins as follows: "It is not necessary, however, for a prince to possess all the good qualities I have enumerated, but it is indispensable that he should appear to have them." According to Cicero's *Laelius de Amicitia* and Sallust's *Coniuratio Catilinae*, you should be, not seem to be. According to Machiavelli's *Principe*, though, you should seem to be, not be. Likewise, a Machiavellian businessperson, like a Machiavellian prince, would not necessarily possess or strive to possess good qualities, but would definitely strive to appear to possess them. Differently put, a businessperson or company needs a further, independent reason to actually do business in an ethical manner. Without it, economic reasoning and the profit motive alone would recommend Machiavellism. Glaucon's challenge would sadly carry the day.

Yet, there is an important qualification, which Boardman sensibly brings up in these lectures, *The Bible in the Counting-House*. It stems from the present dearth of magic rings like Gyges's. Suppose a businessperson decides to decide on a course of action on expediency considerations only. Upon some reflection, he comes to the conclusion that the most expedient course of action is to take advantage of his customers. That seems to be what will best promote the businessperson's material interests. However, this is the case as long as one condition obtains: that he will not get caught. For if he ended up getting caught, then that course of action would not be the most expedient one for him after all: a reputation for being a cheat is often very costly, and doing twenty-four years in the Federal Correctional Institution, Englewood, is always very costly.[34] What is a businessperson to do, then? As Boardman points out, businesspeople driven by the motive of expediency or policy should simply "enter into their . . . calculations" this factor, namely, the

---

33 Ibid., pp. 43–44.
34 Previously, I bracketed the odds of getting caught by law enforcement as a reason not to act unethically (assuming that unethical and illegal behavior coincide). I did that for the sake of the argument. But business ethicists, who aim to actually affect behavior, reasonably and unsurprisingly tend to resort to this prudential threat as a persuasive device.

probability of getting caught. This is just one additional factor that they should take into account, even if the math gets a little more complicated.

Needless to say, Boardman is not satisfied with this Machiavellian outcome. It may happen that a businessperson both conducts his business in a moral fashion and has a reputation for conducting his business in a moral fashion. That is, it may happen to be the case that reality and appearance coincide. But this coincidence is not necessary. Then, causal claim (1), the claim that acting ethically will pay in dollars and cents, seems to be in need of an amendment. What will pay in dollars and cents is not acting ethically, but appearing to act ethically. This is because the causal chain or causal mechanism at play normally involves third parties, such as customers, employees, the community, and regulatory agencies. In certain (though not all) lines of business, the "ethical company" will have more business, it will recruit more talented employees than its competitors, its employees will be more motivated and loyal, the community will be more cooperative, and pesky regulatory agencies and very pesky leftist social movements will interfere less with its operations. Yet, these third parties are normally unable to tell appearance from reality. Or, at least, it would be too costly for it to be worth their while, even when they in principle could obtain the information needed. Hence the Machiavellian amendment:

(1') Empirical: Appearing to act ethically pays.

If, as Machiavelli would have it, this proposition were true, it would be a troubling amendment. It would fly in the face of and be unacceptable to any type of business ethics, Christian or otherwise. Boardman's lecture went on to censure Machiavelli and his system based on "policy as opposed to principle," and to lament the fact that there were "many Machiavellian merchants." For "[t]hey have no conception of a virtue which brings no cash with it. 'Honesty, like every other commodity, has its market value. 'Too much honesty won't pay'."[35] That is not the right way to think about virtue and honesty, whether it brings cash with it, whether one is using too much of it.

The phrase, "the market value of honesty," might have sounded cacophonous to Boardman's audience in the 1850s. But it sounds perfectly normal to anyone who reads the newspapers and business press in the 2010s. In fact, to anyone who reads the newspapers and business press in the 2010s, Boardman's worries about Machiavellism in the 1850s must sound like old news. In chapter 2 we saw that the business ethicists of today try to "[convince] you that you can and should brand and communicate your CSR."[36] So did the business ethicists of yesterday, who tried to convince you that "it pays to tell the public about it." Writing in

---

35   Boardman, *Bible*, p. 45.

36   McElhaney, *Just Good Business*, p. 4. See also Shuili Du, C. B. Bhattacharya, and Sankar Sen. 2010. "Maximizing Business Returns to Corporate Social Responsibility (CSR): The Role of CSR Communication." *International Journal of Management Reviews* 12(1):8–19; Kellie McElhaney. 2009. "A Strategic Approach to Corporate Social Responsibility." *Leader to Leader* 52:30–36.

1917, William Rowland Hotchkin, "ten year Advertising Manager for John Wanamaker," put it straightforwardly:

> Now, while thousands of people have discovered for themselves that John Wanamaker is honest and his goods reliable, it is my definite belief that his widely acknowledged and widely KNOWN reputation for honesty and reliability has grown to its present proportions only because *he hasn't been too modest to widely exploit his principles and policy.* [. . .] So I think it has been abundantly proved that it not only pays to be honest and square with the public, but *it pays to tell the public about it.*
>
> It is a psychological fact that people very largely think the things that we tell them to think. If we talk about our belief in honesty and how we apply it to our business, they will believe that we are honest and that our business is more honestly conducted than other businesses that don't do so much talking about it—provided, of course, that our business ACTS do not belie our words.[37]

Of course, Hotchkin's "of course" is not warranted. Things would be much easier if it were. Of course, neither the business ethicists of today nor those of yesterday mean to suggest that business ethics is *only* a public relations matter. Rather, they insist that a businessperson's acts should not belie her words. For example, *in addition to* planting trees, a firm should tell its customers that it has or will. But cynics and critics of business ethics and CSR are not persuaded that this is what most firms do in reality. Hence the accusation that business ethics and CSR are empty rhetoric, hot air, hypocrisy, and Machiavellism. According to this view, if what makes a bottom-line difference is being believed to behave ethically, or having a reputation for behaving ethically, is it reasonable to expect that firms will actually behave ethically? If this is not a reasonable expectation, then business ethicists are only making things worse. For they are supplying businesspeople with knowledge and techniques that increase the odds of their getting away with lip service and hypocrisy.

Despite these serious concerns and complaints, however, Boardman was still unwilling to give up claim (1). Indeed, later on in that very lecture he assured the merchants in the audience that "high-toned integrity" *was* profitable:

> This may seem to imply a doubt as to the *profitableness* of high-toned integrity. It is put in this form only to give the statement the greater strength. A host of merchants could be cited to show from their own books that honesty is, in the long run, the best policy, and that godliness hath the promise of the life that now is, as well as of that which is to come. But waiving this, the question of right must always take precedence of the question of interest.[38]

Acting ethically does pay after all! Ethics pays not only in the other world, but it pays in this world as well. Besides scriptural authority (1 Timothy 4:8),

---

37   W. R. Hotchkin. 1917. *Making More Money in Storekeeping.* New York: Ronald Press Company, p. 271.

38   Boardman, *Bible*, pp. 64–65.

Boardman even invokes empirical evidence to support claim (1): the books of "a host of merchants." True, rightness and godliness "must always take precedence" over self-interest. But it so happens that rightness and godliness will also result in profits, so self-interest need not worry, even if it is not given precedence. Then, where does Boardman end up standing with regard to claim (2)? Is there not a tension in his claims?

The tension seems even tenser in light of an earlier sermon of Boardman's, which he delivered to the Philadelphia Young Men's Society in 1834, when he was himself a young man in his mid-twenties. Forcefully titled *Piety Essential to Man's Temporal Prosperity*, Boardman discussed the verse that he would cite in 1853 as well, 1 Timothy 4:8: "Godliness is profitable unto all things, having promise of the life that now is, and of that which is to come."[39] The point of the sermon, at least at first, seems to be a defense of both causal claim (1) and normative claim (2). According to Boardman, "[t]he best interest of every young man for the present life, will be greatly promoted by personal piety." How so? What are the causal mechanisms that connect piety and "temporal prosperity"? First, "[r]eligion imparts to every young man who embraces it, much KNOWL-EDGE which is indispensable to his highest temporal interests and happiness." This useful knowledge comprises both self-knowledge and "knowledge of the world." Further, "personal piety is advantageous to young men, in preparing and disposing them to SELECT THE BEST AND NOBLEST OBJECTS OF PURSUIT."[40]

To be sure, these claims differ from the simple "acting ethically pays." They are about being religious, attending to religion, or leading a religious life. Moreover, up to this point their connection to temporal prosperity seems at best indirect.[41] Eventually, though, Boardman presents to these Philadelphian businessmen a more direct connection between piety and prosperity:

Personal piety is especially valuable to Young Men, *inasmuch as it both qualifies and disposes them* TO FORM THOSE HABITS WHICH ORDINARILY INSURE SUCCESS IN BUSINESS.

The Bible is so perfectly adapted to our character and circumstances, that even on the principles of mere human expediency, it would be politic for every man to adopt its maxims and precepts in his secular employment. [. . .] [T]he most valuable qualities for the management of business, are the appropriate fruit of religious principles. Such qualities are prudence, frugality, diligence, industry, and stern, unyielding rectitude.[42]

---

39   Henry A. Boardman. 1834. *Piety Essential to Man's Temporal Prosperity*. Philadelphia: Printed by William F. Geddes, p. 7. Cf. Pointer, "Philadelphia Presbyterians, Capitalism," pp. 182–83.

40   Boardman, *Piety*, pp. 9, 10, 14.

41   Boardman was aware of this issue, and tried to address an imaginary objector as follows: "Are you ready to say, that this view of the subject, however just, is not essentially connected with man's *temporal* interests? I reply by asking whether those interests are not indissolubly associated with the ultimate objects of his pursuits." Ibid., p. 15.

42   Ibid., p. 18.

Thus, the causal chain or path that Boardman suggests is as follows:

(3) Causal chain: religious principles or piety → prudence, frugality, diligence, industry, and rectitude → business success, temporal prosperity, good consequences in this world.

This causal mechanism makes sense and is familiar terrain—both for several observers at that time, and for retrospective historical and sociological observers, including Weber and the Weberians. But it is remarkable that Boardman is analyzing consequences; indeed, the consequences of a person's actions for herself. His reasoning and perspective seem downright egoistic, not utilitarian or something of that sort. More important, on the face of it Boardman seems to be encouraging merchants to be pious *in order to* succeed. In other words, this looks like a defense of expediency as a motive or reason for action, even if qualified as "mere human expediency." Indeed, as a motive or reason to adopt the principles of the Bible. First impressions to the contrary, that impious destination is not where Boardman was headed. For he adds right away:

Now granting that these qualities [prudence, frugality, diligence, industry, and rectitude] are sometimes found disconnected with piety, it is obvious that in that case their only basis is self-interest, and that consequently, they are rather the counterfeit semblances of the virtues whose name they bear than the virtues themselves. In the one case, you have men who are amiable, active, and honest, from a mere regard to reputation or profit, and who under any mutation of fortune, would not hesitate to assume another livery . . . In the other case, you have men who are honest, because it is right to be honest; who are faithful to their engagements, because God requires it; and who render to every one his due, because they hate injustice and love equality.[43]

This is the pious destination where Boardman was headed. It is not a moderate position, because he builds into the very concept of virtue the requirement that its "basis" not be self-interest. If an action is done from regard to reputation or profit, then whatever it is and whatever it brings about, it is not virtue, but a "counterfeit semblance" thereof. This is surely an unambiguous statement on Boardman's part. Clever conceptual moves notwithstanding, though, the tension is still lurking. After all, the sermon was titled, "Piety Essential to Man's Temporal Prosperity," and it spelled out what about religion led to profitability. Yet, on the other hand, it denied that regard to temporal prosperity could be a basis for morality at all.

3.4 Compromises

We have thus come to see a fundamental tension in Christian business ethics. At the end of the day, Henry Boardman, and Christian business ethicists in general, had to live with and face up to it. Generally speaking, they did not wish to and did

43   Ibid.

not try to refute empirical claim (1), to the effect that business ethics pays. Given their job description and audience—active businesspeople, young business-people, "practical men"—it would have been unadvisable to do so. Or, in plain English, it would have been stupid. It would have been equally unadvisable to give the impression that Christian ethics was positively detrimental to temporal pros-perity (which, as we will see in a moment, is a related yet distinct causal claim). More generally, the church, like any institution, must accommodate itself to the social and historical context in which it operates, lest it stop being relevant and ultimately viable. If the sermons and pronouncements of a minister systematically alienated his congregation and the community at large, they would undermine their own possibility (or, more precisely, persistence into the future). For this rea-son, my historical data put my arguments to a tough test. If a minister's audience is composed largely of seminary students or senior citizens, it might be easier to dissociate religion and ethics from temporal prosperity. It is a different ball game altogether to say that sort of thing to people for whom temporal prosperity—some temporal prosperity anyway—is a good to be pursued, something they may attach meaning to, even a life project.

This tension in some cases resulted in cumbersome views, in some cases re-sulted in downright logical inconsistencies, yet in some cases was more cleverly and successfully dealt with. The history of the Christian accommodation to the possession and pursuit of wealth, and to capitalism more generally, has been well studied both in Europe and the United States. It is a colorful, multifaceted history: one can find total rejection of capitalism and the market as evil and the work of Satan, total acceptance as saintly and mandated by God, and many original mix-tures and shades of gray. Yet, the history of this more specific accommodation or equilibrium—challenging (2), but not challenging (1), or not *really* challenging (1)—has not been thematized as such. How did Christian business ethicists in the United States deal with it in their work?

One possible approach was the differential allocation of time, attention, and emphasis in a sermon, lecture, pamphlet, article, book, curriculum, informal con-versation with the mayor of the city, or yearly schedule of activities at the church. This is what Boardman did. For him an assault on (2) would do. He could still mention (1), e.g., the fact that honesty is in the long run the best policy. Yet a lec-ture to merchants was to be mostly devoted to persuading them that they ought to act from rightness and godliness and love of God, and that not any motive would do. In this sense, Boardman is representative of Christian business ethicists. They stressed that the profitability of moral behavior is not an acceptable reason to be-have morally. But they did not deny that moral behavior was profitable. Or if they did, they did it *sotto voce*, or at least not very loudly, nor at much length. It was a pragmatic compromise of sorts.[44]

44 Comparably, historian Richard Pointer notes this "irony": "Alongside their case for Christian piety as a defense against selfish materialism, Presbyterians ironically juxtaposed arguments promot-ing piety as an essential asset in achieving economic success. Typical was Ashbel Green's claim that 'true religion has no tendency to diminish, but on the contrary, a direct tendency to increase, the

Here is a good example of this pragmatic compromise, whose ingenious phrasing illustrates the point well. It is an excerpt from a short article titled "Business Morality," which appeared in 1878 in the *Messenger*, a periodical publication of the Reformed Church in the United States denomination:

Religion bids men to be honest, not because honesty is the best policy merely; be truthful not because lying is unmanly only; be temperate, not because intemperate habits weaken the intellect and impair the vital energy, and in short, put you outside the pale of society; but be all these from one supreme, absorbing motive, the fear you have of offending a loving God. It will be the thought of God and of Christ which will alone make us true to man.[45]

Merely! On the one hand, the *Messenger* gets to tell its readers about the good or bad practical effects of their actions on their personal welfare: honesty *is* the best policy, and too much whiskey *does* "weaken the intellect and impair the vital energy" (the "unmanliness only" of lying may require a different interpretation). Honesty and temperance pay. On the other hand, though, you should be honest, truthful, and temperate "from one supreme, absorbing motive": fear of offending a loving God. It seems the *Messenger* manages to have it both ways. In fact, this is reminiscent of a situation we already saw. To be more precise, what we saw was the opposite situation. We saw contemporary business ethicists who instruct businesspeople to act ethically because it pays, that is, normative claim (2). Yet, while they emphasized this motive—and elaborated on why it pays, and how it pays, and how much it pays—they mentioned that it is the right thing to do as well. The discrepancy between these two groups of business ethicists, then, is one of emphasis. Both maintain that both motives are at work, even if one of them is evil or ungodly, or one of them is of lesser importance and is mentioned in passing. In other words, business ethics is motivationally overdetermined. The two kinds of motives pull in the same direction, even though any one of them would have sufficed to give the businessperson reason to follow the ethical course of action. Once again, what a wonderful world.

---

stock of present fruition.' In a city afflicted with capitalist fever these evangelical Protestants were not about to suggest that Christianity was an obstacle to earning a good living." However, Pointer's reading seems to me inaccurate. For the *Christian Advocate* article he quotes is about the enjoyment of material possessions, not their acquisition. More generally, while the evangelical Protestants who suggested that Christianity was an obstacle might not have made it very far, Pointer places excessive weight on one side of the equation—namely, the piety-essential-to-man's-temporal-prosperity side. Pointer, "Philadelphia Presbyterians, Capitalism," pp. 182–83. Cf. [Ashbel Green.] 1873. "Victory Over the World." *Christian Advocate*, November, 1829, pp. 487–91; [Ashbel Green.] 1873. "Victory Over the World." *Christian Advocate*, December, 1829, pp. 536–39.

45 "Business Morality." *Messenger*, January 9, 1878, p. 1. This article was not written by the editor of the *Messenger*, Rev. Dr. P. S. David (cf. Joseph Henry Dubbs. 1885. *Historic Manual of the Reformed Church in the United States*. Lancaster, PA: n.p., p. 334). Rather, it was reprinted from *Sunday at Home*, the London magazine published by the Religious Tract Society. *The Friend* reprinted it, too: "Business Morality." *The Friend*, vol. 51, no. 21, Seventh-Day, First Month 5, 1878, p. 166.

In this respect, both groups are heirs to the doyen of business ethics manuals, Reverend Richard Steele's *The Trades-man's Calling*.[46] Steele's manual was first published in London in 1684, and a second edition appeared in 1698. His aim was "to guide the honest-minded Tradesman in the right way to Heaven." But only long after its author's death a revised version of the manual achieved great success, now under a new title, *The Religious Tradesman; Or, Plain and Serious Hints of Advice for the Tradesman's Prudent and Pious Conduct*, and with a "recommendatory preface" by Isaac Watts (dated 1747). This version was published in many places in Britain and the United States, including Newburyport, Massachusetts (178–?), London (1792), Charlestown, Massachusetts (1804), Philadelphia (1807), and Trenton, New Jersey (1823). As most business ethicists, Steele asked, too, why be moral. Specifically, in the chapter, "Of Justice," Steele discussed why "the religious tradesman" should be just.[47] First things first: "The *moral law* of GOD obliges us to the practice of *justice*." But there is a second reason: "And not only duty and conscience, but *present interest* obliges men to the exercise of *probity* and *justice*: it is the surest and safest way to prosperity, and has a natural tendency to promote it." Likewise, why should the religious tradesman be truthful? "Religion certainly lays us under the strongest obligations to truth and sincerity. [. . .] And not only reason and religion, but honour and interest should engage men to be exactly true and upright in their words." The tradesman should be truthful "from conscience to God, and a love to virtue. To this he is bound by the rules of reason and religion, of honor and interest." Reverend Steele's manual stresses proper religious conduct, motives, duties, salvation, and the role of God. It is after all the work of a clergyman of the seventeenth century. Still, he did not forget to remind his readers that "present interest" recommends just the same courses of action as Christian duty and godliness.

---

46 Richard Steele (1629–1692) was an English minister, not to be confused with his namesake, the Irish essayist and playwright Sir Richard Steele (1672–1729). Tawney writes about him that "after being deprived of a country living under the Act of Uniformity, [Steele] spent his declining years as minister of a congregation at Armourers Hall in London, and may be presumed to have understood the spiritual requirements of the City in his day, when the heroic age of Puritanism was almost over and enthusiasm was no longer a virtue. [. . .] In reality, however, the characteristic of the *Trades-man's Calling*, as of the age in which it was written, is not the relics of medieval doctrine which linger embalmed in its guileless pages, but the robust common sense, which carries the author lightly over traditional scruples on a tide of genial, if Philistine, optimism. For his main thesis is a comfortable one—that there is no necessary conflict between religion and business." R. H. Tawney [1926] 1998. *Religion and the Rise of Capitalism*. New Brunswick, NJ: Transaction Publishers, pp. 243–44.

Another significant early-modern manual—though more interested in the practical than in the ethical side of business—is Daniel Defoe. [1726] 1738. *The Complete English Tradesman*. 4th ed. London: Printed for C. Rivington.

47 Richard Steele. 1804. *The Religious Tradesman; or, Plain and Serious Hints of Advice for the Tradesman's Prudent and Pious Conduct: from His Entrance into Business to his Leaving it off*. Charlestown: Printed by Samuel Etheridge, pp. 96–97.

Table 3.1: The Consequences of Piety

	Human Causal Mechanisms	Divine Causal Mechanisms
Consequences in this World	(3′) businessperson acts piously / obeys God → frugality, temperance, and industry → business success, temporal prosperity, good consequences in this world (4) businessperson acts piously / obeys God → no negative effect on, decrease in the odds of, etc., business success, temporal prosperity	(5) businessperson acts piously / obeys God → divine intervention/providence → business success, temporal prosperity, good consequences in this world
Consequences in the Hereafter	—	(6) businessperson acts piously / obeys God → divine intervention/providence → good consequences in the hereafter

THE CONSEQUENCES OF PIETY

Thus far I have looked at Christian business ethicists who rejected normative claim (2), but did not reject empirical claim (1). They underscored their rejection of (2) and the importance of acting from certain motives and not from certain others, even when they acknowledged that (1) might be true, or at least might be true sometimes. The historical picture becomes even more instructive for the student of the moral background once we introduce two other families of causal claims, which Christian moralists also employed. They focus on the consequences of moral and immoral actions, or the consequences of piety and impiety. Table 3.1 and table 3.2 present these claims and put them on the same map as Boardman's causal chain (3).[48]

Claim (3′) is similar to claim (1), and oftentimes they were used interchangeably, although only (3′) refers explicitly to piousness, and the causal mechanisms are slightly dissimilar. In (1) the mechanism involves a third party, such as customers' preferring to stay away from dishonest merchants, or employees' preferring to stay away from exploitative employers. As we saw, the truth-value of (1) is controversial. In (3′) the mechanism is based on a simpler, probably uncontroversial fact: prosperity is more likely if you are thrifty and frugal, not hung over every other day, and not in debt due to your fondness for luxurious automobiles. This part of the story has a distinctively Franklin-cum-Weber flavor. While Christian business ethicists surely resorted to (3′), in certain contexts they also resorted to its weaker variant (4): Christian religion is at least not inconsistent with business success. Logically, (4) is entailed by (3′). It is also just a negative proposition: $\neg p$ (it is not the case that p). Accordingly, the pragmatic objective of (4) was generally negative as well: deny that, given the ruthless, competitive, and heartless character of the business world, only irreligious people could make it. Differently put, proponents of (4) were content with a conservative claim: religion has no independent negative causal effect. Both religious and irreligious people may possess

---

48   To be exact, table 3.1 uses (3′), which is a slightly amended version of Boardman's causal chain (3), as outlined in the previous section. Still, (3) and (3′) essentially convey the same point.

Table 3.2: Empirical and Normative Business Ethics Claims

(1) Empirical: Acting ethically pays

(1′) Empirical (Machiavellian amendment): Appearing to act ethically pays

(2) Normative: Because acting ethically pays, you should act ethically

(3) Causal chain: religious principles or piety → prudence, frugality, diligence, industry, and rectitude → business success, temporal prosperity, good consequences in this world

(3′) Causal chain (slight amendment): businessperson acts piously / obeys God → frugality, temperance, and industry → business success, temporal prosperity, good consequences in this world

(4) Causal chain: businessperson acts piously / obeys God → no negative effect on, decrease in the odds of, etc., business success, temporal prosperity

(5) Causal chain (divine mechanisms): businessperson acts piously / obeys God → divine intervention/providence → business success, temporal prosperity, good consequences in this world

(6) Causal chain (divine mechanisms): businessperson acts piously / obeys God → divine intervention/providence → good consequences in the hereafter

(7) Normative: Because acting piously and obeying God pays in this world, you should act piously and obey God

(8) Normative: Because acting piously and obeying God pays in the hereafter, you should act piously and obey God

the qualities that are causally effective—acumen, intelligence, industriousness, or whatever it may be. This conservative claim was especially useful in contexts in which the opposite was believed to be the case.

By contrast, claims (5) and (6) introduce another sort of causal mechanism. Sometimes God punishes immoral behavior and rewards moral behavior in this world; sometimes he punishes immoral behavior and rewards moral behavior in the afterlife. Obviously, eternal reward and punishment are incommensurably more consequential than temporal reward and punishment, even if one must wait a little longer for it to come around. But either in terms of one's soul's fate or in terms of one's bank account's balance, piety will have good consequences and impiety bad ones. And that thanks to God.[49] As an 1865 newspaper article explained, the bad effects of impiety in business on the soul were not negligible: a "life-partnership" with "his satanic majesty".

> Dishonesty, on the other hand, will not pay, under any circumstances. It never did pay, in a single instance. A man may make what he calls a good bargain by using a little deception—by being a *little* dishonest; and he may for the time being, think it pays. But he forgets that every lie told is on its way to tophet. [. . .] And when it has got his satanic majesty's endorsement upon it, which is found upon every lie not repented of, it will come back again upon the vender of it, demanding payment in the shape of a life-partnership, and will secure it too, by a soul mortgage, unless the lie is confessed, restitution made, and the wrong charged upon the devil as its real author.[50]

---

49 I am omitting an additional complication here: God might be said to be ultimately causally responsible for the "human mechanisms" as well. Perhaps God originally arranged human psychology, institutions, economic laws, cultural practices, etc., in such a way that piety will pay in this world, without his more direct or immediate intervention?

50 G. C. 1865. "Will Honesty Pay?" *Circular*, June 5, 1865, p. 94.

Something like claim (6) occurs in many sermons and writings, as a general theological principle upon which the author's more specific ideas about business ethics are built. After all, it is a fundamental Christian belief that God will reward piety and will punish sin and disobeying of the gospel (e.g., Matthew 6:6; 2 Thessalonians 1:8). The wicked are "cursed, into everlasting fire, prepared for the devil and his angels" (Matthew 25:41); they "shall go away into everlasting punishment: but the righteous into life eternal" (Matthew 25:46). As if that did not suffice, the life of the righteous will be longer (Proverbs 10:17). Although wickedness and sin are available in several different flavors, the New Testament singles out the punishment of greed, avarice, and covetousness.[51] For instance, in the parable of the rich man and Lazarus (Luke 16:19–31), the beggar Lazarus was "carried by the angels into Abraham's bosom," whereas the rich man ended up in hell. "And in hell he lift up his eyes, being in torments, and seeth Abraham afar off, and Lazarus in his bosom. And he cried and said, Father Abraham, have mercy on me, and send Lazarus, that he may dip the tip of his finger in water, and cool my tongue; for I am tormented in this flame." At this point, the causal link between life and afterlife, the eventual coming of justice in the afterlife, becomes apparent: "But Abraham said, Son, remember that thou in thy lifetime receivedst thy good things, and likewise Lazarus evil things: but now he is comforted, and thou art tormented" (Luke 16:23–25).

The meaning and implications of these and similar biblical passages, along with Patristic, Scholastic, and modern commentaries and elaborations, were theologically contentious. Yet, ordinary pastoral and educational work could still appeal to divine retributive justice under some guise or another. Take the widely read *Lectures on Christian Theology* of Georg Christian Knapp (1753–1825): "When God exhibits his approbation of such actions as correspond with his laws, and his displeasure at such actions as he has forbidden, we see his retributive justice. This approbation which he expresses of what is morally good, is called *reward*; his disapprobation expressed against what is evil, *punishment*. [. . .] The full display of the divine justice, either in rewards or punishments, is not seen in the present life; but is reserved, as we are taught in the Bible, for the future world."[52] Knapp describes this doctrine as "one of the chief doctrines of Christianity, from which everything proceeds":

This consoling doctrine respective the future life and retribution beyond the grave, is one of the chief doctrines of Christianity, from which everything proceeds, and to which everything is referred; and the writers of the New Testament constantly make use of it, and seek to comfort the pious by the truth that divine justice will not be fully exhibited until the future state shall commence,

---

51   See, e.g., James Davis. 2011. *Medieval Market Morality: Life, Law and Ethics in the English Marketplace, 1200–1500*. Cambridge, UK: Cambridge University Press; Richard Newhauser. 2000. *The Early History of Greed: The Sin of Avarice in Early Medieval Thought and Literature*. Cambridge, UK: Cambridge University Press; Mark A. Noll, ed. 2001. *God and Mammon: Protestants, Money, and the Market, 1790–1860*. Oxford: Oxford University Press.

52   Knapp, *Lectures on Christian Theology*, p. 120.

and that then the righteous shall be richly recompensed, by the exceeding greatness of their future reward, for all the evil they have suffered.[53]

Like anybody else, unrighteous businessmen shall be punished and righteous businessmen shall be rewarded. Then, it is plausible to suppose that the persuasive powers of Christian business ethicists could be improved by invoking God's "retribution beyond the grave." This supposition is plausible as long as two assumptions are made. The first is a not really demanding psychological assumption: that people might fear the beyond and God's retribution. The second is an assumption about sermon audiences and Christian publication readers: that they might give some credence both to what a Christian moralist says and to the idea of retribution beyond the grave in particular. If these assumptions are true, it must have been tempting for a Christian business ethicist to appeal to these considerations to try to persuade his audience to be good and godly in their business pursuits.

DIVINE AND HUMAN MECHANISMS

Pious behavior, in business as much as anywhere else, has beneficial effects either on your temporal concerns, or on your soul, or on both. Both divine causal mechanism and human causal mechanisms can bring this about. Luckily, Christian business ethicists could combine both into a single narrative, since they are not incompatible. Take a sermon on business ethics preached by Alvan Lamson (1792–1864), longtime pastor of the Unitarian First Church and Parish in Dedham, Massachusetts. Besides his pastoral work, Lamson was involved in many pursuits and projects, from local education to independent scholarly research; he was also a Harvard overseer, and from 1844 to 1849 co-editor of *The Christian Examiner*, with Ezra Stiles Gannett.[54] In his sermon, "Supremacy of Conscience.— Business Morality," Lamson said that both causal factors were at work:

[B]esides that wealth gotten by deceit is more likely to prove a curse than a blessing, I do not believe that deception and trickishness [sic], all the cases being taken into view, prove in general to be the road to success, but the reverse. For I believe in the power of truth and justice, and in a retributive Providence. But I am now speaking of facts. Persons, I repeat, love to deal with those they can trust; and let them be once deceived by having a bad article put off upon them, or short weight or measure given them, or by misrepresentation of

---

53 Ibid., p. 251.

54 Cf. Frank Luther Mott. 1928. "The Christian Disciple and the Christian Examiner." *New England Quarterly* 1(2):197–207. Lamson was born in Weston, Massachusetts in 1792, and attended Harvard College (graduating in 1814), and the Harvard Divinity School (graduating in 1817). His pastorate at the First Church and Parish in Dedham extended for 42 years, from 1818 to 1860. In addition to *The Christian Examiner*, Lamson also more briefly co-edited *The Unitarian Advocate* (with Samuel Barrett) and the *Boston Observer* (with George Ripley). "Alvan Lamson." *The Dedham Historical Register*, vol. 12, no. 2, April 1901, pp. 35–38.

any sort, they will leave the person so practising imposture upon them, and in future go elsewhere to obtain what they want.[55]

Although in this passage Lamson's human mechanism is that of (1) more than that of (3′), the basic point remains the same. "A retributive Providence" and "facts" about persons both point in the same causal direction.[56] What is more, Lamson went on to argue for a version of claim (4). Perhaps it may seem logically awkward that he made this more conservative claim at that point. To make things logically worse, he somewhat unclearly mixed together arguments and evidence for (4), (3′), and (5). However, there is nothing pragmatically awkward about this. It makes much pragmatic sense given the question Lamson is addressing and his starting point in this part of the sermon. He starts by considering a specific objection: "do we not see your honest, truthful, Christian men poor? Do they not often fail of success in business?" Lamson was more skilled at understanding relative frequencies and drawing causal inferences than this objector:

> Undoubtedly they do [fail of success in business], but not on account of their honest and Christian qualities, but because they have not skill or business talent, or enterprise, or industry, or judgment, such as we occasionally see, which is all but infallible.
>
> [...]
>
> It does not follow because he is a good man that he has a talent for business,—shrewdness, caution, the capacity of rapid and unerring perception and combination ... A man of moral worth, high-souled, pure, may or may not possess acuteness of intellect, enterprise, untiring industry, and sound judgment, without which great success is not, in ordinary cases, to be looked for. There is no indissoluble connection, and no incompatibility, between the two classes of qualities.[57]

On the one hand, "the real cause of [a Christian's] want of success" is not her being Christian.[58] On the other hand, Lamson's argument is not just that correlation does not imply causation. He did not think there was even an observable correlation, as long as the sample was not skewed: "Do we not see upright, Christian men poor? Certainly we do. But do we not see your rogues poor also?"

This all sounds very reasonable. Unfortunately, trouble looms on the horizon again. The problem is that claims (3′), (4), (5), and (6) are just empirical claims,

---

55　Alvan Lamson. 1857. "Supremacy of Conscience.—Business Morality." Pp. 91–106 in *Sermons*. Boston: Crosby, Nichols, and Company, p. 100.

56　Here Lamson is talking about mechanism (1), but elsewhere in this sermon he talks about mechanism (3), too (e.g., p. 102).

57　Ibid., pp. 101–2.

58　As regards the real causes of success, a businessman might be compared to a poet or a painter. It is not whether they are pious or morally good, but whether they are skillful or technically good at what they do: "A man may set up for a poet; but however good he may be, if he have no inspiration, he will not be read. [...] Or is there any incompatibility between Christian goodness and an eye for colors, or skill, or knowledge of perspective, or of the effects of light and shade, so that a person is less likely to make an eminent painter because he is a good man?" Ibid., p. 103.

much like (1). They are descriptive statements about the nature of the world, or rather worlds, the one we live in and the beyond. By themselves, as they stand, they make no normative demands on a Christian businessman. But such normative demands seem to be a short step away. As table 3.2 shows, empirical claims (5) and (6) have their corresponding normative claims (7) and (8), parallel to the relationship between empirical claim (1) and normative claim (2). In other words, (2) is to (1) as (7) is to (5). Likewise, (2) is to (1) as (8) is to (6):

(7) Normative: Because acting piously and obeying God pays in this world, you should act piously and obey God.

(8) Normative: Because acting piously and obeying God pays in the hereafter, you should act piously and obey God.

Alas, here the tension between an empirical claim about causes and a normative claim about reasons resurfaces—and this time around it strikes with special force. We saw a tension between (1) and (2), and now we see an analogous tension between (5) and (7), and between (6) and (8). Much like advancing (1) does not logically commit one to advancing (2), empirical claims such as (5) and (6) do not logically commit one to normative claims such as (7) and (8). For example, in a sermon he delivered in 1869 in Brooklyn's Plymouth Church, Henry Ward Beecher warned his parishioners: "Religion must not be selfish—not even if it be the selfishness of the highest quality. We have no right to be Christians simply on the ground that so we shall save our souls. We *shall* save our souls; but to come into religion as a mere soul insurance, is selfishness."[59] Along the same lines, Archbishop Whately's dictum might be rephrased as follows: acting piously pays both in this world and in the other world, but he who acts from that principle is not a pious man. As he says in his *Introductory Lessons on Morals*:

If any persons tell you that our first notion of right and wrong is entirely derived from the Divine Law, and that those words have no meaning except obedience and disobedience to the declared will of God, you may ask them whether it is a matter of *duty* to obey God's will, or merely a matter of *prudence*, inasmuch as He is able to punish those who rebel against Him? Whether they think that God is *justly entitled* to obedience, or merely that it would be very *rash* to disobey one who has power to enforce his commands?

They will doubtless answer, that we *ought* to obey the divine commands as a point of duty, and not merely on the ground of expediency; that God is not only powerful, but good; and that conformity to his will is a thing right in itself, and should be practised, not through mere fear of punishment, or hope of reward, but *because* it is *right*.[60]

---

59   Henry Ward Beecher. [1869] 1873. "Scope and Function of a Christian Life." Pp. 91–108 in *The Sermons of Henry Ward Beecher in Plymouth Church, Brooklyn*. New York. J. B. Ford & Company, p. 102.

60   Richard Whately. 1856. *Introductory Lessons on Morals and Christian Evidences*. Cambridge [MA]: John Bartlett, pp. 7–8.

Whately's view is uncompromising. Perhaps someone might respond that (8) is not as bad as (2)—or as (7), for that matter. Other-worldly payments might be seen as more morally worthy than this-worldly ones. And they are certainly more worth one's while, as they are higher, greater, and eternal. However, the deeper trouble remains. For it lies not in the moral worthiness of the consequences one wishes to maximize: the odds of getting rich, the odds of getting into the kingdom of heaven, or the odds of something else. The deeper trouble lies, rather, in the very activity of weighing consequences to choose a course of action—particularly if the choice is whether or not to obey God and do as he says. As we will see shortly, this is comparable to both qualms about Pascal's wager (where the choice is whether or not to believe in God) and qualms about paying too much attention to certain business ethics issues. In the case at hand, the trouble is that the central action-question would not be anymore what the businessperson ought to act out of, and whether these motives are properly Christian, but how the consequences of various possible courses of action compare to one another. Or, to put it differently, people's motivations would become oriented to or shaped by actions' consequences: fear of punishment and hope of reward, divine or otherwise. But this would not do as an exemplar of a good Christian and a good Christian businessman. Then, again, Christian business ethicists had to find pragmatic compromises to alleviate this tension. Just like they did with (1) and (2), they found ways to voice the undoubtedly true causal claim (6)—about consequences in the hereafter—yet without voicing the troublesome normative claim (8)—about the reason to be pious.

3.5 Duties and Motives

The present and the previous chapter have been oriented toward the first dimension of the moral background. I have raised the question of why a businessperson should do business in an ethical manner at all, which is a practical question for business ethicists. For this is something a businessperson may reasonably ask them. And he may reasonably expect an answer both from the prudential point of view—e.g., the odds of ending up in jail—and from the moral point of view, after controlling for prudence, as it were. In the previous chapter I looked at business ethicists who maintained that business ethics pays, and that is the reason why a businessperson should do business ethically. In this chapter I have thus far looked at worries and reservations about that kind of approach, as expressed by Christian business ethicists in the second half of the nineteenth century. This discussion paves the way for a more general argument about the moral background. It is not an accident that Christian business ethicists would object in the way that Presbyterians Henry Boardman and Theodore Cuyler, Quaker Charles Rhoads, and Congregational Joshua Wellman did. Despite the differences between these four men's opinions—and the differences between their denominations' practices and doctrines—they manifested the same moral background elements. These elements include ontological ones, e.g., what there is in the world (dimension: metaphysics), as well as epistemological ones, e.g., what makes a moral claim valid

or acceptable (dimension: method and argument). They also include the normative theories business ethicists explicitly or implicitly draw upon to offer grounds
or reasons. As I argued in chapter 1, these elements underlie business ethicists'
first-order moral claims, doctrines, accounts, and injunctions. Put differently, a
particular answer to "why do business ethically?" is embedded in and dependent
on broader metaphysical, epistemological, and moral understandings. It does not
follow deductively from them: more than one first-order answer is compatible
with a particular background configuration. But they do shape it decisively.

Therefore, Boardman's, Cuyler's, Rhoads's, and Wellman's reaction to normative claim (2) must be understood in the context of a long Christian tradition of
moral thinking—in particular, the moral views and theories that, over the centuries, had become weaved into Christian doctrine, practice, and organization. This
tradition tended to rely on deontological theories to tell ethical from unethical
courses of action, and on divine command theories to support its judgments and
principles. What are "deontological theories" and "divine command theories"?
Take the Decalogue that God gave to Moses on Mount Sinai, and in particular the
commandments, "You shall not murder" and "You shall not steal" (Exodus 20:13,
15; Deuteronomy 5:17, 19). These commandments forbid murdering and stealing
categorically. There might be disagreements about what counts as an instance of
murder and what counts as an instance of killing in self-defense, and clearly the
King James Bible rendition of "לא תרצח" as "Thou shalt not kill" is misleading.
Yet, given an adequate demarcation of the kind of action, these commandments
forbid murdering and stealing always, come what may, without regard to consequences. At least, that would be their deontological interpretation. On the strict
deontological interpretation, stealing is forbidden even if your stealing a loaf of
bread would save a starving person's life. Even if your stealing not one loaf but
one crumb of bread would somehow save not one but one million lives. Even
if your stealing one crumb of bread from Eichmann's pantry would somehow
save six million lives. For a deontological normative theory, stealing and murdering are morally wrong in themselves or intrinsically; they are wrong *simpliciter*,
period. Not conditionally or hypothetically, but categorically, to use Kant's terms.
And because they are morally wrong they should not be done. Differently put,
deontological normative theories hold that the moral status or standing of an
action—usually its moral rightness or wrongness—is intrinsic to it. These theories are often couched in the language of duty, as suggested by the etymology of
"deontology." "You shall not murder" and "You shall not steal" are your categorical
duties. Deontological theories might be theistic, but, as Kant himself illustrates,
they need not be.[61]

Consequentialists believe deontologists are crazy. According to consequentialist normative theories, goodness determines rightness. The extent to which

---

61   The role of God in Kant's deontological ethics is a controversial subject. What is not controversial is that in this context the word "Kant" is not specific enough: it depends on what part of Kant's
oeuvre is being talked about. Cf. R. T. Nuyen. 1998. "Is Kant a Divine Command Theorist?" *History of
Philosophy Quarterly* 15:441–53.

an action promotes some good or goods determines whether it is morally right, or morally ought to be done: "[t]he right option . . . is that which maximises [*sic*] objective probable value, that which promotes the best objectively probable consequences."[62] Consequentialists do not agree on the kinds of goods and consequences of actions they take into account, the algorithms or functions that produce the moral judgment or decision, and who or what is relevantly affected by those consequences. You may consider actions in terms of the amount of pleasure and pain they bring about, thus equating good with pleasure, as in Bentham's "felicific calculus" in his *Introduction to the Principles of Morals and Legislation* (1789). You may consider actions' actual or expected consequences. You may consider actions' impact on you only, your family, the entire population of Uruguay, all human beings, all living creatures, or all living creatures and the environment.

This is how consequentialism would deal with a concrete situation. Take one well-known form of consequentialism, act-utilitarianism, which roughly prescribes the course of action that results in the greatest good for the greatest number of people (good need not be specified here). Suppose the American army captures a dangerous Uruguayan terrorist. Her terrorist cell has planned a deadly attack on America that will kill thousands of churchgoing and taxpaying citizens. This terrorist is known to be in possession of information that would allow America to prevent this terrorist attack. Suppose the terrorist, upon being politely questioned, is unwilling to volunteer that information. Act-utilitarians believe that in this situation it is morally permissible to torture her as much as needed. Indeed, if still needed and known to be an effective way of breaking her down psychologically, it is morally permissible to torture her beloved toddler, or even to kill him. Indeed, in a situation like this it is morally required or obligatory to torture or to kill. It would be morally wrong not to do something that would have saved thousands of lives (American or otherwise). The suffering and pain of one person is very bad, the death of one person is terribly bad, but the alternative outcome, the death of thousands of people, is even worse. Unfortunately, the toddler may have to be killed.

Deontologists believe utilitarians are crazy. Even if utilitarians' ambitions and hopes may be praiseworthy, which is also debatable, they in any case end up with horrific prescriptions. As one famous deontologist, Charles Fried, objects, "there are some things which a moral man will not do, no matter what. The harming of innocent people, lying, enslavement, and degradation—these are all things decent people shrink from, though great good might seem to come in particular cases from resorting to them."[63] According to another famous deontologist, a moral man will not ever tell a lie, even from philanthropic motives or "*Menschenliebe*."[64] How about Christian moralists? They believe utilitarians are crazy, too. While the class of Christian moralists is large and diverse, they have tended not to sympa-

---

62   Philip Pettit and Geoffrey Brennan 1986. "Restrictive Consequentialism." *Australasian Journal of Philosophy* 64(4):438–55, p. 438.
63   Charles Fried. 1978. *Right and Wrong.* Cambridge, MA: Harvard University Press, p. 5.
64   Kant, "On a Supposed Right to Lie from Altruistic Motives."

thize with the utilitarian approach and temperament. Some of them have condemned it as the epitome of the corruption of modern, secular morals. Instead, they have tended to sympathize with versions of the deontological approach and temperament. Evidently, unlike non-theistic deontologists, Christian moralists base their deontology on God and the divine will.

Specifically, God and the will of God can play two types of role. First, Christian moralists may subscribe to a "divine command theory," according to which "it is necessary that something is morally good if and only if God commands (wills, loves, approves of) that thing."[65] Differently put, "all of our obligations are due to God's commands"; "[f]or example, if an act is obligatory, then it has the property of being obligatory in virtue of having the further property of being commanded by God; and if an act is wrong, then it has the property of being wrong in virtue of having the further property of being forbidden by God."[66] Why is it wrong to steal? Stealing is wrong because God forbids it. In theistic ethical systems the wrongness of wrong actions has divine sources, and thus divine justification or validation. Of course, there is the further question of why God forbids stealing (whereas he does not forbid playing soccer). And then there is the lurking threat of "the Euthyphro dilemma," i.e., whether the pious is pious because the gods love it, or the gods love it because it is pious.[67] Yet, with regard to practical or applied Christian morals, it suffices that God be the source of morality and confer normative status on actions, which non-theistic deontologists must get from elsewhere.

Second, not only is God the source of morality and moral principles. God also provides people with reasons and motives to act in accordance with morality and moral principles. The question here is not why stealing is wrong, that is, in virtue of what it is wrong, or what makes it wrong. Rather, *given* that it is wrong, the question is why a person ought not to steal, what reason she has not to steal, or what motive she ought to act from. The question looks not at the moral status of an action or state of affairs, but at the individual's action. And it looks not at the motives people actually act from, as an empirical psychological and sociological phenomenon, but normatively at the motives people ought to act from.[68] Why ought a person not to steal? A non-theistic deontologist may reply, "Because stealing is an intrinsically morally wrong action." Or she may reply, "For its own sake," or "From duty." Or she may say that virtue is it own reward. In any of these cases, the fact that stealing is morally wrong gives her reason not to steal. While a theistic deontologist does

---

65 Richard Joyce. 2002. "Theistic Ethics and the Euthyphro Dilemma." *Journal of Religious Ethics* 30(1):49–75, p. 49.

66 Edward Wierenga. 1983. "A Defensible Divine Command Theory." *Noûs* 17(3):387–407, p. 388.

67 *Euthyphro* 10a. Cf. D. M. MacKinnon and Hugo Meynell. 1972. "The Euthyphro Dilemma." *Proceedings of the Aristotelian Society*, supplementary volumes 46:211–34; Philip L. Quinn. 1978. *Divine Commands and Moral Requirements*. Oxford: Clarendon Press.

68 These sentences skirt relevant philosophical issues such as the relations between reasons for action and motivation, and the debates about it between internalists and externalists. However, I think I have some good reasons to skirt them, given my aims and space constraints. These reasons motivated me to do so.

have recourse to this answer, Christian moralists—including business ethicists—can add a further reason. You should act from or out of the love of God.

Christian love is quite a complex concept. *A fortiori*, the love of God is quite a complex motive.[69] Some complexities have to do with its relationship to: self-love;[70] fear of God—in the sense of the Hebrew word "יְרֵא," i.e., fear, respect, awe, which is a property of a person; and the wrath of God—in the sense of divine justice, punishment, retribution, which is a property of God. Some other complexities have to do with the distinction between a person's loving God on the one hand, and her being loved by God, or God's love, on the other. Yet some other complexities have to do with the nature of a love whose object is God vis-à-vis a love whose object is a neighbor. While none of these complexities can be dealt with in this chapter, the historical significance of the love of God is undeniable. Its scriptural credentials are impeccable. For instance, there is the dictum in Deuteronomy 6:5, Matthew 22:37, Luke 10:37, and Mark 12:30, "Thou shalt love the Lord thy God with all thy heart, and with all thy soul, and with all thy mind." There is also the Gospel of John 14:15–31, especially Jesus' quotable request, "If ye love me, keep my commandments" (John 14:15) (even though its interpretation is complicated by the next verses).[71] Then, medieval, modern, and contemporary theologians have turned the love of God into a building block of their moral systems and demands. Indeed, they might have gone too far: love might be too central in their work.[72] Further, they have usefully contrasted it with bad motives, such as pride, vanity, or love of praise. Methodist founding father John Wesley (1703–1791) spells out this contrast in an illustrative manner: "Yea, two persons may do the same outward work; suppose, feeding the hungry, or clothing the naked: and, in the mean time, one of these may be truly religious, and the other have no religion at all: for the one may act from the love of God, and the other from the love of praise. So manifest it is; that although true religion naturally leads to every good word and work, yet the real nature thereof lies deeper still, even in 'the hidden man of the heart'."[73] From

69   Colin Grant. 1996. "For the Love of God: Agape." *Journal of Religious Ethics* 24(1):3–21; C. S. Lewis. 1960. *The Four Loves.* New York: Harcourt, Brace; Anders Nygren. 1953. *Agape and Eros.* Translated by Philip S. Watson. Philadelphia: Westminster Press; Gene H. Outka. 1972. *Agape: An Ethical Analysis.* New Haven, CT: Yale University Press.

70   Thomas M. Osborne, Jr. 2005. *Love of Self and Love of God in Thirteenth-Century Ethics.* Notre Dame: University of Notre Dame Press.

71   See also 1 John 5:3: "For this is the love of God, that we keep his commandments: and his commandments are not grievous."

72   Cf. Tony Lane. 2001. "The Wrath of God as an Aspect of the Love of God." Pp. 138–67 in *Nothing Greater, Nothing Better: Theological Essays on the Love of God,* edited by Kevin J. Vanhoozer. Grand Rapids, MI: Wm. B. Eerdmans. As Lane notes, the role you can give to love depends on your conception of God, e.g., whether you are a Marcionist: "Marcion differentiated between the wrathful God of justice revealed in the Old Testament and the merciful God of love revealed in those parts of the New Testament that remained after he had, as Tertullian put it, exercised textual criticism with the knife rather than the pen. [. . .] Marcion views God as a being of simple goodness, to the exclusion of other attributes (like his wrath), which are transferred to the Creator God" (p. 142).

73   John Wesley. 1826. *The Works of the Rev. John Wesley. In Ten Volumes.* Volume V. New York: Printed and Sold by J. & J. Harper, p. 65.

the outside, these two persons are doing exactly the same thing; their bodies are moving in exactly the same ways. But the invisible spring of action is not the same: love of praise is bad and love of God is good.

This is the crucial feature that the Christian business ethics tradition shares with Kant and the deontological tradition in philosophy. Despite obvious differences in the metaphysical foundations of their respective ethical systems, concept of God, and the nature and role of reason and rationality, for both traditions it is crucial what a person acts from or out of. In Kant's vocabulary, an action might be in conformity with duty (*pflichtmäßig*), without it having been performed from duty (*aus Pflicht*). Remarkably, one of Kant's most influential examples in the *Groundwork of the Metaphysics of Morals* (or *Grundlegung*) has to do with business ethics. Kant raises the question of "whether the action which accords with duty has been done from duty or from some purpose of self-interest." And he imagines a shopkeeper who may overcharge an inexperienced customer or a child:

> E.g., it certainly conforms with duty that a shopkeeper not overcharge his inexperienced customer, and where there is much commerce, a prudent merchant actually does not do this, but keeps a fixed general price for everyone, so that a child may buy from him just as well as everyone else. Thus one is served *honestly*; but this is not nearly enough for us to believe that the merchant proceeded in this way from duty and principles of honesty; his advantage required it; it cannot be assumed here that he had, besides, an immediate inclination towards his customers, so as from love, as it were, to give no one preference over another in the matter of price. Thus the action was done neither from duty, nor from immediate inclination, but merely for a self-interested purpose.[74]

For Kant, this shopkeeper's prudent one-price policy is not morally satisfactory. His action was driven or motivated by a profitability calculation—just like Robert Reich and others say Starbuck's "special commitment to society" is.[75] Hence, such actions do not have what Kant calls "moral worth." Nor does he attribute moral worth to actions driven or motivated by self-preservation, happiness, fear of punishment, hope of reward, or sympathy—and, least of all, by the agent's inclinations, what she would be inclined to do anyway—even if they happen to produce identical actions and outcomes. According to Kant, only actions driven by duty can be said to have moral worth. The bottom line is that "an action from duty has its moral worth not in the purpose to be attained by it but in *the maxim*

74 Immanuel Kant [1785] 2012. *Groundwork of the Metaphysics of Morals*. Translated and edited by Mary Gregor and Jens Timmermann. Cambridge, UK: Cambridge University Press, p. 13.

75 "'High ideals don't have to conflict with the bottom line,' says Starbucks in one of its many advertisements touting its special commitment to society. 'When we started providing health coverage to our part-time employees, we noticed a lot less turnover.' That's precisely the confusion. If Starbucks's bottom line is improved because it provides health coverage to part-timers, Starbucks is not acting out of high ideals—regardless of the worthy motives of its founder. Starbucks is acting for the benefit of Starbucks's consumers and investors. The extra costs are more than justified by the savings. It's called smart business." Robert B. Reich. 2007. *Supercapitalism: The Transformation of Business, Democracy, and Everyday Life*. New York: Alfred A. Knopf, pp. 172–73.

in accordance with which it is decided upon."[76] But these decisions that guide a person's action are private. While they may be made public, they are essentially mental states; they take place in her mind.

Then, Christian business ethicists have a problem that their consequentialist counterparts do not have—and a big problem at that. The consequentialist business ethicist focuses on a businessperson's observable behavior and its effects, be it on others, on the community, or on herself. It is irrelevant what mental state the businessperson was in when she gave a large donation to a Costa Rican community of coffee growers, raised the daily wages of her factory workers in Coahuila or Guangzhou, or refrained from shortchanging her inexperienced customer. The action's effects are the same regardless. Therefore, the consequentialist does not need to get into the messy and spooky business of mental states. Alas, Christian business ethicists such as Boardman, Cuyler, Rhoads, and Wellman cannot say the same. Their business ethics is based on concepts of good and bad motives, yet, unfortunately, people's motives are not visible or knowable from the outside. They are not deducible from behavioral evidence. Indeed, it is quite unclear what they are and where they are to begin with, assuming they exist at all—as the last hundred years of psychological science and philosophy of mind demonstrate. Luckily, here the moral background of ministers Boardman, Cuyler, Rhoads, and Wellman can intervene. The "business ethics of the Christian" is based on the metaphysical assumption that she has a heart or conscience. Further, there is the metaphysical assumption that there is an omniscient God who sees everyone's hearts. No minister could know if a particular businessperson acted ethically from the love of God, as she ought to. But God did know that. And ministers were sure to tell businesspeople that he did know that.

3.6 The Religion of the Heart

"Another fact in relation to the religion of the Bible is, that *it is the religion of the heart*. It is an inward religion, and not the religion of mere outward forms."[77] Thus spoke in 1847 Gardiner Spring, the legendary pastor of the Brick Presbyterian Church in New York City from 1810 until his passing in 1873. Spring went on to note that the Christian religion's "object is to carry the heart": "It everywhere insists upon right intentions as indispensable to the performance of any and every

---

76 It should be added that an action's not having moral worth does not mean Kant believes it is bad, morally condemnable, or ought not to be done. Yet, it still does not meet the very specific conditions the *Grundlegung* demands. Marcia Baron. 1984. "The Alleged Moral Repugnance of Acting from Duty." *Journal of Philosophy* 81(4):197–220; Marcia Baron. 1995. *Kantian Ethics Almost Without Apology*. Ithaca: Cornell University Press; Barbara Herman. 1981. "On the Value of Acting from the Motive of Duty." *Philosophical Review* 90(3):359–82; Robert N. Johnson. 2009. "Good Will and the Moral Worth of Acting from Duty." Pp. 19–51 in *The Blackwell Guide to Kant's Ethics*, edited by Thomas E. Hill, Jr. Chichester, UK; Malden, MA: Wiley-Blackwell; Samuel J. Kerstein. 2002. *Kant's Search for the Supreme Principle of Morality*. Cambridge; New York: Cambridge University Press.

77 Gardiner Spring. 1847. *The Bible not of Man: or, the Argument for the Divine Origin of the Sacred Scriptures, Drawn from the Scriptures Themselves*. New York: American Tract Society, p. 154.

duty. It looks to the springs of action. [. . .] However fair the outward appearance it makes no account of the most fair and unblemished exterior, unless it flows from right principles and impulses."[78] In other words, as the Quaker periodical *The Friend* put the point some twenty-five years later, there is a crucial "distinction between *outward* or *ceremonial* religion, and *inward* religion or *that of the heart*."[79] Or, in the influential words of Hannah More, there is a crucial distinction between "external profession" and actions on the one hand, and "inward devotedness" and heart on the other.[80] Joshua Bates's *A Discourse on Honesty in Dealing* agrees: "the eye of civil law, which is obliged to regard principally the outward appearance" may not discern your immoral action. "But in the view of Him, who looketh on the heart," it is immoral nonetheless.[81]

Spring, *The Friend*, More, Bates and many others have depicted Christianity as "the religion of the heart." It has even been said that "of all the words that are crucial to biblical anthropology, the word 'heart' is by far the most important."[82] In the King James Bible it occurs more than eight hundred times. Semantically, though, these hundreds of tokens do not always have the same meaning. Romantic relationships and Christian theology are in this respect surprisingly alike: matters of the heart are always complicated. For "heart" is used in several different ways in the Bible, and not all of its senses overlap in English, Hebrew ("לב" [lebh]), and Greek ("καρδία" [kardia]), so there are translation issues involved, too. At any rate, one of the distinct biblical meanings of "heart" is something like a person's moral center and seat of moral understanding and self-consciousness. The *International Standard Bible Encyclopedia* explicates this meaning as follows:

---

78   Ibid., p. 155. Spring's (pp. 101–102) discussion of "the Moral Law" (i.e., the Ten Commandments) further clarifies his point about the heart: "[The Moral Law] extends itself to *the heart*, and does not stop short of the inward *principles and motives* of human conduct. It does not sever the outer from the inner man; but regards his principles and motives as the germ of which his outward conduct is the development. It reaches the fountain, and gains nothing, and cares for nothing, until it carries the heart. It identifies the love of God with keeping his commandments, and keeping his commandments with the love of God."

79   "The Religion of the Heart." *The Friend*, vol. 48, no. 7, Seventh-Day, Tenth Month 3, 1874, p. 52.

80   Hannah More. 1812. *Practical Piety; or, the Influence of the Religion of the Heart on the Conduct of the Life*. New York: Published by Richard Scott, p. 11.

81   Joshua Bates. 1818. *A Discourse on Honesty in Dealing*. Middlebury, VT: J. W. Copeland, pp. 10–11. Orville Dewey (1794–1882) makes the same point about the reach of the law: "Legal expediency, then, is not to be so construed as to warrant the supposition, that it lends a sanction to what is wrong. It may, from necessity, permit or protect fraud, but does not abet it. A man is not to consider himself an honest man, simply because the law gives him deliverance. For the law *cannot* take cognizance of the secret intentions, nor of slight deviations from truth." Orville Dewey. 1838. *Moral Views of Commerce, Society, and Politics. In Twelve Discourses*. 2nd ed. New-York: David Felt & Co. Stationers' Hall, pp. 19–20.

See also Frank W. Ballard. 1865. *The Stewardship of Wealth: As Illustrated in the Lives of Amos and Abbott Lawrence. A Lecture Delivered Before the New York Young Men's Christian Association, January 4th, 1865*. 2nd ed. New York: John Medole, printer, p. 16; R. Heber Newton. 1876. *The Morals of Trade, Two Lectures: I. An Inquiry into the Actual Morality of Trade. II. An Inquiry into the Causes of the Existing Demoralization and the Remedies therefor. Given in the Anthon Memorial Church, New York*. New York: T. Whittaker, p. 23.

82   David K. Naugle. 2002. *Worldview: The History of a Concept*. Grand Rapids, MI: Wm. B. Eerdmans Publishing, p. 268.

As the central organ in the body, forming a focus for its vital action, it [the heart] has come to stand for the center of its moral, spiritual, intellectual life. "In particular the heart is the place in which the process of self-consciousness is carried out, in which the soul is at home with itself, and is conscious of all its doing and suffering as its own" (Oehler). [. . .] God is represented as "searching the heart" and "trying the reins" (Jeremiah 17:10 the King James Version). Thus, "heart" comes to stand for "conscience," for which there is no word in Hebrew, as in Job 27:6, "My heart shall not reproach me," or in 1 Samuel 24:5, "David's heart smote him"; compare 1 Samuel 25:31. [. . .] From this it appears, in the words of Owen: "[. . .] Generally, it [the heart] denotes the whole soul of man and all the faculties of it, not absolutely, but as they are all one principle of moral operations, as they all concur in our doing of good and evil."

Thus, in the Bible's moral teachings the concept of the heart occupies a prominent place. The heart is a person's moral center, where God has written his moral law (Hebrews 8:10; Romans 2:12–16). God sees and knows people's hearts. The scriptural credentials of this idea are solid, too. It is not just God's good old omniscience, that is, his seeing and knowing "what is done in secret" (e.g., Matthew 6:4, 6:6, 6:18), and that "[n]othing in all creation is hidden from God's sight" (Hebrews 4:13). To be sure, this sort of visual imagery, God's sight and God's eyes, "the eyes of him to whom we must give account," is omnipresent. However, there is a more specific idea: he sees and knows people's heart inside and their inner thoughts, intentions, and motives. God "[searches] the heart" (Jeremiah 17:10) and "pondereth the hearts" (Proverbs 21:2) and "weighs the motives" (Proverbs 16:2);[83] "*the LORD seeth* not as man seeth; for man looketh on the outward appearance, but the LORD looketh on the heart" (1 Samuel 16:7). Then, unlike men, and unlike Christian business ethicists, God does possess reliable evidentiary bases to make moral evaluations—"God knows your hearts. What is highly valued among men is detestable in God's sight" (Luke 16:15).

Thousands of pages of theology have discussed, interpreted, and elaborated on these verses. Here one influential early American example will do. Jonathan Edwards (1703–1758) is one of the country's great colonial theologians. A leader of the First Great Awakening, he is sometimes remembered by the rhetoric of his sermon, *Sinners in the Hands of an Angry God*. This is his "brilliant, vivid, and terrifying" 1741 sermon, delivered in Enfield, Connecticut, which emphasized God's wrath, and "made the congregation scream for fear of hell."[84] My example is how-

---

83 While I am generally quoting from the King James Bible, here I make an exception and quote from the New American Standard Bible. This is admittedly a bit of rhetorical trickery on my part, because the King James Bible's translation is "weigheth the spirits." The original Hebrew word is "רוחות" (plural of "רוח")—which in many other biblical contexts clearly means spirit or spirits, and literally means wind or breath.

84 Thomas S. Kidd. 2007. *The Great Awakening: The Roots of Evangelical Christianity in Colonial America*. New Haven, CT: Yale University Press, p. 105. Cf. Douglas L. Winiarski. 2005. "Jonathan Edwards, Enthusiast? Radical Revivalism and the Great Awakening in the Connecticut Valley." *Church History* 74(4):683–739.

ever from a later sermon, titled either "Nothing Can Make Up for Want of Sincerity in the Heart" or "The Greatest Performances or Sufferings in Vain Without Charity" (depending on the edition). Here Edwards insists on the fundamental distinction between the external or outward and the internal or inward, between sincere and hypocritical actions, and on the Christian virtue of love.

It is not the external work done, or the suffering undergone, that is in itself anything worth in the sight of God. The motions and exercises of the body, or anything done by it, if considered separately from the heart, the inward part of the man, are no more worth in the sight of God than the motions of anything without life. [. . .] And as there is nothing profitable to God of men's performances, so there can be nothing amiable in his sight in a mere external work without sincerity of heart; for God sees not as man seeth. He sees the heart; that is as naked and open to him as the external actions. And therefore he sees our actions not merely as external motions as of a mere machine, or piece of clock-work; but as human actions, or the actions of rational, intelligent creatures, and voluntary or free agents; and therefore there can be no amiableness in his eyes without sincerity of heart.[85]

The agent's "heart" or "inward part" is directly apprehended by God and constitutes the agent's act from God's perspective. The analogy between the "motions and exercises of the body" and the "external motions . . . of a mere machine, or piece of clock-work," or something "without life," are philosophically significant— e.g., as regards dualism in the philosophy of mind. Still, note that Edwards's words are not extracted from a philosophical piece, but from a sermon he preached in Northampton, Massachusetts, where he occupied the pulpit from 1729 to 1750.

Many popular Christian writers and preachers stressed God's seeing people's hearts and motives. In turn, they could put God's knowledge of people's hearts to fear-of-punishment uses. For instance, they might remind their audiences about God's system of punishment. Or they might remind their audiences that they should "fear" God, taking advantage of the ambiguity of the verb "to fear" in that context. Whatever the case was, their writings and speeches were also underlain by the particular metaphysical picture I have been fleshing out. To take a very popular example, consider Albert Barnes's *Notes on the New Testament*. Born in Rome, New York in 1798, and educated at Princeton Theological Seminary, Barnes became a pastor in Presbyterian churches in New Jersey and then Philadelphia. He wrote his series of notes from 1832 until 1851 for use in "Sabbath-school and Bible classes." As it turns out, they eventually became a huge best seller

---

85 Edwards [1749], pp. 178–79. I am quoting from the *Works of Jonathan Edwards* online, maintained by Yale University's Jonathan Edwards Center. "Nothing Can Make Up for Want of Sincerity in the Heart" is the third sermon in the "Charity and its Fruits" series, included in Edwards's *Ethical Writings*, edited by Paul Ramsey. The first two sermons are on love, respectively titled "Love the Sum of All Virtue" and "Love More Excellent Than Extraordinary Gifts of the Spirit."

On some common misconceptions about Edwards's economic thought, see Mark Valeri. 1991. "The Economic Thought of Jonathan Edwards." *Church History* 60(1):37–54.

and a classic of American popular theology.[86] Commenting on 2 Corinthians 5:11 ("Knowing therefore the terror of the Lord, we persuade men; but we are made manifest unto God; and I trust also are made manifest in your consciences."), Barnes writes:

> But we are made manifest unto God – The meaning of this is, probably, that God sees that we are sincere and upright in our aims and purposes. He is acquainted with our hearts. All our motives are known to him, and he sees that it is our aim to promote his glory, and to save the souls of people. This is probably said to counteract the charge which might have been brought against him by some of the disaffected in Corinth, that he was influenced by improper motives and aims. To meet this, Paul says, that God knew that he was endeavoring to save souls, and that he was actuated by a sincere desire to rescue them from the impending terrors of the day of judgment.[87]

As discussed earlier, the question is what "actuates" people, so as to distinguish proper from improper motives. God knows, because he "is acquainted with our hearts." A conceptual relative of the Christian's heart is the Christian's conscience. Like its relative, it has multiple meanings, connotations, and functions. Like its relative, it has an extensive and intricate historical trajectory.[88] Conscience might be described in various ways. It might be "an inner source of moral authority that judges and guides us,"[89] "an internal (God-given) judge," or "a faculty of the human mind . . . [whose] principal functions [are] to represent to the individual the universal laws of moral behavior, apply them in specific cases, and punish the individual for going against them."[90] Or it might be simply described as a moral arbiter.

---

86 The *American National Biography* entry for Albert Barnes says that 400,000 volumes had been sold by 1856. According to another source (though perhaps less reliable), as of 1901 "more than one million volumes" had been sold. Joshua L. Chamberlain, ed. 1901. *University of Pennsylvania: Its History, Influence, Equipment and Characteristics.* Boston: R. Herndon Company, p. 319.

87 Albert Barnes. 1962. *Barnes' Notes on the New Testament.* Grand Rapids, MI: Kregel Publications, p. 850.

88 As Lacoste writes, "[t]he concept cannot simply be explained through the history of terms (conscience, *Gewissen, conscientia, synt[d]eresis, suneidesis*) because their meaning vary depending on their contexts. One must look at what determine [sic] conscience in each case and especially at the concept of personality and the type of society that are involved" (p. 339). Two milestones in the history of conscience are the twelfth-century turn towards inwardness, intentions, the *forum internum,* and hence a new sort of "*conscientia,*" and Luther's departure from the scholastics by switching the object of conscience to "the person as a whole, the agent of the actions, rather than simply the actions themselves." Michael Baylor. 1977. *Action and Person: Conscience in Late Scholasticism and the Young Luther.* Leiden: Brill, p. 210; Giles Constable. 1998. *The Reformation of the Twelfth Century.* Cambridge; New York: Cambridge University Press, pp. 271–72; Jean-Yves Lacoste. 2005. *Encyclopedia of Christian Theology.* Volume 1. New York: Routledge, p. 339; C. S. Lewis. 1967. *Studies in Words.* 2nd ed. Cambridge; London: Cambridge University Press, pp. 181–213; Timothy C. Potts, ed. 1980. *Conscience in Medieval Philosophy.* Cambridge; New York: Cambridge University Press.

89 Lacoste, *Encyclopedia of Christian Theology,* p. 339.

90 Douglas C. Langston. 2001. *Conscience and Other Virtues: From Bonaventure to MacIntyre.* University Park: Pennsylvania State University Press, p. 8.

Here I can safely set aside the theological history of conscience, the exact nature of this concept, and the exact nature of the relationship between conscience and the heart. It suffices to underscore that both of them have been central concepts throughout the history of Christian theory and practice, including the history of Christian business ethics theory and practice. Christian business ethicists used them to attack Machiavellian, reputation-based arguments, and the outward identity between actually acting morally and having a reputation for acting morally. The aforementioned doyen of the business ethics manuals, Richard Steele's *The Religious Tradesman*, is the doyen of this useful use, too:

> Reflect on your past conduct as to this great duty of justice. Perhaps your injustice has been so secretly managed, that your reputation is not injured by it; but what says conscience? Does not that remember the unconscionable bargains, the faulty wares shuffled off by deceit and falsehood; the unjust weights and measures used in trade; or the oppression and unmercifulness with which it has been conducted. Let conscience survey the foregoing particulars, and see wherein you have been guilty; and give it leave to speak, while it acts the part of a friendly monitor.[91]

You bet conscience remembers the faulty wares and the unjust weights and measures! That is its job! Nineteenth-century Christian business ethicists in the United States followed in Steele's footsteps. As Massachusetts Unitarian Alvan Lamson did in his sermon, "Supremacy of Conscience.—Business Morality," they were able to "apply" the Christian doctrine of conscience "to the business concerns of life,–or what may be called business morality." Thus, they might insist on "the rightful supremacy of conscience," and on keeping a "clear conscience" with regard to one's business activities. This in turn brought up a traditional Christian economic ethics theme, recurrently called up in the crusade against Mammonism: the comparative assessment of the worth of spiritual matters and material matters. There is a hierarchy of goods. Evidently, a pure soul and a clean conscience are more important than wealth, success, and admiration in this world. Lamson's sermon on 1 Peter 1:7, "Better than Gold," said it well: "Gold can do much, but it cannot do everything." "Peace of mind, content, riches of soul, are better, far more precious." Most evidently, riches of soul are far more precious than gold "[w]hen thou art stretched on thy dying bed." "When thou art stretched on thy dying bed, and memory calls up the sins of thy life, will gold purchase for thee the pardon of the least of those sins? Canst thou with gold bribe the recording angel? Or wilt thou say, Here, Lord, is my gold, the fruits of my lifelong toil,—here is my gold,—accept it, I pray thee, and Heaven be merciful to my soul?"[92]

Regrettably, the alignment of heart and conscience with God's omniscience—or, differently put, the recruitment of God's omniscience to enforce moral dictates—was not free from troublesome consequences. Conscience and the heart are

91 Richard Steele. 1823. *The Religious Tradesman*. Trenton: Francis S. Wiggins, pp. 115–16.
92 Lamson, "Supremacy of Conscience.—Business Morality," pp. 95, 98, 105, 197, 198.

consistent with a full-fledged deontological approach. Indeed, conscience might be seen as favorable to a full-fledged deontological approach—e.g., "do not cheat your customers, because conscience says you ought not to do it, period." By contrast, omniscience lent itself to consequentialist fear-of-punishment and hope-of-reward uses—e.g., "God is watching, he knows what you are thinking, so even in your thoughts you should not sin"; "do not have sinful thoughts and intentions, do not have improper, unworthy, or unchristian springs of actions, or else you'll be punished." Business ethicists have a practical, not theoretical, job, so they no doubt profited from these uses. Yet, the moral problem is that they smack too much of surveillance, total and perfect, by a powerful authority figure, which will eventually result in punishment, should you fail to do what you ought to. The idea and imagery of a day of judgment provide additional rhetorical impetus to these accounts, be it their Christian version, traditional Greek mythology, Plato's, or any other. One day you will have to account for your actions and thoughts, even though God knows what these are already. Are these practical uses theologically and morally kosher?[93]

Whether or not they are kosher, omniscience and surveillance can be effective motivational devices—presumably more effective than love and inherent rightness and goodness. Unlike ministers and moralists, ordinary businesspeople do not need to worry about doctrinal or theological *kashrut*. So, perhaps on average they feel freer to appeal to omniscience and surveillance when they give moral advice. An illustrative—though much earlier—expression of these feelings toward God's omniscience and surveillance is due to Boston merchant Thomas Walley. In 1790, he gave the following piece of advice to his son and nephew: "1. Observe the strictest honor, and integrity, in all your transactions; remembering you are to be accountable hereafter, for all your conduct, while on the stage of life, to that Omniscient Being, who is perfectly acquainted with your most secret motives and springs of action."[94]

Walley was a merchant in Boston in the second half of the eighteenth century. The Walley family was a renowned one in Boston, some of whose members were,

---

93 In principle, omniscience could be understood and utilized differently. For instance, instead of focusing on God's seeing your thoughts in general, you might focus on God's seeing your springs of action in particular. On the other hand, this leads to an infinite regress. You should act from the right motives, such as love of God, lest God punish you for not acting from them. But then the motives for acting from the right motives—call them meta-motives—would be selfish: not the love of God but fear of punishment. And what should your motives for having these meta-motives be, that is, your meta-meta-motives?

94 Thomas Walley. 1790. *Sundry directions, necessary to be attended to, on your setting out in Business*. Unpublished letter. Massachusetts Historical Society. Underlining in original. Walley also warned them against misrepresenting their products and anti-competitive practices: "21. Never enter into any combination, or agreement, with persons in the same line of business with yourselves, to raise, or keep up, the price of any particular article; if you do, you may depend upon it, you will be deceived, and suffer by it; I have often tryed [*sic*] it, in the course [illegible] business, and as often been deceived, and suffered thereby; let your own judgment; [illegible] making all the enquiries which are necessary, and sell as you shall think best; but never suffer yourselves to [be] bound, by any agreement, to ask a particular price, for any article, you have to sell."

had been, or would become ministers.[95] Born in 1725, Thomas did not become a minister, but he was a devout Christian man nonetheless. On October 1, 1790, he appealed to his extensive business experience to advise his son, Thomas, Jr., and his nephew, William Furness. He appropriately titled his handwritten note, *Sundry directions, necessary to be attended to, on your setting out in Business*. It consists of twenty-four numbered tips, of which I quoted the first. This first tip illustrates the potential role of the (underlining in original) "<u>Omniscient Being</u>," and particularly his acquaintance with our secrets. Walley was a devout Christian man, but his advice was consequentialist. Indeed, the reason for being moral that he gives to his son and nephew is an instance of (8): Because acting piously and obeying God pays in the hereafter, you should act piously and obey God.

In sum, Christian business ethicists could count on a terrific metaphysical resource. Non-theistic business ethicists do not have hearts. They do have hearts themselves, in their chests, of course. But there are no such objects in their ontology, in the sense that Christians' ontology has them. It is true that conscience has evolved into and has long existed as a non-theistic concept, too. For instance, a present-day, religiously agnostic business ethicist, teaching at a business school, may talk about conscience. She may talk about the need for businesspeople to consult their consciences before they make a consequential decision. This would be perfectly intelligible to her business students, or to the readers of a business magazine. In fact, many present-day business ethicists, pundits, and consultants do talk about a conscience that needs no religion. That said, these non-theistic consciences, without the background Christian worldview, seem to come about out of thin air, like a creation *ex nihilo*. If looked at from a distance, they appear metaphysically disconnected or aloof—much like talk about souls appears within a scientific worldview. Ultimately, it is perhaps just a way of speaking: a present-day business ethicist's mentioning your conscience might be nothing more than a way of saying, "take morality into account."

There is one last important difference. Without the Christian worldview, there is no omniscient God to be acquainted with motives and hearts, and to be represented as punishment, reward, or enforcement agent. Then, people's motives become completely opaque. Indeed, for all we know, they may not exist. For instance, motive may be a confused folk concept, which science will do away with, as in the past it did away with the concept of impetus.[96] If so, all we can do is to observe actions as physical movements. Moral judgments must be based on these observations. The Christian worldview has a more compelling way of morally

95   Thomas Bridgman. 1856. *The Pilgrims of Boston and their Descendants*. New York: D. Appleton and Company, pp. 33–36; Hamilton Andrews Hill. 1890. *History of the Old South Church (Third Church) Boston, 1669–1884*. Volume I. Boston and New York: Houghton, Mifflin and Company; Cambridge, MA: Riverside Press; Justin Winsor, ed. 1901. *The Memorial History of Boston. Including Suffolk County, Masschusetts. 1630–1880*. Vol. II. The Provincial Period. Boston: James R. Osgood and Company.

96   Cf. Patricia S. Churchland. 1986. *Neurophilosophy: Toward a Unified Science of the Mind/Brain*. Cambridge, MA: MIT Press; Paul M. Churchland and Patricia S. Churchland. 1998. *On the Contrary: Critical Essays, 1987–1997*. Cambridge, MA: MIT Press.

evaluating actions, thanks to the heart-conscience-omniscience triad—as long as you accept its theistic premises.

3.7 One Question Too Many

Let us recapitulate. Many present and past business ethicists have tried to convince businesspeople that business ethics makes business sense—that is, empirical claim (1). Next, they have claimed, or at least implied, that this purported empirical fact is the reason why a businessperson should do what morality dictates—that is, normative claim (2). Taken together, (1) and (2) provide a basic framework for business ethicists' cultural and organizational work. However, both of these claims have been contentious. Those business ethicists who disagree with them have pursued two lines of attack. First, they have quarreled with the purported empirical fact that ethics pays. Granted, ethics may pay sometimes. But it does not always pay. Therefore, the motive of self-interest is not a reliable foundation for business ethics; only sometimes will it produce the desired result. Second, they have quarreled with the moral standing of the motive of self-interest. There is something intrinsically good or praiseworthy about being driven by certain motives, and something intrinsically bad or blameworthy about being driven by certain other motives. Self-interest is morally problematic, independently of its consequences, even in a possible world in which it reliably prevented businesspeople from lying, cheating, and stealing. This second objection is characteristic of Christian business ethicists in the second half of the nineteenth century in the United States. Importantly, it is embedded in their particular background ontology, according to which: there is an all-knowing, all-powerful, and all-loving God; each person has a soul, a heart, and a conscience; and people act from distinct motives or springs of action, which God is naturally able to see. As chapter 7 will address at greater length, it is also embedded in their particular epistemology or style of moral thinking, according to which only certain kinds of moral claims, evidence, and questions are acceptable, interesting, and even meaningful. In brief, first-order disagreements about claims (1) and (2) are partly the result of the second-order moral backgrounds that underlie them.

Thus, Christian business ethicists' approach and work at that time suggest another conclusion. They engaged in the project of advocating and promoting their views about how business ought to be conducted, in particular through pastoral and educational work. They tried to have a positive impact on behavior. They assessed business ethics understandings, institutions, and practices, some of which they approved of and preached for, and some of which they disapproved of and preached against, on moral grounds or otherwise. But Christian business ethicists engaged in an additional project as well: that of assessing business ethics issues and questions, and approving of them as relevant, important, and worth raising and thinking about, or rather disapproving of them as irrelevant, unimportant, and not worth raising and thinking about. In between these extremes they could accept an issue or question partially or conditionally, as long as it was adequately amended.

For example, it should be adequately framed, posed in its correct form, its most significant aspects brought to the fore, and its least significant and uncomfortable aspects disregarded. They could also accept a question or issue to some extent, as long as it was put in its proper place, or it was not emphasized too much, given too much attention and importance, or spent too much time on, vis-à-vis those that did deserve more time, attention, and importance. Like things in general, questions and issues have their proper place in the divine order.[97]

Christian business ethicists directed considerable attention to and invested considerable energy in assessing, approving, rejecting, and amending the nature of issues and questions. Logically, this is prior to their being substantively addressed and discussed (empirically, by contrast, the two processes are simultaneous). Therefore, they tried to shape the questions and issues available at the time: not only what is good to ask and discuss, but also what there is to be asked and discussed at all. What is more, in so doing Christian business ethicists operated *qua* recognized representatives of organized religion in the United States, and operated on the basis of that institutional and cultural framework. I am not referring to any one denomination or church, but to the heterogeneous conglomerate of organizations that socially count as representing the church in this country. Culturally, institutionally, and materially, they privileged certain kinds of issues and questions over others, in terms of their subject matter, form, and implications.

Two aspects of this process should be stressed. First, this is not a black-or-white, all-or-nothing affair. That a question is considered to be bad does not necessarily mean that it should be forbidden altogether, placed on something like the Catholic *Index*. It does not necessarily mean that it is considered wholly impious, unchristian, or a mortal sin to think about it. Second, this was only to some extent an intentional project on the part of the church and its representatives. As such, it is an ordinary characteristic of public opinion and cultural battles that one central question be what the central questions ought to be (so it would be unfair to represent it as the censurable project of censorship). Yet, whatever intentionality might have been involved, this was also an unintentional reflection of moral background elements that Christian business ethicists shared. In particular, the dimensions repertoire of moral concepts and object of evaluation turned certain questions into non-questions, and raised certain questions that could not have been raised from outside that metaphysical perspective or location.

Then, the preceding discussion can sharpen my account of Christian business ethicists' complex relationship to empirical claim (1), the claim that acting

---

97 On the study of questions (though in the case of science), see Nicholas Jardine. 1991. *The Scenes of Inquiry: On the Reality of Questions in the Sciences*. Oxford: Clarendon Press; New York: Oxford University Press.

For instance, Jardine writes: "The shift . . . I advocate is from scientific doctrines to the questions posed in the sciences—from the ways in which answers gain credence in the sciences to the ways in which new questions are brought into being and old ones dissolved. Such a shift brings into view, I shall suggest, a series of new and fascinating issues concerning the formation, maintenance and deconstruction of scientific disciplines" (p. 3).

ethically pays in dollars and cents. Or, more colloquially phrased, the enthusiastic exclamation: business ethics is good for you, American businessman! These statements are answers to the questions, respectively, "Does acting ethically pay (in dollars and cents)?" and "Is business ethics good for you (in dollars-and-cents terms)?" These are questions that today, in the twenty-first century, we are used to hearing and discussing. From our present-day perspective, it seems natural to ask and answer them. Indeed, it seems foolish not to do so. As I showed in the previous chapter, there are legions of business ethicists, pundits, scholars, and journalists for whom they are a central concern. There are legions of organizations that encourage their analysis and discussion in seminars, conferences, newspapers, radio shows, and political arenas. Does ethics pay or not? Does business ethics make business sense? We want to know.

Few Christian business ethicists felt that way. Instead, there was a persistent uneasiness about the very raising of this sort of question—at least in some prominent pulpits and forums. There is something not quite right with your Christian morals and faith if you are the kind of person who needs to ask about the payoffs of ethics in order to decide whether to act ethically. The act of asking—this speech act—is not morally neutral. Still, suppose you did ask a Christian business ethicist whether morality in general and business ethics in particular brought about material rewards. Then, his answer would probably be in the affirmative. However, his advice would be that, first, you should reconsider whether you want to spend your time on that question, and give more thought to the motives from which you ought not to lie, cheat, and steal. If you really, really want to spend your time on that question, though, because of an urgent practical need or a burning curiosity or whatever, at least it should not be loudly asked or prominently displayed. It should never become more important than your love of God, obedience, love of doing the right thing for its own sake, or will to act solely for the glory of God. And your answer should not be too enthusiastic or wholehearted; it probably should be somewhat euphemistic or elliptical. And it might be followed by a "but," specifically about there being good and bad motives, and even about the appropriateness of asking the question you have just answered. For asking whether business ethics is good for you does not bespeak the attitude or disposition of a good Christian.

For instance, consider the sermon, *The Duty of the Christian Business Man*, by Boston Episcopal minister Phillips Brooks (1835–1893). Brooks seemed to be dismayed by people's asking self-interested questions and making self-interested calculations about obeying Jesus—in particular, self-interested questions about the costs of not obeying. Obedience should be an automatic reaction or disposition. In fact, the good Christian does not have to fight against his "impulse and desire" in order to obey God; his very impulses and desires lead him to do so:

> I amaze myself when I think how men go asking about the questions of eternal punishment and the duration of man's torment in another life, of what will happen to any man who does not obey Jesus Christ. Oh, my friends, the soul is all wrong when it asks that. Not until the soul says, "What will come if I do obey Jesus Christ?" and opens its glorified vision to see all the great things

that are given to the soul that enters into the service of the perfect one, the perfect love, not until then the perfect love, the perfect life, come in. A man may be—I believe it with all my heart—so absolutely wrapped up in the glory of obedience, and the higher life, and the service of Christ, that he never once asks himself, "What will come to me if I do not obey?" any more than your child asks you what you will do to him if he is not obedient. Every impulse and desire of his life sets toward obedience. And so the soul may have no theory of everlasting or of limited punishment, or of the other life.[98]

In brief, "the soul is all wrong when it asks that." Its asking that already reveals its corruptness. According to Christian business ethicists, there are moral constraints on the kinds of questions that should be asked, the kinds of considerations that should be entertained, and the kinds of methods that should be employed. Just like there are moral reasons for a businessperson not to shortchange his customers or dilute butter with lard, there are moral reasons for him to spend his time on worthwhile pursuits and address himself to worthwhile questions.

The question then becomes if you should ask whether business ethics is good for you. Whether they realized it or not, Christian business ethicists were offering a variation on an old theme. In the seventeenth century, Blaise Pascal attempted to demonstrate that it was in a rational person's self-interest to believe in God.[99] Pascal set up the problem thus: "'God is, or He is not.' But to which side shall we incline? Reason can decide nothing here. There is an infinite chaos which separates us. A game is being played at the extremity of this infinite distance where heads or tails will turn up. What will you wager? According to reason, you can do neither the one thing nor the other; according to reason, you can defend either of the propositions." Since we are inescapably in the dark about what really is the case, we must wager. Then, as any good seventeenth-century game theorist or decision theorist knew, a rational person should weigh the costs and benefits of both actions (believing and not believing) in both situations (God turns out to exist and God turns out not to exist). Logically, Pascal concludes: "Let us weigh the gain and the loss in wagering that God is. Let us estimate these two chances. If you gain, you gain all; if you lose, you lose nothing. Wager, then, without hesitation that He is." Wagering that he is, is the player's dominant strategy in this game.

I am not interested in the logic of Pascal's argument, but in its moral status. Numerous writers have wondered whether there might be something wrong with Pascal's posing this question in this way, asking us to wager, and relying on these methodological techniques to make a decision about belief in God or faith. Voltaire, for example, found it "indecent and puerile," and ill suited to the "gravity of

98   Phillips Brooks. 1900. "The Duty of the Christian Business Man." Pp. 71–101 in Phillips Brooks. *Addresses*. Rahway, NJ: Mershon Company, pp. 94–95.

99   Blaise Pascal, *Pensées* §233. Cf. Ian Hacking. 1975. *The Emergence of Probability: A Philosophical Study of Early Ideas about Probability, Induction and Statistical Inference*. London; New York: Cambridge University Press, pp. 63–72, Alan Hájek. 2003. "Waging War on Pascal's Wager." *Philosophical Review* 112(1):27–56; Jeff Jordan. 2006. *Pascal's Wager: Pragmatic Arguments and Belief in God*. New York: Oxford University Press; Jordan Howard Sobel. 1996. "Pascalian Wagers." *Synthese* 108:11–61.

the subject."[100] William James likewise complained: "We feel that a faith in masses and holy water adopted willfully after such a mechanical calculation would lack the inner soul of faith's reality; and if we were ourselves in the place of the Deity, we should probably take particular pleasure in cutting off believers of this pattern from their infinite reward."[101] James's malicious punishment aside, the idea is that a conclusion may be all right, it may follow from the premises, and it may be morally acceptable. However, the process through which it was arrived at, the activities, practices, methods, and speech acts involved in this process, should not be free from moral evaluation. Moral errors may have been committed along the way, even at the very beginning, when the problem was set up and the project was embarked upon.

This is the same sort of issue Bernard Williams once raised in a different context: a moral agent can have one thought too many. You are morally permitted to save your wife's rather than a stranger's life. Yet, perhaps the "motivating thought" should not be that "in situations of this kind it is permissible to save one's wife," but simply the thought that she is your wife, period.[102] Much like a moral agent can have one thought too many, she can ask one question too many. She may ask a bad question. This was the Christian business ethicists' point.

100   M. de V. [Voltaire]. 1734. "Vingt-cinquième lettre sur les pensées de M. Pascal." Pp. 273–354 in *Lettres philosophiques*. Amsterdam: Chez E. Lucas, au Livre d'or, pp. 285–86.

101   William James. [1896] 1908. "The Will to Believe." Pp. 1–31 in *The Will to Believe and Other Essays in Popular Philosophy*. New York: Longmans, Green, and Co., p. 6.

102   Williams imagines a situation in which a person can save either the life of a stranger or his wife's but not both. It is hard to deny that it would be at least permissible for him to save his wife. Yet, Williams observes, "this construction provides the agent with one thought too many: it might have been hoped by some (for instance by his wife) that his motivating thought, fully spelled out, would be the thought that it was his wife, not that it was his wife, and that in situations of this kind it is permissible to save one's wife." Bernard Williams. 1981. "Persons, Character, and Morality." Pp. 1–19 in *Moral Luck: Philosophical Papers 1973–1980*. Cambridge, UK: Cambridge University Press, p. 18.

4

The Good of American Business

Thruout [*sic*] the country there exists an idea that Wall Street is a very wicked place and that the New York Stock Exchange is a den of gamblers who would not hesitate to ruin the country if they thereby could make a dollar. [. . .] A demagogue can always win votes by denouncing the conspiracies, the trickery, the deceit, the corruption, which are alleged to exist in Wall Street.
The popular idea of Wall Street and its practice is entirely erroneous.

—Joseph French Johnson, 1917[1]

When we turn from these high-sounding and pleasantly worded codes of ethics to the concrete forms of business behavior, what do we find? To begin with, the actual world of business experience is plainly a cutthroat, "dog-eat-dog" proposition. The business man not only admits this, but like the Irishman accused of being drunk, he claims it and boasts about it and chuckles over it. [. . .] [T]o regard business ethics as merely the declaration of a code is unsatisfactory, for many such a code is a hypocritical camouflage or a stupid smoke-screen, including what Justice McReynolds calls "smug preambles," "pious protestations," and "artful gestures."

—Carl F. Taeusch, 1926[2]

4.1 The Pesky Calf

On June 5, 1926, a strip titled "The Pesky Calf" appeared in *Nation's Business*, the official organ of the Chamber of Commerce of the United States. Tellingly, the strip accompanied an article penned by Secretary of Commerce Herbert Hoover. "BUSINESS" is represented by a pesky, misbehaved calf, which crawls through a fence it should not crawl through. This act of the calf allegorically represents the avoidance of "legitimate methods" and "square dealing" in business—i.e., unethical business practices. The cowboy, who represents the U.S. government, is then compelled to intervene. He will "fix" the pesky calf. The fix is a very heavy collar, "government control," which will prevent the calf from misbehaving again— i.e., from crawling through the fence. The literary sophistication of the allegory leaves much to be desired, but the message is absolutely clear nonetheless (or, rather, precisely because of that). As if the strip were not clear enough, a caption reinforces the message: "While we hesitate to compare business to a calf, what

---

1 Joseph French Johnson. 1917. *Business and the Man*. New York: Alexander Hamilton Institute, p. 124.

2 Carl F. Taeusch, 1926. *Professional and Business Ethics*. New York: Henry Holt and Company, pp. 260, 264.

Figure 4.1. The pesky calf.
Source: *Nation's Business*, June 5, 1926, p. 11. Retrieved from ProQuest Historical Database.
Legends on poles: "legitimate methods" and "square dealing"
Caption: "While we hesitate to compare business to a calf, what happens to the skittish creature will also be the fate of business, if business doesn't rule itself."

happens to the skittish creature will also be the fate of business, if business doesn't rule itself."

The U.S. Chamber of Commerce worked hard to preempt government regulation, through both public opinion campaigns and lobbying strategies, so the "Pesky Calf" strip is standard fare for this organization. From a moral background perspective, though, it is remarkable that "BUSINESS" shows up as both moral subject and object. Or, linguistically, it is both agent and patient. First, business is a sufficiently coherent entity, such that *it* can act, not use legitimate methods, rule itself, and so on. Second, business has the capacity for agency. Not only does it exist, not only is it a sufficiently coherent entity, but a sufficiently coherent entity that can do things, such as crawling through fences. Third, business is an object or patient, that is, it can be acted upon. *It* can be fixed and punished. Fourth, business has the capacity for being a *moral* agent and an object of *moral* evaluation. These actions, of which business is the agent or the patient, can have a moral character; they can be morally assessed.

Yet, what on earth is that thing called "BUSINESS"? In the Heideggerian terms presented in chapter 1, business or American business shows up as something that can have interests, needs, and desires. How can this be? How can it be capable of agency, responsibility for its actions, and moral praise or criticism? A Martian, wholly unacquainted with life on Earth, must find it puzzling that business can be an entity in our social ontology. That this entity, business, can be a moral agent and can be morally responsible for its actions may convince her that earthlings are crazy.

This chapter gives an account of the constitution of business as moral object and moral subject in the United States in the first decades of the twentieth century. Of course, businessmen and their companies had always done morally good and bad acts, and had always been morally responsible, praiseworthy, or blameworthy for their acts. But now this became increasingly true of business as a whole, on occasion tellingly capitalized ("Business"), on occasion tellingly accompanied by the adjective "American" ("American business" or "American Business"). The protagonist of my historical narrative is the U.S. Chamber of Commerce, which, drawing on Spillman, I view as a cultural institution—producing and legitimizing understandings, meanings, accounts, and "cultural infrastructures."[3] Established in 1912, this association worked organizationally and culturally for the constitution, organization, and concerted action of American business, such that it would become a meaningful entity. That was part of its mission. Moreover, it fought public opinion wars to improve the reputation of American business, and convince "the public" that business could regulate itself. These wars led the Chamber into the field of business ethics, telling businesspeople that they should be more ethical, and telling public opinion that businesspeople had in fact become more ethical. My narrative documents how it did so, with special emphasis on the third dimension of the moral background: object of evaluation. The foremost moral agent and object in this chapter is American business, not the individual American businessman. In turn, the third dimension of the moral background impinges on the first one: the reasons that American business has to be ethical are not necessarily shared by every individual American businessman.

In addition, this chapter's historical account is partly oriented toward the fourth dimension of the background: method and argument. I look at the multiplication and prominent public presence of codes of business ethics in the 1920s, including the Chamber's own—which was a *primus inter pares*. I argue that codes of ethics are a special kind of moral tool or instrument.[4] Their first-order prescriptions and principles are normally dull, predictable, and unpersuasive, if not downright platitudinous. To take a more-or-less random historical example, a member of the National Automobile Dealers Association "advertises truthfully"; "[h]e reflects his personal integrity in every transaction"; and "[h]e believes in the Golden Rule."[5] Of more sociological value are the formal properties of codes, their rhetorical uses, and the background elements they are underlain by. The way in which they make and express business ethics claims and demands is a distinct one, distinct from, say, a sermon, speech, or article. So is their "materiality"—that is, the kind of physical objects they are, which, for instance, may be posted on the wall of a business or office.[6] Indeed, the very fact that codes of ethics exist and prosper in a society is symptomatic of a particular conception of what ethics is and does, and how you go about doing ethics.

Besides these moral background dimensions, this chapter tells a story about an organization, the U.S. Chamber of Commerce, which produced and reproduced particular moral background elements. While this is not its chief object,

---

3 Lyn Spillman. 2012. *Solidarity in Strategy: Making Business Meaningful in American Trade Associations.* Chicago: University of Chicago Press.

4 Cf. Andrew Abbott. 1983. "Professional Ethics." *American Journal of Sociology* 88(5):855–85; Spillman, *Solidarity in Strategy*, pp. 161–63, Viviana A. Zelizer. 2011. *Economic Lives: How Culture Shapes the Economy.* Princeton: Princeton University Press, pp. 440–57.

5 Edgar L. Heermance. 1924. *Codes of Ethics: A Handbook.* Burlington, VT: Free Press, p. 36.

6 Pinch and Swedberg, *Living in a Material World.*

the chapter still speaks to the relationship between organizations and moral backgrounds. How do organizations produce, support, promote, diffuse, legitimize, and institutionalize particular background elements? When can we say that we are in the presence of a causal relationship, not just correlation or elective affinity? My ambitions in this area are modest, however. I am not interested here in the traditional interest of the sociology of knowledge: what the social causes or determinants of "mental productions" are.[7] I am not interested in making a general statement about the causes of moral background elements or the conditions under which they emerge. Instead, I locally look at how one organization, or a few organizations, may produce or strengthen a particular background element. For instance, they may actively raise and try to get people interested in particular moral questions in the public sphere, which are questions of particular forms, which refer to particular objects, and so on. Or they may use a particular moral method, tool, or kind of argument, which is based on a particular background property. In other words, moral backgrounds may not be intentionally campaigned for as such—they are after all abstract and esoteric—but they can be strengthened as a by-product of other intentional campaigns. Thus, this and the next chapter reveal how the Chamber of Commerce and some high-status business schools partook in this process: their business ethics work helped strengthen particular moral background elements. Subsequently, chapter 6 analytically brings together these elements as a distinct type of moral background, which I call the Standards of Practice type. Finally, chapter 7 addresses the moral background elements I find in different quarters: Protestant organizations, publications, and pulpits. This type of moral background I call the Christian Merchant type.

One caveat remains to be made before turning to the empirical meat of this chapter. I would like to recall here what I said before: my concern is not individuals' real beliefs or true motives. It is important to recall this point here, given who plays the business ethicists part in this chapter. They are mostly businessmen and business association leaders, that is, businessmen whose job description reads: you must advance the interests of business, bolster its reputation, and influence politicians' and policy makers' decisions. Then, in this chapter the difficulty seems more acute than if the business ethicists were Protestant ministers or business school educators. What should we make of a famous businessperson's publicly emphasizing the importance of business ethics, the social responsibilities of business, including its responsibilities to labor and the environment? Perhaps he is not telling the truth and he is just a hypocrite (which you would discover if you could eavesdrop on his private conversations or read his mind)? How can we know if we can believe what he is saying or not? Or perhaps he does think business ethics is important, but his motivation is to appease the oppressed masses, and support moderate over radical labor leaders?

Furthermore, duplicitous behaviors are arguably more likely if the economic interests of a class are at stake, and deceiving people into the belief that business takes ethics seriously would further these interests. Setting aside real beliefs and

---

7   Robert K. Merton. 1968. *Social Theory and Social Structure*. New York: Free Press, p. 514.

true motives, there is the structural point that business ethics may be functional to capitalists. For instance, it may in fact strengthen the reputation of business and increase the odds of business-friendly legislation (or lack of legislation, where appropriate). So it seems to follow that business ethics does advance the interests of business. I mention these issues because they have been of much interest to many historians and social scientists in the past. In particular, much work about the Progressive Era has focused on them. By contrast, I bracket them entirely. It is not my question here whether the business ethicist is a hypocrite, much less how to discover empirically whether the business ethicist is a hypocrite. My object of inquiry is neither the relations between business and government per se, nor the conflicts between capital and labor per se—historically fundamental though these surely are. Rather, my object of inquiry is the moral background that underlies first-order business ethics understandings, statements, tools, and projects. Duplicity and hypocrisy may be properties of first-order business ethics, but they do not apply to the second-order background properties that underlie them.

4.2 The Chamber

The Chamber of Commerce of the United States was established in 1912, thanks to the concerted efforts of some prominent businessmen and Department of Commerce officials. The Chamber was in some senses a new kind of organization and in some senses an old one. By the end of the nineteenth century, there already existed in the country a large number of business associations. These organizations may be classified in various ways, a common one in the literature being what their objectives were. Now, if they are classified according to what they were associations of, or what they claimed to be representative of, three main kinds emerge. First, organizations that represented a local or regional constituency—such as the San Francisco Chamber of Commerce (1851), the Charleston Chamber of Commerce (1773), or the Chamber of Commerce of New York (1768) (the state).[8] Second, organizations that represented a local or regional constituency *and* a specific line of activity or business. Third, organizations of a national character that represented a specific line of activity or business—such as the American Bankers' Association (1875), National Association of Life Underwriters (1890), United States Brewers Association (1862), Carriage Builders National Association (1872), American Paper and Pulp Association (1878), Laundrymen's National Association of America (1883), National Association of Brass Manufacturers (1886), National Wholesale Lumber Dealers Association (1894), and National

---

8   Lee M. Friedman. 1947. "The First Chamber of Commerce in the United States." *Bulletin of the Business Historical Society* 21(5):137–43; Charles King. 1855. "History of the New York Chamber of Commerce, with Notices of Some of its Most Distinguished Members." In *The Charter and By-Laws with a History of the Chamber of Commerce of the State of New-York*. New York: Published by Order of the Chamber; Kenneth Sturges. 1915. *American Chambers of Commerce*. New York: Moffat, Yard and Company.

Association of Retail Grocers (1896).[9] As historian Robert Wiebe notes, "[l]ocal chambers of commerce and boards of trade comprised the largest number," yet "[p]articularly in the major cities, businessmen often belonged as well to organizations more directly reflecting their self-consciousness as specialist."[10] Unlike the first and second kinds, the third kind of business associations, being of a national character, could speak and lobby on behalf of, say, American laundrymen or American wholesale lumber dealers. Yet, naturally, they could not claim a right to speak and lobby on behalf of American business as a whole.

Although the Chamber was not truly the first of its kind, it was the first reasonably successful and effective attempt at bringing together and legitimately claiming to represent such a large and diverse constituency as American business *tout court*.[11] It is another question whether the Chamber actually represented such a constituency or not (and yet another question what it takes to be actually representative of a constituency). In any case, it did get to be seen by many actors as doing so, and hence it got to interact with them as if it did.[12] As we will see, the Chamber is a key actor in my story because of its business ethics advocacy in the public sphere. Publicly construing itself as a business ethics advocate was a means to advance its mission. It presented business ethics as a form of self-regulation, which would prevent unwanted government regulation, as well as unwanted public criticism and disapproval.

Let me first provide some historical background. What are the origins of the U.S. Chamber of Commerce? What was it meant to do? To what extent was its conception and establishment linked to the ethics of business and moral considerations more generally? The story begins at the beginning of the Progressive Era, in the late nineteenth century. As historian Richard Hume Werking writes:

> With growing frequency, certain officials in the executive branch urged the creation of a national commercial organization, one that would inform the government of business needs with a single voice and would serve as a means of channeling government information to businessmen. It was the smaller and medium-sized firms, of the kind already associated with state and local chambers of commerce or boards of trade, that were thought to need an institutionalized relationship. The larger firms, such as U. S. Steel and International Harvester, already had personal entré [*sic*] to the high levels of government.

9   Emmett Hay Naylor. 1921. *Trade Associations: Their Organization and Management.* New York: Ronald Press Company, p. 23.

10   Robert H. Wiebe. 1967. *The Search for Order, 1877–1920.* New York: Hill and Wang, p. 123.

11   The National Commercial Convention and the National Board of Trade are oft-mentioned antecessors. On the foundation of the former, see "Action of the Boston Board of Trade." *Chicago Tribune*, December 20, 1867, p. 2; *Proceedings of the National Commercial Convention.* 1868. Published by Order of the Convention. Boston, Massachusetts: J. H. Eastburn's Press. On the foundation of the latter, see "Meeting of the National Board of Trade at Philadelphia." *New York Times*, June 3, 1868, p. 1; "National Board of Trade." *Chicago Tribune*, June 5, 1868, p. 1.

12   Cf. William H. Becker. 1982. *The Dynamics of Business-Government Relations: Industry & Exports, 1893–1921.* Chicago: University of Chicago Press, p. 121.

Frederic Emory, chief of the State Department's commercial office from 1894 to 1905, hinted at the need for such an institution as early as 1897.[13]

The Department of Commerce and Labor was created in 1903 (Commerce and Labor were split in 1913). One of its most notable divisions was the Bureau of Corporations, which President Theodore Roosevelt hoped would be a way to control, scrutinize, and regulate big business—that is, bad big business.[14] After the short tenures of George B. Cortelyou (1903–1904) and Victor H. Metcalf (1904–1906), Oscar S. Straus was sworn in as Secretary of Commerce and Labor on December 17, 1906.

Straus wished to make the national business association a reality. As per Werking's account, in September 1907, Straus met with his bureau chiefs, and he told them they should be

"guided by the real public sentiment of the United States; the valuable public sentiment of the United States; the active business men, manufacturers, etc." Unfortunately, Straus explained, it was impossible to establish the proper relationship through letters, because anybody could write them. Letters came to the department "from men who could not earn enough to wear decent shoes, and want to manage the whole Government." If the department was to be of use to what it considered its proper constituency, it needed to know just who comprised that constituency and what their needs were. Thus the department had to keep in touch systematically with the nation's business community through an institution created for that purpose.[15]

Straus then took some concrete steps in the direction of a national business body, but they were ultimately unsuccessful. The most noteworthy of them is the meeting of business associations of December 1907. On December 5, "delegates from thirty-four leading commercial bodies of the thirty-four leading cities of the United States" assembled in Washington, in response to Straus's invitation.[16] At the meeting, they were addressed by Straus and by Secretary of State Elihu Root, and were received by President Roosevelt in his office. The attendees founded the

---

13   Richard Hume Werking. 1978. "Bureaucrats, Businessmen, and Foreign Trade: The Origins of the United States Chamber of Commerce." *Business History Review* 52(3): 321–41, p. 323. As Werking explains in a footnote, this "commercial office" was called "Bureau of Statistics" until 1897, "Bureau of Foreign Commerce" between 1897 and 1903, and "Bureau of Trade Relations" afterward.

On the origins of the Chamber, see also Robert H. Wiebe. 1962. *Businessmen and Reform: A Study of the Progressive Movement*. Cambridge, MA: Harvard University Press, pp. 33–41.

14   See, e.g., Arthur M. Johnson. 1959. "Theodore Roosevelt and the Bureau of Corporations." *Mississippi Valley Historical Review* 45(4): 571–90.

The potential of the Bureau of Corporations was recognized at the time. For instance, according to the *New York Times*, "undoubtedly the most important work it [the Department of Commerce and Labor] can perform is in the Bureau of Corporations, at the head of which Mr. Garfield is placed." The *Times* was skeptical, however, regarding the actual results that Garfield would be able to accomplish. "The Department of Commerce and Labor." *New York Times*, February 19, 1903, p. 8.

15   Werking, "Bureaucrats, Businessmen, and Foreign Trade," p. 328.

16   John Corrigan, Jr. 1907. "Commerce Body for the Nation." *Atlanta Constitution*, December 6, 1907, p. 9.

National Council of Commerce, and elected Gustav H. Schwab as chairman of its advisory committee.[17] However, in practice, the National Council of Commerce never really took off. But it did signal the trend toward the unification of business. This is illustrated by a resolution the Council adopted on December 6, in which it appreciates "the high motives and constructive genius of the Secretary of Commerce and Labor in first perceiving the practical need of uniting the business forces of the country for the furtherance of their best interests, and the national progress in harmonious and close relations with this department and the national government."[18]

The Secretary of Commerce and Labor who followed Straus was Charles Nagel (March 6, 1909–March 4, 1913). He would push the national business association idea with more astuteness, determination, and perhaps also fortune than his predecessor. Against the backdrop of the upcoming 1912 elections, Nagel encouraged President Taft to mention the issue in his December 1911 annual message to Congress. Which Taft did:

In the dissemination of useful information and in the coordination of effort certain unofficial associations have done good work toward the promotion of foreign commerce. It is cause for regret, however, that the great number of such associations and the comparative lack of cooperation between them fails to secure an efficiency commensurate with the public interest. Through the agency of the Department of Commerce and Labor, and in some cases directly, the Department of State transmits to reputable business interests information of commercial opportunities, supplementing the regular published consular reports. Some central organization in touch with associations and chambers of commerce throughout the country and able to keep purely American interests in closer touch with different phases of commercial affairs would, I believe, be of great value.[19]

The need to promote foreign commerce was clear; equally clear were the tensions between the departments of Commerce and State, and the appropriateness of bringing up "purely American interests" in a message to Congress. Either way, the organization of this "central organization" was soon under way, under the leadership of Nagel, Bureau of Manufactures chief Albertus H. Baldwin, and some prominent businesspeople, including the future first president of the organization,

---

17   "Root Talks on Trade." *Washington Post*, December 6, 1907, p. 11. This article speaks of "delegates of the boards of trade of forty-six cities," which is considerably different from what the *Atlanta Constitution* affirmed. The *Atlanta Constitution* article is signed by John Corrigan, Jr., and the first line of the text runs: "Washington, December 5.—(Special.)—" I'm therefore inclined to give more credence to this source, despite the fact that the *Washington Post* probably had better sources in the capital. See also National Council of Commerce. 1907. *Proceedings of a meeting of delegates from the Chambers of Commerce, Boards of Trade, and Trade Organizations of the leading cities of the United States in conference with the Secretary of Commerce and Labor, December 5 and 6, 1907.* Washington, DC: Government Printing Office.

18   "Praise Secretary Straus." *Washington Post*, December 7, 1907, p. 11.

19   "Taft Discusses Our Foreign Relations." *New York Times*, December 8, 1911, p. 6.

Harry Wheeler. This group drafted a constitution, and in March 1912, Nagel sent invitations to about a thousand business associations for a conference to establish a national business association.

The conference took place at the New Willard Hotel in Washington, DC, on April 22 and 23, 1912. Business associations were extremely responsive this time: according to several reports, approximately seven hundred delegates attended.[20] On April 22, President Taft gave a brief welcome address, which touched on the objectives of the conference:

> Even regulating measures which have been adopted in the past may have suffered for lack of advice from those who should be best qualified by experience and training to give it. Now that we enter upon the broad field of constructive legislation, the need for that counsel is absolutely apparent to all of us. Specialized investigation and learning may evolve theories. Those theories no doubt provide proper foundation for new measures. But in the last analysis every thought must stand the test of actual use. With respect to that test, the disinterested advice of those who are to live by the proposed measures is of first importance. You gentlemen are most concerned to have rules of action formulated and adopted that are calculated to insure fair dealing on the one hand and allow and promote legitimate expansion and development upon the other.
>
> To that end you and the government must cooperate. This you cannot accomplish so long as you are disorganized. The advantage of one interest is sure to work to the disadvantage of another.
>
> The government cannot favor separate interests: but it should promote commerce and industry as a whole.[21]

Three aspects of Taft's address are of special significance here. First, it distinguishes theory and practice, and argues that businessmen can and should give their input on the latter. He does value "specialized investigation and learning" and "theories" that "provide proper foundation for new measures." But the ultimate test, he believes, should be "actual use." Americans are a practical people, for whom the proof of the pudding is in the eating, and this should apply *a fortiori* to American businesspeople. Second, Taft talks about "*fair* dealing." Fairness is of course a moral concept. But Taft's use of the expression "fair dealing" does not refer to an abstract, armchair discussion in ethics. Rather, it refers to one recurrent public issue in the late nineteenth and early twentieth centuries: what constitutes "unfair" methods of competition and of doing business. Third, Taft rhetorically framed his call as a call for assistance. This framing should be

---

20 According to the *Washington Post*, the meeting "was attended by nearly 700 delegates of American commercial bodies." The same figure was given by a "staff correspondent" of the *Chicago Daily Tribune*. The *New York Times* reported that "[s]even hundred and fifty delegates, representing 250 commercial bodies," attended the meeting. Werking speaks of 700 hundred delegates representing 392 associations, based on an official pamphlet, *The National Commercial Conference*. "Heads Trade Body." *Washington Post*, Apr il 24, 1912, p. 1; "Plan Future of U.S. Trade Board." *Chicago Daily Tribune*, April 23, 1912, p. 13; "Must Help Trade to Expand Legally." *New York Times*. April 23, 1912, p. 16.

21 "Unite for Business." *Washington Post*, April 23, 1923, p. 3.

flattering and hence less likely to alienate businesspeople, given the recent history of antagonisms, especially during the Roosevelt administration: "We want your assistance in carrying on the government in reference to those matters that affect the business and the business welfare of the country, and we do not wish to limit your discretion in that matter. We wish that your advice should be as free and unrestrained as possible, but we need your assistance and we ask for it."[22]

This April 1912 conference was a success: the Chamber of Commerce of the United States of America was successfully founded. The news was well received. Many commentators, businesspeople, and politicians had long applauded organization in general, as an admirable contemporary tendency. And they had long called for the organization of American business in particular, which was said to facilitate cooperation and communication between government and business.[23] So the press applauded the new business organization. Its first president was a Chicagoan: Harry A. Wheeler, "of the Union Trust company and ex-president of the Chicago Association of Commerce."[24] Wheeler was an intelligent leader, who did his utmost to maintain a balance between all the potential factions and special interests. For example, regional balance was conscientiously sought. A list of officers shows: J. N. Teal of Portland, Oregon (vice president for Pacific slope); Asa G. Chandler of Atlanta, Georgia (vice president for South); A. B. Farquhar of York, Pennsylvania (vice president for East); John Joy Edson of Washington, DC (treasurer); and J. Francis Burke of Pittsburgh, Pennsylvania (consul).[25] And a list of member associations as of September 1912 shows regional diversity, too.

Furthermore, while politically Wheeler was a Republican, he was committed not to let the association take sides on partisan issues. Unlike the National Association of Manufacturers, the Chamber welcomed people like Wilson and Brandeis, and some of its leaders were Democrats. Unlike some of its European counterparts, the Chamber made a commitment to independence from the state, including but not limited to a commitment to financial independence. As Wheeler

---

22 "Plan Future of U.S. Trade Board." *Chicago Daily Tribune*, April 23, 1912, p. 13. Nagel's address similarly argued that, rather than "specialized interests," "we must have a common judgment of commerce and industry, and to get that common judgment we must have a common representation. This is the meaning of the organization which is here proposed." And he added: "[T]o my mind it is true beyond the possibility of refutation that by some means we must establish a common commercial representation, which shall sustain a relation to the Government for purposes of general advice and intelligent direction with respect to proposed measures and the administration of existing laws." "Must Help Trade to Expand Legally." *New York Times*, April 23, 1912, p. 16; "Business Men in Conference." *Los Angeles Times*, April 23, 1912, p. 14.

23 In this sense, the Department of Commerce had its own self-regarding objectives and agenda. It was beneficial for it to have a clearly identifiable constituency and publicly legitimate interlocutor. This could help it accomplish its goals, such as enlarging the volume of exports and foreign trade, expand its power, improve its standing within the state system (e.g., in its competition with the Department of State), and thus increase its resources.

24 "Business, Commercial and Financial Section." *Chicago Daily Tribune*, April 24, 1912, p. 13.

25 "Heads Trade Body." *Washington Post*, April 24, 1912, p. 1.

stressed in a speech at the Union League Club of Chicago (May 14, 1912): "The strength in this country of ours, of a Chamber of Commerce that shall truly represent all interests and all sections will lie in the fact that while it will co-operate with every executive department of the government, it will accept neither appropriation nor subvention from the government, but will find a way to support itself and carry on its work solely by the contributions of its members. More than that, it will not permit upon its board of directors or in its controlling force representatives of either the executive or legislative branches of the government, but will stand in an advisory capacity."

What part (if any) did ethics play in this story? Although not wholly unprecedented, the U.S. Chamber of Commerce was a new public actor, in some ways unprecedented. As any new public actor that is in some ways unprecedented, it had to define, describe, and present itself. How did it do so? In particular, to what extent (if any) did it describe itself as being concerned with moral aims and the common good? This question has to do with public normativity, so one place to look for evidence about it is the Chamber's foundational moments. For they generally carry much symbolic baggage and require formal statements of purpose. They generally bring out, too, excitement, overambitious and overoptimistic goals, and inflated rhetoric. An official report was published in the first issue of the *Nation's Business*, the periodical created to be the official organ of the new organization. First, I will look at this report, authoritatively titled, "Organization and Purposes of the Chamber of Commerce of the United States." Second, I will look at the first *Nation's Business* editorial. It is common practice that the first editorial of a periodical be a statement of purpose. It is common practice *and* people know it is common practice, so this is an excellent empirical locus to observe an organization's public face. Taken together, these two documents show how the Chamber presented itself in the public sphere, what it claimed to be, and what it claimed to be in the business of. To use Goffman's dramaturgical terminology, they show the organization's front-stage and presentation of self in public life.[26]

The "Organization and Purposes" report is not about ethics at all. According to it, the Chamber of Commerce "is organized to accomplish much that is specific, and three general purposes, each necessary and each hitherto neglected":

In the first place, it is to be a clearing house for business opinion, business methods, and such efforts of organized commercial bodies as have suggestive importance in relation to the work of other organizations.

In the second place, it will furnish to the public, and to the government at Washington that correlation which has hitherto been lacking in the activities of the government. It will be a correlating force, thus enabling all the people to learn through an official organization just exactly what is available in the way of knowledge from a government that is very highly ramified and scientifically specialized

26 Goffman, *Presentation of Self*.

In the third place, it is to secure by means of referendum vote an intimate knowledge of the business sentiment of the United States on all important subjects affected by national legislation.[27]

In these three general purposes, knowledge and information are prioritized. There is no reference to moral considerations, let alone moral objectives. The Chamber construes itself as a vehicle for useful information for the public, government, and business. That said, the potential ethical usefulness of the Chamber would soon come to the fore on another occasion. Right after its foundation, the Chamber tried to obtain a federal charter, "following the advice of the Secretary of Commerce and Labor." *Nation's Business* narrates the process thus: "A bill was, therefore, prepared and introduced in the House of Representatives on June 4 [of 1912] and referred to the Committee on the Judiciary, which committee promptly reported the bill back to the House 'with the recommendation that the bill do pass' and with the following significant comments."

"While we have many commercial bodies in the country, known as chambers of commerce and commercial clubs of one sort or another, they are all purely local in their character, intended only to benefit the particular communities in which they are located, we have no organization of a national or quasi national character, such as it is proposed in this bill to organize. [...]"

"Its possible usefulness is practically unlimited, both as to our domestic and foreign commercial relations."

"In the collection, publication and distribution of the latest commercial statistics alone it can do incalculable good."

"It can and ought to greatly increase the commercial standing and importance of the United States among foreign nations by materially extending our foreign trade and by creating a higher standard of business ethics."

The House of Representatives Committee on the Judiciary mentions the Chamber of Commerce's "creating of a higher standard of business ethics." It mentions, too, the effect of business ethics on the international "standing and importance" of the United States. And it is also noteworthy that it speaks of "business ethics"— rather than, say, "commercial morality" or "trade morals."

What about *Nation's Business*'s first editorial? What did it say the nation's business was? It was titled, precisely, "The Nation's Business." While it was published unsigned, its author was most likely the editor, G. Grosvenor Dawe, or the editor along with the publication committee (John H. Fahey of Boston, Frederick Bode of Chicago, and H. E. Miles of Racine, Wisconsin). Perhaps the president of the Chamber, Harry Wheeler, gave his input (I have no evidence either way, though). As befits a new periodical publication, much emphasis was placed on its utility to transmit information: "Its [*Nation's Business*'s] editorial motive is to place before the editorial writers of the country and the officials of organized efforts the

---

27 "Organization and Purposes of the Chamber of Commerce of the United States." *Nation's Business*, September 2, 1912, p. 8.

constantly varying phases of development connected with the resources of the nation, so that knowledge may be widely increased and constructive suggestions become quickly known in every nook and corner of our far-flung territory." However, the editorial only marginally touched on the common good and moral aims:

> The nation's business is to learn the extent of our resources and to understand the interests of our population, without whose activities resources have no value.
>
> The nation's business is to regard the use of resources as better than either waste or disuse, and therefore to move for conservation that shall safeguard the future while serving the present.
>
> [...]
>
> The nation's business is to believe that all who render service are entitled to reward, and to implant the element of hope and courage in every human being who, in his place, is doing his duty well.
>
> [...]
>
> The nation's business is to safeguard from exploitation all who come from foreign lands to throw in their lot with us, and to impart immediately to their children the sense of actual inheritance in all the deeds and growth and successes that have been ours since we first breathed the breath of life as a nation.[28]

These considerations—the interests of "our population," "conservation" (that is, business's impact on the environment), and safeguarding foreigners from exploitation and educating and socializing their children—do not have to do with the selfish interests of business or businesspeople, narrowly conceived. Rather, they are meant to imply that "the nation's business" is related to the common good. Moral overtones are also implied by a human being's "duty"—though here it acquires a corporatist ring, even redolent of Plato's *Republic* (a human being must be in his proper place). Likewise, as we will see in chapter 6, the word "service" was a code word at the time; it had a special meaning. *Nation's Business* was thereby giving a nod to a particular current of business opinion, for which "service" was a mantra of sorts. According to it, profit had to be made by rendering a service—although what this meant was underspecified. That was the morally good way of making profit, in contrast not only to the immoral, Robber-Baron or Bernie-Madoff way, but also to a morally neutral way.

Claims of this sort are expected to show up in the genesis of an organization like the U.S. Chamber of Commerce. Surely it had to declare it had the common good in mind; surely it wished to underscore its having selfless rather than selfish objectives. However, these were not elaborate or extensive statements. Except for once, business ethics per se was largely absent from these presentations of self in 1912. Things would soon change, though. For business ethics would come in very handy in the fight against government regulation the Chamber undertook— one of its principal preoccupations. Preventing regulation is both a private and a public affair. Privately, there are the familiar lobbying strategies of corporations, associations, and pressure and interest groups. These take place behind closed doors: in luxurious offices, living rooms, restaurants, and hotels. That these strategies can be effective is arguably a structural feature of the capitalist state, and is arguably proven by their lasting existence. Yet, public officials in liberal democracies have other incentives and constraints, too (assuming things are working the way they theoretically should). These incentives and constraints are set not only by formal rules and laws (assuming these are effective), but also by political actors' electoral and political goals and thus by public opinion (assuming a more-or-less functioning public sphere). Under these conditions, preventing regulation is a public game as well, in which the strategic moves are speeches, articles, editorials, lectures, conferences, interviews, TV and radio shows, and public relations campaigns. I want now to argue that the Chamber used business ethics in this way, as a public tool against regulation, which is most visible in the 1920s.

4.3 Government Will

Business associations and big businessmen in the Progressive Era had much work to do to improve their public image, good name, or reputation.[29] Criticism and condemnation, spearheaded by the investigative journalism of the muckrakers, was not in short supply.[30] Then, as historian Morrell Heald observes, "[a] s criticism mounted, businessmen began to display a new sensitivity to public opinion."[31] The response of some large firms and businessmen was to individually take the "public relations" route.[32] But this route was not an option for smaller firms. Moreover, while the public relations initiatives of a firm could indirectly contribute to the reputation of all American firms, they could do so only indirectly. The aim of a firm is typically to improve its own image only; indeed, the market may give it an incentive to harm the image of other firms. By contrast, the Chamber of Commerce concerned itself with the public image, good name,

---

29   Cf. Sigmund Diamond. 1955. *The Reputation of the American Businessman*. Cambridge, MA: Harvard University Press; Louis Galambos. 1975. *The Public Image of Big Business in America, 1880–1940: A Quantitative Study in Social Change*. Baltimore and London: Johns Hopkins University Press.

30   See, e.g., David Mark Chalmers. [1964] 1970. *The Social and Political Ideas of the Muckrakers*. Freeport, NY: Books for Libraries Press; Louis Filler. 1976. *The Muckrakers*. University Park: Pennsylvania State University Press (this is a revised edition of *Crusaders for American Liberalism*, originally published in 1939); C. C. Regier. 1932. *The Era of the Muckrakers*. Chapel Hill: University of North Carolina Press; Harold S. Wilson. 1970. *McClure's Magazine and the Muckrakers*. Princeton: Princeton University Press.

Useful documentary collections include: Herbert Shapiro, ed. 1968. *The Muckrakers and American Society*. Edited with an introduction by Herbert Shapiro. Boston: D. C. Heath and Company; Arthur Weinberg and Lila Weinberg, eds. 1961. *The Muckrakers: The Era in Journalism That Moved America to Reform. The Most Significant Magazine Articles of 1902–1912*. New York: Simon & Schuster; Morgen Witzel, ed. 2002. *Big Business and the Muck-Rakers*. 4 volumes. Bristol, UK: Thoemmes Press.

31   Morrell Heald. [1970] 1988. *The Social Responsibilities of Business: Company and Community, 1900–1960*. New Brunswick and London: Transaction Publishers, p. 21.

32   Marchand, *Creating the Corporate Soul*.

and reputation of American business as a whole. That it did have reasons to be concerned, President Harding reminded it in 1922.

On Thursday, May 18, 1922, President Warren Gamaliel Harding addressed the annual meeting of the Chamber. Harding, a Republican from Ohio and a member of the Rotary Club of Washington, spoke about "Commerce with a Conscience."[33] He made the familiar point that "those who do not have conscience" bring criticism on "American activities": "While I am speaking very briefly, I wish to speak for a commerce with a conscience. If I were to bring only one admonition to you, I would like to charge you men and women of influence and responsibility with the task of eliminating from American commerce those who do not have conscience, whose conscienceless practices bring that criticism which sometimes attends our American activities."[34]

Harding did speak briefly, as he had promised he would. But he still got to mention, almost in passing, a main worry of the Chamber at the time. If there are persistent unethical practices in business, which business itself does not take care of, and public opinion does not tolerate, then government must step in. Whether you like it or not. As he said: "Something has been said, and I think opportunely said, that we want a period in America with less government in business and more business in government. If the commerce of America were always conscientious, there never would be a single excuse for government in American business." And he added: "There is not an agency in American life which can so quickly put an end to abuses and offenses in American commerce as those who are conspicuous in the leadership of that commerce."

The theme raised by the president of the United States was picked up on by the president of the Chamber, Julius Howland Barnes. Born in 1873 in Little Rock, Arkansas, Barnes had great success in the grain brokerage business in the 1910s. Once the United States entered the Great War, he was called to Washington to serve as "head of [Herbert] Hoover's Cereal Division and later as president of the Food Administration Grain Corporation, the agency using government funds and trade agreements to maintain a fixed price for wheat and to intervene in other grain markets."[35] In this 1922 address at the meeting, Barnes said the Chamber had been working since its foundation on the "foundations of a splendid tradition of commerce with a conscience." And he denied that "business and industry were solely occupied with the sordid details of making profits." The following excerpt must have been perceived as especially significant, because it was reproduced as an epigraph atop the table of contents in the same issue of *Nation's Business* (June 5, 1922):

33 *The Rotarian*, vol. 18, no. 3, March 1921, p. 100; "Honesty in Business President Harding Pleads." *Wall Street Journal*, May 19, 1922, p. 13; "Harding Asserts Honest Commerce is Nation's Need." *New York Times*, May 19, 1922, p. 1.

34 Warren Gamaliel Harding. 1922. "Commerce with a Conscience." *Nation's Business*, June 5, 1922, p. 9. I said that some uses of "conscience" do not carry the Christian baggage discussed earlier, this seems to be one such instance.

35 Ellis W. Hawley. 2000. "Barnes, Julius Howland." *American National Biography Online*, February 2000.

No man could be called to the leadership of an association such as this, representative of nation-wide business and industry, without a sense of responsibility. If we had ever had a doubt about the basis for that responsibility in business and industry, if we had ever been inclined to feel that business and industry were solely occupied with the sordid details of making profits, the demonstration of the last few years of what it cost in individual distress and loss and suffering when industry recedes, when the processes of trade are broken down, would bring that responsibility home to us at this time as never before.

For ten years the National Chamber has been building the foundations of a splendid tradition of commerce with a conscience; and at this time, in embarking on a new year with a most hopeful atmosphere for business development and restoration, it becomes me to pledge to you in the spirit of that tradition an effort to preserve and to develop it, and to call upon you for service and for helping the preservation and maintenance of that same tradition.[36]

On these ideas—and on moral and public interest considerations in general— Barnes insisted in many of his speeches. For instance, on November 20, 1922, he spoke at the Luncheon Meeting of the Chamber of Commerce of Dallas, Texas, and his subject was "Organization and Fair Play." At the Annual Meeting of the National Association of Insurance Agents, on August 22, 1923, his subject was, "The Service of Organized Industry." Barnes argued that "[o]rganized industry is clearly possessing itself . . . [of] a higher conception of the ideals properly comprised in public service. If you doubt this idealism, think back conscientiously to the code of business ethics commonly accepted, without general protest, as late as ten, and twenty, and thirty years ago."[37]

These snippets from 1922 and 1923 illustrate a more general feature of the public statements of the Chamber of Commerce and its leaders. One recurrent set of issues was the obligations and responsibilities of American business, why it ought not to be selfish, and why ethics and honesty were needed in business. While there was no agreement regarding what to do or what the duties of business were, these issues were not neglected or waved away. Indeed, it would have been against the interests and objectives of the Chamber to neglect them or wave them away. The 1924 annual meeting offers several good illustrations of this pattern.

The twelfth annual meeting of the Chamber took place in Cleveland, from Tuesday, May 6 to Thursday, May 8, 1924. It was very well attended: according to Elmer Murphy, "upward of two thousand business men"[38]; according to the *Boston Daily Globe*, three thousand.[39] Three main topics were selected for discussion: "Business and Agriculture," "European Readjustment," and "The Responsibility

36   "In This Number." *Nation's Business*, June 5, 1922, p. 5.

37   Julius H. Barnes. 1923. "The Service of Organized Industry." In: Chamber of Commerce of the United States of America. *Addresses by the Presidents of the Chamber of Commerce of the United States*. Volume 1, p. 7.

38   Elmer Murphy. 1924. "Business Speaks with One Voice." *Nation's Business*, June 5, 1924, p. 5.

39   "Filene Urges Joining of Stores in Chains for Mass Buying." *Boston Daily Globe*, May 6, 1924, p. 16A.

and Integrity of Business." President Barnes explained the importance of the third topic as follows:

American business standards today condemn practices of undue influence in the securing of trade, and American business will unhesitatingly condemn anything which savors of undue influence in the conduct of industry, or in the relations of government and industry.

But American business has learned to be fair and restrained as well, and guilt must be ascertained by the orderly processes which protect the unjustly accused innocent. Business will not condemn solely on the unproven charges of malice and slander alone. The history of business standards and business practices for the last generation is one of constant advance, and the record of business year by year justifies increasing confidence and securely based pride in the character and the accomplishments of business.[40]

The president of a business association should be careful to distinguish justified condemnation of the ethics of business from malice and slander, lest she alienate her constituency. Barnes was careful to do so. The muckrakers' accusations against business in the early twentieth century were malicious and slanderous. They were not praiseworthy exposés of unethical business practices. More important, Barnes's statement is typical of business leaders' statements about business ethics in three ways. First, there is the trope of "constant advance," "year by year," in business ethics. Worry not: things are getting better. Second, grammatically, "American business" and "business" are the subjects of the sentence; they are agents that can learn, condemn, and so on. Ontologically, they are entities, which have real existence, much like other collective entities—e.g., society, the economy, labor, the State, the American nation, the public interest, the public, or public opinion. Third, the words "ethics" and "morality" are not used. "Business standards" and "business practices" are used in their stead. "Ethics" and "morality" sound a bit too moralistic. "Standards" and "practices" are suitably aseptic.

The first day of the 1924 annual conference featured speeches by President Barnes and Boston retailer Edward Filene—another leading advocate of business ethics and enlightened self-interest, who in the 1930s would deliver one of the Barbara Weinstock Lectures on the Morals of Trade, and who has been described as an "American Owenite."[41] Being the spokesperson for U.S. business, Barnes made predictable statements against "unwise tax laws which might tend

40 "Business at the Annual Council Table." *Nation's Business*, May 1, 1924, p. 60.
41 "Filene Urges Joining of Stores in Chains for Mass Buying." *Boston Daily Globe*, May 6, 1924, p. 16A; Filene, *Morals in Business*; Edward A. Filene. 1939. *Speaking of Change: A Selection of Speeches and Articles*. New York: Published by Former Associates of Edward A. Filene; Kim McQuaid. 1976. "An American Owenite: Edward A. Filene and the Parameters of Industrial Reform, 1890–1937." *American Journal of Economics and Sociology* 35(1):77–94; Kim McQuaid. [1986] 2003. *A Response to Industrialism: Liberal Businessmen and the Evolving Spectrum of Capitalist Reform, 1886–1960*. Washington, DC: Beard Books. On Filene's enlightened self-interest, see Heald, *The Social Responsibilities of Business*, pp. 88–89.

to frighten a large section of the reinvestment capital" and "the lethargy of government politics"; as well as predictable statements for "the methods of the open shop in industrial relations" and "the driving force of private initiative and private enterprise." Barnes also advocated "intelligent team play between Government and industry." That is why he invited his friend, Secretary of Commerce Herbert Hoover, to address the Chamber.[42]

On the conference's second day it was Secretary of Commerce Hoover's turn to speak on "Some Phases of the Government in Business."[43] That was the title of his oral address. Yet, it was published in *Nation's Business* under the more biting (and intimidating) title, "If Business Doesn't, Government Will."[44] Because of both content and context, this is a significant moment and document in the history of business ethics in the United States. Hoover's address deals with the relationship between government and business. He recounts that in one state "more than 1,000 laws and ordinances have been added in the last eight months." He adds the quite businesslike comment that "a large part of them will sleep peacefully in the statute book." And then he raises a key question:

> The question we need to consider is whether these rules and regulations are to be developed solely by government or whether they cannot be in some large part developed out of voluntary forces in the nation. In other words, can the abuses which give rise to government in business be eliminated by the systematic and voluntary action of commerce and industry itself? This is indeed the thought behind the whole gamut of recent slogans, "Less Government in Business," "Less Government Regulation," "A Square Deal," "The Elimination of Waste," "Better Business Ethics," and a dozen others.
>
> National character cannot be built by law. It is the sum of the moral fiber of its individuals. When abuses which rise from our growing system are cured by live individual conscience, by initiative in the creation of voluntary standards, then is the growth of moral perceptions fertilized in every individual character.

Somehow these unethical practices and abuses ought to be eliminated. Who is going to do it? Is it going to be government or business itself? The law and law enforcers or "better business ethics"? According to Hoover, the situation can be described thus. First, there is a choice. Second, the agent who must make a choice is business (he uses the expression "commerce and industry" here, but "business" elsewhere in the article). Indeed, business has a will; it can choose "voluntarily." Third, the choice is between two options, one of which is patently undesired by the agent. Fourth and finally, moral properties, such as "national character," "moral fiber," "conscience," and "moral perceptions" are involved, which the law cannot reach. The obvious implication is that the agent should choose the option that is not undesirable, that is, "systematic and voluntary action."

---

42 Julius H. Barnes. 1924. "Government, Business and Good Sense." *Nation's Business*, June 5, 1924, p. 9.

43 "Business Must End its Wrongs or Law Will, Hoover Warns." *Washington Post*, May 8, 1924, p. 1.

44 Herbert Hoover. 1924. "If Business Doesn't, Government Will." *Nation's Business*, June 5, 1924, p. 7.

Hoover wanted to be even clearer. Business decries government's tightening its regulation of the economy. However, regulation "might have been unnecessary had there been a higher degree of responsibility to the public, higher standards of business practice." "Higher standards of business practice" being the aseptic, businesslike way of talking about morality or ethics, without using these words. Aseptic and businesslike lexical semantics aside, Hoover is putting forward a consequential causal claim here. He does so by means of a counterfactual conditional, that is, a conditional whose antecedent is contrary to fact. For instance, if Socrates had not drunk the hemlock, he would not have died. But in fact he did drink it, so he did die. Therefore, the hemlock is causally responsible for the death of Socrates. Similarly, Hoover claims that business is causally responsible for government's regulation (at least, regulation "*might* have been" unnecessary), because of its failure to be more responsible and have higher standards. Then, he considers what solutions there might be "outside of government regulation":

> *First*, there must be organization in such form as can establish the standards of conduct in this vast complex of shifting invention, production, and use. There is no existing basis to check the failure of service or the sacrifice of public interest. Someone must determine such standards. They must be determined and held flexibly in tune with the intense technology of trade.
>
> *Second*, there must be some sort of enforcement. There is the perpetual difficulty of a small minority who will not play the game. They too often bring disrepute upon the vast majority; they drive many others to adopt unfair competitive methods which all deplore; their abuses give rise to public indignation and clamor which breed legislative action.
>
> I believe we now for the first time have the method at hand for voluntarily organized determination of standards and their adoption. I would go further; I believe we are in the presence of a new era in the organization of industry and commerce in which, if properly directed, lie forces pregnant with infinite possibilities of moral progress.

The "perpetual difficulty," then, is the "small minority" that "bring[s] disrepute upon the vast majority" and "public indignation and clamor." In turn, this "breed[s] legislative action." That small minority provokes a race to the bottom as regards "unfair competitive methods" as well. Individual businessmen may think to themselves: everyone's doing it, so I must do it, or else I'll be driven out of business. Hoover was still optimistic, though. The answer was organization: "I believe that we are, almost unnoticed, in the midst of a great revolution—or perhaps a better word, a transformation—in the whole super-organization of our economic life. We are passing from a period of extremely individualistic action into a period of associational activities." Hoover observed that "[p]ractically our entire American working world is now organized into some form of economic association." Then, the central actor is not anymore the individual, but the association. Luckily, associations have very different inclinations and interests than individuals.

Corporatist or "associationist" notes ring now distinctly in Hoover's words. In fact, Hoover had definite convictions and an agenda in this respect. Two years earlier, he had published his short book *American Individualism*, in which he saw "[o]ur mass of regulation of public utilities and our legislation against restraint of trade" as "proof that we have a long way toward the abandonment of the 'capitalism' of Adam Smith." While he did not like the capitalism of Adam Smith, he did like capitalism. As Fausold and Mazuzan put it, Hoover "always opposed statism, yet he was no advocate of laissez-faire." According to him, "a proper blend of organized expertise, systematized associationalism, and enlightened individualism would provide the ideal blend of order and freedom." The solution, as Ellis Hawley points out, "lay in the development and proper use of cooperative institutions, particularly trade associations, professional societies, and similar organizations among farmers and laborers. [. . .] Unlike the earlier trusts, these newer institutions would preserve and work through individual units, committing them voluntarily to service, efficiency, and ethical behavior and developing for them a new and enlightened leadership capable of seeing the larger picture."[45]

Of course, Hoover's corporatist inclinations should be seen in their historical context: the political economy of the Progressive Era. Hoover was after all the Secretary of Commerce; his job was to represent the state and further its interests and objectives. Calls for cooperation, "industrial conciliation," ethical behavior, and social responsibility were characteristic of the *Zeitgeist* and of what James Weinstein called "corporate liberalism."[46] The National Civic Federation, established in 1900, is one well-known instantiation of this spirit; these groups and individuals worked "[t]o the end that tranquility in the industrial world may prevail."[47] Remarkably, in 1914 the National Civic Federation instituted a "Special Committee on Business Ethics," chaired by Cincinnati banker

45   Martin Fausold and George Mazuzan. 1974. "Introduction." In *The Hoover Presidency: A Reappraisal*, edited by Martin Fausold and George Mazuzan. Albany: State University of New York Press, p. 25; Ellis W. Hawley. 1974. "Herbert Hoover, the Commerce Secretariat, and the Vision of an 'Associative State,' 1921–1928." *Journal of American History* 61(1):116–40, p. 117; Herbert Hoover. 1922. *American Individualism*. Garden City, NY: Doubleday, Page & Company, p. 53; Howard J. Wiarda. 1997. *Corporatism and Comparative Politics: The Other Great "Ism."* Armonk, NY: M. E. Sharpe, p. 135; William Appleman Williams. [1961] 1966. *The Contours of American History*. Chicago: Quadrangle Books, p. 385. See also Michael J. Hogan. 1990. "Corporatism." *Journal of American History* 77(1):153–60.

46   James Weinstein. 1968. *The Corporate Ideal in the Liberal State, 1900–1918*. Boston: Beacon Press. See also Gabriel Kolko. 1963. *The Triumph of Conservatism: A Re-Interpretation of American History, 1900–1916*. New York: Free Press of Glencoe; Gabriel Kolko. 1965. *Railroads and Regulation, 1877–1916*. Princeton: Princeton University Press.

Let me reiterate here that, unlike many historical and sociological studies about this period, my concern is not the backstage relationships between progressivism and big business and business associations (e.g., whether these actually supported the policies they publicly resisted). Nor is it the real motives and intentions of politicians and businesspeople. For an argument against the focus on the "conscious intent of corporate leaders," see Fred Block. 1977. "Beyond Corporate Liberalism." *Social Problems* 24(3):352–61, p. 360; Fred Block. 1977. "The Ruling Class Does Not Rule: Notes on the Marxist Theory of the State." *Socialist Revolution* 33:6–28.

47   *Industrial Conciliation: Report of the Proceedings of the Conference Held under the Auspices of the National Civic Federation*. 1902. New York and London: G. P. Putnam's Sons, p. 270.

J. G. Schmidlap.[48] Indeed, the U.S. Chamber of Commerce itself was conceived and created by the Department of Commerce and business leaders under the influence of this sort of spirit. This also applies to the efforts of the Federal Trade Commission to prevent "unfair methods of competition," such as the "trade practice submittals" starting in 1918, and "trade practice conference rules" starting in 1926. In turn, these supervised voluntary agreements contributed to the multiplication of ethical codes, which I discuss later.[49]

In his speech at the 1924 Chamber of Commerce meeting, Hoover said that organizations were the answer—or part of the answer anyway. Specifically, he said that organizations are able to turn slogans such as "Less Government in Business" and "Better Business Ethics" into reality: "With these agencies [trade associations] used as the machinery for the cultivation and spread of high standards and the elimination of abuses, I am convinced that we shall have entered the great era of self-governing industry and business which has been a dream to many thinkers. A self-governing industry can be made to render needless a vast area of governmental interference and regulation which has grown up out of righteous complaint against the abuses during the birth pains of an industrial world." The abuses are a consequence of the "birth pains of an industrial world"; they are to be expected. Still, complaints against them are righteous. Something ought to be done.

For this purpose, associations are especially helpful, because they can take care of the two practical tasks that standards of practice involve. Not only can they determine standards; they can also enforce them:

> These associational activities are the promising machinery for much of the necessary determination of ethical standards, for the elimination of useless waste and hardship from the burden of our economic engines. Moreover, we have in them not only the agencies by which standards can be set, but by cooperative action among the associations representing the different stages of production, distribution and use we can secure a degree of enforcement far wider than mere public opinion in a single trade.
>
> When standards are agreed upon by the associations representing the manufacturer and distributor, and by those representing the user, we have a triple force interacting for their enforcement.

In the terms of the fifth dimension of the moral background, Hoover is not a metaethical realist. Standards of practice or business ethics principles are not to be *found*. What is just, fair, or morally right to do cannot be discovered upon investigation and reflection. Rather, standards are determined or agreed upon by representative bodies, which meet under fair institutional conditions and

---

48   Jesse H. Bond. 1915. *The Teaching of Professional Ethics in the Schools of Law, Medicine, Journalism and Commerce in the United States*. Ph.D. dissertation. Madison: University of Wisconsin, p. 47; Richard Salvato. 2001. *Guide to the National Civic Federation Records, 1894–1949*. New York Public Library, Humanities and Social Sciences Library, Manuscripts and Archives Division, p. 32.

49   Cf. Federal Trade Commission. 1925. *Trade Practice Submittals*. Washington, DC: Government Printing Office; Richard C. Cabot. 1926. *Adventures on the Borderlands of Ethics*. New York and London: Harper & Brothers, pp. 76–80.

something like impartial governmental supervision. At first glance, these standards seem wholly conventional and arbitrary, like the rules of soccer or checkers. It looks as though, substantively, any rule would be fine, as long as the interested parties agreed on it. But is this really what Hoover meant?

Take the example of the somewhat peculiar question Hoover and his staff worked on for several years: "how many inches is an inch?" In his address at the Chamber meeting, Hoover decided to offer his audience some "illustrations from real life," so that nobody thought that his "feet [were] not on the ground in all this." The first example he offered was the lumber industry conferences.[50] These conferences were held by the Department of Commerce "at the request of the lumber industry." The objective was "to discuss the rules of the road in that industry and its relations to the other industries and the common good. The problem was to establish more general and more constructive standards of practice, ethics, and waste elimination."[51]

In the toil of formulating these standards there arose a question of how thick a 1-inch board should be. It sounds easy. But it quickly developed to be a question whether it should be 1 inch thick when it was green, after it was dried, when planed on one side, or when planed on both sides. It developed not only that a choice had to be made among these four alternatives, but also that this choice had to be based upon a proper consideration for the conservation of our forests on one hand and the provision of a material of such structural character as to constitute a square deal to the consumer on the other.

As Hoover pointed out, "there were 32 different thicknesses of a 1-inch board in current use." Some lumber manufacturers "in the drive of unfair competition were gradually thinning the board until it threatened to become paper." The solution was a collective agreement. Importantly, there were external constraints on the solutions, such as the "conservation of our forests," and, more predictably, fairness to the consumer. As they said at the time, that the consumer should get "a square deal." Thus, the standards were procedurally conventional; they were valid insofar as they were agreed upon, and hence valid relative to this particular

50   On the May 1922 conference, see, e.g., "To Standardize Lumber." *New York Times*, May 29, 1922, p. 2. On the December 1923 conference, see, e.g., "Lumber Standards Set at Conference." *Atlanta Constitution*, December 14, 1923, p. 9; "Wins Point in War on Waste." *Boston Daily Globe*, December 20, 1923, p. 3; "Standards for Lumber Altered." *Los Angeles Times*, December 23, 1923, p. V12.

51   Standardization, waste elimination, and simplification were of interest to Hoover, the Department of Commerce, and several business associations, because of their beneficial economic effects, irrespective of their moral or business ethics aspect. Hoover even created a "Division of Simplified Practice" within the department's Bureau of Standards (which had been established in 1901). George K. Burgess. 1933. "The National Bureau of Standards." *Scientific Monthly* 36(3):201–12; Ray M. Hudson. 1928. "Organized Effort in Simplification." *Annals of the American Academy of Political and Social Science* 137:1–8; E. W. McCullough. 1928. "The Relation of the Chamber of Commerce of the United States of America to the Growth of the Simplification Program in American Industry." *Annals of the American Academy of Political and Social Science* 137:9–12; "The National Bureau of Standards." 1901. *Science* (New Series) 13(325):474–75; William J. Quinn, Jr. 1928. "Standardization and Waste Elimination." *Annals of the American Academy of Political and Social Science* 137:220–22.

framework. However, they were not wholly arbitrary. All in all, the lumber industry conferences bring out Hoover's threefold approach: cooperation is fundamental in contemporary societies; cooperation should result in conventional, agreed-upon standards and practices; and cooperation should be oriented by moral considerations or principles, beyond the benefit of the parties involved.

4.4 The Principles of Business Conduct

Edwin B. Parker was born in Shelby County, Missouri in 1868. In 1889 he received a law degree from the University of Texas, after which he practiced law in Houston for several years. During the Great War he was priorities commissioner of the War Industries Board, and afterward the chairman of the United States Liquidation Commission. Based in Washington, DC since 1923, Judge Parker, as he was usually called, would continue to have an active public life until his premature death in 1929. Among his many positions, he was chairman of the board of directors of the Chamber of Commerce of the United States (1927–1928); umpire of the Mixed Claims Commission of the United States and Germany; commissioner of the Tripartite Claims Commission of the United States, Austria, and Hungary; war claims arbiter under the settlement of war claims act of 1928; director of the Riggs National Bank; and trustee of George Washington University.[52]

In 1924, the U.S. Chamber of Commerce appointed Judge Parker as the chair of an unprecedented committee: the "Committee on Business Ethics." Besides Parker, its other members were: "Paul W. Brown, editor of America at Work of St. Louis; William Butterworth, President of Deere & Co. of Moline, Ill.; Henry S. Dennison, President of the Dennison Manufacturing Company of Framingham, Mass.; Noble Foster Hoggson, President Hoggson Brothers of New York; James R. MacColl, President of the Lorraine Manufacturing Company of Pawtucket, R. I.; Henry T. Noyes of Rochester, N. Y., and George Rublee of Washington."[53] This committee prepared a report entitled "Principles of Business Conduct," and it is a plausible conjecture that Judge Parker actually drafted the text.[54] On April 21, 1924, several newspapers already published it.[55] On May 8, the last day of the Cleveland annual meeting, it was presented to the members of the Chamber.[56]

---

52 Edwin M. Borchard. 1930. "In Memoriam: Judge Edwin B. Parker." *American Journal of International Law* 24(1):139. 43; "Judge E. B. Parker Dies at Home Here." *Washington Post*, October 31, 1929, p. 4; "Judge E. B. Parker is Dead at Capital." *Atlanta Constitution*, October 31, 1929, p. 4; "Judge E. B. Parker Dies in Washington." *New York Times*, October 31, 1929, p. 20; "A Loss to Business." *Nation's Business*, December 1929, p. 11.

53 "Formulates Code of Business Ethics." *New York Times*, April 21, 1924, p. 19.

54 Cf. "A Loss to Business." *Nation's Business*, December 1929, p. 11.

55 "Ethics in Business Arranged as Code for U.S. Chamber." *Washington Post*, April 21, 1924, p. 10; "Formulates Code of Business Ethics." *New York Times*, April 21, 1924, p. 19; "Code of Business Ethics is Now Ready for Framing." *Atlanta Constitution*, April 21, 1924, p. 12.

56 "Will Government Be Kept Out of Business?" *Outlook*, May 21, 1924, p. 86.

The principles were accepted and published as the second "resolution" of the meeting (which overall made twenty-five resolutions).

The "Principles of Business Conduct," the Chamber's code of ethics, consisted of fifteen principles preceded by a short introduction. As a statement made by "American Business" through its legitimate voice or spokesman, it became an influential understanding of the relationship among business, ethics, and government. It was much discussed in the public sphere. It was adopted by numerous business associations. It was even referred to as "the code of codes"—for, "[m]odern principles of business conduct have nowhere been better set forth."[57] For the historical researcher, the Principles of Business Conduct is a terrible source regarding business practice, but it is a terrific source regarding public normativity.

Nation's Business published the Principles in an article penned by Judge Parker, "The Fifteen Commandments of Business." Along with each of the fifteen principles, Parker provides its rationale, as understood by the Committee on Business Ethics.[58] The article uses the word "commandments," but these are certainly not the commandments God gave to Moses on Mount Sinai: the source of their validity is elsewhere. The actual principles are preceded by a telling foreword:

> The function of business is to provide for the material needs of mankind, and to increase the wealth of the world and the value and happiness of life. In order to perform its function it must offer a sufficient opportunity for gain to compensate individuals who assume its risks, but the motives which lead individuals to engage in business are not to be confused with the function of business itself. When business enterprise is successfully carried on with constant and efficient endeavor to reduce the costs of production and distribution, to improve the quality of its products, and to give fair treatment to customers, capital, management, and labor, it renders public service of the highest value.
>
> We believe the expression of principles drawn from these fundamental truths will furnish practical guides for the conduct of business as a whole and for each individual enterprise.[59]

Parker's distinction between "business *itself*" and the "individuals [who] engage in business" is ontologically significant. For "business itself" suggests that "business" is more than the sum of the individuals who engage in business. Business is a separate entity, and it has a function. Indeed, "business as a whole" has a conduct. It can conduct itself well or badly; it is therefore an agent. You can ask *it* to do something or to refrain from doing it. Second, Parker maintains that, when properly conducted, "business enterprise" "renders public service of the highest value." Parker develops the point further by means of a frequent analogy at the

---

57 James Melvin Lee. 1926. *Business Ethics: A Manual of Modern Morals.* New York: Ronald Press Company, p. 182.

58 Judge Edwin B. Parker. 1924. "The Fifteen Commandments of Business." *Nation's Business,* June 5, 1924, p. 16.

59 "The Resolutions of the Meeting." *Nation's Business,* June 5, 1924, p. 26.

PRINCIPLES OF BUSINESS CONDUCT
of the
CHAMBER OF COMMERCE OF THE UNITED STATES

I

THE FOUNDATION OF BUSINESS IS CONFIDENCE, WHICH SPRINGS FROM INTEGRITY, FAIR DEALING, EFFICIENT SERVICE, AND MUTUAL BENEFIT

II

THE REWARD OF BUSINESS FOR SERVICE RENDERED IS A FAIR PROFIT PLUS A SAFE RESERVE, COMMENSURATE WITH RISKS INVOLVED AND FORESIGHT EXERCISED

III

EQUITABLE CONSIDERATION IS DUE IN BUSINESS ALIKE TO CAPITAL, MANAGEMENT, EMPLOYEES, AND THE PUBLIC

IV

KNOWLEDGE—THOROUGH AND SPECIFIC—AND UNCEASING STUDY OF THE FACTS AND FORCES AFFECTING A BUSINESS ENTERPRISE ARE ESSENTIAL TO A LASTING INDIVIDUAL SUCCESS AND TO EFFICIENT SERVICE TO THE PUBLIC

V

PERMANENCY AND CONTINUITY OF SERVICE ARE BASIC AIMS IN BUSINESS, THAT KNOWLEDGE GAINED MAY BE FULLY UTILIZED, CONFIDENCE ESTABLISHED, AND EFFICIENCY INCREASED

VI

OBLIGATIONS TO ITSELF AND SOCIETY PROMPT BUSINESS UNCEASINGLY TO STRIVE TOWARD CONTINUITY OF OPERATION, BETTERING CONDITIONS OF EMPLOYMENT, AND INCREASING THE EFFICIENCY AND OPPORTUNITIES OF INDIVIDUAL EMPLOYEES

VII

CONTRACTS AND UNDERTAKINGS, WRITTEN OR ORAL, ARE TO BE PERFORMED IN LETTER AND IN SPIRIT. CHANGED CONDITIONS DO NOT JUSTIFY THEIR CANCELLATION WITHOUT MUTUAL CONSENT

VIII

REPRESENTATION OF GOODS AND SERVICES SHOULD BE TRUTHFULLY MADE AND SCRUPULOUSLY FULFILLED

IX

WASTE IN ANY FORM—OF CAPITAL, LABOR, SERVICES, MATERIALS, OR NATURAL RESOURCES—IS INTOLERABLE AND CONSTANT EFFORT WILL BE MADE TOWARD ITS ELIMINATION

X

EXCESSES OF EVERY NATURE—INFLATION OF CREDIT, OVER-EXPANSION, OVER-BUYING, OVER-STIMULATION OF SALES—WHICH CREATE ARTIFICIAL CONDITIONS AND PRODUCE CRISES AND DEPRESSIONS ARE CONDEMNED

XI

UNFAIR COMPETITION, EMBRACING ALL ACTS CHARACTERIZED BY BAD FAITH, DECEPTION, FRAUD, OR OPPRESSION, INCLUDING COMMERCIAL BRIBERY, IS WASTEFUL, DESPICABLE, AND A PUBLIC WRONG. BUSINESS WILL RELY FOR ITS SUCCESS ON THE EXCELLENCE OF ITS OWN SERVICE

XII

CONTROVERSIES WILL, WHERE POSSIBLE, BE ADJUSTED BY VOLUNTARY AGREEMENT OR IMPARTIAL ARBITRATION

XIII

CORPORATE FORMS DO NOT ABSOLVE FROM OR ALTER THE MORAL OBLIGATIONS OF INDIVIDUALS. RESPONSIBILITIES WILL BE AS COURAGEOUSLY AND CONSCIENTIOUSLY DISCHARGED BY THOSE ACTING IN REPRESENTATIVE CAPACITIES AS WHEN ACTING FOR THEMSELVES

XIV

LAWFUL COOPERATION AMONG BUSINESS MEN AND IN USEFUL BUSINESS ORGANIZATIONS IN SUPPORT OF THESE PRINCIPLES OF BUSINESS CONDUCT IS COMMENDED

XV

BUSINESS SHOULD RENDER RESTRICTIVE LEGISLATION UNNECESSARY THROUGH SO CONDUCTING ITSELF AS TO DESERVE AND INSPIRE PUBLIC CONFIDENCE

These Principles of Business Conduct have been adopted by the
CHAMBER OF COMMERCE OF NEW BRITAIN,
CONNECTICUT

Figure 4.2. Principles of business conduct.

Source: *Nation's Business*, September 1924, p. 66. Retrieved from ProQuest Historical Database. Note: The figure shows the Principles of Business Conduct as they appeared in various magazines, newspapers, and pamphlets, and as a separate sheet for distribution. Please see the appendix to this chapter for a partial transcription of this document.

time.[60] He compares the distinction between businessmen's motives and business's function and "the legal, the medical, the educational, the political or the engineering professions":

> In considering them [the Principles of Business Conduct] it is important at the outset to have clearly in mind the function of business. It is essentially creative and constructive in its nature. Its function is to produce, distribute and provide for all the material requirements of man and to increase the wealth of the world and the value and happiness of life.
>
> The successful performance of this function is a high order of public service. Individual profit is its direct reward. But it is important that the function of business should not be confused with the motives which may prompt an individual to engage in it, just as the functions of the legal, the medical, the educational, the political or the engineering professions should not be confused with the motives which prompt individuals to engage in them.
>
> Where an individual engages in business or enters and pursues the professions of law, medicine, or engineering, if he has ability and employs it unremittingly and efficiently, he may make money; but that is not the reason for, or the measure of, his success.
>
> Business in the abstract, as distinguished from the individual enterprise, must have a basic purpose, which is to provide for the material needs of mankind. The immediate end may be profit to the individual engaged in serving the public. But whenever a business institution ceases to perform the basic function of business, then it is no longer entitled to exist.

Parker is thus quick to distinguish service from profit. He can then associate the functions of business with the former, and the motives of businessmen with the latter. Making money is a reward to the individual. But it has nothing to do with his success, which presumably has to do with service. Indeed, he makes the rather extreme point that a "business institution" that does not perform the "function of business" (i.e., public service) is not "entitled to exist." At this point the analogy with the professions was helpful. Think of physicians. Making money is a by-product of their being good at healing people and saving lives. Perhaps making money is for the businessman a by-product of their being good at rendering the service they render, too?

In either case, the first principle does not refer to individual motives, but to one fundamental macro-level factor: confidence or trust. Judge Parker rehearses a common historical argument: trust is a consequence of, or has become necessary because of, the impressive development and growth of business. "Implicit confidence between producers, distributers and consumers is the bulwark of modern commerce. This requires honest effort and scrupulous accuracy in the representation of the product." From these facts the first principle follows: "*The Foundation of business is confidence which springs from integrity, fair dealing, efficient service, and mutual benefit.*" While the first principle has to do with the moral concept

---

60 Cf. Khurana, *From Higher Aims to Hired Hands*, passim.

of trust, the second principle has to do with the moral concept of fairness. What counts as "fair profit" and "reasonable returns"? Why would a businessman not try to obtain larger profits and returns should he be able to? Once again, Glaucon's challenge haunts the businessman and the business ethicist:

> The policy of charging the public "all the traffic will bear" if in excess of a reasonable profit, is unsound in principle; and while in isolated and unusual cases it may bring temporary prosperity, it cannot last, for sooner or later an outraged public will take measures to prevent it. The effort should rather be to sell at as low a price as possible to enable the producers to realize cost, plus a safe reserve, and a fair profit, taking into consideration all elements of foresight exercised and risk involved.
>
> [...]
>
> It is in the public interest that a business enterprise should accumulate a reserve sufficient to enable it to continue successfully performing a service notwithstanding adverse conditions, of depression or otherwise, over which it has no control. Therefore, in measuring the reasonableness of returns all of the enumerated factors must be taken into account. Hence the second principle:
>
> *The Reward of business for service rendered is a fair profit plus a safe reserve commensurate with risks involved and foresight exercised.*

Parker agrees with the business ethicists discussed in previous chapters: there is a significant positive relationship between one's ethics and one's bottom line. Ethics makes bottom-line sense, at least in the long run. And the "outraged public" is the crucial causal link. Much like unethical practices, unreasonable prices "cannot last, for sooner or later an outraged public will take measures to prevent it." Thus, an argument about unfairness ends up appealing to businessmen's self-interest. An argument about business ends up talking about individual businessmen. In fact, Parker began this very article by making this very point: "Business has formed and is forming habits of straight thinking and right acting because they are in the last analysis economically sound habits."

The third principle of business conduct pursues this idea, specifically using the expression "enlightened self-interest," and asserting that fair dealing pays. It also introduces the idea of the obligations of business toward other social actors—or its social responsibilities to its stakeholders, as we might say now:

> Every business enterprise necessarily utilizes capital, management, the service of employes [sic], and deals with the public. It, therefore, has obligations to capital, management, employes and the public. No business enterprise is entitled to survive, much less to prosper, without discharging its obligations to each of these classes, and enlightened self-interest should prompt each class to deal fairly with all others, because to do so ultimately pays. But when to the gain motive there is added an earnest desire to be of service each to all others, there is begotten a spirit of harmony and cooperation which makes for increased success. From this is deduced the third principle:

Equitable Consideration is due in business alike to capital, management, employes and the public.

You might be motivated by enlightened self-interest, because you know that dealing fairly will pay. However, if you are motivated by an "earnest desire to be of service," that will pay even more. This statement is like a film spoiler. Spoilers give away the *dénouement* of a film, so reading it beforehand prevents you from fully enjoying watching it. It spoils the experience. Similarly, the very fact of knowing that an "earnest desire to be of service" will be very profitable seems to introduce self-interested considerations that prevent you from earnestly desiring to be of service. Put less in cinematographic and more in logical terms, awareness of these facts is self-undermining. At any rate, cinema and logic aside, you are not "entitled to survive" if you don't discharge your obligations—whatever kind of "entitlement" this might be. Indeed, these are obligations that business has to the public.

Judge Parker put the point even more straightforwardly a few lines down: "The interest of a business enterprise is necessarily that of the community of which it is a part. Enlightened self-interest, as well as consideration of public service, will therefore prompt it to exercise economy in all that contributes toward the creation of wealth." Like "to spring," "to prompt" is a verb that indicates motivation. Both kinds of motives work together: enlightened self-interest and consideration of public service. Moreover, Parker equates the interests of a business enterprise and its community, and this equation, he says, is a necessary one. This is a strong and contentious claim. Surely you can come up with situations where the interests of a business enterprise and the interests of its community diverge, can you not? How much semantic gymnastics do you need to do with the definition of the word "interests" to avoid this undesirable argumentative outcome?

The Principles of Business Conduct deal with business behavior in several domains. The eleventh principle focuses on a particular domain or problem, which had been particularly troublesome in the recent history of business in the United States, and which arguably must be particularly troublesome in a radical free-market nation such as the United States. This problem is how businesspeople and companies relate to one another; the problem of unfair competition or unfair "competitive methods": "*Unfair Competition, embracing all acts characterized by bad faith, deception, fraud or oppression, including commercial bribery, is wasteful, despicable and a public wrong. Business will rely for its success on the excellence of its own service.*"

Last but not least, the fifteenth commandment addresses one consideration that provides the fifteen commandments with their rationale in the first place: government regulation. The last of a list of principles or statements normally enjoys a special rhetorical force, and the Committee on Business Ethics used this opportunity wisely. It wisely picked up Secretary of Commerce Hoover's gauntlet, which reflected more widespread worries in Washington and repeated public opinion complaints. Government says: if business doesn't, government will. Business replies: perhaps business hasn't, but it can and will, so government won't have to:

The growth and development of business and the progress and well-being of society as a whole, demand unhampered opportunity for individual effort and initiative, which is rendered increasingly difficult in proportion to the increase in government regulation of business. On the other hand, methods and practices designed to secure immediate gains, without reference to their effect on the general public or their ultimate effect on the business itself, sometimes render imperative restrictive and regulatory legislation in the public interest. Business impatiently resents such legislation. The remedy lies in its own hands. It can, if it will, be governed and regulated by its own rules and principles of business conduct enforced by the most effective of all sanctions—a wholesome public opinion—created and fostered by business itself. Therefore,

Business should render restrictive legislation unnecessary through so conducting itself as to deserve and inspire public confidence.

The Committee on Business Ethics and the Chamber of Commerce more generally are speaking here to business. Grammatically, the subject of the last few sentences is "business." Or "Business." Business resents regulation. The remedy lies in business's "own hands." Yet, whose hands are these, exactly? Luckily, enforcement responsibilities are in someone else's hands—those of a wholesome public opinion. Seen from the point of view of individual businessmen, however, there is an evident collective action problem. Restrictive legislation would be rendered unnecessary by the conduct of *business*, to which the conduct of one businessman makes little difference (except for a really big businessman or company). So the reason Parker gives to individual businessmen to be ethical does not seem to be a reason for them to be ethical at all.

In sum, the Committee on Business Ethics of the Chamber of Commerce made a significant public statement. Where does its significance lie? For good or bad, public statements are essentially just that: statements. No more, no less. Statements' inflamed rhetoric, high-mindedness, and optimistic righteousness are often dissociated from the people they claim to be speaking on behalf of (such as the rank-and-file of an organization, a whole ethnic or occupational group, the general public, or the citizens of a country). These ordinary persons do not find these public statements to be outrageous, absurd, or objectionable. Rather, they find them to be irrelevant, impractical, or out of touch with reality. Perhaps they do not find them anything at all, because they are not even aware of their existence. Further, even if thousands of people can be shown to have noticed a public statement or ethical code, nothing follows about their eventual behavior. As I said before, the Principles of Business Conduct are a tool in the realm of public normativity, where people fight about what ought to be the case.

At the same time, though, public statements may self-referentially state that they are not mere statements. They claim to reach reality, both describing what is and prescribing what ought to be. They call for action, foresee their world-shattering effects, value deeds not words, and try to pervade people's lives and be lived by. In other words, these public statements tell us nothing about what people actually believe or do. Yet, the statements themselves do not admit that this is the case. Such admission would go against their very nature and point. My argument may be especially applicable to statements made by the most practical of groups: businessmen. In this sense, the Chamber of Commerce hoped that its Principles of Business Conduct would be "constantly striven for in a practical way every day in the year":

> It is the aim of this statement of principles of business conduct to reduce the ideal to practical terms. In this statement the trails are clearly blazed. Practical men can follow them. Let these principles be the creed of American business. Let them be an expression of our ideals to be constantly striven for in a practical way every day in the year. Let them be printed and conspicuously displayed in every business office, counting-room and shop throughout the length and breadth of the land, that every man and woman in business may absorb and live them; that they may form the warp and the woof of the great fabric of our nation's business and extend their influence to other lands.
>
> [. . .] Business has accepted the imperious challenge to correlate and harmonize the conflicting forces in commerce, trade, and industry. That challenge is to the business man, not to the politician, the schoolmaster, the preacher, the lawyer, or the engineer.
>
> These principles simply express the practical idealism implanted in the minds and hearts of successful American business men, and remove the conventional screen which hides it from general view.

4.5 Codes of Ethics

Although in 1924 it was only twelve years old, the U.S. Chamber of Commerce looked more mature than its age. It had already attained considerable public visibility, organizational resources, and centrality in several networks. These facts partly account for the attention the Principles of Business Conduct or "business commandments" received. They were much talked about in the public sphere, and became a symbol of the campaign for better business ethics that the Chamber promoted. One report in *Nation's Business* mentions "300 clippings of editorial articles" only a few months after their publication:

> A surprising amount of public interest has been shown in "The Principles of Business Conduct." Some 300 clippings of editorial articles discussing them have been received by the Chamber between the time of their first publication in May and the first of August. Almost without exception the editorial comment has been favorable, not only to the idea in general, but to the particular form which this code takes. In a few isolated instances, there was a tendency to make light of them on the ground that, after all, they did nothing more than "endorse the Ten Commandments." The answer to this, of course, is that it is necessary in any code compiled by an organization such as the National

Chamber to make its principles general, leaving, as has been said, the task of making them specific to separate organizations.[61]

Undoubtedly, the accuracy of this piece of information is doubtful, because of the potential biases of its source. *Nation's Business* had a vested interest in the amount of public interest's being "surprising," and the editorial comment's being favorable "almost without exception." On the other hand, while the figure of 300 clippings may be an exaggeration, it is unlikely to be extremely far from the truth or completely made up.[62] Either way, *Nation's Business* continued to report on the reception of the Principles. Sometimes authority was appealed to. For instance, the authority of Carl F. Taeusch, who, as we will see in the next chapter, was a professor at Harvard University. As of 1928, he was a professor of business ethics and the first holder of the Business Ethics chair at the business school. In May 1928, *Nation's Business* gives another "indication of how highly they [the Principles of Business Conduct] are esteemed": "a recent letter from Professor Taeusch, of the Harvard School of Business Administration." This is what Professor Taeusch's letter is said to say: "I have for some time regarded your 'Principles of Business Conduct' as one of the best of the many codes which have been drawn up. That this is not flattery, you may know from the fact that I made the statement in my 'Professional and Business Ethics,' which was published in 1926, and in which I sketched the problems of business ethics largely on the basis of your 'Principles'."[63]

Nation's Business carefully reported the adoption of the Principles of Business Conduct by business associations around the country. An "Honor Roll of Those Adopting 'The Principles of Business Conduct'" was published in the September 1924 issue. Subsequent issues published similar reports.[64] According to historian Morrell Heald, "[b]y 1925, this statement of principles had been approved by over 750 member organizations with some 300,000 members."[65] According to an article in *Nation's Business*, as of August 1926 the Principles of Business Conduct had been adopted by 812 chambers of commerce and trade associations, and more than 200,000 copies had been requested.[66] The same article adds that "[i]n addition to this distribution by the National Chamber a great many firms have made reprints in placard form and have distributed many thousands to customers

61   "Almost 300 Ratify Code of Ethics." *Nation's Business*, September 1924, p. 66.

62   While the possibility of an outright big lie cannot be discarded, the historian might conjecture that, if only ten clippings had been in possession of *Nation's Business*, they would have been unlikely to say that they had received 300.

63   "News of Organized Business." *Nation's Business* May 1928, p. 170. Cf. Taeusch, *Professional and Business Ethics*, esp. ch. 8.

64   "Honor Roll of Those Adopting the 'Principles of Business Conduct'." *Nation's Business*, September 1924, p. 68; "Another 150 Names Added to Roll of Honor." *Nation's Business*, October 1924, p. 76; "Code of Ethics Gets 67 More OK's." *Nation's Business*, November 1924, p. 74; "Code of Ethics OK's Pass 500 Mark." *Nation's Business*, December 1924, p. 58; "News of Organized Business." *Nation's Business*, January 1915, p. 68.

65   Heald, *The Social Responsibilities of Business*, p. 93.

66   "Conduct Principles Widely Adopted." *Nation's Business*, August 1926, p. 81.

and employes [*sic*]. In some cases business firms have had the code printed in display form in local newspapers." Not only firms, but also business schools were said to be interested: "Colleges and universities are taking an active interest. In 37 such institutions the Principles of Business Conduct have been used in courses on business administration as an example of the underlying philosophy that is guiding business in America. Several of these schools announce their intention to make this a part of their curriculums."[67] According to a later report, by May 1928, 849 organizations had adopted the Chamber's principles: "More than 250,000 copies of 'Principles of Business Conduct' have been distributed since their adoption by the National Chamber in 1924. Eight hundred and forty-nine chambers of commerce and trade associations have officially adopted them."[68]

Some business associations adopted the Principles of Business Conduct; some other business associations adapted the text to their singularities. In fact, this is how the Chamber retorted to the criticism that the Principles were vague: each industry will have to work out the suitable details as they see fit. The Principles were also criticized for allegedly being obvious or platitudinous: "Is there any interest in an effort to formulate rules of business conduct? What's the sense of trying to put down in black and white things which every man knows he ought to do and which most men do?"[69] Apparently there was. The best rejoinder to this criticism was freely provided to the Chamber by its environment. It just had to look around and claim to be doing what other reputable actors were doing.

In the 1910s and 1920s, ethical codes were common documents, issued by many organizations and professional associations, notably in the medical and legal professions, but also in business. In the early 1920s they seemed ubiquitous, even fashionable. For example, the May 1922 issue of the *Annals of the American Academy of Political and Social Science*—titled, "The Ethics of the Professions and of Business"—shows that librarians, ministers, teachers, accountants, engineers, and others partook in the moral feast. Physicians and lawyers, for their part, had long been in the ethical codes business. In the United States, for instance, medical codes of ethics predate the Declaration of Independence. As Albert Jonsen notes in his history of medical ethics, "[p]hysicians in New Jersey organized a Medical Society in 1766 and immediately promulgated a code of ethics, urging medical practitioners to attain learning and to consult only with learned colleagues."[70] One of the first things that the American Medical Association did was to issue a code of ethics (1847). In turn, this American code was greatly influenced by a famous British one: Thomas Percival's (1802). The American Medical Association had an ethics committee as early as 1858. And in the second half of the nineteenth century the ethics of medical practice was a notorious public issue.

---

67   Ibid.

68   "News of Organized Business." *Nation's Business*, May 1928, p. 170. Again, this estimate of copies distributed is likely an exaggeration; the claim that 849 organizations "officially" adopted the principles seems more reliable.

69   "Almost 300 Ratify Code of Ethics." *Nation's Business*, September 1924, p. 66.

70   Albert R. Jonsen. 2000. *A Short History of Medical Ethics*. New York: Oxford University Press, p. 64.

Besides the "learned professions," the Principles of Business Conduct were pre-dated by many business codes of ethics, from regional chambers of commerce to particular trades and industries. Arguably the Principles crystallized an already-present sentiment among businesspeople and business associations, which may partly account for the attention they were afforded. Put differently, they were to some extent cause and to some extent effect as well. Consider, for instance, Edgar L. Heermance's 1924 *Codes of Ethics: A Handbook*. Published a couple of months after the Cleveland meeting of the Chamber (the preface is dated July 11, 1924), Heermance's 525-page tome is a collection of about 250 codes from busi-ness and professional organizations.[71] While not exhaustive, this is a broad and well-researched collection.[72] The ethical codes that Heermance compiled range from local to national associations. They range from the succinct, such as the Master House Painters and Decorators of Connecticut's, to the thorough, such as the National Peanut Butter Manufacturers Association's. They include all kinds of lines of business—from the American Bottlers of Carbonated Beverages to the National Association of Building Owners and Managers; from the Associated Knit Underwear Manufacturers of America to the American Society of News-paper Editors. Likewise, ethical codes had been a major preoccupation for Rotary, whose own code was adopted in 1915.[73] So much so that "[w]hen [Guy] Gun-daker rose to the international presidency in 1923, Rotary's campaign for codes of correct practice became the major activity for the year."[74]

I have said that codes of ethics may or may not make an actual difference to the ethics of day-to-day business practice. What their effects are, if any, is an empirical question, which requires adequate methodological tools and sampling strategies. Presumably, this is a case-by-case question. For the answer should be a function of the organizational and cultural contexts of the business or businesses in ques-tion. Yet, the student of public moral normativity can reliably observe that in the first decades of the twentieth century codes of ethics were both: (1) *said* to make a difference and be an ethical step forward by some people; and (2) *said* not to make any difference, due to inadequate enforcement, or vagueness and excessive

---

71 Heermance, *Codes of Ethics*. For other useful collections of codes of ethics, see (1) the ap-pendix to the volume 101 of the *Annals of the American Academy of Political and Social Science*, a special issue titled "The Ethics of the Professions and of Business" (May 1922); (2) the appendix to Lee, *Business Ethics*, pp. 187–304; and (3) the unpublished list of codes compiled by the Metropolitan Life Insurance, *Codes of Business Ethics: A List of References. Compiled by the Library of the Metropolitan Life Insurance Company*. See also Mary Ellen Oliverio. 1989. "The Implementation of a Code of Ethics: The Early Efforts of One Entrepreneur." *Journal of Business Ethics* 8(5):367–74.

72 The meticulousness of Heermance's work can be gleaned from a typewritten list, currently in possession of Yale University Library, titled: "Ethical Standards: Revised list of codes of ethics col-lected by Edgar L. Heermance to September 6th 1936."

73 Chesley R. Perry. 1923. "Rotary Code of Ethics." *The Rotarian*, vol. 22, no. 1, p. 20.

74 Jeffrey A. Charles. 1993. *Service Clubs in American Society: Rotary, Kiwanis, and Lions*. Ur-bana: University of Illinois Press, p. 49; Guy Gundaker. 1922. "Campaign of the International As-sociation of Rotary Clubs for the Writing of Codes of Standards of Practice for Each Business and Profession." *Annals of the American Academy of Political and Social Science* 101:228–36.

generality, or both, by some other people.[75] These two positions could sometimes be reconciled by claiming that ethical codes did not make a difference by themselves, but did make a difference with the help of enforcement mechanisms. For example, Secretary of Commerce Hoover found a "steady improvement in business ethics" from 1900 to 1926, which he attributed partly to "business codes," prudently mentioning "their enforcement" as well:

> The great majority [of trade associations] today recognize a responsibility to the public as well as to their own interest. They represent a movement toward a more efficient, more ethical, business practice and a better synchronizing of the parts of the economic machine.
>
> I could point out a thousand accomplishments during the past five years of cooperation, serviceable not only to themselves but to the public. The improved employment relations are one reflection of this new spirit of cooperation. Another has been the steady improvement in business ethics through the establishment of business codes and their enforcement. No one can review the situation today in comparison with that of 25 or 30 years ago without a sense of deep relief.[76]

The president of the National Association of Real Estate Boards, Robert Jemison, made a similar remark. In an article tellingly titled, "Self-Government Must Be Deserved," Jemison wrote that the ethical code of his association was "more than a mere pious expression of good intentions":

> That the code is more than a mere pious expression of good intentions, is indicated by the fact that it is obligatory upon each of the real estate boards affiliated with the National Association to adopt the Code of Ethics formally as a part of its by-laws and to enforce the code on its individual members without fear or favor, on penalty of expulsion from the Association.
>
> An increasing number of our boards are establishing regular committees before whom any person who has a complaint against any member of the Board has an opportunity to state his case and to have any wrong that has been done righted without the delay and expense involved in seeking legal redress.
>
> We shall not try to usurp the functions of the courts, but we shall by the discipline which we impose upon our own members and which they impose upon themselves through our local organizations strive to rectify every wrong that is done in violation of the standards the vocation has established.[77]

---

75 See, e.g., "Codes of Ethics." *The Independent*, December 13, 1924, p. 503; W. Brooke Graves. 1924. "Codes of Ethics for Business and Commercial Organization." *International Journal of Ethics* 35(1):41–59; Edgar L. Heermance, 1925. "Letters to the Editor. Honor and Brickbats." *The Independent*, January 17, 1925, p. 84.

76 Herbert Hoover. 1926. "We Can Cooperate and Yet Compete." *Nation's Business*, June 5, 1926, p. 11.

77 Robert Jemison, Jr. 1926. "Self-Government Must Be Deserved." *Nation's Business*, June 5, 1926, p. 21.

To conclude, whatever else the Principles of Business Conduct and the other codes of business ethics were or did, and whatever their effectiveness was, they have one methodologically invaluable property. They are capable of revealing to us normative expectations: what the ideal to be striven for is; what ought to be the case, whatever actually is the case. They do so as a public performance, part of whose very point is to be morally well regarded or make a good moral impression. Thus, the Chamber of Commerce made a statement before public opinion about the new ethics of business, which hopefully would positively affect the reputation of American business. Further, codes of ethics have physical incarnations or materiality. At least some of them were beautifully printed, using attractive designs and typography, and were then framed and displayed in stores, clubs, associations, and other public spaces. They were meant to be seen. And they were meant to affect public opinion. While a storekeeper in a small town might have had his own reputation in mind, the Chamber of Commerce had in mind the reputation of American Business. Apparently, it was the reputation of American Business that had causal effects on the odds—or "hazard ratios"—of government regulation. Yet, to return to the question with which we started, what is that thing called "American Business," really?

4.6 American Business

The public work of the Chamber of Commerce, its initiatives and its statements, took American business to be a moral object and a moral agent. It was built into the very objectives of the association that American business was a thing about which one could ask what its moral standing was, how it was doing (ethically and otherwise), what its interests were, and whether business ethics was good for it. To be sure, the Chamber sometimes asked, too, individual-level questions, such as whether business ethics was good for each individual businessman. In fact, there was no need to make a choice. They could simply assert both that business ethics was good for you, American businessman, and that business ethics was good for you, American business. Then, depending on the context and the audience, they could place more emphasis on one, on the other, or on both equally. For example, the annual meetings of the Chamber of Commerce tended to elicit questions about the problems of "American Business," whereas addresses at local chambers and smaller associations tended to elicit more questions about the problems of ordinary businessmen. This is no doubt to be expected from business leaders who must strengthen their individual position, the position of the association they represent, and who try to recruit new members and garner public support.

In visible and high-status public loci the Chamber placed more emphasis on the question of whether business ethics was good for American business as a whole. It is easy to understand why: this question was much closer to the Chamber's mission, being the kind of organization it was. This is what it should be asking and discussing, given its role before government and other organizations and groups as the legitimate representative of American business. Yet, these straight-forward facts may make us forget that the expression "American business" does not have an immediately obvious referent. It is not like "American universities," "the tallest giraffe in the world," or "Thelonious Monk." Nor can it be immediately equated with the sum of all the individuals who own a business in the United States. American business is supposed to be a collective and abstract entity, much like American society or the economy. For it to exist it must be believed to exist. It is ontologically subjective, as Searle would say.[78] Then, how did this entity come into being, historically?

The constitution of American business involved at least five general pro-cesses. First that merchants, financiers, manufacturers, etc., hang out together, form networks, exchange ideas. Second, their recognizing one another as peers, members of the same class in both the logical and the Marxist sense, identify-ing their common interests, goals, problems, etc., developing an identity. Third, their starting to use, even if not always, the word "business" and "businessmen" to refer to themselves. Fourth, external observers' (say, politicians, journalists, lexicographers) recognizing merchants, financiers, manufacturers, etc. as peers, members of the same class, having common interests, an identity, etc. Finally, their starting to use, even if not always, the word "business" and "businessmen" to refer to them. While this is not the place to tell a comprehensive history of the constitution of American business, two aspects of it are most significant for my purposes: the organizational and the conceptual work that were simultaneously required.

First, there are the organizational processes through which an organization comes to be able to claim to represent a collective social actor. As the Chamber of Commerce developed organizationally, it increased its public legitimacy, prestige, and involvement in important matters *qua* representative of American business as a whole. Second, the concept of American business came into being in terms of social ontology, that is, widespread understandings about what there is, or what things the social world contains. In other words, it was an accomplishment that people came to be able to speak of American business's having a particular prop-erty (e.g., being unethical or being good for America) or having acted in a par-ticular way (e.g., selfishly, greedily, or courageously).

Part of the conceptual work consisted in subsuming agriculture, mining, manufacturing, transportation, distribution, finance, and so on, under one label: American business. Or, the label *Nation's Business*, as the official organ of the Chamber was suitably named in 1912. Part of the practical organizational work consisted in business leaders' telling businessmen about the selfish benefits that organization, cooperation, and ethics entailed, and sweeping the free-rider prob-lem under the carpet. In this sense, the problem of American business is similar but more serious than the problem of any one industry or local trade association. As one business leader, the active Ernest F. Dubrul, put it in 1926:

---

78 Searle, *The Construction of Social Reality*; John Searle. 2010. *Making the Social World*. Oxford: Oxford University Press.

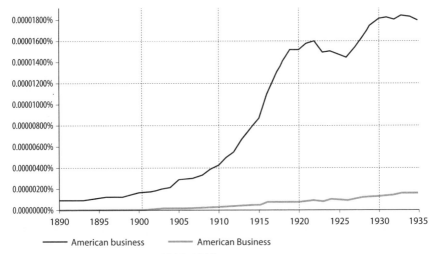

Figure 4.3. American business I, 1890–1935.
Source: Google Books Ngram Viewer. Corpus: American English; Smoothing: 3. http://books.google.com/ngrams

Take any list of bad business practices that, in isolated instances and in isolated places, have crept into any industry. Any one with any business sense will say that if every competitor were to indulge in all these bad practices for a period of thirty days, the whole industry would be so demoralized that they would simply have to right-about-face, or be in the hands of the sheriff in less than a year.[79]

Yet, the free-rider obstacle remains untouched. Bad business ethics, insofar as they are publicly exposed, might be bad for the collective, be it the American metallurgical industry, or American business as a whole. It may affect its reputation and "public confidence" in it. But any particular businessman, if selfish and rational, has reason to prefer to benefit from the collective good—the good reputation of the industry or of business in general—without doing his costly part. American business is especially at risk, because it is a large and abstract entity, which is more distant from the day-to-day practice and imagination of any ordinary American businessman.

Written language use is the main kind of historical evidence to look at processes of conceptual constitution. As figure 4.3 shows, the general pattern is that the expressions "American business" and "American Business" became increasingly used from 1890 till 1935. "American Business," with a capital b, indicates its conceptualization as a proper noun, like Thessaloniki or Theophrastus. It indicates its status as an entity (although "American Business" is less common than "American business"). What stands out in this figure is that the use of "American business" increased steeply in the 1910s and remained at relatively high levels in the 1920s. On

79 Ernest F. Dubrul. 1926. "Business Ethics and Balance Sheets." *Nation's Business*, February 1926, p. 76.

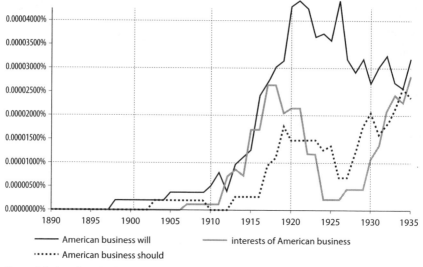

Figure 4.4. American business II, 1890–1935.
Source: Google Books Ngram Viewer. Corpus: American English; Smoothing: 3. http://books
.google.com/ngrams

the other hand, these curves show *that* "American business" was increasingly used, but they do not show *how* it was used. In particular, whether it was seen as an object with properties but without agency—say, like the sun or a banana, which have the property of being yellow. In grammatical terms, figure 4.3 does not tell us whether these phrases' role in relation to the verb is that of a patient or of an agent. In the sentence, "Mary criticized John," Mary is the agent and John is the patient. Was American business conceptualized only as John, the patient, an entity that was acted upon? Or was it also conceptualized as capable of doing things, the way the president of Paraguay might play "Blue Monk," or Thelonious Monk might travel to Asunción?

Figure 4.4 shows an increase in the use of American business as agent. This figure is good at showing change over time. However, the overall occurrence or importance of a concept in a society is more difficult to assess, because what this database is representative of is debatable. Further, searching for the expressions "American business will" and "American business should" unfortunately picks out sentences that are not of interest here, such as, "Some of the criticisms of American business should not be directed to . . ." But it seems reasonable to assume that in general it picks out uses of American business as an agent. Searching for "interests of American business" reveals another interesting property of American business: *it* has interests, much like individual businesses and individuals.

I am now in a position to weave together the arguments presented in the previous sections. The organizational and conceptual constitution of American business is key to understand the history of business ethics in the Progressive Era, because of the following reason. Once there was such a thing as American business in the shared social ontology, it was incorporated into a popular causal

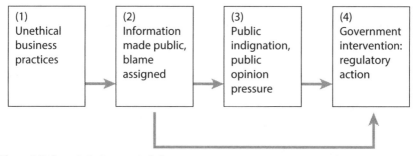

Figure 4.5. Causal stories people tell

story, in which it was accused of bad business ethics, bad business ethics was said to have bad consequences for it, and it was called to act to minimize these bad consequences. In particular, American business was called to govern or regulate itself: that is, to engage in self-government or self-regulation. In this sense, these reflexive verbs, as in the claim that "business must regulate itself," imply that business is an entity or a unit. Further, they imply that business is an agent that can do things, such as regulate, police, or govern. This causal story involving business ethics and American business was a straightforward, even commonsensical one. It was commonly heard in the first decades of the twentieth century, voiced by business leaders, politicians, and journalists alike. And it framed much of the business ethics debates and initiatives to improve it at the time. Figure 4.5 represents the basic form of this causal story.

The causal chain begins with unethical business practices. Then, they are made public and blame is publicly assigned.[80] For example, these morally questionable practices could be exposed by a muckraking journalist in a series of widely read articles in a widely read magazine. At the time there was no scarcity of exposés of this sort, as the Progressive Era was also "the era of the muckrakers."[81] No doubt, at first concrete allegations ought to be directed at particular firms—say, Rockefeller's Standard Oil—or at particular lines of activity—say, the railroads or the Chicago meatpacking industry. But they easily spilled over to the entire class of business, due to the fact that public actors tend to make unwarranted generalizations, and public debates are notorious for their logical carelessness. The crucial intermediary variable was public sentiment or public opinion, and in particular public indignation. Government may intervene independently of public sentiment, but public sentiment can make intervention seem inevitable. In contemporary democratic polities, public opinion can have this sort of force (although, obviously, it does not always have it, and it can also be overridden by other forces). The endpoint or outcome of this causal chain is regulatory action. Even when this causal story did not involve business or American business as a whole, but only one industry or line of business, the unwarranted logical

80 Cf. Tilly, *Credit and Blame*.
81 Regier, *The Era of the Muckrakers*.

jump was tempting—and many were indeed tempted by it. That is, the storyteller jumped from illustrative empirical evidence about unethical practices to more general empirical claims about the ethics of a line of business, or even of business as a whole.[82]

Let me make clear what figure 4.5 is doing for my argument—and hence where my argument is not going. One may raise questions about what really happened at the time. Is the sort of causal chain represented in figure 4.5 empirically true or false? Did journalists' exposés actually have a causal effect? Is this not in fact a case-by-case question, to be considered one piece of regulation at a time, as to what its causes were? Yet, these are not the questions this chapter tries to answer. I do not assess the truth of the causal story shown in figure 4.5. Rather, my point is that this sort of causal chain sounded plausible then, and that many actors voiced it and used it to serve their purposes. The Secretary of Commerce used it to publicly threaten American business, and the Chamber of Commerce used it to advance its public campaign against regulation. In the standard counterfactual conditional fashion, both politicians and business leaders could claim that if (1) had not occurred, then (4) would not have occurred either. Then, they could try to convince businesspeople with arguments of this kind:

(Premise 1) If unethical business practices, then regulation

(Premise 2) No unethical business practices

(Conclusion) Therefore, no regulation

Logically, denying the antecedent is a formal fallacy: the conclusion does not follow from the premises. Deductive logic and syllogisms aside, though, you may argue that unethical business practices is one of the causes of regulatory action, and hence a decrease in unethical business practices will likely decrease the odds of regulatory action. If so, then American business has reason not to engage in unethical business practices. This is just what the Chamber of Commerce argued, even if it reasonably cared more about rhetorical persuasiveness than the logical rigor of its arguments. The main concepts it mobilized for this purpose were self-regulation and self-government (and sometimes self-policing and self-cleansing, too). Most notably, these concepts were examined and emphasized *ad nauseam* in its 1926 annual meeting, whose theme was precisely "Self-Government in Business." In response to warnings like Hoover's—"if business doesn't, government

---

82   One good example is the causal story told about the Pure Food and Drug Act of 1906 (which, however, refers only to the particular lines of business involved). In 1904, 1905, and 1906, Samuel Hopkins Adams, Charles Edward Russell, and Upton Sinclair published the results of their investigations on patent medicines, the beef trust, and the Chicago meatpacking industry. "The Greatest Trust in the World" began in *Everybody's* in 1904 and appeared as a book in 1905; "The Great American Fraud" series ran in *Collier's* from October 1905 to September 1906; *The Jungle* came out in January 1906. Then, the public was enraged and aroused. Then, Congress passed the bill in June 1906. Cf. Upton Sinclair. 1905. "Is Chicago Meat Clean?" *Collier's*, April 22, 1905:13–14; Upton Sinclair. 1906. "The Condemned Meat Industry." *Everybody's*, May 1906:608–16; Upton Sinclair. [1906] 1988. *The Jungle*. Urbana: University of Illinois Press.

will"—American business considered whether self-government was a good thing, and what self-government should be like. The former question turned out to be easier to answer than the latter.

The general tone of the meeting is well summarized by Albert Cabell Ritchie's address: "Business Can and Must Rule Itself." Ritchie was a lawyer and a Democratic politician, who had been the Chief Council of the War Industries Board, and then was the governor of Maryland from 1920 until 1935. Thus, he spoke as a politician and holder of public office, not as a businessman or business leader. Ritchie believed that "government should keep its hands off business so long as business keeps its hands off government and engages in no practices which are unfair or stifling to others." Moreover, business should be more effective than government at this job, and government will be happy to be relieved from it: "Business should so regulate itself as to relieve the government of the need of doing so. It is developing its own ethics, its own philosophy, its own ideals, it should develop its own self-government. Organized business is often more effective to prevent abuses and punish wrong-doing in its own ranks than is the government armed with the letter of the law."[83] Like Ritchie's, the titles of other presentations illustrate well the tone of the 1926 meeting: "Home Rule for Business" by Merle Thorpe; "Self-Government in Business" by former President Julius H. Barnes; "Self-Government Must Be Deserved" by Robert Jemison, Jr.; "Coal Thrives When Let Alone" by Walter Barnum; and "Washington Can't Do It All" by Ogden L. Mills.

The ideas of self-regulation and self-government were most articulately discussed by Merle Thorpe, editor of *Nation's Business*. Reporting on the Chamber's meeting, Thorpe presented the problem thus: "Self-regulation in business! If business doesn't keep its affairs in order, Government will step in and arbitrarily regulate business. What can business do to bring about such self-regulation as to keep in check government regulation? Those were the ideas that dominated the Fourteenth Annual Meeting of the Chamber of Commerce of the United States, held in Washington May 10 to 13 at the home of the organization."[84] But what does self-government and self-regulation involve? Everybody knew, or roughly knew, what government regulation involved. But it was much less clear what self-regulation might involve or require. What is it? How do you do it? Can it actually work?

Thorpe did not really answer these questions, but he reflected on what ought to be accomplished; what the task ahead was. First, he made the customary optimistic remarks to the effect that much progress had been made already: "if sometimes those who are fighting for the home rule of business grow discouraged, it is well to recall that it is only a few generations since business was expected to be dishonest, when the bad old rule, 'Let the buyer beware,' was accepted, when the man who bought a horse or a pair of shoes would have been laughed at had he complained that the horse was blind or the shoes ill-sewn." Needless to say, one should not trust Thorpe's analysis of moral trends, because he was doing

83   Albert C. Ritchie. 1926. "Business Can and Must Rule Itself." *Nation's Business*, June 5, 1926, p. 19.

84   Merle Thorpe. 1926. "Home Rule for Business." *Nation's Business*, June 5, 1926, p. 9.

politics, not historical scholarship. So his optimism is just predictable. Then, he presented self-government as business "policing itself," and thereby driving out or getting rid of crooks and profiteers: "[b]usiness has gone a long way on the road to self-government—a long way in the task of getting rid of crooked methods and crooked men—but it still has far to go." Similarly, "profiteers should be driven out. There's a job for business of policing itself!" Last, Thorpe's report on the conference asked what the attendees took home from it. It seems that the point could hardly be exaggerated: "The delegates took back, too, to their organizations the story of the main purpose of the meeting, this question of self-regulation, the doctrine that 'if business doesn't, government will'."

While he was perhaps more articulate than other members of the Chamber, substantively Thorpe was no exception: self-government was obsessively taken up and dwelt on. It was imagined to be a magical potion that would solve American business's troubles. Further, the Chamber widely publicized what had been already accomplished: "how business is policing itself," as per the title of an article in *Nation's Business* by P. G. Agnew.[85] This publicity should not be surprising, as it advanced the agenda of the organization. But the core of my argument is best represented by the word "itself." Business can police. It can be policed. It can police itself. It shows up as an entity capable of moral action and capable of being morally evaluated.

4.7 The Uses of Ethics

In this chapter we have seen that preventing regulation was a priority on the agenda of the U.S. Chamber of Commerce in the 1920s. Its standard public narrative about this issue went something like this. We admit that American business has sometimes conducted itself unethically and hence government felt compelled to intervene. The solution we propose is that business should try to eliminate unethical practices by itself and hence avoid public indignation and unwanted intervention. As the fifteenth commandment in the Principles of Business Conduct states: "Business should render restrictive legislation unnecessary through so conducting itself as to deserve and inspire public confidence." In this narrative the central moral actor, agent and patient, was American business—or, if not *American* business, business *tout court*. Business had interests, business had a will, conducted itself unethically, was blamed by the public, its reputation and good name were harmed, was negatively affected by regulation, and ought to govern itself.

This is the context in which the Chamber of Commerce got involved in the ethics business. The nice thing about ethics is that it seemed to be useful in many ways at the same time; it could help attain many desired outcomes. Ethics could contribute to the combat against the evil of government regulation, partly through an increase in public confidence and good will. Here ethics refers, first, to the

---

85 P. G. Agnew. 1925. "How Business Is Policing Itself." *Nation's Business*, December 1925, p. 41.

condemnation and proscription of patently immoral practices, such as deception, fraud, and bribery. Second, ethics refers to good practices to be fostered, such as the vague "ideal of service," service to the customer, service to society, service to the country. Duties toward society and the country became most salient after the United States entered the Great War (April 2, 1917). Then, the special historical circumstances put an additional negative mark on unethical and self-regarding behavior on the part of business. More generally, service was used as a moral ideal, and the businessman guided by the ideal of service served as the polar opposite of the Robber Baron.

Under a slightly different cover, ethics could help thwart the two most evil evils businessmen feared at the time: labor unrest and the advancement of leftist ideas and groups in society at large. These were times of forceful and fateful strikes—the 1892 Homestead strike, the 1894 Pullman strike, the 1902 anthracite coal strike, the 1913 Paterson silk strike, the 1913–1914 Colorado coal strike, and after the war the 1919 steel strike, the 1922 railroad strike, and so on and so forth. These were the times of the National Civic Federation, the Commission on Industrial Relations (Walsh Commission), and numerous efforts toward "industrial peace" and "conciliation." Strikes and unionization were major concerns for business associations, the best example of which is the National Association of Manufacturers. Thus, it would be hard to exaggerate the efforts of business and government to preserve the established order. While the conflict between capital and labor is not my focus here, the worry about the good name of American business had much to do with the worry about labor. The idea was that if American business was believed to be driven by moral aims, ethical intentions, and the common good, then more workers would be more content, labor organizations less powerful, labor more docile, and public opinion and government more tolerant of morally questionable and exploitative policies. In addition to the labor evil, there was the (related) advancement-of-radicalism-in-society evil. Then, business ethics could be said to be good for American society—as the next chapter documents.

Under yet a slightly different cover, ethics could help combat the twin evils of the Scylla of monopolistic combinations and trusts, and the Charybdis of unrestricted, destructive, zero-sum competition—which were persistent political and legal problems in the period under examination, and which the leaders of business associations obviously had to address in some fashion. In these contexts, "individualism" and "selfishness" were repeatedly condemned. People did not speak so much of ethics here, but of cooperation, confidence or trust, and fair play. Indeed, the "fair play" analogy seemed to sound highly plausible and persuasive. Chamber of Commerce President Wheeler discussed "Fair Play and the National Spirit" in 1913, former President Barnes discussed "The Philosophy of Fair Play" in 1926, and Wainwright Evans discussed "Fair Play in Business" in 1929.[86] The predictable ambiguity of "fair play" was in fact an asset, because it could be used

---

86   Harry Wheeler. 1913. "Fair Play and the National Spirit." *Nation's Business*, August 15, 1913, p. S5; Julius H. Barnes. 1926. "The Philosophy of Fair Play." *Nation's Business*, June 1926, p. 36; Wainwright Evans. 1929. "Fair Play in Business." *Nation's Business*, August 1929, p. 60.

to speak to the self-interest of an individual businessman, as well as to the fairness of the "game" as a whole.

Moreover, fair play comprises a gentlemanly and honor component, too, which accorded with the gender and class dispositions and views of businessmen then—"the code of a gentleman," as Evans put it. Naturally, playing a game necessitates clear rules, "the rules of the game." It necessitates "sportsmanship," too. Ethics is "a sporting proposition"; good ethics is "sportsmanlike" and bad ethics is "unsportsmanlike."[87] Without ethics, business is like "pugilism before the days of the Marquis of Queensberry rules."[88] For instance, in 1925 the active business and advertising leader, E. St. Elmo Lewis, affirmed:

> Business, commerce, and industry (and I shall lump them all under the one name of business)—business requires many things that cannot be covered by the cold inequities of the law. As soon as men can get to the point where they love the game, where they have a common heritage of a sportsmanlike regard for the game of life and business—they shall not require so many laws . . . We shall learn to play the game like gentlemen.

In turn, the idea of a game entailed the idea of the rules of the game: "For a few minutes let us look at just a few of the fundamental rules, as I see them, of good sportsmanship, and we can see where they apply in business. These rules have greater power some times than statutes—because they are more fundamental. I should like to set down two fundamental things in a game: The first fundamental is—*there must be rules of the game.*" [89] Similarly, in an address he gave at Cornell University in 1917, Rockefeller Junior said that "in the game of business, the same rules of sportsmanship should prevail as in a boxing bout, in a match at golf, or a football game. Play fair and observe the rules. Let the contest be clean,

---

87 Edgar L. Heermance. 1925. "What Can the Club Business Methods Committee Do to Promote Improvement in Business and Professional Standards." Pp. 355–58 in *Proceedings: Sixteenth Annual Convention of Rotary International*. Chicago: Rotary International, p. 356; Albert T. Perkins. 1922. "Sportmanship [sic] in Business and Public Life." *Bulletin of the School of Mines and Metallurgy, University of Missouri* 14(3):3–8.

88 Both Frederick and Heermance stress the sports analogy. According to Heermance: "The code, in other words, is a sporting proposition. Without it, as Mr. Frederick has said, an industry is a good deal like pugilism before the days of the Marquis of Queensberry rules, when nothing was barred. Football would not be the sport it is, if each side made its own rules. After ten minutes of wrangling, the game would degenerate into a slugging match, from which both players and spectators would withdraw in disgust. Business today faces much the same situation." Heermance, *The Ethics of Business*, pp. 22–23.

According to Frederick: "The interesting thing is that this tendency [toward higher business standards] increases alike the pleasure, profit and public service of business. The reasons are, after all, simple; the parallel may be found in athletics. Before the Marquis of Queensberry rules were devised for pugilism, there were slugging matches but no real fistic sporting events. The old-time champions fought haphazardly before audiences of one or two hundred people; today pugilism is a science with careful rules of sportsmanship, and millions of the public as well as the players like the game. The same is true of football, baseball and tennis." Frederick, *Book of Business Standards*, pp. 17–18.

89 E. St. Elmo Lewis. 1925. "Are You a Square-Shooter?" *The Rotarian*, vol. 26, no. 5, May 1925, pp. 11–13, p. 12.

gentlemanly, sportsmanlike, a contest always having regard for the right of the other man."[90]

In sum, ethics was believed to serve all of these useful functions at the same time. The Chamber was not the first organization of businessmen to get involved in the ethics business and make public campaigns about moral needs in these ways. Nor was it the first to get involved in the ethics business with these aims in view. But the Chamber was unique, because of its comprehensive and national scope, and its privileged access and connections to powerful actors and the state. Further, it represented and defended that relatively new entity, American business, which it actually helped constitute and strengthen. Because of these organizational conditions, the concern of the Chamber was not primarily the effects of ethics at the individual level—even though it sometimes had to pay some attention to that, too. Instead, much like the Department of Commerce and the state in general, the Chamber wanted to raise the question of whether ethics was good for business, American business, or American Business. And it wanted to answer that indeed it was.

Finally, regarding the moral background, I have argued that the Chamber of Commerce raised a particular question, which made use of particular concepts, and was about a particular object. It also used particular moral methods, such as codes of ethics. In this way I have brought out some background elements that underlie the business ethics work of the Chamber. The one I afforded most attention to in this chapter is the constitution of American business—or American Business—as a moral entity, both as a moral patient and a moral agent. Once upon a time, "the pesky calf" had been morally bad, it had not "dealt squarely," it had avoided "legitimate methods," and it was blameworthy for all of that. Fortunately, it was now changing its ways, and it had already made some moral progress. There was no need for the cowboy to fix "the skittish creature."

Appendix

PRINCIPLES OF BUSINESS CONDUCT

I. The foundation of business is confidence, which springs from integrity, fair dealing, efficient service, and mutual benefit.

II. The reward of business for service rendered is a fair profit plus a safe reserve, commensurate with risks involved and foresight exercised.

III. Equitable consideration is due in business alike to capital, management, employees, and the public.

IV. Knowledge—thorough and specific—and unceasing study of the facts and forces affecting a business enterprise are essential to a lasting individual success and to efficient service to the public.

---

90   John D. Rockefeller, Jr. 1917. *The Personal Relation in Industry.* New York: n.p., pp. 27–28.

V. Permanency and continuity of service are basic aims of business, that knowledge gained may be fully utilized, confidence established and efficiency increased.

VI. Obligations to itself and society prompt business unceasingly to strive toward continuity of operation, bettering conditions of employment, and increasing the efficiency and the opportunities of individual employees.

VII. Contracts and undertakings, written or oral, are to be performed in letter and in spirit. Changed conditions do not justify their cancellation without mutual consent.

VIII. Representation of goods and services should be truthfully made and scrupulously fulfilled.

IX. Waste in any form, of capital, labor, services, materials, or natural resources, is intolerable and constant effort will be made toward its elimination.

X. Excesses of every nature, inflation of credit, over-expansion, over-buying, over-stimulation of sales, which create artificial conditions and produce crises and depressions are condemned.

XI. Unfair competition, embracing all acts characterized by bad faith, deception, fraud, or oppression, including commercial bribery, is wasteful, despicable, and a public wrong. Business will rely for its success on the excellence of its own service.

XII. Controversies will, where possible, be adjusted by voluntary agreement or impartial arbitration.

XIII. Corporate forms do not absolve from or alter the moral obligations of individuals. Responsibilities will be as courageously and conscientiously discharged by those acting in representative capacities as when acting for themselves.

XIV. Lawful cooperation among business men and in useful business organizations in support of these principles of business conduct is commended.

XV. Business should render restrictive legislation unnecessary through so conducting itself as to deserve and inspire public confidence.

5

The Good of American Society

[A] young man need not feel that the lack of a college education will stand in any respect whatever in the way of his success in the business world. No college on earth ever made a business man.

—Edward Bok, 1894[1]

[A revolution] can be avoided only if our business leaders recognize their responsibility and both think and act wisely in carrying it out. No dam-building process such as that which preceded the French and Russian revolutions will serve to defend the present against the future. Channels and ditches must be dug, to the end that greater happiness and greater security may flourish where social disintegration and economic insecurity now make life an arid desert for vast numbers. [...] The solution, if any is possible in time to save our western civilization, lies in this field of business ethics.

—Wallace Donham, 1929[2]

5.1 Inculcating Ethics

In the evening of April 27, 1931, Nicholas "Miraculous" Butler, president of Columbia University, addressed the Alumni Association of the Columbia School of Business. The occasion was the annual dinner of the association, which took place at the Columbia University Club on 4 West 43 Street in Manhattan.[3] Butler, Columbia's president from 1902 to 1945, was a well-known public intellectual, who that very year received the Nobel Peace Prize. The subject of his address that evening was "business as a university subject," and he reflected on the relationship between practical subjects and higher education. The "medieval university" concerned itself not only with "philosophical and fundamental" subjects, but also with "departments of human interest, of human knowledge, of human action":

> When the medieval university was formed, there were three of those departments of knowledge and action that were outstanding and preëminent [sic]. There was theology, there was law and there was medicine. [...]

---

1 Edward Bok. 1894. "The Young Man in Business." *Cosmopolitan*, vol. 16, no. 3, January 1894, pp. 332–39, p. 338; Edward Bok. 1900. *The Young Man in Business*. Boston: L. C. Page & Company, p. 22.

2 Wallace B. Donham. 1930. "Business Ethics as a Solution to the Conflict between Business and the Community." Pp. 28–48 in *The Ethical Problems of Modern Finance*. New York: Ronald Press Company, pp. 33–34.

3 "Dr. Butler Extols Dignity of Business." *New York Times*, April 28, 1931, p. 19; Nicholas Murray Butler. [1931?]. *Business as a University Subject*. n.p. (According to this pamphlet the day of the address was April 26, but I think the *New York Times* date is more reliable.)

If one had proposed to organize in the University of Bologna, nine hundred years ago, or in the University of Paris, seven hundred years ago, or in the University of Oxford, nearly seven hundred years ago, a faculty of engineering or a faculty of business, he would have been accounted as something more than a lunatic, simply because those subjects did not exist, either in the consciousness of men or in the practical life of men, as organized and delimited fields of knowledge and activity which could provide the subject matter for such study.[4]

This is an insightful observation: engineering and business did not exist in the twelfth or thirteenth centuries. As long as they were not "subject matters" "in the consciousness of men or in the practical life of men," a university could not possibly teach them. Butler made the analogous insightful observation that "the word 'business' as I am using it, as we use it on Morningside Heights, as it is used in the title of the school of which you are graduates, is a new word. You will not find it usually or even commonly understood in that sense much more than sixty or seventy years ago."[5] Fortunately, though, the United States in the late nineteenth century diverged from Bologna, Paris, and Oxford in the High Middle Ages. "Business" already was, or was becoming, a distinct concept and a "delimited field of knowledge and activity." By the 1920s, many universities—including Butler's own Columbia, of course—had a separate school of business or commerce, whose object of scholarship and instruction was that delimited field of knowledge and activity. As of June 17, 1916, they were also collectively organized as the American Association of Collegiate Schools of Business.[6] The history of "business as a university subject" was well on its way.

Next, Butler reflected on the aims of business schools and the aims of business. The *New York Times* summarized his reflections as follows: "Now in the university school of business three things are essential. The first essential is that students should have that amount of preparation for the study of those special groups of subjects with a foundation in the liberal arts and sciences. The second essential is the severely scientific discovery and philosophic discussion of these discoveries, not only their relationship but their inter-relationship. The third essential is that a university school of business must see to it that the aim of service is kept predominant in the thought of its students. Service to the whole community in the largest, fairest and justest sense is the chief aim of business."[7] Butler did not dismiss the "gainful motive," but he did subordinate it to "service": "Satisfy the gainful motive, of course, but not in spite of service, not with failure of service, not with imperfect

---

4 Butler, *Business*, p. 3. In his 1932 report to the trustees, he made the same point, except that he spoke of being "looked upon as of disordered mind" instead of "being accounted as something more than a lunatic." Nicholas Murray Butler. 1932. "Report of the President of Columbia University. For the Year Ending June 30, 1932." Pp. 5–55 in *Annual Report of the President and Treasurer to the Trustees. With Accompanying Documents. For the Year Ending June 30, 1932*. Morningside Heights, NY: Columbia University in the City of New York, p. 29.

5 Butler, *Business*, p. 5.

6 *The American Association of Collegiate Schools of Business, 1916–1966*. Homewood, IL: Richard D. Irwin, Inc.

7 "Dr. Butler Extols Dignity of Business." *New York Times*, April 28, 1931, p. 19.

service, but secondary to and subordinate to service."[8] While the precise meaning of "service" was seldom clear (see chapter 6), it belonged to a family of moral concepts and ideas that frequently showed up in the early history of business schools, and which were employed in similar ways and for similar purposes—including "the social point of view," "social responsibility," and "business ethics." So most people must have gotten Butler's basic point.

In this chapter I argue that these two stories that Butler brought up in his 1931 address—that of business education and that of business ethics—were intertwined in one significant way. In previous chapters I looked at some business ethicists who vociferously announced that business ethics was good for the individual businessman, and some who vociferously announced that business ethics was good for American business. These were their answers to the tough question of why one should forego unethical business practices at all. This chapter looks at early business school leaders who made a different sort of claim about business ethics, and put business ethics to a different sort of use. Their arguments did not primarily refer to the individual businessman. Nor did they primarily refer to American business as a whole. Instead, they picked out another object for which business ethics was beneficial: business ethics was good for American *society*. It was good for the national or common good. Then, they explained why this was the case—usually in terms of the moralizing and civilizing effects of business activity, the demoralizing effects of unethical business, and ultimately their undermining the legitimacy of the capitalist system.

Consequently, proponents and supporters of business schools were in a position to argue that they could make a contribution to society *through* business ethics—or through its cousin concept, social responsibility. These novel educational institutions had, should, or would have social aims, and they were or would become an asset for American society. They were not mere technical instruments to increase the future material well-being of their students. Rather, they would "inculcate and impress upon the students"[9] the importance of ethics, responsibility, and "the social point of view" in business. They would teach young businessmen what counts as ethical and responsible behavior in the first place. As one writer on commercial education put it in 1904—at a time when only a handful of business schools were already in existence:

> Business Ethics.—Wherever schools of commerce are established, whatever their local problems, their supreme aim should be the production of those who have the ballast of integrity of purpose, whose ships of life shall be ever on the even keels of strict morality. [...] Business men, then, need a training which will enable them to see in their occupation much more than the giving or taking advantage. As their service is great, so they may expect large returns. The

---

8 Butler, *Business*, p. 7.
9 *Education of Business Men. An Address before the Convention of the American Bankers' Association at Saratoga, September 3, 1890, by Edmund J. James. Plan of the Wharton School of Finance and Economy. Proceedings of the Association Relative to the Address of Professor James, and upon the Founding of Schools of Finance and Economy.* 1891. New York: Published by W. B. Greene, p. 33.

proper attitude will come neither from instinct nor custom. Charles the Great, in the capitulatory directing the foundation of schools, pertinently said, "Right action is better than knowledge; but in order to do what is right we must know what is right."[10]

By the 1900s this kind of argument, connecting business education and ethics, already had a distinguished lineage in this country. In fact, it was advanced in the very first issue of *Hunt's Merchants' Magazine* in 1839—in the "Introduction" where Freeman Hunt introduced the "objects" of the new magazine.[11] Some time later this kind of argument would help tackle a difficult practical question: why a university should establish a business school; what the *raison d'être* of a university-based business school was. This question was of great consequence in the early years of the business school movement. It required a persuasive answer. One of these persuasive answers was as follows: if good business ethics are good for American society, and if business schools can inculcate into their students (and the business community) good business ethics, then business schools are good for American society. A business school was worth establishing, supporting, and maintaining for social or moral reasons, because of their social or moral function, and their contributions to American society and the commonweal.

In the following sections of this chapter I examine this "ethical argument," focusing on its manifestations and uses at the Wharton School of Finance and Commerce, the Harvard Graduate School of Business Administration, and the Northwestern University School of Commerce. Subsequently, I examine the particular conception of the good of American society that it was underlain by—that is, I delve into the moral background realm. But what justifies such a skewed sample of business schools? What is the rationale for my purposive sampling strategy? These are schools at the high end of the status distribution: Harvard, Northwestern, and the University of Pennsylvania. They are obviously not representative of the whole class of business schools. And that is precisely the reason why I picked them. The high end of the status distribution is the best place to study public morality normativity: what is taken to be morally good in a society, what morally admirable individuals and organizations do, and hence what we all ought to do.

5.2 Business Schools

Horace Greeley (1811–1872) is remembered as an influential politician and journalist in New York, founder and editor of the influential *New York Tribune*—and he is materially remembered by the pretty Greeley Square in Midtown Manhattan and a statue in City Hall Park. In 1867, Greeley was invited to speak at Silas Sadler Packard's "Business College," located at 937 Broadway. The subject of his address was to be "Success in Business." Because the talk was a success—the

10   Cheesman A. Herrick. 1904. *Meaning and Practice of Commercial Education.* New York: The Macmillan Company; London: Macmillan & Co., Ltd, pp. 64–65.
11   [Freeman Hunt.] 1839. "Introduction." *Hunt's Merchants' Magazine* 1(1):1–3.

college's "rooms were crowded almost to suffocation"—Greeley "consented to repeat the address at the large hall of the Cooper Union." Because this talk was also a success—"[h]alf an hour before the time, every seat was taken, and finally, every inch of standing space"—Greeley consented to have the address published.[12] What was such a successful talk about? Greeley recalled the common objection "made to our old-fashioned colleges, that they are not practical": "I know there are to-day one thousand college graduates . . . who are walking the stony streets of this New York, and know not how to earn a living. That is a condemnation of our university system." Yet, he added: "I believe the Business Colleges of our time are destined to rectify to rectify this mistake." "What I hope, then from our Business Colleges is, that they shall educate and send out a class of young men qualified to direct the various processes of industry."[13]

The story of education for business in the United States begins considerably earlier than universities' involvement in it. Private business colleges or commercial colleges, such as Packard's, began to emerge in the 1820s. They intended primarily "to give a boy or girl, man or woman, the technical skill needed to become an office clerk, a bookkeeper, or a stenographer-typist. They were trade schools, and as such they trained thousands of slenderly educated students in bookkeeping, penmanship, commercial arithmetic, shorthand, typewriting, and business correspondence."[14] During the Gilded Age, the number of new business colleges and the number of new branches of existing colleges grew enormously, showing that there was much demand for instruction of this technical character. People like H. B. Bryant and H. D. Stratton, S. S. Packard, George W. Eastman, Thomas May Pierce, and Platt Rogers Spencer led this tendency in education, whose main aim was to be "practical."[15]

The business college was but one of the types of training available before the advent of the university-based business school. For one, there were various types of commercial education in secondary schools. As early as 1823, "bookkeeping was first included in the curriculum of the English High School in Boston."[16] By the early twentieth century commercial classes in public high schools had significantly expanded. For example, according to one survey, in 1915, the number of students in commercial courses was over 200,000; from 1893 to 1915 it increased by 1,270 percent (in comparison to a 423 percent increase in high school

12 Horace Greeley. 1867. *An Address on Success in Business. Delivered Before the Students of Packard's Bryant & Stratton New York Business College.* New York: S. S. Packard, Publisher, p. 3.

13 Ibid., pp. 27–28 and 33.

14 Thurman W. Van Metre. 1954. *A History of the Graduate School of Business, Columbia University.* New York: Columbia University Press, p. 3.

15 Jessie Graham. 1933. *The Evolution of Business Education in the United States and Its Implications for Business-Teacher Education.* Los Angeles: University of Southern California Press; Benjamin R. Haynes and Harry P. Jackson. 1935. *A History of Business Education in the United States.* Cincinnati, OH: South Western Publishing, pp. 27–32; Edwin G. Knepper. 1941. *History of Business Education in United States.* Ann Arbor, MI: Edwards Brothers, Inc.; Leverett S. Lyon [1922] 1923. *Education for Business.* Chicago: University of Chicago Press, pp. 279–313.

16 Haynes and Jackson, *A History of Business Education in the United States*, p. 44.

students).[17] In the late nineteenth century, high schools of commerce began to emerge, the earliest of which was the Business High School of Washington, DC, founded in 1890. By the 1920s, there was an active field and burgeoning literature on the subject.[18] Interestingly, ethics was also taught: "[a]s an aid in settling moral ideals which a worker in business should maintain, instruction in business ethics has sometimes been introduced."[19] In fact, the "typical commercial high school program" might be illustrated with a curriculum in which "office deportment and business ethics" was a required class in the first year.[20] Besides, however much actual business ethics instruction there was, there was a good amount of discussion about how much business ethics instruction there should be—which is not surprising, in view of the moral aims or functions of schools.[21]

In addition to business colleges and high schools, formal training could also be obtained at so-called corporation schools, that is, schools "operated by a business enterprise (usually by a corporation) to train people for its own uses and as a part of its business operations." The earliest schools of this type got under way in the 1870s; then, "[n]ot before 1905 did the movement attain any swing, but since that time it has been rapid and of an increasingly substantial character."[22] For obvious reasons, this was a large corporation phenomenon. For instance, in 1913 the president of the National Association of Corporation Schools was Arthur Williams of the New York Edison Company; and its vice presidents were E. St. Elmo Lewis of the Burroughs Adding Machine Company and Charles P. Steinmetz of the General Electric Company.[23] A valuable specimen for the historian of business ethics is John Wanamaker's Commercial Institute and later his American University of Trade and Applied Commerce in Philadelphia, whose aims comprised moral education. Wanamaker's own assessment in 1909 of the first twelve years

17   Leverett S. Lyon. 1919. *A Survey of Commercial Education in the Public High Schools of the United States*. Chicago: University of Chicago Press, p. 2.
18   Joseph Kahn and Joseph L. Klein. 1916. *Principles and Methods in Commercial Education*. New York: Macmillan; Harry D. Kitson, ed. 1929. *Commercial Education in Secondary Schools*. Boston; New York; etc.: Ginn and Company; Cloyd Heck Marvin. 1922. *Commercial Education in Secondary Schools*. New York: Henry Holt and Company; Frederick G. Nichols. 1933. *Commercial Education in the High School*. New York; London: D. Appleton – Century Company; James J. Sheppard. 1913. "The Place of the High School in Commercial Education." *Journal of Political Economy* 21(3):209–20; Frank V. Thompson. 1915. *Commercial Education in Public Secondary Schools*. Yonkers-on-Hudson, NY: World Book Company.
19   Harry D. Kitson. 1929. "Problems of Secondary Commercial Education." Pp. 3–12 in *Commercial Education in Secondary Schools*, edited by Harry Kitson. Boston; New York; etc.: Ginn and Company, p. 5.
20   Nichols, *Commercial Education in the High School*, p. 446. See also Cheesman A. Herrick. 1904. *Meaning and Practice of Commercial Education*. New York: Macmillan Company; London: Macmillan & Co., Ltd., p. 315.
21   See, e.g., Marvin, *Commercial Education in Secondary Schools*, pp. 5–6, 7, and 140; Thompson, *Commercial Education in Public Secondary Schools*, p. 30.
22   Leverett S. Lyon. 1921. "The Corporation School and Its Place in a Scheme of Business Education." *Journal of Political Economy* 29(9):721–45, pp. 721–22; Lyon, *Education for Business*, p. 328.
23   National Association of Corporation Schools. 1913–1917. *Annual Convention*. New York: Trow Press.

of the Commercial Institute was that "this system of business education . . . has made notable improvements in the methods of work, in the character, outlook and ethics of the personnel in the store."[24] Whether Wanamaker's own assessment is true is of course another matter.[25]

When did universities enter the picture? In 1851, the University of Louisiana (later Tulane University) made the first attempt to establish a business school at a university in this country. As Haynes and Jackson write, "James Dunwoody Brownson De Bow, after great effort, succeeded in having a school of commerce incorporated in the University of Louisiana." Yet, "[u]nfortunately, this project met with little success, and the entire program was abandoned in 1857."[26] The next attempt was in 1869: General Robert E. Lee proposed that a school of commerce be established at Washington College (later Washington and Lee University), of which he was then the president. His proposal, however, never came to fruition.[27] In 1870, the University of Illinois "rearranged its whole curriculum, and the commercial department was thereafter called the 'School of Commerce'." But this school also proved unsuccessful and it was discontinued in 1879.[28] The first successful business school was born in 1881, when the University of Pennsylvania and Joseph Wharton established the Wharton School of Finance and Economy. While courses in business and commerce were offered at numerous universities, there was an interregnum of seventeen years before the University of California founded its College of Commerce in 1898.[29] At the University of Chicago, the College of Commerce and Administration had complicated beginnings, but its establishment may be dated in 1898 (as the business school claims on its website), or, more plausibly, in 1902. The University of Wisconsin (1900), Iowa (1900[30]), New York

24   Joseph Herbert Appel. [1916?]. *American University of Trade and Applied Commerce*. [Philadelphia?]: n.p.; John Wanamaker. 1909. "The John Wanamaker Commercial Institute—A Store School." *Annals of the American Academy of Political and Social Science*, vol. 33, no. 1, January 1909, pp. 151–54, p. 153.

25   One other school of commerce that does not fit into my quadripartite classification is the Alexander Hamilton Institute. Founded in 1909 in New York, "[i]ts aim is to supply a reading course which shall parallel the work in the various university schools of commerce and shall be conducted along the same pedagogical methods, so far as it is possible to that in absentia." Joseph French Johnson. 1917. "The Alexander Hamilton Institute." Pp. 127–33 in *Proceedings of the Second Pan American Scientific Congress. Washington, U.S.A. Monday, December 27, 1915 to Saturday, January 8, 1916.* Washington, DC: Government Printing Office, p. 128.

26   Haynes and Jackson, *A History of Business Education in the United States*, pp. 83–84.

27   C. S. Marsh. 1926. "General Lee and a School of Commerce." *Journal of Political Economy* 34(5):657–59.

28   *Conference on Commercial Education and Business Progress.* Urbana-Champaign: University of Illinois, pp. 1–2.

29   On the College of Commerce at the University of California, see William Warren Ferrier. 1930. *Origin and Development of the University of California.* Berkeley: The Sather Gate Book Shop, pp. 445–48 and 570–71.

30   Strictly speaking, in 1900 the University of Iowa established a School of Political and Social Science. However, its director, Isaac Althaus Loos, was a business education leader, and he led the school in that direction. The word "commerce" was added to its name in 1908, so it became the School of Political and Social Science and Commerce. In 1914 the phrase "political and social science" was dropped, so it became the School of Commerce. *The State University of Iowa Calendar 1900–1901.*

University (1900), Dartmouth College (1900), Michigan (1901), Illinois (1902), Northwestern (1908), Harvard (1908), and others would soon follow suit.

Organization theory has tended to focus on how organizations work, as units, types of units, and ecologically, as well as how organizational forms are adopted, transmitted, transformed, and reproduced. But it has paid less attention to how they come into being in the first place. Fortunately, some organization theorists are now beginning to redress this neglect. As they have convincingly argued, organizational genesis or emergence is a crucial historical moment, whose investigation can offer several unique insights.[31] As it has long been known, the nature of an organization's genesis can leave an indelible mark on its nature and its development: how it was born, the conditions or context in which it was born, and their effects.[32] Besides understanding the organizations or set of organizations in question, emergence can also reveal characteristics of their contexts, much like disasters, unexpected events, and breaching experiments reveal characteristics of the contexts in which they take place.[33] For these reasons, we need more research on organizations' geneses, the work needed to establish them, the people who established them, the cultural tools and material resources they commanded, and the ways in which they articulated and deployed them. Potentially illuminating, too, is to examine whether and how they were resisted, and whether and how resistance was anticipated and combated by organizations' promoters.

Culturally, organizational projects and innovations that relevant others perceive as crazy or useless, or do not make sense to them, are unlikely to be carried through. The character of those projects that do end up being carried through emerges through interactions with their relevant others, and what seems to them

---

Iowa City: Published by the University, p. 178; Clarence Ray Aurner. 1919. "Historical Survey of Civic Instruction and Training for Citizenship in Iowa." *Iowa Journal of History and Politics* 17(2):135–222, p. 204; Norman F. Kallaus and Allen Hall. 1977. *Meeting a Need: A History of Business Education at the University of Iowa.* Iowa City: College of Business Administration, University of Iowa.

   31   Todd H. Chiles, Alan D. Meyer, and Thomas J. Hench. 2004. "Organizational Emergence: The Origin and Transformation of Branson, Missouri's Musical Theaters." *Organization Science* 15(5):499–519; Ryon Andrew Lancaster. 2005. *The Office of St. Peter: The Emergence of Bureaucracy in the English Catholic Church, 1066–1250.* Ph.D. dissertation. Department of Sociology, Northwestern University; John F. Padgett. 2001. "Organizational Genesis, Identity, and Control: The Transformation of Banking in Renaissance Florence." Pp. 211–57 in *Networks and Markets,* edited by James E. Rauch and Alessandra Casella. New York: Russell Sage Foundation; John F. Padgett and Walter W. Powell. 2012. *The Emergence of Organizations and Markets.* Princeton: Princeton University Press.

   32   Victoria Johnson. 2007. "What Is Organizational Imprinting? Cultural Entrepreneurship in the Founding of the Paris Opera." *American Journal of Sociology* 113(1):97–127; Victoria Johnson. 2008. *Backstage at the Revolution: How the Royal Paris Opera Survived the End of the Old Regime.* Chicago: University of Chicago Press; Christopher Marquis. 2003. "The Pressure of the Past: Network Imprinting in Intercorporate Communities." *Administrative Science Quarterly* 48:655–89; Arthur L. Stinchcombe. 1965. "Social Structure and Organizations." Pp. 142–93 in *Handbook of Organizations,* edited by James G. March. New York: Rand McNally.

   33   Elif Kale-Lostuvali. 2007. "Negotiating State Provision: State-Citizen Encounters in the Aftermath of the Izmit Earthquake." *Sociological Quarterly* 48:745–67; Eric Klinenberg. 2002. *Heat Wave: A Social Autopsy of Disaster in Chicago.* Chicago: University of Chicago Press; Kathleen J. Tierney. 2007. "From the Margins to the Mainstream? Disaster Research at the Crossroads." *Annual Review of Sociology* 33:503–25.

doable and worth doing. In the case of business schools in the United States in the late nineteenth and early twentieth centuries, the following questions needed to be settled. Ought a university to offer business education? Why ought a university to offer business education? And why—or why in the world—would a university offer business education anyway? What would be the point of a business school? From an unreflective, present-day perspective, the answers to these questions may seem self-evident. Today the business school is an integral division of the university. Business is an ordinary subject of instruction and research. Of course business can be taught! Are there not hundreds of MBA and undergraduate programs, courses, textbooks, professors, alumni, and students? Of course there can be research on business! Are there not hundreds of journals, grants, and doctoral degrees that resemble physics or political science journals, grants, and doctoral degrees? But this unreflective present-day perspective is of course unreflective. As Carter Daniel has documented, in the early twentieth century the answer to those questions did not seem self-evident at all.[34]

Skepticism about and resistance to university education for business came from both sides of the equation: the business world and the university world. It was a widespread belief among businesspeople that the university provided only useless, theoretical, and unpractical ideas. The university was a place where idle people wasted their time. Even before the existence of the school of business, businesspeople refused to send their children to college, as they deemed it useless as a preparation for business, and a waste of valuable time (and of even more valuable money).[35] They felt that business cannot be taught: you learn your trade in "the school of experience," that is, the old apprenticeship system. In short, as University of Chicago's Harry Pratt Judson observed, they saw an "antagonism . . . between dawdling and doing"; they thought that "higher learning . . . makes its products unpractical, visionary, pedantic, dandified."[36] It was not just that higher learning was not useful or had a zero effect; it actually hurt your chances of success. For example, as historian Irving Wyllie notes:

> In 1881, Edwin T. Freedley, a spokesman for the manufacturing interests of Philadelphia, declared that he doubted that more than six college graduates could be found among the prominent businessmen of the United States. A decade later Edward Bok told the readers of *Cosmopolitan* magazine that of the leading New York businessmen known to him, virtually all had made their way without university training. Andrew Carnegie reveled in the same statistics. After setting down the names of America's leading financiers, merchants, and manufacturers, Carnegie concluded that in every department of affairs

34   Carter A. Daniel. 1998. *MBA: The First Century.* Lewisburg, PA: Bucknell University Press, pp. 15–42.

35   See, e.g., Roger W. Babson. n.d. *Is it Wise to Spend Four Years at College if Planning to Enter Business?* Babson Park, MA: n p ; John A. Broadus. [1875] 1913. *College Education for Men of Business: A Familiar Essay.* Columbia: University of South Carolina.

36   Harry Pratt Judson. [1896] 1911. *The Higher Education as a Training for Business.* 2nd ed. Chicago: University of Chicago Press, pp. 7, 16.

the non-college man took highest honors. Under the one-time clerks and mechanics, college men were working as subordinates, on salaries.[37]

It was not easy to do away with this sentiment. As the *Chicago Daily Tribune* put it in 1907, "[t]he old notion that no special training was needed for such work [business] has been exploded, but the influence of the idea lingers in many places."[38] Similarly, the *Wall Street Journal* wrote in 1903:

> There has long existed a strong prejudice against any special university training for business and journalism. The theory has prevailed that the only training a man needed in these pursuits was actual experience, and that the college was no help and might be a positive detriment to success in either. [. . .] There are still many in business who cling to the old idea that time spent in advanced education is time wasted for a man who intends to make either business or journalism his life pursuit. But the ranks of these are being steadily depleted, and the opinion is gaining force that special training is a needful preparation for a career in either line of endeavor.[39]

Businesspeople had their prejudices about the university. By the same token, university people had their prejudices about business. It was a widespread belief among university people that business was unrelated to scholarship and the pursuit of truth, and it was unworthy of standing side by side with philosophy and the sciences. This belief had an epistemological aspect and a moral aspect.

EPISTEMOLOGICAL CONCERNS

First, there was epistemological skepticism about business knowledge, science, and scholarship, as well as the transmission or teaching of that purported knowledge. Can there be business knowledge? Can there be scientific business knowledge? If so, how can it be obtained? Can business be taught? What can students learn about business in a classroom? And what is the connection between knowledge and instruction? Insofar as business was not a scholarly discipline yet, there was no research, no research problems, no research methods, no data, and no field of knowledge yet. But there was not even a basic sense of what business knowledge might be, let alone what scientific business knowledge might be. This was a good reason to question the establishment and existence of schools of business at universities, which, if other departments of the university were any indication,

---

37 Irvin G. Wyllie. 1952. "The Businessman Looks at the Higher Learning." *Journal of Higher Education* 23(6):295–300+344, pp. 295–96. Indeed, "[c]lassical learning might fit men for life upon some other planet, the steelmaster contended, but it had nothing to do with life on earth. Carnegie claimed he had known few young men intended for business who had not been injured by college training: ' . . . college education as it exists seems almost fatal to success in that domain'." Cf. Andrew Carnegie. 1902. "How to Win a Fortune." Pp. 103–22 in *The Empire of Business*. New York: Doubleday, Page & Co., pp. 109–14.

38 "A School of Commerce." *Chicago Daily Tribune*, January 19, 1907, p. 8.

39 "Schools of Business and Journalism." *Wall Street Journal*, October 10, 1903, p. 1.

should be able to produce and transmit scientific knowledge about business. This is no wonder: the first organization of a kind generally faces these special challenges. Thus, the Wharton School faced considerable opposition from the faculty of the University of Pennsylvania in the 1880s and 1890s. As its dean, Edmund J. James, recalled years later:

> The members of the faculty were men whose education had been primarily classical; whose instincts were against the attempt to make university education practical, and who looked upon all such attempts as this proposed by Mr. Wharton as covert attacks upon the very principle of higher education itself. [...]
>
> [...] The other departments in the University and most of the other members of the faculty were bitterly opposed to the whole project. And even if they did not actually interfere to prevent the progress of the work, they stood with watchful, jealous eye to see that no concession of any sort should be made to these new subjects which, in their opinion, might in any way lower the level of scholarship as the ideal had been accepted by the upholders of the traditional course [40]

Low levels of scholarship might be due to scholars' incompetence. But it might also be due to uncertainty about the kind of knowledge that business scholarship should be looking for. For knowledge about how to make a fortune as fast as possible could not be its ambition. If there is a science of business, its lessons should presumably not be just about increasing individuals' financial success and things of this sort. Yet, as late as 1930, one of the most influential critics of business schools claimed that that was precisely what they did. Abraham Flexner's book, *Universities, American, English, German*, published in 1930, does several things.[41] One of them is to criticize American universities as a whole, as he had already done in 1908 in his *The American College*.[42] Another one is to attack the American business school, even if he devotes only a few pages to it. Flexner was

---

40 Edmund J. James. 1913. "Origin and Progress of Business Education in the United States." Pp. 51–66 in *Conference on Commercial Education and Business Progress*. Urbana-Champaign, Illinois: The University, pp. 52–53; Frances Ruml. 1928. "The Formative Period of Higher Commercial Education in American Universities." *Journal of Business of the University of Chicago* 1(2):238–63, pp. 247–48.

41 Abraham Flexner. 1930. *Universities, American, English, German*. New York: Oxford University Press. Flexner presented an earlier version of the book as his Rhodes lectures at Oxford in 1928. He was most recognized for the 1910 "Flexner Report" on medical education, *Medical Education in the United States and Canada: A Report to the Carnegie Foundation for the Advancement of Teaching*. Cf. Paul Starr. 1982. *The Social Transformation of American Medicine*. New York: Basic Books, pp. 116–27.

42 In 1908, having spent some time at the universities in Berlin and Heidelberg, Flexner "venture[d] to declare without fear of contradiction that in point of scholarship and trained capacity the American college graduate of three-and-twenty is sadly inferior to the German student, some three years younger. [...] The important thing is to realize that the American college is deficient, and unnecessarily deficient, alike in earnestness and in pedagogical intelligence; that in consequence our college students are, for the most part, emerge, flighty, superficial and immature, lacking, as a class, concentration, seriousness and thoroughness." Abraham Flexner. 1908. *The American College: A Criticism*. New York: The Century Co., pp. 10–11.

especially worried about business schools at the graduate level, and attacked with special gusto the Harvard Graduate School of Business Administration—"[m]ore pretentious and for that reason more dangerous."[43] He wrote:

> That business is a phenomenon of major importance is undeniable; that, therefore, it behooves universities interested in phenomena and in problems to study the phenomena and problems of business is clear. It is one thing, however, for economists and sociologists to study the phenomena of modern business in a school of business or in a department of economics, and it is quite another thing—and, in my judgment, an irrelevant and unworthy thing—for a modern university to undertake to "shortcircuit" experience and to furnish advertisers, salesmen, or handy men for banks, department stores, or transportation companies.
>
> [. . .]
>
> There are in the Harvard School of Business men of scientific turn of mind—students of economic history, of the phenomena of economics, transportation, and banking, for example. While then the scholars on the staff of the Harvard Business School are really and critically interested in phenomena, the main emphasis of the School from the standpoint of its administration is concentrated in "getting on"—the canker of American life.[44]

Economists and sociologists, like chemists and psychologists, have a legitimate scientific interest in business and its constituent parts; they produce knowledge of the kind universities should produce. In contrast, the business school, or at least the administration of the business school at Harvard, is in the business of practical training or "getting on." According to Flexner, this should "belong to technological schools or must be left to apprenticeship." When he gets to advertising, his sarcasm reaches an apex: "Advertising *research!* The '*science* of advertising!' What do the real scholars and scientists on the Faculty of Harvard University think of the company in which the University thus places them? The question does not seem to have occurred to the trustees of an institution whose seal continues to contain the word, "*Veritas.*" "*Veritas*" has little to do with the case! The new seal of Harvard University may some day contain the words—*Veritas et Ars Venditoria!*"[45]

Whether they liked to admit it or not, business educators and business school leaders were themselves unsure about the nature of the knowledge they had and the knowledge that could be had. Nor were they sure about the scholarship needed to acquire it, or its usefulness to their students. Yet, unlike their contemporary critics, we should be charitable: how could they be? When trying to raise

---

43 Ibid., p. 162. But see footnote 104 at page 168.

44 Ibid., pp. 165–66.

45 Ibid., p. 168. Flexner's engagement with the business school was incidental to his main argument about universities. He believed that "universities need not and should not concern themselves with miscellaneous training at or near the vocational level." Instead of business schools, he could have made the same argument about "schools of pharmacy, library science, town-planning, social service, etc." Ibid., p. 172. See also Khurana, *From Higher Aims to Hired Hands*, pp. 132, 173–74.

funds for a new school of commerce or when making a case before administrators and trustees, appearance of absolute certainty and absolute self-confidence are *sine quibus non*. But, in fact, that is not a reasonable demand to a new organization and field. That there was much doubt and little certainty can be gleaned from the early conferences on business education, such as the conferences at the University of Michigan in 1903 and at the University of Illinois in 1906.[46] The former was the first national conference on higher commercial education, and it was held in February 1903. Its announcement confessed business schools' "greatest embarrassments":

> The three subjects which have occasioned the greatest embarrassment in organizing university courses in higher commercial education have been made the topics for three of the sessions. At the Friday morning session "The Relation of Commercial Education to the General Educational System and to Industrial Organizations outside the Universities" will be discussed; Friday afternoon "The Educational Requirements of Practical Business Life, so far as they may be met by University Instruction" will claim attention; and Friday evening "The Extent to Which and the Manner in which Students of Commerce should study Science" will be considered.[47]

These sources of embarrassments are alive and well: the Friday morning session on the relation of commercial education to industrial organizations outside the universities would no doubt be useful today. Not even the legitimacy of the scientific credentials of business schools has been completely settled. In the late nineteenth century, the members of the Penn faculty asked Edmund James and his colleagues at Wharton how they could think business an academic discipline. In the early twenty-first century, in his keynote speech at the 2005 meeting of the European Academy of Management, JC Spender asked: "Are we really happy when otherwise friendly people ask us, 'How can you think business an academic discipline?'"[48] Nowadays this question is often asked by scientists or people with science envy. In James's time the question was also asked by classicists or people with classics envy—"men whose education had been primarily classic." In both cases, doubt is cast on business scholarship, knowledge, instruction, and science. Something like 125 years after Wharton, those voices have not been assuaged.

46   *University of Illinois. Installation of Edmund Janes James, Ph.D., LL.D. as President of the University. Part III. Proceedings of the Conference on Commercial Education. October 19–20, 1905, 1906.* Edited by George M. Fisk. Urbana: University of Illinois.

47   "Higher Commercial Education Conference." 1903. *University of Michigan News-Letter*, Number 120, January 17, 1903, p. 1.

48   "Are we really happy when otherwise friendly people ask us, 'How can you think business an academic discipline?' Suspecting us of science envy, they drive the spike deeper, agreeing that economics is a discipline founded on fundamental axioms and susceptible to rigorous analysis, and asking us about business's axioms and what our research reveals. [. . .] So what are we really doing, and whom do we serve? And on what basis, other than sheer opportunism? Are we doing more than selling prayer wheels to those visiting the temples of capitalism?" JC Spender. 2007. "Management as a Regulated Profession: An Essay." *Journal of Management Inquiry* 16(1):32–42, pp. 32–33.

MORAL CONCERNS

Second, besides epistemological concerns, there were moral concerns about business—particularly, about academics' mingling with businesspeople and the spirit and values of business. This reaction was nothing but predictable. Scholars in the United States in the late nineteenth century were simply reenacting, whether knowingly or unknowingly, the very same misgivings that scholars have had in many places and times about business. Merchants and the pursuit of profit have little moral value. Trade and money corrupt. The merchant's life is intrinsically inferior to the examined or philosophical life. Plato and Aristotle worried about "*kapēlikē*" (trade), "*chrēmastikē*" (something like wealth-getting), and unnatural uses of money. Plutarch worried about "*pleonexia*" (covetousness or avarice) in "On the Love of Wealth" in the *Moralia*.[49] Ever since, these concerns have often shaped scholars' identities, self-understandings, and worldviews. One forceful exponent of this sentiment in the Progressive Era is economist and sociologist Thorstein Veblen, especially his combative 1918 book, *The Higher Learning in America: A Memorandum on the Conduct of Universities by Business Men*. Veblen despises the "conduct of universities by business men," a patent sign of which was the emergence of business schools:

> [The] incursion of pecuniary ideals in academic policy is seen at its broadest and baldest in the Schools of Commerce,— "Commerce and Politics," "Business Training," "Commerce and Administration," "Commerce and Finance," or whatever may be the phrase selected to designate the supersession of learning by worldly wisdom. Facility in competitive business is to take the place of scholarship, as the goal of university training, because, it is alleged, the former is the more useful.[50]

Veblen conceded that the business school did not stand alone "as the exponent of worldly wisdom in the modern universities": in this regard it was comparable to the other professional schools. However, it did stand out from them partly because "the proficiency given by training in the other professional schools, and required for the efficient pursuit of the other professions, may be serviceable to the community at large; whereas the business proficiency inculcated by the schools of commerce has no such serviceability, being directed singly to a facile command of the ways and means of private gain." Indeed, Veblen further claimed that business schools decreased the welfare of the rest of the community in a zero-sum

---

49   Aristotle, *Politics* I.8–10 and *Nicomachean Ethics* V.5; Plutarch, *Moralia* 523C–528B. Cf. Lianna Farber. 2006. *An Anatomy of Trade in Medieval Writing: Value, Consent, and Community*. Ithaca: Cornell University Press, pp. 12–37; M. I. Finley. 1970. "Aristotle and Economic Analysis." *Past and Present* 47:3–25; Scott Meikle. 1995. *Aristotle's Economic Thought*. Oxford: Clarendon Press; New York: Oxford University Press; Scott Meikle. 1996. "Aristotle on Business." *Classical Quarterly* 46(1):138–51; Edward N. O'Neil. 1978. "De Cupiditate Divitiarum (Moralia 523C–528B)." Pp. 289–62 in *Plutarch's Ethical Writings and Early Christian Literature*, edited by Hans Dieter Betz. Leiden: Brill.

50   Thorstein Veblen. [1918] 1965. *The Higher Learning in America: A Memorandum on the Conduct of Universities by Business Men*. New York: Hill and Wang, p. 149.

fashion: "[t]he greater the number and the higher the proficiency of the community's businessmen, other things equal, the worse must the rest of the community come off in that game of skilled bargaining and shrewd management by which the businessmen get their gains."[51]

Veblen was not alone in this sort of criticism. He was not alone then, in the first decades of the twentieth century. And he is still in good company—for, in the almost 100 years since he wrote that book, his worries have only become more worrisome. Much like critics of capitalism and the market have continuously argued that its spirit and values corrupt the morals of society, critics of the business school have continuously argued that its spirit and values corrupt the morals of the university. If market values have "destructive" effects on society and "colonize the lifeworld," they likewise have such effects on the university. If the market leads to the morally reprehensible commodification of everything—from "the services of an Indian surrogate mother to carry a pregnancy" to "the right to immigrate to the United States"—it likewise leads to the morally reprehensible commodification of knowledge and education.[52]

The business school has had the dubious honor of being commonly associated with these aspects of marketization and commodification under capitalism. It has even been viewed as an informal associate or representative of the market and its values, which dwells within the walls of the ivory tower, and which threatens to conquer and transform the *ethos* of scholarship and the pure pursuit of truth. Again, the point is not whether this might have been accurate, but rather that it was represented as such. That this representation could show up in humor reveals that it was indeed a common one, which everybody would get, whether they agreed with it or not (humor is in this sense uniquely telling). In 1925, a whole issue of the *Harvard Lampoon* was devoted to lampooning the business school. Here again a picture is worth a thousand words (see figure 5.1).

The contrast between the university president of yesterday and the university president of tomorrow suggests another dimension of the clash between the scholar and the businessman, which was salient in the debates about university-based business schools. Businesspeople are eminently practical people, while scholars are eminently impractical people, even suspicious of anything too practical. This suspicion may be built into their identity. They may even be proud of their practical incompetence. For instance, Harry Pratt Judson describes this view of the scholar (with which he disagrees) as follows:

51 Ibid., pp. 151–153.
52 Fourcade and Healy, "Moral Views of Market Society"; Steven Lukes. 2005. "Invasions of the Market." Pp. 289–312 in *Worlds of Capitalism: Institutions, Governance and Economic Change in the Era of Globalization*, edited by Max Miller. London; New York: Routledge; Margaret Radin. 1996. *Contested Commodities: The Trouble with Trade in Sex, Children, Body Parts, and Other Things*. Cambridge, MA: Harvard University Press; Sandel, *What Money Can't Buy*, p. 3. On universities in particular, see Derek Bok. 2003. *Universities in the Marketplace: The Commercialization of Higher Education*. Princeton: Princeton University Press; Sheila Slaughter and Gary Rhoades. 2004. *Academic Capitalism and the New Economy: Markets, State, and Higher Education*. Baltimore: Johns Hopkins University Press; Jennifer Washburn. 2005. *University, Inc.: The Corporate Corruption of Higher Education*. New York: Basic Books.

The University President of yesterday and—

The University President of tomorrow

OVERHEAD

INFLATION

UNDERHAND

DEFLATION

Figure 5.1. The *Harvard Lampoon* lampoons business education.
Source: *Harvard Lampoon: Business School Number*, vol. 88, no. 8, January 28, 1925. Figure is at pp. 360–61. Thanks to the *Harvard Lampoon* for permission to reproduce this illustration.
(Left) The University President of yesterday. This is Harvard President (1869-1909) Charles William Eliot, although the *Harvard Lampoon* does not explicitly say it.
(Right) The University President of tomorrow. This is Wallace B. Donham, Dean of the Harvard Graduate School of Business Administration (1919-1942), although the *Harvard Lampoon* does not explicitly say it.

Clergymen and authors and college professors sometimes take a sort of pride in being unpractical. They live in a land of dreams, but the butcher and the baker will not take their pay in dreams. Yet the habit of "high thinking" apparently takes these dreamers so very high in the air that they have learned a lofty contempt for the ground. "Mere material considerations" are vulgar. A new aristocracy has grown up among us—the aristocracy of "culture." And just as the old French noblesse disdained manual labor as a peasantly employment, so our modern intellectual noblesse are apt to despise all business as uninteresting, sordid, common. "Practical"—this word to numbers of our educated men, especially in their earlier years, is like a red rag to a bull.[53]

53   Harry Pratt Judson. [1896] 1911. *The Higher Education as a Training for Business*. 2nd ed. Chicago: University of Chicago Press, pp. 7–8.

This description brings out what businesspeople found wanting in and complained about college graduates in general—not only "clergymen and authors and college professors." On the other hand, their complaint loses some force in light of American universities' not fitting very well the prototype of an impractical institution. For one thing, they have provided moral education and guidance rather than purely theoretical knowledge—including but not limited to the traditional college. For another, they have provided applicable and "useful knowledge," even materially useful, rather than purely theoretical knowledge—especially some universities and in some regions, e.g., those established under the auspices of the Morrill Land Grant Act (1862).[54] Plus, the American universities are a diverse class, so few generalizations seem possible. Even the great transformations in higher education of the late nineteenth century did not intend to do away with morality, but rather to reconstitute it in a way compatible with the scientific worldview and the emerging model of a university. Even if the capstone senior moral philosophy class was done away with, extracurricular activities were thought to replace its moral influence.[55] In these regards, the American university is exceptional. Its culture and organizational identity have not always relied on the idea of an ivory tower, disassociated from the contingencies and urgencies of real life.[56] Then, how should Judson's point be interpreted? Perhaps the right inference from it is not that most authors and college professors had "a lofty contempt for the ground." It might rather be that such contempt, when it existed (and, indeed, it did), provoked opposition. For example, in other nations such contempt on the part of authors and college professors might have been taken for granted, or seen as a good thing, or at least as unchangeable, and therefore not opposed.

Apprehensions of this sort would not dissipate any time soon, even after business schools had granted thousands of degrees, their holders had successful careers in business, and their faculty had produced an enormous amount of scholarship. Their persistence in the face of these degrees, curricula, professors, conferences, lavish endowments, and impressive buildings—not to mention the income they generate—is an indicator of their potency and resonance. Nor would the "watchful and jealous eye" of business school professors' colleagues dissipate any time soon. They could even turn into hostility and humiliation, or, as

54   Roger L. Geiger. 2000. "The Rise and Fall of Useful Knowledge: Higher Education for Science, Agriculture, and the Mechanic Arts, 1850–1875." Pp. 153–68 in *The American College in the Nineteenth Century*, edited by Roger Geiger. Nashville, TN: Vanderbilt University Press; Roger L. Geiger 1986. *To Advance Knowledge: The Growth of American Research Universities, 1900–1940*. New York: Oxford University Press; George M. Marsden. 1994. *The Soul of the American University: From Protestant Establishment to Established Nonbelief*. New York: Oxford University Press; Julie A. Reuben. 1996. *The Making of the Modern University: Intellectual Transformation and the Marginalization of Morality*. Chicago: University of Chicago Press; Laurence R. Veysey. 1965. *The Emergence of the American University*. Chicago: University of Chicago Press.
55   Reuben, *The Making of the Modern University*, p. 255 and *passim*.
56   On organizational identity, see Andrew D. Brown and Ken Starkey. 2000. "Organizational Identity and Learning: A Psychodynamic Perspective." *Academy of Management Review* 25(1):102–20; Dennis A. Gioia, Majken Schultz, and Kevin G. Corley. 2000. "Organizational Identity, Image, and Adaptive Instability." *Academy of Management Review* 25(1):63–81.

significantly, fear and myths of hostility and humiliation. This is well illustrated by Abraham Gitlow, former dean of the New York University business school. In his 1995 "centennial" retrospective of his school, Gitlow tells the following "apocryphal story" about Dean Madden (1925-1948):

> An apocryphal story about Dean John T. Madden circulated among the faculty when I came to the School of Commerce in 1947. The story captured and revealed a significant segment of the range of attitudes about undergraduate professional education for business which characterized the Faculty of Arts and Sciences and the Faculty of Commerce at the time.
>
> It was said that at a meeting of deans, Dean Madden was chided by his Arts and Sciences colleagues for presiding over a school that prostituted higher education. To which Dean Madden was reported to reply that there was one thing worse than being a prostitute, and that was to be the pimp living off her earnings.[57]

5.3 The Intellectual and the Ethical Arguments

Novel, original, unprecedented social things rarely have an easy time of it—be it in the realm of education, culture, politics, organizations, philosophy, or science. Unlike that which is only partially novel or original, that which is truly novel or original may not make any sense to people. They may not know what to do with it; it may even offend their sensibilities. Besides, it must overcome routines and inertias, behavioral and cognitive. As if that were not enough, it might also conflict with the interests of powerful gatekeepers. The university-based business school was no exception. In view of all the resistance, skepticism, and cultural and institutional obstacles that the previous section presented, how come universities *did* establish business schools in the end? As I put it earlier: Ought a university to offer business education? Why ought a university to offer business education? And why (in the world) would a university offer business education anyway?

There are two different historical issues that these questions bring up, only one of which concerns public moral normativity. Universities have rules that stipulate how decisions are made. To be able to make the decision to begin to offer business education, you must occupy the position that the organization's rules stipulate. The people who occupy these positions have interests, goals, and constraints. So does a university *qua* organization. So, the first issue is what caused or motivated these people to do the actions that resulted in business schools being founded.

57 Abraham L. Gitlow. 1995. *New York University's Stern School of Business: A Centennial Retrospective.* New York; London: New York University Press, p. 19. Gitlow goes on to comment that the school's "cash cow" status did lessen the opposition: "[w]hile the rejoinder was clever, note that it chose to attack the morals of the accuser rather than reject the substance of the accusation. Indeed, it is probably true that a substantial part of the Arts and Sciences shared the sentiment that undergraduate professional education for business was inferior and tolerated only because it generated large tuition revenues for the university."

What made a professor of political economy show up at the office of the president of Erehwon University and say something like, "I think it'd be a good idea to establish a school of commerce, because of this-and-that reason."[58] Or what made a wealthy banker write a check to underwrite a new business school. These are why-questions about motives.[59] What did these people act from or out of? What psychological mechanisms, conscious or unconscious, help explain their doing what they did? Logically, the next question is what made the professor of political economy, the president, and the banker think it a good idea to establish a school of commerce. Here two sociological factors suggest themselves. First, the effective existence of a demand for business education, which the business community effectively made known. Second, the increase in the proportion and absolute numbers of college graduates who went into business rather than the traditional professions (which, in turn, is partly accounted for by the expansion of higher education in the Progressive Era). Thus, the professor of political economy might have realized that a business school should have high enrollments and predicted that in the long run it would be financially profitable. Or he might have predicted that a younger generation of businessmen would be more likely to hire someone who could produce an Erehwon University diploma. These realizations motivated him to show up at the office of the president.

The second issue is the justification of business schools in the public sphere: what arguments were advanced and defended as to why a university ought to offer business education. Organizations need culturally satisfactory reasons and justifications to implement change. In fact, it is only through cultural lenses or prisms that societies as well as organizations come to identify their needs or "objective functional requirements" in the first place. More generally: from time to time, under certain conditions, in particular situations, questions arise as to why social things are the way they are, or will change in the proposed manner, or why you performed or will have to perform a certain action. These questions call for explanations, accounts, reasons, and justifications. These justifications range from minor, run-of-the-mill policies and actions, to the most basic foundations of a society—for example, how existing institutions and inequalities are justified each time it is politically or socially necessary to do so; or why people who are born economically disadvantaged or physically handicapped are not properly compensated, given that it is not their fault but sheer chance.

For a university to establish a business school in the early years of the field—before it became evident that that was an acceptable course of action—it needed a publicly valid reason to do so. As economist Harvey Wooster, then of the University of Missouri and soon of Tufts College, put it in 1919: "We are so constituted that any innovation must justify itself before it becomes a recognized part of

58 I borrow the name of this university not from Samuel Butler but from Leon Marshall: L. C. Marshall 1926 "The Collegiate School of Business at Erehwon." *Journal of Political Economy* 34(3):289–326.

59 Cf. John Levi Martin. 2011. *The Explanation of Social Action*. New York: Oxford University Press.

our established institutions."[60] But this was not a one-off affair. Once established, the business school, like many organizations, had to periodically reaffirm its legitimacy and usefulness. It needed arguments and reasons consonant with public normativity, including prevalent conceptions about the role of a university. And it had to be the sort of arguments and reasons that a respected higher education institution in this country was permitted and expected to have. In this regard, it would have sufficed neither to invoke the demands from business circles, nor the existence of a demand for the new "product." These were reasonable *pro tanto* reasons, but they only went so far. Nor would it have sufficed to invoke the benefits drawn by American business as a social sector or class—else, business schools would be merely "servants of the business group to be supported at the expense of business for its own benefit."[61]

Much less would it have sufficed to invoke the benefits drawn by individual students—as Northwestern's Ralph Heilman noted, "[m]erely training young men to increase their earning capacity does not constitute adequate justification for the inclusion of business instruction in university curricula." The interpretative emphasis should be placed on the word "merely," which Heilman was not alone in choosing to use.[62] For example, we find the same telling word choice in the book, *University Education for Business*, by Wharton's James Bossard and Frederic Dewhurst: "Surely the universities, and especially the professional schools preparing young men for future business leadership, would be derelict in the discharge of their responsibilities unless they placed primary emphasis upon these broader ethical responsibilities rather than upon the mere technique of money-getting."[63] Likewise, the financial benefits that a university might potentially reap from its business school—the "cash cow" argument—did not qualify as a satisfactory public reason either (besides, they could not be certain that the business school would turn out to be financially profitable).

No doubt, some people did talk about a "pressing need," which they took to be a significant consideration. Actually, it would have been crazy not to. But this did not seem to suffice by itself to justify such a contentious educational innovation. Further, perhaps the demand for business education could have been met by the vocational business colleges and commercial high schools that proliferated at the time. Indeed, this very argument was appealed to in the late nineteenth century by Columbia University to decline the New York Chamber of Commerce's offer to support "adequate commercial training."[64] Why should that demand be met by pres-

---

60   Harvey Alden Wooster. 1919. "University Schools of Business and a New Business Ethics." *Journal of Political Economy* 27(1):47–63, p. 47.

61   Ibid., p. 53.

62   Ralph E. Heilman. 1930. "Ethical Standards in Business and in Business Education." Pp. 3–27 in *The Ethical Problems of Modern Finance*. New York: Ronald Press Company, p. 21.

63   James H. S. Bossard and J. Frederic Dewhurst. 1931. *University Education for Business: A Study of Existing Needs and Practices*. Philadelphia: University of Pennsylvania Press, pp. 14–15.

64   As Columbia economist Edwin R. A. Seligman recounted, "[t]oward the end of the last century the interest [. . .] became so strong that the Chamber of Commerce of New York was ready to grant an annual subvention to Columbia if it should be decided to develop courses of the desired

tigious academic institutions, which apparently are primarily (even if not solely) devoted to the acquisition and dissemination of knowledge and science and truth?

THE ARGUMENTS

What reasons and justifications did business school advocates put forward in the late nineteenth and early twentieth centuries, then? Why, according to them, ought the university to offer business education? I argue that two arguments were most prominent in public debates and representations, and appeared to do the justificatory trick. The first I call "the intellectual argument," and had to do with business having recently become an intellectual endeavor, due to economic, social, and technological transformations. The second I call "the ethical argument," and had to do with business ethics in two complementary ways: business being by nature an ethical endeavor and businesspeople not being ethical enough. There was certainly no agreement regarding the relative weights of these two arguments. In fact, some people rejected the former as an insufficient foundation for a business school. Some other people did not take the latter into account at all. Yet some other people combined the two in one way or another, sometimes helping themselves to a helpful analogy. A profession, says a standard definition, must be based on a body of esoteric knowledge, and must be oriented toward service or moral aims, not self-interest or profit-making. Rhetorically, drawing an analogy between business and medicine, law, and theology proved quite persuasive. As Louis Brandeis—and literally hundreds of others—said time and again, "[b]usiness should be, and to some extent already is, one of the professions." Like in the other professions, "[i]n the field of modern business . . . mere money-making cannot be regarded as the legitimate end."[65]

The intellectual argument went something like this. The world in general and the business world in particular have recently undergone significant changes. In particular, they are much more complex than ever before. In the nineteenth century one could successfully run a business without any formal training. Moreover, businesses were generally small organizations, and were generally managed by their owners. By contrast, in the twentieth century success in business requires a great deal of knowledge. To quote Wharton's dean Edmund J. James, "[m]odern business is becoming more complex and requires a higher order of talent and a higher degree of preparation in order to secure success than ever before."[66]

character." Ccligman mentions several reasons why Columbia decided to decline the offer: the demand was not big enough, lack of qualified instructors and literature on the subject, Columbia's desire at the time to emphasize its political science instruction, and the belief that commercial high schools could fill the gap by themselves. Edwin R. A. Seligman. 1916. "A University School of Business." Reprinted from *Columbia University Quarterly*, vol. 18, no. 3, June 1916; T . W. Van Metre. 1954. *A History of the Graduate School of Business, Columbia University*. New York: Columbia University Press, pp. 13–14.

    65   Louis D. Brandeis. [1912] 1914. *Business—A Profession*. Boston: Small, Maynard & Company, pp. 1, 5. Cf. Khurana, *From Higher Aims to Hired Hands*, passim.

    66   Edmund J. James. 1901. "Relation of the College and University to Higher Commercial Education." *Publications of the American Economic Association*, 3rd Series, vol. 2, no. 1, pp. 144–65, p 155.

Crucially, knowledge does not mean technique. That could be offered by a business college or commercial high school. Rather, it means knowledge of business facts and theories; of social relations, political economy, history, and the law. This knowledge is necessary for the businessperson to understand the complex business world, and hence for them to be able to make the right business decisions. Therefore, business has become an intellectual endeavor, which must be taught in the most intellectual of institutions: the university.

An instructive illustration of the intellectual argument is provided by Leverett S. Lyon, author of the comprehensive, 600-page volume, *Education for Business* (1922):

> The mental equipment of a business man needs to be greater to-day than was ever before necessary. Just as the sphere of a business man's actions has broadened with the advent of rapid transportation, telegraphs, cables, and telephones, so has the need for broad understanding of sound principles increased. It was steam processes of transportation and production that really made technical education necessary. The electric dynamo created the demand for technically educated electrical engineers. So the railroad, the fast steamship, the electric current in the telephone and cable, and the great economic fact of gigantic and far-reaching business combinations, are making the science of business a different thing of any conception of commerce which could have been had when Girard was the most successful of American business men. The enlarged scope of business is demanding better trained men—men who understand principles. New forces have made possible large scale production, and we need men who can comprehend the relation of that production to the world's markets. There has been introduced such complexity into modern business, and such a high degree of specialization, that the young man who begins without the foundation of an exceptional training is in danger of remaining a mere clerk or bookkeeper. Commercial and industrial affairs are conducted on so large a scale that the neophyte has little chance to learn broadly either by observation or experience.

Lyon takes Philadelphia merchant and banker Stephen Girard (1750–1831) to exemplify the times gone by. Girard did well in the past, but today his innate intuition or skill would not have sufficed. Today success requires acquaintance with "the science of business." For "[c]onditions have vastly changed. A new order of equipment is demanded. The staunchness of character, the same intrepid will, today will play their part as they played it then, but in addition there is now demanded a breadth of technical knowledge, a fund of specialized information, a comprehension of intricate relations, and an understanding of broad principles which the conditions of a century or even a generation ago did not make imperative."[67] If business was so complex, if business relations were so intricate, then high-quality thought and research was needed to understand it. It is after all

---

67 Lyon, *Education for Business*, pp. 103–4. Lyon says he is paraphrasing ("adapted from") Vanderlip: Frank A. Vanderlip. 1907. *Business and Education*. New York: Duffield.

little wonder that business researchers and educators, like Lyon, thought business research and education were needed.[68]

The bottom line is that the university should be in charge of discovering these "broad principles," the principles of "the science of business," and then teach them to future businessmen. This intellectual argument was a staple of business education discussions and proposals, and it did sound sensible and convincing. Yet, as far as public normativity is concerned, it was typically believed to be a necessary but not a sufficient one. What was also necessary was the ethical argument. A 1903 article in the *Wall Street Journal* (on schools of both business and journalism) summarizes this belief:

> There are still many in business who cling to the old idea that time spent in advanced education is time wasted for a man who intends to make either business or journalism his life pursuit. But the ranks of these are being steadily depleted, and the opinion is gaining force that special training is a needful for a career in either line of endeavor. [. . .]
>
> But schools of business and schools of journalism will miss their highest calling if they are restricted simply to instruction in the mere technique of business, or even in the history and principles of political economy. That is necessary, indeed, but much more is demanded. There has been no lack of strong and able men in business and journalism without the facilities provided by these schools. Their highest use will be, first, in the training of the mind in accurate and concentrated thought; and, second, in the training of the consciences of their students in habits of spontaneous morality.

What does the *Wall Street Journal* mean by "the training of the consciences of their students in habits of spontaneous morality"? The article does not get into too much detail, but it does describe what the desirable business school graduate looks like: "We want a race of young men who have been trained in the idea that success is not the only test by which life shall be judged." And if that were not clear enough, it adds a strong claim as to the social function of businessmen: "The banker and merchant are not mere agents for the supplying of the material needs of mankind. They, too, may be, and in fact should be, preachers in action, and nowhere are the highest ideals of truth and honesty more essential than in the commercial life."[69]

The *Wall Street Journal* represents public opinion and a public expectation. The proponents, founders, and early leaders of business schools, too, repeatedly expressed the same idea. To take a relatively late illustration, on June 16, 1927, only a few days after the dedication of Harvard's Soldiers Field campus, Northwestern dedicated Wieboldt Hall on its downtown Chicago campus. One of the guest speakers was Edwin Gay, the first dean of Harvard's Graduate School of Business

---

68 Lyon was then Professor of Political Economy and Dean of the School of Commerce and Finance at Washington University. Previously, he had been at the University of Chicago's business school. N. H. Engle. 1959. "Leverett Samuel Lyon." *Journal of Marketing* 24(1):67–69.

69 "Schools of Business and Journalism." *Wall Street Journal*, October 10, 1903, p. 1.

Administration from 1908 to 1919. Gay rehearsed the standard argument about the professionalization of business. Then, he argued that the main purpose of the business school should not be to give technical tools to its students. Instead, he underscored its moral contributions: "the intellectual and moral requirements of modern business organization" and "the genuine spirit of service, intelligent and sympathetic." Indeed, he identified the "chief contribution" that business schools had made and could make as follows:

> Business men have found, and they will in the future discover even more clearly, that the graduates of these schools [the schools of business] bring more to business than a preparatory technical equipment, with some insight into the methods and problems of business. They bring from their training an enhanced respect for the intellectual and moral requirements of modern business organization, and they may be counted on to coöperate [sic] in that which our best business leaders regard as the cornerstone upon which public respect for the profession of business must rest, namely, the genuine spirit of service, intelligent and sympathetic. This steady flow from the reservoirs of idealism, which the schools of business temper and strengthen by knowledge, coming to reinforce the rising standards which business itself is creating, must be thought of as the chief contribution which these professional schools are making and will continue even more to make. They are helping to mould the new ethics of business.[70]

Underemphasizing the importance of the "preparatory technical equipment," and overemphasizing the "spirit of service," "idealism," "rising standards," and "the new ethics of business" was the public norm. For the ethical argument had one particular feature that the intellectual argument did not have. The intellectual argument is mostly based on the students' interest: the complexity of modern business makes knowledge necessary to them. It is in the students' interest to acquire this knowledge, which will increase the likelihood of their future success in business. This is why it was viewed as suspect when considered from a broader, social point of view. Crucially, universities were supposed to be guided precisely by this broader, social point of view, not by individuals' interest. On the other hand, the intellectual argument, while based on the students' interest, cannot be reduced to the "money-making argument": that the justification of the business school lies in increasing its students' "earning capacity." This was surely not a good justificatory argument. By contrast, the intellectual argument did work and did matter—and then money-making could be described as an incidental by-product.

Still, when business schools had to be justified and legitimized—internally within the university and externally before public opinion—the ethical argument

---

70 Edwin F. Gay. 1927. "Social Progress and Business Education. An address delivered on the occasion of the Dedication of Wieboldt Hall, Northwestern University. June 16, 1927." Baker Library Historical Collections. Box ARCH GB2.C.11. Folder GB2.418, pp. 14–15. The same address can be found in *Proceedings of the Northwestern University Conference on Business Education. Held in Connection with the Dedicatory Exercises of Wieboldt Hall. McKinlock Memorial Campus. Lake Shore Drive and Chicago Ave. June 16 and 17, 1927*. Chicago: Northwestern University.

was typically necessary. The evidence for this is abundant, as we shall see. There was a wide public consensus on this sort of ethical foundation for business schools: from university deans and presidents to the periodical press; from politicians to donors like Joseph Wharton or George Baker. As the dean of the University of Chicago's College of Commerce, Leon C. Marshall, put it in 1913: "the college assumes that, at the last analysis, its justification must be a social justification; that, however important it may be to turn out business men who can make money . . . the most important task of all is to aid in promoting the progress and welfare of society." Then, business schools "will miss their purpose if, either by intention or through neglect, the individual, money-making side is permitted to have the ruling hand."[71]

GREAT EXPECTATIONS

In the next section I examine the prehistory, foundation, and early history of the business schools at the University of Pennsylvania, Harvard University, and Northwestern University. I pay particular attention to the character and purpose of moral arguments and reasons in each of these three places. To what extent were business ethics considerations mobilized? To what extent did they carry weight? My narrative, then, is about one business school at a time: what its local context was like, who led the efforts to establish it, what obstacles they encountered, and so on. These are three case studies, if you will, that have intrinsic historical value. However, these case studies can also reflect broader public moral normativity patterns. Take the reports and commentaries of a high-status newspaper about a high-status school's policy or about a high-status dean's address. These pieces of data can help discern normative views and expectations about the emerging type of educational institution. Ultimately, these are two sides of the same coin: normative expectations about business schools as manifested in the press, and public sayings and doings of business schools' representatives and official voices. For, the latter are likely to anticipatorily conform to the former; they have reason to say and do what is publicly acceptable and desirable.

The data show that high-status periodical publications expressed moral expectations about the emerging business schools time and again. Not only publications addressed to businesspeople but also major newspapers hoped that business schools would act as beneficial moral forces. Hopefully, they would have a salutary effect on the morals of business. The same hope could be expressed by saying that business schools should and would professionalize business, which was meant to encompass both the epistemic and the moral requisites for professional status. We have already seen that the *Wall Street Journal* found the intellectual argument to be insufficient and the ethical argument to be necessary. Similarly, when in September 1908 Harvard officially announced its graduate program in business, the *Chicago Daily Tribune* expressed its wishes as follows: "Should [Harvard's] work

---

71 Leon C. Marshall. 1913. "The College of Commerce and Administration of the University of Chicago." *Journal of Political Economy* 21(2):97–110, p. 101.

prove successful and be imitated by other collegiate institutions, it may effect a radical change in business methods. It cannot alter the fundamental laws of profit and loss or of supply and demand, but it may work some ethical changes which are much needed."[72]

The same month, September 1908, the *New York Times* celebrated the moral influence the new schools of business could have. Using the common analogy with lawyers, it hoped schools would provide ethical standards to assess the worth of a businessman's work, other than his bottom line or bank account. On the other hand, the article reflected both optimism and cynicism about the possibility of "a righteous Mammon" and "untainted" dollars, manifesting a reasonable measure of skepticism for someone writing in 1908:

> This is a remarkable series of developments to occur amid our abounding talk of the tainted dollars of trade. Presumably these teachers of our youth think that there is or may be a righteous Mammom [sic], and that the dollars made by their graduates will be untainted. Will there ever come a day when we may develop a class of the educated rich, which shall rank with other learned professions in the development of a class spirit as to how money may be made with credit, and how it should be used after it is made? [. . .] [Hitherto] [s]uccess has too often been held to cure all undiscovered faults, and has been measured by the apparent size of the pile. It will be a happy day if these schools set up a standard by which business men may be tested as lawyers are tested.
>
> [. . .] There is need of many graduates of such schools, and need of many qualified teachers in them, to whom as well as to their graduates the community may look for business ideals, as well as instruction in commercial methods.[73]

This *New York Times* article suggests a broader point: not everyone was equally taken by the ethical argument. Further, not all situations and contexts required that it be appealed to. I argue that business ethics played an important role as a justification for the establishment of business schools, as a rationale for their existence, purpose, and mission, or as an account of their *raison d'être*, especially in their early years. That was certainly the case in the schools my narrative concentrates on. Nevertheless, there are other schools in whose early history business ethics does not show up very much, or not at all. In some contexts, this was because there was little justificatory work to be done. For example, after a good number of first-class universities had already established a business school, the only reason needed was: all of these first-class universities already have a business school; so it must be a good thing; so we should have one as well. This is just a basic organization theory point: under such conditions the whole problem of justification disappears. In fact, it is turned on its head: an organization must justify why it does not have or do that which others do. In some other contexts, however, the intellectual argument took the driver's seat: for example, where schools could be more avowedly technical, either because

---

72 "Harvard's Business School." *Chicago Daily Tribune*, September 6, 1908, p. G4.
73 "College Men in Business." *New York Times*, September 27, 1908, p. 10.

of the university context, or because of their catering to active businessmen, or because of idiosyncratic conditions. This is yet another reminder of the heterogeneity of the university field in the United States, of the need to take the local context into account, and of the probabilistic character of all social scientific propositions.

The probabilistic character of my arguments goes all the way down, because the kind of argument observed is also a function of the pragmatic context of the utterances, and what they were meant to accomplish. Sometimes both the ethical and the intellectual arguments were pragmatically out of place. Indeed, not always was the importance of business school graduates' increasing their "money-making" or "earning capacity" played down. And what was played down and what was played up naturally depended on the context and the audience. Most obviously, prospective students were likely to be interested in the effects of a business degree on their earning capacity.

On October 5, 1908, Northwestern ceremonially launched its School of Commerce. As the *Chicago Daily Tribune* reported, "[a] 'new thing' in Chicago's educational world was launched last night in Booth Hall of the Northwestern University building at Dearborn and Lake streets. The birth of the infant school was presided over by the president of a university and celebrated by addresses by a banker, a business man, an expert accountant, and professors from two great institutions of learning." One of these professors from a great institution of learning was Joseph French Johnson, dean of New York University's School of Commerce, Accounts, and Finance. Johnson, who could not be said to be unfamiliar with the ethical dimensions of business, chose however on this occasion to stress other dimensions.[74] First, he sensibly stressed that business was a science: "'Business is today more of a science than medicine was twenty-five years ago . . .'" Second, he sensibly asked, rhetorically, whether it would pay to study business:

"But will it pay? This is what every prospective student here tonight is asking. And that is what every student ought to ask. Will this knowledge increase my earning capacity?" [. . .] Dean Johnson then stated with supporting statistics and instances gathered at his own school that it would. He gave as his shining example a young man aged 27, who had taken the course and not only increased his earning capacity from $15 a week to $3,500 a week, but had won "a pretty girl with more money."[75]

The causal effect of a business education on romantic success was likely statistically tenuous (once taken into account the appropriate controls); and the experience of this young man aged twenty-seven was likely an exception rather than the norm. Equally exceptional was Johnson's candid analysis of what prospective students likely wished to know—exceptional, that is, given the formal, august, ceremonial context. That should have been discussed instead at a private meeting,

---

74   Joseph French Johnson. 1917. *Business and the Man.* New York: Alexander Hamilton Institute, esp. pp. 111–29.
75   "University to Teach Trade." *Chicago Daily Tribune,* October 6, 1908, p. 10.

in which a prospective student is informed about the school by an administrator or faculty member, as they try to convince him to enroll.[76]

5.4 Ethics at Work

Let me now turn to my three case studies. What work was the ethical argument made to do in the prehistory and early history of the Wharton, Harvard, and Northwestern business schools? How did these schools appeal to it to make a case for their significance? How did they appeal to it to justify their establishment and existence, explicate their usefulness and point, and legitimize their teaching and research activities?

THE WHARTON SCHOOL OF FINANCE AND ECONOMY

Even though in 1881 Joseph Wharton was not "accounted as a lunatic" (to use Butler's terms), he might have come close to that. His proposal for a school of commerce was an original and brave one—even if strictly speaking not the very first of its kind. It has seemed natural to some historians to ask, then, why he did what he did. For example, in the first page of his 1954 history of Columbia University's business school, Thurman Van Metre considers Wharton's "purpose," and singles out a moral one: "Wharton's purpose in founding the School was in a larger measure traceable to his desire to promote a higher standard of morality in American business than that commonly exhibited in the decades immediately following the Civil War."[77] Likewise, historian Morrell Heald considers Wharton's "motives," and singles out a moral one (which "foreshadowed a significant theme in the development of American business education"): "[T]he motives of the donor [Joseph Wharton] foreshadowed a significant theme in the development of American business education. Wharton expressed a desire that emphasis be laid upon 'the immorality and practical inexpediency of seeking to acquire wealth by winning it from another, rather than by earning it through some sort of service to one's fellow men'; and the school's curriculum included courses in philosophy, history, and the social sciences."[78] Ethics shows up in both Van Metre's and Heald's historical accounts—but note just what makes that noteworthy. Van Metre and Heald are interested in what Wharton's motives and purpose really were. I am interested in what Wharton publicly said or implied his motives or

---

76 Daniel similarly notes that "[m]oney earning . . . was seldom mentioned during these years as a reason for studying business, almost as if it was too embarrassing a subject. A couple of times New York University's School of Commerce, Accounts, and Finance issued public relations releases that named salary figures . . . But except for these breaches of unwritten etiquette, one would have thought that business education, the fastest growing phenomenon in American colleges, was strictly a civic-minded undertaking." *Pace* Daniel, I think this was not a breach of etiquette, but a moral one. Daniel, *MBA: The First Century*, p. 48.

77 Van Metre, *A History of the Graduate School of Business, Columbia University*, p. 3.

78 Heald, *The Social Responsibilities of Business*, p. 71.

purpose were, what his motives or purpose were believed to be at the time by his contemporaries, and what they were or are believed to have been by retrospective observers, like Van Metre and Heald are.

This is how the story unfolded. In 1881, Joseph Wharton presented the University of Pennsylvania with a gift of $100,000 to support the creation of "The Wharton School of Finance and Economy"—the precise name he chose for the school.[79] Born in 1826 in Philadelphia, Wharton was a noted industrialist and a religious man of (Hicksite) Quaker faith. In addition to his multiple industrial and commercial pursuits, most notably in the nickel, iron, and steel industries, he had several other interests and participated in several other activities. He was one of the founders of Swarthmore College, a published writer about both scientific and economic issues, as well as a published poet.[80] In the years leading to his 1881 proposal, Wharton had spent much time thinking about the education of the businessman. Thus, along with the pecuniary endowment, he presented the trustees of the university with a thought-out vision for the new school. As historian Fritz Redlich puts it, Wharton "was not only the financier of this new type of school, but also the driving force."[81] Wharton's document, the "Plan of the Wharton School," contains a rationale as to why the university should embark on such an enterprise. It also discusses what the goals of the school should be, how it should be organized, and even what it should teach.

What was Wharton's stated "object" for the Wharton school? In the first place, naturally, it was to provide education—a liberal education—in finance and economy. Yet the goals he stated were also distinctly moral ones:

1. *Object.* To provide young men special means of training and of correct instruction in the knowledge and in the arts of modern Finance and Economy, both public and private, in order that, being well informed and free from delusions upon these important subjects, they may either serve the community skillfully as well as faithfully in offices of trust, or, remaining in private life,

---

79   Wharton wrote to the trustees of the University of Pennsylvania: "These considerations, joined to the belief that one of the existing great Universities, rather than an institution of lower rank or a new independent establishment should lead in the attempt to supply this important deficiency in our present system of education, have led to the suggestion of the project herewith submitted for the establishment of a School of Finance and Economy as a Department of the University which you now control, and which seems well suited to undertake a task so accordant with its general aims. In order that the university may not, by undertaking it, assume a pecuniary burden, I hereby propose to endow the school with the securities below named, amounting to $100,000, and yielding more than $6,000 annual interest   [   ]To commemorate a family name which has been honorably borne in this community since the foundation of the city, I desire that that School shall be called 'The Wharton School of Finance and Economy'." *Education of Business Men*, pp. 29–30. Also quoted in Steven A. Sass. 1982. *The Pragmatic Imagination: A History of the Wharton School, 1881–1981.* Philadelphia: University of Pennsylvania Press, p. 23.

80   W. Ross Yates. 1987. *Joseph Wharton: Quaker Industrial Pioneer.* Bethlehem, PA: Lehigh University Press; London: Associated University Press.

81   Fritz Redlich. 1957. "Academic Education for Business: Its Development and the Contribution of Ignaz Jastrow (1856–1937) in Commemoration of the Hundredth Anniversary of Jastrow's Birth." *Business History Review* 31(1):35–91, p. 82.

may prudently manage their own affairs and aid in maintaining sound financial morality: in short, to establish means for imparting a liberal education in all matters concerning Finance and Economy.[82]

Young men might choose to devote themselves to public or private affairs, but both required some specialized knowledge. The latter required both prudent management and "sound financial morality." The former meant to "serve the community": "skillfully" and "faithfully."

Unlike subsequent business school designers and architects, Wharton's blueprint was not so much the existing professional schools, where the traditional professions of law, medicine, and theology were taught. Instead, it was the existing technical and scientific schools:

> The general conviction that college education did little toward fitting for the actual duties of life any but those who purposed to become lawyers, doctors, or clergymen, brought about the creation of many excellent technical and scientific schools, whose work is enriching the country with a host of cultivated minds prepared to overcome all sorts of difficulties in the world of matter.
>
> Those schools, while not replacing the outgrown and obsolescent system of apprenticeship, accomplish a work quite beyond anything that system was capable of. Instead of teaching and perpetuating the narrow, various, and empirical routines of certain shops, they base their instruction upon the broad principles deduced from all human knowledge, and ground in science, as well as in art, pupils who are thereby fitted both to practice what they have learned and to become themselves teachers and discoverers.[83]

In 1847 and 1854, respectively, Harvard and Yale established their scientific schools, respectively named Lawrence and Sheffield. In 1875, the Towne Scientific School was established at the University of Pennsylvania. Wharton observed this local development with great interest. As historian Steven Sass writes (regarding the modernization of Penn's curriculum and the adoption of the elective system): "With the establishment of the Towne School in 1872, the scientific offerings of the university were revitalized and organized into a three-year course of study that prepared students in chemistry and engineering. When Wharton designed his school, a decade later, he conceived of business education as a three-year elective. And in his formal communications with the trustees, he explicitly used the Towne program as his model."[84]

---

82 *Education of Business Men*, p. 30. Also quoted in Sass, *The Pragmatic Imagination*, p. 21. (Sass is quoting from the "Minutes of the University Trustees" for 1881, though, which I have not had a chance to look at.) Also quoted in Ruml, "The Formative Period of Higher Commercial Education in American Universities," p. 247.

83 *Education of Business Men*, p. 28.

84 Sass, *The Pragmatic Imagination*, p. 32. (The date given by Sass is not accurate: what was established in 1872 was the "Department of Science"; the "Towne Scientific School" was established in 1875.)

Wharton's thinking went beyond the usefulness for individuals of their acquaintance with "broad principles deduced from all human knowledge, and ground in science, as well as in art." He also thought about the usefulness for society of this type of instruction, and the resulting "opportunity for good" before him and the university: "As the possession of any power is usually accompanied by taste for its exercise, it is reasonable to expect that adequate education in the principles underlying successful business management and civil government would greatly aid in producing a class of men likely to become most useful members of society, whether in private or in public life. An opportunity for good seems here to exist, and fairly comparable with that so largely and profitably availed of by the technical and scientific schools."[85]

The project Wharton presented to the Penn trustees was far from an abstract sketch. Instead, it went into much detail. It specified the number and nature of professorships, and even specified the content of professors' teaching and the "general tendency of instruction." This tendency was naturally not only ethical, but it did comprise two moral objectives:

4. *General tendency* [*sic*] *of Instruction.* This should be such as to inculcate and impress upon the students:

(*a*) The immorality and practical inexpediency of seeking to acquire wealth by winning it from another, rather than by earning it through some sort of service to one's fellow-men.

[…]

(*e*) The necessity of rigorously punishing by legal penalties and by social exclusion those persons who commit frauds, betray trusts, or steal public funds, directly or indirectly. The fatal consequences to a community of any weak toleration of such offenses must be most distinctly pointed out and enforced.[86]

It was largely uncontroversial that the school should "inculcate and impress upon the students" these lessons. Disagreements could arise at the level of specifics—for example, what proportion of "legal penalties" and what proportion of "social exclusion"; what proportion of "immorality" and what proportion of "practical inexpediency." Either way, it was evident that morality was part of the plan.

While points (a) and (e) might have been uncontroversial, Wharton also built into his proposal some definitely contentious matters, such as his protectionist creed and other economic and political views he favored. For example, the "Professor or Instructor upon Industry, Commerce and Transportation" should teach, among other things, "how a great nation should be as far as possible self-sufficient . . . supplying its own wants"; and "how by suitable tariff legislation a nation . . . may keep its productive industry active, cheapen the cost of commodities, and oblige foreigners to sell to it at low prices while contributing largely toward defraying the expenses of its government." He should also teach "the necessity, for modern industry, of organizing under single leaders and employers great amounts

85 *Education of Business Men*, p. 29.
86 Ibid., p. 33.

of capital and great numbers of laborers, and of maintaining discipline among the latter"; and "the nature and prevention of 'strikes'." The "professor or instructor upon money and currency" should teach "the meaning, history, and functions of money and currency, showing particularly the necessity of permanent uniformity or integrity in the coin unit upon which the money system of a nation; how an essential attribute of money is that it should be hard to get"; and so on.[87] These were not minor, in-passing comments. Even the last point in the section on the "general tendency of instruction" was about "national self-protection": "(g) The necessity for each nation to care for its own, and to maintain by all suitable means its industrial and financial independence; no apologetic or merely defensive style of instruction must be tolerated upon this point, but the right and duty of national self-protection must be firmly asserted and demonstrated."[88]

In this sense, Joseph Wharton's project was much influenced by the local context—which, as Charles Camic has argued, a social scientist can ignore only at her own peril.[89] Wharton was involved in Philadelphia's and Penn's political economy and social science circles. Philadelphia was home to Henry C. Carey, the influential nineteenth-century political economist, author of *The Principles of Political Economy* and *The Principles of Social Science*, and champion of protectionism. Wharton attended the "weekly discussions [Carey held] in his Philadelphia home, usually on Sunday afternoons"—and which Carey called "vespers."[90] Wharton was also involved in the active Philadelphia chapter of the American Social Science Association.[91] Social science in the late nineteenth century did not look like the abstract and value-free social science that predominates nowadays. Instead, as Haskell observes, "[n]ew ventilation or drainage techniques for the city dweller; new legal forms for the industrial corporation; a new theory of rent or prices; a new way to care for the insane or to administer charity – all of these were equally valuable contributions to 'social science.'"[92] Many of the

---

87   Ibid., pp. 32, 31.

88   Ibid., p. 34.

89   Charles Camic. 1995. "Three Departments in Search of a Discipline: Localism and Interdisciplinary Interaction in American Sociology, 1890–1940." *Social Research* 62(4):1003–33. In this article Camic is thinking of the university as the context; my sentence refers both to the university (Penn) and the city (Philadelphia). See also Charles Camic and Yu Xie. 1994. "The Statistical Turn in American Social Science: Columbia University, 1890 to 1915." *American Sociological Review* 59(5):773–805, pp. 781–84 and *passim*.

90   Yet, "[h]ow often Wharton participated in the vespers and how long he continued coming are unknown." In any event, Yates presents more evidence about the relationship between Wharton and Carey, including a letter where the latter invites the former to "take a glass of wine" at his home. Yates, *Joseph Wharton: Quaker Industrial Pioneer*, p. 180.

91   In 1870, Wharton appears as a new member of the Philadelphia Branch of the American Social Science Association, as reported in the *Journal of Social Science*, the association's organ. Cf. "List of New Members." 1870. *Journal of Social Science* 2:294–96 (Wharton's name is at p. 296). In 1873 he appears as a member of the Executive Committee. Cf. "The Philadelphia Social Science Association." 1873. *Journal of Social Science* 5:202–4 (Wharton's name is at p. 204).

92   Thomas L. Haskell. [1977] 2000. *The Emergence of Professional Social Science: The American Social Science Association and the Nineteenth-Century Crisis of Authority*. Baltimore: Johns Hopkins University Press, p. 87. See also Dorothy Ross. 1991. *The Origins of American Social Science*. Cambridge; New York: Cambridge University Press.

variegated investigations that got called "social science" had a conspicuous moral component—for instance, those related to civil service reform. These influences were manifest in Wharton's project, as well as in the early years of the school.[93] At the University of Pennsylvania, Robert Ellis Thompson, a Presbyterian clergyman and a disciple of Carey's, was the first instructor and professor of "social science" in the United States. He began teaching social science in 1869, and the professorship was formally created in 1874.[94] Edmund Janes James, Wharton's first director and its central figure until his dismissal in 1895, was similarly involved in local social science and reform affairs.[95] This included notably the Philadelphia chapter of the American Social Science Association; the Municipal League of Philadelphia and then the National Municipal League (which concerned itself with city government); and the American Academy of Political and Social Science (which James founded in 1889). James was in favor of the state's intervention in the economy, too. So was his successor, Simon Nelson Patten, a historical economist, trained at Halle, who "in conservative circles . . . was often considered 'a radical'—strange—and unsafe."[96]

To sum up, Joseph Wharton advanced a moral argument for the establishment of a school of commerce. Whatever private conversations took place at the University of Pennsylvania, whatever psychological process caused a trustee to be persuaded by the proposal, morality was much involved in its public representation, justification, and legitimization. In fact, the whole framing of Wharton's project, as he presented it to the University of Pennsylvania, was a moral one. No doubt, the new school would be in the business of teaching business, providing students with knowledge about commerce and finance, and so on. Yet, the point of the school, its *raison d'être*, lay elsewhere. As Wharton put it: "Evidently a great boon would be bestowed upon the nation if its young men of inherited intellect, means and refinement could be more generally led so to manage their property as, while husbanding it, to benefit the community, or could be drawn into careers of unselfish legislation and administration."[97] This is a theme he insisted on. The school was meant to benefit the community and the nation. It would foster probity and unselfishness in private and public affairs. The work of a business school would be good for American society.

93 Cf. Roswell C. McCrea. 1913. "The Work of the Wharton School of Finance and Commerce." *Journal of Political Economy* 21(2):111–16.

94 James H. S. Bossard. 1929. "Robert Ellis Thompson—Pioneer Professor in Social Science." *American Journal of Sociology* 25(2):239–49.

95 See, *The Pragmatic Imagination*, p. 05.

96 "Memorial to Former President Simon N. Patten. Addresses by Friends of Dr. Patten at the Annual Meeting Held in Chicago, December 29, 1922." *American Economic Review* 13(1) suppl.:257–93, p. 289; Simon N. Patten. 1890. *The Economic Basis of Protection*. Philadelphia: J. B. Lippincott; Simon N. Patten. 1899. *The Development of English Thought: A Study in the Economic Interpretation of History*. New York: Macmillan. See also Marion Fourcade and Rakesh Khurana. 2013. "From Social Control to Financial Economics: The Linked Ecologies of Economics and Business in Twentieth Century America." *Theory and Society* 42(2):121–59; Martin Meyerson and Dilys Pegler Winegrad. 1978. *Gladly Learn and Gladly Teach: Franklin and His Heirs at the University of Pennsylvania, 1740–1976*. Philadelphia: University of Pennsylvania Press, pp. 145–55.

97 *Education of Business Men*, p. 29.

THE HARVARD GRADUATE SCHOOL OF BUSINESS ADMINISTRATION

As the oldest university in the country, established in 1636, Harvard's institutional traditions, practices, and ways of doing things were arguably heavier and stickier than elsewhere. It was also seen as representing the intellectual elite of a reputedly practical and not particularly intellectual nation—and its organizational culture and identity drew on this fact. Harvard was at the antipodes of the "Western" universities, which had but recent traditions, and which were receptive to and even oriented by practical concerns. In brief, a priori Harvard did not seem to be the kind of higher education institution where business and businesspeople would be particularly welcome. And yet, as of 1908, Harvard had its own business school. Because of these special conditions, Harvard is a good place to explore the justification and legitimization of a business school—and, in particular, whether and how the ethical argument might have been needed to supplement the intellectual argument.

On May 16, 1916, Harvard's President Emeritus Charles W. Eliot addressed the annual dinner of the students of the business school. Eliot had been Harvard's president for forty years: from 1869 to 1909. So he was a central actor in the process that resulted in the school's foundation in 1908. In his address he discussed why the Harvard Corporation decided to establish a business school. He did mention the intellectual argument to the effect that "large business had become a highly intellectual calling." Yet he also saw "quite clearly" that "the leading motive in the establishment" of the school was "ethical progress":

> I think the [Harvard] Corporation made up their minds that the University was not giving as much attention as it should to the very important profession of business. Everybody who watched the development of American industries since the close of the Civil War knew that large business had become a highly intellectual calling, and called for well-trained minds. Yet the University was not contributing to the training of young men for that particular calling at all as it was training men for other professions. [. . .] But when I look back to the leading motive in the establishment of this School of Business Administration I think I see quite clearly that the strongest motive was ethical progress.[98]

I do not take Eliot's retrospective statement about the corporation's leading or strongest motive to be evidence about the corporation's leading or strongest motive. Rather, given the context of the utterance, I take it to be evidence about the public acceptability and desirability of motives for establishing a business school—such as "ethical progress." Whatever happened in the years leading up to 1908, this is the message Eliot conveyed to his audience in 1916. That is presumably how he wanted the history of the school to be viewed and remembered.

---

98 "Concluding remarks of President-Emeritus Eliot to the students of the Harvard Graduate School of Business Administration, at annual dinner." HBS Dean's Office Correspondence. 1919–1942. Box 37. School Correspondence. 1927–1937. Folder Harvard University – President, Eliot, C. W., 1908–25.

A few years later, banker and philanthropist George F. Baker manifested a comparable orientation toward business ethics when he announced his $5 million gift to the business school. At least, a comparable orientation was manifested by words attributed to Baker. In the early 1920s, the school was working to raise funds to build a new campus. This is the Soldiers Field campus, across the Charles River, where it is still located today. The chair of the fundraising campaign, Bishop William Lawrence, approached Baker, whose son was a member of the Harvard College Class of 1899.[99] This is how Lawrence recalled Baker's response to the effect that he would contribute the whole amount needed: "If . . . by giving five million dollars I could have the privilege of building the whole School, I should like to do it. If it were one of several such schools or an old story, I should not care to do it, but my life has been given to business, and I should like to found the first Graduate School, and *give a new start to better business standards*."[100] These words have been attributed to Baker, by Bishop Lawrence, by the Harvard professor and historian of the business school Melvin Copeland, and by many others over the years. It does not matter here whether Baker actually uttered these words, or whether he rather said to Lawrence, "Here's your bloody check—will you stop harassing me now?" In either case, these are the words the Harvard business school, the institution, has made a point of remembering—or perhaps "remembering." It has also made a point of prominently exhibiting them—for example, in an official history of the school, such as Copeland's, or in the new buildings' dedication ceremony, where Lawrence spoke "in behalf of Mr. Baker."

The first dean of the Graduate School of Business Administration was Edwin Gay (1908–1919). Gay was an economic historian who studied under Schmoller in Berlin, and who was much interested in the social, historical, and ethical aspects of business. Indeed, in 1915–1916 he and Arch Shaw co-taught a course titled "Social Factors in Business Enterprise."[101] The next dean, Wallace B. Donham (1919–1942), would take things further. Donham's work reveals that he gave a lot of thought to these issues. He made several public statements about the responsibilities of business and the teaching of ethics, and in 1928 he instituted a Professorship of Business Ethics.[102] As he unambiguously put it, "[t]here is no calling whose fundamentals should rest on a higher ethical basis than business,

99   Jeffrey L. Cruikshank. 1987. *A Delicate Experiment: The Harvard Business School, 1908–1945.* Boston: Harvard Business School Press, p. 101; Samuel Eliot Morison. [1936] 1964. *Three Centuries of Harvard, 1636–1936.* Cambridge, MA: Harvard University Press, p. 472.

100   Quoted in Melvin T. Copeland. 1958. *And Mark an Era. The Story of the Harvard Business School.* Boston: Little, Brown and Company, pp. 69–70. Emphasis added. Also in "Dedication of the Business School." *Harvard Alumni Bulletin*, June 9, 1927, p. 1010. Harvard Archives. GSBA. Clippings, 1924–29.

101   On Gay, see N.S.B. Gras. 1946. "Obituary Notice: Edwin Francis Gay." *Economic History Review* 16(1):60–62; Earl J. Hamilton. 1947. "Memorial: Edwin Francis Gay." *American Economic Review* 37(3):410–13; Herbert Heaton. 1952. *A Scholar in Action: Edwin F. Gay.* Cambridge, MA: Harvard University Press.

102   See, e.g., Wallace B. Donham. n.d. "Putting Ethics into Business." *Harvard Alumni Bulletin.* Harvard Archives. GSBA. Clippings, 1924–29.

and none is more worthy the attention of the University."[103] Furthermore, a considerable amount of business ethics work—teaching, lectures, advocacy, and even some consulting—was carried out during Donham's years.[104]

For the purposes of this chapter, the exercises of dedication of the school's new campus, on June 4, 1927, are especially relevant. For this ceremonial and grandiose occasion was a special public moral normativity moment—as rituals of this sort always are. Prominent newspapers wrote stories about it.[105] Eminent politicians, businesspeople, and academics showed up: "Among those attending the ceremonies were the Hon. Carter Glass, U. S. Senator from Virginia . . . , and the Hon. Frederick W. Dallinger, Congressman from Massachusetts, representing the Federal government. Among the prominent business men were J. P. Morgan and Thomas W. Lamont, of J. P. Morgan & Co.; Gerard Swope, president of General Electric Co.[;] Howard Elliott, chairman of the Northern Pacific Railway and president of the Board of Overseers of Harvard College; Herbert N. Straus of R. H. Macy & Co. and James Simpson, president of Marshall Field & Co., of Chicago."[106] It was also attended by "the President and Fellows of Harvard College, members of the Board of Overseers, representatives of the State and of the cities of Boston and Cambridge, the presidents of several New England Colleges, and the members of the Faculty of the Business School and other Departments of the University."[107] Further, there was a stage on which the speakers stood, so that they could be seen and heard—which contributes to the symbolic significance of the ritual.

There were two themes that kept coming up throughout the day: the new profession of business, and the ethics and responsibilities of business. The *Harvard Alumni Bulletin* reported on the event as follows:

> The new buildings of the Harvard Business School were dedicated on Saturday, June 4. The exercises began at 11 o'clock in the morning and, after an interim for luncheon, went on at 2.30 in the afternoon; they were held on the north side of the Baker Library, where a platform had been erected, facing seats for the several thousand people who had gathered to witness the ceremony and listen to the distinguished speakers. Perfect weather prevailed.
>
> In the morning, Mr. George F. Baker, whose generosity made the new plant possible, formally presented the keys of the buildings to President Lowell and the latter responded in behalf of the University. At the morning exercises, also, Mr. Owen D. Young, chairman of the board of the General Electric Co.,

---

103 Wallace B. Donham. [1922?] "Fitting the College Man into Business." Baker Library Historical Collections. Wallace B. Donham. Articles and speeches of. Archives GB2.332. Box 1. Folder Donham, W. B., Addresses and Lectures, 1922–1925.

104 Abend, "The Origins of Business Ethics."

105 "Harvard School Gets $2,000,000." *New York Times*, June 5, 1927, p. E1; "$2,070,000 Is Given Harvard University." *Washington Post*, June 5, 1927, p. 7; "Million-Dollar Gift to Harvard University." *Wall Street Journal*, June 6, 1927, p. 11.

106 "Million-Dollar Gift to Harvard University." *Wall Street Journal*, June 6, 1927, p. 11.

107 "Dedication of the Business School." *Harvard Alumni Bulletin*, June 9, 1927, p. 1010.

made the principal address of the day. The Harvard Alumni Chorus sang at the morning exercises.

President Lowell presided in the afternoon; the speakers were: Rt. Rev. William Lawrence, a Fellow of Harvard College; Professor Edwin F. Gay, who was the first dean of the Business School; and Professor Wallace B. Donham, the present dean of the School. The Harvard Glee Club sang in the afternoon.[108]

Fortunately for the organizers, perfect weather prevailed. Fortunately for the organizers, too, Owen D. Young had agreed to be the keynote speaker. Young (1874–1962) was a lawyer and businessman, whose "phenomenal rise" to the chairmanship of General Electric in 1922 was lauded and admired by the business press.[109] In his speech at Harvard, Young underscored the business-is-a-profession argument. Much like the U.S. Chamber of Commerce, of which he was a distinguished member, he took "business" to be a distinct, unified agent. Therefore, it could have moral obligations and responsibilities:

Today the profession of business at Harvard formally makes its bow to its older brothers and holds it [sic] head high with the faith of youth. Today we light the fires in the temple which it is the trust of Harvard to maintain and from which may be renewed through generation after generation the high ideals, the sound principles, the glorious traditions, which make a profession. Today and here business formally assumes the obligations of a profession, which means responsible action as a group, devotion to its own ideals, the creation of its own codes, the capacity for its own discipline, the awards of its own honors, and the responsibility for its own service.[110]

Wallace Donham's address had a special public significance. For, generally, the leader of an organization has unique symbolic powers in the public domain, and a unique capacity to represent and speak on behalf of the organization itself. Donham was sure to make the business-is-a-profession argument, too. Then, he took that argument in a particular ethical direction:

It is not enough that a social consciousness shall develop speedily and widely in this new profession. The social consciousness must be backed up by competently equipped intelligence and wide wisdom. Especially is it necessary if we are to socialize these rapidly developing instrumentalities of science, that

108   Ibid., p. 1009.

109   "The Phenomenal Rise of Owen D. Young Explained." Forbes, June 10, 1922, p. 217. Cf. Josephine Young Case and Everett Needham Case. 1982. *Owen D. Young and American Enterprise: A Biography*. Boston: D. R. Godine; McQuaid, *A Response to Industrialism*; Ida M. Tarbell. 1932. *Owen D. Young: A New Type of Industrial Leader*. New York: Macmillan. See also Owen D. Young. 1929. "What is Right in Business." *Bulletin of the Harvard Business School Alumni Association* 5(5):188–93.

110   Owen D. Young. 1927. "Dedication Address." *Bulletin of the Harvard Business School Alumni Association* 3(6):179–189, p. 189; Owen D. Young. 1927. "Dedication Address." *Harvard Business Review* 5(4):385–94; "The New Management." *New York Times*, June 5, 1927, p. E10. See also Khurana, *From Higher Aims to Hired Hands*, pp. 117–18 and 376–78. The quotation on page 118 of Khurana's book is slightly different from mine, probably because he uses a different primary source (see pp. 410, 481).

we fix for business the foundation stones of the specialized ethics which are characteristic of all professions.

In my judgment one of the major fields in which these new principles must be sought is in the ethics of business, the field which deals both with biologically stable human nature, and with rapidly changing environment. We must by study and research, rather than by the slow sifting of social evolution, develop a specialized ethical system for this new profession.

Dohman tried to develop this specialized ethical system in various ways, including the aforementioned business ethics professorship. In any event, in this inauguration speech he gave ethics a central role. It was part of what the business school at Harvard University was all about. Both intellectual and ethical advancement were the *raisons d'être* of the school. Both were desired by its benefactor, Mr. Baker. In closing, Donham thanked Baker thus:

> Mr. Baker, on behalf of the Faculty of Business Administration and especially on my own behalf, may I thank you from the bottom of our hearts for the opportunity and for the deeply felt responsibility you have placed on us, and may we renew once again the pledge we know you wish from us—that we will, so far as lies within our capacities, advance the intellectual and ethical basis of this new profession of business, thereby fulfilling your generous gifts and carrying on, as lesser men may, your lifelong example.[111]

THE NORTHWESTERN UNIVERSITY SCHOOL OF COMMERCE

The birth of the Northwestern University School of Commerce in 1908 was not preceded by discussions and arguments concerning the ethical aspects and social responsibilities of business, or the potential contributions of business ethics education to American society. As far as my data allow me to determine, business ethics issues were not present. Instead, discussions and arguments centered on the needs and demands of organized business and accountants in the city of Chicago. Privately, there were also discussions and arguments about competition with the University of Chicago and the University of Illinois to meet these needs and demands. It makes sense, then, that the school began in 1908 as an evening school for working businessmen. It also makes sense that it was located not in Evanston, where Northwestern's main campus was, but on its downtown Chicago campus.[112]

However, a few years after its establishment, moral questions about business and business education started to be raised. In the mid-1910s the school publicized in various places its "three fundamental aims." The first and second aims

---

111   Wallace B. Donham. 1927. "The Emerging Profession of Business." *Harvard Business Review* 5(4):201–405, p. 405.

112   For a short account, see Harold F. Williamson and Payson S. Wild. 1976. *Northwestern University: A History, 1850–1975.* Evanston, IL: Northwestern University, p. 119. For a long account, see Willard E. Hotchkiss. 1941. *Northwestern University School of Commerce: The Pioneer Decade.* Chicago: Northwestern University.

are based on the intellectual argument; the third aim is based on the ethical argument. I quote from a typewritten memo that appears to have been written in 1916:

Educational Policy

Business is infinitely complex and specialized, and requires a power of analysis which nothing so well as a comprehensive scientific training can give. With this complexity there exist in a modern business, far reaching public relations demanding a liberal culture and the finest qualities of mind and spirit.

Instruction in the School of Commerce is based on three fundamental aims; first, to give students a comprehensive, many-sided survey of business facts and experience; second, to develop a power of accurate analysis which will prepare the student to think complicated business problems through the end; third, to maintain an atmosphere in which large business problems will be regarded in a public-spirited way.[113]

These three "fundamental aims" appear verbatim elsewhere, e.g., in the pamphlet *Training Business Executives*,[114] and in the *Northwestern University Bulletin* for 1915–1916.[115] The school's first dean, Willard Hotchkiss, must have been partly or wholly responsible for these statements about aims. Hotchkiss was at Northwestern from 1905 until 1917, and then again from 1921 until 1925. From 1917 until 1919 he was at the University of Minnesota. And from 1925 until 1932 he was the first dean of Stanford's Graduate School of Business.[116] Hotchkiss presented his thinking about the Northwestern school in a 1913 article in the *Journal of Political Economy*, which was titled, precisely, "The Northwestern University School of Commerce." It analyzed the tensions between "the acquisitive side of business" on the one hand, and "public welfare," "the socially productive," and "national efficiency" on the other:

In conclusion, permit me to say a word concerning the desirability, from a public viewpoint, of segregating the field of business for special study. Professor [Leon C.] Marshall [of the University of Chicago] has implied that the professional study of business would necessarily direct itself in large measure at least to the acquisitive side of business and that, as a corrective to this, simultaneous attention should be given to matters of public and social administration. I am in entire sympathy with the proposition that emphasis must be placed upon the socially productive rather than upon the acquisitive aspects of any subject whether it be business, agriculture, law, medicine, or any other human pursuit. I am not, however, convinced that it is impracticable to develop work in business administration with a constant emphasis upon the public and social

113 Northwestern University School of Commerce." [1916?] Northwestern University Archives. General Files. Folder: School of Commerce – History – General.

114 *Training Business Executives*. Northwestern University Archives. General Files. Folder: School of Commerce/Business – General (1912–1949).

115 "School of Commerce. Announcements 1915–1916" *Northwestern University Bulletin*, vol. 15, no. 45, July 23, 1915.

116 "Stanford Will Open Graduate Business School." *Los Angeles Times*, June 22, 1925, p. 6.

aspects of business. Indeed, if my analysis of the present conditions is correct, the only kind of training which will make for continued efficiency in business is a training which carries with it a capacity to grasp the ultimate and public aspects of business situations and to harmonize efficiency with considerations of public welfare.

While Hotchkiss agreed with Marshall that "emphasis must be placed upon the socially productive," he wanted to make a further claim. He claimed that "continued efficiency in business" depends on "considerations of public welfare." Then he added:

> If we apply to business the scientific and cultural methods employed in the best university instruction, I am of the opinion that we shall not only promote efficiency through the development of definite professional standards, but that in the long run we shall go far toward removing the conflict between business and ethics. [...]
>
> After all, the greatest problem from a public point of view, which the study of business in a fundamental way may help to solve, is the problem of national efficiency. While we recognize the need of studying business from the point of view of the individual who wishes to make himself efficient, it may be doubted whether the subject will ever become an important factor in national education unless it is able to justify itself from the point of view of the community as a whole.[117]

Hotchkiss's point, then, is specifically about the justification of business schools. This justification requires that they take "the point of view of the community as a whole." They should have a positive impact on national efficiency and the community as a whole, as opposed to the selfish interests of individual students. On the other hand, Hotchkiss did "recognize the need of studying business" of "the individual who wishes to make himself efficient." The first-person plural pronoun—"we recognize"—suggests that Hotchkiss was speaking on behalf of the Northwestern School of Commerce. And this is indeed the balance that the school struck: they did recognize the individual's point of view, even if the ultimate justification had to be a social one. Perhaps this recognition still had to do with the demands and desires of Chicago businessmen and business associations, including the school's donors and guarantors, which had to be paid heed to.

Yet, Hotchkiss would soon go further. In 1919, he made a presentation at the first meeting of the American Association of Collegiate Schools of Business, hosted by Harvard University, which prioritizes business ethics and public welfare to the detriment of the individual businessperson or future businessperson. Hotchkiss identifies "five outstanding ideas which it would seem the curriculum of a collegiate school of business should reflect." The first duty of business schools is "to promote sound business"—"sound" being a common euphemism for ethical

---

117   Willard E. Hotchkiss. 1913. "The Northwestern University School of Commerce." *Journal of Political Economy* 21(3):196–208, pp. 207–8. Footnote omitted.

business practice. He also subordinates "the individual success of its graduates" to the school's public duty: individual rewards are an incidental by-product. As he said:

> *Public responsibility.*—Collegiate education, whether general or professional, and whether supported by the state, or by private endowment, is a public function, and it owes its first duty to the public. Schools of business are in no different situation in this regard from schools of law, medicine, or engineering. Their first duty is to promote sound business, remembering always that business is a function of the national life. A school of business, unless it is a purely research school, can scarcely promote sound business without educating its students to become good business men. If it does this successfully it will incidentally promote the individual success of its graduates, but in any case sound business rather than individual rewards is the first concern of a collegiate school of business.[118]

After Hotchkiss and Arthur E. Swanson's brief tenure, Ralph E. Heilman became the third dean of the Northwestern School of Commerce in 1919. Heilman insisted that business ethics and social responsibility were of great importance, and business schools should make an ethical difference. Indeed, in 1928 he instituted the William A. Vawter Foundation and Lectures on Business Ethics.[119] At the same time, Heilman developed and reinforced Hotchkiss's conception about the point and objectives of business schools. For instance, at the 1928 annual meeting of the American Association of Collegiate Schools of Business, hosted by Northwestern on its downtown Chicago campus, Heilman delivered an address entitled, "A Reevaluation of the Objectives of Business Education." He argued that business education had three types of objectives: "the objectives from the standpoint of the general public; second, from the standpoint of our own students; third, from the standpoint of the entire system of higher education in America."[120] Regarding the first type, he said:

> The test is—Do we perform a service which is socially desirable? The existence of schools of commerce . . . and the expenditure of large sums of money for their maintenance . . . cannot be justified merely by virtue of the fact that we enable our students and graduates to increase their earning capacity. The justification must rest on a broader basis. It must be found in the fact that the

118 Willard E. Hotchkiss. 1920. "The Basic Elements and Their Proper Balance in the Curriculum of a Collegiate Business School." *Journal of Political Economy* 28(2):89–107, pp. 89–90.

119 Northwestern University Archives. J. L. Kellogg Graduate School of Management. Faculty Meeting Minutes. Box No. 1. Folder: Faculty Minutes 1912–1922. March 31, 1928, p. 10; "Gift to Endow Business Ethics Course." *Northwestern University Alumni News*, April 1928. See also Michael W. Sedlak and Harold F. Williamson. 1983. *The Evolution of Management Education: A History of the Northwestern University J.L. Kellogg Graduate School of Management, 1908–1983.* Urbana: University of Illinois Press, p. 62.

120 Ralph E. Heilman. 1928. "A Reevaluation of the Objectives of Business Education." *The Ronald Forum. Proceedings of the Tenth Annual Meeting of the American Association of Collegiate Schools of Business.* Northwestern University, Chicago, Illinois. May 3, 4 and 5, 1928, p. 1.

training provided is socially desirable, that it contributes to social well-being, social progress and human welfare.[121]

Heilman's view is straightforward—and here he echoes his predecessor Hotchkiss. It is a fact that schools of commerce increase their students' "earning capacity." But this fact does not justify their existence. Their justification requires something "broader"; something that relates to "social well-being, social progress and human welfare." Next, Heilman singled out five more specific social objectives for business education: "to promote an increase in the productive capacity of society"; "to promote the more effective distribution of the fruits and products of industry"; "to promote equality of economic opportunity"; "promoting the establishment of standards of business conduct"; and "to contribute, through research, publication and public service, to the solution of important social, economic, and management problems."[122] In sum, Heilman's policy recommendations are clear. Business education ought to develop "a strong sense of social and ethical obligation." It ought to introduce "into business an endless procession of young men who have acquired the social point of view and an understanding of the social obligations and public relations of business."[123] According to him, it was business schools' responsibility to do so.

Heilman continued to think and speak about these issues, and advanced similar arguments on several occasions. For example, in his introduction to Edwin Gay's speech at the Northwestern conference on business education of June 1927, he said:

> Friends and Guests of Northwestern University: Training young men merely to increase their earning capacity does not constitute an adequate justification for the inclusion of business instruction in university curricula. The justification for the expenditure of large sums by state and endowed institutions for instruction in business subjects must rest on a much broader basis. The maintenance of colleges of commerce and business administration is justified only in so far as such institutions promote an increase in our productive capacity and an equitable distribution of the products of industry.
>
> Every college and university is primarily a public service agency, and must be judged as such. All instruction offered must contribute to public well-being. Schools of Commerce are therefore to be judged by precisely the same standard as are schools of arts, science, medicine, theology, engineering, education. The question is, do they perform a service of value, not exclusively for their students, but for society? Is the training which is offered by them socially desirable? Will it make a contribution to social progress and human welfare?[124]

---

121   Ibid., p. 2.

122   Ibid., pp. 2–3. (Note that "to promote an increase in the productive capacity of society" is the kind of objective that allows for students' interest to be recast in socially useful terms.)

123   Ibid., p. 3.

124   *Proceedings of the Northwestern University Conference on Business Education. Held in Connection with the Dedicatory Exercises of Wieboldt Hall. McKinlock Memorial Campus. Lake Shore Drive and Chicago Ave. June 16 and 17, 1927.* Chicago: Northwestern University, p. 75. See also Ralph E. Heilman. 1930. "Ethical Standards in Business and in Business Education." Pp. 3–27 in *The Ethical Problems of Modern Finance.* New York: Ronald Press Company.

Would it make such a contribution? Did schools of commerce perform a service of value for American society?

5.5 The Good of America

In the preceding section we saw the ethical argument at work in the early history of Wharton, Harvard, and Northwestern. We saw how the leading figures and founders of these business schools represented them as being driven by moral or social aims, contributors to the public good, and socially useful and desirable organizations. My account concerned public representations about what schools were driven by and what their point was, or what they ought to be driven by and point should be—not whether these public representations matched their actual priorities, teaching, or policy decisions. Now I wish to look at another source of data, which provides a valuable complementary perspective—and some more external validity.

In 1925–1926, the American Association of Collegiate Schools of Business undertook a large research project on several aspects of higher business education. It was carried out by a "Commission on Correlation of Secondary and Collegiate Education, with Particular Reference to Business Education," chaired by Leon C. Marshall of the University of Chicago. The investigation covered various areas, such as business schools' admission requirements, courses offered, "the outstanding problems in collegiate business education," and "guiding principles for the organization of the collegiate curriculum."[125] One part of the project was a survey, which was sent to the faculty, deans, and presidents of the thirty-three members of the association. More than 250 people responded. The first question of the questionnaire read—"Which ones of the following do you accept as representing the appropriate aims or purposes of collegiate education for business?" Then, respondents were presented with five possible aims, whose appropriateness they had to successively assess. Table 5.1 shows the results, broken down by the respondent's position in the school.

Business school deans, instructors, and university presidents widely agreed that "preparing persons for executive positions in business" and "preparing persons for professional careers in business, e.g., accountants, statisticians, etc." were appropriate aims or purposes. By contrast, "preparing persons for routine positions in business" was not. More relevant here are sections (d) and (e). Their results are unambiguous, too. "Introducing persons with a social point of view into business" was an appropriate aim according to more than 85 percent of the respondents. By contrast, "[p]reparing graduates to 'make money'" was an appropriate goal according to only 25 percent of them.[126] These opinions might or might not have been

---

125   R. E. Heilman, W. H. Kiekhofer, C. O. Ruggles, I. L. Sharfman, and L. C. Marshall. 1928. "Collegiate Education for Business." *Journal of Business of the University of Chicago* 1(1):1–59, pp. 28–29.

126   However, conclusions about "making money" should be conservative, because of a methodological mistake made by the survey researchers, which they only later realized: "This question, unfortunately, was framed in such a way as probably to stimulate negative answers." Ibid., p. 30. The report does not elaborate on this framing error, but one may wonder why "make money" is in quotation marks.

Table 5.1: Survey on Aims or Purposes of Business Education

1. *Which ones of the following do you accept as representing the appropriate aims or purposes of collegiate education for business?*

   a) *Preparing persons for executive positions in business.*

	Yes	No	Doubtful	Total
Presidents	22	..	..	22
Deans	42	3	1	46
Instructors . . .	171	10	25	206
Total	235	13	26	274

   b) *Preparing persons for professional careers in business, e.g., accountants, statisticians, etc.*

	Yes	No	Doubtful	Total
Presidents	22	..	1	23
Deans	44	..	3	47
Instructors . . .	178	12	19	209
Total	244	12	23	279

   c) *Preparing persons for routine positions in business.*

	Yes*	No	Doubtful	Total
Presidents	4	11	4	19
Deans	13	23	5	41
Instructors . . .	25	123	31	179
Total	42	157	40	239

* Some persons apparently voted "yes" in the sense that there should be preparation for routine positions in order to enable the graduates to make a start in business.

   d) *Preparing graduates to "make money."*[11]

	Yes	No	Doubtful	Total
Presidents	2	16	2	20
Deans	16	13	10	39
Instructors . . .	41	98	32	171
Total	59	127	44	230

[11] This question, unfortunately, was framed in such a way as probably to stimulate negative answers.

   e) *Introducing persons with a social point of view into business.*

	Yes	No	Doubtful	Total
Presidents	18	2	1	21
Deans	41	2	1	44
Instructors . . .	174	11	20	205
Total	233	15	22	270

Source: Heilman, R. E.; W. H. Kiekhofer; C. O. Ruggles; I. L. Sharfman; and L. C. Marshall. 1928. "Collegiate Education for Business." *The Journal of Business of the University of Chicago* 1(1):1–59. Tables are at pp. 29–31.

translated into actual policy. But in either case they reveal a normative consensus about the desirable purposes of business education. Plus, unlike public addresses, survey responses may reveal, at least to some extent, the internalization of public moral normativity. In turn, these normative understandings became useful argumentative tools in discussions about the place of business in the university. They were weapons wielded in the public battle against skeptics, who, like Abraham Flexner, questioned their point and utility. At a deeper level, they were useful tools to publicly define the nature of business schools. Organizations cannot be reduced to a set of things, say, buildings, pieces of furniture, human beings, rules, and routines. They are also constituted by representations of what these things taken together are, what they are for, and what they are all about. These representations are not epiphenomenal, like an optional discursive ornament. Rather, they make that particular conjunction of buildings, pieces of furniture, human beings, rules, and routines be the particular organization that they are. In this sense, business ethics was constitutive of business schools.

Business schools proclaimed that business ethics was good for American society. But why was business ethics good for American society? This question connects the arguments of this chapter to the moral background framework developed in chapter 1. For I am now raising a question about the first dimension of the moral background: the grounding of first-order morality. As I argued there, these are the grounds or reasons that social actors rely on and may need to produce. In practice, people and organizations tell—and sometimes must tell—moral from immoral actions, just from unjust institutions, cruel from magnanimous rulers, and worthwhile from worthless life-projects. Presumably, they then make choices accordingly, say, they choose worthwhile life-projects and do not choose cruel rulers. But what makes moral actions moral, just institutions just, cruel rulers cruel, and worthwhile life-projects worthwhile? In virtue of what conception, theory, or understanding are they moral, just, cruel, and worthwhile? The second-order moral background contains resources with which these grounds or reasons are constructed, and which people and organizations can appeal to whenever needed in actual social life, e.g., when someone actually wants to know what these grounds are.

This is precisely the question that business schools were confronted with—as well as anyone else who claimed that business ethics was good for America. If you say that something is good for American society, you must be able to say why that is so; in virtue of what it is good. And only certain reasons and grounds will work, in the sense of their being acceptable, not sounding crazy, and getting the organizational or practical job done. In fact, these first-order moral claims are dependent on background elements in two ways. Giving grounds as to why something is good for America necessitates a conception of the good and what makes a thing good—say, something like an ethical view or theory (though not a formal, systematic, explicit one). But it also necessitates a conception of the good society in general and American society's good in particular—something like a political view or theory, or rather an applied political view or theory (though, again, not a formal, systematic, explicit one). Whether consciously adopted or unconsciously assumed, there must be something like this. It turns out, then, that we are dealing with a version of the grounding problem addressed earlier in this book. To be more precise, the two problems are importantly similar and importantly dissimilar. In chapters 2 and 3 the problem was at the individual level, and the question was why an individual businessman ought to be ethical. One answer was that business ethics was good for him because it was financially profitable. In this chapter the problem is at the social level, and the question is what makes business ethics good for American society. What answers were given to this?

First, business activity and enterprise of the right kind is a morally beneficial force; it improves American society materially and morally. This is a variation on a classic capitalist theme: markets as moralizing and civilizing, and "money-making and commerce as innocent and *doux*."[127] Second, bad business ethics is bad for American society, because it causes government intervention in the economy. In turn, this is bad for the whole of American society (not just bad for American business, in the sense discussed in chapter 4). This is a variation on a classic capitalist theme: the demand, as worded by Bentham, that government should "be quiet."[128] Naturally, this demand is based on a particular view of what the good society is, along with its political and economic implications. Third, unethical and socially irresponsible business practices undermine the foundations of American society, institutions, and our cherished way of life. They do harm to the moral foundations of the capitalist, free-market system. They open the way for external moral criticism, that is, criticism from outside capitalism. They also open the way for the internal moral criticism that honest, hard-working, law-abiding, and well-meaning participants in the economic and political game are taken advantage of by cheaters, profiteers, and free-riders. Ultimately, unethical and socially irresponsible business practices threaten the stability of the system. Maybe some other way of arranging our society, economy, and polity can fare better in these respects? This is a variation on a classic capitalist theme: the vindication of capitalism against rival systems and views of the good society. In the history of American capitalism this vindication has been both national and international. It has involved cultural work, rhetoric, and consumer goods aplenty, but also embargos, tanks, and aircrafts aplenty.

Let us look again at Charles Eliot's 1916 address to the Harvard business school students. I mentioned Eliot's account about how the school had been founded. Then, from the past of the school he turned to recommendations for the future. He exhorted students to "go out into business . . . with a clear conception . . . of what we mean by business men promoting and bringing into practice sound ethics":

> It is quite astonishing to see the change that has come over the business community, since I was a boy, in regard to this promotion of human welfare. We have come to realize, I think, that the keeping on of everything we most value

---

127 Hirschman, *The Passions and the Interests*, p. 56. Cf. Fourcade and Healy, "Moral Views of Market Society."

128 Jeremy Bentham. [1798] 1839. *A Manual of Political Economy*. In *The Works of Jeremy Bentham*. Part IX. Edinburgh: William Tait, p. 33.

in the organization of American society and the protection and safeguarding of our institutions depend upon the success of the business man in the American community in the promotion of human welfare. In no other way will the American people be able effectually to overcome the evils of the factory system. Ministers have contributed very much to this protection of American society; lawyers have contributed; legislators have contributed; but no one so much as the active, alert, leader in business.

You young men ought to go out into business with these standards before you; with a clear conception of what we mean in these days by a successful man of business; what we mean in these days by a public spirited man; what we mean by business men promoting and bringing into practice sound ethics.[129]

Eliot claims that business ethics (in a particular sense of the expression) is good for American society. The Paterson silk strike (1913) and the Ludlow Massacre (April 10, 1914) were still fresh in people's minds—perhaps most especially in the mind of someone according to whom unions were a threat "to personal and public freedom, to progress, and to the common well-being," and "the scab was a pretty fair type of hero."[130] Thus, "our institutions" appeared to be in jeopardy. Business can "protect" and "safeguard" "everything we most value in the organization of American society." It can do that more effectively than ministers, lawyers, and legislators. But not any kind of business or businessman could succeed at this task: only a new kind of "successful man of business," who promotes and practices "sound ethics." In brief, the more "human welfare" there is, the smaller the odds of social discontent and turmoil. Hence, it is in American society's interest— understood as the preservation of the social and political status quo—that business ethics be promoted and business schools turn out ethical businessmen.

A few years later, protecting and safeguarding everything we most value in the organization of American society might have seemed all the more urgent. In the aftermath of World War I and the Russian Revolution, the United States experienced its first (yet sadly not last) "Red Scare." Agrarian populists, muckraking journalists, and progressive reformers had all, in their different ways, protested against certain aspects of the social order—including business immorality in its various guises. Wealth was said to stand against commonwealth, as Lloyd put it in the 1890s.[131] Brutal factory conditions and child labor were denounced. Prominent businessmen were accused of greed and selfishness. That was the tone

---

129   "Concluding remarks of President–Emeritus Eliot."

130   Charles W. Eliot. 1905. "Employers' Policies in the Industrial Strife." *Harper's Magazine*, March 1905, pp. 528–33, p. 529; Harry B. Taplin. 1904. "President Eliot Before the Boston Labor Union." *The Commons*, vol. 9, no. 4, April 1904, pp. 139–40, p. 140; "His Objections. Former President Eliot of Harvard Criticises Unionism." *The American Employer*, vol. 2, no. 8, March 1914, p. 456. See also Charles W. Eliot. 1919. "Road Toward Industrial Peace." *New York Times*, September 21, 1919, p. 38. An earlier speech of Eliot's about business ethics, "The Ethics of Managing Large Corporations," he gave at the Merchants' Club of Chicago in 1906. "Honesty in Business the Plea of Dr. Eliot." *New York Times*, March 11, 1906, p. 6.

131   Henry Demarest Lloyd. [1894] 1963. *Wealth Against Commonwealth*. Edited and with an Introduction by Thomas C. Cochran. Englewood Cliffs, NJ: Prentice-Hall.

of the Progressive Era. However, some overlaps notwithstanding, the reds that America was scared of constituted a more radical challenge to it. After all, a robust regulatory apparatus, improved labor conditions, and curbs on big business, trusts, combinations, and monopolies actually strengthen capitalism.[132] The actual threat came from people and groups whose inspiration and aspiration was an alternative type of social, political, and economic arrangement altogether, oriented by an alternative conception of the good life altogether. After the "ten days that shook the world," they had an actually existing model to be based on and receive support from. They then had, too, an actually existing model of access to power through violent means, chopping heads off along the way if need be— which liberal democracies were naturally eager to forget they had had to use once themselves. Further, organized labor and its allies could have substantial power in an industrial nation—which liberal democracies were naturally eager to try to subdue or domesticate. Attorney General A. Mitchell Palmer's "Raids" in late 1919 and early 1920 dramatized and sensationalized a more profound cultural pattern. More significant than its occasional dramatic and hysteric symptoms is the ingrained and durable pattern, the defense and vindication of the American institutions and way of life, which Cold War dynamics only intensified. In this sense, the good of America was tied to the reinforcement and legitimization of free-market capitalism and rugged individualism, and the rejection and delegitimization of socialist ideas, institutional arrangements, and of course Soviet-style communism. And here business schools could play an important role, and they hastened to say that they could play an important role.[133]

In a recent article, business historian Bert Spector argues that "the roots of [the] current corporate social responsibility movement can be traced to the decade-and-a-half following World War II" and that "the advocacy of business responsibility, as well as the opposition to that view, was profoundly shaped by and reflected a pervasive Cold War ideology."[134] According to Donald K. David, dean of Harvard's Graduate School of Business Administration from 1942 to 1955, businessmen should "serve the interests of society against the threatened encroachment of Communism." Businessmen should, Spector continues, "help to correct the misdirection away from free-market capitalism and toward socialism

---

132   As mentioned earlier, historians have ardently debated whether progressivism was in fact progressive or conservative, whether Teddy Roosevelt and his associates said one thing in public and another thing in private, and the like. In addition, the concept of progressivism itself has turned out to be problematic. See, e.g., Peter G. Filene. 1970. "An Obituary for 'The Progressive Movement'." *American Quarterly* 22(1):20–34; Kolko, *The Triumph of Conservatism*; Michael E. McGerr. 2003. *A Fierce Discontent: The Rise and Fall of the Progressive Movement in America, 1870–1920*. New York: Free Press; Daniel T. Rodgers. 1982. "In Search of Progressivism." *Reviews in American History* 10(4):113–32.

133   Given this conception of America's good, there is an overlap between the idea that business ethics is good for American business, and that business ethics is good for American society. Yet, unlike business associations, it was morally problematic for business schools to present themselves as advancing the interests of one particular group. Ultimately, the end ought to be the good of society, to which the good of American business was only a means.

134   Bert Spector. 2008. "'Business Responsibilities in a Divided World': The Cold War Roots of the Corporate Social Responsibility Movement." *Enterprise & Society* 9(2):314–36, pp. 315, 316.

that David saw as a dangerous threat throughout the Cold War world." In fact, this phenomenon was already evident much earlier than the post-war era—at Harvard and elsewhere. As Spector himself aptly observes (though does not explore), David "stood . . . on the shoulders of his immediate predecessor, Wallace B. Donham."[135]

As we saw, Donham was not one to give short shrift to the ethics and responsibilities of business. He participated in business ethics projects and discussions. He pondered what the place of these subjects in the business school curriculum should be. Eventually, he decided to institute a chair of business ethics at Harvard. As it turns out, he was worried not only about the good of America, but also about the future of "our western civilization," and specifically about how to "save" it. In 1929, Donham was invited to speak at the William A. Vawter Foundation on Business Ethics, the series of lectures hosted by the School of Commerce at Northwestern. The suggestive title he chose was "Business Ethics as a Solution to the Conflict between Business and the Community." After noting the great "changes in the environment wrought by science," he affirmed:

The effective control of the mechanisms which produce them [those changes] lies not in the scientist, who rarely has any control over the results of his own thinking, but with the business group. Such control must be exercised with a responsible sense of accountability to the community as a whole or we face either revolution or a feudal system based on business overlordship. The last is unthinkable; the former can be avoided only if our business leaders recognize their responsibility and both think and act wisely in carrying it out. No dam-building process such as that which preceded the French and Russian revolutions will serve to defend the present against the future. Channels and ditches must be dug, to the end that greater happiness and greater security may flourish where social disintegration and economic insecurity now make life an arid desert for vast numbers. The task is stupendous, the time elements all too short. The solution, if any is possible in time to save our western civilization, lies in this field of business ethics.[136]

There is no doubt that Donham called a spade a spade. A "revolution" "can be avoided only if our business leaders recognize their responsibility." "Channels and ditches must be dug," but do not even try "dam-building," or you may end up like Louis XVI or Nicholas II. As he explained elsewhere, such dams would be "antisocial"; they "would inevitably help to accumulate a flood of discontent fraught with increasing dangers. The profession of business . . . must avoid the kind of reactionary attitude which strengthens the forces of discontent and revolution."[137] In addition, Donham puts forward the bold suggestion that if there is a solution, it

135 Ibid., p. 321.
136 Donham, "Business Ethics as a Solution," pp. 33–34; Wallace B. Donham. 1929. "Business Ethics—A General Survey." *Harvard Business Review* 7(4):385 94, p. 288. See also John O. Knutson. 1928. "The Cash Value of Ethics." *The Rotarian*, April 1928, pp. 8–9, 59–60.
137 Wallace B. Donham. 1927. "The Social Significance of Business." *Harvard Business Review* 5(4):406–19, p. 413.

"lies in [the] field of business ethics." It turns out that business ethics is our hope to "save our western civilization." The stakes are high indeed.

Although from a different perspective, and somewhat less dramatically, Northwestern's Ralph Heilman similarly claimed that business ethics was essential for the good of American society. Without it, "the result may be disastrous." In fact, business schools may be causally responsible for this disastrous result. As he said in 1928:

> A better knowledge of business methods may prove a curse rather than a blessing, if used simply to obtain personal advantage of competitors, customers, employees and the community.
>
> If departments of commerce in our colleges and universities provide the rising generation with a greater mastery of business technique and methods without developing a strong sense of the moral obligations of the business man, the result may be disastrous. University education for business aims to provide the young man with better tools of business; but if he is to have better tools there must be provided a strong control of the use of such tools. It is of the utmost importance that there be developed in the business leaders of tomorrow a strong ethical sense and a keen realization of the social obligations of business.[138]

Heilman feared the potential dangers of the "greater mastery of business technique and methods." Supposedly, a "strong sense of the moral obligations of the business man" would prevent the disaster of letting that mastery loose, so to speak. This is a bit like the typically modern apocalyptic fears of letting science loose, without ethical and political oversight, as in science fiction dystopias.[139] In other words, Heilman believes that, without something like business ethics, business schools would not be useless and hence a waste of time and effort, but effectively counterproductive. Their effects on society would not be zero, but negative: "[t]o the extent that graduates of our collegiate schools of business use their training for purposes of this kind, it will be worse than useless, from the social point of view."[140]

---

138 "Gift to Endow Business Ethics Course." *Northwestern University Alumni News*, April 1928.

139 Heilman also discussed this fear in his report to the president of Northwestern University for the year 1928–1929, where he formally announced the Vawter gift and lectures: "In the movement for making effective a higher level of ethical conduct in business relations, the higher institutions of learning must perform an important function. A better knowledge of business may prove a curse to society rather than a blessing, if used simply to obtain personal advantage of customers, employees, and the community. University education for business aims to provide the young man with better tools for business, but if he is to have better tools, there must be inculcated in him a strong sense of social obligation in his use of such tools." *Northwestern University Bulletin. The President's Report for 1928–1929*, vol. 30, no. 32, April 14, 1930, pp. 119–20. See also Heilman, "Ethical Standards in Business and in Business Education"; Ralph E. Heilman. 1931. "Personal Qualities Requisite for Success in Business and the Rôle [*sic*] of the School of Business in their Development." *Journal of Business of the University of Chicago* 4(3):11–22, pp. 21–22; Ralph E. Heilman 1932. "Can Business Be Taught?" *Journal of Business of the University of Chicago* 5(4):9–10.

140 *Northwestern University Bulletin* 1930, pp. 119–20.

In sum, I have looked at a peculiar sample of business schools in the late nineteenth and early twentieth centuries, and I have found that these high-status institutions mobilized both the intellectual and the ethical arguments. However, for certain purposes and in certain contexts, only the ethical argument seemed to be able to do the trick. These business schools presented themselves as adopting and advancing the social point of view, the interests of American society. This was to some extent their *raison d'être*. Whatever transpired in deans' offices and board of trustees' rooms, business schools' policies and decisions had an inescapable public dimension. Public opinion would be aware of and pass judgment on them. They were associated with prestigious institutions, such as the University of Pennsylvania, Harvard University, or Northwestern University. The emerging business schools existed in a space of public moral normativity, to which reasons were in principle owed, and in which not any reason was acceptable. For example, it was not acceptable to be oriented toward or guided by the individual, "selfish" point of view—e.g., the maximization of students' future income. Finally, I have argued that business schools' orientation toward the good of American society depended on a particular conception of it—according to which the American capitalist institutions and way of life ought to be "safeguarded." Fortunately, they could help. "The safeguards of the future of private business are the men in its ranks who believe its fundamental purpose is to serve society," as Wigginton Creed, of the Pacific Gas & Electric Company, said.[141] Then, business schools could help enlarge the number of such men.

For the reasons outlined in the introduction, I have focused on public reasons and representations rather than the work of the young business schools to advance the cause of business ethics and social responsibility. What (if any) ethical instruction did they try to "inculcate and impress upon the students"?[142] What (if anything) did they do outside the university to promote business ethics? I did mention, more or less in passing, the chair of business ethics at Harvard, and the William A. Vawter Foundation and Lectures on Business Ethics at Northwestern.[143] I mentioned, too, the Barbara Weinstock Lectureship on the Morals of Trade at the College of Commerce of the University of California. Endowed by Harris Weinstock, "the purpose of the lectureship is stated by the founder to be the education of young men 'to the belief that success in business is more probable and more lasting if conducted upon a high ethical plane, and that true success lies in developing character rather than in

141   Wigginton E. Creed. 1923. *Safeguarding the Future of Private Business*. Boston and New York: Houghton Mifflin, p. 34. This is Creed's 1921 Barbara Weinstock Lecture on the Morals of Trade at the University of California. Creed was described by B. C. Forbes as "the most dynamic directing genius of the colossal and rapidly expanding Pacific Gas & Electric Company." B. C. Forbes. 1923. *Men Who Are Making the West*. New York: B. C. Forbes Publishing, p. 143.

142   *Education of Business Men*, p. 33.

143   Cf. *Official Register of Harvard University*, vol. 25, no. 12, March 24, 1928; Northwestern University Archives. J. L. Kellogg Graduate School of Management. Faculty Meeting Minutes. Box No. 1. Folder: Faculty Minutes 1912–1922. March 31, 1928; Sedlak and Williamson, *The Evolution of Management Education*, p. 62.

heaping up gold'."[144] This series of lectures began in 1904 and has existed ever since. As of this writing the most recent lecture was delivered in 2011 by former Secretary of Labor Robert Reich. A similar initiative was the Page Lecture Series at the Sheffield Scientific School of Yale University, which began in 1908. These lectures dealt "with the question of right conduct in business matters"; they were "given to the members of the Senior Class toward the end of their college year," although "it was intended that the course should not be restricted to them but should be open to all members of the University who might desire to attend."[145] With regard to teaching in the classroom, Harvard was not alone. As of 1931, "a number of schools have come to develop formal instruction on the ethical aspects of business conduct. Such instruction varies from a few lectures to a fully developed course. These courses are given under various terms such as 'business ethics,' 'business procedure,' 'business conduct,' and 'business standards.'" As for their content, "they deal with such matters as standards of right and wrong, and of good form as applied to business, sanctions under which business institutions and methods have developed, ideas of justice in the distribution of wealth—in short, an examination, wholly or in part, of the self-regulatory functions of business."[146]

Taken together, these courses, lectures, foundations, and projects are of much historical significance, and not only because they predate present-day courses, lectures, foundations, and projects by nine or ten decades. Hence, they merit a full-blown historical account that I am unable to offer here.[147] Still, probably no business school ranked business ethics and related subjects among their priorities—in terms of instruction, research, and outreach and public work alike. Take instruction. One section of the study, *University Education for Business*, by Bossard and Dewhurst, examines the curricula of the thirty-eight undergraduate schools in the American Association of Collegiate Schools of Business in the late 1920s. The results show that only 3,815 class hours in the curricula of these schools were devoted to "business and the public" courses—comprising business ethics, social and economic reform, business regulation, and trusts and combinations. In comparison, accounting classes accounted for 22,259 hours, distribution classes 17,986, banking and finance 16,584, economics 14,476, transportation and public utilities 9,544, and management 9,263. By itself, business ethics accounted for

144   University of California. 1904. *Register 1903–1904*. Berkeley: University Press, pp. 103–4; University of California. 1915. *Circular of Information Concerning the Colleges of Letters and Science, Commerce, Agriculture, Mechanics, Mining, Civil Engineering, and Chemistry, the Schools of Architecture, Education and Jurisprudence, and the First and Second Years of the Medical School, 1915–1916*. Berkeley: University of California Press, p. 159; Harris Weinstock. 1904. "The Founder's Preface." Pp. v–viii in Albert Shaw. 1904. *The Business Career in its Public Relations*. San Francisco: Paul Elder and Company.

145   Sheffield Scientific School. 1909. *Morals in Modern Business. Addresses delivered in the Page lecture series, 1908, before the senior class of the Sheffield scientific school, Yale University*. New Haven, CT: Yale University Press, p. v.

146   Bossard and Dewhurst, *University Education for Business*, p. 410.

147   Cf. Abend, "The Origins of Business Ethics."

only 287 class hours.[148] At the same time, though, as far as public representations, presentations of self, self-understandings, and normativity go, ethics and the public good continued to loom large. These normative understandings constituted U.S. business schools as the kind of organization they were, no matter where, to what extent, and how teaching and research practices kept up with them.

148   Bossard and Dewhurst, *University Education for Business*, pp. 290–91.

6

Standards of Practice

> And it is strange, that while every profession, every mechanical art has its theory, no one has as yet attempted to construct the Science of Business. Such a system would embrace a code of business, including the Morals and Manners of Trade, the *rationale* of business management, and a course of business education, including the study of the resources of nations, and Commercial Geography, the processes of production, and the Laws of Wealth, or Political Economy.
>
> —Freeman Hunt, 1856[1]

6.1 Types

The moral background is a conceptual tool that allows us to see the history of business ethics in a new light. As any social science concept, one of its criteria of success is utility: whether it helps us perceive and understand phenomena that we had not properly perceived and understood before. According to my conceptual framework, first-order morality comprises individuals' behaviors, understandings, views, and judgments, as well as society's norms and institutions. These are the sorts of facts that scientists of morality have investigated up to now. In this book I argue that this first-order, surface level is enabled, supported, and facilitated by an underlying second-order level—even if it might not be immediately apparent to the naked eye. This framework oriented my historical narrative in chapters 2 through 5. It directed my attention to the grounds or reasons given as to why businesspeople should be moral, along with the broader understandings and theories that those reasons were in turn based on. It also directed my historical attention to other dimensions of the background: business ethicists' preferred concepts, the objects they morally evaluated, and the moral methods and arguments they used.

In the present and the next chapters I would like to exploit the full potential of the moral background concept to reveal what is going on underneath first-order morality. More specifically, I want to bring out a difference between two types of moral background in the history of business ethics. What follows, then, is an analytical comparison of background elements. While I do not abandon the narrative presentation of historical events, the emphasis is placed on dissecting and scrutinizing the substance of the moral background. In a nutshell, my argument is that underneath durable normative continuities and stability there lie fundamental background discontinuities and variation. The history of business ethics

---

1 Freeman Hunt. 1856. *Worth and Wealth: A Collection of Maxims, Morals and Miscellanies for Merchants and Men of Business*. New York: Stringer & Townsend, pp. vi–vii.

and business ethicists' work is, at the first-order morality level, largely monotonous. Normatively, there are no significant differences between the prescriptions and recommendations of, say, seventeenth- and eighteenth-century manuals of business ethics, early-twentieth-century ethical codes, and early-twenty-first century speeches about business immorality. The social and economic details have changed a lot, of course. But the normative bottom line remains the same: be honest; do not cheat, lie, or steal; you have obligations to you stakeholders; you have obligations to the environment; and so on. This stability cuts across organizational and cultural settings. It cuts across business ethicists' cultural provenance and religious leanings. As mentioned in the introduction, business ethics' first-order monotony comprises the content and tone of complaints about business morals; the content and tone of business ethicists' prescriptions, principles, and recommendations; and the story of scandals and public outrage that seems to repeat itself every so many years. However, once we look at the history of business ethicists' work through the prism of the moral background, what stands out is discontinuity and change. This is where the action is. This is where we find radically different metaphysical pictures, moral methods, objects of evaluation, conceptual repertoires, reasons to be moral, and understandings about the meta-ethical status of business ethics.

In the present and the next chapters I identify and analyze two types of moral background—the Standards of Practice and the Christian Merchant types. My typology is based on the conceptual framework presented in chapter 1. Each type is characterized by a distinct pattern of values on the six moral background dimensions. Table 6.1 summarizes the main characteristics of the Standards of Practice and Christian Merchant types. The next sections of this chapter will mostly flesh out the former; the next chapter will mostly flesh out the latter. Then, unlike chapters 2 through 5, chapters 6 and 7 are organized around specific background dimensions, comparisons, and contrasts, whose empirical manifestations—that is, the historical evidence—I analyze in depth. However, my discussion of these dimensions will not be exhaustive: I only address the most instructive ones. In this chapter my analysis of the Standards of Practice type underscores its scientific worldview and its consequences, its tendency to take actions, decisions, and cases as its objects of moral evaluation, and its tendency toward moral relativism—which is at odds with the moral objectivism of the Christian Merchant type. In the next chapter my analysis of the Christian Merchant type underscores its demanding and consequential metaphysical picture; the status and role of Mammon; the stewardship concept and doctrine; the moral evaluation of a Christian life as a whole; and the applicability of Christian ethics no matter where you are, what you are doing, or whether it is Sunday or Monday.

Three methodological preliminaries remain to be addressed. First, I talk about two types of moral background, but what are types of moral background? How does a social scientist come up with a typology? What makes one typology better than another? My answer draws on Stinchcombe, according to whom "[a] *type-concept* in scientific discourse is a concept which is constructed out of a *combination of the values of several variables*. Sometimes we find that in the world a whole

Table 6.1: Two Types of Moral Background

Background Dimension	Specific Variable	Christian Merchant Type	Standards of Practice Type
Grounding	Why be moral?	- Because it is right, love of righteousness, love of God - Omniscient being knows motives - It will pay in hereafter	- Because it will pay the individual businessperson, American Business, and American society
Grounding & method and argument	Moral theory	Both deontology and (in one particular context) consequentialism	Consequentialism
Object of evaluation	Object	Both ethics of being and ethics of doing	Only ethics of doing
Object of evaluation	Main ethical questions	- What ought I to be? - How does business fit in this life?	- What ought I to do? - What is the ethical "decision" in this particular "case"?
Method and argument	Evidence	- Bible, theology - Anecdotes	- Science, empirical data - Anecdotes
Method and argument	Kind of arguments	- Metaphysical arguments - Biblical exegesis	- Empiricism, inductivism, and scientism - Case method and decision
Repertoire of concepts	Key business ethics concepts	Golden Rule, service	Golden Rule, service, profession
Repertoire of concepts	Kind of concepts	- Theoretical - Theological	- Scientistic - Professional
Metaethical objectivity	Truth-aptness of morality	Generally yes, absolute terms	Generally yes, sometimes relativist terms
Metaphysics	Elements in metaphysical picture	- God - God's ownership of creation - God's omniscience - Heart and soul - Two kinds of time	- Scientific naturalism - Secular time

series of variables has a set of values which are all the same in a large number of observations, and that if we find that one of the variables has a different value then all of them have different values." And he adds: "Whenever a large number of variables go together, so that specific values of one are always associated with specific values of the others, the creation of *typologies*, or sets of type-concepts, such as the chemical elements, is scientifically useful."[2] I draw on this account of Stinchcombe's, but I do not endorse his adverb "always." Chemical elements

2 Arthur L. Stinchcombe. 1968. *Constructing Social Theories*. Chicago: University of Chicago Press, p. 43. I prefer Stinchcombe's to Durkheim's or Weber's classic accounts of types, since they have much methodological and metaphysical baggage that I had rather not carry about. Durkheim, *Rules*; Max Weber. [1904] 1949. "'Objectivity' in Social Science and Social Policy." Pp. 49–112 in *The Methodology of the Social Sciences*. Translated and edited by Edwards A. Shils and Henry A. Finch. Glencoe, IL: Free Press.

are natural kinds; they purportedly carve nature at its joints. The values of these various variables are constitutive of what it is for something to be gold or rubidium.[3] Social types, like my types of moral background, have to have more modest ambitions. This is so both empirically and ontologically. Empirically, I simply wish to highlight probabilistic associations between values of variables. Nothing of importance hangs on just what the probability ought to be; there is no objective threshold that an association must reach to attain type status. Ontologically, social types are not entities that exist independently of us, and hence cannot be empirically discovered the way chemical elements arguably can. Rather, I take them to be just observed empirical patterns or conjunctions, which can be represented as a type for particular purposes, such as comparative arguments. In short, I am a nominalist and a pragmatist about types of social things (just like I said I am about the background in chapter 1).

Second, where are the Standards of Practice and Christian Merchant types to be found? What are their social and organizational locations or roots in the United States in the late nineteenth and early twentieth centuries? Typically, I came across Christian Merchant elements at Protestant churches, groups, meetings, and publications. And I came across Standards of Practice elements in the business press, popular business publications, and the work of business associations, business schools, and some public agencies and officials. This is where I was more likely to find them in my historical research. However, these associations are probabilistic as well. Even more, given a particular organization, both types may coexist within it. And even more, it is neither unthinkable nor uncommon for a single individual to rely on resources and assumptions from both. My claim is not simply that a single individual or organization may be drawing on either type, depending on whom they are talking to, how old she is, or how she is feeling that afternoon. That is certainly the case, but my claim is also that an individual or organization may do that on the same occasion, and even combine their elements for a particular practical purpose—say, a public address or a new policy. Therefore, the Standards of Practice and the Christian Merchant types might coexist in one code of ethics, syllabus, speech, or statement. Pure empirical manifestations of a type are more the exception than the rule. For good or bad, this is how social things are. Then, my speaking of, say, a Standards of Practice business ethicist or organization is but a stylistic shortcut; it means a business ethicist or organization whose work as a rule manifests Standards of Practice elements.

Third, my historical account deals neither with types' social or public preponderance, nor with change over time, nor with the explanation of change over time. My argument is not that one type was hegemonic in this particular period, and then gradually lost its ascendancy until another type took its place. Much less is

---

3 On natural kinds, see, e.g., Joseph Keim Campbell, Michael O'Rourke, and Matthew H. Slater, eds. 2011. *Carving Nature at Its Joints. Natural Kinds in Metaphysics and Science*. Cambridge, MA: MIT Press; André Kukla 2000. *Social Constructivism and the Philosophy of Science*. London; New York: Routledge; Joseph LaPorte. 2004. *Natural Kinds and Conceptual Change*. Cambridge and New York: Cambridge University Press.

my argument comparable to Kuhn's, where paradigms become dominant after a revolution, which is a radical break with the past. Much, much less is my argument a causal explanation of moral background differences across organizations or individuals. Instead, my aims are essentially typological. As I said in the introduction, the logical form of my historical argument is simply that there is a difference or set of differences here. Yet, as this and the next chapters show, this is an illuminating set of differences, which sheds new light on the history of business ethics. It is also a generative set of differences, which paves the way for future research on the moral background level. I hope that this future research will take up questions of preponderance, change, and explanation, which this book is unable to.

6.2 The Science of Ethics

Materialists like Marx and Dr. Johnson fervently oppose idealists like Hegel and Bishop Berkeley—and sometimes refute them by kicking stones. Scientific socialists like Marx and Engels fervently oppose utopian socialists like Saint-Simon, Fourier, and Owen—and charge them with being, precisely, too utopian. Similarly, Standards of Practice business ethicists have little sympathy for "idealists," "utopians," "sentimentalists," and "social dreamers." To begin with, these people's diatribes against business and bad business ethics are naïve and vague. Their demands and proposals are nebulous and softheaded; they do not understand pressing real-world pressures and realities. Businesspeople are busy and have no time or patience for unpractical, unbusinesslike demands and proposals. Furthermore, the methods and evidence of utopian and idealist business ethicists are faulty, too. From the Standards of Practice perspective, they are not systematic enough, not objective enough, and not scientific enough. Especially not scientific.

The Standards of Practice type is characterized by its enormous faith in science: the institution of science, scientific knowledge, and the amenability of all human affairs to scientific methods—human affairs, including ethics and business ethics in particular. The moderate thesis here is that scientific methods can help determine what is good and bad, right and wrong, and permissible and impermissible. The radical thesis is that business ethics can be turned into a science, essentially like physics or biology.[4] Scientific methods can determine what is good and bad, right and wrong, and permissible and impermissible, in business and anywhere else. This is not only a methodological view. It is also an ontological view to the effect that reality consists entirely of particles in fields of force; there

---

4 This is a familiar chapter in the history of the social sciences: all of them have played up their scientific credentials, all of them have had every so often physics envy, and all of them have been every so often accused of "scientism" (up to this very day and for very good reasons). See, e.g., F. A. v. Hayek. 1942. "Scientism and the Study of Society." *Economica* 9(35):267–91; Jürgen Habermas. 1971. *Knowledge and Human Interests*. Boston: Beacon Press. On analytic philosophy's scientism, see Joseph Margolis. 2003. *The Unraveling of Scientism: American Philosophy at the End of the Twentieth Century*. Ithaca: Cornell University Press; Tom Sorell. 1991. *Scientism: Philosophy and the Infatuation with Science*. London; New York: Routledge.

are no supernatural entities, no minds, souls, spirits, fairies, or Platonic objects outside space and time. Therefore, science can in principle provide an exhaustive account of the universe, and science and only science can provide a satisfactory understanding of the universe. Following common practice, I refer to these methodological and ontological views taken together as "scientific naturalism"—which is a moral background feature of the Standards of Practice type.

Good examples of this kind of scientific naturalism in the business world are easy to come across in the activities and documents of Rotary and the business schools. Both of them granted a special institutional and cultural place to science. And, when they engaged in business ethics work or advocacy, they tried to make it more scientific, or at least to be based more on science. Take Rotary first. As we saw in chapter 2, it was born in Chicago in 1905, it rapidly expanded to other towns, and it viewed itself as having a moral mission. Rotary was also born under the influence of the scientific worldview, in part due to its founder and leader, Paul Harris. Harris repeatedly underscored that business should be "scientized"—a process that luckily, he added, was already under way. His 1912 presidential annual report illustrates this view: "As we have said, this is a scientific age and we have scientized almost every step on the route of human progress. Business was one of the last to come into its own; but now that business procedure is being scientized, now that we have scientized our methods of manufacture, sale and delivery, why not go a step further and scientize the very fundamental principles of business success? Let us scientize our methods of acquaintance-making and service-giving."[5] But how can science help make acquaintances and help give service? Harris addressed the former issue as follows:

> The Rotarian plan of acquaintance-making is the latest word in the science to date. [. . .] As an acquaintance-making machine Rotary possesses 100 per cent efficiency. It does easily, smoothly, economically and directly that which is a recognized part of the world's work, a part which has hitherto been done in a far from scientific manner. It reduces waste of time and money to the minimum and produces an acquaintance product scientifically and rationally adjusted to the needs of men.[6]

These statements attest to the centrality of networking in Harris's mind.[7] Along with Rotary's "limited and representative membership," it was a controversial stance. In terms of ethics, acquaintances seem to be treated as mere means to the selfish end of business success. In terms of political economy, it seems to encourage collusion and discriminatory economic practices. Harris did anticipate and try to meet these objections. In any event, the point here is the thorough influence

5 Paul P. Harris. 1912. "Annual Report of President Paul P. Harris." *The Rotarian*, vol. 3, no. 1, pp. 19–25, p. 22.

6 Ibid., p. 23.

7 Indeed, here Harris was arguing for one of the "objects" of the Rotary Club: "To promote the scientizing of acquaintance as an opportunity for service and an aid to success." "Pertinent Facts." 1918. *The Rotarian*, vol. 12, no. 3, p. 82.

of the scientific point of view; the approval and excitement commanded by that which is scientific and rational.

Arthur "Fred" Sheldon, another leader of Rotary in its early years, felt the same way about science. As we saw, Sheldon coined the motto, "He Profits Most Who Serves Best," and ran the Sheldon School of Scientific Salesmanship, a business college in Chicago. The word "science" was in the name of Sheldon's school, as well as in the title of its multi-volume textbook, *The Science of Business.*[8] It was also in the motto of his magazine, *The Business Philosopher*: "A Magazine Devoted to the Science of Business and the Principles Determining the Evolution of Success." In fact, perhaps *The Business Philosopher* is a less appropriate title for the magazine than *The Business Scientist* would have been. Even more, Sheldon held strong deterministic views about universal natural laws that regulate human behavior. For example, an ad for his business college that appeared in several issues of *The Rotarian* in 1916 and 1917 read: "Life in all its phases is governed by Natural Law, not Luck. Successful salesmanship is no exception. It is a matter of Conscious or Unconscious Obedience to Universal Rules of Action or Conduct Prescribed by Nature herself." Sheldon's school, of course, "Makes the Fundamental Laws of Nature Plain." In short, as Seattle Rotarian E. L. Skeel put it, Rotary "[sought] to help each member to do what every business man has long been trying to do for himself, viz., to make his business a science and to study and develop it as such."[9]

Given these commitments to science in relation to business in general, it is not surprising that they would manifest themselves in the business ethics domain, too. Fred Sheldon was committed to science and the scientific perspective; he was committed to using the scientific perspective to address ethical questions as well. Yet, how was this to be done? In the 1921 Annual Convention of Rotary, in Edinburgh, Scotland, Sheldon delivered an address titled "The Philosophy of Rotary." This address was given much symbolic importance by the organization, perhaps because of the high status of the speaker, and perhaps because of its ambitious aspirations and self-aggrandizing, philosophical tone. This tone seems to have impressed Rotarians even in 1976, when a retrospective account in *The Rotarian* saw Sheldon as a "logical man" on the basis of his 1921 address.[10] As reported in the *Proceedings* of this 1921 conference, "for some forty-five minutes [Rotarian Sheldon] held the rapt attention of the convention." "His address was liberally punctuated with applause many times, and at its close an ovation was given which left no room for doubt as to the reception of the message. The audience rose en masse and remained standing and cheering until Mr. Sheldon responded by rising and acknowledging the ovation."[11] This account might be more rhetorical hyperbole

8   Arthur Frederick Sheldon. [1904] 1917. *The Science of Business. Being The Philosophy of Successful Human Activity Functioning in Business Building or Constructive Salesmanship. Lesson Five. Man Building. Reliability Development.* Chicago: n.p.

9   E. L. Skeel. 1914. "Greater Rotary." *The Rotarian*, vol. 5, no. 6, pp. 13–21, p. 15.

10   "Arthur Sheldon: He Made a Motto." 1976. *The Rotarian*, vol. 128, no. 2, pp. 44–45, p. 44.

11   Arthur Frederick Sheldon. 1921. "The Philosophy of Rotary." Pp. 109–45 in *Proceedings. Twelfth Annual Convention of the International Association of Rotary Clubs.* Chicago: International Association of Rotary Clubs, pp. 112 and 110.

than literal truth. But this is precisely the point, because the *Proceedings* show the public face of the organization.

The pillars of Sheldon's "Philosophy of Rotary" were his epistemology and philosophy of science, according to which there exist social laws, or, as he calls them, "wholly natural laws of human relationships." One of these laws, indeed a basic one, turns out to have to do with business ethics: "[L]et us establish the fact that the '*Principle of Service*,' for which Rotary stands, does actually . . . represent a natural law, or rather *the basic law of harmonious and profitable human relationship*" (p. 115). Not only does Sheldon believe in social laws. He also believes that these are universal laws, which, like the laws of physics, are necessarily at work whether anyone recognizes it or not. The "principle of service" is one of them: "Whether the world does, or will, for a long time, recognize the fact or not, the *Principle of Service*, for which Rotary stands, represents a *fact* in Nature. In fact it represents *the controlling or governing law of harmonious and profitable human relationships*." And he adds: "The basic fact for which Rotary stands, '*The Principle of Service*,' is not a *new* fact. The fact is that this, like all other natural laws and principles, has always existed. But the *discernment* of this fact, as a law of human nature, is relatively new" (p. 113).

While many of Sheldon's arguments are unclear, and some are hopelessly confused, his metaphysical commitments regarding the status of these laws of nature are easy to discern. These commitments are even easier to discern when he explicitly alludes to physics, chemistry, and mathematics:

> Man is well acquainted with the law of the compass and the laws of mathematics, and of mechanics and of chemistry. He utilizes them and recognizes the fact that he *must work in harmony with them*, if he expects to get results in the realm of their operation.
>
> It is high time for man to recognize the fact that there are *natural laws of the Kingdom of Man*, and that as such they are universal in their application.
>
> And the "*Principle of Service*" is to the natural laws of human relationships exactly what the law of gravitation, or principle of attraction, is to material bodies. (p. 116)

Sheldon's philosophy of science is surely not his forte. Even if it were logically and substantively straightened out, it would be far from inherently valuable or original. He patently fell prey to several confusions. If you wish to fly across the Atlantic Ocean, then you "must work in harmony" with the laws of physics. But this is so because you have that conscious goal; you wish to "get results in the realm of their operation." Otherwise, the individual's consciousness has nothing to do with the laws of physics. In any event, it is revealing that Sheldon equates the "principle of service" to the laws of physics. He no doubt felt strongly about this issue. Then, what is the content of this principle, similar to the law of gravity? What does it explain and predict, according to Sheldon?

> First: It is perfectly natural for a motionless body, heavier than air, to gravitate toward the earth when the support is removed from it.

Second: It is perfectly natural for trade, in any given line of business, to gravitate to the institution in that line of business which, best serves the world with its products.

Third: It is perfectly natural for the right kind of employees to gravitate toward, be attracted by, the institution in any line of business which, broadly speaking, truly serves its employees the best.

Fourth: It is perfectly natural for increased monetary reward and desirable promotions to gravitate to the individual in any given organization who really and truly serves that institution the best.

Thus do we see that there is no sickly sentiment about the natural law of Service. It is the basic law of sound economics. (p. 116)

This is quite underwhelming, unfortunately. Sheldon does not properly defend this account of the "natural law of Service," or the mechanisms that mediate between causes and effects. Nor does he clarify what work the phrase "perfectly natural" is supposed to do.[12] His metaphors—e.g., "to gravitate" and "to be attracted by"—might be rhetorically clever, but argumentatively will not do. Which becomes even more plain later on: "As certainly as the ripe apple gravitates towards the earth when ready to fall, so does 'trade,' and all the good things of life gravitate toward the individual or institution" whose morals are good (p. 128). The image of an apple under the force of gravity, even if it is Newton's apple, does not really improve the argument.

In any case, what Sheldon viewed himself as advancing was a scientific account of business ethics. And this is probably what he was viewed as advancing. No "sickly sentiment" here, but only "sound economics." We are talking about the "mathematics of life," as he said later (pp. 125 and 140). Much of Sheldon's address does not stand logical scrutiny, and much of it does not stand empirical scrutiny. But the Rotary annual meeting was not an academic seminar room, but a gathering of businesspeople. They were unlikely or unable to assess Sheldon's arguments logically or empirically. He was probably believed to be an intellectual providing profound truths about business ethics. Moreover, what these businesspeople probably took away were basic, rough ideas and memorable words and phrases. That is what they were up to. And this basic, rough idea was roughly as follows: there are scientific principles about the ethics of business; scientific research can lead to business ethics truths. Business ethics was catching up with contemporary science.

Sheldon represents a broader phenomenon in business ethics in the first decades of the twentieth century: the persistent attempts to base it on scientific principles, utilize scientific methods, and arrive at scientific truths. Typical of this

---

12   Having already implied that what is natural is good, Sheldon took the evolutionary analogy further, connecting it to enlightened self-interest: "The law of the survival of the fittest is not the law of the survival of physical and mental strength selfishly exercised. It is the law of the survival of the *most serviceable*, and spiritual power, or *righteousness*, is one of the natural elements in *might*.

He profits most and *survives* best, who serves best. The way to preserve self is to serve others. Service to others is enlightened self-interest. Selfishness is the road to self-destruction. Service to others is the road to self-construction; the preservation of self-interest" (p. 117).

way of conceiving of business ethics is the work of Edgar Laing Heermance in the 1920s. While not as preeminent a Rotarian as Fred Sheldon, Heermance still achieved some fame as a Rotarian, too.[13] He was born in White Plains, New York in 1876, the son of a minister, and the grandson on his mother's side of the long-time president of Yale University, Theodore Dwight Woolsey.[14] Having studied at Yale and the University of Edinburgh, in 1902 he was ordained to the ministry and became the pastor of the First Congregational Church in Mankato, Minnesota.[15] After seventeen years in Minnesota, he returned to New Haven, gave up the ministry, "dropped the title of 'Reverend'," and "turned his full time to forestry."[16] Or so an obituary states—that forestry occupied his "full time" is doubtful, because Heermance also had time to be an active Rotarian. And he also had time to do research and write several books, some of which were on business ethics: *Codes of Ethics, a Handbook* (1924), *The Ethics of Business* (1926), and *Can Business Govern Itself?* (1933).[17]

In chapter 4 we encountered Heermance's 1924 handbook, which is a large collection of codes of ethics. These are codes adopted by various associations in various industries, such as ice cream supplies, advertising agencies, detective agencies, petroleum, automobile manufacture and retail, among many others. Heermance was evidently impressed by what he saw as "a remarkable ethical movement." In the book, the collection of codes is preceded by a short introduction, which begins thus: "The ethical movement of the present generation is part of the adjustment of our race to the particular kind of world in which we live. We have been learning that there are laws of Ethics, as well as of Physics and Biology, and that they operate in much the same way." Thus, Heermance stated right away one of his commitments regarding the metaphysics of ethics or the nature of ethics. Next, he stated his commitments regarding ethical theory or what makes something good from an ethical point of view: "Practices are ethical if, in the long run, they make for the well-being of the human species and for normal human relations. If there is friction and social loss, it is a sign of unethical conditions."[18] So, Heermance turns out to support consequentialism. Positively and optimistically assessing the situation up to that point, he concludes: "We have begun to gather the experience out of which may come in time a science of Social Ethics."[19]

---

13 Hubert Sedgwick. 1928. "Among European Rotarians: Random Rotary impressions of a Connecticut Yankee." *The Rotarian*, vol. 33, no. 4, pp. 15–16, p. 15.

14 William P. Bacon. 1897. *Fourth Biographical Record of the Class of Fifty-Eight, Yale University*. New Britain, CT: Adkins Printing, pp. 129–31.

15 Susan Grigg. 1979. *Guide to the Edgar Laing Heermance Papers*. New Haven, CT: Yale University Library, Manuscripts and Archives; Thomas William Herringshaw. 1914. *Herringshaw's American Blue-Book of Biography: Prominent Americans of 1914*. Chicago: American Publishers' Association, p. 492; Albert Nelson Marquis. 1907. *A Biographical Dictionary of Leading Living Men of the State of Minnesota*. Chicago: A. N. Marquis & Company, p. 222.

16 "Heermance, Author, Dies in Hamden." *The Hartford Courant*, May 18, 1953, p. 4.

17 Heermance, *Codes of Ethics*; Heermance, *The Ethics of Business*; Edgar L. Heermance. 1933. *Can Business Govern Itself? A Study of Industrial Planning*. New York, London: Harper.

18 Heermance, *Codes of Ethics*, pp. iii, 1.

19 Ibid., p. 4.

Naturally, the "science of Social Ethics," like any other science, required systematic data collection.

Two years later, in 1926, Heermance published a book titled *The Ethics of Business*, where his scientific inclinations and ambitions would become more conspicuous.[20] In fact, *The Ethics of Business* was the introduction to "social ethics" that *Codes of Ethics* had been envisioned as a supplement to. The official organ of Rotary, *The Rotarian*, endorsed it enthusiastically. It underscored the book's opposition to "sentimentalism" and its consistency with Rotarianism: "If you believe in sentimentalism, do not read 'The Ethics of Business'—you might not like it. [. . .] If you believe the Rotary Motto and the Rotary Code of Ethics are pretty phrases to toy with but not suited to the crush and jam of modern business, avoid this book—your theory of life might not withstand the force of the facts Mr. Heermance commands."[21] The following year, the annual convention of Rotary International was held in Ostend, Belgium. Heermance's book was mentioned and "Rotarian Heermance," who was in attendance, spoke on the relationship between competitors on the June 7 session.[22] *The Rotarian* also published ads for the book, whose slogan was "NOT a sermon but an exposition of FACTS."[23] This is a good piece of evidence about what readers did and did not appreciate, because ads are specifically designed to appeal to the inclinations of readers. So it is a reasonable inference that they wanted facts, not sermons. If so, the fact that Heermance had been a pastor was not a fact they would have wanted to know. At least, that would not have been the best publicity for the book.

The most remarkable thing about Heermance's 1926 *The Ethics of Business* is its threefold relationship to science. First, its arguments are themselves based on empirical research, which is said to have followed the scientific method. Second, it argues that ethics is a science and its claims have scientific status. Third, its ethics specifically draws on ideas and concepts from physics and biology. To take the first point first, right at the beginning of the book Heermance tells the reader about the method through which he arrived at his conclusions. He impartially analyzed empirical data. In his own words: "My function is that of an impartial interpreter. We are dealing largely with official documents [codes of ethics], and for every point I endeavor to refer to chapter and verse. This method makes it possible to treat the subject as the scientist would treat any other group of social facts." As any good scientist would, Heermance rejects received opinion; he finds it "necessary to base our conceptions of right and duty on experience rather than tradition."[24] As any good promoter of a new science would, he underscores its infancy: "Social accommodation has lagged behind our knowledge of physical

---

20   Heermance, *The Ethics of Business*.

21   R. V. W. [Russell V. Williams.] 1926. "About a Business Methods Book." *The Rotarian*, vol. 29, no. 1, p. 42.

22   *Proceedings. Eighteenth Annual Convention of Rotary International*. 1927. Chicago: Rotary International, pp. 94–99.

23   [*Ethics of Business* Ad.] 1926. *The Rotarian*, vol. 28, no. 6, p. 54.

24   Heermance, *The Ethics of Business*, pp. viii, vii.

forces. But an applied science of Social Ethics is probably no more difficult than the problem of power transmission or the navigation of the air would have appeared a hundred years ago" (p. 204). Not only research, but also the "teaching of Ethics" ought to be scientific: "Standards of practice in industry are the material to be studied and analyzed, as one would interrogate specimens in other science work" (p. 201).

Perhaps most revealing of what Heermance is after is what he is *not* after. There are certain things that "we cannot" do "for the present scientific age":

> For the present scientific age we cannot deduce the laws of conduct from abstract principles, or from the words of an authoritative teacher. To do so would be as futile as to take our astronomy on authority, or to learn anatomy from some arbitrary notion of the human body. The historical treatment of moral standards and ethical standards is interesting and important. It helps us to keep a proper sense of perspective. But such a study should follow first hand investigation rather than precede it; the history of physical theories is not the way we take to advance our knowledge of physics. It will be necessary to follow the inductive method that has proved so fruitful in other lines of research. (p. 192)

Heermance sounds like Robert K. Merton's dismissal in the 1940s of past social theory as scientifically useless: "[s]chools of medicine do not confuse the history of medicine with current theory, nor do departments of biology identify the history of biology with the viable theory now employed in guiding and interpreting research."[25] Likewise, while he does give it a little pat on the back, Heermance views the history of ethics as secondary. Nor does he accept abstract principles or authoritative teachers. In fact, that the laws of conduct be given by authoritative teachers seems to be a common practice, then and now. And it is tempting to mention the words of religious authoritative teachers as a prominent example, Heermance's earlier occupation notwithstanding. By contrast, on his account, ethics is similar to astronomy, anatomy, or physics, which do not care about their history and do not listen to authority. Instead, what is needed in ethics is facts: "first hand investigation" and "the inductive method that has proved so fruitful in other lines of research."

According to Heermance, the inductive method is not merely going to tell us what the laws of conduct are believed to be, in the way an anthropologist may report on what the laws of conduct are believed to be among the Yanomani, the Azande, or the Uruguayans. Rather, first-hand investigation promises to tell us what the laws of conduct actually are. Thus Heermance denies that there is a gap between fact and value. This point is even starker in his discussion of what "a science of Ethics" concerns itself with: "A science of Ethics, as I conceive it, is concerned solely with the question of what is ethical. The further and pressing problem of applied ethics, how to get people to do what is ethical, I must leave

---

25   Robert K. Merton. 1948. "Discussion." *American Sociological Review* 13:164–68, p. 165. Cf. Gabriel Abend. 2008. "The Meaning of 'Theory'." *Sociological Theory* 26(2):173–99.

to the psychologist and the educator" (p. 190). In brief, rather than a dichotomy between fact and value, he maintains that facts established by science can help establish what is and what is not ethical.

I have argued that one main claim of Heermance's *The Ethics of Business* is that ethics is a science and its claims have scientific status. Along the same lines, the businessperson and business ethicist Edward Page said in his 1914 book, *Trade Morals*, that ethics was "the science by which we endeavor to discover principles governing human conduct when appraised as either right or wrong." The revised second edition of Page's book, published in 1918, even had a new subtitle to emphasize the point: *Trade-Morals: Their Relation to the Science of Society.*[26] For his part, Heermance emphasizes the parallels with physics and biology, which provide ethics with concepts and ideas. This happens in two ways. On the one hand, he compares claims about ethics to claims about physics, saying or implying that the analogy should give more credence to the former. For example: "Good-will is not a beautiful but rather utopian ideal. It is one of the most practical realities of social relationship [*sic*]. Every action brings its reaction, and in Ethics, as in Physics, action and reaction are more or less equal. Good-will, expressed in fairness, courtesy and consideration, brings in return the good-will of the customer, which is the greatest asset in any business" (p. 63). The analogy, then, is between the claim that ethics pays and Newton's third law of motion. Logically, however, the analogy does not really constitute evidence for the claim that action and reaction are equal *in ethics*. Which is reminiscent of Sheldon's rhetorical moves.

On the other hand, Heermance tries to make ethics fit into the physical and biological universe. Indeed, this is the way in which he derives the normative content of his business ethics. Specifically, he asks the reader:

> Look at the matter, for a moment, from the broad standpoint of Biology. The problem of right conduct is the problem of evolving life, in its highest phase. All living beings must adjust themselves to their environment. [. . .] The human race, whatever its advantage over lower species, is subject to the same fundamental law. [. . .] This biological approach, which I regard as fundamental, clears up a good many of the difficulties that have beset the path of ethical theory. It gives us a functional conception of ethics, as the art and science of social adjustment.

Heermance then concludes: "There is probably a close correlation between what we are accustomed to call moral, psychological and physiological laws. The function of ethics is to shape the behavior patterns of the group in such a way as to promote normal and efficient living." Thus, "the ethical is that which has positive social value" (pp. 195–97). This should be familiar ground to anyone familiar with late-nineteenth and early-twentieth-century attempts to ground ethics in

---

26 Edward D. Page. 1914. *Trade Morals: Their Origin, Growth and Province.* New Haven, CT: Yale University Press, pp. 6 and 16 (see also pp. 4–5); Edward D. Page. 1918. *Trade-Morals: Their Relation to the Science of Society.* New Haven, CT: Yale University Press.

biological concepts and theories.[27] The evolutionary framework, along with the concepts of survival/extinction, normality/abnormality, and fitness/pathology, seemed to promise a solid foundation upon which to build scientific truths about social life as well. There is still more good news. If ethics is on the side of empirical science rather than philosophy and metaphysics, you get to use objective tests: "Here is an objective test which is capable of the widest application. It may be used to cover any type of group relations. I would put this standard of measurement in the form of two practical rules. They apply to a community quite as much as to a trade association or profession. *First, what is the effect on our own group of the line of conduct under consideration; is it favorable or unfavorable? Second, what is its effect on the wide community with which we are in contact?*" (p. 199).

While "favorable" and "unfavorable" are ambiguous words, a group-level evolutionary framework, along with the "functional conception of ethics," gives them definite content. For example, Heermance has in mind things like "the effect of members' behavior on the standing and prosperity of the group" (p. 197). In turn, this shows that his conception of ethics is a wholly and profoundly consequentialist one. What matters—all that matters, it seems—are the effects of lines of conduct. There are different ways of talking about these effects: "positive social value," "favorable effect," "good consequences," and so on. But they all point in the same direction and reveal a strong commitment to consequentialism. If the effect of a practice on the group and the community is favorable, then *ipso facto* that practice would be ethical (even, apparently, if one or two people had to be sacrificed for the good of the greatest number). As we saw, this consequentialism contrasts with the deontology that ought to guide the Christian businessman.

Heermance's "objective test" is not an abstract, philosophical proposal, or the product of pure reason or theoretical reflection. In accordance with his scientific approach, it is the product of empirical observation: the observation of the actual activities of business and professional associations. As it happens, this is what these associations themselves were doing in order to come up with their codes. They turned out to be as devoted to consequentialism as Heermance was:

It [the unwritten code of conduct in an industry] represents a fresh induction from experience. The practices put under the ban are those which have been found to jeopardize that industry. The practices endorsed are essential to its standing and efficiency. The trade association, in other words, has followed a rough process of social evaluation. Group action and reaction are noted and appraised. Conduct is judged by its consequences. If the reaction on the group is favorable, the practice in question is regarded as ethical. If the reaction is unfavorable, it is unethical. (p. 194)

27 Frances Cobbe. 1872. *Darwinism in Morals and Other Essays*. Edinburgh: Williams and Norgate; L. T. Hobhouse. 1906. *Morals in Evolution*. 2 vols. New York: Henry Holt; Charles Letourneau. 1887 *l'évolution de la morale*. Paris: A. Delahaye et É. Lecrosnier; Jacob Gould Schurman. 1887. *The Ethical Import of Darwinism*. New York: Charles Scribner's Sons; Herbert Spencer. 1879. *The Data of Ethics*. New York: D. Appleton; Alexander Sutherland. 1898. *The Origin and Growth of the Moral Instinct*. 2 vols. London, New York: Longmans, Green.

The confluence of scientific propositions and sensibilities and business propositions and sensibilities, which formed the scientific business ethics of the early twentieth century, produced a reviled enemy. That is the conception of business ethics in a "theoretical" and "abstract" manner; anything that reeks of "preaching," "sentimentalism," or "impracticality." Take Justus George Frederick's 1925 *Book of Business Standards*. The book was published under the auspices of the Commercial Standards Council—an association established in New York City in 1922, which "[bound] together commercial organizations of many types in many fields, and also firms and individuals interested in better business ethics," "[f]or the purpose of fostering higher business standards and eliminating business malpractices."[28] Frederick was a member of the executive board of the Commercial Standards Council, founder of the New York "vigilance committee" that worked for "truth in advertising," former editor of *Printer's Ink* and *Advertising and Selling*, and founder of a marketing research, consulting, and publishing company, The Business Bourse—or "Research and Sales Counsellor [*sic*]."[29] Fortunately for his pecuniary interests, the approach of Frederick's book was properly scientific and properly businesslike: "This is not a book of theory, nor a 'preachment.' It is compiled and written for practical guidance, in the interest of better business. It is a business fact book, not an ethical essay." That should make sense to businesspeople, but nothing makes as much sense to businesspeople as "hard-headed business common sense": "Business executives or business firms will, I hope, find definite, practical value from use of this book, for it is the only broad attempt yet made to codify and interpret the fair rules of business in its various phases. The wider application and use of practical codes is not a moralist's dream, but already a partly accomplished fact, as a result of hard-headed business common sense."[30]

So far this does sound like the sort of book a hardheaded and busy businessman might want to purchase, which Frederick, an expert on advertising and marketing, could hardly fail to be aware of. Yet, in case that was still not clear enough, or in case the hardheaded and busy businessman was still not persuaded, Frederick distances himself from "Sunday schools" and "abstract ideals of conduct."

They [the codes of ethics and standards of practice already so widely adopted] have tended to take off the sharp, crude edges of competitive malpractice and substitute the role of reason and fair play, as well as higher efficiency, which is in reality the mainspring of the whole movement. No one wishes to make Sunday schools out of trade association gatherings, or to impose any laws and precepts for the sake of any abstract ideal of conduct. The guiding thought has

28   Williams Haynes. 1922. "Better Ethical Standards for Business: The Purpose of the Commercial Standards Council." *Annals of the American Academy of Political and Social Science* 101:221–23, p. 221.

29   J. George Frederick. 1920. *The Great Game of Business: Its Rules, Its Fascination, Its Services and Rewards*. New York and London: D. Appleton; J. George Frederick. 1937. "New Uses for Marketing Research." *Journal of Marketing* 2(2):132–33; Lawrence C. Lockley. 1950. "Notes on the History of Marketing Research." *Journal of Marketing* 14(5):733–36.

30   Frederick, *Book of Business Standards*, p. 9.

been the riddance of business barnacles, the "cleaning up" of objectionable, harmful factors, and the speeding up of prosperity and profit thereby. (p. 39)

Now the hardheaded businessman cannot fail to be persuaded. It turns out that the point of the whole business ethics movement is to increase profits! Yet, remarkably, something substantive has changed as a consequence of this scientific and businesslike approach. It seemed we were talking about business *ethics* and *ethical* problems, but it turns out that, in fact, we are not. Not really, or not anymore. According to Frederick's *Book of Business Standards*, "[i]t isn't a matter of 'ethics' or 'morals' at all. To good business men it is, in fact, *more like mathematics than like morals*. To be straightforward takes fewer footsteps than to be crooked. To tell the truth requires less energy than to tell lies and keep them covered up. [. . .] Honor in business is a sheer labor-saving device. To attempt to do without it would be incalculably costly. To use it is to reap the benefit of modern science of inter-relationships" (pp. 23–24).

The simultaneously businesslike and scientific tone displayed by Frederick takes us back to the beginning of this section. Scientific naturalism is an underlying moral background feature, but its manifestations are visible on the surface in the form of language use patterns, particularly lexical inclinations, disinclinations, and taboos. In this regard, scientific-sounding words were dear to Standards of Practice business ethicists. Similarly, business ethics is an ethics for business, so Standards of Practice business ethicists employed, whenever possible, businesslike language. Richard C. Cabot tellingly reports that businesspeople were wary of the very word "ethics," due to its "scholastic connotations."[31] Judge Parker's article about the Principles of Business Conduct, "The Fifteen Commandments of Business," is equally telling. Parker distinguishes two ways of going about doing business ethics, a good one and a bad one:

> It will be noted that all of these principles of business conduct have their source in motive [*sic*] of ultimate enlightened self-interest. They do not spring, in whole or in part, from the emotionalism or the altruism of the social dreamer, who dimly glimpses a distant vision but point us to no road whereby to reach it. Yet when the objective sought is closely examined, it bears a striking likeness to the vision of the dreamer. By different routes the same end is reached.[32]

The word "altruism" did not sound quite right to Parker and his audience of businesspeople. It sounded moralistic. So did the words "emotionalism," "idealism," and "sentimentalism." The language of business ethics ought to be ethically aseptic. It ought to be scientific and naturalistic. This is why "standards of practice" and "business conduct" went down much better than "business ethics" or "trade morals." Similarly, "ethics," "ethical principles," "moral ideals," and "moral duties" had been lost from sight. Indeed, they were almost absent. "Standards of practice," "codes of conduct," "fair play," and "competitive malpractice" were very

---

31 Cabot, *Adventures*, p. 62.

32 Edwin B. Parker. 1924. "The Fifteen Commandments of Business." *Nation's Business*, June 5, 1924, p. 26.

much present. That is a linguistic fact about this kind of business ethics work, underlain by Standards of Practice background elements. More generally, this is consistent with the fact that businessmen are practical men, so they are not interested in the ideals of "social dreamers," but in tangible results. Enlightened self-interest promises to deliver tangible results. Long live Mandeville!

6.3 Science and Ethics at the Business School

In the mid-nineteenth century, Freeman Hunt, publisher of *Hunt's Merchant's Magazine*, lamented that "no one has as yet attempted to construct the Science of Business."[33] Indeed, as early as 1839, in the very first article of the very first number of his renowned magazine, he already referred to this science: "Commerce is not only a business, but a science, extremely intricate in some of its developments, and calculated to elevate the mind, and enlarge the understanding, when pursued upon legitimate principles, and with high and honorable views."[34] Yet, long after Hunt's calls, in the early twentieth century, the construction of the "Science of Business" could not be said to be too far along. For the young university-based business schools, this seemed a matter of life and death. The existence of business schools seemingly required that there existed something like a science of business, or at least that a science of business be possible and its construction under way. This science should distinguish itself from unscientific and journalistic accounts about business, for the same reason that political science, sociology, and economics distinguish themselves from unscientific and journalistic accounts about politics, society, and the economy. The legitimacy of the science of business required, too, that it could distinguish itself from neighboring sciences, such as economics or political economy, so that it could bring something new to the scientific table.

Much like other social science disciplines and departments of the university, business schools thoroughly embraced the scientific worldview and epistemological principles, no questions asked. As Khurana has documented, they associated "management with the moral authority vested in science and the perceived objectivity of the scientific method."[35] This is noticeable almost everywhere in their early institutional history, research, and curricula, including their interest in Taylor's "scientific management."[36] For a good illustration, consider how the scientific spirit manifests itself in the *Harvard Business Reports*, a short-lived series launched in 1925 at Harvard's business school. These were "case books," much like legal ones, presented to the reader as useful experience to be drawn upon. They were "authentic records of real (not fictional) business concerns under actual (not theoretical) business conditions. For the most part, they consist of 'cases,' with commentaries upon them ..." Practically, they should help active businesspeople make decisions

33 Hunt, *Worth and Wealth*, pp. vi–vii.
34 [Freeman Hunt.] 1839. "Introduction." *Hunt's Merchants' Magazine* 1(1):1–3, p. 1.
35 Khurana, *From Higher Aims to Hired Hands*, p. 92 (see pp. 51–64, 91–100).
36 Daniel Nelson. 1992. "Scientific Management and the Transformation of University Business Education." Pp. 77–101 in *A Mental Revolution: Scientific Management since Taylor*, edited by Daniel Nelson. Columbus: Ohio State University Press.

on the basis of those "business precedents." But Dean Donham thought the reports could have a theoretical payoff as well: the "series [was] designed to help develop the theory of business."[37] The scientific theory of business, of course.

Arch Wilkinson Shaw, the business education leader and business publisher, who published the *Harvard Business Review* and the *Harvard Business Reports*, stressed the novelty of the scientific investigation of business:

> It is only within the past twenty-five years or so—a very short period of time— that business men have had really intelligent guidance on which to rely in planning their business courses. For it is only within that comparatively short space of time that the domain of business has been *scientifically* explored.
> [...]
> Business is now scientifically studied. Its facts are collected, classified, an- alyzed. Its underlying principles are emerging in the form of rules, or laws, which have research and reason behind them, instead of merely tradition. With more and more scientific principles to follow, business is becoming very much like a profession.[38]

Once scientific knowledge helped medicine become a true profession; now scientific knowledge would help business become a true profession. What does the scientific perspective involve? First, it rejects any tradition or authority, and traditional ways of doing things, in business or anywhere else. Instead, it rests on empirical evidence or experience; it succeeds or fails on its ability to pass empiri- cal tests. It makes discoveries about the world. Whenever possible, it discovers laws that explain and predict the behavior of atoms, comets, grocery shoppers, or factory workers, as the case may be. It seeks what Williams calls the "absolute conception" of reality.[39] At the university, all of business and management were penetrated by the influence of the scientific worldview: production, distribu- tion, marketing, finance, labor relations, and so on. Business ethics was, too. Ac- cording to the Standards of Practice type, business ethics should be investigated scientifically. These investigations should yield scientific truths about it, just like it was yielding scientific truths about production or marketing. New York University psychologist James E. Lough put the point concisely at a 1915–1916 "commercial education" conference: "We now realize that business is a science and that it is founded on certain general principles. These principles apply to all business operations and include among other topics business ethics and business psychology."[40]

37   Quoted in Jeffrey L. Cruikshank. 1987. *A Delicate Experiment: The Harvard Business School, 1908-1945.* Boston: Harvard Business School Press, p. 143.

38   A. W. Shaw Company. n.d. *Business Precedents and How to Use Them.* Chicago: A. W. Shaw Company, pp. 4, 2-3.

39   B.A.O. Williams. 1978. *Descartes: The Project of Pure Enquiry.* Hassocks: Harvester Press. See also Thomas Nagel. 1986. *The View from Nowhere.* New York: Oxford University Press.

40   James E. Lough. 1916. "Business Ethics and Psychology." Pp. 61–62 in Glen Levin Swiggett. 1916. *Commercial Education. A Report on the Commercial Education Subsection of the Second Pan American Scientific Congress. December, 1915-January, 1916.* Washington, DC: Government Printing Office, p. 61.

Unfortunately, these scientific principles "apply" more straightforwardly to other business operations, even to business psychology, than to business ethics. Therefore, business ethicists had to find a way to work out this "application." They asked, like many philosophers had asked, how exactly science and ethics relate to each other. This was a tough question, especially for business ethicists at business schools. Journalists, trade association leaders, and popular writers and speakers about business ethics can get away with relatively loose arguments. Trade book readers and trade association audiences are unlikely to critically scrutinize the nature of the connection between science and ethics. They may be pleased to hear that science is somehow contributing to the development of better business ethics, or that business ethics has somehow scientific foundations. That is a great thing, they may think to themselves, given that we live in a scientific age. By contrast, the scholarly context of business schools' business ethicists required better arguments. Not only because of their own scholarly disposition or *habitus*, developed over many years of formal education and informal socialization, but also because of the more academic audiences they addressed orally and in print.

Then, the specific problem was how the scientific perspective could and should contribute to business ethics arguments, discussions, and eventually practice. That science can have something to do with production, marketing, or distribution is easy to see. For instance, scientific work can help maximize efficiency and minimize costs through better machines, algorithms, drugs, or energy drinks. It is not so easy to see how science can have something to do with business ethics. Still, many people at the time were trying to build bridges or close the gap between science and ethics. They were trying to come to terms with the omnipresence of science and its impact on society and social life. In that early-twentieth-century context we find, for instance, Felix Adler's somewhat idiosyncratic Society for Ethical Culture in New York, and Albion Small's somewhat idiosyncratic sociology-cum-ethics in Chicago.[41] The relationships between science and ethics were addressed, too, by early social scientists such as Spencer, Comte, Sumner, Durkheim, Lévy-Bruhl, and Charlotte Perkins Gilman.[42]

For scholars whose understanding of society was shaped by Darwin's evolutionary theory, it was perhaps natural to "appeal to biology or evolution for human guidance," as one commentator put it in 1899.[43] In addition to appeals

41   See, e.g., Felix Adler. 1905. *The Religion of Duty*. New York: McClure, Phillips & Co; Felix Adler. 1918. *An Ethical Philosophy of Life: Presented in its Main Outlines*. New York and London: D. Appleton and Company; Felix Adler. 1921. "An Ethical Programme for Business Men." *The Standard* 7(9):253–58; Albion W. Small. 1902. *The Significance of Sociology for Ethics*. Chicago: University of Chicago Press.

42   Charlotte Perkins Gilman. [1914] 2004. *Social Ethics: Sociology and the Future of Society*. Westport, CT: Praeger.

43   Robert Mackintosh. 1899. *From Comte to Benjamin Kidd: The Appeal to Biology or Evolution for Human Guidance*. New York: Macmillan; London: Macmillan & Co., Ltd. Cf. Robert C. Bannister 1979. *Social Darwinism: Science and Myth in Anglo-American Social Thought*. Philadelphia: Temple University Press; Mike Hawkins. 1997. *Social Darwinism in European and American Thought,*

to biology in particular, there were appeals to science in general. Spencer's 1879 *The Data of Ethics* called for "the establishment of rules of right conduct on a scientific basis"; the epigraph of George Gore's 1899 *The Scientific Basis of Morality* was, "The Great Laws of Science are the Chief Guide to Life."[44] Calls for a science of ethics or morals, which hopefully would have policy implications, were common—just like they are common today, one might add. University of Chicago-trained sociologist Edward Cary Hayes published a book in 1921, *Sociology and Ethics*, whose subtitle summarizes the general tendency: *The Facts of Social Life as the Source of Solutions for the Theoretical and Practical Problems of Ethics*.[45] Of course, like today, there was no agreement about the meaning of the expression "science of morality." Like today, there were many proponents, but also many opponents. Some of them insisted, with Hume, that "ought" can never follow from "is." Science is logically incapable of determining what is morally right and good, what we ought to choose, or what is beautiful.[46]

Business ethicists grappled with these problems and debates as well. Especially if based at business schools, they lived in the midst of them. Further, as practical ethicists, they had a special interest in the relationship between science and ethics. One of the most insightful of them was Carl Frederick Taeusch. A native of Ohio, Taeusch did his undergraduate studies at Princeton University (1914), and obtained his doctorate in philosophy at Harvard University (1920), with a dissertation titled, *An Analysis of the Categorical Judgment*. Then he taught philosophy at the University of Chicago (where his colleagues included Tufts and Mead), Tulane University, and the University of Iowa.[47] In 1928, Wallace Donham hired him to work at the Harvard business school, where he taught for the next seven years as Assistant and then Associate Professor of Business Ethics, and became the managing editor of the *Harvard Business Review*.[48] Even though his business ethics class was not required, Taeusch's views were very visible, given his location in the business school field. He was an intelligent observer and analyst, who read broadly and widely, and whose arguments were nuanced, reasonable, and sometimes sophisticated. Taeusch's work is largely academic in spirit and tone.

1860–1945: Nature as Model and Nature as Threat. Cambridge; New York: Cambridge University Press; Richard Hofstadter. 1955. *Social Darwinism in American Thought*. Rev. ed. Boston: Beacon Press.

44 G. Gore. 1899. *The Scientific Basis of Morality*. London: Swan Sonnenschein & Co.

45 Edward Cary Hayes. 1921. *Sociology and Ethics: The Facts of Social Life as the Source of Solutions for the Theoretical and Practical Problems of Ethics*. New York and London: D. Appleton and Company.

46 See, e.g., Henry Sidgwick. 1876. "The Theory of Evolution in its Application to Practice." *Mind* 1(1):52–67; Henry Sidgwick. 1880. "Mr. Spencer's Ethical System." *Mind* 5(18):216–26; Henry Sidgwick. 1899. "The Relation of Ethics to Sociology." *International Journal of Ethics* 10(1):1–21; Henry Sidgwick. 1902. *Lectures on the Ethics of T. H. Green, Mr. Herbert Spencer, and J. Martineau*. London: Macmillan and Co.; New York: Macmillan.

47 The University of Chicago. 1920. *Annual Register*, p. 61.

48 Taeusch "left Harvard in 1935 to become an official of the Federal Department of Agriculture," and, after the war, he taught at the American University in Biarritz, France, at the University of Ankara, Turkey, and at St. Louis University. "Dr. Carl Taeusch, Ex-Professor, 72." *New York Times*, September 23, 1961, p. 19; Copeland, *And Mark an Era*, p. 365.

Unlike Sheldon or Heermance, he was first and foremost a scholar. He was not the kind of person who would jump on a popular bandwagon, just because of its popularity, even if it had to do with science and the promise of science. For instance, despite its popularity, he insisted that the word "service" was "hypocritical and misleading." The slogan "service is above profit" was nonsense, too: "Plainly, the fact is that *profit* always has been, and is always bound to be, the motive of business enterprise. [. . .] When business men lose sight of this patent fact, and sentimentally assert that 'service is above profit,' their statements are meaningless or misleading."[49]

Taeusch was a business ethicist much unlike Sheldon or Heermance, but he agreed with them about the need for an empirical science of business ethics. In his 1926 book, *Professional and Business Ethics*, Taeusch expressed skepticism about how much "arm-chair philosophy or empty metaphysics" could accomplish—two customary archenemies of scientism. Instead, he encouraged "empirical study," "comparative analysis," and "experimental inquiry" in ethics. Thus, he anticipated today's experimental philosophy movement by roughly eighty years, by asking philosophers to get their hands dirty and carry out empirical work.[50]

> The historical and philosophical interpretation of ethical situations alone can avoid the inevitable difficulties which arise from attempts to formulate explicit rules of conduct. Not that these difficulties are to be disposed of by "arm-chair" philosophy or empty metaphysics. For philosophical ethics employs as one of its methods the comparative analysis of all existing codes in order to determine the essentials of a workable code, and it recognizes the necessity of taking into account peculiar conditions surrounding the various professional and business activities. Coupled with this empirical study and comparative analysis of codes is the practical problem of administration. Pragmatism insists that a code is valuable only in so far as it "works." What are the elements which make a code workable? What are the specific sanctions which make a code operative? These are matters of experimental inquiry, and involve a study of cases that are actually and constantly arising.[51]

Taeusch defines ethics as "the science of right human conduct," and argues that "professional and business ethics" should be regarded "as a source of social materials which is coming to be of increasing importance and which is fruitful with implications and amenable to a strict methodological treatment." The next question is what the empirical objects of inquiry of such an empirical business ethics are: "The methods employed by business and the professions in establishing standards and inducing conduct give the cue to methods requisite

49 Taeusch, *Professional and Business Ethics*, p. 258.
50 Granted, 80 years is not a big deal, given that the precursors of experimental philosophy include Aristotle and Hume. Anthony Appiah. 2008. *Experiments in Ethics*. Cambridge, MA: Harvard University Press; Joshua Knobe and Shaun Nichols, eds. 2008. *Experimental Philosophy*. New York: Oxford University Press; J. Knobe, W. Buckwalter, S. Nichols, P. Robbins, H. Sarkissian, and T. Sommers. 2012. "Experimental Philosophy." *Annual Review of Psychology* 263:81–99, pp. 95–96.
51 Taeusch, *Professional and Business Ethics*, p. 5.

for studying them. Empiricism is the keynote of both. The immediate objective of the empirical study of ethics is the codes and standards." Unfortunately, the usual problem resurfaces for Taeusch as well: it is not entirely clear how to move from sociological descriptions of codes to ethical arguments or conclusions. What is entirely clear, though, is Taeusch's empiricist approach: "Strict empiricism does not go beyond the facts, and such empiricism is the heart of the methodology of ethics."[52] His empiricism is likewise patent in his later book, *Policy and Ethics in Business* (1931), which begins with a sociological analysis of "the land and the people" of the United States, as the causal factors or antecedents that account for their business ethics.[53] This was an example of what an empirical, scientific, methodologically rigorous approach to business ethics should look like.

The scientific spirit and worldview of the Standards of Practice type is not a first-order phenomenon. It does not consist in or entail any first-order normative business ethics principle or view. Rather, it is a moral background phenomenon. It is a set of concepts, tools, assumptions, and sensibilities on the basis of which a business ethics approach might be built. It enables and constrains it. The good news is that business ethics and business ethicists could benefit from their association with science. They could benefit from its prestige and from its methods. Associating oneself with science is also known to entail risks, though. There is no scarcity of historical examples of advocates of the scientific worldview who become excessively self-assured and militant about its powers and potentials—and sometimes even arrogant and intolerant. Anything that is not scientific is mere subjective opinion or obscurantism. Even more, anything that is not scientific is just meaningless, as the logical positivists affirmed. Science is able to determine not only what there is, but also what can be said.

Disciplines that are insecure about their scientific powers and whose scientific credentials are not universally recognized are more vulnerable to scientism. They may be more vulnerable, too, to the more-royalist-than-the-king syndrome. They need more "boundary work" to demarcate scientific from non-scientific accounts about their objects of inquiry.[54] For instance, the knowledge claims about politics of politicians, political activists, and journalists are not properly scientific; the knowledge claims about politics of political scientists are. In these respects, the history of the science of business and the history of the science of business ethics clearly fit the bill.

52 C. F. Taeusch. 1927. "An Approach to the Science of Ethics." *International Journal of Ethics* 37(3):269–87, pp. 269, 270–71, 283, and 284. On the relationship between social and natural science, see Taeusch, "An Approach to the Science of Ethics," pp. 285–87; C. F. Taeusch, 1928. "The Logic of the Case Method." *Journal of Philosophy* 25(10):253–64, pp. 253–55; C. F. Taeusch. 1932. "Business Ethics." *International Journal of Ethics* 42(3):273–88, p. 276. On the relationship between ethics and science, see C. F. Taeusch. 1927. "The Significance of Professional and Business Ethics." *Philosophical Review* 36(6):552–61, pp. 559–60.

53 Taeusch, *Policy and Ethics in Business.*

54 Gieryn, "Boundary-Work"; Gieryn, *Cultural Boundaries*; Lamont and Molnár, "The Study of Boundaries in the Social Sciences."

6.4 Cases

There are moral questions and judgments that are primarily about what to do. For instance, a person may have a choice before them, like Jean-Paul Sartre's student: whether to join the army to fight an evil enemy, or to stay at home to care for an ailing relative.[55] Or, like Philippa Foot's trolley driver, a person may have a few seconds to decide whether to run over five workers on the tracks, or turn the trolley and run over one other worker instead.[56] The moral question, then, is what this person should do, or what it would be right, permissible, or obligatory for him to do, morally speaking. However, not all moral questions and judgments are about what to do: some of them are about what or how to be. What kind of person should you be? What kind of life should you lead? As discussed in chapter 1, this is sometimes referred to as the distinction between the ethics of doing (which asks what to do) and the ethics of being (which asks what to be).[57] For example, you may ask whether you should be a courageous, pious, modest, or loving person. Someone may be considered to be a good, bad, vain, generous, fair, open-minded, or irresponsible person. Or as someone who has guts, has integrity, or is depraved, sly, or manipulative.

What is the connection between being and doing? Judgments about being and character are based, inductively, on individual instances of doing. The way you know someone is a courageous or generous person is through seeing they have done several courageous and generous acts. But a person's courageousness or generosity is more than the sum of the many courageous or generous acts they have done. Being and character cannot be translated into a set of concrete and exhaustive judgments, principles, or action-maxims. While you can develop some rules of thumb, they will be somewhat imprecise and not exhaustive, and their application will require *phronēsis* or practical wisdom. Differently put, the ethics of being has changed the question, the primary subject matter, or the order of the factors—which here does change the product. First, you should strive to be a loving or generous person. *Then*, you should lead your life doing the things loving or generous persons do, and making the choices loving or generous persons make. That will take care of the dilemmas you may have to face. But the ethics of being is not concerned with establishing whether an individual act is right or wrong, permissible or impermissible—not even loving or unloving, or generous or ungenerous—as an end in itself.

What about U.S. business ethicists in the period under scrutiny? Were their questions mostly about being or about doing? I argue that the Standards of Practice type is all about doing. Indeed, it is all about a specific kind of doing: making a decision in a particular situation or case. On this view, business ethics works

---

55   Sartre, *L'existentialisme.*

56   Foot, "The Problem of Abortion."

57   William K. Frankena. 1970. "Prichard and the Ethics of Virtue: Notes on a Footnote." *Monist* 54(1):1–17; William K. Frankena. 1973. "The Ethics of Love Conceived as an Ethics of Virtue." *Journal of Religious Ethics* 1:21–36; Stanley Hauerwas. 2001. *The Hauerwas Reader.* Durham, NC: Duke University Press; Mayo, *Ethics and the Moral Life.*

roughly like this. You are a business executive or manager. You are presented with a case, which has many dimensions or elements, some of which are ethical ones. You must single out all of the relevant factors. Then you must decide what you should do. And then you do it. The inclination toward ethics-of-doing questions and an ethics-of-doing style of thought is most evident in the emerging business schools. It is most evident in the "case system" or "case method," promoted by Wallace Donham at Harvard, and progressively adopted in many other universities.

In 1925, Stanford University established its Graduate School of Business—part of the impetus for which had been given by Stanford trustee Herbert Hoover, as President Wilbur later recalled.[58] Stanford's business school was modeled after Harvard's, as a professional, graduate institution. In March 1926, a conference was held at Stanford to celebrate the recent addition to the university, as well as to discuss the subject of business education. One of the presenters was Donham, and his remarks, "University Training for Business in the Light of Harvard [sic] Experience," were followed by an interesting discussion. The first question was asked by Henry S. Dennison, a Boston manufacturer associated with the scientific management school and the Harvard business school.[59] "May I ask Dean Donham if he believes specifically that the ethics of business can be embodied in a course, or in any other way, in a graduate school of business?" Donham said he was not sure (that was in early 1926, yet, as we saw, he would soon come to the conclusion that it could). At that point, "President Morgan" interjected. President Morgan was Arthur Ernest Morgan, president of Antioch College, engineer by profession, and perhaps best known as the first chairman of the Tennessee Valley Authority from 1933 to 1938.

President Morgan: May I break in on this? I started out with the thought that business ethics should not be taught. But as students come in touch with business problems I am more and more convinced that it takes more than good will to make good ethics. We are beginning to admit that business can be taught. Business ethics is something which you too often approach by intuition or a "hunch," and that hunch is ultimately going to be no more authoritative in business ethics than it is in business management. It is highly valuable, but needs the correction of analysis and evidence. If we have gone too far with analysis in business education, we have not gone far enough in business ethics.[60]

Business ethics could profit, too, from "analysis and evidence." Morgan continued by analyzing how business ethics might be taught:

---

58   Ray Lyman Wilbur. *The Memoirs of Ray Lyman Wilbur*. Edited by Edgar Eugene Robinson and Paul Carroll Edwards. Stanford: Stanford University Press, p. 297.

59   Kyle Donovan Bruce. 1999. *Activist Management: The Institutional Economics of Henry S. Dennison*. Ph.D. dissertation. Department of Economics, University of Wollongong; Kim McQuaid. 1977. "Henry S. Dennison and the 'Science' of Industrial Reform, 1900–1950." *American Journal of Economics and Sociology* 36(1):79–98.

60   W. B. Donham. 1926. "University Training for Business in the Light of Harvard [sic] Experience." Pp. 51–62 in *Proceedings of the Stanford Conference on Business Education*. Stanford: Stanford University Press, pp. 59–60.

I think if there is any place in the world where the "case method" is fully appropriate, it is in teaching business ethics. I am coming to believe a course in business ethics built on the case method—where cases in which moral principles are emphasized are brought up—is going to be necessary, because intuition is going to be as vulnerable there as anywhere else.

Saying business ethics cannot be taught is putting ourselves just where people were twenty-five years ago who said business could not be taught. It is one more of the fields which have to be brought into the field of research. It seems to me the time is going to come when we are going to tackle the proposition of business ethics.

Donham responded that he was "entirely in accord with that," although it is unclear to me with what exactly he was entirely in accord, whether the last bit or all of Morgan's arguments. In either case, Morgan's interjection brought up the case system or method. Of all people, Donham did not need to be persuaded of its value. The "problem" or "laboratory" method had been used at the Harvard business school since its very first days.[61] However, Dean Donham institutionalized the case "system" or "method" and strengthened its standing as *the* teaching method of the school. He also had the Harvard Bureau of Business Research collect empirical data in the field, "from the actual experience of the business world," and he had them published as the *Harvard Business Reports*. Being a graduate of Harvard Law School, Donham was familiar with and inspired by Dean Christopher Columbus Langdell's pedagogical innovation for law school teaching.[62] He wrote in 1922: "Fifty years ago when Professor Langdell introduced the use of selected reported decisions of the courts into the Harvard Law School as the basis of classroom instruction, his idea was not received with the greatest confidence, nor was it immediately adopted by the other law schools."[63] Eventually, though, Langdell's idea became more and more confidently received, and was adopted by more and more law schools. Donham speculated—it turns out, correctly—that the same would be true of the case method in the business school. While there were significant dissimilarities between law cases and business cases, Donham thought the similarities were more significant and the analogy still held water.

In this institutional context, the case method addressed pedagogical and epistemological questions that the business school was forced to address. How do you teach business knowledge? What is business knowledge to begin with? These are practical needs implied by the undertaking of running a university-based business school. Thus, the case method was introduced as a general teaching method, that is, for the teaching of all subjects. Much of the discussion about the case

61 Copeland, *And Mark an Era*, pp. 27, 227.

62 Bruce A. Kimball. 1999. "'Warn Students That I Entertain Heretical Opinions, Which They Are Not to Take as Law': The Inception of Case Method Teaching in the Classrooms of the Early C. C. Langdell, 1870–1883." *Law and History Review* 17(1):57–140; William P. LaPiana. 1994. *Logic and Experience: The Origin of Modern American Legal Education*. New York: Oxford University Press.

63 Wallace B. Donham. 1922. "Business Teaching by the Case System." *American Economic Review* 12(1):53–65, p. 53.

method had to do with pedagogical objectives and effectiveness. The case method also had an impact on business schools' research work, because cases ought to be empirically collected. Even high-status institutions realized that collecting these data was tricky. Yet, whatever the practical concerns and pedagogical needs out of which it arose, the case method smuggled in with it a lens or prism through which business reality was apprehended. Looking at it through this prism, business can be "reduced to the making of decisions":

> [N]otwithstanding the difficulties, one thing is encouraging. As more and more cases are developed the teaching of business gets very close to business itself. Practically all business not of a routine nature may be reduced to the making of decisions based on specific sets of facts. [. . .] The overwhelming complexity of modern business and social organization makes it almost certain that some new variable, some new combination of facts, will distinguish the new situation from the old. The business school should furnish a background of facts and general principles upon which the mind trained in the solution of executive problems by the educational process of the school may react, and the training is of far greater importance than the background. The case system is particularly adapted to these ends.[64]

That decision-making is at the heart of business and of business instruction may sound commonsensical, even platitudinous to contemporary Western sensibilities like ours. What else if not decision-making, rational and efficient decision-making, could business possibly be about? Being a good manager means being a good decision-maker. Further, we are accustomed to there being departments and centers of decision-making at universities, journals of decision-making, and methodological and theoretical advances in the "science of decision-making." We have grown accustomed to decision-centered conceptions of economic and political life, and even to decision-centered conceptions of ordinary life—which is exploited and reproduced by trade books on how to make good decisions. In academia, we have grown accustomed to rational choice as a theoretical and methodological paradigm in political science, international relations, sociology, and beyond. According to this paradigm, individuals choose presidents and spouses in the same way they choose detergents and automobiles. However, despite their popularity in many university departments, we should not forget that these are particular conceptions of the world, comparable to prisms or grammars, through which you see the world or with which you talk about the world. Like prisms and grammars, there are many of them out there. Yet, none of them is capable of truth or falsehood; they are not truth-apt.

The case method contributed to business schools' construal of business as "reducible to the making of decisions." The business ethics subfield was no exception. Much like other subfields of business, business ethics was reduced to a matter of cases and decisions. Business ethics issues were defined as cases: cases in which a business executive has to make a decision that somehow had an ethical dimension. If that is so, then the case method is the best way to teach and learn business ethics.[65] Richard Clarke Cabot was both an observer and a participant in this process. Cabot was a man of many interests and talents, professor of medicine and then of social ethics at Harvard from 1903 to 1934, and an advocate of the case method.[66] He used the case method in the medical school, and occasionally at the business school as well:

> [In 1922] I first learned of the project to introduce the teaching of business ethics into the Harvard School of Business Administration. The way in which they purposed to introduce it was of particular interest to me because of my long and enthusiastic acquaintance with the "case method" of teaching. Most of the teaching in the Harvard School of Business Administration has been for years carried on by the case method which I introduced twenty years ago in the teaching of the Harvard Medical School on the suggestion of Professor Walter B. Cannon and have used there ever since, following the much older tradition of the Harvard Law School. Dean Donham of the Business School has been planning since 1922 to have business ethics taught in the Business School by the case method and in that year he was polite enough to ask my advice about the ethical problems or questions to be sought for in the concrete life of industry and brought back to the school for the use of students. He wishes to follow, in relation to ethics, the plan long used in other departments of the Business School, namely, that of gathering from industry concrete cases, problems, difficulties to be written out and presented in case books to the students.[67]

As discussed before, starting in 1928 the Harvard Graduate School of Business Administration began to offer an elective business ethics course, which Carl F. Taeusch was responsible for. In the intervening years, however, business ethics was taught by Cabot, as an invited instructor. As Assistant Dean William D. Kennedy explained to a correspondent, "[l]ast year in this course [business policy], Dr. Richard Cabot took the entire second year class for about five weeks for a discussion of business ethics. I personally went through a very large number of cases in the files of the Bureau of Business Research, and selected a number which appeared to have ethical phases. These Dr. Cabot discussed with the students in the class, and arrived, I think, at some very interesting conclusions."[68] Cabot also

---

65 For a divergent position, see Heermance, *The Ethics of Business*, pp. 202–3.

66 "Cabot's teaching career spanned nearly four decades. At Harvard, he was Lecturer on Philosophy (1902–1903), Instructor in Clinical Medicine (1903–1908), Assistant Professor of Clinical Medicine (1908–1913), Assistant Professor of Medicine (1913–1918), Professor of Clinical Medicine (1918–1933), and Professor of Social Ethics (1920–1934). From 1935 to 1939, he was professor of natural theology at the Andover-Newton Theological School." Harvard University Archives. Richard C. Cabot. 1868–1939. *Papers of Richard Clarke Cabot: an Inventory.* Cf. T. Andrew Dodds. 1993. "Richard Cabot: Medical Reformer during the Progressive Era." *Annals of Internal Medicine* 119(5):417–22; Gary Dorrien. 2009. *Social Ethics in the Making: Interpreting an American Tradition.* Chichester, UK; Malden, MA: Wiley-Blackwell, p. 34.

67 Cabot, *Adventures*, pp. 68–69.

68 Letter of William D. Kennedy to Mr. Black. December 10, 1925. HBS Dean's Office Correspondence. 1919–1942. Box 23. 1923–27. Folder 23-16. So-Ss. Society for Ethical Culture.

recalled these invited classes and his use of cases in his 1926 book, *Adventures on the Borderlands of Ethics*: Dean Donham "has been good enough to allow me to give each year a few case-teaching exercises before students of the Business School and has furnished me, from his own collection, some cases which, though originally written out to exemplify a problem in business management or business policy, seemed to involve primarily questions of ethics." Cabot's book also advances an important substantive point about the role of cases in ethics. The case method of teaching business ethics entails that a business ethics problem is basically a decision problem. But it does not entail that no principles are involved. This is not the "ethics without principles" of Jonathan Dancy.[69] Rather, principles will emerge eventually: "I have already tried it [the case method in business ethics] out enough to convince me that it is the proper way to proceed. It is perfectly possible to build up one's principles of ethics in the classroom with the advice and consent of the student body, rather than to enunciate those principles at the outset. Ethical principles can be made to emerge from any dispassionate consideration of the concrete problems which come up in business, as they do in medicine, in education, or in social work." The endpoint, Cabot made clear, were "ethical principles," and, indeed, "a system of ethics."[70]

Donham was of course the mastermind here, and he provides additional evidence about the relationship between business ethics and the case method. In 1924 he wrote four short pieces for publication in various newspapers as an advertising campaign for the school. The title of the series was "A Professional Education for Business." The first three installments delved into "Business Fundamentals," "The Case Method," and "The Value of Theory." The fourth and last installment was "Building a Code of Ethics":

> The whole problem of teaching business ethics has been much in our minds. From our standpoint it is not enough to deliver to a group of active young men about to enter business a series of talks or lectures with a high ethical purpose. To be effective, instruction or guidance in business ethics must be so handled that the student faces under school conditions, where he has time to think over the problems and to formulate principles from his own thoughtful experience, actual questions involving ethical considerations.[71]

As per the case method, "actual questions" means real-world cases, except that real-world businessmen do not have the benefit of "time to think over the problems." The situation involves complex moral issues and a decision must be made. Donham words it in a revealing manner: businessmen in real life and business students at school have to face "ethical dilemmas."

---

69 Jonathan Dancy. 2004. *Ethics without Principles*. Oxford: Clarendon Press; New York: Oxford University Press.

70 Cabot, *Adventures*, pp. 70–71.

71 Wallace B. Donham. 1924. "A Professional Education for Business. By Dean W. B. Donham. Installment Four. Released for Publication in Newspapers of June 11, 1924. IV-Building a Code of Ethics." Baker Library Historical Collections. Wallace B. Donham. Articles and speeches of. Archives GB2.332. Box 1. Folder Donham, W. B., Addresses and Lectures, 1922–1925.

What we can do in the business school is to give the student practice in handling the same type of dilemmas which he will face later in business life. The only effective way, we think, to help business men of the future in this respect is to give them . . . practice in considering concrete cases which have actually arisen in business. In our courses at the present time cases are frequently brought up involving problems of this nature. This type of problem is not discussed as a thing apart, but as an integral part of all business experience. Thus, we try to develop the power of discrimination between what is right and what is wrong.[72]

That these are "concrete cases which have actually arisen in business" is a significant feature of the case method approach. Standards of Practice business ethicists did not seem to tire of the word "concrete." Yet, how exactly they can "develop the power of discrimination between what is right and what is wrong" is unclear and unspecified. That these are "dilemmas," "ethical dilemmas," is significant as well. This expression did not randomly show up in this piece of business school publicity. Consider a private letter Donham wrote in 1921 to the aforementioned Henry S. Dennison of Dennison Manufacturing Co. The letter is about the lawyer, businessman, and author Waddill Catchings's visit to Harvard: "I have already arranged with him [Catchings] for his work when he is here in the Spring and he may be unwilling to divert his attention from that particular topic. I have asked him to devote his time to an intensive treatment on the case system of the ethical dilemmas in which business men find themselves. You might call it a week's course in Business Ethics."[73] Similarly, consider a letter Donham wrote in 1931 to the British Fabian Graham Wallas, much of which is about the subject of business ethics. Here he spoke of the "ethical dilemmas which are involved in advertising and raising the level of both integrity and research in this field."[74] In these pieces Donham represents the tendency of business ethicists to think in terms of dilemmas. But note that a dilemma is a very particular kind of thing. It is a problem in which a decision-maker has two options, neither of which is entirely unproblematic. Like all cases, perhaps even more than other kinds of cases, they wholly turn ethics into an ethics-of-doing affair. That is built into their nature. They are to be analyzed one at a time. They are compiled in casebooks. All other things ethical are left out of the picture. The ethics-of-being problem of what kind of person one ought to be—which other traditions see as *the* central problem of ethics—is rendered invisible altogether.

It comes as no surprise, then, that Taeusch's business ethics course should be described as a course about cases. This is its description in the 1928 *Official Register of Harvard University*:

The main object of this course is to acquaint the student with cases involving the self-regulatory functions of business: the development of business

72 Ibid.

73 Letter of Wallace B. Donham to Henry S. Dennison. December 13, 1921. HBS Dean's Office Correspondence. 1919–1942. Box 10. 1919–23. Folder 10-20. Dennison Mfg. Co.

74 Letter of Wallace B. Donham to Dr. Graham Wallas. March 25, 1931. HBS Dean's Office Correspondence. 1919–1942. Box 53. School Correspondence. 1927–1937. Folder 53-16. Wa-Ware.

knowledge and integrity, commercial arbitration, association and corporation policies, and the elimination of trade abuses and of unsound promotion
schemes.

Only second-year students may enroll for the first half-year course, in
which attention will be given to the ethical problems arising in marketing, to
trade-association functions and institutes, and to governmental agencies concerned with business ethics.

Both first-and [sic] second-year students may enroll for the second half-
year course. The ethical problems of banking and financial promotion will be
studied, together with methods of business bureaus and problems of organization and labor.[75]

Taeusch had himself given much thought to the case method and its relation
to business ethics. In his 1926 book, *Professional and Business Ethics*, he discussed
"the necessity of the case method." And he already had a clear idea about how
to use cases in business ethics practice (as opposed to business school instruction): "The pressing necessity is for some organization—Rotary, Kiwanis, Lions,
Conopus—to accumulate well-defined cases of business conduct; to rest content
with only a few such cases in the next several years; to have a representative, authoritative, and respected body of men interpret the situation; and then to record
these findings in such a way that they can constantly be referred to, by number, for reference and comparison."[76] The idea is a system based on precedent,
something like accepted customs or the *stare decisis* principle in the common
law. Taeusch continued to develop his arguments about these problems in "The
Logic of the Case Method" (1928) and "Business Ethics" (1932). While he used
the case method as a method of instruction, he found it useful, too, for "generating a science": "It is on this point, of the relation of opinion to social facts, that
the distinction must be made between the employment of the 'case method' as a
pedagogical device and its use as an instrument for generating a science of social
phenomena."[77]

Remarkably, Taeusch's article on "Business Ethics" begins by explicitly rejecting an ethics-of-being sort of question: "One frequently hears the remark that
the whole of ethics, of whatever sort, can be summarized in a single statement:
'Be a gentleman.' The difficulty is not only that, in times of crisis when such a
simple rule could be tested, there are no 'gentlemen'—the same remark applying to 'gentlemen's agreements'—but also that, even in the ordinary problems of
daily life, people differ as to what constitutes a 'gentleman.'"[78] While the passage is
too concise to draw any conclusive inference, Taeusch does come across as being
committed to the ethics-of-doing approach. The ethics-of-being answer, "be a
gentleman," does not produce unambiguous rules to guide a moral agent; it does
not tell her what to do. This is a classic objection leveled at virtue ethicists. And
this is just how Taeusch seems to feel. You tell me that I should be a gentleman,

75 *Official Register of Harvard University*, vol. 25, no. 12, March 24, 1928, p. 40.
76 Taeusch, *Professional and Business Ethics*, p. 271.
77 Taeusch, "The Logic of the Case Method," p. 257.
78 Taeusch, "Business Ethics," p. 273.

but in this particular situation I am now in, not only is it unclear to me what a gentleman should do, but I do not even know how to go about finding out what a gentleman should do.

In sum, in the present and the preceding sections I have examined two characteristics of the Standards of Practice type of moral background: its commitment to the scientific perspective and its commitment to the ethics of doing. My historical data have shown how they manifested themselves in the business school field in the first decades of the twentieth century, e.g., in business ethics thinking and research about cases and decisions, and in business ethics teaching through the "case method" or "case approach." Cases helped business schools solve practical and organizational problems, such as what to teach students tomorrow. In this sense, they were devices with lowly origins, as Nietzschean and Foucauldian scholars like to say. They were organizationally viable solutions thanks to the successful experience of law schools and medical schools—the traditional professions that business schools were trying to emulate. I have also argued that this background-level conception of ethics is not innocuous, but decisively loads the dice. It constrains not only the business ethics policies and strategies that are likely to be implemented, but also the business ethics questions that are found worth raising and discussing, and the business ethics claims that are found interesting and even meaningful. For example, Aristotle, his students, and many of his Greek contemporaries would find the Standards of Practice ethical problems to be useless and a waste of time. Maybe they would not even recognize them as ethical problems at all.

6.5 Metaethics

Business ethicists say that cheating on taxes and Ponzi schemes are morally forbidden and the one-price policy and environmental responsibility are morally required. They demand that businesspeople act accordingly. But what are these demands based on beyond convention, mores, and the law of the land? If Uruguayans denied that Ponzi schemes were wrong, would they be in error, objectively? Or is that just like a custom in their culture, like drinking *mate* and "[looking] at hedgehogs in the light of the moon"?[79] Chapter 1 introduced metaethical objectivity as the fifth dimension of the moral background. First-order morality is underlain by an assumption about its ability to attain objectivity or truth—simplifying somewhat, whether it can or it cannot. The morally realist assumption is that it can, and moral disagreements are like disagreements about factual matters—who the King of Spain was in 1701, or how far is Montevideo from Bilbao. The morally skeptic assumption is that it cannot, and moral disagreements are like disagreements about matters of taste—whether cauliflowers are yummy, Julio Sosa was handsome, or van Gogh's "Starry Night" is beautiful. The morally relativist assumption is that morality is capable of truth, but in a

79 Philippa Foot. 1958. "Moral Arguments." *Mind New Series* 67(268):502–13, p. 512.

peculiar way: "eating people is wrong" might be true for me, but not for you; or true for Americans, but not for the Aztecs. Few people are acquainted with this philosophical distinction and terminology, but the social scientist may still figure out what side they are on.

Here there is a significant difference between the Christian Merchant and Standard of Practice types. Historically, most Christian theologians and moralists have been realists and anti-relativists. That is, they have asserted that moral statements are capable of truth and objectivity, and that true moral statements are true for everyone. In turn, the objectivity and universality of moral statements has been backed up by their conception of God and his divine commands. These are general Christian leanings that the Christian Merchant type of business ethics manifests. By contrast, the Standards of Practice type leans toward moral relativism. While they might not have articulated a consistent and forceful version of relativism, some business ethicists' relativistic tendencies and sympathies are unmistakable. In both cases, these are metaethical assumptions that underlie first-order business ethics work. Business ethicists' *métier* does not comprise metaethical analysis and discussion. They do not need to be aware of the metaethical status of their views, claims, or recommendations. They do not even need to realize that there is a metaethical realm, on which they are taking sides.

Let me illustrate first the Christian Merchant stance via Henry Boardman's 1853 "course of lectures to merchants," *The Bible in the Counting-House*. In the second lecture, "The Standard of Commercial Rectitude," Boardman laments the "lax morality which has so entrenched itself in the business-world as to hamper the freedom even of those who abhor it. And this, in turn, is to be traced to the substitution of false standards of virtue, for the law of God."[80] Boardman goes on to say that the law of God is eternal and universal:

> This law has suffered no abatement in consequence of the coming of Christ. It is as much a rule of duty to us as it was to the generations that lived before the advent. He came, not to destroy, but to fulfil [sic] it. And, in his exposition of it, he has not only ratified every jot and tittle [sic] of the decalogue, but added a "new commandment." "Thou shalt love the Lord thy God with all thy heart and with all thy soul and with all thy strength and with all thy mind; and thy neighbour as thyself." "All things whatsoever ye would that men should do to you, do ye even to them: for this is the law and the prophets." This is the Scripture code. It is no local or temporary enactment. It extends to all times, all countries, all classes, all transactions. (pp. 41–42)

The issue is not what this moral law is, but its universal status. Boardman finds the point worth insisting on. According to relativists, a certain moral obligation or principle may apply to Indians and in India, but not to Americans and in America. According to Boardman, God's law applies even "on the banks of the Ganges": "It is no chameleon-like scheme, which takes its hue from the interests with which it may happen to come in contact. It knows no variableness, nor shadow of turning.

80   Boardman, *Bible*, p. 41.

It speaks the same language in the palace as in the cottage, on the banks of the Ganges as on the banks of the Delaware." In sum: "*This* is the august and immutable standard of morality, which demands the homage of the eager tribes of commerce, of whatever clime, or tongue, or occupation. Impressed with the image and superscription of the only Lord of the conscience, it claims to be installed in every counting-room, and wheresoever men may meet for traffic" (pp. 42–43).

As revealing as what Boardman proposes is what Boardman condemns: "the disposition to make the community itself the arbiter in questions of morals." Custom and convention are often equated with morality, which is terribly misguided. From the Christian Merchant perspective, questions of morals cannot be up to the community. Unlike dress codes and table manners, they are not merely conventional. There are metaphysical reasons for this: "Considering what man is, it would be a marvel, if codes of morals formed in this way were not radically defective: for the stream cannot rise higher than its fountain. In some communities they are, of course better than in others. There is scarcely any class or association which is without its peculiar code, its body of unwritten maxims and usages, which, like the common law, has been handed down from one generation to another, and is clothed with all the authority of regular statutory enactments" (p. 54). Even the "*Bar*, it is alleged, has a traditionary [*sic*] code not coincident in all respects with the Sermon on the Mount, and tolerant of some customs which an advocate like Paul would hardly have resorted to, either before the Sanhedrim or the Areopagus." And, of course, "Commerce also has its conventional standards of morality," which are not all in agreement with "the law of God" (pp. 55–56). Needless to add, Boardman deplores all of these facts. Yet, conventionality about morals—and a community's autonomy to ascertain right and wrong, permissible and impermissible—is just what the Standards of Practice type defends.

The moral relativism of Standards of Practice business ethicists is normally a tendency or intuition, not a full-fledged metaethical view, let alone a consistently articulated and defended one. But it is nonetheless discernible and ubiquitous. Boston retailer Edward A. Filene put it concisely in the course of his 1934 Barbara Weinstock Lecture on the Morals of Trade at the University of California: "Morals are temporal and local. They are local because people live in different times and times change."[81] Despite its conciseness, Filene's statement also illustrates a common ambiguity in standard Standards of Practice relativism. An even more clear illustration is due to Ralph E. Heilman, dean of Northwestern's business school: "Business ethics are clearly relative to the environment in which they are nurtured and to the times, the conditions, and the prevailing type of economic organization."[82] The ambiguity is this: are these statements to be interpreted as descriptive or normative? Are Filene and Heilman merely noting the empirical fact that the ethics of business have varied a lot across time and place? This is an indisputable fact, comparable to the fact that beliefs about the shape of the earth

81   Filene, *Morals in Business*, p. 13.
82   Ralph E. Heilman. 1930. "Ethics Standards in Business and in Business Education." Pp. 3–27 in *The Ethical Problems of Modern Finance*. New York: Ronald Press Company, p. 7.

and women's rights have varied a lot across time and place. Historians and anthropologists have discovered that in some places and times the earth was believed to be a flat disk, and the subordination of women was morally and religiously sanctioned. Or, rather, do Filene and Heilman mean to build on their descriptive statement to make a normative one? If so, their claim would be that, for instance, the "type of economic organization" determines what actually is morally right and wrong. What is wrong here and now may not be wrong elsewhere, because we have a specific type of economic organization. Regrettably, where Filene and Heilman stand is underdetermined by the evidence.

The purported "relativity of business morals" is the focus of an earlier Barbara Weinstock Lecture on the Morals of Trade. This is indeed the title of this 1927 lecture, delivered by California businessman and banker Henry M. Robinson.[83] Robinson began by telling his audience that "we must look upon the morals of business as a relative matter—something to which the doctrine of relativity applies, as it does to all the phenomena of Nature and the handiwork of man, and even to our conceptions of time and space." By now it is evident that Robinson was impressed by "the Einstein philosophy": "The doctrine of relativity asserts that there can be no such thing as absolute position, absolute movement, absolute space, or absolute time; it contends that space and time are interdependent phenomena, not independent; and that everything in Nature is relative to something else. If this be true of the physical world, may it not also be true in its application to the imponderable things of life, including the morals of business?"[84] Robinson's actual application to the morals of business is intellectually dissatisfying. But his basic intent comes through repeatedly: "business morality" "is related to the time, the community, and to the particular branch of business that is concerned"; "business morals are affected by tradition, by racial traits, by the economic conditions of individual communities, by prevailing religious influences, and by various other factors"; and "[t]here is also, of course, a wide and natural divergence in standards as between the large urban communities and the rural districts" (pp. 14–15, 16, and 17).

83   Born in Ohio in 1868, Henry Mauris Robinson attended Cornell University, then worked in corporate law in New York, and in 1906 moved to Pasadena, California. In addition to his successful business activities, he occupied many public posts, through which he made friends with politicians of the stature of Herbert Hoover. Even though at the University of California he lectured on business morals, his own business morals were not free from suspicion, especially in connection with the 1927 Julian Petroleum scandal: "Many southern Californians saw Robinson's arguments as an apologia for the Julian affair, others derided the very notion that the president of Pacific Southwest would dare lecture the nation on business morals." Jules Tygiel. 1994. *The Great Los Angeles Swindle: Oil, Stocks, and Scandal During the Roaring Twenties.* Berkeley and Los Angeles: University of California Press, p. 273.

84   Henry M. Robinson. 1928. *Relativity in Business Morals.* Boston and New York: Houghton Mifflin Company, pp. 1, 2–3. I am presenting Robinson's arguments more coherently than he himself does. In fact, the interpretation of this text can be tricky. For example, he mentions the Golden Rule twice, once at the very beginning and once at the very end (and at the beginning he presents it as an "absolute concept"), which is hard to square with some of his arguments. While there are good grounds to read these Golden Rule references as reverential hat tips, this is still an interpretative judgment on my part.

Moreover, Robinson shows himself to be a true moral relativist about business ethics—rather than, say, a moral skeptic. This is not because he is a sophisticated thinker; he is surely not even aware of the distinction between relativism and skepticism. Still, his intuitions reliably lead him to relativist positions. Recall that relativism does not mean rejection of the predicates "is true," "is correct," "is good," "is right," and so on. It rather means that these predicates are not to be used universally. An action can be right or a thing can be good relative to a framework. In this regard, Robinson is not unlike a Durkheimian "normative relativist": within any given social type there is objective moral good and objective moral progress. Within it, goodness and progress can be objectively established.[85] Thus, Robinson does talk about "better" and "worse" business ethics, "progress" and "improvement" in business morals, and "a higher conception of correct business practice," referring to the 1920s in comparison to the late nineteenth century (pp. 20, 36, and *passim*). In short: "Business morals will doubtless continue to improve, but they will continue to be relative to time and place, and to the circumstances under which each branch of business is carried on at any given time."

The university provided the institutional context not only for Dean Heilman's intervention, but also for Filene's and Robinson's: these were business ethics lectures at the University of California. The university also provided the institutional context for the following three exponents of Standards-of-Practice relativism: James Melvin Lee at New York University, Carl Frederick Taeusch at Harvard University, and Edward Day Page at Yale University. Lee was a "Lecturer on Business Ethics" at New York University in the 1920s. Lee was also the director of the Department of Journalism, and his most significant piece of scholarship was his 1917 history of journalism, based on the class he taught at New York University's School of Commerce, Accounts and Finance.[86] In 1926, Lee published the book, *Business Ethics: A Manual of Modern Morals*, a manual in which "the case system [was] followed wherever possible."[87] In the chapter, "Business Ethics—its Aims and its Principles," Lee emphasizes that business ethics is a relative matter: "One matter can not be overemphasized, the morals of business men as well as those of other individuals must be judged by the standards obtaining in their day. The bewigged and beknickered [sic] business man of Colonial days was strict in his observance of Sabbath, but he favored the lottery as the most practical method of erecting a church building, a bridge, forming a city library, etc. Today the lottery is not only unethical but illegal." However, we are left once again with the same ambiguity. Is Lee's relativism descriptive or normative? Lee adds that "[m]oral standards in the church have been subject to many changes." But it is unclear if he

85   Gabriel Abend. 2008. "Two Main Problems in the Sociology of Morality." *Theory and Society* 37(2):87–125; Roger Cotterrell. 2011. "Justice, Dignity, Torture, Headscarves: Can Durkheim's Sociology Clarify Legal Values?" *Social Legal Studies* 20(1):3–20.

86   James Melvin Lee. 1917. *History of American Journalism*. Boston and New York: Houghton Mifflin Company.

87   Lee, *Business Ethics*, p. v.

intends these changes to justify that "[i]n Colonial days, the minister might drink six days of the week."[88]

For his part, the above-mentioned business ethics professor Carl Taeusch takes "generally accepted standards" to have normative force in business. They are enforceable and should be enforced. Taeusch imagines these standards becoming something like the medieval *Lex Mercatoria* or Law Merchant, which merchant courts enforced. Unfortunately, business practices do not naturally produce "decisions" in the legal sense. Businesspeople obviously make business or executive decisions, but these are not the normative decisions about right, obligatory, or forbidden that a business ethicist would need. In light of this difficulty, Taeusch calls for a committee of notables to make these decisions retrospectively, so that they can be used as precedents:

> The workable, controllable, and desirable project would seem to be . . . the collection of cases which have actually been experience by business men; their analysis, interpretation, and adjudication by a responsible committee, such as is exemplified in the Rotary International Business Methods Committee; and orderly arrangement of these cases and decisions so as to provide for a cumulative set of well-defined precedents; constant codification of these practices—as was done, for example, in the Law Merchant of England several centuries ago—and code accommodations to new situation; and some means of enforcing the generally accepted standards, whether through statutory enactment and legal agencies or by means of sanctions controlled by business organizations themselves.[89]

The committee of notables' "adjudications" will help build the "cumulative set of well-defined precedents," which would change business ethics in practice. The metaethical point, though, is that these notables will consult the accepted standards and discover what is good and right at that time and for that community. Discovering what is good and right is a matter of empirical research. Yet, findings do not generalize beyond the community under investigation.

Not all manifestations of the Standards of Practice type are explicitly associated with a broader social theory, which might entail relativist consequences and commitments. You do not need to talk about social theory to talk about business ethics. But some manifestations do show such association—an instructive example of which is Edward Day Page's business ethics, as presented at Yale University in the late 1900s and early 1910s. Unlike Lee and Taeusch, Page was not a university professor. Rather, he was a "merchant, capitalist, scientist, and patron of art," who "had wide business interests and was also much interested in civic affairs."[90] He was born in 1856 in Haverhill, Massachusetts, graduated from Yale

---

88 Ibid., p. 27.

89 Taeusch, *Professional and Business Ethics*, pp. 264 65.

90 "E. Day Page Dies at Dinner Table." *New York Times*, December 26, 1918; "Edward D. Page." *American Wool and Cotton Reporter*, vol. 33, no. 1, January 2, 1919, pp. 54–55; "Edward Day Page." *Phi Gamma Delta*, vol. 41, no. 4, February 1919, pp. 348–50.

University's Sheffield Scientific School in 1875, and after graduation entered the New York and Boston wholesale dry goods commission firm Faulkner, Page & Company. In 1896, he took residence in Oakland, New Jersey, where he became a prominent citizen and mayor (1909–1911). Page was an intellectually and ethically curious person, one of whose concerns was the ethics of business. Thus, in the summer of 1907, he endowed a series of lectures at his alma mater on "the question of right conduct in business matters."[91]

The "Page Lectures on Business Ethics" began in 1908.[92] Their intended audience was not only "the members of the Senior Class toward the end of their college year," but all of the members of the Yale community. Then they were also "offered to the public" in book form.[93] As the 1914–1915 *Catalogue of Yale University* describes the course, it offered instruction in "Commercial Ethics":

> A course of five lectures (the Page lectures) is given to the entire Senior class during the second term. These lectures deal with the ethical side of business life, and are given by men of experience in mercantile, financial, and legal pursuits. They embrace the following or similar topics: the morals and ethics of production and transportation; the morals and ethics of purchase and sale; the morals and ethics of credit and banking; the morals and ethics of public service; the morals and ethics of corporate and other trusts.[94]

Benefactor Edward Page contributed an introduction to the first series, delivered in the spring of 1908, which he titled "The Morals of Trade in the Making."[95] Three years later, in 1911, he took it upon himself to deliver the whole series, which he eventually published as the book, *Trade Morals: Their Origin, Growth and Province.* Apparently, there was "demand for another printing of this little book," so a second, revised edition came out in 1918. This was in keeping with his

91 The idea might not have been Page's own, though: "For some time prior to [1908] the authorities of the Sheffield Scientific School had been considering the possibility of a course of five lectures dealing with the question of right conduct in business matters, to be given to the members of the Senior Class toward the end of their college year. While these addresses were to be in a sense prescribed study for members of the Senior Class, it was intended that the course should not be restricted to them but should be open to all members of the University who might desire to attend. Through the generosity of Mr. Edward D. Page, of New York City, a graduate of the Sheffield Scientific School in the Class of 1875, this course, now named for the founder, was established in the summer of 1907; and in the spring of 1908 the first lectures in the series were delivered . . ." [Publishers.] 1909. "Publishers' Note." Pp. v–vi in Sheffield Scientific School. 1909. *Morals in Modern Business. Addresses delivered in the Page lecture series, 1908, before the senior class of the Sheffield scientific school, Yale University.* New Haven, CT: Yale University Press, p. v.

92 *Yale Scientific Monthly,* vol. 16, no. 3, December 1909, p. 148.

93 Ripley Hitchcock. 1909. "Introduction." Pp. vii–viii in Sheffield Scientific School. 1909. *Morals in Modern Business. Addresses delivered in the Page lecture series, 1908, before the senior class of the Sheffield scientific school, Yale University.* New Haven, CT: Yale University Press, p. viii.

94 Yale University. 1914. *Catalogue of Yale University. 1914–1915.* New Haven, CT: Published by the University, p. 354.

95 Edward D. Page. 1909. "The Morals of Trade in the Making." Pp. 1–22 in Sheffield Scientific School. 1909. *Morals in Modern Business. Addresses delivered in the Page lecture series, 1908, before the senior class of the Sheffield scientific school, Yale University.* New Haven, CT: Yale University Press.

intention to reach a broad audience: not to address "only college professors," but "[lead] people generally to think about conduct."[96]

Page's relativism starts with his identification of six distinct "business groups": industrial, trading, transportation, financial, laboring, and professional. Then he argues that "[e]ach group has class-ways, class-customs and, therefore, group morals peculiar to itself, which do not always accord with folkgroup morals" (p. 158). Page's relativist idea is that there are "group morals derived from class-customs." On the other hand, he holds that there are also "universal morals derived from folk-custom," which "are recognized by society as obligatory upon all of its members" (p. 152). That said, Page is still proposing a relativist picture, according to which some courses of action are right and obligatory for one group, but are wrong and impermissible for another group. And group here can refer to being an industrialist rather than a financier: there is no need to be an indigenous "culture" in a faraway jungle to be granted the right to some "group morals peculiar to itself."

Furthermore, Page's relativist business ethics account was embedded in broader social theory accounts: he was influenced by his reading of Darwin, Spencer, Wundt, Edward B. Tylor, and William Graham Sumner. In particular, he borrowed the concept of folkways from Sumner's 1906 *Folkways: A Study of the Sociological Importance of Usages, Manners, Customs, Mores, and Morals*, which had been recently published. Sumner was a professor at Yale starting in 1872—and a charismatic and popular one to boot.[97] While I have no evidence about this, maybe Page met him and/or heard him talk about folkways during his time as a student in New Haven. Either way, Sumner puts folkways to relativist ends. He argues that "[t]he notion of the right is in the folkways. It is not outside them, of independent origin, and brought to them to test them. In the folkways, whatever is, is right. [. . .] World philosophy, life policy, right, rights, and morality are all products of the folkways."[98] Sumner does not apologize for his relativism; on the contrary, he boldly asserts that "for the people of a time and place, their own mores are always good, or rather that for them there can be no question of the goodness or badness of their mores. The reason is because the standards of good and right are in the mores."[99] Following Sumner, Page employs the concept of folkways—and the derivative neologisms "folk-custom," "folk-feeling," "folkgroup," "folklaw," "folkspeech," "folkfaith," "folkweal," and "folkwill"—to construct his account about

96   Edward D. Page. 1918. *Trade-Morals: Their Relation to the Science of Society*. New Haven, CT: Yale University Press, pp. ix, xvii.

97   Cf. Robert C. Bannister. 1987. *Sociology and Scientism: The American Quest for Objectivity, 1880–1940*. Chapel Hill and London: University of North Carolina Press, pp. 87–110; B. Nadya Jaworsky. 2007. "Sumner's Tales: Reflections on 133 Years of Sociology at Yale." *Footnotes* 35(7):7–8; B. Nadya Jaworsky and Jeffrey C. Alexander. 2007. "The Secret History of Sociology at Yale: 'Billy' Sumner's Charisma and its Problematic Institutionalization." Unpublished manuscript; Everett W. Hood. 1930. *An Introduction to the Study of Business Ethics*. Buffalo, NY: R. W. Bryant, p. 36.

98   William Graham Sumner. 1906. *Folkways: A Study of the Sociological Importance of Usages, Manners, Customs, Mores, and Morals*. Boston: Ginn and Company, pp. 28–29.

99   Ibid., p. 58.

business ethics. Predictably, the resulting business ethics are relativist; they are necessarily relativist.

Finally, the relativism of the Standards of Practice type was bolstered by another frequent conceptual move: the equation of good business ethics with fair play and sportsmanship. As we saw earlier, this means that businesspeople should abide by the "rules of the game," which are essentially analogous to the rules of boxing, chess, or soccer. Rules of games are obviously nothing but conventions, as are the conventions of driving on the right or left side of the road. Whether you should drive on the right or left side depends on where you are. And that is that. What constitutes a cautionable foul or a sending-off foul in soccer has changed, since the International Federation of Association Football has changed the rules every once in a while. Different soccer associations may have slightly different rules, so what is permissible and prohibited depends again on where you are. These are all relative normative questions. So are business ethics questions. What constitutes unethical business behavior depends on the convention that has been agreed upon in the place where you happen to be.

From a Christian Merchant point of view, however, all of this is nothing short of crazy. For instance, for a moral objectivist like the Presbyterian pastor Henry Boardman, it is crazy to imagine that convention provides the foundations for morality. How in the world could "the community itself [be] the arbiter in questions of morals"? The arbiter is God and the divine law, whatever the community says. Whatever the Sodom and Gomorrah communities say. Now, Boardman was a churchman and a churchman of the nineteenth century. The strongest versions of business ethics relativism had not been formulated yet. So, perhaps a more instructive source of evidence would be an opponent of these later and stronger versions. Perhaps even better would be an actual opponent, outlier, or defector, who developed a divergent understanding in close contact with her relativist antagonists—to use Bernard Williams's useful distinction, someone who faced a "real" (as opposed to "notional") confrontation with them.[100]

One such person was the already mentioned Richard C. Cabot, a devout Christian, who "[u]ntil his last year in college . . . planned to follow a career either as a Unitarian minister or a philosopher."[101] In the end, he became a physician instead, and eventually a member of the Harvard medical faculty in 1903. Yet, his career changed in 1920, as he became a professor of social ethics, also at Harvard. Cabot did not accept much of the ethics accepted and taught as good in his time, especially in professional and business milieus. Relativism included: "trade customs, legal enactments of attraction or repulsion are not sufficient guides to conduct in business—or anywhere else." While "a close understanding of trade customs" is important, it is crucial to still "distinguish ethics from the compilation and registering of trade customs. For those customs may be mischievous, harmful, and wrong, even in the opinion of those governed by them. Agreement between the

---

100 Bernard Williams. 1974–1975. "The Truth in Relativism." *Proceedings of the Aristotelian Society* New Series 75:215–28.

101 T. Andrew Dodds. 1993. "Richard Cabot: Medical Reformer during the Progressive Era." *Annals of Internal Medicine* 119(5):417–22, p. 417.

members of a trade does not in itself make anything right or wrong." Is it not implausible to say that "whatever is is right"?[102]

This is anti-moral relativism and anti-moral subjectivism 101. Cabot's ideas are in some ways peculiar. To be sure, he does not represent the Christian Merchant type as well as, say, Boardman. But this is a textbook example of the anti-relativist stance anyway.[103] In the next chapter I will show where the anti-relativist metaethics of the Christian Merchant type comes from. Christian business ethicists stood on the shoulders of the Christian ethical and metaphysical traditions. So it is necessary to explore the genealogy of their understandings, concepts, and tools to better understand the nature and bases of their rejection of relativism.

6.6 Service and the Golden Rule

In the preceding sections of this chapter I discussed some moral background features that are characteristic of the Standards of Practice type. In the next chapter I will discuss some moral background features that are characteristic of the Christian Merchant type. By contrast, in this section I wish to discuss some elements that are characteristic of both—which therefore serve as a transition from this chapter to the next. My constructing and analyzing types obviously foregrounds the differences between them. But there are similarities and overlaps as well. There are moral background elements that are very widespread in the last decades of the nineteenth and first decades of the twentieth centuries, and thus are equally likely to co-occur with any other element, or to show up in any social or organizational context. At least, this is what I have found in the business ethics field. If they were usable elements, like a concept or a theory, then almost everybody used them. Nobody would have been unable to use them, due to inconsistencies with their background metaphysics, ethics, or style of thinking.

The best examples are the ubiquitous concept of service and the ubiquitous Golden Rule—along with the moral theories and ways of thinking about morality they give expression to. I have already mentioned the extent to which business ethicists insisted on the "ideal of service": the idea that the aim of business is service to the customer, the community, society, or "the public."[104] Service had

---

102   Cabot, *Adventures*, pp. 65–66, 75, 86.

103   I cannot elucidate here Cabot's metaethical views and their Christian underpinnings. Nor can I do justice to the complexity of his arguments. For example, he goes on to deny that people know what they want: "[C]an anyone seriously maintain that people *want* all the wildcat stocks, all the bad whiskey, all the rotten drama and music, all the lying newspaper headlines which they pay for? What other evidence have we that they want them except the fact of payment. In one sense of course the morphinist '*wants*' his dope . . ." This may sound like false consciousness or revealed preferences, but Cabot is headed toward a "Christian ethics," which goes beyond people's "obvious desires," and satisfies instead their "real, deep, and permanent desires." Cabot, *Adventures*, pp. 87–89.

104   The ubiquity of service was not limited to business and the professions. For example, the "professional reformers" of the Progressive Era were also "imbued with the ideal of service—service to the ill-housed and ill-fed and to the community." Roy Lubove. 1962. *The Progressives and the Slums: Tenement House Reform in New York City, 1890–1917*. Pittsburgh: University of Pittsburgh Press, p. 214.

several Christian readings and usages, as well as several non-Christian readings and usages. As we saw, Rotary was one organization captivated by or even obsessed with it. According to Rotarian philosophy, "service is the basis of all business." Thus the slogans, "he profits most who serves best," and "service above self." Likewise, the slogan of its official publication, *The Rotarian*, was "the magazine of service." Rotarian conferences were rife with discussions about service and "service talk." It was a panacea to business-government troubles, business-business troubles, business-customer troubles, and business-labor troubles alike. Rotary surely fell under the spell of service, but surely it was not alone.

It was in the same boat as businessmen like E. St. Elmo Lewis, Edward Filene, and John Wanamaker, the department store pioneer and devout Presbyterian in Philadelphia.[105] Lewis believed that there was a "law of service." Service "*is doing things for others* in recognition of your moral obligation to do more than the letter of your contract if you are in business." "You can't dodge it; it is the law; and prosperity follows the law."[106] For his part, Filene summarized his "simple code of business ethics" thus: "1. A business, in order to have the right to succeed, must be of real service to the community"; and "2. Real service in business consists in making or selling merchandise of reliable quality for the lowest practically possible price, provided that merchandise is made and sold under just conditions."[107] These businessmen were in the same boat as business school leaders such as Leon Marshall and Willard Hotchkiss. Service was at the center of Marshall's curriculum at the College of Commerce and Administration at the University of Chicago. It was also prominent in Hotchkiss's Weinstock Lecture on the Morals of Trade, *Higher Education and Business Standards*.[108] Because service was one of the aims of the traditional professions, business school leaders sought to make the case that service was one of the aims of business as well. It would be hard to exaggerate how often they sought to do so. All in all, B. C. Forbes, the successful business journalist, eloquently summed it up in the 1910s: "SUCCESS, HERETOFORE SPELT $UCCE$$, COMING TO BE SPELT SERVICE—NOT WHAT A MAN MAKES FOR HIS OWN POCKET, BUT WHAT HE CONTRIBUTES TO HIS FELLOW MEN. [. . .] The big man of the future is to be the one who DOES MOST FOR MANKIND, not the one who takes most FROM mankind." From which he concluded, on a pragmatic and prudent note: "To 'put it over' someone is not clever. It is a pinheaded shortsightedness—if you want to keep out of the bankruptcy court. The keynote of modern commerce is SERVICE."[109]

105   *Golden Book of the Wanamaker Stores*. 1911. n.p.; John Wanamaker. 1923. *Maxims of Life and Business*. New York; London: Harper & brothers. Cf. Joseph H. Appel. 1930. *The Business Biography of John Wanamaker, Founder and Builder*. New York: Macmillan.

106   E. St. Elmo Lewis. 1915. *Getting the Most out of Business: Observations of the Application of the Scientific Method to Business Practice*. 2nd ed. New York: Ronald Press Company, p. 468.

107   Edward A. Filene. 1922. "A Simple Code of Business Ethics." *Annals of the American Academy of Political and Social Science* 101:223–28, p. 228.

108   Hotchkiss, *Higher Education*; Marshall, "The College of Commerce."

109   B. C. Forbes. 1916. *Finance, Business and the Business of Life*. 3rd ed. New York: B. C. Forbes, pp. 218 and 220.

It goes without saying that "service" was a vague word, whose meaning could be stretched and manipulated. Take this article by retailer Otho Mooney in *System*, the magazine edited by Arch W. Shaw: "It pays to be of service to the community. And conversely, it does not pay to sell the community a lot of things that are not needed. We could, I have no doubt, work off a lot of stuff which our public would buy if we advertised and displayed it well. But we have held to the ideal of service to the community."[110] In this fragment "service to the community" seems to mean simply not selling to "the community . . . things that are not needed," even if a little advertising could have deceived it into believing that they are. I think that no lexicographer would assent to this definition, however. Still, whatever it meant, and whatever it could be made to mean, the word "service" was pleasing to many ears in the public sphere. Associating yourself or your company with this string of sounds was well regarded and might have reputational benefits. This probably accounts for its having been so widely used by business ethicists, businesspeople, and business associations. But, then, overuse and overextension caused it to become almost empty of meaning.

For its part, the Golden Rule is "the precept that one should do as one would be done by"; it "is perhaps humanity's most familiar ethical dictum."[111] The idea that undergirds this dictum, sometimes referred to as "the ethic of reciprocity," has had innumerable religious and non-religious incarnations. Their diversity is impressive: they can be found in Confucian, Zoroastrian, Islamic, Buddhist, Jewish, and Christian sacred texts alike. They come in both positive-form versions and negative-form versions, such as the "Silver Rule." "What is hateful to you do not do to your neighbor," as Hillel puts it in the Babylonian Talmud (Shabbat 31a). There are also several early versions from Classical Antiquity: for instance, in Homer's *Odyssey*, Herodotus, Isocrates, and even Thales (according to Diogenes Laertius). Despite these variegated genealogical lineages, in the United States in the late nineteenth and early twentieth centuries the Golden Rule had a Christian ring to it. Its ordinary wordings were those of the New Testament, one from the Sermon on the Mount, and the other from the Sermon on the Plain: "Therefore all things whatsoever ye would that men should do to you, do ye even so to them: for this is the law and the prophets (Matthew 7:12); and "And as ye would that men should do to you, do ye also to them likewise" (Luke 6:31).

This was in keeping with earlier business ethics history. The Golden Rule was an essential business ethics principle in Richard Steele's manual, *The Religious Tradesman*, whose first edition appeared in London in 1684.[112] It was an essential business ethics principle, too, to the earliest business ethicists on this side of the Atlantic. For example, New England Puritan minister Cotton Mather declared "the just rules of commerce" in the early eighteenth century: "The *Busineß* of the

110 Otho Mooney. 1921. "Building Beyond Our Narrow Bounds." *System. The Magazine of Business*, July 1921, pp. 28–30, 70, p. 29.

111 Jacob Neusner and Bruce Chilton, eds. 2008. *The Golden Rule: The Ethics of Reciprocity in World Religions*. London and New York: Continuum, p. 1; Jeffrey Wattles. 1996. *The Golden Rule*. Oxford and New York: Oxford University Press, pp. 28–31.

112 Steele, *The Religious Tradesman*, p. 84.

CITY, shall be managed by the *Golden* Rule"; "*I am to Deal with every other man, as I would have another man to Deal with me*. Mark it; I don't say, *I am to deal with others, as they have dealt with me*."[113] Steele and Mather illustrate the fact that the Golden Rule was always part and parcel of Christian moralists' practical work. It was part and parcel of Christian business ethicists' practical work in particular as well. They said it worked. As Reverend Charles Dole said in *The Golden Rule in Business*, "[w]e are ready to show that the Golden Rule is no idle 'Counsel of perfection,' no mere theory or imaginary ideal, but the highest actual law of human life here and now."[114] The Golden Rule was in turn said to present the church with an opportunity: "the Opportunity of Establishing Christ's Supreme Law as the Basic Principle of Commercial Life."[115]

The devout and active Christian businessman Arthur Nash (1870–1927) is another good example. Nash was the owner of the Nash Clothing Company in Cincinnati, Ohio, and formerly had been a Seventh-day Adventist minister. He prided himself in conducting his business activities as a Christian. And he was vocal about his business philosophy and its Christian inspiration: *The Golden Rule in Business*.[116] Indeed, he became "widely known as 'Golden Rule Nash'."[117] But he was not the only Christian businessman whose nickname was "Golden Rule"; curiously, not even the only one in the state of Ohio. Samuel M. Jones (1846–1904), owner of the Acme Sucker Rod Company and mayor of Toledo from 1897 to 1904, was widely known as "Golden Rule" Jones, too.[118] And for the same reason: the application of the Golden Rule in their relationships to customers, employees,

---

113   Cotton Mather. 1710. *Theopolis Americana: An Essay on the Golden Street of the Holy City*. Boston: Printed by B. Green, p. 4; Cotton Mather. 1705. *Lex Mercatoria: Or, the Just Rules of Commerce Declared*. Boston: Printed and sold by Timothy Green, p. 10. See also Joshua Bates. 1818. *A Discourse on Honesty in Dealing*. Middlebury, VT: J. W. Copeland, p. 25; Henry W. Bellows. 1848. *The Christian Merchant: A Discourse Delivered in the Church of the Divine Unity, on Occasion of the Death of Jonathan Goodhue*. New York: C. S. Francis & Co., p. 18; Andrew P. Peabody. 1837. *Views of Duty Adapted to the Times: A Sermon Preached at Portsmouth, N.H. May 14, 1837*. Portsmouth: J. W. Foster, J.F. Shores and Son, p. 10; Jason Whitman. 1837. *The Hard Times: A Discourse, Delivered in the Second Unitarian Church, and Also in the First Parish Church, Portland, Sunday, January 1st, 1837*. Portland, ME: Arthur Shirley, Printer.

114   Charles F. Dole. 1895. *The Golden Rule in Business*. Meadville: Flood and Vincent, p. 17.

115   Arthur Holmes. 1922. "Business Must Have the Golden Rule." *Christian Herald*, February 11, 1922, pp. 101–2.

116   Arthur Nash. 1923. *The Golden Rule in Business*. New York, Chicago, London, and Edinburgh: Fleming H. Revell. Cf. Willard E. Atkins. 1922. "The Personnel Policies of the A. Nash Company." *Journal of Political Economy* 30(2):212–28; Silas Bent. 1926. "The Golden Rule, Plus Sound Business." *Nation's Business*, August 1926, p. 18.

117   Albert Sidney Gregg. 1925. "'Golden Rule' Nash and his Millions." *McClure's Magazine*, October 1925, p. 936.

118   Samuel M. Jones. 1899. *The New Right: A Plea for Fair Play through a More Just Social Order*. New York: Eastern Book Concern. Cf. Robert H. Bremner. 1949. "Samuel M. Jones: The Man without a Party." *American Journal of Economics and Sociology* 8(2):151–61; Peter J. Frederick. 1976. *Knights of the Golden Rule: The Intellectual as Christian Social Reformer in the 1890s*. Lexington: University Press of Kentucky; Marnie Jones. 1998. *Holy Toledo: Religion and Politics in the Life of "Golden Rule" Jones*. Lexington: University Press of Kentucky; Gary Scott Smith. 2000. *The Search for Social Salvation: Social Christianity and America, 1880–1925*. Lanham, MD: Lexington Books, pp. 283–332.

and competitors. While they were both uncommon men in several regards, Nash and Jones represent the class of businessmen who struggled to be morally good Christian businessmen. For this purpose, the Golden Rule seemed to them a most helpful tool. And straight from the Bible!

However, despite its historical and psychological associations with Christian traditions, institutions, and vocabularies, the Golden Rule was not out of place in secular forums. Much to the contrary, it was appropriated, reworked, and deployed in meeting rooms of business associations, business school classrooms, and mainstream newspapers and magazines. Business ethics accounts that drew on the Golden Rule were ubiquitous in these places, even if little or no attention might be paid to its Christian version and Gospel references. Edward Page's 1907 "The Morals of Trade in the Making" illustrates this widespread phenomenon. Page practically "dechristianized" the Golden Rule by invoking "rational consideration of this principle" and by crediting Confucius with its invention (and by not mentioning Jesus or any Christian source):

> The basic idea of Duty, applicable to business as to all other kinds of social conduct embraced within the definition of Morality has been found with singular unanimity by all teachers of mankind in the golden rule, first propounded by Confucius—that each one should treat others as himself. Rational consideration of this principle with respect to any given act or line of conduct will do much to eliminate that degree of selfish interest which we all recognize as antisocial and morally reprehensible.[119]

The codes of ethics of business associations were also replete with references to the Golden Rule. According to Richard Cabot's content analysis, 40 "codes of business ethics" mentioned it, out of the 198 codes he considered (these were the codes included in Edgar Heermance's collection). Not surprisingly, "service" got the silver medal: 36 codes mentioned it.[120] As in the case of service, examples about Golden Rule usage could be multiplied ad infinitum. As in the case of service, the overextension of the Golden Rule meant substantive thinning and conceptual vagueness. Anybody could liberally use it the way they pleased and for what they pleased. It was then no actual panacea. It was rather a cliché, without much agreed-upon meaning.[121]

---

119   Edward D. Page. 1909. "The Morals of Trade in the Making." Pp. 1–22 in Sheffield Scientific School. 1909. *Morals in Modern Business. Addresses delivered in the Page lecture series, 1908, before the senior class of the Sheffield scientific school, Yale University*. New Haven, CT: Yale University Press, pp. 19–20.

120   Cabot, *Adventures*, p. 80.

121   For additional examples of Golden Rule advocacy, see, among many others, William Patrick Clarke. [1920]. "The Golden Rule in Business. Address Made Before the National Association of Manufacturers of Pressed and Blown Glassware Pleading for Betterment of Working Conditions." Pp. 125–35 in *Speeches and Addresses of William P. Clarke*. Toledo, OH: n.p.; Witt K. Cochrane. 1913. "The Golden Rule." *The Rotarian*, vol. 3, no. 8; "The Golden Rule in Action." 1916 *The Rotarian*, vol 9, no 5, November 1916, pp. 447–49; Wilfred Currier Keirstead. 1923. "The Golden Rule in Business." *Journal of Religion* 3(2):141–56; Orison Swett Marden. 1903. *The Young Man Entering Business*. New York: Thomas Y. Crowell & Co.; "Owen D. Young's Business Sermon." *Nation's Business*, April 1929, p. 161.

All the same, business ethicists' appeals to both service and the Golden Rule are sociologically significant, because they can be understood as performative utterances, to use J. L. Austin's avowedly "ugly word."[122] *In* uttering those words, business ethicists were doing something—they were performing illocutionary acts. And *by* uttering those words they were trying to bring about something—they were performing perlocutionary acts.[123] Hence, instead of seeing such appeals as empty substantive arguments or communications, we might consider what the speakers were doing with these words, "service" and the "Golden Rule," given the particular pragmatic contexts in which they used them. First, these might be illocutionary acts expressing allegiance to and support for the business ethics movement, or agreement with the importance of the problem about which something ought to be done. While not as evidently as performative verbs (to name, to promise, to apologize, etc.), speakers were still declaring themselves members of this group of people, or participants in this movement, however informal and unstructured it was. Here the special connection between language use and collective identity becomes evident. Business ethicists in the first decades of the twentieth century began to recognize one another partly through the use of specific linguistic expressions and ways of speaking. Eventually, an informal network began to take shape and solidify: they met at various places, they invited one another to various events, and they cited one another in their speeches and writings. Second, as perlocutionary acts, these utterances might try to get people to do something—namely, to worry more about the business ethics problem, do something about it, sympathize with and provide funding for business ethicists' work, and so on. To quote Austin, these acts tried to "produce certain consequential effects upon the feelings, thoughts or actions of the audience."[124] Service and the Golden Rule were seen as morally good things, businesspeople should want to render a service and follow the Golden Rule, so hopefully these perlocutionary acts would make a practical difference.

That business ethicists began to establish connections among themselves takes us back to one of the backbones of this book: the distinction between morality, moral life, and moral institutions on the one hand, and the underlying background or para-moral elements on the other. It suggests an important historical phenomenon: this network of business ethicists could practically transcend the moral background and metaphysical differences that I have been documenting and examining. By "practically" here I mean in practice, for practical purposes: most of them agreed on most first-order business ethics prescriptions, rules, laws, or institutions. After all, *that* was their primary work—to promote, publicize, and persuade about first-order morality. Although there were exceptions, they could build on one another, or draw on one another whenever convenient, despite their

122   John L. Austin. 1979. "Performative Utterances." Pp. 233–52 in *Philosophical Papers*, edited by J. O. Urmson and G. J. Warnock. Oxford: Clarendon, p. 233; John L. Austin. 1962. *How to Do Things with Words*. Oxford: Clarendon.

123   Cf. John R. Searle and Daniel Vanderveken. 1985. *Foundations of Illocutionary Logic*. Cambridge; New York: Cambridge University Press.

124   Austin, *How to Do Things with Words*, p. 101.

moral background divergences. For example, a secular business school professor could be found drawing on and praising a Protestant minister, and a Protestant minister could be found drawing on and praising a secular business school professor. While at some point the deeper divergences might come into view, there were significant practical overlaps nonetheless. In this sense, this business ethics situation is analogous to the human rights situation depicted by Charles Taylor. As I discussed in chapter 1, Taylor argues that a broad world consensus might be attained despite incommensurable moral, metaphysical, and religious backgrounds.[125] Put differently, it is possible to reach first-order agreements despite second-order disagreements. Or so one hopes.

125   Taylor, "Conditions of an Unforced Consensus on Human Rights."

7

The Christian Merchant

Money, in the sight of Him who made *it* and *us*, is but one of the atoms of His creation; and the idolatry that worships Mammon, amid the light and knowledge of our age—and especially, within the pale of the modern Church—must inevitably draw down the lightning-stroke of Him with whom we have to do. The possessions we lay claim to, and assume to make the ministers of our selfish whims, are but accommodation loans made us by Him who has also loaned us our lives. Both property and life and our account of them—with principal and interest—are subject to his call and liable to His demands.

—Frank Ballard, 1865[1]

Every sphere of life develops thus of necessity a special morality. This customary morality may, however, lose vitalizing connection with higher than utilitarian standards, may fail to root itself in ethical principles, and so may be low in its ideals, weak in its motivities [*sic*]. It is needful in every sphere, and especially in the realm of business, where selfishness most powerfully depresses and deflects conscience, to bring the customary morality frequently before the court of ethical law, in order to ascertain its shortcomings, to correct its deviations, to vitalize anew its principles.

—R. Heber Newton, 1876[2]

7.1 Moral Exemplars

November 24, 1848. New York City. The merchant Jonathan Goodhue passed away at sixty-six years of age. Goodhue was regarded as "one of the first merchants in New-York" for two kinds of reasons:

We and many others—all indeed who knew him, either personally or by reputation—have been wont to regard him as one of the first merchants in New-York; and not solely by reason of his extensive mercantile operations, or of the enterprise and intelligence by which they were guided, but equally, and even in a greater degree, by the integrity, the large and liberal spirit, the enlightened conscientiousness, which governed them, and which long since gained, and permanently secured to Mr. Goodhue the unqualified respect of his fellow merchants and fellow-citizens, and made his name as it were

---

1 Ballard, *The Stewardship of Wealth*, p. 5.
2 R. Heber Newton. 1876. *The Morals of Trade. Two Lectures: I. An Inquiry into the Actual Morality of Trade. II. An Inquiry into the Causes of the Existing Demoralization and the Remedies therefor.* Given in the Anthon Memorial Church, New York. New York: T. Whittaker, p. 11.

a synonim [*sic*] for all that is honorable and estimable in the mercantile profession.[3]

Obituaries, which always praise the exceptional morals of the deceased, unanimously praised the exceptional morals of Goodhue. Associations such as the Chamber of Commerce of the City of New York and the Grocers of the City of New York made resolutions to publicly express their condolences. The former additionally appointed a committee "to procure a portrait or bust of Mr. Goodhue for the Chamber of Commerce," and the latter declared "the death of Mr. Goodhue . . . a public calamity."[4]

A memorial sermon was delivered on Sunday, December 3, at the Church of the Divine Unity in New York—in the elegant building the congregation had recently relocated to on Broadway between Spring and Prince Streets.[5] The pulpit was occupied by Henry Whitney Bellows. Bellows was then in the early stages of his influential career as pastor of that congregation, eventually rechristened Unitarian Church of All Souls, founder and editor of the *Christian Inquirer*, and leader of American Unitarianism. As a contemporary of his observed, he was "a ready extempore speaker and a popular lecturer," who spoke and published "his views freely upon the prominent topics of the day, and inclines to deal with current interests rather than with scholastic studies."[6]

Bellows's eulogy of Goodhue, *The Christian Merchant*, appeared in several periodicals and was published soon afterward as a booklet.[7] It is instructive for at

---

3 "General Intelligence." *New York Evangelist*, November 30, 1848, p. 191.

4 "Obituary. Jonathan Goodhue." *New York Municipal Gazette*, vol. 1, no. 52, January 18, 1849, pp. 880–81; Jonathan Sturgis. 1848. "Jonathan Goodhue." *Christian Inquirer*, December 2, 1848, p. 30. See also "Jonathan Goodhue." *New-York Daily Tribune*, December 4, 1848, p. 1; "Mercantile Biography. The Late Jonathan Goodhue." 1849. *The Merchants' Magazine* [*Hunt's*], vol. 21, no. 1, pp. 40–49; Hunt, *Lives of American Merchants*.

5 "All-Souls' Church, Corner of Fourth Avenue and Twentieth Street, N.Y." *Ballou's Pictorial*, vol. 17, no. 8, August 20, 1859, p. 117; Jonathan Greenleaf. 1846. *History of the Churches, of all Denominations, in the City of New York*. New York: E. French; Portland: Hyde, Lorde & Duren, p. 375; Benson J. Lossing. 1884. *History of New York City*. Volume 2. New York: Perine Engraving and Publishing Co., p. 575; *A Picture of New-York in 1846; with a Short Account of Places in its Vicinity; Designed as a Guide to Citizens and Strangers: with Numerous Engravings, and a Map of the City*. New-York: C. S. Francis & Co., pp. 133–34.

Founded in the early nineteenth century, this congregation was referred to by different names throughout its history: First Unitarian Church, Church of the Divine Unity, and eventually Unitarian Church of All Souls, its most recognizable (and current) name. Before Henry Bellows, its pastors were William Ware and (for a brief period) Charles Follen.

6 George Ripley and Charles A. Dana, eds. 1870. *The New American Cyclopædia. A Popular Dictionary of General Knowledge*. Volume III. New York: D. Appleton and Company; London: 16 Little Britain, p. 107.

Bellows (1814–1882) graduated from Harvard Divinity School in 1837, and his long pastorate at the Church of All Souls in New York lasted from 1839 until his death in 1882.

7 Henry W. Bellows. 1848. *The Christian Merchant: A Discourse Delivered in the Church of the Divine Unity, on Occasion of the Death of Jonathan Goodhue*. New York: C. S. Francis & Co; Rev. Henry W. Bellows. 1848. "A Discourse Occasioned by the Death of Jonathan Goodhue. Delivered at the Church of the Divine Unity, on Sunday, December 3, 1848." *Christian Inquirer*, December 9, 1848, pp. 33–34; "The Christian Merchant." *Christian Register*, December 30, 1848, p. 1.

least two reasons. First, it illustratively manifests the traditional ambivalence of Christian moralists regarding business, commerce, and money-making. Bellows did not find anything wrong with business in and of itself. Much to the contrary. After all, was he not talking about a businessman and to businessmen? In this sense, selection into this group—speakers at a memorial of this sort—accounts for the observed outcome. Yet, characteristically, Bellows did find morally good and bad ways of going about engaging in business. Second, the sermon illustrates the construction of "the Christian Merchant" as a moral exemplar—which, I argue, is underlain by specific moral background elements. Bellows said:

> What we particularly need . . . is the example of men who are thrown into the hottest part of this furnace, and yet come out unscathed! Men who enter into the arena of business, seek its rewards, wrestle with its competitors, experience its temptations, taste its disappointments and its successes, its anxieties, and its gratifications; pass through its crises of panic, and of bubble-prosperity, and yet through all, uphold a character and reputation for unspotted honor and integrity, for equanimity and moderation, and for qualities of mind and heart, to which worldly success is manifestly and completely subordinated. (pp. 7–8)

One such Christian Merchant was Goodhue: "My brethren, we have had such an example before us, in a distinguished merchant of this community, and an honored member of this Christian Society, recently departed from among the living." An exemplar such as the Christian Merchant was intended to set a normative standard to be followed or an ideal to be approached: "Brethren, I have thus imperfectly, but truthfully set forth this example of a Christian Merchant, especially addressed to you as business men, in the hope that it may win your serious and profound attention, and with the prayer that through its contemplation, the words of the text may be verified: 'That thou mayest walk in the way of good men, and keep the paths of the righteous'" (pp. 11 and 27). This verse, Proverbs 2:20, encapsulates my point about moral exemplars. They are tools or devices whose point is to affect moral convictions, behaviors, and institutions. In the words of the *Herald of Gospel Liberty*, "[n]othing speaks more loudly for the Christian life than a real Christian life."[8] Exemplars have been long put to these practical uses—harking back to hagiographers' "lives" of the saints, or Plutarch's *Parallel Lives*. Plutarch's lives are moral lives; Plutarch, much like Bellows, is "far more moralist than historian."[9] Furthermore, clergymen did not monopolize this tool: neither among U.S. business ethicists nor elsewhere. The above-mentioned *Lives of American Merchants*, by John Frost and by Freeman Hunt, are biographies of merchants "eminent for integrity, enterprise and public spirit," as per the subtitle

---

8 "Business Men and the Christian Life." *Herald of Gospel Liberty*, November 9, 1916, p. 1411.

9 Bernadotte Perrin. 1914. "Introduction: Plutarch's Life and Writings." In *Plutarch's Lives*. With an English translation by Bernadotte Perrin. London: William Heinemann; New York: The Macmillan Co, p. xi. Cf. Tim Duff. 1999. *Plutarch's Lives: Exploring Virtue and Vice*. Oxford: Clarendon Press; New York: Oxford University Press; Peter France and William St Clair, eds. 2002. *Mapping Lives: The Uses of Biography*. Oxford; New York: Oxford University Press for the British Academy.

of the former.[10] They have a moral point. So do ordinary periodicals' obituaries of eminent businessmen.[11]

Bellows's "Christian Merchant" illustrates how business ethicists utilized this moral exemplar to further their practical projects. Not all of them attributed the exact same characteristics to the exemplar. And some of them referred to it, perhaps more accurately, as "the Christian Business Man" or "Christian man of business"—as clergymen Phillips Brooks and John De Witt respectively did toward the end of the nineteenth century, for example.[12] However, some common characteristics of this moral exemplar were as follows. The Christian Merchant or Christian Business Man is a good businessman and a good Christian. In fact, he does not lead his life as though business and Christianity were two separate spheres or compartments of it. Morally speaking, it makes no difference whether it is Sunday and he is at the church or it is Monday and he is at the counting house, office, or factory. His behavior is guided by the same principles and convictions. The Christian Business Man does not cheat or lie to his customers. He does not use false weights and measures or adulterate his products. If he is an agent, he never tries to deceive his principal. He does not cheat on his taxes or misrepresent his financial statements to the shareholders and state agencies. Why? The reason is not that business ethics is good business. Rather, he does it from his love of God and his neighbor. Furthermore, the Christian Business Man believes he has responsibilities toward his community. He has responsibilities toward his workers and toward the poor. Why? The reason is that he is just a steward or trustee of riches that are not his but God's.

In this chapter I spell out the Christian Merchant or Business Man exemplar, and the normative demands and ideals it sets forth. This is what actual Christian merchants were urged to strive for. This is what they should try to be or become. Then, I spell out the moral background elements that underlie these first-order normative demands and ideals. These elements can be grouped together as a type of moral background, the Christian Merchant type, which I contrast to the Standards of Practice type analyzed in the previous chapter (see table 6.1).

One methodological clarification before moving on: I do not mean to imply that there was a homogenous group of Christian business ethicists, nor that they necessarily agree at the first-order or second-level levels. To begin with, the "tradition" on which I say Christian business ethicists drew is a great simplification. There are differences across denominations and groups, given the characteristic "Protestant pluralism" of the United States.[13] Thus, "Christian," "Protestant,"

---

10 Frost, *Lives of American Merchants*; Hunt, *Lives of American Merchants*. Note that one of Hunt's eminent American merchants was Goodhue.

11 Cf. Diamond, *The Reputation of the American Businessman*.

12 Brooks, "The Duty of the Christian Business Man"; John De Witt. 1885. "The Relations of Religion and Business." Pp. 150–65 in *Sermons on the Christian Life*. New York: Charles Scribner's Sons, p. 164. See also Carlos Martyn. 1890. *William E. Dodge: The Christian Merchant*. New York and London: Funk & Wagnalls.

13 Cf. Richard W. Pointer. 1988. *Protestant Pluralism and the New York Experience: A Study of Eighteenth-Century Religious Diversity*. Bloomington: Indiana University Press. (Pointer's book is about New York only, though.)

"Christian business ethicists," and "Protestant business ethicists" are broad, catch-all labels, which conceal a lot of internal variation. This is so regarding ordinary practices and institutions, as well as the various branches of theology: Christology, soteriology, pneumatology, ecclesiology, eschatology, and anthropology. Besides, there is the simple fact that Christian business ethicists might have different views about things, some of which can sort them into subcategories, and some of which are idiosyncratic. Even if patterns exist, all social patterns have exceptions, and Christian business ethicists are no exception. Last, I pay little attention to changes over time and geographical differences. That said, typologies are analytical tools, which necessarily simplify reality. So the question is what they were designed to be useful for. Despite the diversity of the class of Christian business ethicists, in this book my interests and objectives lie elsewhere. Where you should stand to look at the world, and whether you should look at it with a microscope, the naked eye, or a telescope, do not depend on the nature of the world itself, but on what you are up to.

7.2 Mammon

January 31, 1875. New York City. "Christ Church, corner of Fifth avenue and Thirty-fifth street, was filled . . . by a cultivated audience to hear the fourth of the course of sermons on 'Christianity and Social Morals.' Rev. R. Heber Newton, of the Anthon Memorial Church in West Forty-eight street, preached the sermon upon the Morals of Trade." What did that cultivated audience hear on that winter evening? Reverend Newton's sermon addressed various topics: "overcharging, undermeasurement, undervaluation in invoices, lying advertisements, and gambling speculations," the need for "a code of trade ethics," "financial crises," and how "Wall street [was] hypocritical in covering its gambling transactions with the flimsy veil of commercial or financial operations." Wall Street notwithstanding, God's blessing and the millennium of trade were not unreachable, though. There should be hope: "When selfishness was turned into justice, competition into reciprocal interest, and the greatest good—not for the greatest number—but for all, became the maxim of those engaged in trade, then would God's blessing be given, and the millennium of trade be at hand."[14]

Christ Church, despite its "modest, unecclesiastical looking" abode, was a traditional institution in New York. It had been in existence since 1793; indeed, it was "the first Protestant Episcopal parish formed in this city after the Revolution."[15] The speaker, Richard Heber Newton, was the rector of another Episcopal congregation in the city, Anthon Memorial Church (All Souls'), at the time located at West 48 Street and Sixth Avenue.[16] Newton was a popular and controversial

---

14 "The Importance of Commercial Morality." *New York Times*, February 1, 1875, p. 5.

15 William J. Davies. 1888. "Historical Sketch of Christ Church, New York City." *Magazine of American History with Notes and Queries*, vol. 19, no. 1, January 1888, pp. 58–64, p. 58.

16 All Souls' Church was established in 1859 under the leadership of Henry Anthon—it was then referred to as the Anthon Memorial Church, and it was located at 139 West 48 Street at Sixth Avenue. Led by R. Heber Newton since 1869, in 1889 it merged with the Episcopal Church of the Holy

clergyman: Social Gospel leader, Society of Christian Socialists leader, and social reformer—a "stout champion of social-moral reform," as Rabbi Stephen Wise said in his memorial service.[17] His opinions on social, political, and theological matters were contentious—so much so that he was even charged with heresy.[18] Being a Social Gospel leader, he always attended to current social problems and public issues, including "wickedness in high positions" and "epidemics of fraud."[19]

Since at least 1874, Newton lectured in various cities on business ethics, culminating in the two lectures he delivered to his own congregation, Anthon Memorial Church, in the spring of 1876. These were titled, "An Inquiry into the Actual Morality of Trade," and "An Inquiry into the Causes of the Existing Demoralization and the Remedies Therefor," and they were published together in book form that very year, along with fifteen appendices. Aptly, the title of the book is *The Morals of Trade*, which Newton borrowed from Herbert Spencer's 1859 essay.[20]

The Morals of Trade deals with several issues related to business ethics: *laissez-faire* economic policies, women's economic and moral roles, greenback currency, trade associations, among others. Like many Christian business ethicists, Newton morally differentiates "wealth well won and used" on the one hand, from the "altar of Mammon" and the "order of the Almighty Dollar" on the other:

Society is to-day realizing the satire of one of [Thomas] Nast's cartoons, its beauty and fashion falling down in homage before the altar of Mammon. Wealth well won and used deserves deference. It is the sign of ability and character, in which inhere the roots of all genuine aristocracies. Wealth in itself may mean the accident of birth, the luck of rascality. To pay court to the

---

Spirit and it moved to Madison at East 66 Street. After Newton's departure to Stanford University, it merged in 1906 with the Church of the Archangel and it moved to Harlem, 88 St. Nicholas Avenue at 114 Street, where it still is today. "Anthon Memorial Church. Rev. R. Heber Newton's Congregation." *New York Times*, December 7, 1874, p. 2; "Proposed Union of All Souls' and the Church of the Archangel." *New-York Tribune*, December 9, 1905, p. 11; "Old Church Joined to New." *New-York Tribune*, March 16, 1906, p. 3.

17 *A Service to Honor the Memory of The Rev. R. Heber Newton, D.D. And to Help Perpetuate the Ideals to which his Life was Dedicated.* 1915. New York: G. P. Putnam's Sons, p. 61.

Richard Heber Newton (1840–1914) was an Episcopal clergyman, the son of Episcopal clergyman Richard Newton. He attended the University of Pennsylvania and the Philadelphia Divinity School. In 1869 he became the rector of All Souls' Church in New York, a position he occupied until 1902. He "was perhaps the second most prominent figure in the early development of social Christianity [after Gladden]. A champion of liberal, evolutionary theology, Newton reached a wide audience with his sermons and frequent periodical publications." Henry F. May. [1949] 1967. *Protestant Churches and Industrial America.* New York, Evanston, and London. Harper & Row, p. 170. See also Clyde C. Griffen. 1967. "Rich Laymen and Early Social Christianity." *Church History* 36:45–65; Arthur M. Schlesinger. [1932] 1967. *A Critical Period in American Religion, 1875–1900.* Philadelphia: Fortress Press, p. 36.

18 R. Heber Newton. 1887. "The Religious Aspect of Socialism." Pp. 259–96 in *Social Studies*. New York & London: G. P. Putnam's Sons; R. Heber Newton. 1887. "Communism." Pp. 297–355 in *Social Studies*. New York & London: G. P. Putnam's Sons. Cf. "Charged with Heresy. A Presentment against the Rev. R. Heber Newton." *New York Times*, April 26, 1883, p. 8; "Charges against Dr. Newton." *New York Times*, April 30, 1895, p. 8; "Dr. Heber Newton, Noted Rector, Dies." *New-York Tribune*, December 20, 1914, p. 11; "R. Heber Newton, Noted Divine, Dead." *New York Times*, December 20, 1914, p. 15.

19 "The Epidemic of Fraud." *New York Herald*, October 11, 1886, p. 8.

20 Spencer, "The Morals of Trade."

empty-headed son of a millionaire, to smile upon the successful sharper, is in fact to create an aristocracy based on neither power nor merit, to set up a plutocracy whose only standard is money, an order of the Almighty Dollar. [. . .] When society accredits money as a valid passport, it gives as its all-influential counsel the advice of the old man, "My son, get money; get it honestly if you can; but get it."

This is the evil, not indeed of our really best society, but of that which passes for such, which is accredited "good." The old traditions of respectability and worth are giving way before the weight of the plutocracy. [. . .] Our parlor conversation is full of one subject, money: the wealth of Mr. A, the costliness of Mrs. B's dresses, the money spent upon somebody's entertainment, the price paid for somebody else's last picture. It is

"Gold, gold, nothing but gold.
. . . .
Our daughters sing to their harps of gold,
'O bella eta del' oro'!' " [*sic*][21]

Both how wealth is won and how it is used are subject to moral scrutiny. Are you doing both things well? If you pass the two tests, you can be a good Christian Merchant (more on this in my discussion of stewardship). Wealth well won and used receives Newton's moral praise: not just deference, but *deserved* deference.[22] Ability and character are its morally legitimate causes. Yet, Newton is unforgiving about wealth badly won and used. The objects of his diatribes include the "empty-headed son of a millionaire," "the successful sharper," a "society [that] accredits money as a valid passport," as well as the recurrent evils of luxury and extravagance. These were classic enemies of Christian moralists; that "childish and inexcusable extravagance," "[v]ulgar pleasure-seeking and wild extravagance," as Francis Wayland put it.[23] Newton submits that "[i]t is becoming extremely hard for the great majority of men to pay honestly for the lavish establishments, the costly dressing, the expensive entertainments, the wasteful management of families who aspire to follow the customs of society. If women insist upon 'keeping up appearances,' their husbands will very likely fail to pay, or fail in paying" (p. 76).

Newton's *Morals of Trade* worries about and inveighs against "Mammon." Its spirit is that of Jesus' Sermon on the Mount: "No man can serve two masters. [. . .]

21   R. Heber Newton. 1876. *The Morals of Trade. Two Lectures: I. An inquiry into the actual morality of trade. II. An inquiry into the causes of the existing demoralization and the remedies therefore. Given in the Anthon memorial church, New York.* New York: T. Whittaker, pp. 77–78. Newton's footnote reads: "Hood's Poems: Miss Kilmansegg and her Golden Leg, stanza 9." Thomas Hood (1799–1849) was a British poet, best known for his comic work, of which *Miss Kilmansegg and her Precious Leg* (1840) is one of the best known. Thomas Nast (1840–1902) was a cartoonist and political satirist, known as "the father of American caricature," and best known for his attacks on the "Tweed Ring."

22   See also "The Epidemic of Fraud." *New York Herald*, October 11, 1886, p. 8.

23   Francis Wayland. [1835] 1841. *The Elements of Moral Science*. Boston: Gould, Kendall, and Lincoln, p. 248; Francis Wayland. [1837] 1879. *The Elements of Political Economy*. New York: Sheldon & Company, p. 352.

Ye cannot serve God and mammon" (Matthew 6:24; Luke 16:13). Indeed, is it not "easier for a camel to go through the eye of a needle, than for a rich man to enter into the kingdom of God" (Matthew 19:24; Mark 10:25; Luke 18:25)? And is Paul's first epistle to Timothy not clear that "the love of money is the root of all evil" (1 Timothy 6:10)? Newton's business ethics account did not reject business activity per se, but criticized much actual business, which he thought was infested with mammonism: "[i]n every sphere of business this decadence of honor is the characteristic sign of the times" (p. 23). Now, because Newton was a Social Gospel minister, his attitude may be taken to be an expression of this movement, concerned as it was with social and economic problems, and sympathetic as it was to socialist or socialist-leaning ideas. So what is the role the Social Gospel is playing here? To what extent is Social Gospel anti-Mammonism an upshot of their anti-business views—given that "Business life is the unregenerate section of our social order" and "It is in commerce and industry that we encounter the great collective inhumanities that shame our Christian feeling"?[24] Were they not "in the trenches with Jesus and Marx"?[25] As historians have extensively documented, Social Gospel leaders did worry about and inveigh against Mammon. But their worry was not unique: this enemy transcended denominational, theological, geographical, and historical boundaries—and the historical aspect will be important momentarily.

Francis Greenwood Peabody (1847–1936) and Walter Rauschenbusch (1861–1918) were two noted Social Gospellers. Peabody was a Unitarian minister who taught theology, ethics, and homiletics at Harvard Divinity School. His influential 1900 book, *Jesus Christ and the Social Question*, repeatedly condemns "the mammonism . . . of modern life" (p. 32), "the enshrining of Mammon" (p. 176), "the attendants of the god Mammon" (p. 212), "the altar of Mammon" (p. 214), "the service of Mammon" (p. 221), and the "gospel of Mammonism" (p. 244). What is more: "Prosperity, he [Jesus] preaches, is not sign of Divine acceptance; on the contrary, it is one of the most threatening obstructions of the spiritual life." Then, the Christian must make a choice: "Let them [the poor] realize how hard it is for a rich man to enter into the kingdom. There is but one supreme end for the life of rich and poor alike,—the service of the kingdom; and there is but one fundamental decision for all to make,—the decision whether they will serve God or Mammon."[26]

---

24 Walter Rauschenbusch. 1913. *Christianizing the Social Order*. New York: The Macmillan Company, p. 156.

25 At least, this has been said of one Social Gospeller: Methodist and Union Theological Seminary professor Harry Ward. David Nelson Duke. 2003. *In the Trenches with Jesus and Marx: Harry F. Ward and the Struggle for Social Justice*. Tuscaloosa: University of Alabama Press.

26 Francis Greenwood Peabody. 1900. *Jesus Christ and the Social Question: An Examination of the Teaching of Jesus in its Relation to Some of the Problems of Modern Social Life*. New York: The Macmillan Company, p. 207. On Francis G. Peabody (not to be confused with Andrew P. Peabody), see Barton J. Bernstein. 1963. "Francis Greenwood Peabody: Conservative Social Reformer." *New England Quarterly* 36(3):320–37; Jacob H. Dorn. 1993. "The Social Gospel and Socialism: A Comparison of the Thought of Francis Greenwood Peabody, Washington Gladden, and Walter Rauschenbusch." *Church History* 62(1):82–100; Jurgen Herbst. 1961. "Francis Greenwood Peabody: Harvard's Theologian of the Social Gospel." *Harvard Theological Review* 54(1):45–69.

Rauschenbusch, a Baptist minister, preached in Hell's Kitchen in New York and taught at the Rochester Theological Seminary. His influential 1907 book, *Christianity and the Social Crisis*, interrogates the foundations of "our system":

> If it were proposed to invent some social system in which covetousness would be deliberately fostered and intensified in human nature, what system could be devised which would excel our own for this purpose? Competitive commerce exalts selfishness to the dignity of a moral principle. It pits men against one another in a gladiatorial game in which there is no mercy and in which ninety per cent of the combatants finally strew the arena. [...] Our business life borders so closely on dishonesty that men are hardly aware when they cross the line.[27]

Rauschenbusch lamented that "covetousness," "commercialism," "materialism," and "mammonism" were rampant. Regrettably, American society was at a deep moral loss: "If a man sacrifices his human dignity and self-respect to increase his income, or stunts his intellectual growth and his human affections to swell his bank account, he is to that extent serving mammon and denying God. Likewise if he uses up and injures the life of his fellow-men to make money for himself, he serves mammon and denies God." What is to be done, then? Rauschenbusch responds: "The spiritual force of Christianity should be turned against the materialism and mammonism of our industrial and social order."[28]

Newton, Peabody, and Rauschenbusch were Social Gospel clergymen in the late nineteenth and early twentieth centuries. Both academic and popular narratives about this movement highlight its attention to social, economic, urban, and labor issues, as well as its attunement to the *Zeitgeist* of the Progressive Era.[29] Sometimes it is even "described as the religious expression of progressivism in the early twentieth century."[30] In some respects, then, the ideas and proposals of Rauschenbusch, Peabody, Newton, Josiah Strong, Washington Gladden, Harry Ward, Lyman Abbott, or the "lay spokesman" Richard Ely[31] represent a marked departure from traditional Christian theologians, moralists, and preachers. Thus, the Social Gospel, in both its politically moderate and politically radical versions,

27 Walter Rauschenbusch. 1907. *Christianity and the Social Crisis*. New York: The Macmillan Company, pp. 265–66.

28 Ibid., p. 369.

29 Cf. Charles H. Hopkins. 1940. *The Rise of the Social Gospel in American Protestantism, 1865–1915*. New Haven, CT: Yale University Press; London: Oxford University Press; Robert T. Handy, ed. 1966. *The Social Gospel in America, 1870–1920*. New York: Oxford University Press; May, *Protestant Churches*; Gary Dorrien. 2001. *The Making of American Liberal Theology: Imagining Progressive Religion, 1805-1900*. Louisville, KY: Westminster John Knox Press; Gary Dorrien. 2003. *The Making of American Liberal Theology: Idealism, Realism, and Modernity, 1900–1950*. Louisville, KY: Westminster John Knox Press; Gary Dorrien. 2009. *Social Ethics in the Making: Interpreting an American Tradition*. Chichester, UK; Malden, MA: Wiley-Blackwell.

30 Susan Curtis. [1991] 2001. *A Consuming Faith: The Social Gospel and Modern American Culture*. Columbia: University of Missouri Press, p. 2.

31 Benjamin G. Rader. 1966. "Richard T. Ely: Lay Spokesman for the Social Gospel." *Journal of American History* 53(1):61–74. Cf. Richard T. Ely. 1889. *Social Aspects of Christianity and Other Essays*. New York: Thomas Y. Crowell & Company.

has been depicted as a unique, revolutionary, idiosyncratic movement in the religious history of the country. In other respects, however, it is continuous with its Christian past. In particular, with respect to Mammon, there was nothing original about the otherwise original Social Gospel. Thus, Newton's, Peabody's, and Rauschenbusch's distress over the extreme "covetousness" and "mammonism" of the age was shared by Christian business ethicists of most persuasions, across denominations, regions, and social and political orientations. Nor were their anxieties unique to the new industrial times they were living in: their distress over the extreme "covetousness" and "mammonism" of the age would have been at home in any age. For Christian business ethicists have always placed covetousness at the heart of the business ethics problem—as Richard Steele advised the tradesmen who consulted his manual in the seventeenth, eighteenth, and nineteenth centuries: "Subdue covetousness. He that loveth money better than God and conscience, will for money displease God and conscience, by this or any other sin. Covetousness is the root of falsehood, and many other vices."[32]

These observations bring up an important component of the argument of this chapter. Christian business ethicists—high-status theologians and professors as much as ordinary pastors and popular writers—were building on and operated in the context of a millenarian tradition of theory and practice. Without proper awareness and understanding of this tradition, it would be hard to understand and make sense of many events that constitute the history of Christian business ethicists' work. It would be hard to understand, say, a Christian minister's sermon or a Christian newspaper's editorial about growing business dishonesty and selfishness in nineteenth-century New York. In particular, it would be hard to understand their underlying moral background. The Christian Merchant type has old roots; much older roots than their Standards of Practice counterparts. Throughout this extensive historical trajectory, background elements could get built into Christian institutions, practices, and concepts—such as Mammon. Mammon is a consistently salient theme in the history of the relationship between religion and economic activity, reacted to and dealt with in various ways, but consistently salient nonetheless. It represents one of the constitutive tensions of business ethics in the West, which preoccupied the Fathers, the Scholastics, modern theologians, preachers, rulers, and judges, and which the rise and triumph of capitalism only exacerbated.

In brief, to borrow the *Annales* school's expression, we are talking about a *longue durée* process.[33] As it happens, the study of moral backgrounds calls for a long-term—or least medium-term—perspective. In the area of morality, a history of events (*histoire événementielle*) is analogous to the study of first-order actions and judgments, which may be caused by as immediate and accidental a factor as whether an individual's desk is dirty and messy.[34] By contrast, the historian of

---

32 Steele, *The Religious Tradesman*, p. 140.

33 Fernand Braudel. 1958. "Histoire et sciences sociales: La longue durée." *Annales. Économies, Sociétés, Civilisations* 13(4):725–53.

34 Simone Schnall, Jonathan Haidt, Gerald Clore, and Alexander Jordan. 2008. "Disgust as Embodied Moral Judgment." *Personality and Social Psychology Bulletin* 34(8):1096–1109. In this paper the "disgust condition" was as follows: "An old chair with a torn and dirty cushion was placed in front

the moral background often addresses *longue durée*, structurally ingrained patterns, which by their very nature move slowly. In addition, some dimensions of the background are not up to individuals. They cannot be affected by what one individual does, feels, or says, let alone by the dirtiness and messiness of her desk. They are already there.

7.3 Ambivalence

It is beyond the remit of this chapter to present a *longue durée* history of Christian business ethics and its conceptions of Mammon. However, I should underscore and we should keep in mind that there is such a history, of which the aforementioned nineteenth-century New York minister is but a late chapter. For that minister could not but operate within that tradition or framework. To make a long story short, in the Middle Ages avarice—sometimes referred to as covetousness, cupidity, greed, or mammonism—became a central sin.[35] "[B]etween the eleventh and fourteenth century," avarice gradually displaced pride as "the worst of all vices" in the Christian hierarchy of evils.[36] "Quite literally," Langholm writes, "in the medieval configuration of vice, avarice was the stem from which all specific economic vices branched off."[37] Sadly, we witness around us that all too often money conquers, money reigns, money rules ("*nummus vincit, nummus regnat, nummus imperat*"). But good Christians should combat this unjust conquest, reign, and rule. Then, one of medieval business ethicists' responsibilities was to condemn and curb avarice, along with its kindred vices, usury and unjust prices. The good news for them was that social misgivings about money and trade were common. As Baldwin writes: "Characteristically during the Middle Ages economic theories

---

of a desk that had various stains, and was sticky. On the desk there was a transparent plastic cup with the dried up remnants of a smoothie, and a pen that was chewed up. Next to the desk was a trash can overflowing with garbage including greasy pizza boxes and dirty-looking tissues" (p. 1101).

35 Avarice, mammonism, covetousness, cupidity, love of money, and greed are kindred concepts, but each has had its own distinct historical trajectory. The Greek words used in the New Testament are "pleonexia" and "philargyria." As Barclay notes, "pleonexia" "occurs in Mark 7.22; Luke 12.15; Rom. 1.29; II Cor. 9.5; Eph. 4.19; 5.3; Col. 3.5; I Thess. 2.5; II Pet. 2.3, 14." The words "philargyria," "philargyros," and "aphilargyros" also occur, although they are somewhat less common: 1 Tim. 6:10; Luk. 16:14; 2 Tim. 3:2; 1 Tim 3:3; Heb. 13:5. Translations into Latin were not consistent, but the Vulgate generally renders "pleonexia" as "avaritia," and "philargyria" as "cupiditas." In English, "pleonexia" has been translated as "avarice" and "covetousness," but also "greediness," and even "lust." William Barclay. 1974. *New Testament Words*. Louisville, KY: Westminster John Knox Press, p. 233; Richard Newhauser. 2000. *The Early History of Greed: The Sin of Avarice in Early Medieval Thought and Literature*. Cambridge, UK: Cambridge University Press, p. 92.

36 Lester K. Little. 1971. "Pride Goes before Avarice: Social Change and the Vices in Latin Christendom." *American Historical Review* 76(1):16–49, p. 16. Cf. Jacques Le Goff. 1986. *La bourse et la vie. Économie et religion au Moyen Age*. Paris: Hachette; Lester K. Little. 1978. *Religious Poverty and the Profit Economy in Medieval Europe*. Ithaca: Cornell University Press.

37 Odd Langholm. 1998. "The Medieval Schoolmen (1200–1400)." Pp. 439–502 in *Ancient and Medieval Economic Ideas and Concepts of Social Justice*, edited by S. Todd Lowry and Barry Gordon. Leiden; New York: Brill, p. 446.

were discussed against a background of general suspicion towards merchants and mercantile activity. To a large extent this attitude was transmitted to the Middle Ages through the revered writings of the ancient Church Fathers."[38]

In the early-modern period the Reformation gave new meanings to worldly success, work, and wealth—or so Weber's thesis goes. Still, as Weber himself and many others have pointed out, these new meanings did not mean giving up the "cries of antimammonism."[39] It was still the case that avarice and its attendant evils were condemned—though there were new opportunities to assess and contest what counted as avarice and what did not. Economic pursuits remained a source of danger to both the temporal and the eternal interests of the Christian. The outcome was new equilibriums, adaptations, and institutions, and finer distinctions between good and bad motives, and good and bad courses of action. As Tawney argues in *Religion and the Rise of Capitalism*:

> [Calvinism] no longer suspects the whole world of economic motives as alien to the life of the spirit, or distrusts the capitalist as one who has necessarily grown rich on the misfortunes of his neighbor, or regards poverty as in itself meritorious, and it is perhaps the first systematic body of religious teaching which can be said to recognize and applaud the economic virtues. Its enemy is not the accumulation of riches, but their misuse for purposes of self-indulgence or ostentation. Its ideal is a society which seeks wealth with the sober gravity of men who are conscious at once of disciplining their own characters by patient labor, and of devoting themselves to a service acceptable to God.[40]

To be sure, there have been many scholarly disputes around these issues. The arguments of Weber, Tawney, and their followers have been criticized by many. There have been questions about the extent to which the Reformation was a break with the past in terms of its economic ethics, and the extent to which the Reformation was a cause of economic and social change. Yet, whoever got these points right, it is clear that the traditional Christian anxieties about Mammon did not disappear after the Reformation—even when temporal success was accepted, promoted, or celebrated.[41]

---

38 John W. Baldwin. 1959. "The Medieval Theories of the Just Price: Romanists, Canonists, and Theologians in the Twelfth and Thirteenth Centuries." *Transactions of the American Philosophical Society* New Series 49(4):1–92, p. 12.

39 Malcolm H. MacKinnon. 1993. "The Longevity of the Thesis: A Critique of the Critics." Pp. 211–43 in *Weber's "Protestant Ethic": Origins, Evidence, Contexts*, edited by Hartmut Lehmann and Guenther Roth. Washington, DC: German Historical Institute; Cambridge; New York: Cambridge University Press, p. 216. This is "an apparent contradiction in ministerial writing" that Weber tried to "explain away": "On the one hand, this writing exhorts followers to pursue profit assiduously in a worldly calling; on the other hand, this same writing is crammed with cries of antimammonism, that the accumulation of riches is evil in the eyes of the Lord."

40 Tawney, *Religion and the Rise of Capitalism*, p. 105.

41 Here historians have taken usury to be a test case of sorts, including much productive scholarship about the establishment of *montes pietatis* or *monti di pietà* starting in the fifteenth century, the economic role of the Jews, and the ways in which money-lending was affected by the Reformation, in theory and in practice. See, e.g., Hans-Jörg Gilomen. 1990. "Wucher und Wirtschaft im Mittelalter."

In this respect, colonial America and the early Republic are strategic empirical loci: the New World, a land of political and religious freedom, where apparently old traditions, hierarchies, and institutions would not impede progress, and where apparently an "entrepreneurial spirit" could develop at ease.[42] Here recent historical scholarship has found more nuances and complexities than earlier accounts had had room for. There were various ways in which Christianity and capitalism—religion and business activities, the interests of community and the interests of individuals, spiritual and material pursuits, piety and profit—were interwoven, interacted, and shaped each other. To take colonial New England as an example, historians such as Peterson have rejected "the myth of declension," and historians such as Valeri have rejected the traditional dichotomy of individualism versus communal values.[43] It turns out that there were various kinds of religious understandings of business and various kinds of business understandings of religion, which cannot be mapped onto one dimension. Further, neither purported camp is homogenous: there were various kinds of businesspeople and commercial institutions, and various kinds of clergymen and religious institutions. Finally, the process was not linear from, say, colonial times to the early twentieth century; its character changed over time.

After all is said and done, Christian business ethicists' relationship to business and market capitalism has been characterized by ambivalence, tension, uneasiness,

---

Historische Zeitschrift 250(2):265–301; David W. Jones. 2004. *Reforming the Morality of Usury: A Study of the Differences that Separated the Protestant Reformers.* Lanham, MD: University Press of America; Norman L. Jones. 1989. *God and the Moneylenders: Usury and Law in Early Modern England.* Oxford; Cambridge, MA: B. Blackwell; Eric Kerridge. 2002. *Usury, Interest, and the Reformation.* Aldershot; Burlington: Ashgate; Odd Langholm. 1984. *The Aristotelian Analysis of Usury.* Bergen, Norway: Universitetsforlaget; Jerry Z. Muller. 2010. *Capitalism and the Jews.* Princeton: Princeton University Press; Benjamin Nelson. [1949] 1969. *The Idea of Usury: From Tribal Brotherhood to Universal Otherhood.* 2nd ed. Chicago and London: University of Chicago Press; John T. Noonan. 1957. *The Scholastic Analysis of Usury.* Cambridge, MA: Harvard University Press; Joseph Persky. 2007. "From Usury to Interest." *Journal of Economic Perspectives* 21(1):227–36; Joseph Shatzmiller. 1990. *Shylock Reconsidered: Jews, Moneylending, and Medieval Society.* Berkeley: University of California Press

42 John Frederick Martin. 1991. *Profits in the Wilderness: Entrepreneurship and the Founding of New England Towns in the Seventeenth Century.* Chapel Hill: University of North Carolina Press; Edwin J. Perkins. 1989. "The Entrepreneurial Spirit in Colonial America: The Foundations of Modern Business History." *Business History Review* 63(1):160–86.

43 Mark A. Peterson. 1997. *The Price of Redemption: The Spiritual Economy of Puritan New England.* Stanford: Stanford University Press; Mark Valeri. 2010. *Heavenly Merchandize: How Religion Shaped Commerce in Puritan America.* Princeton: Princeton University Press. See also Bernard Bailyn. 1979. *The New England Merchants in the Seventeenth Century.* Cambridge, MA: Harvard University Press; Patricia U. Bonomi. [1986] 2003. *Under the Cope of Heaven: Religion, Society, and Politics in Colonial America.* Updated edition. New York: Oxford University Press; Richard L. Bushman. 1967. *From Puritan to Yankee: Character and the Social Order in Connecticut, 1690–1765.* Cambridge, MA: Harvard University Press, pp. 107–43; Jon Butler. 1990. *Awash in a Sea of Faith: Christianizing the American People.* Cambridge, MA: Harvard University Press; Charles L. Cohen. 1997. "The Post-Puritan Paradigm of Early American Religious History." *William and Mary Quarterly* 54(4):695–722; Charles L. Cohen. 2003. "The Colonization of British North America as an Episode in the History of Christianity." *Church History* 72(3):553–68; Stephen Innes. 1995. *Creating the Commonwealth: The Economic Culture of Puritan New England.* New York: W.W. Norton.

and anxiety. This is a *longue durée* pattern, which is true of the period under consideration here as well. As a meta-analysis of historians' and sociologists' numerous investigations might show, favorable and unfavorable views have generally coexisted. They have also coexisted with many views that are neither straightforwardly for nor straightforwardly against. So, overarching general statements cannot do justice to reality in this area. Sometimes, in certain forums, on certain occasions, one heard about capitalism as a beneficial moral force, the religious meaning of success in this world, the practical benefits of piety, God as well disposed toward businessmen, and so on. Sometimes, in certain forums, on certain occasions, one heard about capitalism gone sour, piety as a moral force that can counteract the love of money, God as not so well disposed toward businessmen, the dangers posed by Mammon, extravagance, materialism, and so on. Sometimes, in certain forums, on certain occasions, one heard complex combinations and arrangements of these and other elements. In fact, this ambivalence can be traced back to the Bible: either side can produce its legitimate scriptural credentials.[44] One might refer, among other things, to camels that are unable to go through eyes of needles.[45] The other might refer, among other things, to wicked and slothful servants who fail to put talents to work.[46] This ambivalence becomes even more significant in the United States in the nineteenth century, and especially in the wake of the economic and social changes brought forth by the market revolution.[47]

However capitalism and religion accommodated to each other, however they were brought into harmony, however much business got to be seen as morally legitimate and socially beneficial, Mammon remained a source of concern and anxiety. However much Jesus or Paul were represented as "men of affairs,"[48] religion

44 Cf. Zelizer, *Morals and Markets*, p. 75.

45 Matthew 19:24; Mark 10:25; Luke 18:25. See also Hebrews 13:5; Matthew 5:3; Luke 6:24–25; and the parables of the rich fool (Luke 12:13–21) and of Dives and Lazarus (Luke 16:19–31).

46 Defenders of money-lending have often recruited the help of the Parable of the Talents (Matthew 25:14–30) and the Parable of the Minas (Luke 19:12–27). On the other hand, Jesus says in the Sermon on the Plain: "And if ye lend to them of whom ye hope to receive, what thank have ye? for sinners also lend to sinners, to receive as much again. But love ye your enemies, and do good, and lend, hoping for nothing again; and your reward shall be great, and ye shall be the children of the Highest: for he is kind unto the unthankful and to the evil" (Luke 6:34–35). Then, the question has become whether the injunction to lend hoping for nothing again—usually cited in Latin: "*mutuum date, nihil inde sperantes*"—is meant to be about lending money in particular (see also Matthew 5:42). Besides wicked and slothful servants who fail to put talents to work, this side could also refer to injunctions not to be "slothful in business" (Romans 12:11). It should be noted, though, that this is the King James Bible's rendering of this phrase, and other English translations are quite different: "not lagging behind in diligence" (New American Standard Bible); "in carefulness not slothful" (Douay Rheims Bible); "in diligence not slothful" (American Standard Version); "never be lazy" (New Living Translation); and "do not be slothful in zeal" (English Standard Version).

47 Cf. Mark A. Noll, ed. 2002. *God and Mammon: Protestants, Money, and the Market, 1790–1860*. New York: Oxford University Press.

48 Bruce Barton. 1925. *The Man Nobody Knows*. New York: Grosset & Dunlap; Austin Bierbower. 1898. "Jesus as a Man of Affairs." *Biblical World* 11(1):17–27; A. C. Zenos. 1891. "St. Paul as a Business-Man." *The Old and New Testament Student* 12(2):71–78. Cf. Leo P. Ribuffo. 1981. "Jesus Christ as Business Statesman: Bruce Barton and the Selling of Corporate Capitalism." *American Quarterly* 33(2):206–31.

was represented as a "business proposition,"[49] and the "theology of success" became successful itself,[50] Mammon remained a threat to the Christian Merchant
exemplar. Even apologists of wealth, such as the Episcopal Bishop William Lawrence and the Baptist minister Russell Conwell, had to acknowledge that it was
"a source of danger" and grappled with the interpretation of 1 Timothy 6:10.[51]
Over time, the courses of action that were morally and legally permitted, the defi-
nitions of avarice and usury, religious practices, theological arguments, and the
social and economic contexts changed dramatically. But business ethicists kept
having to come to terms with Mammon. Covetousness and selfishness continued to set moral limits. They continued to symbolize business gone awry, the
Christian Merchant who lost his moral compass regarding wealth acquisition or
use, his relations to competitors, the community, or the church. Likewise, broader
Jeremiads about the degeneration of social morals might single out for special
mention the vices of mammonism, commercialism, materialism, and selfishness.
Money was said to contaminate and corrupt several aspects of people's lives, notably intimacy. That these are "hostile worlds" is a "longstanding and persistent"
assumption, as Zelizer has shown.[52]

These anxieties and ambivalence vis-à-vis Mammon existed in the late-
nineteenth, in the mid-eighteenth, and in the early-seventeenth centuries alike.[53]
As Wuthnow argues in *God and Mammon in America*, they still exist today:

> [W]e still express much of our ambivalence towards economic conditions in
> the language of morality. On the one hand, we continue to regard hard work as
> a moral virtue and laziness as a vice; we consider it not only a matter of expedi-
> ence but of moral duty to pass on the opportunity for economic prosperity to
> our children; we have spent much of this century arguing that capitalism was
> morally superior to communism and have viewed the collapse of communism
> in Eastern Europe and the Soviet Union as a moral victory. [. . .] On the other
> hand, we express our concerns about economic conditions in moral terms as
> well. We decry the expansion of advertising and of the mass media because it

---

49   "Booming Religion as a Business Proposition." *Christian Century*, May 21, 1925, pp. 658–59.

50   Irving G. Wyllie. [1954] 1966. *The Self-Made Man in America: The Myth of Rags to Riches.*
New York: Free Press, p. 64. Cf. Judy Hilkey. 1997. *Character is Capital: Success Manuals and Man-
hood in Gilded Age America.* Chapel Hill: University of North Carolina Press, p. 88. *Contra* Wyllie,
Weiss argues that "[c]lergymen who wrote success tracts considered God and Mammon absolutely
incompatible and repeatedly said so. Mammonism and success were very different things in the
minds of nineteenth-century Christian moralists." Richard Weiss. [1969] 1988. *The American
Myth of Success: From Horatio Alger to Norman Vincent Peale.* Urbana: University of Illinois Press,
pp. 125–26.

51   William Lawrence. 1901. "The Relation of Wealth to Morals." *The World's Work*, vol. 1, no. 3,
pp. 286–92; Russell H. Conwell. [1890] 1915. *Acres of Diamonds.* New York and London: Harper &
Brothers, pp. 22–24; Russell H. Conwell. 1917. *What You Can Do with Your Will Power.* New York and
London: Harper & Brothers, p. 8.

52   Viviana A. Zelizer. 2005. *The Purchase of Intimacy.* Princeton: Princeton University Press,
p. 23. Cf. Zelizer, *Economic Lives*, pp. 151–53.

53   On seventeenth-century America, see E.A.J. Johnson. 1961. *American Economic Thought in
the Seventeenth Century.* New York: Russell & Russell, esp. pp. 83–100, 123–36.

corrupts the morals of our children; we talk about the self-interestedness that markets encourage as if this were an immoral orientation and lament the ways in which economic conditions continue to undermine communities. When loopholes in our codes of professional ethics allow doctors or stockbrokers to reap huge earnings, we put these offenders on display as examples of immorality and greed.

This is indeed a "lasting ambivalence."[54] The market, profit-making, and money find themselves in a complex and awkward moral position, and in complex and awkward moral relationships to other social practices and institutions. To see the profundity and durability of this phenomenon, consider an early-eighteenth-century, Puritan illustration. I mentioned earlier Cotton Mather's sermons, *Lex Mercatoria: Or, the Just Rules of Commerce Declared* (1705) and *Theopolis Americana: An Essay on the Golden Street of the Holy City* (1710). What was the point of lecturing about "just commerce," that is, the ethics of business? According to Mather, "[t]here is abundance of Wickedness, thro' a Thirst of Dishonest Gain, Committed among us. A Testimony Publickly given against all such Wickedness may be of some Use, if the Glorious Lord please to make it so, to bring some Slaves of *Mammon* to an Amendment of their wayes, and to stop others from running into the *Pathes of Unrighteousness*."[55] Or take Benjamin Wadsworth's (1670–1737) sermon on "fraud and injustice" from 1712. Wadsworth was the First Church of Boston pastor and the president of Harvard College from 1725 to 1737. In his sermon, he put forward "Directions" to prevent one's wronging and defrauding others, the first of which was: "*Let us Mortifie our Coveteousness* [sic]. Coveteousness, or excessive Love to the World, puts persons on many methods of unrighteousness." After quoting the entire 1 Timothy 6:9–10 passage, Wadsworth added: "Since love to the World is so great a Sin, so dangerous a snare, it should be carefully subdued."[56]

Wadsworth and Mather would have hardly recognized America one hundred years later, when, in the midst of the market revolution, the crisis of 1837 wreaked economic havoc. It also caused a great deal of anxiety.[57] In its wake, several pastors addressed themselves to the disastrous economic situation and the "hard times" their parishioners and communities were going through.[58] One of the issues they

54 Wuthnow, *God and Mammon in America*, pp. 27, 26. Cf. Robert Wuthnow. 1996. *Poor Richard's Principle: Recovering the American Dream through the Moral Dimension of Work, Business, and Money*. Princeton: Princeton University Press, pp. 59–82.

55 Mather, *Lex Mercatoria*, p. 6.

56 Benjamin Wadsworth. 1712. *Fraud and injustice detected and condemned: In a lecture sermon in Boston, Feb. 28. 1711,12. / By Benj. Wadsworth, A.M. Pastor of a church of Christ in Boston, N.E.* Boston: B. Green, p. 26.

57 Jessica M. Lepler. 2008. *1837: Anatomy of a Panic*. Ph.D. dissertation. Department of History, Brandeis University; Jessica M. Lepler. 2012. "'The News Flew Like Lightning'." *Journal of Cultural Economy* 5(2):179–95.

58 Leonard Bacon. 1837. *The Duties Connected with the Present Commercial Distress. A Sermon, Preached in The Center Church, New Haven, May 21, 1837, and Repeated, May 23*. New Haven, CT: Hitchcock & Stafford; N. L. Frothingham. 1837. *The Duties of Hard Times. A Sermon, Preached to the First Church, on Sunday Morning, April 23, 1837*. Boston: Munroe & Francis; Andrew P. Peabody. 1837. *Views of Duty Adapted to the Times: A Sermon Preached at Portsmouth, N.H. May 14, 1837*.

addressed was "the causes that may have concurred to produce any particular pressure in the times"—as worded by N. L. Frothingham in his sermon, *The Duties of Hard Times*. Frothingham's view was that "moral causes have been chiefly operative in the disastrous result. Those causes may be founded in greedy passions, and ambitious indulgences, and the haste to be rich, and headlong schemes, and strange delusions."[59] So, economic crises are said to have moral causes, just like they are said to have in the twenty-first century.

Just three years later, in 1840, Ezra Stiles Gannett's *Sermon on the Arrival of the Britannia* sums up the issue: business is not intrinsically a bad thing, but it is morally dangerous, and hence it leads to worry and anxiety. The ship Britannia was then making its maiden voyage from Liverpool and was due to arrive in Boston, which prompted Gannett to reflect on the advancement of communications, business, and technology: "That this increase of business will have its advantages, it would be useless to deny. Money, commerce, industry, are among the means which the Divine Providence has embraced in its plan of education for man. But there are also temptations, dangers and evils incident to prosperity; and it is more important that we should contemplate these than that we should be busy in arranging our hopes."[60] So, Gannett makes his priorities clear: being watchful against the dangers and temptations is more important than "arranging our hopes." Then, he goes on to warn against "unreasonable calculation, extravagant enterprise, (with extravagant expenditure too,)" and one particularly troubling danger:

> Especially is there danger, that business, as it shall become more active and profitable, will engross the minds of the people, and they will think of little else than their worldly affairs. Let then the word of Christian counsel be heard at this moment. [. . .] –Beware of the dangers by which you will soon be encompassed. Go into them with your eyes open and your consciences awake. Do not regard wealth as an end; it is only a means. Understand its value as a means—not to luxury, not to self-indulgence, not to the vain acquisition of

---

Portsmouth: J. W. Foster, J.F. Shores and Son; George Ripley. 1837. *The Temptations of the Times. A Discourse Delivered in the Congregational Church in Purchase Street, on Sunday Morning, May 7, 1837*. Boston: Hilliard, Gray, and Company, p. 6; Jason Whitman. 1837. *The Hard Times: A Discourse, Delivered in the Second Unitarian Church, and Also in the First Parish Church, Portland, Sunday, January 1st, 1837*. Portland, ME: Arthur Shirley, Printer.

59 Frothingham, *The Duties of Hard Times*, pp. 11–12. Nathaniel Langdon Frothingham (1793–1870) was a renowned Unitarian minister in Boston, where he occupied the pulpit at the First Congregational Church of Boston from 1815 to 1850. Octavius Brooks Frothingham. 1890. *Boston Unitarianism, 1820–1850: A Study of the Life and Work of Nathaniel Langdon Frothingham*. New York and London: G. P. Putnam's Sons; J. W. T. 1870. "Ministers Gone." *Monthly Review and Religious Magazine*, vol. 43, no. 5, May 1870, p. 496.

60 Ezra S. Gannett. 1840. *The Arrival of the Britannia: A Sermon Delivered in the Federal Street Meeting-House, in Boston, July 19, 1840*. Boston: Joseph Dowe, p. 13. Ezra Stiles Gannett (1801–1871) was the longtime minister of the Federal Street Church in Boston, occupying that pulpit from 1824 to 1871. Educated at Harvard College and the Harvard Divinity School, he was involved in the founding of the American Unitarian Association in 1825, and was the editor of the *Christian Examiner* from 1844 to 1849. Cf. William C. Gannett. 1893. *Ezra Stiles Gannett: Unitarian Minister in Boston, 1824–1871*. 3rd ed. Boston: American Unitarian Association.

influence—but a means to self-denial and to usefulness. Let your industry cover opportunities of doing good, and your ambition aspire to spiritual improvement. Be honest, moderate, devout, whether the tide of prosperity ebb or flow. Keep your Christian character unstained and unimpaired by its exposure to the influence of worldly success.[61]

Similarly, Henry Bellows, in his above-mentioned *Christian Merchant* sermon, observes that business is here to stay, *nolens volens*, whether you like it or not: "Merchants, in the largest use of the word, are a necessary and most important class—a fixed, indispensable, and permanent class—in the divisions of society. There is no prospect whatsoever that the pressure of care, the competitions of trade, the increase of wealth, or the growth of private fortunes, will diminish in a place like this [the city of New York]."[62] Unfortunately, though, business is dangerous: "We live confessedly in the midst of great temptations and seductions. There is nothing, perhaps, concerning which men doubt each other more than in regard to their power to withstand the temptation of money" (pp. 6–7). Next, Bellows eloquently spells out these dangers:

Amid the competitions and collisions of mercantile enterprise, pressed by the necessity and the difficulty of speedily succeeding, in order to maintain the expensive position here assumed; surrounded by examples of crowds, whose confessed and only object is accumulation; supported in lax practices by the maxims of the careless; tempted now by the glittering prizes of rapid success, and then by the imminent perils of sudden failure; excited by the triumphant speculations of the adventurous, and dazzled by the social splendors of the prosperous; conversant all the day long, for at least six days in the week, with the plans and project, the conversation and spirit of money-making, what wonder is it, that riches come to stand for the principal thing, and that the laws and spirit of Christian virtue are so often found to be withes of straw in the fires of worldly ambition and business enterprise? (p. 7)

Thus, Bellows chastises "the conversation and spirit of money-making" and "the fires of worldly ambition and business enterprise," due to which "riches come to stand for the principal thing." But that is not his bottom line. His bottom line is rather that business has the capacity for both good and evil; it can be either morally good or morally bad. In other words, there is no "intrinsic immorality" in business. It is a mistake to "[attribute] to wealth itself all the evils which come from the passionate 'love of money'" (p. 8). The distinction is crucial: wealth itself is not intrinsically immoral; wealth itself should not be confused with love of money or avarice. Then, Christian business ethicists' morally accepting business and the pursuit of wealth leaves them with the worry that it might degenerate into love of money. That means more attentive vigilance is required. And that means more work is required.

61 Gannett, *The Arrival of the Britannia*, p. 14.
62 Bellows, *The Christian Merchant*, p. 9.

Gilded Age manifestations of ambivalence and anxiety with regard to the market and profit are equally numerous. One good illustration is the May 1888 issue of the *Methodist Review*, edited at the time by J. W. Mendenhall, which carried an editorial on business ethics.[63] It was titled, precisely, "Christianity and the Ethics of the Business World." It was about Mammon. It began by identifying the main enemy of Christianity at the time: "Has spiritual Christianity any stronger, any more dangerous, foe than 'Mammon' in these modern days and in our own land?" This foe is "subtle and deadly," because of his covert or indirect tactics: "But Mammon is a subtle and deadly foe, who makes his attacks not directly on Christian truth, but on that divinely created love for God and man which is the essence of all spiritual life. As the malaria of a marshy country is more destructive to an army than the bullets of its foes, so is the self-loving spirit of the world often vastly more injurious to the life and progress of the Christian Church than all the arguments that skeptical philosophers and scientists can invent."[64] Mammon is a god, who tempts people to get the "filthy lucre" the Bible (1 Timothy 3:3; 1 Timothy 3:8) talks about:

> In his [Mammon's] unhallowed temple men are taught how to frame plausible theories in defense of gambling speculations, "corners," "trusts," "combinations," "pools," briberies, railway-wrecking, betrayals of official obligations, adulterations of food, fraudulent manufacturing, dealing in things injurious to health and public morals, and similar methods of gaining wealth by wronging other men. And having reduced these theories to practice, and reaped "filthy lucre" thereby, they move among other men, crying, in the spirit of the ancient Ephesians respecting their goddess Diana, "Great is Mammon, by whose favor we heap up much treasure!"

The editorial, then, worries about "the ethics of the business world," including the common business ethics worries of the day: trust, combinations, and restraint of trade, and the adulteration of food products. Yet, reasonably, it worries more about the Church. It turns out that business ethics is "a question of life or death to the Church." For the editorialist sees a special connection between business ethics, Mammon, "selfism," and "preserving the existence" of the Church, as this passage shows:

> The drift of the Mammon worship of to-day is to corrupt this divinely born affection, and to restore the reign of selfism. It aims to strike the Church where she is most vulnerable. Discerning the "heel of Achilles" in the liability of this affection to be alienated, the "god of this world" seeks, by manifold and novel devices, to inflict a deadly wound upon the Church by alienating it. And therefore it is that a question of life or death to the Church is involved in her conflict with the excessive activity and abnormal devices for the rapid acquisition of

---

63 Frank L. Mott. 1930. *A History of American Magazines, 1741–1850*. New York, London: D. Appleton, pp. 299–301.

64 "Christianity and the Ethics of the Business World." *Methodist Review*, May 1888, pp. 452–59, p. 452.

wealth which now give character to the doings of the business world. If her members who are men of business generally succumb to the law of selfism now prevailing in the world, they must inevitably lose their spiritual life, and thereby deprive her a measure of her power. [. . .]

To preserve her own existence, therefore, the Church of Christ needs to stem, as best she can [sic], the swelling tide of immoral methods of business, which is threatening to sweep honor, honesty, truth, justice, and fair dealing from our markets, manufacturing establishments, railway corporations, and business exchanges. (p. 456)

All in all, the *Methodist Review*—as well as Ezra Gannett, Henry Bellows, the Social Gospellers, and Wadsworth and Mather much earlier—illustrate two of the backbones of Christian business ethics. First, while moral wrong does not inhere necessarily in business, it is still morally dangerous, especially as profits and hence temptations increase. For, "a life of business, in these days, is full of dangers."[65] Second, wealth should not be an end in itself, but a "means to self-denial and to usefulness." From these principles a standard inventory of prescriptions usually follows: do not ever forget your Christian duties; avoid extravagance and ostentation; be honest; remember Proverbs 28:20 and reject "the fiery haste to be rich, so characteristic of our people to-day," which "is destroying the higher life of thousands"; and so on.[66] Listen to God and beware of Mammon. But this is a demanding demand. More generally, the work of Christian business ethicists reflects the tension, ambivalence, and sometimes anxiety about the role and function of business enterprise in capitalist societies. Because of the nature of their job, they suffer it first-personally, if anyone does. They, more than anyone, must pay heed both to the demands of the capitalist system and to the demands of Christian morals; they can afford to alienate neither the businessman nor the moralist.

Let me end this section with another story. The 132nd annual banquet of the Chamber of Commerce of the State of New York took place on November 20, 1900, at the renowned restaurant Delmonico's. That was two weeks after Republican William McKinley defeated Democrat William Jennings Bryan, so the event, as the *New York Times* reported, "resolved itself largely into an affair of congratulation over the election of Mr. McKinley and the triumph of sound money." After dinner, "[w]ith the coffee and liqueurs came the speech making." One of the speakers was Bishop Lawrence. He was introduced by the chamber's president, Morris Ketchum Jesup, as follows: "Is it not true that religion has been the pioneer of our civilization and our commerce throughout the world? The toast that I will now give you is 'The Relation of the Material Prosperity of a People to Their Morality.' This toast will be responded to by the Right Rev. William Lawrence, D. D., Bishop of Massachusetts." Then, at the annual banquet of the New York Chamber

---

65 T. L. Cuyler. 1883. *"Business is Business."* Philadelphia: Presbyterian Board of Publication, p. 5. Cf. Henry Ward Beecher [1844] 1890. *Lectures to Young Men on Various Important Subjects.* New York: John B. Alden, Publisher, p. 59.

66 John De Witt. 1885. "The Relations of Religion and Business." Pp. 150–65 in *Sermons on the Christian Life.* New York: Charles Scribner's Sons, pp. 159–60.

of Commerce (of all places!), Bishop Lawrence (of all clergymen!) gave expression to the ambivalence this section has explored. He did reassure his audience (and his powerful and generous hosts) first:

> To seek for and earn wealth is a sign of a natural, vigorous, and strong character. Wherever strong men are there they will turn into the activities of life. The race is to the strong. The search for material wealth is, therefore, as natural and necessary to the man as is the pushing out of her roots for more moisture and food to the oak. This is man's play, his exercise, the expression of his powers, his personality. [. . .] You know better than I that for one man who seeks money for its own sake there are ten who seek it for the satisfaction of the seeking, the power there is in it, and the use they can make of it. [. . .] The massing of great wealth in corporations has come to stay. It is a new, a necessary, and, on the whole, a beneficent instrument in civilization.

If it was natural to search for wealth, it had to be good. Large corporations were not bad, at least "on the whole." However, Lawrence immediately added that "the people, the great common people, are suspicious that some great corporations and masses of wealth are protected, or their interests advanced, in ways that are inconsistent with the rights of the people." He conceded that they "may have no material grounds for their suspicions, but they are suspicious," and then, "[c]ivilization cannot go on where there is mutual suspicion, and prosperity cannot go on long while the people feel or think that the reverence for law by which property is safeguarded is not upheld." Lawrence concluded his address by reminding his audience about "[o]ne other point of danger, and I am done—the spirit of commercialism, the test of value by money, the gauging of social position by fortune, the loss of pity for the failures in life, the figuring of National highness by National wealth and the getting of the foreign markets."[67]

7.4 Metaphysics

The preceding section focused on Christian discussions about the morality of wealth, profits, and capitalism. However, in this book these discussions are means, not ends. Looking at first-order morality is a means to identify background elements that distinguish the Christian Merchant type from the Standards of Practice type. The present section focuses on this task, specifically as regards the sixth dimension of the moral background, metaphysics. In chapter 1 I said that metaphysical pictures manifest themselves in ordinary social practices, institutions, and understandings—from art criticism to neuroscience to the modern state. In this regard, religious practices and institutions are particularly fruitful objects of

---

67 William Lawrence. 1901. "Speech of the Right Rev. William Lawrence, D. D., Bishop of Massachusetts." Pp. 62–66 in *Forty-Third Annual Report of the Corporation of the Chamber of Commerce of the State of New-York, for the Year 1900–1901*. New York: Press of the Chamber of Commerce, p. 66; "Chamber of Commerce Dinner a Love Feast." *New York Times*, November 21, 1900, p. 1.

inquiry. For, however defined, religions' characteristic duties comprise designing and providing metaphysical accounts that make sense to ordinary people. Within these metaphysical pictures human life makes sense, and they, in turn, give meaning to human life. For instance, the metaphysics of Abrahamic religions center on their God, who is eternal, omniscient, omnipotent, and omnibenevolent. Their associated cosmology explains what the origin, nature, and purpose of the universe is, and what the place of human beings in it is. Then, cosmological accounts have institutional, doctrinal, and liturgical embodiments, at which point the discrepancies across Abrahamic religions and sects become conspicuous—even where there are metaphysical overlaps.

I have argued that U.S. Christian business ethicists partook in a longstanding theoretical and practical tradition. One of the constitutive components of this tradition is its metaphysical picture, one of whose foundations is the Christian concept of God hinted at above: the eternal, omnipresent, omniscient, and omnibenevolent creator of the universe.[68] Then, how did Christian metaphysical fundamentals manifest themselves in business ethics work? Did these background elements make any difference to the demands, prescriptions, and claims made by business ethicists on the ground? The most consequential principle, itself omnipresent, is simply the very existence and omnipresence of God. This may seem to be an obvious, commonsensical point. Yet, it is a most consequential one nonetheless, whose implications for the Christian Merchant type must be carefully thought through. Consider, for example, the business ethics ideas of Reverend Charles Fletcher Dole, as expressed in an 1895 pamphlet, *The Golden Rule in Business*.[69] Dole, a Unitarian minister in Jamaica Plain, Boston, starts out with the deep metaphysics on the basis of which his business ethics stand:

> There is a growing suspicion that the fine teachings of our Sunday-schools . . .
> fail to make valid connection with practical life. Young people are taught to
> recite the Beatitudes or to tell the story of Jesus, without being made to think
> what these magnificent ideas and this splendid example have to do with or-
> dinary buying and selling, or with voting, on occasion, against the unworthy
> candidates of one's own party.

---

68 "The Christian concept of God" is a rough simplification, which circumvents many theological disputes. Is God immanent or transcendent? Is God one person or three (Father, Son, and Holy Spirit)? What are God's attributes? What is meant by his simplicity, timelessness, immutability, impassibility, sovereignty, incomprehensibility, compassion, and aseity? As Protestants' rejection of transubstantiation and papal infallibility exemplifies, these theological disputes can have large social and political effects. Not to mention the large effects of the internal theological disputes for which Protestantism is known on the schisms for which Protestantism is known. Cf. Gerard J. Hughes. 1995. *The Nature of God*. New York: Routledge; Anthony Kenny. 1979. *The God of the Philosophers*. Oxford: Clarendon Press; Alvin Plantinga. 1980. *Does God Have a Nature?* Milwaukee: Marquette University Press; Richard Swinburne. 1994. *The Christian God*. New York: Oxford University Press.

69 Charles Fletcher Dole (1845–1927) was a Unitarian minister, pastor of the First Congregational Church in Jamaica Plain, Boston. A graduate of Harvard and the Andover Theological Seminary, he was the grandson of Wigglesworth Dole, the son of Nathan Dole, a minister, and the father of James D. Dole (the "Hawaiian pineapple king," as the *New York Times* called him).

This pamphlet is prepared with the purpose of showing what our Christianity has to do with the familiar practices of business. It is written in the conviction of the most impressive fact that has ever dawned upon the mind of man. This fact is, that *we live in a divine universe*. It is a realm of beneficent law, extending to every particle of matter and to every event and moment of life. [. . .] The whole visible world . . . is only a vast system of parables, illustrations, and object lessons of the vaster world of thought—the moral and spiritual world—to which men belong.[70]

That "we live in a divine universe" is a fundamental belief or premise, in both senses of "fundamental." As a consequence, the "whole visible world" becomes merely epiphenomenal. It is as though there were a world of intelligible reality or essences, and a world of visible appearances. Yet, as in Plato's allegory of the cave, we mistakenly take appearances or shadows to be reality.[71] That is a big metaphysical error, Reverend Dole would maintain. While Reverend Dole's view is not a moderate one, its characteristic antagonist shows no moderation either: materialism, naturalism, or physicalism. This is the view that "[u]ltimate reality . . . is the reality described by chemistry and physics"; "the universe consists entirely of entities that we find it convenient . . . to call 'particles' in fields of force."[72] There is nothing else in the universe. Reality is identical with physics' final, comprehensive account of it, which will be arrived at sometime in the future.

As table 6.1 shows, the Christian Merchant and the Standard of Practice types of moral background stand on opposite sides of this divide. Much follows from accepting either premise. To begin with, much follows about the meaning and point of life and our attitude toward it—including the meaning and point of our business life and our attitude toward it. In this regard, Boston Trinity Church minister Phillips Brooks had a point to make.[73] In his sermon, *The Duty of the Christian Business Man*, delivered in 1891, he insisted that "however He may be hidden from our sight God is the ultimate fact and the final purpose and power of the universe, and . . . everything that man tries to do for his fellow-man is but the expression of that love of God." What are the implications of God's being "the final purpose and power of the universe"?

70 Dole, *The Golden Rule in Business*, pp. ix–x.

71 *Republic* 514a–520a.

72 John Searle. 1998. *Mind, Language, and Society*. New York: Basic Books, pp. 32 and 40; John Searle. 1992. *The Rediscovery of the Mind*. Cambridge, MA: MIT Press, p. 28.

73 Episcopal minister Phillips Brooks (1835–1893) was rector of the Church of the Holy Trinity in Philadelphia (1862–1868), rector of Trinity Church in Boston (1868–1893), Bishop of Massachusetts (1891–1893), and a member of Harvard's Board of Overseers (1870–1891). He has been described as "undeniably one of the most popular preachers of Gilded Age America." Gillis J. Harp. 1998. "The Young Phillips Brooks: A Reassessment." *Journal of Ecclesiastical History* 49(4):652–67, p. 652. Cf. Alexander V. G. Allen. 1900–1901. *Life and Letters of Phillips Brooks*. 3 volumes. New York: E. P. Dutton and Company; William Lawrence. 1893. "Phillips Brooks." *Andover Review,* March/April 1893, pp. 183ff.; William Lawrence. 1903. *Phillips Brooks: A Study*. Boston: Houghton, Mifflin; William Lawrence. 1930. *Life of Phillips Brooks*. New York; London: Harper & Brothers; "Phillips Brooks.—A Tribute and a Study." *Christian Advocate*, February 2, 1893, p. 65; Julius H. Ward. 1892. "Bishop Brooks." *Andover Review,* May 1892, pp. 433ff.

We moralize, we philosophize about the discontent of man. We give little reasons for it; but the real reason of it all is this, that which everything lying behind it really signifies: that man is greater than his circumstances, and that God is always calling to him to come up to the fullness of his life. [. . .] Sad will be the day for every man when he becomes absolutely contented with the life that he is living, with the thoughts that he is thinking, with the deeds that he is doing, when there is not forever beating at the doors of his soul some great desire to do something larger, which he knows that he was meant and made to do because he is the child of God.[74]

Brooks penetratingly observes that it would be sad if (what we call) scientific naturalism turned out to be true. A disenchanted world—to use Max Weber's and Charles Taylor's term—would seem to have no meaning.[75] That would be sad. But Brooks believes that, in fact, it is *not* true: man is "the child of God," he is "greater than his circumstances," and he can do something larger than himself. Interestingly, though, in a disenchanted world Mammon would not exist either. Since the Middle Ages, Mammon had been commonly represented as a demon. As Peter Lombard said in the twelfth century: "Riches are called by the name of a devil, namely Mammon, for Mammon is the name of a devil, by which name riches are called according to the Syrian tongue."[76] Thus, enchantment brings with it both good and bad. This metaphysical picture is a precondition for the very existence of that traditional enemy of the Christian Merchant: the love of money. The social ontology of the Christian Merchant type, then, has Mammon in it—a demon that causally interacts with human beings.[77]

Further, Brooks's metaphysics—according to which "God is the ultimate fact and the final purpose and power of the universe"—involves a teleological understanding of the social world, human history, and human lives. A person's life has a *telos*, destination, or finality. This is "the chief end of [our] being."[78] A life is going somewhere, toward something—toward which it is meant to go, and in relation to which it is intelligible. Likewise, there is a *telos*, destination, or finality to the lives of all of us taken together. We are going somewhere—e.g., toward the Second Advent, the Millennium, and the world to come. This narrative may sound strange to some ears, especially some contemporary ears, because teleology is at odds with scientific naturalism. For it, the idea of a historical destination or direction makes no sense. Yet, it has made total sense to many societies and thinkers

74　Brooks, "The Duty of the Christian Business Man," pp. 75–76. Reprinted as Phillips Brooks. n.d. *The Duty of the Christian Business Man.* New York: Dodge Publishing. Partly published in "The Life with God." *Friends' Intelligencer and Journal,* Fourth Month 4, 1891, p. 209.

75　Taylor, *A Secular Age.*

76　Cited in Deborah Valenze. 2006. *The Social Life of Money in the English Past.* New York: Cambridge University Press, p. 95.

77　See also Henry Ward Beecher. [1869] 1873. "Scope and Function of a Christian Life." Pp. 91–108 in *The Sermons of Henry Ward Beecher in Plymouth Church, Brooklyn.* New York: J. B. Ford & Company, p. 104.

78　Van Doren, *Mercantile Morals,* pp. 23, 29, 33.

throughout history, of which the Aristotelian, Hegelian, and Marxist traditions are the best known.[79]

Then, Brooks maintains that a person can interpret her own past life from the standpoint of the future, and thereby understand what was really going on before: "When a man comes forth into the fullness of that life with God, when at last he has entered God's service and the obedience to God's will and the communion with God's life, then there comes this wonderful thing, there comes the revelation of the man's past." Thus, "[a] marvelous revelation that is to come to him of how all his past has been filled with the power of that spirit with which he has at last entered into communion, to which he has at last submitted himself."[80] One's life becomes retrospectively intelligible; a new light is shed on it and a true understanding is obtained of it. Regrettably, Brooks did not work out the specific implications of his teleology and eschatology for the "Christian Business Man"— even though he should have, given what his sermon was about and whom it was addressed to. For instance, it could have said that human beings and human institutions, business included, have a purpose or function, which is to contribute to the realization of God's plan for the world. But then *this* is what they should be ultimately guided by or oriented toward.

In brief, according to the metaphysics and eschatology illustrated by Dole's 1895 *The Golden Rule in Business* and Brooks's 1891 *The Duty of the Christian Business Man*, an almighty God created and rules the universe, and he has a plan in relation to which human lives have meaning. The "dying testament" of Jonathan Goodhue, the "Christian Merchant" eulogized by Henry Bellows, sums it up:

> [T]he Great, Omnipotent, Omnipresent, and Perfect Being, the Great First Cause, the Creator and Ruler of the Universe—our Father, Preserver, and Benefactor; and to keep habitually in view the obligations I owe to him of perfect obedience in all things. What these duties are, I think are more plainly shown in the life and precepts of the Great Teacher, and I wish accordingly to

---

79 Cf. MacIntyre, *After Virtue*, pp. 51–54. While MacIntyre sees "Protestantism and Jansenist Catholicism—and their immediate late medieval predecessors" as a break with the past, "the contrast between man-as-he-happens-to-be and man-as-he-could-be-if-he-realized-his-*telos* remains and the divine moral law is still a schoolmaster to remove us from the former state to the latter" (pp. 53, 54). See also Kelvin Knight. 2007. *Aristotelian Philosophy: Ethics and Politics from Aristotle to MacIntyre*. Cambridge; Malden, MA: Polity Press.

80 Brooks, "The Duty of the Christian Business Man," pp. 79–80. Brooks's idea is that "[w]hen a man comes forth into the fullness of that life with God, when at last he has entered God's service and the obedience to God's will and the communion with God's life, then there comes this wonderful thing, there comes the revelation of the man's past. We dare to tell the man if he enters into the divine life, if he makes himself a servant of God and does God's will out of obedient love, he shall then be strong and wise. One great element of his strength is going to be this: A marvelous revelation that is to come to him of how all his past has been filled with the power of that spirit with which he has at last entered into communion, to which he has at last submitted himself. [. . .] He sees that back through all the years of his most obstinate and careless life, through all his wilfuness [sic] and resistance, through all his profligacy and black sin, God has been with him all the time, beating himself upon his life."

set all value upon them. These he has said are essentially, love to God, and love to man.[81]

The next question is how this metaphysical picture affects Christian business ethicists' work, injunctions, and arguments. In the next section I present its three chief implications for business ethics. First, the idea that the spiritual is more important than the material, it constitutes a higher plane, so business must be subordinated to religion. Second, the idea that a life has a unity to it, and should be grasped as a whole. There are no discrete compartments or parts to a life, one of which is business. Third, the idea that God is the owner of everything in the universe, so, appearances to the contrary, no human being actually owns anything. We are just stewards or trustees of God's property: our material possessions, bodies, knowledge, even our time are in fact his.

Before turning to that, I wish to indicate two other contributions of Christian metaphysics. First, Christian business ethicists' metaphysical commitments help us better understand my earlier discussion, in chapter 3, about the motives, conscience, and heart of the Christian businessman. There I spent much time on the ways in which business ethicists utilized these concepts. Now we can see a bit more of the big picture into which they fit. Likewise, we can now better understand my earlier discussion, in chapter 6, about metaethical relativism. It was no accident that Christian business ethicists opposed relativism, nor that they opposed it emphatically. It is not simply the case that they happened to find metaethical objectivism a persuasive view. Rather, it was entailed by their metaphysical picture, which required objective standards to "bring the customary morality frequently before the court of ethical law."[82] This is a higher, true, unchanging ethical law, which exists on a different ontological plane than accidental, flimsy, erratic customs. A relativist approach to business ethics would have been incompatible with these fundamental principles, which Christian business ethicists had been taught and into which they had been socialized.

Second, abstract and abstruse though metaphysical issues might sound, they have substantial social and cultural consequences, as Zelizer's *Morals and Markets* shows. Zelizer argues that the nineteenth-century "debate over life insurance was but one expression of a long-lasting dispute concerning the role of Providence in public affairs." It was an expression of a metaphysical dispute over whether Providence was "responsible for a man's family after death," or " 'Providence helps he who helps himself'."[83] Clergymen were at odds about Providence theologically and practically: diverging interpretations of the concept led to diverging

---

81   Bellows, *The Christian Merchant*, p. 25. "After Mr. Goodhue's death, a letter was found, written by him only a few months before, and addressed to his family, which forms such a mirror of the man, and contains so much that is interesting and valuable to us and the community, that every scruple of reserve has given way before the urgency which has sought its publication on the present occasion. It may be considered as Mr. Goodhue's dying testament, as it is, next to his good name, the most precious bequest left to his children" (pp. 22–23).

82   Newton, *The Morals of Trade*, p. 11.

83   Zelizer, *Morals and Markets*, p. 75. Cf. Jacob Viner. 1972. *The Role of Providence in the Social Order: An Essay in Intellectual History*. Princeton: Princeton University Press.

conclusions about the moral status of life insurance. More generally, Zelizer offers a historical account about the moral background. Conceptions about the nature of Providence, chance, and death are background elements, which underlay and shaped first-order moral views, prescriptions, and behaviors. They help explain the obstacles life insurance confronted and its eventual success.

7.5 Stewardship

"Because of his early and seminal work, I would submit that Howard Bowen should be called the 'Father of Corporate Social Responsibility'." Thus writes Archie B. Carroll, former president of the Society for Business Ethics, in his oft-cited 1999 article about the history of CSR.[84] Bowen's paternity is largely due to his book, *Social Responsibilities of the Businessman*, published in 1953 under the auspices of the Federal Council of the Churches.[85] In this book he aimed "to explore the implications of the much-discussed 'concept of social responsibility' as applied to businessmen."[86] Bowen was certainly right that by the 1950s the concept of social responsibility had been much discussed. A few years later, in 1957, historian Morrell Heald made a similar observation regarding "management's responsibility to society": "[m]uch has been written about the contemporary manifestations of this aspect of business thought." However, he added, "[l]ike many other social phenomena it appears, on closer examination, to be not quite so new as the current upsurge of interest and comment may suggest."[87] Heald's historical

84   Archie B. Carroll. 1999. "Corporate Social Responsibility: Evolution of a Definitional Construct." *Business and Society* 38(3):268–95. See also Archie B. Carroll. 2008. "A History of Corporate Social Responsibility: Concepts and Practices." Pp. 19–46 in *The Oxford Handbook of Corporate Social Responsibility*, edited by Andrew Crane, Abigail McWilliams, Dirk Matten, Jeremy Moon, Donald S. Siegel. Oxford; New York: Oxford University Press, pp. 24–27; Archie B. Carroll, Kenneth J. Lipartito, James E. Post, Patricia H. Werhane, and Kenneth E. Goodpaster. 2012. *Corporate Responsibility: The American Experience*. Cambridge, UK: Cambridge University Press, pp. 212–14; Aurélien Acquier, Jean-Pascal Gond, and Jean Pasquero. 2011. "Rediscovering Howard R. Bowen's Legacy." *Business and Society* 50(4):607–46.

85   "This volume forms part of a larger study of *Christian Ethics and Economic Life* which was begun by the Department of the Church and Economic Life of the Federal Council of the Churches of Christ in America in 1949. [. . .] The results of the study are to be presented in six volumes: *Goals of Economic Life, The American Economy and the Lives of People, Social Responsibilities of the Businessman, The Organizational Revolution, American Income and Its Use*, and *Ethics and Economic Life*." Charles P. Taft. 1953. "Foreword." In Howard R. Bowen, *Social Responsibilities of the Businessman*. New York: Harper & Brothers, pp. vii, ix.

86   Bowen, *Social Responsibilities of the Businessman*, p. xi. See also Howard R. Bowen. 1952. "How Public Spirited Is American Business?" *Annals of the American Academy of Political and Social Science* 280:82–89; Howard Bowen. 1954. "Ethics and Economics." Pp. 183–200 in John C. Bennett, Howard R. Bowen, William A. Brown, and G. Bromley Oxnam. 1954. *Christian Values and Economic Life*. New York: Harper & Brothers. Cf. Richard Marens. 2008. "Recovering the Past: Reviving the Legacy of the Early Scholars of Corporate Social Responsibility." *Journal of Management History* 14(1):55–72.

87   Morrell Heald. 1957. "Management's Responsibilities to Society: The Growth of an Idea." *Business History Review* 31(4):375–84, pp. 375, 376. See also Morrell Heald. 1961. "Business Thought in the Twenties: Social Responsibility." *American Quarterly* 13(2):126–39.

research explored these overlooked origins, roughly from 1900 to 1960, and with special emphasis on the 1920s. Heald was aware, too, that the history began earlier: the first chapter of his 1970 book, though short, is devoted to the nineteenth century.[88] In any event, more than fifty years after Heald's and Bowen's observations, they are still right about the 2010s: CSR is "not quite so new as the current upsurge of interest and comment may suggest."

Bowen and Heald realized, too, that a history of corporate social responsibility must start with the Christian doctrine of stewardship. Heald refers to the "doctrine of stewardship and responsibility of the successful for the unfortunate, stemming from centuries of Christian and Jewish teaching" (even though he does not dwell on these teachings).[89] Bowen, in an article published in 1955, writes:

> There is no doubt of an increasing acceptance among businessmen of important obligations toward their diverse clients. The concept of "stewardship" is, of course, an old one, and many businessmen have been thinking in this direction. Especially within the past few years, large numbers of business leaders have publicly acknowledged and actively preached the doctrine that they are servants of society and that management merely in the interests (narrowly defined) of stockholders is not the sole end of their duties.[90]

By "of course," Bowen seems to mean that everybody knows that there exists the concept of stewardship (or the concept of "stewardship") and that it is an old one. In other words, the Christian ring of the word might have been obvious. But is it still obvious today? In the 2010s, the noun "stewardship" is still commonly found in the public sphere. It is commonly accompanied by the adjective "environmental": environmental stewardship is one popular way in which businesspeople, politicians, and journalists talk about companies' environmental policies and environmental legislation. Yet, it is not clear to what extent our contemporary environmental stewardship has been substantively informed and shaped by its Christian counterpart. It is also an open question what the older Christian stewardship and the newer environmental stewardship share, besides their English names' sharing a word. Perhaps contemporary commentators and proponents of stewardship are not well versed in the genealogy of the concept. But perhaps that should be expected: after all, they are not intellectual historians or conceptual genealogists. In any case, what is clear is that the traditional Christian doctrine of stewardship is not principally about natural resources, global warming, or endangered species.[91] Rather, it is a more general and ambitious

88 Heald, *The Social Responsibilities of Business*, pp. 1–19. See also Richard C. Hoffman. 2007. "Corporate Social Responsibility in the 1920s: An Institutional Perspective." *Journal of Management History* 13(1):55–73.

89 Heald, *The Social Responsibilities of Business*, p. 15.

90 Howard R. Bowen. 1955. "Business Management: A Profession?" *Annals of the American Academy of Political and Social Science* 297:112–17, p. 115.

91 More recently, Christian organizations and writers have also applied the concept of stewardship to the environment, often inspired by Genesis 2:15: "And the LORD God took the man, and put him into the garden of Eden to dress it and to keep it." One example is the *Cornwall Declaration*

approach.[92] It addresses not only the proper use of a person's money and material possessions, but also their proper acquisition, as well as the proper use of her talents, time, and soul. As a result, stewardship—sometimes also referred to as trusteeship—became a common tool in the toolkit of the Christian business ethicist.

In the present and the next sections I analyze Christian business ethicists' usage of the doctrine of stewardship, its practical implications, and its metaphysical foundations. Ever since Richard Steele's *Religious Tradesman*, business ethicists have been quick to draw out the implications of stewardship for the businessperson.[93] Seldom have they failed to take advantage of it. For, if certain propositions about stewardship are agreed to, then they have an obvious bearing on a Christian's economic behavior and business activities. My immediate plans are as follows. First, I examine the origins of stewardship, i.e., where it comes from and what its main sources are. Then, I examine its business ethics applications in the United States in the second half of the nineteenth and first decades of the twentieth centuries. Finally, in the next section I examine the relationship between the business ethics uses of stewardship and the metaphysical picture they are underlain by—which is that of the Christian Merchant type of background.

What are the sources of the Christian doctrine of stewardship? First, there are the biblical lessons about God's ownership of the world (e.g., Psalm 24:1), and our role in the world as "good stewards of the manifold grace of God" (1 Peter 4:10; see also 1 Corinthians 4:1–2). Further, there are the interpretations of the controversial parable variously known as the unjust, or dishonest, or shrewd steward, or manager, or servant (Luke 16:1–13). (This difference of nomenclature stems from controversies about the adequate translations of the original Greek words, "*epitropos*" and "*oikonomos*.")[94] Third, there are the interpretations of the Parable of the Talents (Matthew 25:14–30) and the Parable of the Minas (Luke 19:12–27).[95] To

---

on *Environmental Stewardship* (2000) and the Cornwall Alliance for the Stewardship of Creation, "a coalition of clergy, theologians, religious leaders, scientists, academics, and policy experts committed to bringing a balanced Biblical view of stewardship to the critical issues of environment and development." http://www.cornwallalliance.org/site/cornwall-declaration/. Cf. Robert Booth Fowler. 1995. *The Greening of Protestant Thought*. Chapel Hill: University of North Carolina Press.

92   See, e.g., T. K. Thompson, ed. 1960. *Stewardship in Contemporary Theology*. New York: Association Press.

93   Steele, *The Religious Tradesman*, pp. 109, 156.

94   On the concept of *oikonomos*, see Helge Brattgård. 1963. *God's Stewards: A Theological Study of the Principles and Practices of Stewardship*. Translated by Gene J. Lund. Minneapolis: Augsburg Publishing House, pp. 22–64. See also Mark Allan Powell. 1995. *God with Us: A Pastoral Theology of Matthew's Gospel*. Minneapolis: Fortress Press, pp. 89–90. On the disagreements surrounding this parable, see Dennis J. Ireland. 1992. *Stewardship and the Kingdom of God: An Historical, Exegetical, and Contextual Study of the Parable of the Unjust Steward in Luke 16:1–13*. Leiden: Brill.

95   Richard L. Scheef. 1960. "Stewardship in the Old Testament." Pp. 17–38 in *Stewardship in Contemporary Theology*, edited by T. K. Thompson. New York: Association Press; Warren A. Quanbeck. 1960. "Stewardship in the Teachings of Jesus." Pp. 39–53 in *Stewardship in Contemporary Theology*, edited by T. K. Thompson. New York: Association Press; Holmes Rolston. 1960. "Paul's Philosophy of Stewardship." Pp. 54–75 in *Stewardship in Contemporary Theology*, edited by T. K. Thompson. New York: Association Press.

jump to an example from sixteenth-century systematic theology, in the *Institutes* Calvin (1509–1564) invokes the unjust steward parable and claims that "earthly possessions [are] held in trust":

> Scripture has a third rule with which to regulate the use of earthly things. [. . .] It decrees that all those things were so given to us by the kindness of God, and so destined for our benefit, that they are, as it were, entrusted to us, and we must one day render account of them. Thus, therefore, we must so arrange it that this saying may continually resound in our ears: "Render account of your stewardship" [Luke 16:2]. At the same time let us remember by whom such reckoning is required: namely, him who has greatly commended abstinence, sobriety, frugality, and moderation, and has also abominated excess, pride, ostentation, and vanity.[96]

"Earthly possessions" are not really ours; we hold them in trust. Along these lines, Puritan theologian Richard Baxter (1615–1691) made an important connection between stewardship and the obligation to choose the more "gainful way," as the Parable of the Talents would seem to suggest. Baxter's words have become famous thanks to Max Weber, who quoted them as evidence for his famous thesis: "If God show you a way in which you may lawfully get more than in another way (without wrong to your soul or to any other), if you refuse this, and choose the less gainful way, you cross one of the ends of your calling, and you refuse to be God's steward, and to accept His gifts and use them for Him, when He requireth it: you may labour to be rich for God, though not for the flesh and sin."[97]

Along with sixteenth-century Calvin and seventeenth-century Baxter, eighteenth-century John Wesley (1703–1791) found considerable theological merit in the doctrine of stewardship. In his sermon, "The Good Steward," delivered in Edinburgh on May 15, 1768, he takes it one step further. According to Wesley, "[t]he relation which man bears to God, the creature to his Creator, is exhibited to us in the oracles of God under various representations." The argument is that "no character more exactly agrees with the present state of man than that of a *steward*. [. . .] This appellation is exactly expressive of his situation in the present world; specifying what kind of servant he is to God, and what kind of service his divine Master expects from him." Then Wesley makes a metaphysical distinction between temporal things and eternal things: "Eternal things only are our own: with all these temporal things we are barely entrusted by another; the Disposer and Lord of all. And he entrusts us with them on this express condition, that we use them only as our Master's goods, and according to the particular direction which he has given us in his word."

Wesley goes on to enumerate the things "God has entrusted us with": "our souls, our bodies, our goods, and whatever other talents we have received." Thus, "God has entrusted us with our soul, an immortal spirit," along with its associated "powers and faculties" ("understandings, imagination, memory, will, and

---

96 Calvin, *Institutes*, I.x.5.

97 Richard Baxter. 1838. *The Practical Works of Richard Baxter*. Vol. I. London: George Virtue, p. 377.

a train of affections," and so on). God has also "entrusted us with our bodies," "that most excellent talent of speech," and "the use of our hands and feet." He has also "entrusted us . . . with several talents," such as "bodily strength," or "learning and knowledge in their various degrees." It is significant that "worldly goods" and "money" are indeed on the list; they are among the things God has entrusted us with. But they are not the only ones. Wesley's trusteeship or stewardship is global. The question is not only whether throughout our lives we put worldly goods and money to good, godly uses, but also whether we put to good, godly uses all of our talents, our learning and knowledge, our powers and faculties, and our soul. One day, the "Judge of all will . . . inquire":

> How didst thou employ thy soul? I entrusted thee with an immortal spirit, endowed with various powers and faculties, with understanding, imagination, memory, will, affections. I gave thee withal full and express directions, how all these were to be employed. Didst thou employ thy understanding, as far as it was capable, according to these directions; namely, in the knowledge of thyself and Me? [. . .] How didst thou employ the body wherewith I entrusted thee? I gave thee a tongue to praise me therewith: didst thou use it to the end for which it was given? [. . .] How didst thou employ the worldly goods which I lodged in thy hands? [. . .] In what manner didst thou employ that comprehensive talent, money? Not in gratifying the desire of the flesh, the desire of the eye, or the pride of life? Not squandering it away in vain expenses, the same as throwing it into the sea? Not hoarding it up to leave behind thee, the same as burying it in the earth? But first supplying thy own reasonable wants, together with those of thy family; then restoring the remainder to me, through the poor, whom I had appointed to receive it.[98]

Creation comes with instructions for use. The entire endowment—human powers, faculties, learning, knowledge, bodies, and material goods—ought to be handled in accordance with these divine directions. For they have intrinsic ends, determined by God. Importantly, Wesley argues that time is included as well: the "invaluable talent of time . . . God entrusts us from moment to moment." Therefore, "there is no employment of our time, no action or conversation, that is purely indifferent. All is good or bad, because all our time, as every thing we have is not our own."

In sum, stewardship might be theologically understood as a prism through which to see all aspects of a Christian life. I am not interested here in the implications of the doctrine of stewardship for Weberian arguments, but in the metaphysical baggage it carries along. How did its dependence on particular conceptions about the nature of world, the nature of time, and the ends or purposes of things show up in U.S. business ethics? Against this theological backdrop, inherited from Calvin, Wesley, and other old-world writers, new-world moralists

---

98   John Wesley. [1768] 1836. "The Good Steward." Pp. 448–57 in *Sermons on Several Occasions*. Vol. I. New York: B. Waugh and T. Mason, pp. 454–55. See also John Wesley. 1836. "On the Use of Money." Pp. 440–48 in *Sermons on Several Occasions*. Vol. I. New York: B. Waugh and T. Mason.

and preachers—including but not limited to business ethicists—developed their views and tried to profit from the stewardship doctrine. Here, as church historians have argued, a key factor is the need to support churches and missions. Kelly Johnson summarizes the situation thus: "in [the American] context it [stewardship rhetoric] flourished as never before. Sermons, tracts, and even books on stewardship became abundant in mid-nineteenth-century Protestantism in the United States as a way for clergy to raise support for missions and for their own churches . . . This period, called by some 'the great stewardship awakening,' has been pinpointed in several works on stewardship as the emergence of the modern use of the term."[99]

But how exactly was stewardship used? And how were these uses metaphysically loaded? Take first an antebellum antecessor. Leonard Bacon (1802–1881) has gone down in history as the longstanding Congregational minister of New Haven's First Church.[100] A few years after taking that job, Bacon, a young man himself, was asked to address the Young Men's Benevolent Society of New Haven. The "subject respecting which the Committee of the Young Men's Benevolence Society have desired that instruction and counsel may be given on this occasion from the oracles of God,—is THE CHRISTIAN DOCTRINE OF STEWARDSHIP IN REGARD TO PROPERTY. The question is, *What is the right use of property on Christian principles*?" The answer, italicized in the published pamphlet, was basically the standard line: "*Every man is bound to regard all his property, and all the avails of his industry and enterprise, as belonging to God; he is to hold it all, and manage it, as a sacred trust for which he must give account to the supreme proprietor; he is to apply it and dispose of it exclusively as the Lord's servant, and in the work of the Lord.*" [101] This seems a fittingly capitalist turn of events: the supreme creator has become the supreme proprietor.

The doctrine of stewardship was recurrently resorted to by Christian business ethicists in the second half of the nineteenth and first decades of the twentieth centuries. Indeed, the moral exemplar, the Christian Merchant, could be described as a steward. His stewardship was one of his essential properties—as a eulogy of Boston brothers Amos Lawrence and Abbott Lawrence, *The Stewardship of Wealth*, emphasized.[102] While usage expanded, the basic, foundational

99   Kelly S. Johnson. 2007. *The Fear of Beggars: Stewardship and Poverty in Christian Ethics.* Grand Rapids, MI; Cambridge: William B. Eerdmans, p. 89.

100   *Leonard Bacon: Pastor of the First Church in New Haven.* 1882. New Haven, CT: Tuttle, Morehouse & Taylor, printers. Cf. Hugh Davis. 1998. *Leonard Bacon: New England Reformer and Antislavery Moderate.* Baton Rouge: Louisiana State University Press.

101   Leonard Bacon. 1832. *The Christian Doctrine of Stewardship in Respect to Property. A Sermon Preached at the Request of the Young Men's Benevolent Society of New-Haven, Conn.* New-Haven: Printed by Nathan Whiting, pp. 5 and 6–7. A review of the sermon presented Bacon's central "proposition" and commented: "The proof is derived from the Bible—1st, from the parable of the talents—2d, from the numerous passages in the New Testament which speak of the comprehensive duty of being entirely devoted to God—3d, from those passages in which property is directly spoken of, and its uses and abuses expressly stated." "Notices of New Publications." 1832. *The Quarterly Register,* vol. 5, no. 1, August 1832, pp. 74–78, pp. 76–77.

102   Ballard, *The Stewardship of Wealth.*

principles remained relatively constant. To give one late-nineteenth-century il-lustration, in 1895 *The Gospel in All Lands* published an article titled, "Christian Stewardship," pseudonymously signed by "Christian Steward":

1. *Our Property, as well as Ourselves, Belongs to God.* He has given us what-ever we possess. He has the right to take it from us, when and how he will. "The Lord maketh poor, and maketh rich" (1 Sam. 2. 7). "The Silver is mine, and the gold is mine, saith the Lord of hosts" (Hag. 2. 8).
2. *Our Property is to be Used for God's Glory.* All of it—that which we spend upon ourselves and our families, as well as that which we give to the Church and its benevolent work. In other words, we are but stewards, trustees, of that which the Lord puts into our hands. We are to use the tal-ents with which he has intrusted us for him. Occupying till he come again, we are at his coming to give account of our stewardship.[103]

As suggested earlier, stewardship could help with urgent practical matters, particularly urgent material ones. As one writer put it in the 1920s, "Satan seems to realize that money is an indispensable asset to the church. He understands that Christ's work will be delayed and God's program for world redemption indefi-nitely postponed, if he can prevent the church from getting the money with which properly to support and equip those who shall teach and preach and heal and serve in extending the gospel." Satan tempted Christians to "rob God, to neglect their needy world-neighbors, to insult Christ with beggarly pittances."[104] Money was an indispensable asset, but the word "money" did not sound pleasing to the ear, so "stewardship" became something of a euphemism. It was employed by numerous church organizations, groups, departments, agencies, and committees that concerned themselves with church finances, fund-raising (e.g., the "Every Member Canvass"), and stewardship advocacy more generally.[105]

For example, the Baptist General Committee on Christian Stewardship was "organized in 1902 for the purpose of emphasizing regular and systematic giv-ing among Baptists."[106] The Church of the United Brethren in Christ organized

---

103 Christian Steward. 1895. "Christian Stewardship." *The Gospel in All Lands*, December 1895, p. 601. (*The Gospel in All Lands* was the official organ of the Missionary Society of the Methodist Epis-copal Church.) "Christian Steward" continued: "The adoption of the principle of Christian steward-ship, so clearly taught in holy writ, makes all we possess sacred to God. It regulates our personal and household expenses, our pleasures, our expenditures, in every direction. We allow not charges against the fund which we cannot justify when the final accounting is rendered to Him whose trustees we are."

104 Albert F. McGarrah. 1922. *Money Talks*. New York, Chicago, London, and Edinburgh: Fleming H. Revell Company, p. 145. Cf. Rev. J. Ashworth. 1857. *Christian Stewardship: A Treatise on the Scriptural Obligation, Method, Measure and Privilege of Systemized Beneficence.* Auburn: William J. Moses.

105 Cf. James Hudnut-Beumler. 2007. *In Pursuit of the Almighty's Dollar: A History of Money and American Protestantism.* Chapel Hill: University of North Carolina Press, esp. ch. 3 and 5.

106 Department of Commerce and Labor. Bureau of the Census. 1910. *Religious Bodies: 1906.* Part II. Washington, DC: Government Printing Office, p. 52. See also the "Special Issue on Christian Stewardship" of the Baptist periodical, *Missions*, including several articles, a "Stewardship pledge card," and a "message to the pastors from the Stewardship Committee of the Northern Baptist Convention." "Missions' Special Issue on Christian Stewardship." *Missions*, vol. 13, no. 9, October 1922, p. 515.

a Stewardship Commission in 1905,[107] and the Inter-Church World Movement had a Stewardship Department, whose director in 1920 was R. S. Cushman.[108] Presbyterians had comparable agencies, such as the Permanent Committee on Stewardship or Permanent Committee on Systematic Beneficence and Stewardship.[109] The minutes of the 1921 General Assembly illustrate how "stewardship" was used to talk about financial matters in general: "Pastors all over the Church are faithful in teaching the Stewardship of life and possessions, and there is a commendable increase in the number of members who tithe or give a definite proportion of their income, yet not half the churches seem to have paid in full their apportionment for benevolences."[110] Similarly, a 1915 "Stewardship Conference" dealt with "Church finances and methods" and "the financial policy of the church." The conference, luckily, was itself "most satisfactory and profitable."[111] In 1922, a "prize essay on stewardship" was announced by the Stewardship Department, with the "purpose of getting young people to face the claims of Stewardship."[112] And the Stewardship Department of the New Jersey Synod prepared various didactic materials, including stewardship textbooks and "an intimate interview with John D. Rockefeller, Jr., showing how he is bringing up his children in Stewardship."[113]

The Methodist Christian Stewardship League, later renamed Christian Stewardship Movement, was organized in 1916.[114] According to its constitution, "[t]he Christian Stewardship League is formed in order that Christian people may be helped to know the spiritual meaning of ownership, and in order that they themselves may help to establish, in the Church and in society, a Christian attitude toward property, income, wages, and wealth. It is recognized that Christian Stewardship must be of life and opportunity, no less than of possessions; therefore it is the further purpose of the League to emphasize and promote the stewardship

---

107   "The Promoting of Christian Stewardship." 1910. *The Year Book of the United Brethren in Christ 1910.* Dayton, OH: Otterbein Press, pp. 42–43; "The Stewardship Commission." 1911. *The Year Book of the United Brethren in Christ.* Dayton, OH: Otterbein Press, pp. 40–41; *Origin, Doctrine, Constitution and Discipline of the United Brethren in Christ.* 1905. Dayton, OH: United Brethren Publishing House, p. 102.

108   "What is the Interchurch World Movement?" *The Sabbath Recorder,* vol. 88, no. 2, January 12, 1920, pp. 56–57; Stacy R. Warburton, ed. 1920. *Year Book of the Churches 1920.* New York: Fleming H. Revell Company, pp. 271–72.

109   *Minutes of the Sixty-First General Assembly of the Presbyterian Church in the United States.* 1921. Richmond, VA: Presbyterian Committee on Publication, pp. 4, 23–26, 43–50.

110   Ibid., p. 64.

111   "The Montreat Conference." *The Missionary Survey,* vol. 5, no. 9, September 1915, p. 646.

112   "Prize Essay on Stewardship." *Herald and Presbyter,* vol. 93, no. 45, November 8, 1922, p. 18.

113   *Minutes of the One Hundredth Annual Session of the Synod of New Jersey, Held in the First Presbyterian Church, Atlantic City, N. J., October 16–18, 1922.* Newark, NJ: Baker Printing Co., p. 121.

114   "Christian Stewardship League." 1918. *The Methodist Year Book 1918.* Oliver S. Baketel, editor. New York and Cincinnati: Methodist Book Concern, p. 164; "The Christian Stewardship Movement." 1919. *The Methodist Year Book 1919.* Oliver S. Baketel, editor. New York and Cincinnati: Methodist Book Concern, pp. 160–61; Ralph S. Cushman. 1918. *Studies in Stewardship.* New York: Joint Centenary Committee, Methodist Episcopal Church.

of personal Christian service, and of prayer."[115] It is indicative of popular perceptions about stewardship that one of the movement's publications rhetorically asked whether "stewardship and tithing [were] the same," and then answered that they were not. A plausible inference to the best explanation is that the League thought people thought they were.[116]

Besides tithing practice, the Christian Stewardship Movement and other comparable agencies were interested in stewardship theory, so to speak. They attempted to work out, on the basis of both traditional theological arguments and actual historical conditions, what stewardship should involve for a Christian at the time. Further, they put considerable effort into publicity and education, or the promotion of stewardship as an ideal—which no doubt included, but no doubt was not limited to, tithing and giving. Thus, this stewardship theorization illustrates a more general tendency: the expansion of the reach of the concept beyond the use of property—much like in the theology of their founding father, John Wesley.[117] For example, in 1918 the chairman of the Stewardship Movement, Ralph Cushman, published the book, *Studies in Stewardship*. According to him, stewardship should include—and it was already beginning to include—"stewardship in acquiring": "It is one of the happy signs of this day, that there is a growing conviction that good stewardship must reach into the realms of acquiring. This means that no man can be faithful in the administration of his possessions, unless they have first come into his hands by legitimate business transaction."[118] Similarly, in 1914 "Stewardship Secretary" Harvey Reeves Calking published the book, *A Man and His Money*. Calking argues that "stewardship is not 'giving.' [. . .] Stewardship is the recognition that God is the owner of all economic value, and, therefore, that private property can be no other than a sacred trust." Again, popular perceptions to the contrary, stewardship does not simply mean "giving" (quotation marks are Calking's). What does it mean, then? It means everything: "Stewardship is the attitude of a Christian toward his possessions. But it is very much more than this. Stewardship is the Christian law of living. The stewardship of privilege, of opportunity, of experience, of education, of artistic talent, of mental and spiritual gifts, in a word, the whole inclusive stewardship of personality—this, indeed is the Christian life."[119]

---

115 Harvey Reeves Calkings. 1917. *Ganga Dass: A Tale of Hindustan*. New York and Cincinnati: Abingdon Press, p. 82. The constitution of the Christian Stewardship League was printed at the end of this book, since it was part of a "'World-Series' of Stewardship Booklets" the league published; Calking was the series' editor.

116 Ralph S. Cushman. 1919. *The New Christian: Studies in Stewardship (Revised)*. New York: Centenary Conservation Committee, Methodist Episcopal Church, p. 137.

117 This conceptual expansion did not only come from Methodists. For instance, the Stewardship Commission of the United Brethren in Christ stated: "We greatly err when we think that in giving an account of our stewardship it refers only to our temporal affairs. In the teachings of the Man of Galilee we are taught that we are his bond-servants. If we accept him as authority, then whatever we possess, whether of experience, talent, training, time, or property belongs to our Master, and they are ours only to be used for the best possible advantages of his kingdom." "The Stewardship Commission." 1911. *The Year Book of the United Brethren in Christ*. Dayton, OH: Otterbein Press, pp. 40–41, p. 40.

118 Cushman, *Studies in Stewardship*, pp. 84–85.

119 Harvey Reeves Calking. 1914. *A Man and His Money*. New York and Cincinnati: Methodist Book Concern, p. 271.

The preceding discussion sheds light on the lecture from which the epigraph of this chapter is taken, Ballard's *The Stewardship of Wealth*, even though it was delivered half a century earlier. Christian businessmen Amos and Abbott Lawrence were stewards of wealth, they were known for their philanthropic donations, and they deserved credit for that. "It was permitted to Amos and Abbott Lawrence to realize the responsibilities which are inseparable from wealth, and, recognizing their obligations to the Giver, to dispense, as in His sight and for His greater glory, the bounties held by them in trust." However, the Christian's stewardship, as exemplified by the Lawrence brothers, went beyond wealth: "The stewardship, then, of which we speak, is not exclusively a Stewardship of Wealth; it is much more; for it involves the idea of God's ownership of ourselves and *all* we have, and His indubitable right to give and take away and transfer, as may best conduct to His 'greater glory' and the swift furtherance of His providential designs."[120]

7.6 Stewardship Metaphysics

To what lengths could the concept and doctrine of stewardship be pushed? How much theoretical and practical work could they be made to do? Some Christian writers and preachers turned stewardship into *the* central ethical concept, even a keyword or mantra of sorts. One case in point is Reverend Guy Louis Morrill, of the Stewardship Department and Department of Missionary Education of the New Era Movement of the Presbyterian Church. In *You and Yours: God's Purpose in Things* (1922), Morrill starts from the empirical premise that "[o]ur generation believes that in the solution of the problems arising from the possession of riches lies the key to every other social problem. So the bases of the getting and the keeping, the using and the spending of riches, are being extensively and searchingly re-examined." The starting point, then, is the centrality of "riches" and economic life in contemporary societies, as well as the concern of contemporary societies about it. The Christian solution to all of these problems is stewardship: "[t]he new word for the Church today must be this startling word, 'stewardship'." Literally, Morrill writes that "*[s]tewardship* is the answer."[121] And the italics are his. Then, he spells out the doctrine's principles and their scriptural underpinnings:

> The Bible doctrine of stewardship is "The doctrine that God, the Creator, is the only absolute owner of all things or persons—that 'all things come of Him' and are 'His own' and that we men hold what we hold as stewards for the purpose of His kingdom, with only *relative* and *dependent* ownership limited at every point by the purpose for which it was entrusted to us." (Property: Its Rights and Duties.) Its four basic principles stated as a personal creed are: I believe
> That God is the owner of all. (Ps. 24:1; 1 Chron. 29:11–14; Ps. 50:1–, 11; Hag. 2:8.)

---

120 Ballard, *The Stewardship of Wealth*, pp. 48–49, p. 14.
121 Guy L. Morrill. 1922. *You and Yours: God's Purpose in Things*. New York, Chicago, London, and Edinburgh: Fleming H. Revell Company, pp. 5, 15, 7.

That I am His steward and must account for all that I have. (Lk. 16:2; 1 Cor. 4:2.)

That God requires me to give a definite proportion of my income for His service in acknowledgment of His ownership and my stewardship. (Lev. 27:3–32; Mal. 3:8–10; 1 Cor. 16:2; 2 Cor. 8:1–9.)

That I should use all the rest—what I spend and what I save—in ways that are pleasing to God. (Romans 11:16; 1 Cor. 10:31.)[122]

Morrill was a stewardship maximalist. Hence, it is understandable that he should be upset at stewardship reductionism, that is, the reduction of stewardship to tithing or fund-raising: "Much of the superficial writing and talking about stewardship robs the New Testament teaching on this subject of its glory and marvel. Stewardship is too often presented as just a way of raising money, of supporting the Church, of paying the minister, of maintaining missionary work." In contrast, for Morrill, stewardship should not be seen as "a sort of subterfuge for getting money for the Church" at all.[123] It was rather a concept and doctrine that applied across the board, and on the basis of which a good Christian life should be led. The phrasing chosen by the Stewardship Committee of the Northern Baptist Convention in 1922 is unequivocal: "We are His, our time is His, our strength is His, our ability is His, our money is His, our children are His. We hold them indeed, but we hold them for Him. This is what we mean by Stewardship."[124]

Wherever else it is relevant, the doctrine of stewardship is surely relevant to business ethics. It followed from its broad conception that it could and should guide a Christian's business practices and wealth acquisition as much as its use.[125] Indeed, it should guide your whole life. For the actual owner of your talents, skills, knowledge, body, and time is God. We are not even talking about a loan here, because you cannot do with them as you please. Rather, you have to use them according to God's will and plan. Or perhaps they can be viewed as conditional loans, analogous to those of the International Monetary Fund (except for the wisdom and benevolence of the lender). Either way, Christian business ethicists were happy to jump on the stewardship bandwagon and contribute to its development. It provided them with a metaphysical basis for their practical recommendations and prescriptions—and one which, stripped of its more abstruse metaphysical and theological aspects, resonated with businesspeople. You should not use your business skills to deceive customers and crush competitors because they are not

---

122   Ibid., p. 14. Morrill is quoting from the introduction to a 1922 book, penned by the Bishop of Oxford: *Property: Its Rights and Duties. Historically, Philosophically and Religiously Regarded. Essays by Various Writers.* New York: The Macmillan Company, p. xi. In turn, the Bishop of Oxford was himself quoting "Dr. Bartlet, of Mansfield College, Oxford [who] had written a letter to the *British Weekly* strongly urging upon Christians the duty of reconsidering their ideas about property in the light of the Bible doctrine of stewardship."

123   Ibid., p. 199.

124   "The Spiritual Significance of Stewardship. A Message to the Pastors from the Stewardship Committee of the Northern Baptist Convention." *Missions*, vol. 13, no. 9, October 1922, p. 523.

125   On the Bible on acquisition, see Milton G. Evans, 1906. "Biblical Teaching on the Righteous Acquisition of Property." *Biblical World* 27(4):275–85.

yours. In these contexts, trusteeship might replace stewardship: you are a trustee managing property held in trust. Is not a manager accountable to the stockholders? Is not an agent accountable to the principal? Do they not have a fiduciary duty to act for their benefit and maximize their interests? In fact, this analogy was explicitly employed. For instance, Peabody said: "The teaching of Jesus permits in no case the sense of absolute ownership. [. . .] A man does not own his wealth, he owes it. Precisely as a business man says to himself, I must invest and distribute a certain sum with special scrupulousness because I administer it as a trustee . . . , so the disciple of Jesus acts in all concerns of his life as a servant who has heard the great word, 'Be ye also ready: for in an hour that ye think not the Son of man cometh'."[126] In brief, as he said elsewhere, in a lecture at the University of North Carolina in 1913, "[t]his is the paradox of property. To own is to owe. Possession means obligation. [. . .] Ownership is stewardship."[127]

Because it resonates with practices and ideas they are familiar with, the stewardship doctrine—its demands and their rationale—should make sense to businesspeople. They should be able to get it, whether or not they end up complying with its demands. At the same time, this doctrine rests on heavy metaphysical foundations, which are literally foundational, not optional by-products or unintended side effects. Obviously, that the universe belongs to God is a strong metaphysical commitment. It is a commitment that does not simply follow from your believing that God created the universe, established laws of nature and laws of conduct, and will eventually judge your temporal behavior. It is perfectly possible to believe that God gave you your life and your skills, gave you time, and so on, all of which *ipso facto* became yours. This is how giving something normally works. They would be yours even if he commanded you to act in certain ways (piously) and to use them in certain ways (for the glory of God). Moreover, that your stewardship of, say, property should follow God's commandments and plan presupposes that there are such commandments and plan. This may seem commonsensical to anyone with some exposure to the Abrahamic religions, but it is another nontrivial metaphysical commitment

126 Peabody, *Jesus Christ and the Social Question*, pp. 212–13. And he goes on to say: "If in any case riches obstruct the complete dedication of the life, then Jesus has no objection to offer to the most sweeping of modern demands for the abolition of rich men. Indeed, he goes beyond most of these demands. [. . .] [Jesus] does not ask of a man a fair proportion of his personal profits; he asks the whole of one's gains—and the life which lies behind the gains—for the service of the kingdom" (p. 215).

127 Francis Greenwood Peabody. 1915. *The Christian Life in the Modern World*. New York: The Macmillan Company, p. 119.

For his part, Peabody's fellow Social Gospeller Walter Rauschenbusch maintained that "men of wealth" were stewards of both God and "the people": "The doctrine of 'Christian stewardship' . . . is a new formula designed to give our modern men of wealth a stronger sense of responsibility and to induce them to give more largely to the Church and its work. But if a rich man withdraws a million from commerce and gives it to a missionary society or a college, that simply shifts the money from one steward to another, and from one line of usefulness to another. The ecclesiastical idea of stewardship needs to be intensified and broadened by the democratic idea. Every man who holds wealth or power is not only a steward of God, but a steward of the people. He derives it from the people and he holds it in trust for the people." Rauschenbusch, *Christianity and the Social Crisis*, pp. 387–88.

nonetheless. It is even less trivial if this plan contains functionalist concepts and understandings, whereby people and events have purposes, and history has a meaning and direction. God has a plan for our individual lives and for his creation as a whole. As a consequence, a business ethics approach that relies on the doctrine of stewardship confers a distinct status to business activities and products. Their natures are such that they can fit with these broader metaphysical and moral background elements.

No doubt, a business ethicist may advance something like a stewardship doctrine without its theistic components, or at least without any essential theistic components. Many have indeed done so—from the above-mentioned environmental stewardship in the twenty-first century to the late-nineteenth-century "Gospel of Wealth" of steel magnate Andrew Carnegie.[128] Nevertheless, stewardship may not amount to the same thing anymore, even if the word "steward" is still prominently displayed. For it is now uncertain who we are stewards, trustees, or agents of. At least, the intuitive forcefulness of the doctrine is severely weakened. Its plausibility must be derived from some other source—but what source? For instance, it is hard to agree on whom the environment belongs to, or what it means to say that it belongs to future generations or to humanity. It is hard to agree on how society might be the real owner of my hard-won fortune, such that I am in fact society's trustee. It is even harder to pull off a more extended stewardship doctrine, which encompasses a person's time, abilities, skills, and body. Who can possibly be the true owners of these, if not she herself? To be sure, there might be other reasons for a businessperson to put her talents and skills to good moral use, for the benefit of society, the community, or the environment. This is precisely what corporate social responsibility advocates have always tried to argue for. There are many ways in which they have tackled the question of whence the "social responsibility imposed on the business man of today," as Wallace Donham worded it in the 1920s.[129] For instance, you may suggest that corporations are like citizens, speak of corporate citizenship, and derive their duties from an analogy with the duties of ordinary citizens in democratic polities. Or you may suggest that corporations are like neighbors. Or you may imagine tacit contracts and veils of ignorance. Yet, whether these alternative approaches are persuasive or not, the stewardship doctrine would have already dropped out of the picture, and a different set of background elements would now be involved.

Within the general theory of stewardship, the special theory of the stewardship of time is of special interest. This is because from a Christian perspective time has been often viewed as a metaphysically special kind of thing.[130] First,

---

128　Andrew Carnegie. 2006. *The "Gospel of Wealth" Essays and Other Writings.* Edited with an Introduction by David Nasaw. New York: Penguin Books.

129　Donham, "The Social Significance of Business," p. 407.

130　I must ignore an entire literature on time, temporality, eternity, and timelessness here, so the following discussion about Christian time is quite crude, theologically and philosophically. See, e.g., Antje Jackelén. [2002] 2005. *Time and Eternity: The Question of Time in Church, Science, and Theology.* Translated by Barbara Harshaw. West Conshohocken: Templeton Foundation Press; Brian Leftow. 1991. *Time and Eternity.* Ithaca: Cornell University Press; Alan G. Padgett. 1992. *God, Eternity and the Nature of Time.* London: Macmillan.

there are qualitatively different kinds of time, such as profane or ordinary time on the one hand, and higher or sacred time on the other. As Taylor writes, "in earlier ages . . . profane time existed in relation to (surrounded by, penetrated by: it is hard to find the right words here) higher time." The former might be "transcended and held in place by eternity," which is "not just endless profane time, but an ascent into the unchanging, or a kind of gathering of time into a unity."[131] But what is eternity? And does God exist in time or timelessly? The point is that Christian time is more complex and multidimensional than profane, secular time. This is a property of the Christian Merchant type of moral background. There are kinds of time, one of which is special, higher, sacred (which is in turn based on a distinction between the higher and the lower). By contrast, Standards of Practice time is homogeneous—consistent with the secular "rejection of higher time, and the positing of time as purely profane," where "[e]vents . . . exist only in this one dimension."[132] Contemporary, secularized Westerners may even be unable to wrap their mind around the idea that time is not one kind of thing only.

Second, like everything else in the universe, time is God's, not ours. It has not been easy to agree on what this means and entails, exactly. However, it is easy to see that, whatever it means and entails, it sets apart the Christian Merchant from the Standards of Practice type of moral background. To take an instructive medieval example, the usury controversies, one argument against moneylending was that moneylenders were thieves. They were thieves because they sold time. But time did not belong to them but to God; he gave it to all of us in common. Hence, time ought not to be sold.[133] Of course, this argument only works and makes sense given certain premises or starting points, which the Christian Merchant type does start from, but the Standards of Practice type does not. Furthermore, the implications of God's being the owner of time should be more than practical recommendations. According to Christian moralists and business ethicists, you should use your time in accordance to God's will. They might tell you how to use it for God's glory, to thank him, to grow spiritually, what activities you should not engage in, and so on. What you devote your time to is subject to moral evaluation. This is the point at which Weberian and Weberian-like arguments are pertinent, especially once thoroughly religious prescriptions gave way to secularized and semi-secularized advice about intelligent, smart, effective, and productive uses of time.

131 Taylor, *A Secular Age*, p. 195. See also Charles Taylor. 1995. "Liberal Politics and the Public Sphere." Pp. 257–87 in *Philosophical Arguments*. Cambridge, MA: Harvard University Press, pp. 269–71; Taylor, *Modern Social Imaginaries*, pp. 96–99; Taylor, *A Secular Age*, pp. 54–59, 96, 208–9, 712–13.

132 As Taylor says: "Now it seems to have been the universal norms to see the important metatopical spaces and agencies as constituted in some mode of higher time. States, churches, were seen to exist almost necessarily in more than one time-dimension, as though it were inconceivable that they have their being purely in the profane or ordinary time." And he adds: "Modern 'secularization' can be seen from one angle as the rejection of higher time, and the positing of time as purely profane. Events now exist only in this one dimension, in which they stand at greater and lesser temporal distance, and in relations of causality with other events of the same kind. The modern notion of simultaneity comes to be, in which events utterly unrelated in cause or meaning are held together simply by their co-occurrence at the same point in this single profane timeline." Taylor, *A Secular Age*, p. 195.

133 Cf. Le Goff, *La bourse et la vie*; Noonan, *The Scholastic Analysis of Usury*.

Using your time in accordance with God's will does not necessitate that time still *be* his. Perhaps he gave it to you once, along with a letter of intent stating the conditions that it would be prudent for you not to violate. Yet, the claim that time belongs to God further suggests that the nature or essence of time is divine. Metaphysically, it is not an empty time, a neutral container "that things and events contingently fill," as Taylor and Benedict Anderson observe.[134] Rather, it has itself a distinct divine mark or signature. It may further suggest that time is a collective good, which was given to us in common—which would be another reason why you cannot meaningfully speak of *your* time. Of course, ministers can benefit from invoking the stewardship of time in their pastoral and educational work with very worldly, matter-of-fact aims in view. For instance, they can encourage parishioners to devote more time to spiritual concerns and service to the church and less time to intoxicating beverages—just like they encouraged parishioners to give more of their income to the church and less to drinking establishments. But the key point is that time has metaphysical, godly marks, such that there is no time outside God or religion. This is not because, as a matter of fact, all of your time is or should be devoted to religion. Rather, it is because of the very nature of time; what time is. It follows that in practice there is no moral difference between what you do on Monday and on Sunday, or between what you do at the office and at church. You exist in time—this godly time—all the time.

"Christian Stewardship" is the title of a 1920 article in the *Herald of Gospel Liberty*, the periodical publication of the Christian Connexion. Its author, J. W. Stout, begins with standard stewardship fare—the standard broad definition of "stewardship," and the standard analogy that makes sense to businesspeople:

> Christian Stewardship is not solely a relationship between man's pocketbook and God; it is a relationship between man's life and God. [. . .] A Steward is a trustee, accepting the gifts that God has given him, and accepting also the duties of trusteeship that God has imposed.
>
> A Steward is accountable for what has been committed to him. He is to manage or administer it in the interest of the owner. To forget this, and to appropriate and use what God has entrusted to him for himself, is not less a crime than for a trustee of an estate to appropriate the funds entrusted to him for his own profit and pleasure.[135]

---

134 Here Taylor draws on Anderson on time as homogeneous and the concept of simultaneity; Anderson in turn draws on Benjamin: "In *Imagined Communities*, Anderson borrows a term from Benjamin to describe modern profane time. He sees it as a 'homogeneous, empty time.' Homogeneity captures the aspect I am describing, that all events now fall into the same kind of time. But the 'emptiness' of time takes us into another issue: the way in which both space and time come to be seen as 'containers' that things and events contingently fill, rather than as constituted by what fills them. This latter step is part of the metaphysical imagination of modern physics, as we can see with Newton." Taylor, *Modern Social Imaginaries*, p. 206. Cf. Benedict Anderson. 1983. *Imagined Communities: Reflections on the Origin and Spread of Nationalism*. London: Verso.

135 J. W. Stout. 1920. "Christian Stewardship." *The Herald of Gospel Liberty*, December 16, 1920, pp. 1208–9.

Next, Stout spells out what "Christian Stewardship" encompassed. To him, "[e]very believer is a steward of the manifold grace of God [. . .] This Stewardship of the gospel is all-inclusive." It includes time: "There is a stewardship of time. Time is God-entrusted. We have no right to do as we please with it. We are to use it as a part of one great stewardship of the manifold grace of God for the good of men." It also includes "the stewardship of opportunity, and of privilege, and of every blessing that may come into our lives"; "the stewardship of parenthood; the stewardship of good citizenship"; and of course "the stewardship of property or wealth." "Indeed, Stewardship is in every relation of life or death." An all-inclusive stewardship indeed. Stout's next step is crucial:

> When men and women catch the vision and realize the ever-present Christian Stewardship, life to them will no longer be divided into sacred and secular. There will be no line on one side of which he will say, "Here I may be religious," and on the other side of which he will say, "Here I may be worldly." To the true Steward, business is as sacred a thing as a prayer-meeting, and is to be conducted on the strictest lines of honesty and purity. The Christian Steward realizes that he is in partnership with the Father and His Son Jesus Christ, and his business is carried on in relation to that partnership.

Unfortunately, Stout does not explain what he means by "in relation to" in this context. But it seems to mean something like consistent with or guided by that partnership, and what that partnership suggests or demands. Either way, his basic point is that your business activities are not off the moral hook. "Christian Stewardship" is "ever-present," so the distinction between sacred, religious activities and secular, worldly activities is morally irrelevant. True, in one sense there is a distinction: you cannot be in two places at once; you go to church particular days; you pray at particular times; and so on. But the moral applicability of your "partnership" with "Father and Son" is independent of where you physically are or what you are physically doing. Differently put, morally speaking, religion and business are not separate spheres. Morally speaking, your life is a whole thing, and no section or department of it can be exempted from moral scrutiny. You are only one person, a Christian Merchant, all the time.

7.7 Spheres

"One very important department of life where religion is to hold perpetual sway, is that of *business*. 'As the golden sun-light tints the flower, and colors the rock; as it sparkles in the dewdrop, and shines in the broad, magnificent ocean,' so should religion permeate every transaction with our fellow-men. It should go with its possessor into the counting-room, the store, the market, the factory; and its influence should be felt in all places."[136] Poetic metaphors and business ethics are rarely found together, as they were in this *Reformed Church Messenger* article, "Religion

---

136   "Religion in Business." *Reformed Church Messenger*, February 2, 1870, p. 8.

in Business," from 1870. Signed by Rev. John Berg, its motivating concern and rhetorical foe was a familiar one: the apparently widespread fear among businessmen that "a man cannot be a good Christian and a successful merchant."[137] If you were a Christian business ethicist at the time, you would of course categorically affirm that he could; that of course he could. At the very least, religion did not prevent success—which, however, would require you to accomplish and maintain the fragile equilibriums and compromises discussed in chapter 3. While its poetic language might have been atypical, in another respect Berg's article was typical: its making an ethical and metaphysical distinction between the higher and the lower.

> How many are there whose powers are so exhausted by business, as to have neither time, inclination, nor energy, to seek after their own spiritual interests, much less those of their families. But *who* does not perceive that the life of such a man is the life of an idiot? There is, after all, something higher, and nobler, and better, than merely "to buy and sell, and get gain." "For what is a man profited, if he shall gain the whole world and lose his own soul?"

Quoting James 4:13 and Matthew 16:26, Berg presents spiritual interests as "higher, and nobler, and better" than material interests; *mere* material interests such as business, buying and selling. That life is not only a lower life; it is an idiotic one. The reverend's reminder brings up two characteristics of the Christian Merchant type of moral background. First, the fact that there are higher and lower pursuits, projects, and ends, that is, more and less significant, worthwhile vis-à-vis what should really matter. What is higher and significant, and what is lower and less significant, is not a matter of personal preference or liking, let alone pleasure, as a utilitarian might have it. Instead, this distinction is based on objective grounds. We are not talking about higher and more important for me, but higher and more important, period; for instance, pursuits and ends that ought to be more important to everyone. An objective hierarchy of this sort is perfectly at home in Platonic, Aristotelian, Christian, and many other viewpoints and worldviews. However, it is foreign to the Standards of Practice type's consequentialist normative ethics and scientistic metaphysics, according to which ends are subjective and goodness and value do not inhere in objects. They are secondary, not primary qualities. By contrast, it is plain to Reverend Berg that spiritual ends and concerns are more important and higher, and hence everyone should devote most attention to them. Despite the Reformation's "affirmation of ordinary life," it remains true that, at least in this sense, the spiritual is infinitely and eternally more important.[138] Its directives and requirements should take precedence.

Taylor's arguments about the affirmation of ordinary life take us to a second characteristic of the Christian Merchant type. Taylor emphasizes the Protestant rejection of "the notion that there are special places or times or actions where the power of God is more intensely present and can be approached by humans." In

---

137   Cf. John Leonard Cole. 1926. "A Clergyman Looks at Business." *Nation's Business*, September 1926, p. 60.

138   Taylor, *Sources of the Self*, p. 215.

turn, this "led to an enhanced status for (what had formerly been described as) profane life"; it gave "spiritual value [to] lay life."[139] But there is one additional consequence: the "interpenetration" of the sacred and the profane; "lay life" became "a central locus for the fulfilment of God's purpose." Then, "[f]or ordinary life to encompass this spiritual purpose, it had of course to be led in the light of God's ends, ultimately to the glory of God. This meant, of course, that one fulfil God's intention for life, avoiding sin, debauchery, excesses of all sorts. But it also meant that one live it for God."[140] For obvious reasons, business ethicists are specially positioned to reflect this interpenetration—a fact well exploited by Weber and the Weberians. Business ethicists are charged with no easy task. To live your lay life avoiding sin and to the glory of God is difficult enough; to live your business life avoiding sin and to the glory of God seems a whole lot more difficult. In any case, their bottom line is that the aforementioned moral hierarchy of ends and pursuits functions, too, as a hierarchy of authority. The material ends that you pursue in the factory or office are to be regulated or supervised or oriented by the higher spiritual ends. This orientation does include that spiritual meaning and value be given to ordinary life pursuits, but it also includes that ordinary life pursuits be "subordinated" to the higher ends. Thus, while in one sense one speaks of spheres, areas, or departments of life, as an empirical fact about modern societies, these departments should have no normative or moral autonomy.

This is a prominent storyline in the history of business ethicists' work. In the United States, its most widespread incarnation may be called the "business is business" wars, after that most common phrase. "Business is business" is the view that business is and ought to be guided by its own rules; morality may apply elsewhere, but not in business life (more on this in the conclusion). Naturally, Christian business ethicists, actually any business ethicist, should combat it. As the *Christian Science Monitor* wrote in 1912: "'Business is business and religion is religion' is a saying that is used by a great many in the sense that these two are and should be kept separate from each other. A greater mistake could hardly be made. They should, per contra, be so closely associated that the one cannot be thought of without the other."[141] Christian business ethicists fought those wars in their own way. While the enemy was mighty, they had some mighty weapons in their arsenal as well.

Take the fittingly titled 1883 address, *"Business is Business,"* by Theodore L. Cuyler (quotation marks around the title are his). Cuyler (1822–1909) was "the most conspicuous figure among the ministers of Brooklyn, having served as pastor of the Lafayette Avenue Presbyterian Church for thirty years, until he retired in 1890."[142] An influential pastor and prolific writer, he lays out the problem right at the start:

139   Ibid., pp. 216, 217.
140   Ibid., pp. 218, 221.
141   "Religion in Business." *Christian Science Monitor*, September 14, 1912, p. 35.
142   "Dr. Theodore Ledyard Cuyler Dead at Eighty-seven." *New-York Tribune*, February 27, 1909, p. 7: See also Theodore L. Cuyler. 1884, *Right to the Point. From the Writings of Theodore L. Cuyler, D.D.* Selected by Mary Storrs Haynes. Boston: D. Lothrop and Company; "Rev. Dr. Cuyler's Church." *New York Times*, October 26, 1874, p. 2; "Theodore L. Cuyler, D.D." *New York Times*, October 26, 1874, p. 2; "The Rev. Dr. Cuyler Dies at Eighty-seven." *New York Times*, February 27, 1909, p. 9.

"Business is business." Yes, and a sorry business too many people make of it when they consult covetousness rather than conscience. They go on the false principle that there are two separate departments in human life, and that in one of them true religion—Bible religion—has no place. They consider Sunday as the only day and the church the only place for that. [...] [W]hen Monday comes and the church is locked up, they lock up their hearts also, and say to themselves,

"Religion is religion. I had enough of that yesterday; but business is business, and that I am going into to-day. [...]"

They may not say this in so many words, but they practice this principle. They *divorce* religion from business, put the multiplication-table in the place of the ten commandments and study their account-books in place of the Bible. On Sunday they say, "Now let us worship God;" during the week they say, "Now I'll make money; business is business."[143]

Of course, Cuyler thought that "[n]o more fatal blunder could be made than this one." For "there are religious elements in all true, upright, honorable business; and you cannot separate them any more than you can the light and the heat in a sunbeam."[144] What was needed, as he said elsewhere, was "Christ every day!" Sadly, some people, "and quite too many, reserve their piety for the Sabbath and the sanctuary, and on Monday they fold it up, and lay it away with their Sunday clothes." That is a big error: "every day has got to be a 'Lord's day' if we expect to make any real headway heavenward."[145] And this requires a crusade against the "business is business" position and mentality.

A better understanding of this crusade may be gleaned from the work of Presbyterian Henry Boardman, whom we encountered in chapter 3. The very title of his business ethics lectures, *The Bible in the Counting-House*, already begins to illustrate the point. Boardman's volume was meant as a "popular treatise ON THE APPLICATION OF CHRISTIAN MORALITY TO THE AFFAIRS OF COMMERCE"; "the ministers of religion" should "go directly into the abodes of Commerce, and publish to the great army of traffickers the high requisitions of Christianity." The book Boardman "offered to the Mercantile classes with the hope, that, through the Divine blessing, its suggestions may afford them some

---

143 T. L. Cuyler. 1883. *"Business is Business."* Philadelphia: Presbyterian Board of Publication, pp. 3–4. Reprinted in *The Christian Treasury, Containing Contributions from Ministers and Members of Various Evangelical Denominations.* 1883. Edinburgh: Johnstone, Hunter, & Co.; London: Groombridge & Sons. See also Theodore L. Cuyler. 1880. "Over the Stile." *New York Evangelist*, December 23, 1880, p. 1; Theodore L. Cuyler. 1898. "Christ Every Day." *Northern Christian Advocate*, vol. 58, no. 52, December 28, 1898, p. 2.

144 Cuyler, *"Business is Business,"* pp. 4, 5.

145 Cuyler, "Christ Every Day," p. 2. "The periodical piety that goes by the calendar, and only serves the Lord Jesus at set times and places, is of very little value; it is only a perennial piety that possesses both peace and power. He is the only healthy Christian who runs his Christianity through all the routine of his every-day experiences. [...] The busy bustle of the counting-room has not hindered the fellowship with Christ of many a godly-minded merchant who carries his religion into his business and deals by the Golden Rule."

assistance in adjusting the casuistries of trade, and subordinating its aims and implements to the higher ends of life."[146] The image is familiar: there are two kinds of ends; the lower are "subordinated" to the higher. Next, Boardman tries to anticipate the familiar objection:

There may be those who will regard this as delicate ground. The pulpit has itself moulded a public sentiment by which it is watched with a jealous eye, lest it should venture upon themes that lie beyond its jurisdiction. Curiously enough, the territory which it is sought to sequester from all the aggressions of the sanctuary, is that which embraces the actual application of the Gospel to no small portion of the daily avocations of men. Upon the paths which men are treading for six days out of every seven, upon their husbandry and their handicraft, their shops and their warehouses, their hoarding and their disbursing, their legislation and their jurisprudence, there is impressed the brand of a secularity so flagrant that the pulpit cannot venture into this arena, without contracting the taint of a grievous defilement! [. . .] And so it comes to pass, that when a Christian minister propounds for discussion one of these *tabooed* topics, he is quite likely, on the one hand, to wound the sensibilities of certain sincere and excellent people, who tremble to think of his degrading the Gospel into a mere scheme of morals; and, on the other, to disturb the equanimity of certain careless and somewhat unscrupulous devotees of mammon, who think he had better confine himself to his own sphere and leave them to theirs. (pp. 20–21)

The "devotees of mammon" are especially worrisome, because they desire a separation of spheres, such that the moral and the spiritual do not impinge upon the material and the secular. Mammon worshippers fail to see what a reviewer of Boardman's lectures for *The Presbyterian Magazine* found praiseworthy in them: that there should be a relationship of "subordination" between secular and spiritual. Specifically, in these lectures "'[t]he chief end of man' is kept prominently in view; and the necessity of subordinating the secular to the spiritual is inculcated in a winning and forcible manner."[147] In sum, Boardman's bottom line is this: "There may be those who will deem it a very superfluous and a very puritanical procedure to undertake to set up the BIBLE as the grand regulator of commerce. But how is commerce to be exempted from its jurisdiction? Who is empowered to say, 'We will have the Bible in our houses, our schools, our churches, our charities, but it shall not come into our stores. We are quite willing to live by it, and to die by it, and to go to heaven by it, but as to trafficking by it, that is out of the question'."[148] This argument, Boardman says, does not hold water. Why would this one sphere be "exempted from its [the Bible's] jurisdiction"? In fact, precisely because "trafficking" is more morally dangerous than our houses and schools, the Bible is needed there. Or, to put it the way Rev. Edward Sullivan did two decades later, at the 1877 banquet of the Boston Commercial Club: "Will you, as

146 Boardman, *The Bible in the Counting-House*, pp. 15, 25, viii.
147 "Review and Criticism." *The Presbyterian Magazine*, vol. 3, no. 7, July 1853, pp. 338–43, p. 338.
148 Boardman, *The Bible in the Counting-House*, p. 63.

business men, accept a little bit of advice . . . from a clergyman? It is this: If you would give practical effect to the sentiment 'the morals of commerce,' bind up the Decalogue with your ledger and daybook, and turn to it frequently for purposes of reference."[149] Orville Dewey,[150] Charles Rhoads,[151] and many other business ethicists expressed similar opinions and gave similar pieces of advice.

In moral background terms, the Christian Merchant type contains a metaphysically laden hierarchy of ends, the highest and most important of which are religious and spiritual. Further, temporal pursuits and ends—and, in particular, your business life—do fall under the jurisdiction of religion. These pursuits and ends are worthwhile and praiseworthy, sanctioned by God, and may have spiritual significance and be in accordance with God's plan. Precisely for this reason, they should be guided by the Bible, like all of a Christian's life, so that they are properly pursued. A recurring imagery is that of jurisdictions, provinces, departments, and spheres. Unfortunately, business (unjustifiably) attempts to declare its moral, normative, and practical independence and autonomy; businessmen (unjustifiably) attempt to morally isolate their business "life," as though it were a separate sphere.[152] From the Christian Merchant perspective, these attempts are based on a misguided understanding of the nature of a person's life and God's role in it. There is no morally meaningful distinction between departments and spheres: Christian morality is applicable everywhere and all the time. How could it *possibly* not? How could God's eye, law, or jurisdiction *possibly* stop at the doorsteps of business (or anywhere else)? For a Christian business ethicist that is simply absurd. The emphasis is on the word "possibly." The "business of business" doctrine is not merely morally mistaken. That much can be held and is often held by Standards of Practice business ethicists. Rather than mistaken, Christian metaphysics make it impossible and absurd. That business must be subordinated to and supervised by religion is necessitated by the Christian metaphysical and ethical worldview—including its concept of God and God's relationship to his creation. Religion does not happen to be inextricable from business; its inextricability is metaphysically necessary.

Reverend Cuyler's and Reverend Boardman's understandings about the moral wholeness of a Christian life bring us back to a dimension of the moral

---

149 "Commercial Morality." *Chicago Daily Tribune*, January 6, 1878, p. 6.

150 "The question then is—what is the proper range of the pulpit? What is the appropriate business of preaching? The answer is plain—to address the public mind on its moral and religious duties and dangers. But what are its duties and dangers, and where are they to be found? Are they not to be found wherever men are acting their part in life? Are human responsibility and exposure limited to any one sphere of action—to the church or to the domestic circle—or to the range of the gross and sensual passions? Are not men daily making shipwreck of their consciences in trade and politics? And wheresoever conscience goes to work out its perilous problem, shall not the preacher follow it?" Dewey, *Moral Views of Commerce, Society, and Politics*, p. vi (see also pp. vii, 53).

151 "The sum of my argument, then is, this: That we stand in need of a religion that will wear in the counting-house, the market and the workshop, as well as in the sanctuary and home circle. That will stand as a barrier to injustice and fraud both in the small and great affairs of life." Rhoads, *Business Ethics in Relation to the Profession of the Religious Society of Friends* , p. 17.

152 Cf. MacIntyre, *After Virtue*, pp. 204–5.

background we looked at in the previous chapter. What does first-order normative morality take as its object? In particular, does it mostly evaluate "doing" or "being"? We saw that the Standards of Practice moral background can be described as an ethics of doing. Its moral evaluations are largely about individuals' actions or decisions about actions. Business ethics concentrates on actions and choices: the choices businessmen ought to make, morally speaking, given a set of initial conditions. It analyzes ethical "cases," about which it asks what one should do, on what criteria one should choose what to do, what makes an action right or wrong, or what duties one has. By contrast, the Christian Merchant moral background comprises both ethics of doing and ethics of being. Christian business ethicists' tools, accounts, prescriptions, and recommendations do have some room for action-evaluations. But they have much room for life-evaluations as well. They ask what kind of life one ought to lead, what kind of person one ought to be, and what it is for a life to go well. They foreground character—the ideal here being "the possession of a character formed on that of Christ and daily growing more and more like his," as John De Witt said in his sermon on "The Relations of Religion and Business."[153]

Thus, "the Christian life" has been a helpful tool not only for Protestant theologians—standing on the shoulders of Calvin's chapters 6 through 10 in the third book of the *Institutes*—but also for preachers, moralists, and business ethicists on the ground. For example, Henry Ward Beecher, the popular preacher at Brooklyn's Plymouth Church, took up this issue head-on in his 1869 sermon, "Scope and Function of a Christian Life." It is a Christian's life as a whole that Beecher takes as his analytical focus and level of analysis. Moreover, he explicitly disputes the compartmentalization of life: "Men think, 'As long as I am in the world, and doing business, I must perform my business according to the way of the world; and then, when I have got through with the necessary sacrifice to the world, I must wash up, and go to church, and be a Christian.' As if that was something separate and different from the life which they have been living in the world!"[154] Seeing lives as wholes (as opposed to a number of independent compartments) and making evaluations of lives as wholes (as opposed to a number of independent actions) are not the same thing. Yet, they go well with each other.

153   John De Witt. 1885. "The Relations of Religion and Business." Pp. 150–65 in *Sermons on the Christian Life*. New York: Charles Scribner's Sons, p. 163. Born in 1842 in Harrisburg, Pennsylvania, John De Witt (sometimes spelled DeWitt) "graduated at Princeton College in 1861; studied law; studied divinity at Princeton and Union Theological Seminaries," and "was ordained in the Presbyterian ministry in 1865." Then he "served as a minister, with notable success, in churches at Irvington, N.Y., Boston, Mass., and Philadelphia. But though he was an admirable and efficient preacher and pastor (and so long as his strength endured he never gave up preaching), the natural bent of his mind was towards [sic] study and teaching." In 1882 he became a professor of church history at Lane Theological Seminary, in 1888 a professor of apologetics and missions at McCormick Theological Seminary, and in 1892 a professor of church history at Princeton Theological Seminary—a position that he held until his retirement in 1912. "Rev. Dr. John De Witt." *New York Times*, November 20, 1923, p. 19; Henry Van Dyke. 1923. "In Memoriam John De Witt '61, D.D., LL.D." *Princeton Alumni Weekly* 24(9):182–83.

154   Beecher, "Scope and Function of a Christian Life," pp. 95–96.

Furthermore, this tendency toward the ethics of being fits well with another characteristic of the Christian Merchant type, which we looked at in chapter 3. The motive of love is at the heart of the business ethics of the Christian. You should not deceive your customers or exploit your workers out of love of God and love of righteousness, not out of policy or expediency. So far this is a judgment about a class of actions and motives. Yet, more generally, a Christian should strive to be a loving person. Thus, Christian ethics can be characterized as an ethics of love or *agape*.[155] Like all ethics of being, an agapeistic ethics does not tell people what courses of action they should choose and what courses of action they should not choose. Nor does it offer a rule whose application to each particular situation will tell people that. Rather, it tells them to be loving, or become loving, and then simply do what a loving person would do. As Frankena observes, either Augustine or Aristotle can serve as good models here, despite the dissimilarities between the form of their prescriptions. You can say, "much as St. Augustine did, 'Be a bundle a love, and then do as you please,' or perhaps better, 'Become loving, if you are not so already, and do as you then, as loving, please to do.' This will tell us what to do once we are loving, namely, what love (using its head) moves us to do." Alternatively, you can "follow a suggestion of Aristotle's and say, 'Do what the loving man would do'."[156]

Reverend Phillips Brooks's *The Duty of the Christian Business Man* (1891) provides us again with a good illustration. His starting point is a rather ordinary, mundane complaint, familiar to anyone involved in a religious or voluntary organization: people who claim that, because they work so hard and they are so busy, they do not have enough time to be a Christian. A minister should surely worry about this, since the fate of his congregation is at stake. Ministers should get more people to be more devout, to go to church more often, and to devote more of their time to religion. They should also validate and strengthen normative understandings according to which people ought to devote more time to religion, so that if you are presently not paying attention to it, you are at moral fault. Unfortunately for ministers, this is how many people responded:

> I say to my friend, "Be a Christian." That means to be a full man. And he says to me, "I have not time to be a Christian. I have not room. If my life was not so full. You don't know how hard I work from morning to night. What time is there for me to be a Christian? What time is there, what room is there for

155 Nygren, *Agape and Eros*; Outka, *Agape: An Ethical Analysis*.

156 Frankena asks how the ethics of love, being an ethics of being, can work "as a guide to action." His answer is instructive: "[I]t seems to me that an agapistic EV [ethics of virtue] can, in principle at least, answer my question in either of two ways. One is to say, much as St. Augustine did, 'Be a bundle a love, and then do as you please,' or perhaps better, 'Become loving, if you are not so already, and do as you then, as loving, please to do.' This will tell us what to do once we are loving, namely, what love (using its head) moves us to do. [. . .] The other answer is to follow a suggestion of Aristotle's and say, 'Do what the loving man would do.' This formula has the advantage of applying both while we are becoming loving and afterwards—provided one can know in some way, perhaps by studying the life of Jesus and the teachings of his disciples, perhaps by knowing what love is, what it is that the loving man would do." Frankena, "The Ethics of Love," p. 32.

Christianity in such a life as mine?" But does not it come to seem to us so strange, so absurd, if it was not so melancholy [*sic*], that man should say such a thing as that? It is as if the engine had said it had no room for the steam. It is as if the tree had said it had no room for the sap. [. . .] It is as if the man said that he had no room for his soul. It is as if life said that it had no time to live, when it is life. It is not something that is added to life. It is life. A man is not living without it. And for a man to say that "I am so full in life that I have no room for life," you see immediately to what absurdity it reduces itself.

Both Brooks's request and his response are telling. What Brooks asks his friend is that he *be* a Christian. This is the characteristic form that ethicists of being employ. Be loving, or be a loving person, for example. Or, as Bernard Mayo writes, "'Be brave,' or 'Be patient' or 'Be lenient.' We may even say 'Be a man'."[157] Similarly, they may say, be a Christian, and then do as a Christian would. What Brooks responds to his friend is not something like, "Look, you're making a substantive moral mistake here." Nor something like, "You should get better organized, my friend, so you can free up some more time to go to church." Instead, he accuses him of absurdity: a logical or conceptual problem. Brooks appeals to analogies such as engine:steam and tree:sap, and then makes an intelligent conceptual substitution. These moves yield the result that "I have not room for religion" is a logical contradiction. It is not just mistaken but inconceivable. Logical contradictions aside, Brooks's point is that being a Christian is part of your essence, not a specific action or activity, like going to work or having dinner at your mother's house:

> You have got to know that religion, the service of Christ, is not something to be taken in addition to your life; it is your life. It is not a ribbon that you shall tie in your hat, and go down the street declaring yourself that you have accepted something in addition to the life which your fellow-men are living. It is something which, taken into your heart, shall glow in every action so that your fellow-men shall say, "Lo, how he lives! What new life has come into him?" It is that insistence upon the great essentialness of the religious life, it is the insistence that religion is not a lot of things that a man does, but is a new life that a man lives, uttering itself in new actions because it is the new life.[158]

This is a textbook example of the differences between ethics-of-being and ethics-of-doing perspectives, which the Christian Merchant and Standards of Practice types (partly) instantiate. Brooks's moral object is one's life; religion "is not a lot of things that a man does, but is a new life that a man lives." It is what you are, not what you do. In a Durkheimian fashion, he sees a life as more than the sum of a lot of things a person does. Even more, he explicitly makes his point in metaphysical terms by speaking of "the great essentialness of religious life." Then, your life, being what it is, will "glow in every action" or "[utter] itself in new

---

157 Mayo, *Ethics and the Moral Life*, p. 213.
158 Brooks, "The Duty of the Christian Business Man," pp. 84–86. And he goes on to cite John 3:3, the verse about being "born again": " 'Except a man be born again he cannot see the kingdom of God.' So Jesus said to Nicodemus the ruler . . ."

actions." Yet, actions are by-products of lives; for example, a courageous action is the by-product of the agent's being a courageous man or woman—not the other way around. So, we see that business cannot possibly be business. From an ethics-of-being perspective, the purported moral autonomy of business is an absurdity. You should be a kind of person: a Christian or a good Christian. And your Christian being or character, the kind of person you are, cannot be bracketed or selectively utilized in some departments or areas of life only. It is not like a hat that you may wear at will. Nor is it like a "Sunday suit to be laid away during the week."[159] That it "cannot" be bracketed in this context does not mean that it is unadvisable or imprudent to do so. It is impossible. In this sense your essence renders you helpless: a courageous person will act (or at least be strongly inclined to act) in a courageous manner always. And she will not do so following a calculation about the particular choice before her, but driven by her character or disposition.

Which ties the argument of this chapter back to its very beginning. I began this chapter by talking about moral exemplars, and in particular the Christian Merchant as a moral exemplar. While the connection is not necessary, moral exemplars are especially suitable to express and teach ethics-of-being lessons. For they are typically constructed out of someone's entire life, looked at in retrospect, as a whole. This is reasonable if you agree with the old Aristotelian insight that *eudaimonia* (human flourishing or happiness) cannot be assessed until a person is dead.[160] What is more, moral exemplars are also typically constructed in a teleological fashion. In these rational reconstructions, lives are represented as having had a direction, which brought about certain morally good ends. Indeed, bringing them about might have been the point of that life all along. The Christian Merchant is one such exemplar. In this chapter I have examined some main features of this moral background type, some of its main metaphysical commitments, along with their main implications. These moral background elements underlie—enable, facilitate, and support—the work of Christian business ethicists in the United States, the normative accounts they devise, the demands they make, the reasons they offer, and so on. This first-order level work I have deployed not so much for its own sake, but primarily to bring into view the second-order level underneath it.

---

159 Ballard, *The Stewardship of Wealth*, p. 8.
160 *Nicomachean Ethics* 1.10–11.

Conclusion

"Are they not doing good with their property, and am I not aiding a good cause in giving a fair price for the land?"

"That's all nonsense. Business is business. We do not expect to do missionary work when we buy land."

—*Zion's Herald*, 1875[1]

Its Directors [of the Pacific Mail] have been detected in all kinds of transactions which the unsophisticated part of the world generally agree in calling dishonest. It is true that we are often told that there is one standard of honor for private life and another for commercial affairs. A man may do many things without blame as a "Director" which would be disgraceful to him in his private capacity. And we have seen and known of a good many men who insist upon carrying out this theory in their daily pursuits.

—*New York Times*, 1875[2]

1. Business Is Business

Businesspeople are not particularly known for their appreciation of poets' work (and vice versa). There is one poem, though, originally published in January 1917, which did attain a surprisingly wide circulation in the business press. Penned by Wisconsinite poet Berton Braley, it first appeared in *Nation's Business*, the official organ of the U.S. Chamber of Commerce. The poem's title is "Business is Business," and it goes like this (see figure C.1).

The first stanza, the "Little Man," represents the ordinary sense of the phrase, "business is business." This is probably what most people understood by it. Business pursuits are shielded from the demands of morality. Moral considerations do not apply to business, so in business "all that you do is fair." It is a morally separate sphere or domain or part of life. In the next stanza, the "Big Man" makes his triumphant appearance. He also uses the phrase, "business is business," but he interprets it in a different manner. He depicts business as a contributor to the common good. Business is a civilizing force. He does admit that there are still some bad apples, "bandits and buccaneers," but "their number dwindles with passing years." There are grounds for optimism. Finally, the poem's final lines enthusiastically proclaim that the business of "Business is to serve!"[3]

---

1 "Business Ethics." *Zion's Herald*, August 1875, p. 252.

2 "A Great Commercial Scandal." *New York Times*, January 3, 1875, p. 6.

3 In fact, Braley wrote two poems entitled, "Business is Business"; the first one had appeared in April 1914 in *The Caxton Magazine*, and it had also been reprinted in various publications. "Business is Business." *Acetylene Journal*, vol. 17, no. 1, July 1915, p. 25; "Business is Business." *Texaco Star*, vol. 3, no. 2, December 1915, p. 4; Lee, *Business Ethics*, pp. 7–9, 65–66.

"Business is Business," the Little Man said,
    "A battle where 'everything goes',
Where the only gospel is 'get ahead',
    And never spare friends or foes,
'Slay or be slain,' is the slogan cold,
    You must struggle and slash and tear,
For Business is Business, a fight for gold,
    Where all that you do is fair!"

"Business is Business," the Big Man said,
    "A battle to make of earth
A place to yield us more wine and bread
    More pleasure and joy and mirth;
There are still some bandits and buccaneers
    Who are jungle-bred beasts of trade,
But their number dwindles with passing years
    And dead is the code they made!

Figure C.1. Braley's poem.
  Source: *Nation's Business*, January 1917, p. 34. Retrieved from ProQuest Historical Database.

Braley's poem enjoyed considerable success and was reprinted in numerous publications.[4] As per the calculations of the editor of *Nation's Business*, writing in 1924: "[i]n the seven years and seven months that have elapsed [since the poem was published], hardly a week has passed that we have not had requests for reprints of this verse, the copies sent out, to date, totaling in excess of a million." The

4 E.g., *The American Stationer and Office Outfitter*, vol. 82, no. 7, August 18, 1917, p. 6; *Pacific Marine Review*, November 1921, p. 651; *The Rotarian*, vol. 10, no. 4, April 1917, pp. 320–21.

"Business is Business," the Big Man said,
        "But it's something that's more, far more;
For it makes sweet gardens of deserts dead,
        And cities it built now roar
Where once the deer and the gray wolf ran
        From the pioneer's swift advance;
Business is Magic that toils for man
        Business is True Romance.

"And those who make it a ruthless fight
        Have only themselves to blame
If they feel no whit of the keen delight
        In playing the Bigger Game,
The game that calls on the heart and
                head,
        The best of man's strength and
                nerve;
Business is Business," the Big
        Man said,
        "And that Business is
        to serve!"

Figure C.1 (*continued*).

reliability of these estimates is dubious, because the editor, Merle Thorpe, might have had an ax to grind. Either way, he had some more good news to relay to his readers. The business-is-business poetic motif was flourishing: "just the other day, we received another 'Business is Business' poem, suggested by Berton Braley's verse and written by Everett W. Lord, Dean of the College of Business Administration, Boston University." Lord was apparently proud of his poetic composition, because he used it as the epigraph of his book, *The Fundamentals of Business Ethics*, which came out in 1926:

"Business is Business," the Old Man said,
"It's warfare where everything goes,
Where every act that is fair
And all of whom you meet are foes,
It's a battle of wits, a heartless rush—
It's a tearing, wearing fight;
It's a trick of the strong to win from the weak,
With never a thought of the right."
[...]
"Business is Business," the Young Man said,
"A game in which all may play:
Where every move must accord with the rules
And no one his fellow betray.
It's wholesome and clean, and full of good-will
It's an urging, surging game,
It's a mission to serve in your day and age,
And a guerdon to honor your name."[5]

Lord's and Braley's poems are comparable in terms of their artistic value: not very high, I am told. They are also comparable in terms of their historical value, as pieces of historical evidence: much greater, I believe. For both poems informatively depict what business ethicists were fighting for and against. In Lord's case, the bad guy is "the Old Man" and the good guy is "the Young Man"—which already suggests an auspicious demographic trend.[6] This "Young Man" likens business to "a game in which all may play," which is "wholesome and clean, and full of good-will," and where "no one his fellow betray." That was an optimistic young man indeed. It was a useful optimistic young man, too. For instance, because the dean of a business school wrote the poem, it came in especially handy to answer "an oft repeated question as to the aims of our Collegiate Schools of Business."[7]

Lord's and Braley's poems bring out one of the central historical themes of this book: business ethicists' work of advocacy, persuasion, and representation of reality in public forums and the public sphere. In fact, the significance of these poems lies partly in their normality: except for their being in verse, they are standard business ethics devices, which put across standard business ethics messages. They effectively profited from the fact that "business is business" was a common phrase, which everybody would understand. For instance, as figure C.2 shows, in the Ngram Viewer corpus of American English, until the mid-1910s "business is business" is more common than "business ethics."[8] (However, it always lags

5 "Business is Business." *Nation's Business,* August 1924, p. 24; Everett W. Lord. 1926. *The Fundamentals of Business Ethics.* New York: Ronald Press, p. 2.

6 Or "newer ethics of capitalism." Cf. Judson G. Rosebush. 1923. *The Ethics of Capitalism.* New York: Association Press, pp. 162–63.

7 *Idaho Economic Bulletin,* vol. 3, no. 4, December 1924, p. 1.

8 For some standard uses, see, e.g., "Business Ethics." *Zion's Herald,* August 1875, p. 252; "Business is Business." *Everybody's Magazine,* vol. 22, no. 2, February 1910, pp. 287–88; James H. Collins.

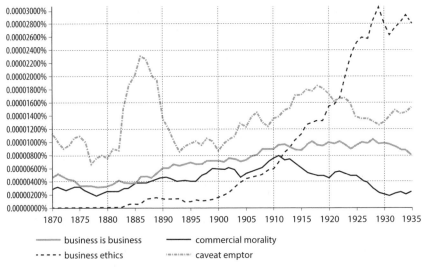

Figure C.2. "Business is business," 1870–1935.
Source: Google Books Ngram Viewer. Corpus: American English; Smoothing: 3. http://books
.google.com/ngrams

behind its cousin, the Latin expression "*caveat emptor*," that is, let the buyer beware.) Tellingly, "business is business" had two distinct uses. First, an exculpatory one: "American business men, while energetic and resourceful, are suspicious, largely unscrupulous and given to the use of questionable methods, too readily excused by the phrase, 'business is business.' The 'business' that is 'business' is usually some kind of knavery or double dealing that 'gets by' because 'nothing succeeds like success.'"[9] Second, an accusatory one: precisely because of its frequent exculpatory uses, business ethicists could single out "business is business" as epitomizing all that was wrong with American business. Rhetorically, due to its pithiness, "business is business" was a good target for attack—which is just what Braley and Lord did. It pithily expressed and justified the old idea that, as Daniel Defoe's *Complete English Tradesman* put it in 1726, "there are some latitudes, like poetical licences in other cases, which a tradesman is and must be allow'd, and which by the custom and usage of trade he may give himself a liberty in, which cannot be allow'd in other cases to any man, no, nor to the tradesman himself out of his business."[10]

1928. "Is Business Business?" *Nation's Business*, September 1928, p. 21; Charles F. Dole. 1902. *What Business is For.* Haverhill, MA: Ariel Press, p. 1; George N. McLean. 1890. *How to Do Business, or The Secret of Success in Retail Merchandizing.* Chicago: Jefferson Jackson, pp. 180–82.

9   Frank Koester. 1913. *The Price of Inefficiency.* New York: Sturgis & Walton, p. 215.

10   To be fair to Defoe, he did add right away: "I say, he may take some liberties, *but within bounds.*" Next he discussed these liberties, such as "[t]he liberty of asking more than he will take," or "appointings and promising payments of money, which men in business are oftentimes forced to make, and forced to break, without any scruple." Daniel Defoe. 1726. *The Complete English Tradesman.* London: Printed for Charles Rivington, pp. 275ff.

"Business is business" thus functioned as one of business ethicists' foremost antagonists; it was the perfect example of an intellectually and morally misguided doctrine. Its implications for the very status of business ethics were probably part of the story. If business and ethics would come to be believed not to overlap, then business ethicists would be superfluous and should be disposed of—which business ethicists naturally did not agree with. In this sense, "business is business" is equivalent to "business ethics is an oxymoron." In any case, the more this doctrine seemed to influence business practice, the more business ethicists tried to combat its influence. The more business ethicists heard that businessmen believed that business is business, the more reason they had to chastise it. This is something that business ethicists of all types and varieties did: from the editor of *Nation's Business*, Merle Thorpe (whom we encountered in chapter 4 promoting American business's self-regulation in the 1920s), to Brooklyn minister Theodore Cuyler (whose 1883 address, *"Business is Business,"* was discussed in the preceding chapter), among many others.[11]

In this regard, there was no significant difference between the Standards of Practice and Christian Merchant types of moral background: condemnations and refutations of "business is business" originated from both. Yet, the empirical investigation of the moral background unearths differences in the ways in which and means through which business ethicists fought that fight. For example, my analysis of the Christian Merchant type in the previous chapter suggests that it is well prepared, morally and metaphysically, to take up the challenge posed by "business is business." If the Christian life is a unity and the spiritual has authority over the material, how on earth can business be business? Differently put, to oppose and fight against "business is business" is in the job description of any business ethicist. It does not matter whether she is an American Protestant, a Buddhist, or an atheist, whether in America or in Uruguay, whether in the nineteenth century or today. However, these various business ethicists differ in their background premises, points of departure, and preferred routes—moral and metaphysical.

More important, in one respect "business is business" is not standard business ethics fare: it is not a first-order moral claim or view. It is not a view about what practices are morally permissible or admirable in business. Rather, it is about who or what is to say what practices are morally permissible or admirable in business. In other words, it addresses a second-order, moral background issue. What principles and criteria apply where and to whom? What is the proper jurisdiction of morality? Does the social world or a person's life consist of several separate spheres or realms? And what principles and criteria are to be employed to answer *these* second-order questions?

I have argued that such moral background elements underlie normative morality—enabling, supporting, and facilitating it. And I have empirically shown

---

11 "'Business is Business.'—is falling into disuse as an excuse for the conscience-pricking business deal. Report of Address by Merle Thorpe." *The Rotarian*, vol. 25, no. 2, August 1924, pp. 27, 54–57; Merle Thorpe. 1930. "Is Business Becoming Civilized?" *The Rotarian*, vol. 36, no. 2, February 1930, pp. 8–10, 53; T. L. Cuyler. 1883. *"Business is Business."* Philadelphia: Presbyterian Board of Publication.

how they underlie the work of business ethicists in the United States, roughly from the 1850s to the 1930s. In particular, I have identified two types of moral background, which differ not at the first-order level of prescriptions and recommendations, but at the second-order, background level. This is not the level of moral claims—e.g., you should not cook the company's books, you should minimize harm to the environment—but that of the methods, tools, concepts, and "machineries" with which moral claims are constructed and put forward.[12] This is not the level of moral evaluations about this or that object—e.g., a cat, a toddler, a corporation, American Business, the working class—but that of the metaphysics that makes these particular objects candidates for moral evaluation in the first place. This is not the level of evaluations about this or that moral quality—e.g., a person's integrity, dignity, or entrepreneurship, a corporation's generous, materialistic, or exploitative practices—but that of the conceptual and institutional conditions that make these moral qualities possible at all. This is not the level of exhortations to be moral, but that of the moral theories on which such exhortations implicitly or explicitly draw.

What are the main differences between the Christian Merchant and Standards of Practice types of moral background? The Christian Merchant type is based on a metaphysical picture or understanding according to which we are divine creatures living in a divine universe. As far as business ethics is concerned, it is key that we have a heart into which God can see. Consequently, action must spring from the right motives. Consequentialist considerations about good effects are trumped by considerations about good motives or springs of action. Moreover, the Christian Merchant type relies on the doctrine of stewardship understood in a literal manner: the universe belongs to God, so we are only temporary stewards of God's property. It also rejects the conception of a life as the conjunction of various activities and actions that take place in distinct areas or spheres. Temporal pursuits and ends—and, in particular, your so-called business life—have no moral autonomy; they necessarily fall under the jurisdiction of religion.

In contrast, the Standards of Practice type is based on a radically different understanding of what there is, what the universe is like, and how to know it. Its commitment to the scientific perspective and scientific naturalism is unconditional. The scientific method is the best way to understand human affairs, ethics and business ethics included. Science can even help us determine what is moral and immoral in business. Further, Standards of Practice favors a particular kind of object for moral evaluation: an individual's action or decision, one individual action or decision at a time. Consequently, business ethicists address themselves to situations or "cases," in which certain conditions are given, and a course of action must be chosen at a specific point in time. They address themselves to the question of what the morally right decision in this case is—unlike ethicists who prefer to look at and think about moral lives as wholes. In addition, Standards of Practice favors external behavioral choices and outcomes over internal motives, reasons, and mental contents. This is congruous with its scientific outlook,

---

12 On epistemic machineries, see Knorr Cetina, *Epistemic Cultures*.

because the latter are apparently invisible and arguably unknowable, whereas the former are visible, knowable, and amenable to scientific observation. Finally, in metaethics the Standards of Practice type favors relativism, and thus is at odds with the objectivism of the Christian Merchant type.

My comparison of the Christian Merchant and the Standards of Practice types offers one additional lesson. Morality is underlain by background elements, whether actors realize it or not, and whether they like it or not. For example, a moral doctrine built on scientific and naturalistic premises and foundations is as dependent on particular metaphysical commitments as a moral doctrine built on theistic premises and foundations. While the self-understanding of science—and of modernity—may say otherwise, no doctrine or system can be metaphysically neutral. In this respect, the only difference between Christian Merchant and Standards of Practice is the former's awareness of its metaphysical commitments. To be sure, the properties of the moral background are revealed to the social scientist by what individuals and organizations do and say. But these properties may bypass people's consciousness altogether. After all, people are unlikely to know much moral philosophy and metaphysics, just like speakers are unlikely to know much grammar, and scientists are unlikely to know much epistemology and philosophy of science. Yet, they can speak and do science just fine anyway.

Having summarized the contrast between the Christian Merchant and the Standards of Practice types of moral background, in the rest of this conclusion I want to consider two broader sets of issues raised by my arguments in this book. First, I want to sharpen and develop my claim that studying the moral background and studying public normativity pay (though admittedly they may not be good business or make bottom-line sense). In the course of this discussion I will also highlight a few empirical avenues that my project did not take, in the hopes that future research will pick up where I left off. Second, I want to reflect on the implications of my conceptual framework for today's science of morality. What does the moral background have to say to current moral psychology and neuroscience (if anything)? If it is true that a second-order background underlies first-order morality, how should that affect psychologists' and neuroscientists' conception of and approach to their object of inquiry (if at all)?

2. Back to the Background

I began this book's introduction by talking about moral accounts of economic and financial troubles—in particular, causal accounts in which moral phenomena partly account for economic and financial outcomes. Economic troubles can make many people and organizations worry, especially in capitalist societies, and especially in societies that venerate the free market and market freedom.[13] Especially in the wake of scandals and crises, one burning question in the public

---

13   On the concept of market freedom, see Eric MacGilvray. 2011. *The Invention of Market Freedom*. Cambridge; New York: Cambridge University Press.

sphere is what is to be done. Moral accounts suggest one obvious (if only partial) solution: improve the ethics of business. This is why the central character of my historical narrative—the business ethicist—is believed to have an important causal role to play. In addition, business ethicists' job comprises providing and validating causal accounts, and, if possible, shaping public understandings and discussions about them. While this book's narrative is largely historical, in this sense the past and the present are not all that different.

For example, in the wake of the Enron and WorldCom scandals, the American Academy of Arts and Sciences, an organization that is always concerned about "the success and stability of America's economic institutions," got even more concerned than usual. Hence, it "initiated a project on corporate responsibility to examine the causes of, and conditions surrounding, the malfunctioning of critical parts of the corporate system. Given its independence and nonpartisanship, the Academy was well suited to explore the institutional foundation on which public trust in our economic institutions is based and to contribute to the public discourse needed to restore that trust."[14] The Academy "convened a group of leaders from law, journalism, government, investment banking, corporate governance, management, and variety of scholarly disciplines to examine the roots of the problems facing American business and to recommend a long-term course of action."[15] Their conclusions about these "roots," also known as causes, appeared in the suitably titled 2005 volume, *Restoring Trust in American Business*. One conclusion was the failure of gatekeepers: regulators, boards of directors, auditors, lawyers, investment bankers, and the business press. Unfortunately, "market pressures . . . undermined their commitment to 'doing the right thing'." The volume also made concrete "recommendations for practice." Recommendations for directors, institutional shareholders, regulators, auditors, journalists, educators, and other relevant actors. Recommendations about "corporate ethics," "executive compensation," "'fair presentation'," "principles-based accounting," "professional standards," "professional education," and other relevant issues.

Another similarly high-status example is the *Principles of Corporate Governance* of the Business Roundtable, whose most recent update was issued in June 2012. The Business Roundtable is "an association of chief executive officers of leading U.S. companies with over $6 trillion in annual revenues and more than 14 million employees." This association is partly in the public normativity business: it states how things—economic, social, political—ought to be. Indeed, the spirit and tone of these *Principles* is distinctly that of the moralist or business ethicist, who assertively tells businesspeople and public opinion what business behavior and organization should be. It touches on both companies' internal workings and their relations to employees, the community, government, shareholders, and "other constituencies." Thus, the Business Roundtable demands that employees be treated

14 http://www.amacad.org/projects/corporate.aspx.
15 Leslie Berlowitz and Andy Zelleke. 2005. "Introduction." Pp. 1–6 in *Restoring Trust in American Business*, edited by Jay W. Lorsch, Leslie Berlowitz, and Andy Zelleke. Cambridge, MA: American Academy of Arts and Sciences and MIT Press, p. 1.

"fairly and equitably," because "[i]t is in a corporation's best interest to treat employees fairly and equitably." It demands that corporations discharge their obligations to the community for the same reason: "Corporations have obligations to be good citizens of the local, national and international communities in which they do business. Failure to meet these obligations can result in damage to the corporation, both in immediate economic terms and in longer-term reputational value."[16]

I cite here these recent instances of business ethics work for two reasons, which highlight two central concerns of this book, and suggest where to go from here. First, they illustrate my claim that, at the level of first-order morality, there is little novelty and originality in the history of business ethics. Normative prescriptions, codes of ethics, business ethics classes, speeches in the legislature, newspaper editorials, and outraged reactions to scandals repeat themselves over and over again. You may view it as a constant *déjà vu*. Even more, arguments, counterarguments, and actions seem structurally predictable: who will say and do what seems determined by their social-structural and cultural location. To be sure, the Business Roundtable's *Principles* in 2012 and the American Academy of Arts and Sciences' recommendations in 2005 had to deal with business ethics' current legal, economic, social, and organizational conditions. These conditions are probably more complex than the conditions any past business ethicist had to deal with. The business ethicists of today need more advanced technical knowledge about economics, finance, technology, the law, organizations, culture, social structures, and social networks to understand unethical practices and how to prevent them— knowledge that was not needed to understand Tigg Montague's Ponzi scheme in *Martin Chuzzlewit*, let alone the grocer who "sand[s] the sugar, and water[s] the vinegar."[17] However, the point and the bottom line of this kind of business ethics work remain basically the same. It tells businesspeople: you have moral obligations to society, your workers, your customers, your competitors, and the environment. You ought to be honest. You ought not to be "tricky." As the above-mentioned Phillips Brooks, an Episcopal minister and Bishop of Massachusetts, said in the late nineteenth century: "If you, in any part of your business, are tricky, and unsound, and unjust, cut that off"; "Stop doing the bad thing which you are doing."[18] Those two contemporary documents conform to this long-term pattern of normative recommendations and principles. What their second-order foundations or presuppositions are like, however, is another question—which a research project about the moral background might profitably explore.

In this book my empirical data have been largely about the past—except for some sections in the introduction and in chapter 2. But I surely hope that future research will investigate contemporary business ethicists' work in terms of the moral background framework that I have put forward. For instance, chapter 2

16 Business Roundtable. 2012. *Principles of Corporate Governance*, Washington, DC: Business Roundtable, pp. 31, 32.

17 Charles B. Tayler. 1835. *Social Evils and Their Remedy*. Vol. III. London: Smith, Elder and Co., p. 79.

18 Brooks, "The Duty of the Christian Business Man," pp. 89, 90.

might suggest the hypothesis that something like the Standards of Practice type is common in the public sphere today. At least, that seems plausible regarding the grounds or reasons to be moral, and the moral theories on which, in turn, these grounds rely. Moreover, future research should quantify the prevalence and influence of different moral background elements in different periods and places. This book has confined itself to two tasks: arguing for a novel object of inquiry, X, and then arguing that A differs from B with respect to X. These tasks are only a first step toward a sociological and historical account of business ethics' moral background. The measurement of prevalence and influence of background elements is a natural and important follow-up task, even though it is conceptually and methodologically daunting.

Equally important is that researchers undertake comparable projects outside the United States. The moral background is shaped by social, cultural, and institutional forces, so comparative studies can discover variations that are beyond the reach of non-comparative work. International and intercultural comparisons may also yield productive surprises: background properties that are unimaginable to us. What awaits us at the second-order level might be like the incredible diversity of moral practices and beliefs that anthropologists, sociologists, and historians have discovered over the years at the first-order normative and behavioral levels. What is more, this might be a reflexively therapeutic project, just like other anthropological and sociological projects about the core categories and practices of Western modernity have been. It should remind us that our social scientific understandings and investigations about moral backgrounds have their own background assumptions—which, like all background assumptions, have causes and histories. Our accounts are not epistemologically "unmarked," as Taylor might say.[19]

The 2012 Business Roundtable's *Principles* and the 2005 American Academy of Arts and Sciences' recommendations lead me to another payoff of this study— which in turn leads me to another gap to be filled by future research. I have chosen to focus on one particular kind of situation and one particular kind of data: situations and data that get at society's public front-stage, normative structure, or public moral normativity. This refers to, for example, societies' moral heroes and villains, which history books, moral education textbooks, and children's stories might reveal. It refers to the courses of action expected from exemplary citizens and organizations, and the sorts of accomplishments that ethics awards are given for, obituaries highlight, and monuments commemorate. Accordingly, I used historical sources such as the official pronouncements of prestigious associations, the published sermons of popular ministers, the addresses of public figures at well-publicized events, and editorials in well-known newspapers—which the interventions of the Business Roundtable and the American Academy of Arts and

---

19   Taylor's argument is about Westerners' belief that only they are "'unmarked' moderns," that is, "the inability of many Westerners to see their culture as one among many." Similarly, science does not acknowledge its own perspective; it sees its accounts—and only its accounts—as unmarked. Taylor, "Conditions of an Unforced Consensus on Human Rights," pp. 143–44. Cf. Abend, "Styles of Sociological Thought."

Sciences represent, too. I have emphasized that these conspicuous situations and data do not tell us much—perhaps nothing at all—about the opinions of ordinary businesspeople, let alone about their ordinary practices. To begin with, they are sometimes not even meant to describe or represent reality, but it is explicitly acknowledged that they are meant to prescribe, persuade, and motivate. They lay out normative principles, rules, and aims. They are calls to action. But even when they ostensibly describe, these purported descriptions should not be taken at face value. Despite grammatical appearances, prescription, persuasion, and motivation may still be the pragmatic point of such public statements, addresses at the annual dinners of prestigious associations, or firms' annual corporate social responsibility reports. At least, that may be one of their intended or unintended effects.

Then, potentially (though not necessarily), there can be a disjunction between words and deeds, between commencement ceremonies on campus and ordinary practice downtown. From the perspective of business ethicists, policy makers, and politicians, this is a terrible state of affairs and a constant worry. From the perspective of critics, this means business ethics and corporate responsibility are sheer hypocrisy and public relations ploys. As far as this book's objectives go, however, this is precisely the kind of data that is needed. I am interested in the fact that societies have such public moral normativity, which is worth studying in itself, as a distinct feature of human groups. Besides its public aspect, I am also interested in the fact that there is such a thing as normativity at all. Is this not a peculiar phenomenon? Not only may people sometimes help strangers, cooperate, reciprocate, conform to rules of right behavior, give to charity, recycle their trash, and demonstrate against unjust institutions in faraway countries. People may also feel that they ought to do these things, independently of whether they actually do them or not, independently of whether most people do them or not, and independently of whether other people know if they actually do them or not. Behavioral patterns are not proofs in this realm. This "ought" is a distinct aspect of moral life; "that short but imperious word *ought*" Darwin was impressed by.[20] Further, this is not just a feeling of obligation or guilt that individuals can have: normativity is built into our practices, interactions, public sphere, and institutional arrangements. There are social and political mechanisms in place to produce, reproduce, and enforce normativity, which a three-dimensional conception of power helps understand.[21] For only the right people should receive moral recognition and awards, only the right people should be invited to deliver keynote addresses, only certain stories should be taught to children, only certain projects should be publicly funded, only certain problems should count as important ones, and only certain sets of events should count as problems. Like everywhere else, social forces manifest themselves not only psychologically, but also through structural mechanisms of selection, status, rewards, and the production of knowledge, categories, and understandings.

---

20 Charles Darwin. [1871] 1872. *The Descent of Man, and Selection in Relation to Sex.* Volume I. New York: D. Appleton and Company, p. 67.

21 Steven Lukes. 2005. *Power: A Radical View.* 2nd ed. New York: Palgrave Macmillan.

Business ethics is a great area to empirically study public moral normativity. Maybe a lot of businesspeople cheat and steal and lie and engage in unethical practices. Or maybe only a few of them do. Yet, except for pathological cases and extreme situations, those who do cheat and steal and lie are not proud of it. They do not speak of it to their aging mothers and young children, much less to a large audience or interviewer on the radio. They may not pass a red-face test. And they may even provide themselves with a moral justification for what they did, for instance, by redescribing their actions in suitably ethical ways. This is a significant psychological phenomenon. The significant sociological phenomenon is that blatantly unethical business practices are socially condemned and negatively sanctioned. These are not facts about individuals' behavior, but Durkheimian social facts. This means that they are condemned by whoever happens to discuss them on well-regarded newspapers, radio stations, and podiums. They are condemned by the morally good businesspeople, politicians, professors, and policy makers; those people who do get invited "to speak at the big, prestigeful [sic], and splashy business conferences," as Harvard's business scholar Theodore Levitt said in the 1950s.[22] These practices are represented as shameful and dishonorable, which moral villains are responsible for. Good citizens and organizations would never do that; it is incongruous with the venerable traditions of this great country of ours. That I spoke of "our country" hints at a further important issue. Public moral normativity does not track the behavior and beliefs of ordinary businesspeople, but it can have a significant impact on institutions: from the law to corporations' organizational practices; from economic policy to business school curricula. For some organizations and individuals are structurally forced (or at least incentivized) to do what is publicly acceptable and desirable, and refrain from what is publicly unacceptable and undesirable. This is a key fact about modern societies.

Thus far I have had some nice things to say about my approach and data—what they do well and are useful for. Now it is time to say some not-so-nice things about them—what they do not do well and are not useful for—so that future work can fill these gaps. Just like the recommendations of the American Academy of Arts and Sciences and the *Principles* of the Business Roundtable, my historical data get at moral backgrounds in a more-or-less congealed state. Take a code of ethics adopted by a business association and posted on many office walls around the country, a sermon about the morals of trade delivered at a Manhattan church and printed for distribution, or a lecture about business ethics given at a business school on the first day of the academic year. These are pieces of business ethics work into whose background properties I have empirically inquired. What kinds of metaphysical assumptions are they underlain by? What kinds of objects are morally evaluated? What kinds of moral methods and arguments are used? What moral concepts are employed? What kinds of reasons and theories help give support to moral claims, judgments, and prescriptions?

---

22 Theodore Levitt. 1958. "The Dangers of Social Responsibility." *Harvard Business Review*, September–October 1958:41–50, p. 42. (In 1958, Levitt had not joined the Harvard faculty yet; he would do so the following year.)

If all goes well, the social scientist should be able to answer these questions by analyzing those documents in their context—as I have done. As a result, types of moral background in the history of business ethics may emerge—as they have in this book. However, only exceptionally do documents of this sort reveal conflict, negotiation, and hesitation about moral background elements. Most times they reveal only the outcome, not the process. But this is surely insufficient. Students of the moral background should also look at explicit confrontations between people, groups, and organizations. For instance, imagine a confrontation between Hernández and Fernández, in which Hernández finds the moral method of Fernández to be a terrible one, or even not to be a moral method at all. For her part, Fernández finds Hernández's moral argument not a meaningful argument at all—that is, her problem is not with the argument's content but with its form. Ideally, Hernández and Fernández would be Paraguayan senators, and their background disagreements would emerge in a legislative debate, where a lot is at stake. Or imagine a confrontation between two organizations in which a concrete decision or material reward is at stake. Suppose this decision requires that an agreement about the measurement of morality be reached. How do you measure a firm's business ethics or corporate responsibility? Do you need to take into account the agents' motives in your measurement? If so, how can agents' motives be empirically discovered and measured? Even more, is morality the sort of thing that can be measured and quantified at all? As it turns out, these two organizations are at odds about these issues and they clash in a public place. For example, they may face off against each other and exchange blows in a televised debate, or they may have to meet in a court of law. The intended take-away point of these thought experiments is straightforward: future work on the moral background should search for and then examine public confrontations like these.

It is true that some of my data contain conflicts about background elements. For instance, controversies in the pages of periodicals in which business ethicists attack the metaphysics, moral theory, or methods of one another. Or a speaker who anticipates potential objections, or discredits the courses of action and currents of opinion he thinks are prevalent, pernicious, and his audience might be seduced by. In these situations, even if the opponents are not physically co-present, they are clashing nonetheless. Examples from my narrative include the controversies over what reason a businessperson has to act ethically. Still, none of this is as methodologically valuable as the direct confrontations I am calling future research to locate and analyze. It is true that explicit confrontations about moral background elements are rare. In fact, sometimes they are simply nonexistent: as I have argued, some dimensions of the background do not ever reach individuals' consciousness or organizations' documents. They enable and facilitate first-order morality, leaving behind only indirect traces of their work. Still, we should look for these traces. With regard to the substantive historical arguments of this book, future work should investigate whether the two moral background types, Standards of Practice and Christian Merchant, publicly fought over background issues. Can we find clashes between business ethicists or organizations that reasonably represent each type, yet clashes not at the level of first-order morality, but at the second-order, background level?

Finally, the study of confrontations can shed light on how moral background elements come into being; how they rise, fall, coexist, compete, and change; what accounts for these processes and phenomena; and what part power plays in them. To take one background dimension as an example, only some objects can be morally evaluated. Only some objects show up for us as the kind of thing that is capable of moral evaluation. But how did this come to be? What processes in the history of our understandings, classifications, styles of thought, and institutions resulted in our grasping them in this way? Now, however it is that background elements historically emerge and diffuse, they end up engendering inequalities. Once they are there, the benefits they offer are unequally distributed, much like the unequal benefits offered by other kinds of culturally accepted and institutionalized beliefs and understandings. A background element can be more functional to particular types of business organizations and social arrangements, which thereby improve their relative standing. It can make things easier and cheaper to some people and organizations to the detriment of others.

For example, the moral background can provide us with a repertoire of concepts you wish did not exist—for now it turns out that you are exploiting your factory workers, and you are a member of a fanatical or terrorist group. It can provide us with methods you wish were not valid—for now policy makers are trying to achieve the greatest good for the greatest number, and by "good" they mean units of pleasure and pain. It can allow us to morally evaluate objects you wish could not be morally evaluated—for certain behaviors that used to be mere breaches of etiquette or bad taste have now become moral wrongs, and hence they carry heavier penalties. Yet, such is life that while you are materially harmed by these facts about the background, some other folks benefit from them. That these concepts exist, these methods are valid, and these objects can be evaluated is in their objective interest—though they may not be aware of this. Thus, future research on the moral background should address, too, these questions about inequality, stratification, interests, and power.

Walter Lippmann made an observation in the 1920s, an analogy with which can illustrate this line of thinking:

> Thus if an organization like the Federal Council of Churches of Christ is distressed by, let us say, the labor policy of a great corporation, it inquires courteously of the president's secretary whether it would not be possible for him to confer with a delegation about the matter. If the churchmen are granted an interview, which is never altogether certain, they have to argue with the business man on secular grounds. Were they to say that the eight-hour day was the will of God, he would conclude they were cranks, he would surreptitiously press the buzzer under his desk, and in a few moments his secretary would appear summoning him to an important board meeting. They have to argue with him, if they are to obtain a hearing, about the effect on health, efficiency, turnover, and other such matters which are worked up for them by economists.[23]

23   Walter Lippmann. [1929] 1982. *A Preface to Morals*. New Brunswick, NJ: Transaction Publishers, pp. 87–88.

In this fragment of *A Preface to Morals*, Lippmann contrasts the will of God on the one hand, and effects on "health, efficiency, turnover, and other such matters which are worked up for them by economists" on the other. All of these—the will of God included—are tools with which claims about labor policy and the length of the workday can be defended. They are grounds or reasons that may be adduced in this imaginary discussion between the churchmen and the businessman. In turn, they stem from theories that tell rightness from wrongness, or permissibility from impermissibility, along with criteria about which theories and considerations are apposite when and where. According to Lippmann, considerations about God's will were out of place in a businessman's office in the 1920s, in the sense that they would have no effect on him; he would not even listen to them.

My analogy is as follows. Claims and views about the length of the workday are roughly like first-order moral claims and views—e.g., whether it is wrong to force factory workers to work twelve hours. The above-mentioned theories and criteria are roughly like second-order, moral background elements—e.g., how you should go about determining whether it is wrong to force factory workers to work twelve hours.[24] With regard to these elements, there is an obvious difference between the churchmen and the businessman in Lippmann's story. But there are also social structural factors, cultural factors, and power differentials, which affect what you may listen to if you wish, what you must listen to and take seriously, or what almost nobody will take seriously. Even more, they affect what people will understand or get, and what will only produce shrugged shoulders or downright puzzlement. Taking now the case of the moral background: it is not randomly distributed across societies and social groups what moral methods and data are considered ridiculous, what moral objects are out of the question, what argumentative forms and inferences will not fly, and what moral theories sound plausible. Rather, these facts can be sociologically accounted for. In this book I have attempted to offer neither such explanatory accounts nor an account of the power dynamics involved. Hopefully, though, I have paved the way for and shown the significance of these research avenues, which others will pursue.

3. The Science of Morality

In this book I have developed a conceptual framework for the empirical study of morality. In addition, since the moral background is not an abstract construct but a practical tool, I have done some empirical work with it. Thus I have tried to demonstrate its utility or practical value. To conclude, I wish to consider what implications my conceptual framework might have for the contemporary science of

---

24 I say "roughly" because the analogy is not perfect. First, Lippmann depicts a private interview, not a public situation. Second, in his thought experiment the issue is not necessarily about morality. The businessman's view seems to be that moral considerations are trumped by health, efficiency, or turnover considerations. This differs from the view that morality is itself to be assessed in terms of health, efficiency, or turnover, rather than divine will—which is what a moral background difference would ideally look like.

morality, as practiced primarily by researchers in psychology and neuroscience. Instead of deploying the moral background to better understand empirical reality, as I did in the previous chapters, I shall now reflect, from the armchair, on what it tells us about morality and the scientific investigation of morality as a whole. How should the background affect our overarching conception of the nature of morality (if at all)? How should it affect our scientific investigations and theories about morality (if at all)? I proceed in two stages. First, I describe how present-day psychologists and neuroscientists go about doing research on morality (a good number of them anyway). Second, I raise two sets of questions about their approach that my moral background framework suggests.

"The idea that morality, for a long time religious or metaphysical, must from now on rest on science, is today very widespread."[25] Undoubtedly, this idea is today very widespread—today, in the 2010s. Yet, this sentence was actually published more than one hundred years ago. It was the very first sentence of Albert Bayet's 1905 book, *La morale scientifique*. At the time, in the first decades of the twentieth century, the science of morality was a burgeoning field.[26] And not only in France: in the middle of the Midwest, University of Illinois sociologist Edward C. Hayes emphasized in 1921 that "[t]he study of ethics here discussed is neither sentiment nor *a priori* speculation. It is a matter-of-fact research."[27] Today the science of morality is a burgeoning field, too. Like Hayes, it prides itself in its mater-of-fact research about ethics. Led by neuroscientists and psychologists, it has also recruited scholars from the fields of primatology, ethology, biology, anthropology, philosophy, law, business, and economics. In the past few years, a large amount of research on morality has been produced, which has received a large amount of public attention as well. Predictably, people soon started to talk about the newness of the new approach and the ways in which it revolutionizes our understanding of morality. Predictably, soon conferences, projects, funding competitions, books, talks, articles, radio programs, and blog posts started to use the expression "science of morality" (or some variant thereof) in their title or description.

In some ways, early-twentieth-century and early-twenty-first-century scientists of morality are unsurprisingly very dissimilar. For instance, one main dissimilarity is the current emphasis on discovering the neural correlates of moral phenomena through brain imaging techniques, such as functional magnetic

25 Albert Bayet. 1905. *La morale scientifique*. Paris: F. Alcan, p. 1. My translation.
26 Albert Bayet. 1925. *La science des faits moraux*. Paris: F. Alcan; Gustave Belot. [1907] 1921. *Études de morale positive*. 2 volumes. Paris: F. Alcan; Célestin Bouglé. 1922. *Leçons de sociologie sur l'évolution des valeurs*. Paris: A. Colin; Émile Durkheim. [1920] 1970. "Introduction to Morality." Pp. 191–202 in *Emile Durkheim on Institutional Analysis*. Edited, translated and with an introduction by Mark Traugott. Chicago: University of Chicago Press; Paul Fauconnet. 1920. *La responsabilité; étude de sociologie*. Paris: F. Alcan; Georges Gurvitch. 1937. *Morale théorique et science des moeurs*. Paris: Presses Universitaires de France; Lucien Lévy-Bruhl. [1903] 1905. *Ethics and Moral Science*. Translated by Elizabeth Lee. London: Archibald Constable & Co; E. de Roberty. 1896. *L'éthique. Le bien et le mal, essai sur la morale considérée comme sociologie première*. Paris: F. Alcan. Cf. Abend, "What's New and What's Old."
27 Hayes, *Sociology and Ethics*, p. 35. See also Small, *The Significance of Sociology for Ethics*; Gilman, *Social Ethics*.

resonance imaging (fMRI). Another main dissimilarity is the current emphasis on one particular phenomenon: an individual's moral judgment. However, in some other ways, early-twentieth-century and early-twenty-first-century scientists of morality are much alike. For instance, they both draw a contrast between two types of approaches to morality, one scientific and one religious, metaphysical, philosophical, or speculative—as the Bayet and Hayes quotations illustrate. They both see the latter as wishy-washy and airy-fairy. And they both see themselves as representatives of science, which tackles morality empirically, objectively, and rigorously, and will soon supersede the failed efforts of religious and metaphysical approaches. As neuroscientist Moll and his colleagues put it in a recent paper: "Morality has been at the center of informal talks and metaphysical discussions since the beginning of history. Recently, converging lines of evidence from evolutionary biology, neuroscience and experimental psychology have shown that morality is grounded in the brain."[28]

No matter what century you happen to live in, though, if you are a scientist of morality, your job is naturally to scientifically investigate morality. If your job is to scientifically investigate morality, you naturally need to know what morality is and what it is not; what it encompasses and what it does not encompass. What is that thing you hope to understand by conducting experiments and analyzing fMRI data (or, for that matter, by analyzing survey data, examining historical evidence, or observing and participating in social practices)? How can you tell moral and non-moral phenomena apart? After all, you wish to help build a science of morality, not a science of etiquette, prudence, politics, or a science of a random collection of things. In brief, what are the objects of inquiry of the science of morality? This question ties the ending of this book to its beginning. Chapter 1 made a distinction between the three levels a science of morality should investigate: the first-order normative level, the first-order behavioral level, and the moral background level (see table 1.1). However, present-day scientists of morality have missed the background level completely—a lacuna that this book begins to redress. Psychologists and neuroscientists have also neglected the behavioral level somewhat, at least in comparison with the attention they afford to the normative level.

The typical object of inquiry in contemporary moral psychology and neuroscience is "moral judgment," understood as an individual's reaction to a stimulus. For instance, experimental subjects are told about a person who must make a really hard decision—to return to the cases mentioned in chapter 1, either join the *Résistance* or stay at home to look after one's ailing mother, either shove a fat man onto the train tracks to save the lives of five workers or stay put.[29] Then, they are asked to make a judgment as to what it would be morally okay for this person do, or what would be morally permissible and impermissible, praiseworthy and blameworthy, appropriate and inappropriate, or right and wrong. Neuroscientists typically study these moral judgments' neural correlates, substrates,

---

28 J. Moll, R. de Oliveira-Souza, and P. J. Eslinger. 2003. "Morals and the Human Brain: A Working Model." *NeuroReport* 14(3):299–305, p. 299.

29 Foot, "The Problem of Abortion"; Sartre, *L'existentialisme est un humanisme*.

or underpinnings: what areas of their subjects' brains are recruited, implicated, or responsible for making these moral judgments. Studies also seek to discover whether different types of moral judgments recruit different areas of the brain. For example, whether philosophers' distinction between deontological and consequentialist judgments translates into distinct patterns of neural activity. In addition, scientists of morality have explored the neurochemistry of moral-judgment making, e.g., specific neurotransmitters' effects (or functions, if they are more metaphysically committed to evolutionary theory).

In contrast, it seems fair to say that recent moral psychology and neuroscience have spent less time and energy studying the first-order behavioral level. Recall that this level refers neither to people's judgments, beliefs, and values, nor to societies' norms and institutions. Rather, it refers to moral action—roughly, actual behavior, what people do in real-life situations, as opposed to either "finger movement" or vocal folds movement.[30] For instance, in social psychology there is an extensive literature on helping strangers, some of which (though not all) is about actual behavior. What these studies investigate is not whether a subject judges that one ought to help a stranger who appears to be in distress, nor whether a subject predicts that she herself would help a stranger who appeared to be in distress, were she to encounter one. Rather, they investigate whether the subject actually helps a stranger who appears to be in distress when she encounters one (but is in fact a confederate of the experimenter).[31] Action was more central in earlier moral psychology than it is today.[32] Action is today more central in sociological research on morality, perhaps because sociologists are less likely than psychologists and neuroscientists to employ experimental methods. Instead, sociologists have undertaken numerous observational studies, ranging from ethnographic observation of places and situations where moral choices are made, to statistical

30 Roy Baumeister, Kathleen Vohs, and David Funder. 2007. "Psychology as the Science of Self-Reports and Finger Movements." *Perspectives on Psychological Science* 2(4):396–403.

31 Classics on helping include John M. Darley and Bibb Latané. 1968. "Bystander Intervention in Emergencies: Diffusion of Responsibility." *Journal of Personality and Social Psychology* 8(4):377–83; John M. Darley and C. Daniel Batson. 1973. "'From Jerusalem to Jericho': A Study of Situational and Dispositional Variables in Helping Behavior." *Journal of Personality and Social Psychology* 27(1):100–8; Alice M. Isen and Paula F. Levin. 1972. "Effect of Feeling Good on Helping: Cookies and Kindness." *Journal of Personality and Social Psychology* 21(3):384–88. More recent studies include Robert A. Baron. 1997. "The Sweet Smell of . . . Helping: Effects of Pleasant Ambient Fragrance on Prosocial Behavior in Shopping Malls." *Personality and Social Psychology Bulletin* 23(5):498–503; Peter Fischer, Tobias Greitemeyer, Fabian Pollozek, and Dieter Frey. 2006. "The Unresponsive Bystander: Are Bystanders More Responsive in Dangerous Emergencies?" *European Journal of Social Psychology* 36:267–78; Jonathan W. Kunstman and E. Ashby Plant. 2008. "Racing to Help: Racial Bias in High Emergency Helping Situations." *Journal of Personality and Social Psychology* 95(6):1499–1510.

32 Augusto Blasi. 1980. "Bridging Moral Cognition and Moral Action: A Critical Review of the Literature." *Psychological Bulletin* 88(1):1–45; Lawrence Kohlberg and Daniel Candee. 1984. "The Relationship of Moral Judgment to Moral Action." Pp. 498–581 in *The Psychology of Moral Development: The Nature and Validity of Moral Stages*. San Francisco: Harper & Row; Herbert D. Saltzstein. 1994. "The Relation between Moral Judgment and Behavior: A Social-Cognitive and Decision-Making Analysis." *Human Development* 37:299–312.

analyses of philanthropy, volunteering, blood and organ donation, and other altruistic behaviors.[33]

What accounts for contemporary moral psychologists' and neuroscientists' tendency to have moral judgment as their object of inquiry? I think their preference is not accidental and could be accounted for by a sociologist of science and knowledge. It is interwoven with a set of assumptions about social and moral life that are common in several scientific disciplines today. These assumptions are well illustrated by economist and neuroscientist Paul Zak's 2012 book, *The Moral Molecule*: "Morality is not wishful thinking—it's biology, specifically, as we now know, the biology of oxytocin. This means the behaviors that align with pro-social behavior, commonly called moral behavior, aren't adapted from a Sunday school lesson but are time-tested survival strategies, shaped by the harshest realist of all, natural selection."[34] The claim that morality *is* biology may be hard to pin down, but it does successfully convey where Zak is coming from and is headed. He is headed to the claim that the kind of behavior that is "called moral behavior" is evolutionarily advantageous. Zak's lab has experimentally investigated the positive effects of "the moral molecule," oxytocin, on "pro-social behavior" in humans. Then, he has tried to fit his experimental findings into a more general evolutionary account. In this account, two key characters are the male prairie vole and the male meadow vole, which are in some respects similar animals, except that the former "are stand-up guys," who "live peacefully in social groups," and "remain with their mates for life," whereas the latter "are loners and players." It turns out that scientists have discovered that "it's the number of oxytocin receptors lining the 'reward' areas of the brain that accounts for how the gregarious and monogamous prairie vole conducts his entire life, and how his anti-social and unreliable cousin the meadow vole conducts his."[35]

I am not interested in the details of Zak's account here, but only in its general orientation, which scientists of morality typically share (even if some do not agree with the substance of his claims). This orientation is comparable to that evidenced by Moll and his colleagues' assertion that "converging lines of evidence from

33   See, e.g., Elijah Anderson. 1999. *Code of the Street: Decency, Violence, and the Moral Life of the Inner City*. New York and London: W. W. Norton; Daniel F. Chambliss. 1996. *Beyond Caring: Hospitals, Nurses, and the Social Organization of Ethics*. Chicago: University of Chicago Press; Healy, *Last Best Gifts*; Carol Heimer and Lisa Staffen. 1998. *For the Sake of the Children: The Social Organization of Responsibility in the Hospital and the Home*. Chicago: University of Chicago Press; Hitlin and Vaisey, *Handbook*; Hitlin and Vaisey, "The New Sociology of Morality"; Jackall, *Moral Mazes*; Robert Zussman. 1992. *Intensive Care: Medical Ethics and the Medical Profession*. Chicago: University of Chicago Press. But note that sociologists have also conducted experimental research on morality, altruism, and cooperation, which typically underscores group-level and social-level factors—see, e.g., Delia Baldassarri and Guy Grossman. 2011. "Centralized Sanctioning and Legitimate Authority Promote Cooperation in Humans." PNAS 108(27):11023–27; Delia Baldassarri and Guy Grossman. 2013. "The Effect of Group Attachment and Social Position on Prosocial Behavior. Evidence from Lab-in-the-Field Experiments." PLoS ONE 8(3); Brent Simpson, Ashley Harrell, and Robb Willer. 2013. "Hidden Paths from Morality to Cooperation: Moral Judgments Promote Trust and Trustworthiness." *Social Forces* 91(4):1529–48; Robb Willer, Matthew Feinberg, Michael Schultz, and Brent Simpson. 2010. "The Trouble with Invisible Men: How Reputational Concerns Motivate Generosity." Pp. 315–30 in *Handbook of the Sociology of Morality*, edited by Steven Hitlin and Stephen Vaisey. New York: Springer.

34   Zak, *The Moral Molecule*, pp. 167–68.

35   Ibid., pp. 35 and 36.

evolutionary biology, neuroscience and experimental psychology have shown that morality is grounded in the brain."[36] While the expression "grounded in the brain" is vague, the basic project is plain: in order to understand human morality, you have to understand its evolutionary roots and its neural bases. Along these lines, the introduction of a recent book, *The Moral Brain*, recommends:

> If we wish to obtain a better understanding of how morality evolved, we must not remain stuck on the most recent strata of the mammalian or primate brain, in which separated structures are indeed exceedingly thorny to uncover. Ancient strata common to all mammals might be equally informative to the evolution of morality. Given that homologous brain structures largely process equal function across species, comparative brain research might reopen the possibility of a deep history of shared moral powers. By pinpointing the brain structures that are essential to moral tasks in man and animals alike . . . we regain the prospect to reconstruct the roots of moral propensities.
>
> Brain imaging research (fMRI, PET, DTI) has to play a key role in this project.[37]

More generally, morality is conceived of as an evolved and hardwired capacity to produce moral reactions, comparable to other capacities that enhanced the reproductive success of our Pleistocene ancestors. I underscore both that morality is conceived of as a *hardwired* and *evolved* capacity, and that morality is conceived of as a hardwired and evolved *capacity*. The implications of describing anything human as hardwired or evolved are historically familiar: they hark back to Plato's nativist theory of recollection (*anamnesis*) in the *Meno*, and more recently they were at the center of debates about sociobiology, evolutionary psychology, and generative linguistics' universal grammar.[38] The implications of describing anything human as a capacity are not innocuous either. By calling something a "capacity for" you are already making substantive commitments about what it is, how it works, and how it is to be studied. For example, according to evolutionary biologist David Sloan Wilson, "[i]f anything, the subjects associated with the humanities should be *easier* to study from an evolutionary perspective than most subjects associated with the social sciences. After all, dance, music, and the visual arts have all the earmarks of genetically evolved capacities: they appear early in life, are intrinsically enjoyable, exist in all cultures, are mediated by ancient neuronal mechanisms, and often perform vital social functions."[39]

36   Moll et al., "Morals and the Human Brain: A Working Model," p. 299.

37   Jan Verplaetse, Johan Braeckman, and Jelle De Schrijver. 2009. "Introduction." Pp. 1–43 in *The Moral Brain*, edited by J. Verplaetse, J. De Schrijver, S. Vanneste, and J. Braeckman. Dordrecht: Springer, pp. 31–32.

38   David J. Buller. 2005. *Adapting Minds: Evolutionary Psychology and the Persistent Quest for Human Nature*. Cambridge, MA: MIT Press; Fiona Cowie. 1999. *What's Within?: Nativism Reconsidered*. New York: Oxford University Press; Jerry A. Fodor. 2000. *The Mind Doesn't Work That Way*. Cambridge, MA: MIT Press; Steven Pinker. 1997. *How the Mind Works*. New York: Norton; Steven Pinker. 2002. *The Blank Slate: The Modern Denial of Human Nature*. New York: Viking.

39   David Sloan Wilson. 2007. *Evolution for Everyone: How Darwin's Theory Can Change the Way We Think about Our Lives*. New York: Delacorte Press, p. 189.

We saw earlier that moral psychologists and neuroscientists tend to do research on moral judgment; now we can see that a moral judgment is what the hardwired moral capacity produces as a reaction to a stimulus. A moral judgment is an individual's positively or negatively valenced response to something that appears before her. It is a quick, brief, automatic, time-bounded, motivating reaction like "yay!" or "boo!"; "ah!" or "yuck!"; "approach!" or "avoid!" Note that these words are not what the person who makes the moral judgment actually says: verbally, these reactions may manifest themselves as judgments about rightness, permissibility, appropriateness, or something else. Or else, the individual may not utter any words, even though she is still making a judgment in her mind or brain. Morality is in any case a universal human capacity; it is a distinctive mark or "signature of the species."[40] Building on this idea, some scholars have proposed that morality is analogous to language—specifically to language as viewed by Chomsky. Then, there would be a moral faculty analogous to the language faculty, and moral judgments would be analogous to grammaticality judgments. According to this "linguistic analogy," "[i]n much the same way that individuals respond to the grammaticality of a sentence, individuals appear to spontaneously and confidently offer moral judgments in response to moral dilemmas. Proponents of LA [the linguistic analogy] contend that these intuitive moral judgments do not typically express reflectively held normative principles."[41] Per the linguistic analogy, the enormous moral differences across cultures and historical epochs are analogous to the enormous differences across natural languages: the switches may be set to different positions, but they are always the same switches nonetheless. The deep structure is universal and hardwired.

The conception of morality that current moral psychology and neuroscience favor suggests another analogy. Morality can be seen as analogous to or continuous with the emotions, even if it is more complex and evolutionarily more recent. Triggered by stimuli, moral judgments are the outcome of affective, automatic, intuitive processes, not reason and deliberation. These are "the dozens or hundreds of rapid, effortless moral judgments and decisions that we all make every day."[42] Then, the primary emotions (e.g., fear, disgust), the moral or social emotions (e.g., shame, guilt, sympathy, empathy), and morality end up on the same theoretical plane or continuum. Although there are some disanalogies, all of them work basically in the same way. First, you smell rotten meat, perceive a mouse, or perceive "a smear of soup on a man's beard."[43] Then, some things happen within

40   Marc D. Hauser. 2006. *Moral Minds: How Nature Designed Our Universal Sense of Right and Wrong.* New York: Ecco, p. 53.

41   S. Dwyer, B. Huebner and M. D. Hauser. 2010. "The Linguistic Analogy: Motivations, Results, and Speculations." *Topics in Cognitive Science* 2(3):486–510, pp. 493–94. See also John Mikhail. 2011. *Elements of Moral Cognition: Rawls' Linguistic Analogy and the Cognitive Science of Moral and Legal Judgment.* New York: Cambridge University Press.

42   Jonathan Haidt. 2012. *The Righteous Mind: Why Good People Are Divided by Politics and Religion.* New York: Pantheon Books, p. 45.

43   Charles Darwin. [1872] 1886. *The Expression of the Emotions in Man and Animals.* New York: D. Appleton and Company, p. 257.

you, in your brain and elsewhere. And then your body reacts in a characteristic manner and you experience disgust.[44] Similarly, you perceive an event, say, a fat man being pushed off a bridge and onto the train tracks, or someone cleaning their toilet with a Paraguayan flag.[45] Then, some things happen within you, in your brain and elsewhere. And then your response is the moral judgment, "It is wrong to do that" or "It is not okay to do that."

4. Whither the Science of Morality?

Admittedly, I have been sketching a picture of the contemporary science of morality that admits of numerous exceptions. Generalizations are hard to make about a field that is not formally established and institutionalized as such, whose boundaries are fuzzy, and which encompasses diverse disciplines and kinds of work. Still, it seems to me uncontroversial that my account represents a widespread approach in the literature on morality, especially in psychology and neuroscience. Then, how can this book's arguments contribute to it? What does the moral background have to say to this approach, its methodological inclinations, and its conception of morality? I think that if my arguments about the moral background are correct, two sets of questions about the foundations and priorities of the field must be addressed. These are tricky questions, though, which I cannot hope to answer in such brief compass as this section. I agree with Kitcher that "[s]ince the late nineteenth century, the relation between biology and ethics has been an alluring swamp in which any number of scholars have floundered."[46] Because I would rather not flounder in this alluring swamp myself, in the last pages of this book my assignment is modest. I outline what these two sets of questions are, in which direction my thought about them might go, and whether the science of morality might need to be amended as a result. But that is all. And I wish to stress that these are only tentative ideas, which I hope to develop in future work, hopefully without drowning in Kitcher's swamp in the process.

Suppose you accept my arguments about the moral background and the fact that it enables, facilitates, and supports first-order morality. It turns out that moral judgments and behaviors are underlain by a level that scientists of morality have so far overlooked. For there to be moral judgments and behaviors at all, there first need to be entities that can be morally evaluated, moral concepts, socially valid methods, valid kinds of arguments, and a distinction between the moral and the non-moral. Then, the first set of questions that arises is how far investigations about the neural correlates of moral judgment and the evolutionary history of the moral capacity can take us, without taking into account the moral background

---

44 Cf. Daniel Kelly. 2011. *Yuck! The Nature and Moral Significance of Disgust.* Cambridge, MA: MIT Press.

45 Jonathan Haidt, Silvia Helena Koller, and Maria G. Dias. 1993. "Affect, Culture, and Morality, or Is It Wrong to Eat Your Dog? *Journal of Personality and Social Psychology* 65(4):613–28.

46 Philip Kitcher. 2006. "Biology and Ethics." Pp. 163–85 in *The Oxford Handbook of Ethical Theory*, edited by D. Copp. Oxford: Oxford University Press, p. 163.

and what it does. Differently put, how far these investigations can take us in understanding how morality works. To what extent do they shed light on morality? If they shed light on one part of morality, what part is this? How does it relate to the whole? These questions do not question the experimental results scientists of morality have obtained in recent times. Rather, they try to specify the nature and reach of these results' contribution to knowledge, given that there is more to the workings of morality than previously acknowledged. Machery and Mallon make a similar point concerning the capacity of evolutionary theory to account for the capacity to make moral judgments: "We do not doubt that there exists some thin description of the class of moral judgments that could be offered such that, under this description, the capacity to make moral judgments would be the product of evolution. We deny the claim that when moral judgments are richly described, the capacity to make them is a product of evolution."[47] Now, you may still choose to offer a thin "description of the class of moral judgments." At first glance it seems that you have the freedom to describe moral judgment as you see fit. Why would you not? Are you not the author of your paper? However, the problem is that then these "moral judgments" of yours might not be recognizable as moral judgments anymore. There are constraints on how you may choose to describe your object of inquiry—how thin would be too thin, for example. And these constraints are partially determined by ordinary language and cultural understandings: we are not talking about a formal language whose author can freely and arbitrarily stipulate the meaning of words. It is not up to you what "moral" and "morality" refer to, and therefore what is and is not a moral judgment or a moral belief (as opposed to other kinds of judgments and beliefs).

One possible response is that the goal of the aforementioned scientists of morality is not to understand morality *tout court*, but only its bases, roots, origins, or "building blocks."[48] This includes both its neural roots and its evolutionary roots, such as empathy and pro-social behavior in rats, or altruistic grooming in non-human primates.[49] If so, they could not be blamed for not having done what they did not set out to do. It may be a good idea for a scientist of morality to make this concession, because it forestalls some philosophical objections that are not easy to meet. Yet, not all of them have been willing to make it. For example, Bekoff and Pierce's *Wild Justice* argues that ethology investigates not "merely building blocks for human morality," but "the real thing": "We believe that there isn't a

---

47 Edouard Machery and Ron Mallon. 2010. "Evolution of Morality." Pp. 3–46 in *The Moral Psychology Handbook*, edited by John M. Doris and the Moral Psychology Research Group. Oxford: Oxford University Press, p. 22.

48 E.g., Jessica C. Flack and Frans B. M. de Waal. 2000. " 'Any Animal Whatever': Darwinian Building Blocks of Morality in Monkeys and Apes." *Journal of Consciousness Studies* 7(1–2):1–29.

49 Inbal Ben-Ami Bartal, Jean Decety, and Peggy Mason. 2011. "Empathy and Pro-Social Behavior in Rats." *Science* 334:1427–30; Jane Goodall. 1986. *The Chimpanzees of Gombe*. Cambridge, MA: Belknap Press of Harvard University Press; N. E. Newton-Fisher and P. C. Lee. 2011. "Grooming Reciprocity in Wild Male Chimpanzees." *Animal Behaviour* 81:439–46; B. M. Spruijt, J.A.R.A.M. van Hooff, and W. H. Gispen. 1992. "Ethology and Neurobiology of Grooming Behavior." *Physiological Reviews* 72(3):825–52; Frans B. M. de Waal. 1989. *Peacemaking among Primates*. Cambridge, MA: Harvard University Press.

moral gap between humans and other animals, and that saying things like 'the behavior patterns that wolves or chimpanzees display are merely building blocks for human morality' doesn't really get us anywhere. At some point differences in degree aren't meaningful differences at all and each species is capable of 'the real thing.' Good biology leads to this conclusion. Morality is an evolved trait and 'they' (other animals) have it just like we have it."[50] Setting aside the issue of how to draw the line between morality and its mere building blocks, scientists of morality may still concede that moral processes and outcomes in a society or group—including their underlying moral background elements—are better accounted for by social than by neural phenomena. They are better accounted for by facts about socialization patterns, social class structures, organizational dynamics, and cultural changes than by facts about oxytocin levels or brain activity. For this purpose, historical research, ethnographic observation, and representative surveys are more adequate than scans. That said, it is still worthwhile that scientists of morality do research on oxytocin levels and brain activity. These are scientifically worthwhile endeavors in themselves. They have yielded and will continue to yield exciting scientific discoveries. On the other hand, journalists, universities, juries, and readers in general should be cautioned that these findings and claims are not about morality proper, and their predictive power in the real world is uncertain. Hence, caution should be exercised when drawing conclusions from experiments about the neural correlates of judgment—just like it should be exercised elsewhere when drawing conclusions from other findings about patterns of brain activation.[51]

In the end, such a pluralist science of morality would have to confront practical trade-offs. Some effort should be put into understanding the neural and evolutionary aspects of morality. Some effort into understanding real-world morality, how it actually works, and what causal relations it enters into—which necessitates that historical and anthropological data be analyzed, and that the behavioral, normative, and background levels be all taken into account. And some effort into deriving the real-world implications and predictions of this work. But how much? How much time and money should the science of morality devote to each of its various objectives and objects of study? How should efforts and grants be allocated? In addition, a pluralist science of morality, just like a pluralist society, would have to figure out how these different parts fit together. In this respect, it will not be easy to figure out how to transition from facts about ancient building

50   Marc Bekoff and Jessica Pierce. 2009. *Wild Justice: The Moral Lives of Animals*. Chicago. University of Chicago Press, p. xi (see also pp. 137–49). See also Marc Bekoff. 2004. "Wild Justice and Fair Play: Cooperation, Forgiveness, and Morality in Animals." *Biology and Philosophy* 19:489–520.

51   See, e.g., Cordelia Fine. 2010. *Delusions of Gender: How Our Minds, Society, and Neurosexism Create Difference*. New York: W. W. Norton; Nikos K. Logothetis. 2008. "What We Can and What We Cannot Do with fMRI." *Nature* 453:869–78; Nikolas S. Rose and Joelle M. Abi-Rached. 2013. *Neuro: The New Brain Sciences and the Management of the Mind*. Princeton: Princeton University Press; Sally Satel and Scott O. Lilienfeld. 2013. *Brainwashed: The Seductive Appeal of Mindless Neuroscience*. New York: Basic Books; Jan Slaby and Suparna Choudhury, eds. 2012. *Critical Neuroscience: A Handbook of the Social and Cultural Contexts of Neuroscience*. Chichester, UK; Malden, MA: Wiley-Blackwell.

blocks to facts about human morality.[52] Is the right image a continuum, at one end of which we find the biological altruism and reciprocity of non-human animals, and at the other end of which we find complex societies' moral practices and institutions? If so, at which point does the moral background begin to show up?

Now, this division of labor would mean that some scientists of morality spend their time analyzing brain imaging data, while some others spend their time analyzing medieval textual data. Yet some other scientists of morality would spend their time trying to piece together findings about trolley problems and findings about medieval practices. This is fine as far as it goes, but maybe something more laborious and profound than an adequate division of labor is needed. I have just raised a first set of questions about the reach of today's science of morality, and whether the picture it has been painting might be incomplete. A second set of questions is more far-reaching, because it has to do with the substantive implications of the moral background for the approach of the science of morality. I have argued that first-order morality is dependent on the moral background, and the background is a social object to be accounted for sociologically and historically. Should these arguments, if true, affect the conception of morality as an evolved, universal, and hardwired capacity? In other words, besides pointing to new research areas and issues, should the moral background affect the conceptual apparatus, premises, and objectives of the whole field?

As we saw, moral psychologists and neuroscientists normally rely on a thin conception of morality. Moral judgments are automatic, positively or negatively valenced reactions to stimuli. They exhibit significant similarities to a surge of epinephrine at the sight of a snake in the desert or a cop in the city. Their triggers may vary across time and place, but the judgments themselves, along with their neural correlates, can be scientifically understood apart from these cultural and social specificities. Cultural and social specificities can and should be bracketed. Methodologically, one advantage of thin morality is its tractability: its operationalization and measurement are more or less straightforward. Substantively, it places morality closer to the concept- and language-free pro-social behavior of non-human primates than to the conceptually and linguistically saturated practices and institutions of human primates. If instances of morality, such as judgments, actions, or norms, can be represented in a formal and content-neutral way, aside from the cultural stuff that fills in the blanks, then a scientific account of a universal and hardwired morality looks like a reachable endpoint.[53] However, my conceptual framework presents a challenge to this plan. For it makes first-order morality dependent on a social object or set of elements, the background, which may thwart the bracketing-the-social or bracketing-the-cultural maneuver.

---

52   Cf. Philip Kitcher. 2011. *The Ethical Project.* Cambridge, MA: Harvard University Press; Alasdair C. MacIntyre. 1999. *Dependent Rational Animals.* Chicago: Open Court.

53   Cf. Chandra Sekhar Sripada and Stephen Stich. 2007. "A Framework for the Psychology of Norms." Pp. 280–301 in *The Innate Mind: Volume 2: Culture and Cognition,* edited by P. Carruthers, S. Laurence, and S. Stich. New York: Oxford University Press.

Dependent? What is the character of the relation between the first-order level and the moral background level? Uruguay, Paraguay, Brazil, Argentina, and Venezuela jointly make up the MERCOSUR regional bloc, but each of them exists independently of the other four. Further, they are all entities of the same kind, sovereign states, which relate to each other as equals (at least, *de jure* equals). By contrast, the normative, behavioral, and background levels are not entities of the same kind. In my view, the background has a special status and a distinct mode of existence. I conveyed this idea in chapter 1 and elsewhere by speaking of an underlying moral background, which enables, supports, and facilitates first-order morality. Let me ignore here the fact that these verbs are not synonymous, and focus instead on the strongest of the three: "to enable." That *A* enables *B*, or makes *B* possible, means that *B* cannot exist without there being *A*. These relations have gotten different names in the history of philosophy and social thought. In fact, this is not one relation with different names, but a family of related relations. One tradition talks about conditions of possibility and transcendental arguments, i.e., arguments about what makes *B* logically possible, what *B* presupposes, or how *A*'s existence is logically entailed by *B*'s existence. Another tradition prefers to talk about conditions of intelligibility, i.e., not what is necessary for *B* to exist, but what is necessary for *B* to be intelligible or make sense in a given context. Arguably, it follows that *A* is necessary for *B* to be what it is, or to exist *qua* what it is. Another tradition talks about constitution, e.g., *A*'s being constitutive of *B*, so there can be no *B* without *A*. Yet another tradition talks about ontological dependence relations. Examples include the ontological dependence of non-empty sets on their members, of holes on their hosts, and of Socrates' life on Socrates.[54]

However it is conceived and whatever it is called, this is roughly the kind of role that the enabling dimensions of the moral background have vis-à-vis first-order morality. They make moral norms, institutions, actions, beliefs, and judgments possible. They make moral phenomena and moral life possible. Given this relation of ontological dependence, it seems that the social nature of the background must also be part of the other two levels of morality. The point is not that there are social or cultural variables that impinge on moral outcomes. For example, they might increase the odds of observing particular judgments, behaviors, or norms, such as that divorced people are likely to say that shoving the fat man is okay, Hopi people are likely to help a stranger, and so on. Important though they are, I am not talking about the social and cultural as external causal factors or contexts. My point is not about causation but about constitution: the social is built into all of moral life. Put differently, it seems that you cannot tease out the social and cultural baggage the background carries with it, so as to grasp, analyze, or explain the automatic

---

54 Roderick Chisholm. 1994. "Ontologically Dependent Entities." *Philosophy and Phenomenological Research* 54:499–50; Kit Fine. 1995. "Ontological Dependence." *Proceedings of the Aristotelian Society* 95:269–90.

reactions (the "yay!" and "boo!") by themselves. It is impossible to disentangle them.[55] Here I am unable to develop a full-fledged argument to that effect. It would take a lot of work to unpack the idea that the background's social nature is "part of" first-order morality, and that that "must" be the case. Nor is it easy to elucidate what should count as "teasing out" or "disentangling" the background's social and cultural baggage, and what exactly it means "to be built" into something. It would take a lot of work, too, to consider separately each of the six dimensions of the moral background as regards their ability to enable first-order morality.

Yet, assume for the moment that something like such an argument can be successfully advanced and defended. One of its important implications would be that the science of morality should make room for the background's social nature within it. Not as an optional supplement, but within its substantive accounts about how morality works, its causes, and effects. Maybe behavioral-level phenomena and even normative-level phenomena are best understood by means of brain imaging studies, maybe they have evolutionary roots and homologues in the animal world, and maybe they are best accounted for by the theories of evolutionary psychology and neuroscience. While it is controversial whether and to what extent this is the case, here these controversies can be put to one side. In either case, a scientific understanding of the moral background calls for a different kind of approach altogether. This approach should allow for social processes to take center stage. Facts about the background cannot be discovered by collecting neural or genetic data, but by collecting sociological, historical, and anthropological data. Whether or not first-order morality is hardwired and universal in some way, this line of thinking is a nonstarter with regard to background phenomena. In practice, not only would the science of morality need to both expand its methods and broaden and thicken its object of inquiry, morality. It would also need to epistemologically come to terms with its newest partners, the disciplines of sociology, history, and anthropology. In order for the research of, say, neuroscientists and historians to contribute to the same body of knowledge, they have to find common ground as to what constitutes knowledge, valuable knowledge, and acceptable proof.

What is more, we have seen that some dimensions of the moral background are such that the proper unit of analysis is not the individual, but a group or society. As my discussion in chapter 1 about conceptual repertoires, object of evaluation, and metaphysics pointed out, these are social-level phenomena or properties. For example, that the concepts of materialism, fanaticism, and dignity are available for people and organizations to use is a property of a collective entity, our society. It is not a property of the individual who happens to use it in a courtroom, legislature, or bar. You cannot individually prescribe what concepts are available any more than Humpty Dumpty can individually prescribe that the word "glory" really means "a nice knock-down argument."[56] Similarly, you cannot individually

55 Cf. John McDowell. 1998. "Non-Cognitivism and Rule-Following." Pp. 198–218 in *Mind, Value, and Reality*. Cambridge, MA: Harvard University Press.

56 Lewis Carroll. [1871] 1902. *Through the Looking-Glass and What Alice Found There*. New York and London: Harper & Brothers, p. 117.

prescribe what objects may be morally evaluated any more than you can individually prescribe how to follow a particular rule.[57] These are all facts about the society in which you find yourself living your moral life. They are bigger than you, if you will. So they cannot be captured by investigations whose unit of analysis is the individual, as is typical in the contemporary science of morality. Even if the task of the experimental subject involves other people, mentally or actually, the conclusions of studies are still based on the sum of individual-level data points. Getting at the moral background demands yet another epistemological and methodological reform, then. (On the bright side, some scientific disciplines have been paying increasing attention to objects that cannot be reduced to the sum of its constituent parts, emergent properties, and complex networks and systems, such as the brain itself.[58])

Another way to put the more general argument is as follows. This book has shown that there is more to moral life than meets the eye. Moral life has unseen pillars or presuppositions, which the moral background concept tries to unearth and grasp. In fact, this argument applies to all of social life and behavior, which is in this regard at variance with non-human animals' life and behavior. Sounds may come out of human beings' mouths, their bodies may move from one place to another, their body parts may come into contact, their neurons may fire in particular ways, but these physical events are not language, action, or interaction. What makes social life unique is that for it to happen, certain prerequisites need to obtain. They need to be already there for sounds to count as language, a promise, or an expression of moral indignation, or for bodily movements to count as a moral action, a flirtatious wink, or an act of resistance against oppression. Thus, human beings have linguistic interactions, abstract thoughts, moral views, and political institutions; these linguistic interactions, abstract thoughts, moral views, and political institutions have social presuppositions. That is, these unseen pillars are essentially social. They are the product of social processes, and they exist in the social (not psychological or biological) world.

All in all, if the preceding arguments hold water, the burgeoning science of morality would be well advised to broaden its horizons—including but not limited to broadening its conception of morality and its methodological toolkit. Perhaps it should take more seriously its ancestors in the early twentieth century, like Durkheim and Lévy-Bruhl, who took seriously the idea that morality is a social phenomenon. Perhaps today's scientists of morality should look beyond the boundaries of individuals' skin or skull, beyond individuals' verbal or behavioral reactions to stimuli, and spend more time observing everyday life and ordinary social processes. Perhaps they should grant more attention to history: the history of societies' practices, institutions, and conceptual repertoires. If the preceding

57 Wittgenstein, *Philosophical Investigations*, §§185–201.
58 E.g., Deborah Gordon. 2010. *Ant Encounters: Interaction Networks and Colony Behavior.* Princeton: Princeton University Press; Nancey Murphy and Warren S. Brown. 2007. *Did My Neurons Make Me Do It? Philosophical and Neurobiological Perspectives on Moral Responsibility and Free Will.* Oxford; New York: Oxford University Press.

arguments hold water, the burgeoning science of morality would be well advised to take these steps in order to develop a satisfactory scientific account of morality—as opposed to a scientific account of one peculiar part of morality, or a scientific account of some of the building blocks of morality. This science of morality would concern itself both with what happens at the behavioral and normative levels, and with what happens at the background level. More generally, I believe that social scientists would benefit from asking transcendental questions and pursuing transcendental lines of inquiry. They should investigate not only what causes social phenomena and behaviors, but also what underlies them and makes them possible. Only then can science be in a position to understand the social for what it is, and how the objects of social science differ from the objects of natural science. Unlike Kant's, though, my transcendental project is not a philosophical or conceptual one. It is not armchair thinkers but empirical scientists who can carry it out—as this book's empirical approach to the background exemplifies. While people's experience of and interaction with the world is blind to the background level, here lie the conditions for the possibility of social life. Social scientists ought to identify, describe, and account for these conditions, without which, nothing.

ACKNOWLEDGMENTS

While I have almost surely completed this book in less time than one million monkeys pounding away at typewriters would have, it was a long road nonetheless, and I have incurred many obligations along the way.[1] Many thanks to Julia Adams, Jeffrey Alexander, Patrik Aspers, Jens Beckert, Yael Berda, Bruce Buchanan, Craig Calhoun, Frank Dobbin, Ron Eyerman, Claude Fischer, Marion Fourcade, Daniel Fridman, Andreas Glaeser, Philip Gorski, Neil Gross, Kieran Healy, Felisberto Hernández, Steven Hitlin, Gregory Jackson, Elif Kale-Lostuvali, Thomas Kemple, Rakesh Khurana, Issa Kohler Hausmann, Greta Krippner, Ryon Lancaster, Wayne Norman, Mario Small, Ann Swidler, Iddo Tavory, Charles Taylor, Jonathan Trejo-Mathys, Stephen Vaisey, J. David Velleman, Samuel Weber, and Christopher Winship for their contributions to the long-term project whose outcome is this book. Rene Almeling, Claudio Benzecry, Charles Camic, Andrew Deener, David Garland, Carol Heimer, Michèle Lamont, Douglas Porpora, Alan Sica, Peter Stamatov, Arthur Stinchcombe, Owen Whooley, Viviana Zelizer, and the reviewers for Princeton University Press generously took the time to give me feedback on parts or the whole of the manuscript. Steven Lukes and Michael Sauder contributed to this book in countless ways, including their detailed comments on both earlier versions of the chapters and the penultimate version of the manuscript.

I am much obliged to Gerardo Caetano, Juan Oddone, and especially José Pedro Barrán, who taught me the *métier* of the historian. I am much obliged to Charles Camic, Bruce Carruthers, Ann Orloff, Arthur Stinchcombe, and especially Carol Heimer, who taught me the *métier* of the sociologist. I am also much obliged to the Paris Program in Critical Theory at Northwestern University (in particular to Samuel Weber); the Max-Planck-Institut für Gesellschaftsforschung (in particular to Jens Beckert and Wolfgang Streeck); the Paduano Symposium in Business Ethics at New York University's Stern School of Business (in particular to Bruce Buchanan and Robert Frank); and the Institut d'études avancées de Paris (in particular to Gretty Mirdal). I owe special thanks to my colleagues at the New York University sociology department for their constant support, friendship, and conversations in the hallway or over lunch; to the graduate students who took my

1 Émile Borel. 1913. "La Mécanique statique et l'irréversibilité." *Journal de Physique*, 5e série, t. III, pp. 189–96, p. 194; Émile Borel. [1914] 1920. *Le Hasard*. Paris: Librairie Félix Alcan, p. 164; A. S. Eddington. [1928] 1929. *The Nature of the Physical World*. New York: The Macmillan Company; Cambridge: The University Press, p. 72.

classes; and to department chairs Dalton Conley, Jeff Manza, and Willie Jasso, who did everything in their power to increase the odds of this book's passing the infinite monkey theorem test.

I am grateful to my editor at Princeton University Press, Eric Schwartz, for his support and insightful substantive suggestions. I have learned a lot from working with him. I would like to express my gratitude, too, to production editor Leslie Grundfest, copyeditor Karen Verde, art director Maria Lindenfeldar, designers Nick Stover and Jessica Massabrook, and editorial assistant Ryan Mulligan. Thanks also to Kay Banning for preparing the index. Earlier on, my historical research was facilitated by archivists Patrick Quinn, Kevin Leonard, and Janet Olson at Northwestern University Archives; Laura Linard and Timothy Mahoney at Baker Library's Historical Collections; Timothy Driscoll, first at Baker Library's Historical Collections, then at Harvard University Archives; Jillian Lohndorf at Rotary International's History and Archives Department; and the Massachusetts Historical Society staff.

Above all, I am thankful to those who have not given me any feedback on the manuscript, but have given me much love along the way. Some of them will not or cannot read this. Some of them are right here. Some of them are far away, in faraway places with strange-sounding names (such as Uruguay). Some of them have passed away. This book is dedicated to my grandparents, *sine quibus non*.

All told, it follows pretty straightforwardly from the above that, as Goffman might say, I alone am not responsible for this book's shortcomings.[2]

---

2   Erving Goffman. 1981. *Forms of Talk*. Philadelphia: University of Pennsylvania Press, p. 5.

INDEX

Note: Italic page numbers refer to figures and tables.

Index | 391

capitalism: and business case for business ethics, 79, 105–6n84, 252; business schools associated with, 221, 257; Christian responses to, 36n11, 133, 315, 317, 318–22, 325, 326; and common good, 25; and function of business ethics, 165, 209, 254–55; and government regulation, 254; and honesty is the best policy doctrine, 89; Hoover on, 180; tension with ethics, 13, 14, 116

Carey, Henry C., 238

Carnegie, Andrew, 215–16, 216n37, 344

Carroll, Archie B., 332

Cartesians, 64

Catchings, Waddill, 288

causation: causal chain of business ethics, 199–200, 199; causal theories and manipulation of environment, 4–5; concept of, 29; and moral background, 60, 364; moral causation, 3, 4, 5, 7, 8–9, 364–65

Center for Business Ethics, 6

Chamber of Commerce of the United States: and business case for business ethics, 100; business ethics advocacy of, 166, 172, 174, 175, 176–77, 179, 181, 190, 202–5; and codes of ethics, 163, 183–95, 205; Committee on Business Ethics, 183–84, 188, 189; and conscience, 175, 175n34, 176, 178; constituency of, 166, 167, 170–71; and enlightened self-interest, 187–88; establishment of, 165, 170; and government regulation, 23, 100, 161, 166, 173–74, 175, 188–89, 195, 200, 202; organizational development of, 196; origins of, 166–67; "Pesky Calf" strip, 161–62, 162; Principles of Business Conduct, 183–95, 185, 202, 205–6; purpose of, 171–73, 181, 195–96, 202; regional balance in, 170; and service, 173, 176, 179, 186, 188, 203

Chandler, Asa G., 170

Chiapello, Eve, 78

Chomsky, Noam, 378

Christian business ethicists: and business case for business ethics, 113–14, 117–19, 130–33, 142, 157–58; compromises of, 132–42, 348; and conscience, 152–54, 152n88, 155, 156; and consequences of piety, 136–39, 136, 136n48, 137n49, 319, 319n46; and consequentialists, 143–44, 148, 154–55, 154n93; and deontology, 119, 143, 144–47, 154, 273; differences among, 309–10; and divine and human mechanisms, 139–42, 140n58; and divine command theories, 143, 145; and empirical and normative claims, 136–38, 137, 141; and ethical questions, 156–60; and expediency, 127–29, 132; and Golden

Rule, 302; and materialism, 133–34n44, 158, 314, 319, 319n46, 320, 326; and millenarian tradition, 315; and morally good motives, 75–76, 119, 122–26, 126n28, 133, 142–48, 145n68, 152, 363; and religion of the heart, 148–56, 149n78, 331; and springs of action, 126, 149, 363

Christian Merchant: ambivalence regarding business, 308, 316–26; and business is business doctrine, 362; and metaethical objectivity, 291, 292, 298, 299, 331, 348, 364; metaphysics of, 27, 261, 299, 326–32, 335, 336, 352, 363, 364; as moral exemplar, 26–27, 306–10, 337, 356; and morally good motives, 75–76; and role of Mammon, 261, 310–16, 316n35, 317, 319–21, 320n50, 324–25, 329, 351; social and organizational locations of, 263; and spheres, 347–56, 352nn150, 151; and stewardship concept, 261, 312, 332–41, 333–34n91, 337n101, 338n103, 340n117, 363; and stewardship metaphysics, 341–47, 343n127; and stewardship of time, 344–47; as type of moral background, 20–21, 25, 164, 261, 262, 308, 315, 328, 363, 370

Christian Stewardship Movement, 339–40

Chrysippus, 18

Cicero, 128

codes of ethics: and business associations, 192–93, 303, 369; and Chamber of Commerce of the United States, 163, 183–95, 205; and Golden Rule, 163, 303; and Heermance, 193, 204n88, 269–70, 303; materiality of, 11, 163, 195, 369; as moral instrument, 163; and public moral normativity, 189, 193–94, 369–70; and service, 300, 303; and Taeusch, 281

Cold War, 254–55

Coleman, George W., 106

Collins, Frank, 109n97

Columbia School of Business, 207, 234

Columbia University, 226–27, 226–27n64

Commercial Standards Council, 274

Commission on Industrial Relations, 203

Committee on Business Methods, 109

common good: and benefits of business ethics, 209; business as contributor to, 357; and business case for business ethics, 96; business schools as contributors to, 210; and Chamber of Commerce of the United States, 173, 203; and enlightened self-interest, 91–92; universities as contributors to, 24, 25

competitive advantage, and business case for business ethics, 80–81, 101

Comte, Auguste, 278

PRINCETON STUDIES IN CULTURAL SOCIOLOGY

Paul J. DiMaggio, Michèle Lamont, Robert J. Wuthnow, and Viviana A. Zelizer, Series Editors